SCIENTIFIC PSYCHOLOGY

SCIENTIFIC
PSYCHOLOGY

Principles and Approaches

BENJAMIN B. WOLMAN

Editor

ERNEST NAGEL

Consulting Editor

BASIC BOOKS, INC., PUBLISHERS

New York   *London*

Second Printing

Copyright © 1965 by Basic Books, Inc., Publishers

Library of Congress Catalog Card No.: 64-24589

Manufactured in the United States of America

Designed by Loretta Li

PREFACE

PSYCHOLOGY BEGAN ITS MODERN DEVELOPMENT less than a century ago when it emancipated itself from traditional speculative philosophy and adopted the methods of "piecemeal empirical research." This revolution transformed psychology into a science that investigates psychological phenomena in laboratories and clinics to the extent that it is feasible to do so and seeks to establish its findings by painstaking observation, controlled experimentation, and quantitative and statistical analysis.

However, empirical data are simply the bricks out of which a science is built; a science of psychology is achieved only when significant relations of dependence are shown to hold among its empirical findings. Accordingly, the rapidly growing body of psychological data must be classified, interpreted, and systematized on the basis of hypotheses or theories and in the light of explicit inferences that these theories make possible.

The present volume was planned on the assumption that, in their continuing endeavors to build a science, psychologists can profit from philosophical analysis whose aim is to clarify epistemological and methodological problems of experimental inquiry and theory construction, rather than to advance the cause of some traditional metaphysical system. The volume should therefore be construed as an attempt to bring about a *rapprochement* between scientific psychology and the philosophy of science. Its thirty original chapters, written by psychologists and philosophers, have been grouped for convenience into three parts. The first deals with broad principles of scientific inquiry applied to psychology; the second examines several theoretical systems of psychology; and the third discusses a number of special issues encountered in empirical and theoretical research in psychology. A selected and briefly annotated bibliography concludes the volume.

B. B. W.
E. N.

New York City
October 1964

THE AUTHORS

AMSEL, ABRAM
Ph.D., State University of Iowa, 1948
Professor of Psychology, University of Toronto
Has published extensively in the areas of learning and motivation theory and experiment

ANSBACHER, HEINZ L.
Ph.D., Columbia University, 1937
Professor of Psychology, University of Vermont
Editor, *The Individual Psychology of Alfred Adler* (1956) (with Rowena R. Ansbacher)
  Alfred Adler, Superiority and Social Interest: A Collection of Later Writings (1964) (with Rowena R. Ansbacher)
  Journal of Individual Psychology

ARMSTRONG, DAVID MALET
Ph.D., Melbourne University, 1960
Challis Professor of Philosophy, University of Sydney
Author, *Berkeley's Theory of Vision* (1960)
  Perception and the Physical World (1961)
  Bodily Sensations (1962)

ATKINSON, RICHARD CHATHAM
Ph.D., Indiana University, 1955
Professor of Psychology and Education, Stanford University

BERTOCCI, PETER A.
Ph.D., Boston University, 1935
Borden Parker Bowne Professor of Philosophy, Boston University
Author, *Introduction to Philosophy of Religion* (1951)
  Personality and the Good (1963) (in collaboration with Richard M. Millard)
  The Empirical Argument for God in Late British Thought (1938)

BEVAN, WILLIAM
Ph.D., Duke University, 1948
Professor of Psychology and Vice-President for Academic Affairs, Kansas State University

Author or co-author of more than one hundred experimental, theoretical, and review papers in psychology; co-editor of *Theories and Data in Psychology* (in press)

CALFEE, ROBERT C.
Ph.D., University of California, 1963
Assistant Professor, Department of Psychology, University of Wisconsin

CUMMING, ROBERT DENOON
Ph.D., University of Chicago, 1950
Professor of Philosophy, Columbia University
Author, "Mill's History of His Ideas," *Journal of the History of Ideas* (1964)
Editor, Plato's *Euthyphro, Apology, Crito* (1956)
    Philosophy of Jean-Paul Sartre (1965)

DAVIS, FREDERICK BARTON
Ed.D., Harvard University, 1941
Professor of Education, Director of the Bureau of Educational Research and Services, University of Pennsylvania
Author, *The AAF Qualifying Examination* (1946)
    Utilizing Human Talent (1947)
    Educational Measurements and Their Interpretation (1964)

DEUTSCH, MORTON
Ph.D., Massachusetts Institute of Technology, 1948
Professor of Psychology and Education, Head of the Doctoral Program in Social Psychology, Teachers College, Columbia University
Author, *Interracial Housing* (1951)
    Research Methods in Social Relations (1951)
    Preventing World War III: Some Proposals (1962)

GANTT, W. HORSLEY
M.D., University of Virginia, 1920
Professor Emeritus of Psychiatry, John Hopkins University
Chief, Psychophysiological Laboratory, and Consultant in Psychiatry, Veterans Administration
Author, *Experimental Basis of Neurotic Behavior* (1944)
    Russian Physiology in the Atomic Age (1955)
    Adaptation and Preventive Psychiatry (1955)
    Physiological Psychiatry (1958)
Editor, *Cerebral Cortex and Internal Organs* (1947)
    American Lectures in Objective Psychiatry (1955)

GRIZE, JEAN-BLAISE
Docteur ès Sc., University of Neuchâtel, 1954
Professor of Logic and History of Sciences, University of Neuchâtel
Author, "L'Implication et la négation vues au travers des méthodes de Gentzen et de Fitch," *Dialectica* (1955)
    "Du groupement au nombre: essai de formalisation," *Études d'épis-*

témologie génétique (1960)
"Remarques sur les limitations des formalismes," Études d'épistémologie génétique (1962)

HENLE, MARY
    Ph.D., Bryn Mawr College, 1939
    Professor of Psychology, Graduate Faculty, New School for Social Research
    Editor, *Documents of Gestalt Psychology* (1961)

KLINEBERG, OTTO
    Ph.D., Columbia University, 1927
    M.D., McGill University, 1925
    Professor of Social Psychology, University of Paris
    Professor Emeritus of Social Psychology, Columbia University
    Author, *Race Differences* (1935)
        Social Psychology (1954)
        The Human Dimension in International Relations (1964)

KOTARBIŃSKI, TADEUSZ
    Ph.D., Lwow University, 1912
    President, Polish Academy of Sciences
    Author, *Lectures in the History of Logic* (1957)
        Treatise on Good Work (1958)
        *Elements of Epistemology, Formal Logic, and Methodology of
        Sciences* (1961)

KUBIE, LAWRENCE SCHLESINGER
    M.D., The Johns Hopkins University, 1921
    Clinical Professor of Psychiatry, University of Maryland, and Lecturer in
        Psychiatry, Johns Hopkins University
    Author, *Practical and Theoretical Aspects of Psychoanalysis* (1950)
        "Problems and Techniques of Psychoanalytic Validation and Prog-
        ress," in *Psychoanalysis as Science* (1952)
        Neurotic Distortion of the Creative Process (1956)

MANDELBROT, BENOIT
    Dr. ès Sc. in Mathematics, Sorbonne, 1952
    Staff Member, IBM Thomas J. Watson Research Center
    Visiting Lecturer on Applied Mathematics, Harvard University
    Author, *The Variation of Certain Speculative Prices* (1963)
        A New Model for Error Clustering on Telephone Circuits (1963)
        *Derivation of Statistical Thermodynamics from Purely Phenomeno-
        logical Principles* (1964)

MORRIS, CHARLES
    Ph.D., University of Chicago, 1925
    Graduate Research Professor in Philosophy, University of Florida
    Author, *Signs, Language, and Behavior* (1946, 1955)
        Varieties of Human Value (1956)
        Signification and Significance (1964)

NAESS, ARNE
  Ph.D., Oslo University, 1936
  Professor of Philosophy, Oslo University
  Visiting Professor, University of California at Berkeley
  Author, *Erkenntnis und wissenschaftliches Verhalten* (1936)
      *"Truth" as Conceived by Those Who Are Not Professional Philoso-
      phers* (1938)
      Democracy in a World of Tensions (1951)
      Interpretation and Preciseness (1953)
      Democracy, Ideology, and Objectivity (1956)

NAGEL, ERNEST
  Ph.D., Columbia University, 1930
  John Dewey Professor of Philosophy, Columbia University
  Author, *Sovereign Reason* (1954)
      Logic without Metaphysics (1957)
      The Structure of Science (1961)

PETERS, RICHARD STANLEY
  Ph.D., University of London, 1949
  Professor of the Philosophy of Education, University of London Institute
      of Education
  Lecturer (part-time) in the History of Psychology, Birkbeck College, Uni-
      versity of London
  Author, *Hobbes* (1956)
      Concept of Motivation (1958)
      Social Principles and the Democratic State (1959) (with S. I. Benn)
      Brett's History of Psychology (1962)

PIAGET, JEAN
  Doctorat en zoologie, University of Neuchâtel, 1916
  Professor of Psychology, University of Geneva
  Director of the International Center of Genetic Epistemology
  Director of the International Bureau of Education
  Author, *Introduction à l'épistémologie génétique*
      Les Mécanismes perceptifs
      La Genèse des structures logiques élémentaires
      The Construction of Reality in the Child (1954)
      The Growth of Logical Thinking from Childhood to Adolescence
      (1958) (with Bärbel Inhelder)

PRIBRAM, KARL HARRY
  M.D., University of Chicago, 1941
  USPHS Research Professor, Departments of Psychiatry and Psychology,
      Stanford University
  Author, *Plans and the Structure of Behavior* (1960) (with Miller and Gal-
      anter)
      "A Review of Theory in Physiological Psychology, *Annual Review of
      Psychology* (1960)

"The Intrinsic Systems of the Forebrain: an Alternative to the Concept of Cortical Association Areas," *Handbook of Physiology, Neurophysiology,* II (1960)

RAPOPORT, ANATOL
Ph.D., University of Chicago, 1941
Professor of Mathematical Biology and Senior Research Mathematician, Mental Health Research Institute, University of Michigan
Author, *Fights, Games, and Debates* (1960)
"Mathematical Models of Social Interaction," *Handbook of Mathematical Psychology,* II (1963)
Strategy and Conscience (1964)

RAZRAN, GREGORY
Ph.D., Columbia University, 1933
Chairman, Department of Psychology, Queens College of the City University of New York
Author, "Conditioned Responses: An Experimental Study and a Theoretical Analysis," *Archives of Psychology* (1935)
"The Dominance Contiguity Theory of the Acquisition of Classical Conditioning," *Psychological Bulletin* (1957)
"The Observable Unconscious and the Inferable Conscious in Current Soviet Psychophysiology: Interoceptive Conditioning, Semantic Conditioning, and the Orienting Reflex," *Psychological Review* (1961)

RITCHIE, BENBOW F.
Ph.D., University of California at Berkeley, 1946
Associate Professor of Psychology, University of California at Berkeley
Author, "The Circumnavigation of Cognition," *Psychological Review* (1953)
"A Logical and Experimental Analysis of the Laws of Motivation," *Nebraska Symposium on Motivation* (1954)

SCRIVEN, MICHAEL
Ph.D., Oxford, 1956
Professor, Department of History and Philosophy of Science, Indiana University
Author, "A Study of Radical Behaviorism," *Minnesota Studies in the Philosophy of Science,* I (1956)
"The Experimental Investigation of Psychoanalysis," *Psychoanalysis, Scientific Method, and Philosophy* (1959)
"Scientific Method in Psychology," *Psychology* (1961)

SEWARD, JOHN PERRY
Ph.D., Columbia University, 1931
Professor of Psychology, University of California
Author, "A Neurological Approach to Motivation," *Nebraska Symposium on Motivation* (1956)
"Basic Issues in Learning Theory," *Current Issues in Psychology*

(1958)

"The Structure of Functional Autonomy," *American Psychologist* (1963)

WARNOCK, GEOFFREY JAMES
M.A., Oxford, 1952
Fellow of Magdalen College, Oxford
Author, *Berkeley* (1953)
    English Philosophy since 1900 (1957)

WOLMAN, BENJAMIN B.
Ph.D., Warsaw University, 1935
Clinical Professor of Psychology, Post-Doctoral Program in Psychotherapy, Adelphi University
Lecturer, Hunter College
Author, *Freedom and Discipline in Education* (1949)
    Contemporary Theories and Systems in Psychology (1960)
Editor, *Handbook of Clinical Psychology* (1965)
    Historical Roots of Contemporary Psychology (in press)

CONTENTS

Preface   v

The Authors   vii

PART I PRINCIPLES

1 Toward a Science of Psychological Science   3
   BENJAMIN B. WOLMAN

2 Psychology and the Philosophy of Science   24
   ERNEST NAGEL

3 Psychology and Philosophy   28
   JEAN PIAGET

4 Psychological Propositions   44
   TADEUSZ KOTARBIŃSKI

5 Science as Behavior   50
   ARNE NAESS

6 The Uses of Mathematics in Psychology   68
   ANATOL RAPOPORT

7 On the Approach of the Experimental Psychologist   88
   WILLIAM BEVAN

8 Some Philosophical and Methodological Problems in Social Psychology   114
   OTTO KLINEBERG

PART II SYSTEMS

9 Pavlov's System   127
   W. HORSLEY GANTT

10 Concerning an Incurable Vagueness in Psychological Theories   150
   BENBOW F. RITCHIE

11 Choice Points in Behavior Research   166
   JOHN P. SEWARD

12 On Inductive versus Deductive Approaches in Neo-Hullian Behaviorism   187
   ABRAM AMSEL

13 Evolutionary Psychology: Levels of Learning—and Perception and Thinking   207
GREGORY RAZRAN

14 Mathematical Learning Theory   254
RICHARD C. ATKINSON AND
ROBERT C. CALFEE

15 On Gestalt Psychology   276
MARY HENLE

16 Foundations of Personalistic Psychology   293
PETER A. BERTOCCI

17 The Scientific Problems of Psychoanalysis   316
LAWRENCE S. KUBIE

18 The Structure of Individual Psychology   340
HEINZ L. ANSBACHER

19 Emotions, Passivity, and the Place of Freud's Theory in Psychology   365
RICHARD S. PETERS

20 The Existentialist Psychology of Action: Art and Theory   384
ROBERT D. CUMMING

21 George H. Mead: A Pragmatist's Philosophy of Science   402
CHARLES MORRIS

PART III ISSUES

22 An Essential Unpredictability in Human Behavior   411
MICHAEL SCRIVEN

23 Proposal for a Structural Pragmatism: Some Neurophysiological Considerations of Problems in Philosophy   426
KARL H. PRIBRAM

24 Genetic Epistemology and Psychology   460
JEAN-BLAISE GRIZE

25 Logical Analysis and the Nature of Thought   474
G. J. WARNOCK

26 A Theory of Perception   489
DAVID M. ARMSTRONG

27 Some Psychological Aspects of Social Interaction   506
MORTON DEUTSCH

28 Interpretation in Measurement   526
FREDERICK B. DAVIS

CONTENTS

29 Information Theory and Psycholinguistics   550
      BENOIT MANDELBROT
30 Principles of Monistic Transitionism   563
      BENJAMIN B. WOLMAN

    SUGGESTED READINGS   586
    INDEX   601

SCIENTIFIC PSYCHOLOGY

PART I PRINCIPLES

1 BENJAMIN B. WOLMAN

TOWARD A SCIENCE OF PSYCHOLOGICAL SCIENCE

ONE MAJOR CONNOTATION of science is research, that is, the knowledge-producing behavior of scientists. Such activity is a legitimate subject for psychological scrutiny; several investigators have devoted their time and talents to the analysis of scientific behavior, that is, to the psychology of science. Since a scientist interacts with other individuals, scientific behavior has also been analyzed by sociologists in a special discipline—the sociology of science. Scientific inquiry has a long past, and its methods and findings have been influenced by and in turn have influenced several areas of human life; thus, the history of science is another discipline concerned with scientific activities.

Besides these disciplines, there is room for a special discipline called the *science of science*. Let us define "science" as "a system of propositions that convey a certain kind of knowledge." The science that studies these scientific propositions is the science of science.

According to this definition, the science of science is a formal discipline. It deals with scientific procedures (research) and scientific results (data and theory). The science of science studies scientific propositions as propositions, as a system of true or false statements in relation to the subject matter of a particular science.

When the science of science analyzes the connection between the set of scientific propositions and the data they are expected to represent, it is equivalent to epistemology. When it analyzes the formal structure of the propositions irrespective of their factual content, it is formal logic; when formal logic operates with mathematical symbols, it is mathematical logic or logistic. When the science of science deals with language problems involved in reporting data and in other verbal activities of science, it is variously semantics, semiotic, logical syntax, or perhaps logic of language. When the science of science analyzes research procedures and theory formation, it functions as methodology of science. When the science of science draws comparisons and makes all-embracing statements based on

3

conclusions derived from research in various areas, it should be called scientific synthesis. Some thinkers, Auguste Comte and Herbert Spencer in particular, hoped for and endeavored to develop an all-encompassing synthetic philosophical system, a kind of common roof for all sciences (Wolman, 1949b).

Following the traditional patterns of our cultural heritage, the science of science would be known as the "philosophy of science." Originally, philosophy included both the search for truth and the analysis of this search for truth. Presently, the search for truth has been relegated to the particular sciences, and philosophy has become the science of science.

The particular sciences are either empirical, like physics, history, biology, astronomy, psychology, and chemistry, or praxiological, like medicine, education, and political science. Empirical sciences operate with propositions, true and false, while praxiological sciences (cf. Wolman, 1949a) use sentences describing what ought to be done and how to do it.

The philosophy of science is neither an empirical nor a praxiological science. It is a *formal* science; the other formal sciences are the various mathematical disciplines. The philosophy of science, or the science of science, can be broken down according to the various sciences it serves. Accordingly, we have the science of physical science, the science of historical science, the science of psychological science, and so on.

The philosophy of physics, that is, the science of physical science, need not be identified with the traditional philosophy of nature or metaphysics. Metaphysics professed to know more than science did; contemporary philosophy of science analyzes the work and products of scientific inquiry but does not substitute for it. For example, the science of psychological science, that is, the philosophy of psychology, does not study conditioned reflexes nor does it substitute another set of propositions instead. It merely analyzes the propositions of psychology and examines the methods of the scientific procedure in this branch of science.

EPISTEMOLOGICAL REALISM

The epistemological assumption underlying this essay is that things are what they are no matter whether someone does or does not perceive them. In other words, the conviction expressed here is that America *was* before Columbus. Columbus did not create America; he merely discovered it. Or, as Einstein (1931) wrote, "The belief in an external world independent of the percipient subject is the foundation of all science."

This position of *radical realism* is far apart from the naïve realism which assumes that things are as perceived. Radical realism is aware of the perceptual inadequacies of a certain biological species that is capable of verbalizing its perceptions. This species, *Homo sapiens,* has no monopoly on perception of the world. The hunter perceives the wolf and acts accordingly; the wolf perceives the hunter and also acts accordingly. If wolves could talk, their theory of human behavior could certainly be enlightening, although it would be greatly influenced by their acuity of sensory perception and ability to reason. Human cognitive talents are likewise limited; human perception and reasoning are often fallacious. There is no reason to assume that our senses never err.

Without the assumption that things and events (that is, what happens with things) are independent of the perceiver, any further discussion of scientific procedures would be rendered useless. Scientific research could be defined as action (behavior) leading toward the development of a system of true propositions constituting science or the scientific system. Should one accept Schopenhauer's epistemological premise that the world is a product of the perceiver's will and imagination, scientific inquiry would become impossible. If the perception of the world as it is were impossible and what we perceive were determined by our mind, "objective research" would be a meaningless term.

Exploration of what the world is like can make sense only on the assumption that the world did not start with *Homo sapiens* and his subjective or absolute or categoric mind. The explorer checks his binoculars before setting forth, but what can he check in order to gain a clearer view of the fata morgana? There is good reason to check the vision of a man applying for a driver's license, but no purpose is served by an eye examination of a hallucinating individual. Small wonder that Kant assigned to empirical psychology (which he called "anthropology") a rather insignificant role in his system. Actually, Kant's *Prolegomena* was not a prolegomena to scientific inquiry but rather a death verdict on any empirical research whatsoever. A consistent Kantian should follow Schopenhauer in seeing the world as an act of imagination and will, join Hegel in his disrespect for reality, or accept du Bois-Reymond's *"Ignoramus . . . ignorabimus."* In any case, scientific inquiry would become senseless.

On the foundation of radical realism, one can build a philosophy of science that examines the accuracy of empirical observations and the usefulness of theoretical explanations. A radical-realistic scientist means business when he seeks to find the chemical composition of a gas and the laws of gases. When humans are the subject matter of his investigation, he is concerned with finding out exactly what is going on in that area of empirical research and how it all can be explained.

EMPIRICAL GENERALIZATION

As a psychologist, I envy the physicists. Physical phenomena apparently make more sense, are more rational and more in agreement with logic and mathematics, than human behavior can ever be. As complex as the physical universe is, it displays regularity and invariability. Physics is indeed a science *sub specie aeternitatis.* Einstein could present important aspects of relativity theory in a simple equation, $E = mc^2$. Whenever physical causality is not applicable to empirical data, statistics and probability calculus bear witness to unity in the diversity of the physical world.

The study of living nature certainly lacks the serenity and clarity that characterize physics and astronomy. Biologists and especially psychologists face immense difficulties whenever they try to order their empirical findings to the superb mathematical models of physical sciences. Yet no science can renounce the desire to present its findings in the most objective, formalized, and quantitative statements.

One can distinguish two levels of general statement in scientific inquiry. At the first level is the generalization from observable data: Archimedes' law of submerged bodies, the boiling point of water, the velocity of sound, or Ebbinghaus' law of forgetting. An empirical generalization is as a rule open to empirical test by observation or experiment. It is validated by such an empirical test, whereas a theory is not open to direct empirical test. A theory *explains* empirical data and is *supported* by empirical generalizations. A theory per se is neither true nor false; it may be useful or useless, depending on how much and how well it explains. Newton's theory of gravitation was useful, but was supplanted by a "better" theory, derived from Einstein's special and general theories of relativity. A theory is not formed in terms of observable data; were observable data self-explanatory, there would be no need for theory.

Empirical generalizations describe observable regularities of nature. Boyle's law of gases, Mendel's laws of genetics, the Weber-Fechner laws of psychophysics, Pavlov's laws of conditioning, Ebbinghaus' law of forgetting, and the Lewin-Zeigarnik law of incompleted tasks are examples of empirical generalizations, describing permanent relationships between observable events. They describe *what* happens and *how* it happens. They do not go beyond the "what" and "how" questions and do not answer the question "why" things happen. They may read as follows: "Whenever this and this happens, such and such is the sequence." Or: "Whenever an event p that belongs to class P takes place, an event q that belongs to class Q must take place." The relationship may or may not be one of temporal sequence. It may be stated in precise terms, or in probabilistic terms such as the dominant-recessive ratio in Mendelian laws.

All generalizations are statements dealing with classes or categories of bodies or events. The term "event" is used here (instead of the ambiguous term "phenomenon") to denote whatever happens to or with bodies.

Some logicians and philosophers of science call these empirical generalizations "empirical laws" (cf. Feigl, 1951) or "experimental laws" (Nagel, 1961). Both "law" and "experimental" are open to objection. It is true that many empirical generalizations have been derived from experimental studies, but one may develop empirical generalizations by using the observational method. Consider such a generalization as "All humans are mortal." Certainly, observation and induction alone offer valid evidence for such an empirical generalization. There are many empirical generalizations that require no experimentation; consider "All men are born," or "All men have two eyes." In this context, the term "generalization" is preferable to the term "law" because "law" may mean a certain relationship in nature that may be discovered by inductive or deductive method, whereas the term "generalization" is explicitly related to the scientific procedures of the research worker.

Experimentation is observation under conditions planned and set by the experimenter. Planned experimentation offers a far superior and much more precise method of research than naturalistic observation. One may notice that the rails of a railroad expand on a hot day or that the highway surface melts under a scorching sun, but only experimentation can give a precise statement in regard to the impact of heat on physical bodies. One may notice that dogs salivate, but it took carefully planned experimentation to determine the laws of generalization, discrimination, and extinction.

Empirical generalizations, whether arrived at by observation or by experimentation, can be validated by controlled observation or experimentation. Empirical generalizations form the bedrock of any science. They may or may not express laws of nature; they may or may not be causal (cf. Mill's division into types of laws). Empirical generalizations are, in any case, milestones in the development of any empirical science.

On the level of empirical generalization, psychology faces problems not encountered in physics or chemistry. This fact is of crucial importance in the study of psychology. Consider such a generalization. "Whenever a rock hit a window pane, the glass broke": "Whenever p then q," or $p \supset q$; p stands for the first proposition, q for the second. Let us substitute an "iron door" for the "window pane." Certainly, "iron" would not break. Thus, "Whenever p, then $not = q$," or $p \supset q'$; p stands for the proposition "A rock hit the iron door," and q' stands for "The iron door did not break."

Now let us substitute a "man" for the "window pane." When "A rock hit a man," what happened? So far as physiology is concerned, the issue might be presented in general terms: "The skin was scratched, there was some bleeding, swelling, and so forth." But this description is far from complete. A man, being a living organism, *acts*.

Were man a simple organism, his reaction would be fight or flight. Men, being what they are, may react in diverse ways in addition to fight or flight. A man may start a verbal fight or a verbal flight, rationalize, negotiate compensation, forgive, postpone revenge, blame himself, take any of several other courses of action, or possibly combine several, in response to the blow. Thus, general statements such as "Men hurt by rocks throw the rocks at the attacker," "Men hurt by rocks cry," "Men hurt by rocks blame themselves," or "Men hurt by rocks forgive" are not true if "men" means "all men." Yet these may be true in regard to "some men"; furthermore, the same men may react differently, depending on who threw the rock, when, why, and so forth.

As has long been observed, some children are thumb-suckers. Investigation reveals several possibilities: (1) Some children suck when the holes in the nipples are too big; they finish their milk too rapidly and go on to suck their thumbs. (2) Some children suck when the holes in the nipple are too small; apparently, they get tired and give the bottle up, but suck their thumbs because they are hungry. (3) When sucking the breast of an affectionate mother, sucking becomes a pleasurable experience; children suck their thumbs any time they are upset, as if seeking the soothing pleasure of sucking. (4) Children who did not suck in childhood or were weaned too early suck their thumbs as if trying to recapture the missed gratification.

All four generalizations are apparently supported in some degree by empirical findings (cf. Farrell, 1954; Halverson, 1938; Isaacs, 1933; Koch, 1935; and others). Thus q (sucking the thumb) follows p_1 (big holes), p_2 (small holes), p_3 (gratification in sucking), and p_4 (deprivation in sucking). Obviously, p_1 contradicts p_2, and p_3 contradicts p_4. If p_1 is a, p_2 is $not = a$; if p_3 is b, p_4 is $not = b$. Yet q follows p_1, p_2, p_3, and p_4.

Let us take another example, this time the highly controversial issue of learning. Experimental animals do not behave, in an unequivocal way, in support of one learning theory and against all other theories. Even a cursory review of the literature bears witness to this highly variated observable behavior. E. L. Thorndike's cat offered support to his master's thesis by prolonged trial-and-error learning (1911), yet Guthrie's cat outdid him in loyalty to his master and learned in one-trial learning (Guthrie & Horton, 1946).

Let us consider the reaction to frustration. In one study (Dollard, Doob, Miller, Mowrer, & Sears, 1939), frustrated children turned aggressive. In another (Barker, Dembo, & Lewin, 1941), frustrated children did not react with aggression but with regression. In Wolman's (1960b) experiments with face-to-face groups, the reaction to failure largely depended upon the objectives of the group.

Clinical observations (Wolman, 1964a) yielded a rainbow variety of reactions. Some patients react to frustration with aggression or regression; others become very depressed. A schizophrenic patient, defeated in her efforts to set fire to the hospital, reacted with obvious relief. As she explained later, she realized she was not so dangerous as she had thought, if one stupid doctor and one moronic attendant could overwhelm her. For a while she screamed "We are outnumbered," but later on she felt happy that finally someone "did not take her nonsense." Apparently her reaction to frustration was ambivalent and included both protest and relief.

Pavlov's dog suffered a "nervous breakdown" when he was exposed to conflicting stimuli in an ellipse approaching a circle (1927, p. 291). Would a man suffer a nervous breakdown if he could not distinguish between his girl friend and her twin sister? Would he not find some way out?

Psychological propositions are exasperatingly variated. Physicists can remove air from a tube in order to find out whether bodies fall with the same speed in a vacuum. Humans do not fit into evacuated tubes; moreover, their behavior is guided by a variety of reasons. They are inconsistent and change their minds; in similar situations they may react in dissimilar ways, and in similar ways in dissimilar situations. Men marry for a variety of rational and irrational reasons; so also do they love, hate, come together, and part. Simple and uniform generalizations do not do justice to the complexity of human behavior.

IDIOPHENOMENA

This diversity of human behavior gives rise to the idea that each human being is unique and each human act an unrepeatable event. It was Wilhelm Dilthey (1883) who started psychology on an idiographic footing. Dilthey deviated from Windelband's division into the idiographic sciences of history and culture (*Kulturwissenschaften*) and the nomothetic natural sciences (*Naturwissenschaften*). Windelband (1915, Vol. 2, pp. 136 ff.) granted that the new experimental psychology as developed by Wundt, Ebbinghaus, and others was a nomothetic science. But precisely this admission perturbed Dilthey. Experimental psychology dealt with sensory perceptions and thresholds but failed to *understand* the man. Shakespeare's dramas *King Lear, Hamlet,* and *Macbeth,* said Dilthey, "contain more psychology than all psychological books together."

Dilthey was opposed to psychological theory patterned after the natural sciences. Natural sciences "explain" (*erklären*) what is going on. There is no need for explanation in psychology because the human mind acts as a whole and there is no need to split it up into components. Psychological processes are lived through or experienced from within (*erlebt*); psychological research needs not to analyze details but to comprehend or understand (*verstehen*) the human mind as a whole. These insights can be traced not only in the works of W. Stern and G. W. Allport and in Gestalt and field theories but also in their impact on the thinking of behaviorists and learning theorists in the molar–molecular issue. Dilthey himself was caught in a conflict between the associationist and neoidealist philosophies (cf. Wolman, 1960a, pp. 399-406).

Although Dilthey's system is itself of little value in contemporary psychological inquiry, the problem that Dilthey tried to solve is still very much alive. In the physical sciences, simple generalizations of observable data are rather uncontroversial; in psychology, even so low a level of generalization as that of simple behavioral patterns is less likely to receive such agreement. The first-level empirical generalization in psychology, exemplified in learning behavior, reaction to frustration, and thumb-sucking, is controversial, whereas experimental generalization in osmosis, genetics, thermodynamics, and hydraulics is generally accepted. Thus one can understand why several brilliant psychologists developed idiographic systems (cf. Allport, 1960, 1961; Lewin, 1935, 1936; and others), in opposition to some oversimplified and unwarranted generalizations of contemporary psychological theory.

The term "idiophenomena" requires further clarification. Unless one assumes the "realist" position in the Platonic sense and ascribes existence to general concepts, the entire issue seems to rest on a misunderstanding. For a "nominalist," there are no other phenomena but idiophenomena. Whatever happens, happens once; whatever happens "for a second time" is no longer what it was before. Not only are historical events idiophenomena, but every drop of rain, every seed and every decay, every fall of a rock and every motion of air are idiophenomena. The idiophenomenon—the single case—is the raw material of science. The work of science starts, but does not end, with the single case. Science compares, abstracts, generalizes, and classifies by common denominators. Nor, in the nature of things, can science exhaust all cases. Newton did not experiment with all falling bodies nor did Boyle study all gases. Darwin and Mendel did not study all biological species or cases.

So with psychology. Every experiment is, in a sense, a case study. But a single observation or experiment is merely the first step. Psychology, like any other science, uses inductive generalization; the individual case study is only the first step, which must lead to classification and generalization. Certainly, psychological phenomena are more complex than those studied by physics and biology, for a human being is a physical body, a living organism, and a personality, all of them at the same time. Thus, generalizations here must be more cautious and more complex.

THEORY FORMATION

Empirical generalizations deal with observable facts. The business of science is to obtain more knowledge, more precise, more open to test and prediction, than daily observation does. But even in daily common-sense observation men go beyond empirical data and try to answer the question "why?" It is not enough to know what happened; it is very important to know why the air conditioner does not work and why the car brakes failed. A mere description is incomplete knowledge; it is necessary to *explain* and to form hypotheses and inferences. When some scientists and philosophers suggest limiting scientific inquiry to description, they may be reducing the adequacy of scientific systems below that of simple common-sense inquiry. "Pure" empiricism does not make science more rigorous; rather, it makes it less adequate. A mere collection of facts is no more a science than a pile of bricks is a house, as Poincaré said (1908).

Were it possible to build a scientific system by empirical generalization, there would be no need for theoretical propositions. Unfortunately, such a purely empirical system is impossible. Consider physics. Gravitation, the corpuscular theory of light, the electromagnetic field theory, and the quantum and relativity theories are *not* empirical generalizations. A statement that all bodies fall with the same speed in a vacuum is an empirical generalization; so is the observation that apples fall but feathers and balloons rise. Had Newton been a pure empiricist, he would have never gone beyond empirical generalization and his contribution would be negligible. Empirical generalizations concern observable facts only; they state what happens and how, but science must reach beyond observable data, develop inferences about unobservables, and discover connections and relationships. These inferences and hypotheses enable us to relate present events to past and future events.

Such a procedure is no longer observation or generalization from observation. It involves filling loopholes in observations, bridging gaps by means of experiments, and relating things that are, as far as empirical data are concerned, not related. It is no longer empirical research; it is theory formation. Modern astronomy and physics are as much indebted to deductive, theoretical concepts as to inductive, empirical generalizations. The discovery of outlying planets in the solar system was brought about by theory. Einstein's relativity theories and the space–time continuum are not direct products of observation or experimentation. Discussing Bridgman's operationism, Einstein (1959) wrote:

> In order to be able to consider a logical system as physical theory it is not necessary to demand that all of its assertions can be independently interpreted and "tested operationally"; *de facto* this has never yet been achieved by any theory and can not at all be achieved (Vol. 2, p. 679).

A theory is a set of hypothetical propositions that are not derived from empirical data. Empirical data are statements of facts; a theory is not a statement of facts but an *explanation of facts*. It is a fact that solid bodies turn into fluids under the impact of heat, but there are tremendous differences as to why ice, copper, and aluminum melt. The "why" is no longer a matter of fact, but an explanation of fact.

Consider learning. Thorndike's cat learned by trial and error, but Guthrie's cat learned at one trial. Why? To answer the question "why" we must go beyond observable data. We leave the domain of empirical generalizations and enter the kingdom of hypotheses and hypothetical systems.

Some scientists prefer to stick to observable data and empirical generalizations. Following the tradition of Hume and Mach, Skinner (1931) maintained that in scientific disciplines "explanation is reduced to description and the notion of function substituted for that of causation. The full description of an event is taken to include a description of its functional relationship with antecedent events."

Skinner (1950) was opposed to interpretations of behavior that went beyond observable data. He saw no point in trying to answer the question *why* positive stimuli are reinforcing and why aversive stimuli are aversive. What is to be studied are the facts: whether these stimuli produce certain reactions, how they are brought about, and to what extent. Psychology has no business going beyond "public" and observable events. For example, Skinner (1953) used the term "drive" merely as a convenient way of referring to "the effects of deprivation and satiation and of other operations which alter the probability of behavior in more or less the same way" (p. 144).

Skinner was opposed to looking "inside the organism," and refused to deal with "private" events. His decision would be commendable were science free to choose its subject matter. However, the task of scientific inquiry is to seek truth, be it visible and observable or private. If there are private events, we must study them. We shall study them as objectively as possible, because science is a quest for objective truth. Science has to study things as they are and cannot reject things because they do not fit into one's intellectual preferences or modes of thinking.

VERIFICATION OF THEORIES

Theory is neither true nor false in the sense that a single observation or a generalized observation can be. Consider the following propositions: (1) This dog salivated when the bell rang, after the bell's ringing and the meat powder coincided *n* times. (2) All dogs salivate under similar conditions. (3) Dogs salivate on bell because of coupling in analyzers. (4) Dogs salivate on bell whenever there has been drive reduction. The first proposition is a description of a single case; the second proposition is an empirical generalization; both can be empirically tested. The third and fourth propositions are not empirical statements, but hypothetical explanations.

Why dogs salivate when the bell rings is a question that can be answered in several ways. Consider the answers given by Pavlov, Thorndike, Guthrie, Hull, and Tolman. Learning, the process of observable modification of behavior, can be explained in more than one way. First, without conditioning: Consider the developmental theories, such as Gesell's principle of maturation and Freud's theory of libido, cathexis, and development. None of these has been "proven," nor have they been adequately refuted.

Learning theorists are no more in agreement among themselves than they are with non-learning theorists. The literature gives ample evidence that all the years of extensive research have not brought us any closer toward the resolution of this controversy (cf. Deese, 1958; Estes, 1960; Hilgard, 1956; Kimble, 1961; Mowrer, 1960).

Hull's theory of reinforcement has been supported by an impressive body of experimental data (cf. preceding references and Spence, 1960). Yet no experimenter was so successful as to eliminate all the alternative solutions nor so unsuccessful as to force Hull's followers to abandon his theoretical framework altogether.

Tolman's school brought substantial evidence that latent learning does not need reinforcement. According to Tolman, drives and the possibility of their satisfaction facilitate learning, yet the learning process itself is a process of organization of cognitive experiences. Latent learning takes place without reward as a result of exploratory activities (Tolman & Honzik, 1930).

It seems that each experimenter has impressive—but not conclusive—experimental data in favor of his hypothesis. Razran (1957) suggested a three-level theory of learning, the first level corresponding to the Pavlov-Ukhtomski viewpoint, the second to the Thorndike-Hull, and the third to the Tolman-Krech. Wolman, after a critical examination of learning theories (1960a, chs. 1-4), introduced an additional variable, namely, the prehedonic, hedonic, and posthedonic levels of behavior (Ch. 15). K. Spence, O. H. Mowrer, N. E. Miller, H. F. Harlow, and others have introduced several new explanations of learning. Although these theories all stem from Pavlov's conditioning, none of their originators accepted Pavlov's neurological theory. They accepted conditioning without the neurological processes of concentration and irradiation, excitation and inhibition in the cortical centers. According to Pavlov (1928), "Nervous activity consists in general of the phenomena of excitation and inhibition. . . . I shall not commit a great error if I liken these two phenomena to positive and negative electricity" (p. 156). Such a hypothesis was apparently unacceptable to learning theorists. Thus K. S. Lashley wrote in a letter to B. P. Babkin:

Paradoxically, many psychologists in whose current work the influence of Pavlov's theories can be most clearly traced, have turned to the development of conceptual systems from which all neurological interpretations are vigorously excluded. Thus the chief influence on psychology in America of conditioned reflex theory seems to have been diametrically opposed to Pavlov's expectation of using his studies as a basis for the physiological explanation of behavior. All this is no fault of Pavlov. He was one of the great pioneers of experimenting and inductive reasoning. But it seems to me that these characteristics of his work which gave him greatest claim to genius have been least influential in American psychology. It has been his misfortune to fall into the hands of philosophers. His influence has been rather that of Descartes than of Pasteur (quoted after Gantt, 1958, p. 244).

To be sure, events can be explained in more than one way, but so many contradictory explanations give point to Skinner's question, "Are learning theories necessary?" (1950). I would add: If they are necessary, which one shall we choose?

There are several criteria for the acceptability of a scientific theory. The first criterion is the principle of *immanent truth,* an outgrowth of the Aristotelian *tertium non datur.* A scientific theory must represent a system of propositions free from inner contradictions.

The second criterion for acceptability of a scientific theory is its *relationship to observable data.* If someone were to explain migratory trends by the influence of invisible little ghosts, there would be no need to refute such a theory. Therefore, the principle of *transcendent truth* requires that the system of propositions be free from contradiction with data obtained by observation or experimentation.

Whereas the principle of immanent truth is self-evident and generally acceptable, the principle of transcendent truth is one of the most controversial issues in contemporary philosophy of science. Certainly, one can hardly expect, from a contemporary philosopher, the reply Hegel gave to the criticism that his theory was contrary to historical facts and reality. Hegel's famous reply was *"Desto schlimmer für die Wirklichkeit"* (too bad for reality).

Yet even the acceptance of the principle of transcendent truth does not solve the problem. The difficulty lies not within the theoretical system but within the empirical data. Some scientists, such as Bridgman (1927, 1936), have insisted that theoretical propositions be checked against data obtained by rigorously controlled experimentation and described in terms of experimental procedures. However, such a demand debars astronomy, geology, paleontology, history, and archaeology from science. Yet, since scientific research activity aims at the discovery of truth, no part of the universe and no event may be excluded from inquiry.

Moreover, even those sciences that operate with experimental method cannot operate with it exclusively. Thus, some aspects of biology are experimental but others are not. It is certainly an unwarranted belief that psychology is par excellence an experimental science, and nothing else. Certain aspects of human behavior cannot be dealt with by experimental methods; ethical reasons eliminate others from consideration.

In some cases, efforts to "check" a theory against experimental evidence either have forced the theory into a Procrustean bed of data obtained by a certain experimenter in a certain setting with certain experimental subjects, or else have failed of conclusive evidence in the direction of either proof or disproof. To the first category belongs the experimental and theoretical work of C. L. Hull (1943, 1952). Hull's impressive theoretical system was checked against certain experiments conducted in a certain way with a certain species (rats). On the other hand, experiments conducted by such experimenters as Tolman, Skinner, Razran, Guthrie, and many others could not be used as empirical evidence for Hull's theory. Thus Hull's theory is "proven" only insofar as it has been found in agreement with *certain* empirical data. Its general validity, for both rats and humans, has been questioned by scores of experimental and theoretical workers.

The second type of experimental evidence that has ended up with inconclusive results is the experimental research in psychoanalysis. One cannot but admire the zeal and thoroughness of the studies conducted by several outstanding workers and yet wonder what proof was expected from these studies. Psychoanalytic theory is a system of hypothetical propositions that deal with a few observable facts or symptoms and with a great many inferred and unobservable facts of unconscious life. Psychoanalytic theory has introduced many, but not always unequivocally defined, logical constructs; and like any other theory, it cannot be directly proven (cf. Nagel, 1959; Wolman, 1964b).

As a set of observational or empirical generalizations, psychoanalysis describes the "ambivalence" of human nature. People do not necessarily either love or hate; they often practice both at the same time toward the same person. People may try hard to attain a goal and at the same time do everything to thwart their own efforts. People may be domineering and subservient, independent and overdependent, gay and sad at the same time and act in a most illogical way. Freud's theoretical work was certainly not rigorous, but when one deals with "the most obscure and inaccessible region of the mind, [the] least rigid hypothesis . . . will be best" (Freud, 1950, p. 2).

Psychoanalysis as a *theory* operates with a complex set of hypothetical constructs and models. For example, the statement that anxiety is a state of tension created by a conflict between the ego and the superego, or the ego and the id, cannot be experimentally or observationally validated. This statement is neither true nor false, because ego and superego are not observable data but hypothetical constructs. But drive, habit, irradiation, and concentration are likewise not empirical facts but hypothetical constructs. Hypothetical constructs cannot be directly validated; there is no shortcut between these and empirical generalizations; special "correspondence rules" must be established. These rules can be formulated in several ways, depending on the nature of the empirical data (cf. Cohen & Nagel, 1934; Nagel, 1961, pp. 97 ff.).

Certain psychoanalytic propositions could and should be validated by controlled observation and experimentation. Consider the origin of neuroses. Karl Abraham (1955) suggested a timetable of fixation as a starting point for the various mental syndromes. Controlled observation must not only state how often fixation occurs, but must also take into consideration a variety of factors: predisposing factors (heredity, prenatal life, conditions attending birth, sociocultural background); precipitating factors; nature and severity of the damage; developmental stage at which these factors acted on the individual; personality structure of the individual at that stage, and his ability to take stress; aggravating factors (lack of support, failure in school); compensatory factors (friends, special talents); nature of the interindividual relations of the patient; cultural and religious factors. Simple correlations and measurements of variability may overlook the most significant and relevant variables.

Some of the difficulties in psychological research stem from lack of precision in experimental designs, lack of clarity and precision in theories, or both. But the peculiarities of the subject matter, that is, human behavior, complicate the task. Predicting the course of a hurricane is not an easy task, but a hurricane of human feeling has to account for even more variables. The complexity of human behavior is a factor psychologists should be keenly aware of. Rash quantification and oversimplified experimentation may produce trivialities.

Men are neither rats nor servomechanisms; experimentation with humans requires sophistication and precision. Kurt Lewin's experiments in "social climate," with allegedly despotic, democratic, and laissez-faire leaders, were not bona fide leadership experiments (Lippitt, 1940; Wolman, 1958). None of the "leaders" was chosen as a leader nor conquered his leadership by any *coup de force*. All of them were *appointed* leaders by the experimenter; thus, their leadership was autocratic. The allegedly "democratic" leader was not truly democratic, for the children knew very well that he had full power to control their behavior; since he was nice to them, he could be classified as a benevolent dictator. The "autocratic" leader was rude and not too bright (dictators rarely are). The "laissez-faire" leader did not lead at all. Thus, Lewin's conclusions with regard to social systems certainly were not borne out in his experiments.

Perhaps N. R. F. Maier's rats needed a goal in their life: they were upset when frustrated (1949). Many retiring but otherwise sensible individuals have no particular goals. Frustration in humans leads to a great many reactions, among them redoubled effort, resignation, projection, increased group cohesiveness, decreased group cohesiveness, aggression, and self-directed aggression. Some people can take frustration in stride with little if any change in their behavior whereas others seem unable to bear even mild frustration.

Empirical generalizations are either true or false and can be validated by controlled observation or experimentation. Theories are neither true nor false, but they can be *useful* or *useless*. A theory is useful when it leads to new discoveries of facts and explains and predicts more facts than any other theory. Certainly, Pavlov's theory is superior to Sechenov's and Freud's to Janet's.

A theory does not deal directly with observables but with "empirically unobservable, purely imaginative or intellectually known, theoretically designated factors, related in very complicated ways to the purely empirically given" (Northrop, 1959). Psychological theory must find its own, very complicated ways or "correspondence rules" between theoretical constructs and empirical generalizations.

THE NEED FOR A PHILOSOPHY

Modern science has broken away from philosophy. Instead of leaning on speculative philosophy, modern physicists have developed their own frame of reference and their own conceptual system. Neither Einstein, Maxwell, nor Eddington could rely on the philosophical systems of Leibniz, Kant, or Bergson. Yet the spectacular development of empirical research required fresh hypotheses and new and bold theories.

In their search for clarity and refinement in the development of concepts and theories, the philosophically minded scientists found reliable support in scientifically minded philosophers. Most of the traditional areas of philosophy are now harnessed for the use of science. The new philosophy is primarily a philosophy of science. This philosophy is not a prolegomena to science but rather an *epilegomena* of the sciences. Philosophy is no longer the proud queen of the sciences but the useful serviceman, the dependable repairman of the sciences. It analyzes the formal content of propositions and checks research methods and concept-formation. The philosophy of science does not prescribe truth, but it checks and analyzes the methods by which the sciences proceed in their search for truth.

The cooperation between scientists and scientists of science, or philosophers, has been beneficial for both. Scientists need a check-up of the tools they use, formal logical analysis of their premises, examination of their research methods, detailed scrutiny of their observational and experimental procedures, and finally, a rigorous critique of their concept-formation and construct- and model-building. The development of theories requires advice from men competent in the formal sciences. Philosophers, by the nature of their discipline, can help to make science more logical, more consistent, more precise.

Conversely, philosophers need the empirical body of scientific data to apply their formal rules of implication, their syllogisms, axiomatics, calculus of classes, and other techniques. Scientists supply the propositions to be analyzed, examined, verified, deduced, and inferred from. Close cooperation between philosophers of science and philosophically minded scientists produces *science without naïveté* and *logic without metaphysics* (Nagel, 1956; Wolman, 1960a).

This rapprochement (the main objective of the editors of this volume) requires a great deal of work on both sides. Philosophers of science must become fully acquainted with the methods and problems of the particular branch of science they intend to serve. Scientists must carefully examine their specific area of research and cautiously elaborate the specific problems.

This has happened in physics. Einstein, de Broglie, Eddington, Jeans, Planck, and Schrödinger carefully examined the problems faced by *physicists*. Their epistemological and methodological inquiries revolved around problems created by the nature of physical science and its subject matter, the physical world. Theoretical physicists developed their own philosophy of science guided by and related to the peculiar problems in their research area. Einstein developed an epistemological system related to physics; nothing of that kind has been done in psychology.

Unfortunately, *some psychologists have adopted concepts and research tools from areas alien to their own research area.* Too often psychologists wear a hat borrowed from the physical sciences, although psychology, by the very nature of its subject matter, is miles apart from physics. Psychology, the study of the behavior of certain organisms, is a specific branch of the biological sciences. The biological sciences, as a study of certain processes of certain objects, are a specific branch of physical sciences. The physical sciences deal with the entire universe.

It is a dubious procedure to apply indiscriminately the rules of a class to a subclass on the assumption that these rules will explain all the processes of the subclass. To be sure, human beings are physical bodies, and the laws of physics and chemistry apply also to them; no man could ever be jailed for a violation of the laws of gravitation or electromagnetism. Yet, as Fenichel (1945) put it, "Mental phenomena occur only in living organisms. The general laws that are valid for life phenomena are also valid for mental phenomena: Special laws that are valid only for the level of mental phenomena must be added" (p. 5).

Human behavior cannot be reduced to and wholly interpreted in terms of physical laws. Nor can the behavior of the experimental rat, cat, dog, or monkey be reduced to physics or chemistry. There are additional variables, discovered by the biological sciences and nonexistent in the nonorganic part of the world: consider birth, sex, reproduction, assimilation, digestion, respiration, growth, and death.

Unfortunately, many modern psychologists are inclined to abandon biology and join the physicists. One form of this practice is an extreme and radical *methodological reductionism*. Instead of developing methods and concepts derived from human life, they imitate the methods and concepts of physical science. More generally, methodological reductionism introduces into one area of research methods and concepts coined in another (cf. Wolman, 1960, pp. 520 ff.). In a second form, *theoretical reductionism,* they reduce psychological propositions to propositions of other sciences.[1]

Quite naturally, one is prone to transfer his observations from the physical world to human beings, and from humans to everything else. Were men exactly the same as all other things, such a "transfer" would be justified. Despite the obvious differences, some authors have practiced *anthropomorphism,* whenever they ascribed their nature to nonhuman objects, and *reimorphism* whenever they ascribed physical nature to themselves. Both types of "morphism" have certainly not promoted the cause of scientific inquiry.

Unfortunately, both tendencies are very much alive in contemporary psychology. When psychologists describe "anxiety," "frustration," or "nervous breakdown" in rats or servomechanisms, at least the language of scientific propositions in comparative psychology becomes suspect; and so does the validity of generalizations which stem from fitting a human hat on a rat's little head and then return it to the human beings.

The impressive precision and achievements of physical science tempt psychologists to view men and their activities in terms of mechanics, electromagnetism, or other physical concepts. Being human, psychologists fall prey to many temptations, including the fantasy of the golem or robot. Certainly, one can program a computer in such a way as to prove his theory. Computers are more obedient than rats and more cooperative in research than hospitalized patients. One wonders whether students of medicine would abandon the study of the organism and dissect statues or electric wires to prove the validity of a theory in anatomy or physiology.

Actually, no psychological theory can ever be finally and completely proven. Every set of observable data can be interpreted in more than one way; obviously, human behavior, largely unobservable and hidden from observation and known only through inference, leaves even more freedom in its interpretation. Unfortunately, some psychologists seem to insist on final and conclusive evidence. For lack of it, they resort to the null-hypothesis method as if this were the best medicine for the troubled research worker. Yet Rozeboom (1960) has raised the most serious doubts about the null hypothesis as a method of inference. Needless to say, the common practices (significance levels 1-5) prove little if anything at all.

Dazzling statistical techniques are no guarantee of proper scientific procedure. Schlaifer (1959) pointed to the common error that occurs "when the statistician delivers a carefully computed solution of the wrong problem" (p. 654). A considerable part of quite precise research in abnormal

---

[1] See Chapter 30, "Principles of Monistic Transitionism."

psychology deals with irrelevant issues in an inconclusive way, probably because the research problem was incorrectly stated.

The "right problem" must be derived from painstaking study of the behavior of a single case. Psychological processes are too complex to be studied by oversimplified and uncritical generalities. Certainly the case study method and uncontrolled observation easily become anecdotic and even misleading. But a controlled observation and/or controlled experimentation must be *preceded* by the most meticulous naturalistic observation of and experimentation with single cases. Because of the high variability of human behavior, the careful study of individual cases is a necessary first step. Observational or experimental case study will *disclose* the variables to be isolated, variated, and controlled in further research. The meticulously conducted case study will point to the relevant problems. Quantification is the indispensable language of science, but it must come at a later stage, after identical elements have been isolated and put into distinct classes.

The men who have contributed most to the development of psychology as a science are undoubtedly Freud, Pavlov, and Piaget. They did not use high-powered statistics nor did they try to validate their generalizations or theories by correlations, null hypotheses, chi square, and the like. Freud, Pavlov, Piaget, and scores of other workers in psychology started from the most detailed case-study observations and experimentations. They drew generalizations, and developed general theories on the basis of relatively small numbers of patients, dogs, and children.

The most intimate knowledge of the individual case is a priceless virtue in all biological sciences. Neurologists, biochemists, histologists, physiologists—all start from the single case. The greatest scientific discoveries in biological science have been attained by this method.

It is patent that no science can stop at the single case. Comparison, abstraction, measurement, classification, generalization, and correlation, as well as postulates, constructs, deduction, and equations, are legitimate tools in any scientific inquiry. Psychologists must study the tools they use in relationship to their empirical data and in regard to their specific problems: Do we psychologists really see what we see and how do we see? To what extent does the observer become a determinant in results of observation when he observes another human?

The quantum theory or the corpuscular theory of light will not make us more sophisticated, more precise workers in our field. Psychology needs its own sophistication, its own precision, its own philosophical refinement.

Theoretical physicists today combine physics with the philosophy of science. Some graduate schools of physics teach the history and philosophy of physics; psychologists seem to be more concerned with the history and philosophy of physical problems than with the history and philosophy of problems specifically psychological.

Physical science gained depth and clarity by philosophical analysis of itself as a science. A similar development is suggested for psychology. While empirical research goes on, analysis of methods and theory-formation require the help of what was called logic, epistemology, semantics, and so on, presently included in the modern philosophy of science. Philosophically minded psychologists and philosophers interested in psychology must re-examine the specific problems of the psychological science. A new branch of the philosophy of science, applied specifically to psychology, is needed, not a science of physical science, ill-translated into psychology. We need a philosophy that has grown up in psychological laboratories and clinics: *a science of psychological science.*

REFERENCES

ABRAHAM, K. *Selected papers on psychoanalysis.* New York: Basic Books, 1955.

ALLPORT, G. W. *Personality and social encounter.* Boston: Beacon Press, 1960.

ALLPORT, G. W. *Pattern and growth in personality.* New York: Holt, Rinehart & Winston, 1961.

BARKER, R. G., DEMBO, T., & LEWIN, K. Frustration and regression: an experiment with young children. *Univ. Iowa Stud. Child Welf.,* 1941, **18,** No. 1.

BRIDGMAN, P. W. *The logic of modern physics.* New York: Macmillan, 1927.

BRIDGMAN, P. W. *The nature of physical theory.* Princeton Univ. Press, 1936.

COHEN, M. R., & NAGEL, E. *An introduction to logic and scientific method.* New York: Harcourt, Brace & World, 1934.

DEESE, J. *The psychology of learning.* New York: McGraw-Hill, 1958.

DILTHEY, W. *Einleitung in die Geisteswissenschaften.* Vol. 1. Leipzig: 1883.

DOLLARD, J., DOOB, L. W., MILLER, N. E., MOWRER, O. H., & SEARS, R. R. *Frustration and aggression.* New Haven: Yale Univ. Press, 1939.

EINSTEIN, A. Maxwell's influence on the development of the conception of physical reality. In *James Clerk Maxwell: Commemoration Volume.* London: Cambridge Univ. Press, 1931. Pp. 66-73.

EINSTEIN, A. Reply to criticisms. In P. A. Schilpp (Ed.), *Albert Einstein: Philosopher-Scientist.* Vol. 2. New York: Harper, 1959. Pp. 663-688.

ESTES, W. Learning theory and the new "mental chemistry." *Psychol. Rev.,* **67,** 1960, 207-223.

FARRELL, B. A. The scientific testing of psychoanalytic findings and theory. In H. Brand (Ed.), *The study of personality: a book of readings.* New York: Wiley, 1954.

FEIGL, H. Principles and problems of theory construction in psychology. In W. Dennis (Ed.), *Current trends in psychological theory.* Univ. Pittsburgh Press, 1951. Pp. 179-213.

FENICHEL, O. *The psychoanalytic theory of neurosis.* New York: Norton, 1945.

FREUD, S. *Beyond the pleasure principle.* New York: Liveright, 1950.

GANTT, W. H. *Physiological bases of psychiatry.* Springfield, Ill.: Charles C Thomas, 1958.

GUTHRIE, E. R., & HORTON, G. P. *Cats in a puzzle box.* New York: Rinehart, 1946.

HALVERSON, H. M. Infant sucking and tensional behavior. *J. genet. Psychol.,* 1938, **53,** 365-430.

HILGARD, E. R. *Theories of learning.* (2nd ed.) New York: Appleton-Century-Crofts, 1956.

HULL, C. L. *Principles of behavior.* New York: Appleton-Century-Crofts, 1943.

HULL, C. L. *A behavior system.* New Haven: Yale Univ. Press, 1952.

ISAACS, SUZANNE. *Social development in young children.* London: Routledge & Kegan Paul, 1933.

KIMBLE, G. A. *Hilgard and Marquis conditioning and learning.* New York: Appleton-Century-Crofts, 1961.

KOCH, H. L. An analysis of certain forms of so-called "nervous habits" in young children. *J. genet Psychol.,* 1935, **46,** 139-170.

LEWIN, K. *A dynamic theory of personality.* New York: McGraw-Hill, 1935.

LEWIN, K. *Principles of topological psychology.* New York: McGraw-Hill, 1936.

LIPPITT, R. An experimental study of the effect of democratic and authoritarian group atmospheres. *Univ. Iowa Stud. Child Welf.,* 1940, **16,** 44-195.

MAIER, N. R. F. *Frustration: the study of behavior without a goal.* New York: McGraw-Hill, 1949.

MOWRER, O. H. *Learning theory and behavior.* New York: Wiley, 1960.

NAGEL, E. *Logic without metaphysics.* Glencoe, Ill.: Free Press, 1956.

NAGEL, E. Methodological issues in psychoanalytic theory. In S. Hook (Ed.), *Psychoanalysis, scientific method, and philosophy.* New York Univ. Press, 1959. Pp. 38-56.

NAGEL, E. *The structure of science.* New York: Harcourt, Brace & World, 1961.

NORTHROP, F. S. C. Einstein's conception of science. In P. A. Schilpp (Ed.), *Albert Einstein: Philosopher-Scientist.* Vol. 2. New York: Harper, 1959. Pp. 385-408.

PAVLOV, I. P. *Conditioned reflexes.* London: Oxford, 1927.

PAVLOV, I. P. *Lectures in conditioned reflexes.* New York: Liveright, 1928.

POINCARÉ, H. *La science et l'hypothèse.* Paris: Flammarion, 1908.

RAZRAN, G. The dominance-contiguity theory of the acquisition of classical conditioning. *Psychol. Bull.,* 1957, **54,** 1-46.

ROZEBOOM, W. W. The fallacy of the null-hypothesis significance test. *Psychol. Bull.,* 1960, **57,** 416-428.

SCHLAIFER, R. *Probability and statistics for business decisions: an introduction to managerial economics under uncertainty.* New York: McGraw-Hill, 1959.

SKINNER, B. F. The concept of the reflex in the description of behavior. *J. gen. Psychol.,* 1931, **5,** 427-458.

SKINNER, B. F. Are theories of learning necessary? *Psychol. Rev.,* 1950, **57,** 193-216.

SKINNER, B. F. *Science and human behavior.* New York: Macmillan, 1953.

SPENCE, K. *Behavior theory and learning.* New York: Prentice-Hall, 1960.

THORNDIKE, E. *Animal intelligence: experimental studies.* New York: Macmillan, 1911.

TOLMAN, E. C., & HONZIK, C. M. Introduction and removal of reward and maze performance in rats. *Univ. Calif. Public. Psychol.,* 1930, **4,** 257-275.

WINDELBAND, W. *Präludien.* (5th ed.) Vol. 2. Tübingen: 1915.

WOLMAN, B. B. Scientific study of educational aims. *Teachers Coll. Rec.,* 1949, **50,** 471-481. (a)

WOLMAN, B. B. Theory of history. *J. Phil.,* 1949, **46,** 342-351. (b)

WOLMAN, B. B. Education and leadership. *Teachers Coll. Rec.,* 1958, **59,** 465-473.

WOLMAN, B. B. *Contemporary theories and systems in psychology.* New York: Harper, 1960. (a)

WOLMAN, B. B. Impact of failure on group cohesiveness. *J. soc. Psychol.,* 1960, **51,** 409-418. (b)

WOLMAN, B. B. Non-participant observation on a closed ward. *Acta Psychother.,* 1964, **12,** 61-71. (a)

WOLMAN, B. B. Evidence in psychoanalytic research. *J. Amer. Psychoanal. Assn.,* 1964. (b)

2 ERNEST NAGEL

PSYCHOLOGY AND THE PHILOSOPHY
OF SCIENCE

LIKE SEVERAL OTHER branches of contemporary science, psychology was for many centuries a province of philosophy, during which its major theoretical distinctions among and generalized accounts of psychological processes were based almost entirely on casual observation, rather than on systematic experimental study. To be sure, ever since the first fruits of modern research into nature during the late Renaissance began to excite men's imaginations concerning the promise of "the new science," students of psychological phenomena have repeatedly urged that psychology pattern itself on the natural sciences by adopting their methods and strategies of inquiry. Indeed, by the eighteenth century some highly influential philosophers believed they were practicing "the experimental method of reasoning" in their own psychological investigations. However, these early proposals to reform psychology, as well as the claims to have accomplished this end, were premature, and psychology remained for many years longer an armchair discipline.

The career of psychology as an experimental natural science did not properly begin until the final quarter of the nineteenth century, but by the beginning of the present one it was well on the way to its current status as a distinctive branch of specialized inquiry. Although as a subject of academic instruction it continued for a time to be housed in departments of philosophy, even this purely formal connection with its ancestral home was eventually broken. Instruction as well as research in psychology is now carried on by men whose primary intellectual loyalties are almost universally to the ideals of natural science, and who are not expected to be even acquainted with the traditional concerns of philosophy. But conversely, with rare exceptions professional philosophers are no longer active contributors to psychological research; and indeed, familiarity with the materials of contemporary psychology is not a requirement for an academic career in philosophy.

Psychology has profited enormously from its emancipation from the

24

tutelage of philosophy. It has made substantial advances in detailed knowledge of numerous psychological processes and their interrelations in both man and the lower animals, and of their dependence on organic as well as environmental conditions (whether physical, social, or cultural). In particular, many age-old distinctions and assumptions bearing on men's psychological capacities have been shown to be inadequate if not basically mistaken. In consequence, widely held conceptions of human nature, inherited from earlier generations and serving as justifications for numerous institutional practices, have been placed on the defensive and have to some extent been modified. Moreover, conclusions drawn from a variety of psychological experiments have provided grounds for initiating policies that often turned out to be effective in dealing with important areas of private as well as public concern. Even philosophy has in a measure been affected by developments in the new psychology, since many questions that are commonly classified as philosophical ones have at least the appearance of involving issues of psychological fact—for example, questions concerning the validity of perceptual knowledge, the nature of the human self, or the conditions of meaningful discourse. In any event, some of these questions as well as the traditional answers to them have been reconsidered in the light of recent work in psychology and either reformulated to meet criticism or amended, if not abandoned in favor of analyses believed to be more consistent with the findings of psychological inquiry.

Nevertheless, the hope shared by many of the founding fathers of experimental psychology that its achievements would soon match those of the older natural sciences has not yet been realized; and the radical separation of psychology from philosophy has not been an unmixed blessing to either discipline. The theories current in psychology are hardly the equals of most of those available in physics and biology either in reliability or range of explanatory power. Indeed, unlike these sciences, psychology is marked by the existence of warring schools, which differ not only in their interpretations of newly gathered empirical data—disagreements on matters at the frontiers of research occur in all branches of science—but are also at odds over the "proper" way of studying as well as interpreting phenomena that have long been subjects of investigation. This persistence of divergent schools of psychology makes evident that the achievement of comprehensive and objectively grounded theoretical knowledge is not assured by formally disavowing all "philosophical" preconceptions when conducting inquiries directed toward that end; for such disavowal is no guarantee that insufficiently analyzed if not entirely tacit philosophical assumptions will not control the scientific enterprise and perhaps even hinder the realization of its major goals. In point of fact, proponents of these conflicting psychological schools are often divided not only by disagreements on substantive issues, but in part also by commitments (sometimes, though not always, explicit) to different philosophical conceptions of what constitutes scientific knowledge and how such knowledge is to be established. These conceptions frequently involve gross oversimplifications and misunderstandings of the logic of inquiry in other natural sciences; in particular, they sometimes contain crude empiricistic notions of scientific research that fail to do justice to the complex substantive and methodological assumptions which enter into the collection and interpretation of empirical data. But in any event, such conceptions are commonly acquired by psychologists from the parochial intellectual traditions which they imbibe in an unquestioning manner during their professional training. Accordingly, it does not seem unreasonable to suppose that the progress of psychology as a natural science would be helped, and the level of its theoretical discussions raised, if psychologists were philosophically more knowledgeable than they usually are and had in particular competence in the logic of theory construction.

On the other hand, despite the fact that psychology has become a discipline independent of philosophy, professional philosophers have not ceased to concern themselves with various psychological notions—such as sensation, memory, motivation, or voluntary action—which enter centrally into their discussions of problems in epistemology, ethics, and social philosophy. Indeed, there has been a vigorous revival of interest in so-called "philosophical psychology" among Anglo-American philosophers during the past two decades, stimulated in part by the belief that many perennial philosophical issues could readily be resolved, if not shown to be entirely spurious, by making explicit the "logic" embedded in the "ordinary" use of key psychological terms. However, whatever new light these recent philosophical discussions may throw on various philosophical problems, the discussions rarely depend on the actual findings of psychological science and reveal little familiarity with the work of experimental psychologists. Current philosophical psychology has refined and sometimes corrected analyses of common-sense psychological concepts which philosophers had proposed during the centuries prior to the birth of experimental psychology. But it is at bottom a continuation of the same type of analysis in which those earlier thinkers were engaged, and present-day contributors to it do not, as a rule, regard the conclusions of experimental psychology as relevant to the business of philosophy. Moreover, although professional philosophers have shown increasing interest in the philosophy of science at least since the term of the present century, attention has been focused mainly on questions raised by developments in the physical sciences. Most philosophers of science have not concerned themselves with comparable issues in the various sciences dealing with human behavior—possibly because there are no comprehensive and generally accepted theories in these disciplines, so that their findings appear to be fragmented and to be too difficult subjects for systematic philosophical commentary. But whatever be the explanation, only a few philosophers of science have occupied themselves seriously with analyzing the structures of various substantive concepts employed in contemporary psychology, or have contributed significantly to the clarification of the logic of psychological inquiry.

In short, although psychology and philosophy in their current forms are distinctive types of inquiry with generally different objectives, each discipline deals with questions that are relevant to some of the issues with which the other is often confronted. The present collection of essays was planned with the intent of exhibiting this relevance clearly, and in order to make evident that, although the formal separation of the two disciplines has produced great enlightenment, psychologists are compelled by developments in their science to come to grips with problems that have a philosophical dimension, as well as that philosophers who are seeking to interpret various forms of human experience in a responsible manner cannot safely ignore pertinent aspects of psychology. Although a number of the essays deal with questions that are associated with particular standpoints in contemporary psychology, not every psychological school is represented in the volume. Nor does the book contain an exhaustive survey of the many substantive and methodological problems raised by contemporary psychological research. But most of the problems that are discussed in the various chapters have a general import for understanding the present state of the science; and the discussions illustrate both the role of as well as the need for philosophical reflection in psychology.

3 JEAN PIAGET

PSYCHOLOGY AND PHILOSOPHY *

ALTHOUGH THEIR ORIGINS depend in part on the history of techniques, the sciences, as theoretical reflection, were almost all initially undifferentiated from philosophy, in other words, were more or less specialized chapters of philosophy: the "physics" of the pre-Socratics and that of Aristotle were linked to a general conception of the world, the mathematics of Pythagoras was connected to a more or less esoteric universal doctrine, and chemistry before Lavoisier and biology until the nineteenth century continued to be steeped in various metaphysics.

One by one the sciences detached themselves from philosophy: mathematics with Greek thought, physics in the seventeenth century, chemistry in the eighteenth century, biology and psychology in the nineteenth. The two principal reasons for this dissociation are complementary. First, science tends to delimit problems in order to define them more clearly, whereas philosophy by its very nature treats reality as a totality both objective and experienced. Second, science tends to achieve objectivity by methods of experimental control or of deductive (algorithmic) technique, permitting a relative unanimity in the solution of sufficiently delimited problems; whereas a general assent is impossible in philosophy, which lacks a method for overcoming irreducible divergences in points of view (for example, between metaphysics and positivism).

This development has been fortunate for psychology, and there is no valid reason for altering it. It will most likely continue irreversibly, as in the case of the other sciences. It is true that certain philosophies occasionally exert a temporary influence on various psychological currents. For example, phenomenology, after having played a role in the formation of Gestalt theory, today inspires a tendency in certain psychologists to set a higher value on consciousness. Logical empiricism exerts an opposite influence on others, and dialectical materialism has led some (though by no means all) investigators to overestimate the role of conditioning. But these

---

* Translated from the French by Richard Howard.

are local or national reactions and not universal or universalizable, so that we may consider them passing episodes in the history of our science.

On the other hand, two new situations have for some time modified relations, not, strictly speaking, between psychology and philosophy, but between certain psychological problems and certain problems, hitherto considered philosophical, which today suggest autonomous investigations of an increasingly scientific character. Hence, this development implies, not a new subordination of psychology to philosophy, but merely an increasing enlargement of the field of scientific research (in accordance with the historical tradition of continual expansion of the sciences), integrating problems hitherto considered "philosophical" with scientific research.

The first such situation is that the advanced sciences are today obliged to construct their own epistemology. Epistemology has classically been regarded as a chapter of philosophy: it is the theory of knowledge as understood by Plato, Descartes, and Leibniz, by Hume and, above all, by Kant. Yet today it is tending to become scientific, in that it becomes an integral part of certain sciences in their spontaneous development. For instance, the problem of the basis of mathematics, which has always been the key problem of epistemology, has become a strictly mathematical problem, studied by the mathematicians themselves. Even if the latter often resort, in this case, to logic alone, following the tradition of Russell and Whitehead (*Principia Mathematica*), they also have occasion to appeal to psychological factors and thereby introduce operative (and psycholinguistic) activities of the subject, following a tradition suggested by the names of Helmholtz, Poincaré, Enriques, Brouwer, Manoury, and Gonseth. Similarly, the problem of the basis of physics is today treated by the physicists themselves, for it has become impossible to establish the conditions of objectivity in microphysics without deriving theory from observation itself, that is, without studying the relations between the observer's actions, which modify the phenomenon, and the object's reactions, which are to be learned through the material or operative manipulations by the subject.

The second key situation that today modifies the relations between the sciences and philosophy is that philosophy itself has been partially dissociated into new disciplines which tend to independence and thereby acquire a properly scientific character. An instance is logistical or mathematical logic, which has become an autonomous and rigorous discipline. Similarly, the epistemology of the sciences tends to become independent not only for the reasons just enumerated, but further by virtue of an increasing specialization within philosophy itself.

In short, the problems of logic and epistemology tend to dissociate themselves from general philosophy and increasingly to unite with scientific problems. Consequently, contemporary psychological research finds itself increasingly in contact with such problems of knowledge. This development does not mean that psychology tends to return to philosophy, from which it has had reason to separate itself, but on the contrary that certain questions, once purely philosophical, tend to be shifted to a scientific level, where they reunite with certain psychological preoccupations.

THE APPROACH TO A PSYCHOLOGICAL EPISTEMOLOGY

But at this point we must be careful to distinguish two possible viewpoints in these interactions between epistemology and psychology. One might first construct the epistemology of psychology, as one might treat the epistemology of, say, mathematics or physics. But one might also (and this second viewpoint is both more fruitful and particular to psychology) attempt to analyze epistemology as radiating outward not from the subject-psychologist, that is, from the scientist as he elaborates his science, but from the focus of the subject as the object of psychology, both in general (child, adolescent, civilized adult) and in particular (as psychology studies the formation of his perceptions, his concepts, his intelligence, in short, his general instruments of knowledge).

Psychology is doubtless insufficiently advanced for discussion of its methods, its principles, and its basis to be, as yet, fruitful for the epistemological viewpoint, for it is when a science has become exact that its epistemology can perform truly general services. It is probable that this will eventually be true of psychology, but it is doubtless too soon to rely, in this regard, on rather generalized attempts. On the other hand, it may even now be useful to reflect on the epistemological bearing of certain principles proper to psychology, such as that of the parallelism (or isomorphism) between the processes of consciousness and the concomitant physiological processes. For example, I have maintained (notably in a symposium held at Princeton by the Macy Foundation on *Problems of Consciousness*) that this principle suggested an isomorphism between processes of an implicative nature and those of a causal nature. Consciousness does not derive, in fact, from relations of causality but from "implication" in the broad sense. The characteristic of states of consciousness is to allow of significations: one signification is not the "cause" of another, but it "implies" the other in varying degrees ranging from designation to implication in the strict sense. The organism, on the contrary, proceeds from causality and not from implication. The principle of a psychophysiological parallelism then proposes an isomorphism between certain causal structures observable in the nervous system and the structures of implication, such, for example, as the logico-mathematical structures. (The fine essay by McCulloch and Pitts on the isomorphism between the logical links of propositions and the various forms of neuronic connections shows the likelihood of such a hypothesis.) If this interpretation of the parallelism were valid, we should then have a first example of a purely psychological principle becoming instructive for epistemology in general.

GENETIC EPISTEMOLOGY

But the specific originality of psychology is to raise problems of knowledge (logical and epistemological) by certain of its results, and not only by its methods. One of the objectives of psychology is, in fact, the study of the *subject* who acts, perceives, and thinks; analyzing this subject's mechanisms of knowledge leads quite naturally to raising the problem of his epistemology. It is true that this subject is, perhaps, not very interesting if we are concerned only with the average adult, who is neither logician nor scientist. But we can go much further: the psychology of development (or genetics) studies the subject as gradually constructing and continually correcting his own knowledge, in part under the influence of the environment but in part spontaneously. By studying the formation and the transformation of knowledge, from birth to adolescence and to maturity, we thereby raise all the problems of knowledge proper to the *subject in general* and not only those proper to the psychologist himself; and we grasp them in the perspective of an "embryogenesis" or of an ontogenesis of knowledge that can perform the same services for epistemology that organic embryology has performed for comparative anatomy and biology in general.

We apply the term "genetic epistemology" to this study of the way in which the subject constructs and organizes his knowledge during his historical development (ontogenetic and sociogenetic). Genetic epistemology presupposes a psychological analysis, but it necessarily leads to an epistemological study treating the great problems of the theory of knowledge. In fact, the study of the construction of a structure of knowledge teaches us something of the nature of this structure, that is, of its epistemological mechanism: whether the structure has been derived from experience or has been constructed deductively; whether it derives from language alone (and thus remains purely analytic) or is synthetic and supposes operations or actions.

In fact, between birth and adolescence, the child constructs, partly by himself, a series of basic structures whose epistemological bearing is considerable. For instance, he constructs an elementary logic whose stages can be followed in detail. Thus there is an age (generally before 7-8 years) when the child does not recognize the transitive nature of equalities ($A = C$ admitted deductively if the subject has empirically discovered that $A = B$ and $B = C$) or of inequalities ($A < C$ if it has been discovered that $A < B$ and $B < C$); whereas after 7-8 years (for lengths and certain other relations, but only after 9-10 years for weights without indications of volume), this transitive nature henceforth appears "necessary" without having been taught. What, then, is the source of this logical necessity which is neither innate nor socially transmitted?

Similarly, the child spontaneously discovers certain arithmetic operations, such as biunivocal and reciprocal correspondence. When asked to reproduce the same group of six or seven tokens arranged in a row, he begins by constructing a row of the same length, but without a term-for-term correspondence. Then he constructs an optical correspondence, but he no longer accepts equivalence if one of the rows is simply squeezed more closely together (without adding or removing anything). Finally, around 7-8 years, he admits that once there is a term-for-term correspondence, equivalence is necessarily maintained even if the spatial arrangement of the elements is modified. Here, then, is another example of logico-mathematical necessity spontaneously discovered, whose source we must attempt to comprehend.

Again, the child discovers certain spatial operations, beginning with operations of a topological character (which he is *not* taught) and continuing with projective and measuring operations combined, these latter leading to the conservation of lengths (not accepted at the start) and to spontaneous measurement.

The child also performs certain temporal operations (seriation of events and relation of intervals or durations) and arrives at an original notion of speed based, at first, not on the relation of space and duration ($v = e/t$), but on purely ordinal spatiotemporal considerations derived from the intuition of passing.

Lastly, we observe a spontaneous development of the ideas of chance and probability, in close connection with the development of the logicoarithmetic operations.

Confronted with such facts, whose variety far exceeds these few examples, we cannot avoid a number of strictly epistemological questions. One which will doubtless be raised from the start is: What are the relations between this logic of the average subject and the logic of logicians, or between the mathematics of the average subject and that of the mathematician? It is clear that the isomorphisms we are here concerned with are far from complete: there actually exist only a few relations between the logician's refined axiomatics and the intuitive and imprecise logic of the average subject. Nonetheless, certain relations do exist, and if the mathematicians may use the phrase "natural numbers" to designate positive wholes, we may speak of a *natural logic* in the same sense, since the series of numbers involves a logic. If no one denies that the equalities $2 + 2 = 4$ or $2 + 3 = 3 + 2$ offer something in common to the average subject and to the mathematician, there is also no doubt that on the most elementary operational levels we find certain fundamental structural characteristics, such as the reversibility of operations (the possibility of making an inverse or a reciprocal correspond to any operation). We can thus show that operations are spontaneously organized according to certain structures (classifications, seriations, correspondences, and so on), whose simplest forms or "groupings" prefigure the very general forms of "groups," "lattices," and other such concepts which constitute the essential architecture of logico-mathematical algebra.

Granted that we can find the roots of logical and scientific thought in the average subject, the basic problem is then to determine the formative processes of such cognitive structures. This is a psychological problem, deriving from experimental analysis alone, yet it is obvious that its study necessarily leads to the most general epistemological problems. For instance, if we could demonstate that the structures of knowledge are constructed by pure learning from the experience of objects alone, this would be a justification of classical empiricism; if we proved that this development results from a combination of physical experiences and linguistic structuration, this would be a verification of the thesis of "logical empiricism"; if we discovered that none of these factors suffice to account for the structures of knowledge, we should be led to justify other forms of epistemology.

On such a basis, we shall distinguish five kinds of formative factors in cognitive structures, each of which affords a specific psychological signification but each of which also involves a different and well-characterized epistemological meaning.

Innateness or *maturation.* Cognitive structures may, in fact, be innate; we do not believe that this is so, but it is possible. In particular, one might interpret logical structures (appearing at a certain age) as the result of new paths of association forming in the mind by internal maturation, or take some similar approach.

Social interactions. Some knowledge may be acquired by educative transmission or, more generally, may be deposited in and conveyed by language itself (compare the role of syntax and semantics in the interpretations of logical positivism).

Physical experience may play a fundamental role. By this term is meant the experience whose results are acquired by abstraction from objects or from events relating to objects.

Another form of experience may play an equally decisive role. This form is also related to objects or their symbolic substitutes, but its results are acquired by abstraction, not from objects as such, but from *actions by the subject upon objects,* which is not the same thing. For instance, arithmetic notions or operations may result not from objects, but from the manner in which we act on them (by combining, ordering, measuring, and so on).

Lastly, mention must be made of what we call the *equilibration factor,* systems of compensation resulting from the subject's actions in a direction contrary to external disturbances (regulations and negative feedbacks). For instance, the reversibility of operations ($5 - 3 = 2$ if $2 + 3 = 5$)

could be due to a process of progressive equilibration (we prefer the term "equilibration" to the static "equilibrium").

By determining the role of these various factors in the formation of knowledge, we may hope to solve certain general epistemological problems, such as that of the origin—empirical, linguistic, or other—of certain notions or even of certain principles.

THE GENESIS OF LOGIC AND KNOWLEDGE IN THE CHILD

Let us select, as a first example, the development of logic in the child (a problem I have studied over forty years without having begun to exhaust it). Initially, we may be sure that even the most elementary logical structures (transitive qualities, inclusion, and so on) are not simply innate in the human being, since we must wait, in our societies, until an average age of 7-8 years for them to be achieved and utilized in a systematic way. We might suppose, it is true, that certain processes of late maturation of the nervous system are involved, processes depending on hereditary factors yet not contemporaneous with birth: but the basic fact which prevents us from adopting this exclusive explanation is the acceleration or the retardation we observe, depending on the different social milieu or the degree of exercise from which the subjects may have benefited. The extension of our experiments by a number of English, American, and Canadian authors (Lowell, Peel, Berlyne, Wohlwill, Elkind, Lunzer, Laurendeau, Pinard, and others) has shown, in fact, that the developmental stages of the logical structures, and notably of the notions of conservation with regard to which the structures become manifest, are to be found with great regularity with regard to the order of succession of the levels concerned, but that delays or accelerations may occur systematically, depending on the milieu. Experiments conducted in Martinique by Canadian psychologists show an average backwardness that may extend as long as four years; in Iran, we find an average gap of two and half years between the results obtained in Teheran and the results of young illiterates in the country.

But if logical structures are not to be explained (or not to be explained exclusively) by innate factors, neither do they depend exclusively on social or linguistic factors. Two observations show decisively that, although the role of language is not negligible, it is just as surely not preponderant. Language is probably necessary to the completion of spontaneous logical structures, that is, to the constitution of propositional operations (around 11-12 years) together with the possibility of reasoning on simple hypotheses stated verbally. But even at this late level, language is not an adequate constitutive condition, for this logic of propositions also presupposes a combinative faculty (*une combinatoire*) as well as a "group" of four transformations which coordinate inversions and reciprocities. These structures mark the completion of the systems of "operations."

Our first observation as to the inadequate character of the linguistic factors is that operations in general (treating not only propositions but, from 7-8 years on, classes, relations, and numbers) have a much deeper source than language: operations (such as combining or ordering) are internalized actions, which language can certainly manipulate symbolically but which proceed from actions that are sensorimotor in source. Long before affording a syntax and a semantics, in the linguistic sense of these terms, logical structures, by the very virtue of their operative character, express the laws of the most general coordinations of actions. There is, then, a logic of coordinations of actions, of which verbal logic is only a particular case, and in studying "the child" before the appearance of language, we find, at the purely sensorimotor levels, the roots of this language of coordinations of actions. The system of sensorimotor "schemes" affords, in fact, the beginnings of classifications, of a sense of relationships, reversibilities, and reciprocities; and these sensorimotor roots of subsequent logical structures are, from all evidence, independent of verbal behavior.

The second observation suggesting the inadequacy of verbal factors is that verbal exercise is not enough to produce the acquisition of a logical structure when it is not yet constructed operationally. On the one hand, we observe children of 7-8 years who use certain verbal expressions involving inclusion (for example, "Some of my flowers are yellow") but without precisely understanding this inclusion (as if the expression meant "All of my some flowers are yellow"): we must wait until the relation of inclusion is acquired in the operational mode ($A < B$ if $A + A' = B$ and if $A = B - A'$) for the adequate comprehension of verbal expression to be possible. On the other hand, if we consider a verbal learning of the operations, as A. Morf has attempted by systematic experiments (for example, on disjunctions, and on inclusion itself), we make only insignificant progress so long as there is no concrete and active manipulation.

What then is the role of experience itself in this constitution of the logical structures? We must first distinguish carefully between two types of experience, of quite different significance, which epistemological empiricism has constantly confused. As we have seen, there is, on the one hand, the "physical" experience, with abstraction from objects; but there is also a second form of experience, which we shall henceforth call "logico-mathematical," whose results are obtained by abstraction from the subject's actions on (real or symbolic) objects.

Physical experience, characterized by that process which specialists in learning call "reinforcement," plays only a secondary role in the acquisition of logical structures, for in order to acquire a logical structure the subject must rely on other, simpler logical structures (and this by indefinite regression to the general coordinations of actions). Several of the collaborators at our Centre d'Épistémologie Génétique in Geneva (P. Gréco, B. Matalon, J. Smedslund, J. Wohlwill) have performed a series of experiments in this regard whose results are conclusive. For instance, after showing that there exists a significant correlation between the conservation of weight (when the form of a lump of modeling clay is changed) and the transitivity of weights, Smedslund obtained an easy learning of the conservation of weights, as a physical observation (verifiable on the scale), yet did not obtain, by the same procedures of empirical verification, a learning of transitivities.

It remains no less true that, at elementary levels, experience is necessary to the subject for him to discover what will subsequently appear from deductive evidence. For instance, as late as 6 years of age, the child needs empirical observation to admit that the combination of classes $A + A'$ $(= B)$ gives the same result as $A' + A$ $(= B)$; or that $2 + 3 = 3 + 2$. But, in such cases, what kind of experience is involved? It is a matter of discovering about objects that their total is independent of the order in which they are taken; yet neither this order nor this total belong, strictly speaking, to the objects, since their order and their total merely derive from the fact that the subject has ordered or combined them in a certain way. Hence experience consists in observing, but on "any" objects, the results of the action of ordering and the action of combining, and in discovering that the result of combining is independent of order! There is indeed a discovery, but with abstraction from action and not from the object!

This fundamental type of experience, which we have called "logico-mathematical" as opposed to "physical," is of obvious epistemological significance: it shows that, even if the subject needs experimental inductions before arriving at pure deduction, he still does not derive his logic from the empirical laws of the object, but gradually abstracts it from the co-ordination of his own actions.

Before drawing other epistemological conclusions from these facts, let us further note that if logical structures thus begin by a kind of experimental induction, with abstraction from the coordinations of actions, the gradual shift to deduction proper is made not by external reinforcements but by a continuous process of equilibration: by studying the transformations due to his actions, the subject discovers that he can compensate for them, and this compensation (which defines equilibration) then leads to the constitution of operative reversibility. Thus every operation, starting from a certain level, affords an inverse or a reciprocal, and it is the functioning of the structural systems thus made reversible which then assures the play of deductions.

There are two conclusions to be drawn from these remarks. The first is that, although symbolic or abstract logic is a logic without subject, there does not exist, psychologically, any subject without logic. It is thus necessary today to reconcile logic and psychology, and the foregoing considerations make this reconciliation easy: psychology studies the formation of operative structures for which logic furnishes an axiomatic or formalized model. Logic is then competent only to determine questions of (axiomatic) validity, while psychology is concerned with questions of fact. As for epistemology, it must account simultaneously for facts and for formal validity, which leads it to restore the role of the subject's activities by linking logic to the general coordination of actions and not only to language.

Second conclusion: for "logical empiricism," logical propositions are essentially "analytic"; only physical statements are "synthetic." The great logician Quine has opposed this absolute dichotomy, using both formal and empirical arguments. The foregoing facts, which we have analyzed at length from this viewpoint at our Centre d'Épistémologie Génétique (*Études d'Épistémologie génétique,* Vol. 4, *Les Liaisons analytiques et synthétiques dans les comportements du sujet*), show that Quine is entirely right; logical statements begin by being synthetic; although they may become analytic, it is secondarily and only when observations have been rendered useless by the advances of deduction. Thus we find every intermediate step between these two kinds of links, not an absolute dichotomy.

Similarly, for mathematical notions, the study of their formation furnishes the opportunity for a number of epistemological reflections.

A first problem is that of the reduction of mathematics to logic, a reduction affirmed by Frege, by Whitehead and Russell in the *Principia,* and by others and denied by Poincaré and by Brouwer. We know today, thanks to Gödel's theorems, that it is impossible to demonstrate the non-contradiction of a structure by its own means or by weaker means, an impossibility which marks the victory of non-reductionism. This point of view offers a rather striking parallel with the genetic approach, since in development, too, a structure never completes itself save by integrating itself into stronger structures, in an endless progression. In a Platonic interpretation, or leaving out of account the subject's constructions, it is difficult to represent this demand for coherence to increasingly stronger structures, which would correspond, if everything were given in advance, to a pyramid suspended at its apex (but from what?) and not resting on its base.

A particular case of this problem of reduction is that of the relations between the whole number and classes, or of asymmetrical relations. Whereas Poincaré and Brouwer believed in a primitive intuition of number, the *Principia* tries to reduce the cardinal number to classes (classes equivalent to classes by biunivocal correspondence) and the ordinal number to transitive asymmetrical relations. As we have seen, the child manages quite soon to construct biunivocal correspondences spontaneously, but we must wait until 7-8 years for him to accept the conservation of numbers when we alter the optical correspondence, which is obviously contrary to the hypothesis of a primitive intuition of number: we must admit that the components of number are entirely logical. On the other hand, there is no separate construction of cardinal numbers from classes and of ordinal numbers from seriation; number results from a new and original synthesis of inclusions and of seriation, the idea of order intervening upon cardination, or else one unit would be indistinguishable from another since they are all equivalent. This psychological hypothesis, which we believe verified by the facts, has elsewhere been formalized from the logical point of view by J. B. Grize, an achievement which furnishes a splendid example of the possible parallel between genetic analysis and logical formalization.

But the basic problem in the epistemology of mathematics reduces to a twofold question: Why can we constitute a "pure" mathematics like a "pure" logic, whereas in other realms deduction must always rely sooner or later on experience? Why does mathematics nonetheless remain adequate to reality, to the point of often anticipating by years or even centuries the deductive framework which physics may subsequently employ? Psychogenetic analysis permits us to answer this double question in the following way. Mathematics, like logic, is applied to reality because both begin by a phase in which experience is necessary, since they derive from the general coordination of actions and, in order to coordinate his actions, the subject must first perform them upon reality. On the other hand, we are here concerned not with a "physical" experience, with abstraction from objects, but with a "logico-mathematical" experience, that is, with abstraction from actions (abstraction which furnishes the ideas of reversibility, of order, of "transformation group," of "lattice," and so forth). At a given level of development, actions on objects are no longer necessary and the subject can manipulate his own operations symbolically. Thus, mathematics becomes "pure" to the degree that it is derived, not from objects, but from the subject's own actions and operations; yet this permits complete objectivity, for the general coordinations of action are common to all subjects and thus characterize what we might call the "epistemic subject" as opposed to the individual subjects, who require a systematic decentration in order to free themselves of their intellectual egocentrism and thereby to arrive at the most general coordinations.

A final problem (among many possible others) which we should like to mention is that of the relations between geometry and arithmetic or algebra. We know that, historically, geometry first took a metric Euclidean form, the only kind known to the Greeks, with a few glimpses of projective geometry. The latter did not develop until the seventeenth century, and we must wait until the nineteenth century for the development of topology (although it was anticipated by Leibniz). From the theoretical point of view, however, topology is fundamental, and from it proceed both general metric and projective geometry, with between them the related geometry, etc. Further, between topology, general algebra, and group theory exist the closest relationships, which have made possible a growing localization of geometry. Now, it is most interesting to note that, genetically, the evolution of the subject's geometries is much closer to theoretical construction than to historical development. The child begins by topological intuitions and from them proceeds to a simultaneous construction of metrical operations (conservation of lengths, proportion, and so forth) and of projective operations that are of an essentially qualitative and logical nature. Proportion is constructed only subsequently, in a manner astonishingly parallel to the construction of number (by synthesis of distribution and order, as number proceeds by synthesis of inclusion and seriation). But space offers this peculiarity, that whereas logic and arithmetic proceed from a purely logico-mathematical experience by abstraction from action, spatial knowledge is developed on two levels, one similarly logico-mathematical, but the other physical (space of the objects themselves) by abstraction from material data as well as from actions.

PERCEPTION

This leads us to further epistemological considerations suggested by the psychogenetic study of physical data, starting from the perceptional data. If there exist a pure logic and a pure mathematics, in the sense of "purely formal," there does not exist, on the other hand, a pure physics in the sense of "purely experimental": every kinematic, mechanical, or physical experience is referred, in effect, to a logico-mathematical framework outside of which the very reading of the experience would be impossible.

Now, this is true genetically as well as theoretically, and is even already true of perception as such. Studying the development of perceptions genetically, we observe in fact that at no level do they constitute a mere "copy" of objects, for they proceed by a random sampling among the group of elements to be apprehended. Perception is thus essentially distorting and achieves a relative objectivity only by the use of multiple activities of decisions, of relating, of pre-inferences, and of schematization. This schematization proceeds by active assimilations as opposed to automatic associations, and, in defining the forms of these perceptional schemata, we find a partial but rather extensive isomorphism with the elementary logico-mathematical schematizations. From the level of perception, therefore, the apprehension of experience appears as something quite different from a simple "reading"; it reveals itself as, on the contrary, a structuration, at the heart of which the data furnished by the object are found to be in continuous interaction with the subject's activities. Empiricist epistemology is therefore based no more on perceptional grounds than on notional ones.

As for the physical notions whose development we can study in the child, they appear as the product of an operational elaboration of the data of perception, an elaboration not just derived from perception (though prepared by it), but involving a restructuring on the level of representations. This restructuring is often very original and, in certain cases, permits unexpected juxtapositions from an epistemological point of view.

Let us take as an example the notion of speed, which presents a double interest from the epistemological point of view. On the one hand, we know that there exists a permanent vicious circle, in the realm of theoretical physics, between speed and time: we define speed by referring to duration, since speed is the relation between the space covered and duration, yet we never measure duration except by referring to speed (whether astronomical or other). On the other hand, epistemological relations between the notions of speed and duration have been modified with the theory of relativity, and this independently of the preceding vicious circle which subsists even in relativity. For classical mechanics, space and time are absolutes, anterior to speed, and speed is only a relation introduced between them and depending on them. For the theory of relativity, on the contrary, time and space are relative to speed, which thus assumes an absolute and anterior character in relation to them.

There is thus a special interest in speculation whether, psychogenetically, the notion of speed is based on that of duration, is anterior to it, or at least remains independent of it. Einstein himself, whom I had once met in Switzerland, had suggested study of this question.

The facts in this matter are quite clear. The metric notion of speed conceived as a relation between the space covered and duration is actually formed quite late and is not worked out before the age of 10-11 years in the child. But, before this, we find a systematic notion of speed based on purely ordinal considerations: the faster of two moving objects is the one that "passes" the other, that is, which was behind it at a previous moment and which is in front of it later on. Passing thus supposes the order of spatial positions (behind, in front) and the order of temporal succession (before, after), but it implies neither the intervention of the space covered (spatial intervals as opposed to ordered positions) nor, above all, that of duration (temporal intervals as opposed to the order of succession of events).

As a result, speed is constituted independently of duration. On the other hand, consideration of the development of temporal notions shows that they are constituted in relation to speed: judgments of simultaneity and equalization of synchronous durations do not raise problems for the young child when it is a question of comparing bodies moving at the same speeds; but once the speeds are different, problems appear, as is true for the establishment of the inverse relation "faster = less time."

These results of psychological research inspired by a reflection on the epistemology of physics have returned to physics in an unexpected way. A French mathematician and a French physicist, J. Abelé and P. Malvaux, attempting to restructure the basic concepts of the theory of relativity while avoiding the vicious circle of speed and time (see *Vitesse et univers relativiste,* Paris, Édit. Sedes), have resorted to psychology to see how this notion of speed was constituted. In possession of our results, they then constructed, by means of the ordinal notion of speed as "passing," a theorem of addition of speeds, introducing a logarithmic law and an Abelian group in order to shift from order to quantity; and this theorem has permitted them to rediscover the laws of relativity. Here we have a fine example of the use of psychogenetic researches for the elucidation of notions which, outside this perspective, have classically involved a vicious circle.

Let us now return to perception in order to define the relation between a physical notion and the corresponding perceptions. We have just offered the hypothesis that the notion was not just derived from perception but involved an operative elaboration, reconstructing (on the broader level of representation) what perception had already elaborated, but on the more restricted level of sensory contact with the object.

The realm of speed furnishes in this respect a very instructive example (but also found in many other cases: space, causality, and the like), for there exists an evident analogy between perceptional construction and notional or operative construction of speeds, without this latter thereby deriving directly from the former.

In terms of perception, we can (1) compare the speeds of two moving bodies, or (2) judge the speed of a single moving body with eyes moving freely, or again (3) judge the speed of a single moving body with eyes motionless. In situation (1), perception is first ordinal, that is, based on the order of positions (passing and so on) without being concerned with the space covered or with duration (there is more than a 50 per cent chance of contradiction between the three kinds of data when evaluated); but perception is also "hyperordinal" (to use Suppes' term), that is, it is also based on the more or less rapidly increasing or decreasing intervals between the moving bodies. The same is true of situation (2), but since there is only a single external moving body, the second moving body is the eye itself. For instance, there is an acceleration effect, upon the appearance of the external moving body in the field of vision, which is due to a speed relative to that of the eye: the eye is late because it lacks immediate adaptation to this appearance. As for situation (3), in which the eye is motionless, two distinct speeds still intervene, that of the beginning and that of the termination of the series of excitations during their passage across the retina. In this case, the moving body seems faster in the fovea than in the periphery because in the latter the persistence of retinal excitations is greater and the termination of the series of excitations is late in relation to the passage of the initial excitations.

Thus we see that the mechanism of the perceptions of speed is indeed comparable to that of the construction of the corresponding notions, since both are of an ordinal nature. But perception initially outstrips the notion, since it reaches a hyperordinal level more rapidly. Afterward, the notion exceeds perception, since it achieves, around the age of 10-11 years, a metric level (spaces related to durations). However, there is a remarkable analogy in the procedures of construction.

But from this analogy in constructive mechanisms we may not conclude that notions, even physical ones, are merely derived from the corresponding perceptions. The relationship between these two kinds of formations is only indirect because they have a common source from which they both proceed; this is the group of sensorimotor mechanisms, from which have come the operative schemata engendering notions and of which the perceptional mechanisms constitute only a particular sector. From the epistemological point of view, it is essential to underline this fact, for the empiricist epistemologies forget the role of the subject's activity when they attempt to explain notions by a simple abstraction from perceptions. When the common source of notional operations and of perceptional mechanisms is to be sought in sensorimotor activities, then the knowledge of the subject and the subject itself, like the object, play a necessary role in such knowledge. We have here, in other words, a verification of the thesis of knowledge as assimilation as opposed to that of knowledge as copying.

CONCLUSION

The great epistemologies of history have all referred to psychology in one form or another, and the empiricist epistemologies, from Locke and Hume to John Stuart Mill or Spencer, have done so quite explicitly in order to justify their particular theses. But the psychology which all of them invoked was that of common sense or of the very beginnings of experimental psychology, and, although every epistemology has defended theses as to the origins of knowledge, all these theses were elaborated before there existed in scientific form a genetic psychology or a psychology of development! The moment has therefore come, now that such a discipline has been constituted and its first results are known, to compare the data concerning the formation of knowledge with the many epistemological hypotheses, classical or recent.

It is such a comparison whose possibility I have attempted to show, quite schematically, in this chapter, and which genetic epistemology has taken as its mission to pursue systematically. The comparison is facilitated by the fact that the study of the formation of cognitive structures in the child raises, of itself and in an intrinsic manner, a series of epistemological questions which converge with the great problems of the philosophy of the sciences: relations of logic with language or with general coordinations of action, intuitive nature or logic of number, deductionism in mathematics or role of the structures according to Bourbaki, perceptional or operative nature of space, relations between speed and time, nature of causality, formation of subjective probabilities, relations between induction and deduction—so many questions, which I have merely touched on or have not even been able to approach.

But from these several indications there has appeared at least one conclusion: that the infinite varieties of knowledge, logico-mathematical or physical, never proceed from ready-made structures innate in the subject, nor from a simple abstraction from objects, but that they always suppose, in varying degrees, interactions between the subject and objects, which makes indispensable, from the epistemological and not only the psychological point of view, the consideration of the subject's activities.

4 TADEUSZ KOTARBIŃSKI

PSYCHOLOGICAL PROPOSITIONS

LET US BEGIN by differentiating among propositions which describe the ways in which animal organism change physically. If a man's head is overexposed to the sun, it gets overheated; if a bird is winged by a shot, it falls to earth: something happens to the head and to the bird. But to become overheated or to fall is not, by any means, to function. However, whenever the wings of a butterfly form in a chrysalis, or phagocytes collect around an infected wound and liquidate the source of infection, then, in each case, a living organism is not only being subjected to physical change: it is also functioning. For what is meant by functioning—the performance of a function? Is this not consonant with changing—but in such a way that the process occurs in a definite direction, that is, in such a way that if no circumstantial obstacles arise, the process of change is denoted by the final phase? In such a conception, functioning is action with an intention, but it is also action, subject to an unintended change, although occurring as if it were the intended action of a motivator.

Let us now differentiate between two types of functioning, internal and external. Growth, the circulation of the blood, digestion, the excretion of bile by the liver—these are all examples of internal functioning. Whereas the accommodation of the ear to catch a whisper, the scratching of an irritated point of the skin, flight from an enemy, chase, the catching of a victim, the building of a nest—these are all examples of external functioning. The former occurs within the organism and is usually concealed from the sight of an onlooker, whereas the latter occurs through the displacement of the whole or part of the organism and is usually externally visible. It is then necessary to differentiate between two types of propositions: propositions describing the internal functions of living creatures, that is, physiological propositions, and propositions describing external functioning.

The propositions describing external functioning should, however, be further classified into two subdivisions. One of these is the description of external functioning taking into account its direction, but not describing it as an activity, since the description is not concerned with the aim chosen by an activator. These are propositions from the science of the behavior of living creatures, that is, behavioral propositions, such as "The dog jumped over the fence" and "The crows are flying to the wood." The second subdivision is that of propositions of external functioning as an activity, that is, taking into account not only their trends, but also the conjectured intention of the motivator and all the experiences by which his externally visible movement can be explained. These are said to be praxiological propositions, propositions of the science of activity: "John took some medicine for his headache'; "People often lie through fear." It should be noted that praxiology is usually to be understood in a narrower sense as the investigation of the conditions of efficient activity; for our present purposes, however, its meaning may be extended to embrace the typology of forms of activity not necessarily considered from the point of view of their efficiency.

Having set out these preparatory definitions, we must now attempt to define psychological propositions. By a psychological proposition, I mean a proposition which contains a description of someone's experiences; but I hasten to explain the meaning of such a laconic interpretation. Let us take "John" as the name of our psychological subject: "John feels pain"; "John dreamed about green fields"; "John is troubled by an uneasy conscience"; "John is fully aware that $2 \times 2 = 4$." There are psychological propositions. Each tells us something about John; they inform us that John is experiencing something since he feels a pain, sees something in a dream, is worried about something, and is aware of something—all are varieties of experience. Within this form I include all cases, but only those cases, in which—to use the expression of an older tradition in psychology—one experiences some psychic acts or some psychic state. But these psychic acts or states differ in the experience which they provide, that is, differ in content of experience. Perhaps the most cautious method of defining psychological propositions would be to say that in essence their differences lie in their portraying somebody as experiencing in some manner. It is obvious that not all psychological propositions are of such extreme simplicity as the examples cited above; on the contrary, some are highly complicated. They embrace all propositions containing the verb "to experience," its synonyms, or any other expression denoting some form of experience ("He is troubled," "He is aware of"). For instance, the following is a psychological proposition: "The people got out of the crowded bus pleased that they had reached their destination after the uncomfortable journey." That this is a psychological proposition is determined by the words "pleased" and "uncomfortable" if the description of the journey is understood subjectively as describing certain experiences by the passengers. Psychological propositions are obviously not limited to descriptions of single facts, but often include generalizations, such as the well-known generalization that in old age people remember comparatively well the content of experiences long past although they often forget the content of recent experiences. There are similar psychological propositions on the ability or tendency to undergo certain experiences and to perform conscious actions. Such propositions concern such matter as the musicality of a given person, the cool nerve of a pilot, ability in mental arithmetic, and the like.

It must be borne in mind that the truth or falsity of a proposition has no bearing on its qualification as a psychological proposition. A psychological thesis does not cease to be psychological even if it is clearly false, as, for example, is the statement that "The majority of five-year-old children can work out differential equations in their heads." The reader may consider an explanation of such a statement superfluous; nevertheless, it would be difficult to deny consideration to the following as psychological propositions: tautologisms, in which the truth is of a formal-analytical character, and absurd statements of such a false type as "John is merry or it is not true that John is merry" (tautology), or "John is merry but it is not true that John is merry" (absurd). It would be possible to refuse to recognise such propositions as psychological since, although psychology is an empirical science, no empirical premises are required to support or refute these statements: they are true or false by their very structure and by the meaning arising from their terms. Such a refusal, however, would go counter to the foregoing criteria. However, the remainder of this chapter will give no further treatment to psychological propositions of such construction.

Are the physiological, behavioral, and praxiological propositions differentiated above psychological propositions? There can be little doubt as to the physiological propositions. They are not psychological since they convey no reference to experience, although physiological functions are sometimes accompanied by experiences which are naturally dependent upon them.

Behavioral propositions, however, require consideration. In sentences such as "The dog is chasing a hare" or "The bird is building a nest," the words "chase" and "build" seem to contain in their meaning the experience characteristic for psychological statements: "To chase" means "to run after in order to catch," implying the desire to catch and, thus, a certain experience. *Mutatis mutandis,* the same must be said of the word "build." However, it has been pointed out that, although behavioral sentences express some definite aim, this aim is taken, merely as stating the objective direction of movements. Let us now consider two ways of expressing this direction. As just delineated, the first method defines a given movement as occurring "as if" the organism were acting with the conscious aim of reaching a defined state. In such a case a behavioral proposition is psychological, since after the phrase "as if" there appears, with varying degrees of definiteness, "it experiences." "Bees breed a chosen grub as queen" may mean that the bees behave as though they wished the chosen grub to grow into a candidate for mother to the hive. And if this behavioral sentence is so understood, then it should be accounted a psychological proposition. However, the second method of understanding behavioral propositions, in describing a given function, without deprecating words of a psychological origin, interprets them in a completely unpsychological manner. The action of eating by an animal, for instance, may be taken to mean simply a series of movements defined by the usual concluding phase in which the animal's digestive organs are filled with food. In this case it is only the direction of the process which is being considered, as one would describe the way in which a plant blossoms and bears fruit, without reference to conscious motivation, even through the agency of the phrase "as if." In such a conception, behavioral propositions are not psychological. However, there is no room for doubt that praxiological propositions are psychological in character.

Having considered the variety of psychological propositions, let us now turn to their construction. However involved a proposition may be, it contains in its composition a straightforward psychological proposition, that is, a proposition equivalent to one with the structure "A experiences this and that," "Every A experiences this or that," or "Some As experience this or that." In short, such a psychological proposition is a subjective sentence with a varying quantification of the subject and corresponding conjugations of a specific psychological verb. Sometimes a simple psychological statement exhausts the whole psychological proposition, as in "John smelled a pleasant fragrance." Simple psychological propositions are often combined, with other elements, in involved, complicated propositions and serve to qualify the whole as psychological propositions. The following may serve as an example: "There have been frequent occasions in history when abundant food supplies have remained unexploited because people were afraid to eat a particular type of food."

Let us now consider the construction of simple psychological propositions (Kotarbiński, 1955, 1958, 1961). They always fall into two parts: that informing that a given person undergoes an experience, and that describing the content of that experience. This may be seen in "John wishes that the frost would end," which may be changed to the equivalent form, "John experiences the wish: Oh, that the frost would end." The sentence "Peter believes that Mars is inhabited," subjected to similar analysis, takes the form, "Peter experiences the belief that Mars is inhabited."

Thus it is not difficult to see that, in a simple psychological proposition, the first part of which signalizes experiences of cognition by such expressions as "assumes that," "believes that," "is aware that," "presumes that," and the like, the second part, carrying information on the content of the cognitive experiences, may be quite disparate as to content, and only in given cases a psychological proposition. The latter is the case, for instance, in the sentence "It is widely known that children like sweets." Generally, however, the content of the second part is not psychological, and is in some way dependent on the field of reality with which the intellectual experiences of the given person are concerned.

Interesting consequences arise from this. When we are interested in people's experiences, we are usually concerned with the value of these experiences; if these are cognitive, their value is often defined by that which is cognitively experienced, for example, by the logical value of the convictions, opinions, assumptions, or ideas of the given person. But this value is, in turn, defined by relations prevailing in the sphere of reality with which the cognitive definitions are concerned. In evaluating them, we must then divorce them completely from the person undergoing the experience, and from his experiences, and transfer our attention to an examination of that sphere of reality itself, which is usually nonpsychological. Four examples will clarify this system of relations.

The first is the surmounting of psychologism in formal logic. Let us take as our point of departure the interest displayed by philosophers in the correctness of human reasoning. To reason is, in a sense, to experience, and investigation of reasoning may be initiated by posing questions expressed in the form of psychological propositions. Thus arose the fallacy of psychologism, which appeared to triumph at one point in the history of logic. The psychologists maintained that, since logicians are concerned with the conditions of correct reasoning and since reasoning is a psychic fact, logic is a branch of psychology and logical theses are also psychological. Psychologism was, however, an erroneous doctrine. Let us take for an example the proposition "If some birds are beasts of prey, then some beasts of prey are birds." To investigate the correctness of this reasoning, it is necessary and sufficient to decide whether, for all cases of A and B, if some As are Bs then some Bs are As. There was then a sliding over from the province of psychological propositions to ontological ones, in which neither the word "experience" nor its synonyms appear.

The second example concerns the comparative estimation of a teacher's qualifications for teaching a given subject in school, that is, what should be undertaken by someone who wishes to become a successful teacher of a given subject, say physics. The initial question is psychological in character since there is a psychological element in the phrase "successful teacher": a successful teacher is one who is able to effect the acquisition of knowledge by a second person. Nevertheless, it cannot be denied that to become a successful teacher of physics it is a primary necessity to concern oneself with physics, that is, to acquire and consolidate answers to questions with a content of physics, such as those concerning the speed of specified vibrations. In such answers one will search in vain for psychological propositions concerned with someone's experiences.

Our third example is derived from the theory of nonmaterial culture. Is it not a commonplace that technology contributes considerably to spiritual culture? and that technique itself considerably advanced by scientific achievements and thus by the contents of propositions expressing cognitive experience? This means that, in setting out to understand the process by which this culture is formed, it is necessary to divorce one's thinking from the people who were concerned with science and from their experiences and to concern oneself in proper, consequent order with that of which they became aware in their experiences, that is, with the most varied domain of extra-psychic reality. Progress in cosmological views is measured by the relation of the contents of the Copernican theory to those of the Ptolemaic theory; in neither of these systems of propositions does there figure the term "experience" or its equivalent, so characteristic of psychological propositions.

For the fourth example, let John be made to talk to Peter, so that Peter will be interested by the conversation. The description of Johns task is then clearly a psychological proposition. In order to fulfill his duty, however, John must choose a topic in which Peter is interested; thus, if Peter is interested in the structure of an engine, this will mean that John is obliged to consider together with Peter a combination of relationships free of psychological content.

Thus relations are strange since at least in some cases of evaluations based on psychological propositions describing some cognitive experiences, the invited psychological issue during the accomplishment of the task must of necessity give place to nonpsychological issues. I take the liberty of calling such a system of relationships "a paradox of cognitive psychological statements." And I pose this question: Is it not this paradox which explains the well-known fact that, both in the history of human abilities and in the art of transferring their results, the role of psychology is of less importance than it would seem to be from the psychological character of the initial issues of these disciplines?

REFERENCES

KOTARBIŃSKI, T. On pansomatism. *Mind*, 1955, **64,** 488-500.
KOTARBIŃSKI, T. Essai de reduire la connaissance psychologique a l'extraspection. *Atti del XII Congresso Internationale di Filosofia*, 1958, **5,** 295-299.
KOTARBIŃSKI, T. *Elementy teorii poznania, logiki formalnej i metodologii mauk.* (2nd ed.) Wroclaw: Ossolineum, 1961. Pp. 406-410.

5 ARNE NAESS

SCIENCE AS BEHAVIOR: PROSPECTS AND LIMITATIONS OF A BEHAVIORAL METASCIENCE

METASCIENCE FROM THE FAR OUTSIDE AND FROM THE NEAR OUTSIDE

The various sciences of religious prayer do not presuppose the existence of any gods. If a religion with a god G is studied, the researcher does not have to be a believer in G. The sentences he writes have meanings, truth-values, and designated objects that are independent of the question whether G exists. The phenomenologist of religion does not study the believer's relation to his god, but the believed relation. If the believer reports that lately his prayers have been heard and rain fell on his lands, this is used as material, as object, for analyses of various kinds. As to the validity or truth of the believer's assertions (insofar as they are assertions), the phenomenologist of religion retains his *epoché*. The same holds good of the existence of any objects of religious worship.

How far is it possible to maintain such a detachment and still understand what is supposed to be studied, namely, religion?

The programs for a science of science that are the primary concern of this discussion are characterized by looking at a scientific enterprise (or a part of it) as an object to be studied "from the outside," not as an undertaking to engage in and improve upon. They are phenomenological insofar as they maintain, more or less, an *epoché* in the sense above.

The qualification "more or less" is essential because there are theoretical as well as practical limits to the degree and extent of attainable alienation from the claims of scientists. Beyond certain limits, it becomes more and more doubtful whether what is studied is still science. After all, the practicing scientist explains what he is doing in sentences presupposing the existence of a vast number of objects—elementary particles, matter waves, stimuli, drives—and what he refers to as the scientific enterprise is defined in terms of intentions and aspirations.

50

On the other hand, the basic aim of metascience as discussed in this chapter is to study a scientific enterprise without engaging in it. The scientist himself not only uses but also mentions sentences in his own discipline. His work consists partly in comparing contemporary theories, thus implying neutrality within certain narrow limits. When these limits are widened, the conception of metascience envisaged in this chapter emerges. An answer to "What is cosmology?"—as a piece of metascience from the near outside—would describe the contemporary cosmological undertaking but would take part in assessing neither the truth-value nor the "fruitfulness" of the different theories, nor of the specific presuppositions of that discipline. This requirement, if stated clearly, implies that the metascience cannot even presume that there is a cosmos such as is described by the cosmology under study.

Falsification and rejection of a particular theory should not occasion retraction of anything said in the genuinely metatheoretic description of the theory and in its prior acceptance. But because the falsification of the theory sometimes also undermines the reasons for accepting the existence of certain objects or entities in terms of which the theory is described, the program of the scientist of science must be to eliminate sentences which presuppose their existence. It will, however, retain names naming the expressions used in the theories studied. In the metavocabulary "cosmology," for instance, may be used as a name of the expression "cosmology" in a cosmological textbook.

In order to avoid the very special problems confronting a "sociology of sociology," a "theory of learning of theory of learning," or a "logic of logic," I shall limit the expressions "a science of a science" or "x-ology of y-ology" to cases where x and y are different. That there are special problems connected with "x-ology of x-ology" does not impress scientists so much as philosophers. Thus E. C. Tolman (1932), the purposive behaviorist, says that he himself asserts "that all human knowledge, including physics and purposive behaviorism and our own present remarks, are but resultant of, and limited by, human behavioral needs and behavioral capacities" (p. 430).

I shall discuss the attempts which have been made to supply the conceptual tools for a certain kind of factual science of science, the behavioral. The discussion will, I think, bring to light considerable theoretical difficulties inherent in the programs of such a science of science. But whatever the ultimate limitations of a molar behavioral view and way of attack, I believe that this approach will continue to be a potent agent in the carving out of new fragments, disciplines, or departments of science.

We are in a position to describe a psychological system as an object only when we place ourselves within a frame of reference which is different from the ultimate, specific premises and rules of that particular system. This does not necessarily force us out of any psychological frame of reference whatsoever (cf. S. Koch's *Psychology: A Study of a Science,* and similar undertakings). The studies from the near outside are not independent as to general presuppositions of the science. The objects of the science are presumed to exist. A revolutionary change in beliefs concerning these objects might therefore affect the acceptance of the metascientific theories from the near outside.

RESEARCH BEHAVIOR UNITS: A LIST OF SCIENTIFIC DOINGS

Behavioral conceptions are generally pragmatic and functional—trying to focus on the deeds of the researcher and describing his theoretical results in terms of achievements and adjustments, such as bringing order into something.

In one sense, the scientific enterprise is described by its practitioners themselves in terms of acts or deeds. These descriptions may be improved upon by researchers looking at other researchers from the outside, but still participating in general. This aspect is what Albert Einstein (1934) had in mind in his maxim: "If you want to find out anything from the theoretical physicists about the methods they use, stick close to one principle: don't listen to their words, fix your attention on their deeds" (p. 30).

The behavioral metascientist will find that the scientists themselves have, in part, a vocabulary which seemingly describes a behavioral aspect of the general scientific enterprise. Let us suppose he takes over the terms in this vocabulary.

The initial behavioral metascientific vocabulary will accordingly contain terms in general use among practicing scientists: observing, experimenting, measuring, classifying, describing (in gestures, writing, or speech), explaining, predicting, discovering, inferring, guessing, interpreting (symbols, processes), proving, deducing, calculating, justifying, presupposing, defining, discussing, refuting, accepting as working hypotheses, posing a problem, proposing conventions, accepting conventions. In what follows I refer to this (fragmentary) list as the list of "kinds of doings."

The terms themselves permit interpretations in different directions, some of which lead outside the behavioral aspect of science. The location of the boundary depends upon the interpretation of the key terms "behavior" and "science." "Located outside" is a strictly logical, or formal logical direction. For example, logicians of science such as Karl Popper stress the view that they are concerned with relations between statements of science, such as implication, and that terms like "observe" and "falsify," as used in the logic of science, have nothing to do with processes in time, as do psychological events. In studies which are not logical in a strict sense, but often so called, the terms of the list of doings are likewise taken in nonbehavioral senses. Rather, one is supposed to study the *logic* of the use of "observe" and "falsify." What the scientist actually does need not be described in the terms of his factual science.

Even when (as throughout this chapter) "behavior" refers to the behavior of *living* beings, there is an institutional, more or less purely sociological sense of each of the words listed which falls outside the behavioral aspect of science. Thus, if one were to contribute to the institutional sociology of science, the accepting or rejecting of conventions would certainly be central themes, but the subject of inquiry would ultimately be defined, not in terms of behavior, but in terms of institutions. Furthermore, there may be a phenomenological interpretation, essentially bound up with the philosophy of Husserl or with related philosophies.

All the terms of the list, however, at least in one plausible interpretation, do refer to doings of human beings as individuals or groups. The characterization of observing, experimenting, and the others as "doings" is appropriate and significant in various degrees. Concerning explaining as a kind of doing one may, for instance, ask: Who was it that explained this phenomenon? Did he explain it completely? When did he start? Has he yet finished? Have others explained the same? How did he explain it? Did he do it well? Did he do any deducing in explaining? Why did he do it as he did? Could it be explained better otherwise?

Approaching his subject, the metascientist announces his intention to study some area or aspect of the scientific enterprise. The words he uses when he does this are not yet those of a metalevel; we may conveniently conceive of him as a scientist announcing his intention to other scientists in their common jargon. He may, for instance, say that he intends to "study our explanations as explanations." In spite of initially *using* the term "explaining," the behavioral metascientist is committed in principle, when carrying out his intention, to taking the occurrences of that term in speech and writing *as objects*.

What this implies is conceived differently by metascientists of different philosophical inclinations. To some it implies abstraction from intended meanings and focusing on the extensional aspects, for instance, on the string of letters e-x-p-l-a-i-n-i-n-g, or on a certain phonetic unity. By others, for instance some phenomenologists of Husserlian inclinations, the object "explaining" is taken as an intended meaning.

If it seems convenient to the metascientist, he will continue to use the term "explaining," but as a common name for occurrences of the term "explaining" in certain scientific contexts, or as a unit of intended meaning. To obtain fluency of use on a new level, he must undergo a process of unlearning or "extinction" which poses practical difficulties that I shall not discuss. Analogous difficulties have been discussed elsewhere, for instance, in literature dealing with the unlearning of natural or physical geometry when starting on pure or abstract or axiomatic geometry. I shall here assume that the extinction problems of a metascientist can be solved and that his objects can be named and identified by using the ordinary terms of the practicing scientist with new metalevel meanings.

One of the best surveys of pertinent behavioral literature is to be found in Campbell (1959). It refers to works by D. Bakan, G. Bergmann, L. Bertalanffy, E. Brunswik, D. T. Campbell, H. Feigl, W. Köhler, K. Lorenz, R. K. Merton, J. Piaget, G. Polya, E. C. Tolman, B. Whorf, and others. Most of these contributions have been made under the spell of a particular ideal, that of nomothetic science. There is a premium on general behavioral *laws,* as these quotations attest: "Categorizing is the means by which the objects of the world about us are identified"; "by categorizing as equivalent discriminably different events, the organism reduces the complexity of its environment." As formal scientists studying the research behavior of a scientist, we should investigate inventions in the light of his discriminatory behavior and capacities in general, his perceptions ("what he sees"), and his discriminations of degrees of convenience: "We invent logical systems such as logic and mathematics whose forms are used to denote discriminable aspects of nature and with these systems we formulate descriptions of the world as we see it and according to our convenience" (cf. Bruner, 1956, pp. 7-21). "Attainment of concepts" is defined as "the behavior involved in using the discriminable attributes of objects and events as a basis of anticipating their significant identity."

It seems more hopeful to look for structural and phenomenological accounts, taking behavioral science of science as primarily an idiographic discipline.[1]

VALUE OF A TOTAL BEHAVIORAL VIEW

By a total view of science, I mean a perspective or vision that, at least implicitly, embraces any part whatsoever of science as well as science as a whole.[2]

The implications of a total view, for instance of a logical or sociological character, may in principle be carried through consistently in the form of an elaborate construct, or emerge without being noticed by those who share the view. Thus, a psychologist immersed in research on general fea-

---

[1] To the above list of works, I should like to add some important ones which either explicitly discuss the possibilities of a behavioral science of science or are pertinent without explicit reference to our theme: Allport (1955), Bruner (1956), Geach (1957), Koch (1959), Kuhn (1962), Lewin (1952), Nagel (1961), Oakeshott (1951), Parsons (1949), Polanyi (1958), Popper (1945, 1957), Ryle (1949), Weber (1922), Winch (1958).

[2] It is, of course, open to doubt whether any author, past or present, is in possession of a total view actually covering all science, and not merely of vivid intentional experiences within which there is nothing which calls for a halt—for exceptions, restrictions, qualifications. I shall, for simplicity, ignore the distinction between a total view and an intentional experience covering a totality.

tures of learning processes, using rats in a more or less natural environment (not inside elaborate machinery as has been done recently), will in
the long run, or remarkably soon if intensively engaged, acquire a very
special way of looking at living beings as systems of behavior. For the
psychologist or philosopher who is interested in basic ways of looking at
and conceiving the world, any special views generalized or inflated into
total ones are of great interest. A behavioral total view has an intrinsic
philosophical interest.

The professional behavioral point of view, like many other professional views, has a strong intuitive component. In some researchers
(Brunswik, Naess, Tolman), it has had the character of a vision. To those
who do not share the intuition, more or less general statements about
science as behavior which are obvious to the behavioral scientist sound far-
fetched and unsound. For example, to look at *proving* as a piece of behavior or doing is rather rare and, to most, rather unnatural. But looked at
freshly and consistently in this way, certain relations are immediately evident, which are sometimes judged to be nonexistent by the philosopher or
the mathematician, who habitually takes a logical point of view in science
of science.

The selection of the terms of rule formulation is made on the basis of
existing rules and habit formations among the prospective users of the
rules by the rule-senders. If any major variation in habits occurs, the rules
will mislead or, rather, result in indefiniteness. This will be discovered,
for example, by a contradiction or a *non sequitur* within the formal system.
"A calculus is never completely regulated [*geregelt*] in the sense that the
rules for manipulating the sign complexes prescribe perfectly unambiguously the way of manipulating" (Naess, 1936, p. 152). Kaila (1941) argued that this view does not make sense, since we have proofs of the
completeness of the calculi or propositions and of the predicates. But
when the rule-giver and rule-follower are seen behaviorally "from the outside," the incompleteness is intuitively clear. It is also clear that "behavioral incompleteness" is different from incompleteness as conceived by
a participant in logical or mathematical research. The argument of Kaila
is conclusive only if the metalevel intended in a consistent behavioral account of rules is utopian or impossible in principle. If the latter is the case,
the behavioral "vision" is self-deceptive, and Kaila's view is correct.

Historically, the behavioral point of view gained its strength from a
dominant trend in psychological methodology stressing the importance of
defining the objects investigated in terms of observables. "Behavior"
came into favor in part because of a kind of maxim that a person's behavior
is completely and conspicuously observable. Because of its genesis, the behavioral point of view might be considered to be infected with a latent
"observationism." There is, however, no necessary connection between
taking a behavioral point of view and "observationism" as defined by

Peters (1951), for example. The behavioral point of view is independent of operationism and logical behaviorism; it does not imply that research activity must start (in time) with observation rather than with formulating a problem, getting an idea or hunch, or with a need to test an idea already there. What is implied in the idea of behavioral science of science seems rather to be a view of the researcher from the outside rather than as a colleague. The expression "from the outside" is to be taken in the metaphorical sense of "as a nonparticipant in his special doings" rather than in the sense of concentrating on the gross overt movements of the researcher.

In practice, for a nonparticipant the possibility of saying anything of interest about the researcher seems to depend upon being or at least having been a colleague. The behavioral "vision" is therefore dependent upon a process of extinction (in the terminology of learning theory); and because of the large scope of this extinction, it is tempting to say it depends upon a process of alienation (*Entfremdung*).

Concluding, the value of a behavioral view as a total view has several components: (1) as a philosophical system or subsystem of the "alienation" class, (2) as a means of keeping apart and working out in isolation the logical, factual, and other aspects of a vague or general question, and (3) heuristically, in suggesting concrete behavioral research projects.

BEHAVIORAL APPROACH AND BEHAVIORISM

The behavioral accounts of science are highly sensitive to the use of the term "behavior" in the conceptual structures of *psychology*. We must tackle the problem of what behaviorists mean by behavior.

In order to eliminate certain confusions, it should be borne in mind that behavioral scientists have not intended to follow the "ordinary usage" of "behavior." In the vernacular, "to behave" is usually qualified without reference to definite forms of behavior. The answer to "How does he behave?" is not "He is running" or "He is testing his hypotheses," but the provision of adverbial qualifications like "admirably," "badly." To report on behavior and separate it from any evaluation is itself to behave rather strangely.

Let us inspect an astute behaviorist's comments on an example of behavior.

According to B. F. Skinner (1953), "Narrative reporting of the behavior of people" is "part of the sciences of archaeology, ethnology, sociology, and anthropology," but "only the beginnings of a science" (p. 15). As an example of narrative reporting about behavior, Skinner uses the following highly instructive sentence: "She slammed the door and walked off without a word." But such a remark is typical of a participator in social events, not of a scientific observer. Two other witnesses might have reported the "same" event as follows: "She ignored his question, moved slowly toward the door without looking at anybody, and disappeared." "After this, she did not do anything—just left."

If every truthful, conscientious participant's account is taken as an observational basis, behaviors will be strange, multidimensional events indeed. But if a certain selection is made, for instance, if "She shut the door" is preferred to "She slammed the door," a process of behavioristic purification is started which seems to lead to absurdities. What would be the correct, nonparticipatory description in which only the public, molar behavior itself is reported?

Let us imagine that an ordinary behavioral description is made more and more detailed and complete. Will it ever include a kinematic description in terms of smaller and smaller segments of behavior? It is, *prima facie,* very unlikely. Let us try to formulate a complete behavior description of an event, starting with an everyday description—let us take "She slammed the door." Is it true, as B. F. Skinner argues, that behavior is a difficult subject matter for science "because it is extremely complex"? It would seem that if the event, which took place within the interval of one-third of a second, were described kinematically in a ten-page report as a *complex movement,* the report, for all its length, becomes no more accurate as a description of her slamming the door. The real complexity is related to the "social structure" which may or may not make an event a case of slamming.

Guthrie (1935, p. 29 *et seq.*) uses terms such as "the continuing flow of behavior" and "total behavior" and suggests that science cannot cope with it in its entirety. This suggests that Guthrie wishes to define behavior in terms of movements.

What is indeed difficult is to make a *report* of the event "itself" which can be used as a *common basis* for various interpretations, some in terms of slamming, others in terms of mere shutting. I suggest that an "objective" report by a specialist in acoustics and a specialist in limb movements, "on the movements and the resulting noise," would scarcely constitute a report that could be used as such a common basis. On the other hand, if the participants' reports are taken as ultimates, one may no longer speak of different accounts or interpretations or meanings of *the same* event or behavior.

It has been stressed by Guthrie (1959, p. 165) that "the hope that response could be treated just as movements in space" failed to carry us very far toward the understanding of behavior. "Patterns of stimuli and patterns of response have their psychological significance and usefulness tied to their patterning—pattern as pattern must be recognized and dealt with." But *can* pattern *as* pattern be recognized? It seems that a pattern must be a pattern *of something* within or on something. Guthrie's critique of "an entire generation" (Koch) of S-R theorists leaves us in doubt as to what will be the subject matter of the next.

There is, of course, no reason a priori why "behavior" and forms of "behaviors" cannot, in spite of unorthodox semantics, be useful key terms within (so-called) behavioral science, suggesting a witness' view from the "near outside." But it must then be dissociated from reports about "movements" and associated intimately with terms such as "doing." "What is he doing now?" rather than "What is his behavior now?" is what is answered by accounts of the kinds that molar behavioral scientists class as observational. The usual answers about what somebody is doing are quite straightforward, in terms of the participator, at the witness level, not at the level of a complete stranger. Projection tests show that different people will answer the question "What is he doing?" very differently, "seeing" different doings. The resulting accounts are understandable and of interest to the acting person as true or false accounts of what he really is doing. If a report on mere movements is offered, he may legitimately protest, for the result is to substitute movements for doings. The same kind of protest is justified if the doings are in terms of other "far-fetched" frames.

Even in the cruder forms of behaviorism, "learning," "searching," "finding," and "making hypotheses" were not defined or conceived as classes of movements. In the field of rat learning, it was early stressed that the learning of a maze is not the establishment of any kind of definite sequence of movements or overt behavior fragments. In certain experiments mazes were inundated, yet rats easily found their food by swimming in spite of having learned them by running. Similarly, a description of research in terms of behavior must not be expected to consist of descriptions of concrete pieces of behavior (behavioral "episodes") corresponding to sentences of the kind "N. N. now falsifies the hypothesis *H*" and other sentences referring to the doings of scientists.

There is some truth in Ryle's contention that there has been a kind of "official" program in psychology to investigate states of consciousness as such, but since the famous article of William James (1904), "Does consciousness exist?" the mind-stuff theory has not had much influence in psychological research. The notion that immediate experience can be investigated as mind-stuff and separated from the "material" world was not taken seriously, and molar behaviorists rejected the dichotomy between "sense data" and "physical reals."

So much in defense of the behaviorist's general view. As regards the *results,* the view suggested by R. Peters (1951), that these psychologists were rather sterile, can scarcely be taken seriously in the light of the history of psychology since World War II (see Steward, 1954).[3]

---

[3] An inspection of recent volumes of the *Psychological Bulletin* reveals the great impact of the rigorous methodologists and system builders. The superiority of be-

My main contention in this section is that certain psychologists who called themselves behaviorists worked within a conceptual framework that proved adequate in dealing with large areas of problems and which directly furnishes a workable research program for a factual science of science. But it will not automatically be a science of science at a genuine metalevel, studying the scientific enterprise as an object, but rather studying additions to science at the object level. A program of step-by-step elimination of participatory assumptions is called for, starting from "nearest outside."

A scientific enterprise is seen from the near outside within a contemporary framework more or less congenial with the enterprise studied. This implies that there is, strictly speaking, no "actual scientific practice," or "methods such as are actually used" to be investigated behaviorally from the far outside. There are only practices as seen by participants in research, more or less colored by definite traditions and schools, and by prevailing terminological and conceptual idiosyncrasies and ideological convictions. The slogan "Do not listen to what the scientist says, but study what he does" is misleading. One must listen and take part.

Later I shall turn to certain grave difficulties confronting those who try seriously to implement a program of a science of science which consistently occupies a genuine metalevel. One of these difficulties can be clearly stated with reference to the notion of "operation," a central notion in behavioral descriptions of the scientific enterprise.

THE BEHAVIORAL APPROACH AND OPERATIONISM

According to operationism as defined by P. W. Bridgman, a concept is identical with a set of operations, and if a term is used for several operations, it expresses several operations.

An operational account of a scientific term or assertion is also a behavioral account, provided an operation is a kind of behavior. Operations are performances; they are carried out correctly or incorrectly and with greater or lesser skill. In order to make operations a subclass of behaviors, this term must presumably be interpreted in the direction of "doings."

Both the theory of relativity and quantum physics have contributed to a strengthening of behavioral tendencies in describing science. Physicists have explicitly distinguished between the intuitive pseudomeaning of a term, based on appeals to the imagination, and physical meaning in terms of certain doings such as measurement, which not only in theory, but also

---

haviorism (identified with the model stimulus-response correlation) to field psychology (response-response correlation) as argued by Burns (1960) does not apply to the behavioristic organism-environment view, because "environment" is analyzed into (1) environment for the observed organism and (2) environment for the observer. Burns writes as if the field concept of stimulus could only comprise (1).

in practice, may be carried out. In the case of quantum mechanics, invocation to manipulate certain equations according to a set of rules has often replaced appeals to the imagination. The retreat from *Anschaulichkeit* has been a retreat from "connotative imagery" in the sense of the behaviorists.

If it were required of all physical theory that all terms be expressive of *physical* operations, modern physics would not fulfill the requirement: some terms are mathematical. Operationists characterize mathematical concepts as sign manipulations. If a physical theory need be testable only as a whole, its terms then need not all be expressive of physical operations. The mathematical manipulations, especially in the form of derivation operations, can be shown to furnish contact between the physical concepts of the theory and the operations of testing, such as measurements. As I understand it, a necessary condition for tenable operationist accounts of modern physics is that testability is required of a physical theory (in the form of a hypothetico-deductive system) only as a whole, not separately of every proposition contained in it. If this weaker requirement is made, the operationist can meet the argument of Einstein (1949, p. 679) against operationism. He complains that operationists overlook the point that a theory, in order to be physical, needs to imply only *some* "empirically testable assertions in general."

The operationist account of physics is clearly different from a logic of physics in that the operations are conceived as observable activities. One is to *look at* the physicist and see how the different kinds of measurements are carried out. The operations are not conceived as rules governing observable activities. If the ultimate characterizations of an operation were to include a reference to a rule, this would spoil the postulate of observability. Rules are not observable activities.

Study of the operationist influence shows very clearly the danger of practicing scientists' taking metascientific theories seriously as guides for their own activity. Thus, the operationist influence in psychology has in part resulted in severe inhibitions of imagination in the researchers. In "heuristics" any kind of introspection, myth formation, or cognitive imagery may be of help to the theorist. And even in taking up the question of testability, there is room for much of this as long as the Einsteinian requirement, broadly approving as empirically testable any theory which connects at least at one point with nonverbal operations, is satisfied.

Strangely enough, it was among scientists of behavior that the idea of Bridgman's operationism as a kind of generalization from observation of scientists gained most enthusiastic support. Thus S. S. Stevens (1953), in a paper avidly read by psychologists, wrote that Bridgman in an "empirical spirit" observes the behavior of his colleagues and finds that what is considered an *explanation* 'consists in reducing a situation to elements with which we are so familiar that we accept them as a matter of course, so that our curiosity rests.' " (p. 160).

With this faith in a nonpsychologist's capacity of observation as a basis, it may be understood that Stevens felt he was "witnessing the birth of a new discipline: the Science of Science. . . . science-makers . . . asking themselves how they make science and turning on that problem the powerful empirical weapon of science itself" (p. 159).

The foregoing metascientific account of explanation implies not only that curiosity in scientists can be identified as a general attitude, but that a behavioral study can reveal the difference between "curiosity whether *p* or *not-p*" and "curiosity whether *q* or *not-q*," where *p* and *q* are sentences in physics. Further, it implies a criterion-measure of "familiarity" and of "reduction of situation." All these concepts would then have to be either defined in terms of scientist's doings or connected into a unified theory from which some empirically testable propositions might be derived (using Einstein's minimum requirement).

It is not here suggested that the idea of an empirical behavioral metascientific discipline of explanation is completely utopian, but that its implementation presupposes questions of observation and testing which must be faced squarely before anything is accepted in the form of general results. Even if, through observation of behavior connected with research occurrences of a term T, we are led—and exclusively led—to observation of operations, tremendous difficulties confront the behavioral observer in deciding what constitute the specific characteristics of a definite kind, B, of behavior unit or doing. The question, "Exactly what is he now doing?" is of a difficult type, normally capable of adequate answer only from extensive knowledge of the situation, which again implies knowledge of many happenings before "now." Operationists presume that they have the capacity of giving adequate (definite) answers, because they presume the existence of an inventory of definite, identifiable operations, each having some unique characteristics: "We must demand that the act of observation equivalent to any concept be a unique set, for otherwise there are possibilities of ambiguity in practical applications which we cannot admit" (Bridgman, 1948, p. 6).

As an example, let us take an answer to "What, exactly, is he *now* doing?" formulated as follows: "He measures the simultaneity or lack of simultaneity of two events far from a stationary clock" (cf. Einstein, 1923, p. 38). Exactly which traits or fragments of an actual sequence of behavior within a specified region of time and space are relevant and which irrelevant? Observing a scientist at work, ten bystanders who are not instructed about what the scientist is doing, or that he is a scientist, may each note down a hundred observations, each from his own perspective or interest, and none referring to any traits mentioned in the ordinary, conven-

tional description of measurements of time. The definition of the behavior
B (or, more precisely, of the kind of behavior) will be able to include
reference to only a small number of traits. A *principle of elimination
of irrelevant traits* is needed, and such a principle cannot be found by
an observer who has no education in physics. Bridgman (1949) indirectly testifies to the difficulty of operational analysis when he credits
Einstein with seeing the importance of certain details in measuring
which "no one had had the imagination to formulate" or "to see that they
might be significant." Normally, students gradually learn to know which
traits of behavior fragments are significant, that is, which traits are considered significant among contemporary experimental physicists. The
learning, however, does not include learning to give a verbal report stating
explicitly which traits are significant. The behavioral metascientist could
not get his data regarding the physicist's doings or behavioral units directly
from the physicist by asking him, even if, as a metascientist, he were able
to do so without giving up his metalevel.

The audible word-event "rascal" varies acoustically in an extremely
complicated way. No researcher has been able to characterize acoustically
the limits of satisfactory pronunciation of that term; the relevant acoustical
studies are guided by phonetic knowledge. Similarly, exploration of forms of
research behavior must proceed from an intuitive understanding as a "colleague" of the researcher studied. The absurdity or at least extreme difficulty of exploring in the other way (starting from more or less narrow behavioral observation and trying to arrive at the description of research
units such as "testing the hypothesis *H*") can be adequately experienced
only by trying to abstract from what our colleagues have "whispered"
about their research objects and research projects. An experiment of this
kind (performed by the author in 1938) consisted in noting down the overt
behavior of a psychologist engaged (he said) in studies of anxiety in rats.
The rat suddenly found itself on an unexplored open space and began
running around. High frequency of defecation and long distances of (be-
wildered) running were taken as manifestations of anxiety. Adopting the
position of (behaving as if) not knowing what the psychologist "had in
mind," the metascientist placed himself "accidentally" in such a way that
the rat could not be seen. He nevertheless succeeded in obtaining an
"observational journal" very nearly isomorphic with that of the psychologist by listing his movements with head, eyes, and hands. But this observational journal could be used for an indefinite number of different
hypotheses about the psychologist, one being that he was practicing certain
rules for coordinating head and eye movements and writing down symbols
for those movements in his protocol.

The lesson from this kind of "wild-life study" [4] of researchers is that one

---

[4] This happy phrase I owe to an amazed listener to the account of the "experiment,"
Prof. P. Suppes.

must be extremely cautious about claiming that an assertion belongs to metascience if (as is here the case) it is thereby claimed that it belongs to a science *studying* science. Suppose the metascientist, uncritically, had introduced his account by stating that the psychologist A was "studying anxiety in rats." Suppose further that he was informed by A, ten years later, that rats of course do not suffer anxiety, but only fright and that A therefore had not studied anxiety in rats ten years previously. The "metascientist" would then in a collegial way *change* his account, a sure sign of sameness of level.[5]

MAZE EPISTEMOLOGY

The shortcomings of attempts to describe the scientific enterprise from the far outside in terms of research behavior can be shown to derive from one fatal flaw, that of "maze epistemology" (Naess, 1936).

A psychologist constructs his mazes and assumes that his own description of them is the correct one. He introduces food or obstacles of various kinds and describes the movements of the rat, freely using references to his maze and the objects in it and postulating a drive and a goal; the rat is said to make correct or wrong turns, to be a fast or slow learner, to make true or false hypotheses, and to make good or bad cognitive maps of the maze.

But what happens if one of them tries to carry over the attitude of unquestioned superiority, or this absolute frame of reference of the experimenter, to the metascientist's studies of the scientist? One notices at once that the metascientist does not, and cannot, make the mazes. What is the scientist looking for? Where are the goal, the cul-de-sacs, the rewards? What is the problem situation? The metascientist must *ask* the scientist for information about the maze.

A description of science or the scientific enterprise may be said to be subject to the *error of maze epistemology* when the (would-be) metascientist announces his descriptions of the object of scientific research as the psychologist announces his description of his experimental setup— the maze, the food, the obstacles—whereas the descriptions are in fact more or less regurgitated information obtained directly from the scientist.

The error of maze epistemology results in the production of a quasimetascience, an ephemeral vision of science in terms of a part of the contemporary beliefs of scientists. In the interest of a genuine, if only fragmentary, behavioral view of the scientific enterprise, a step-by-step elimination of direct information by suitable methods should be carried out before claims to have reached, in part or in approximation, a genuine metalevel, are asserted.

---

[5] The well-known way out of this, to write "A *says* that so and so . . . ," has been sufficiently criticized to be passed over in silence.

The error is not only relevant to a description of contemporary science, but also to historical accounts. It is known in that field as the "error of absolutism" in relation to the scientific beliefs of the historian's contemporaries. Important chapters of the history of science have recently been rewritten by students of history who do not take the victor's account (for instance, Lavoisier's) any more seriously than that of the defeated scientist (the phlogistonist's).

REFORMULATION OF THE PROGRAM OF
BEHAVIORAL SCIENCE OF SCIENCE

Concluding, we may characterize a practicable and consistent program of molar behavioral science of science as follows: it is a program of description and explanation of the scientific enterprise in terms of the scientist's molar behavior units in the sense of doings, not motions, in research situations, using, as far as possible, the methodologies of behavioral science. The frame of reference of the descriptions, that is, of the observational journals, will *not* be independent of the conceptualization of a definite tradition or scientific culture. There will be no description of scientific practice in itself (*an sich*) as something invariable. A radical pluralism is thus called for.

The conclusion that participation is a necessary characteristic of the metascientist's relation to the scientist and his enterprise is of special significance to psychologists, because their own relation to the subject matter of psychology, the human being, is of the same kind. This structure of participation might be further developed as a supplement to the less fundamental discussion on formal aspects of psychological methodology.

BEHAVIORAL SCIENCE, LOGIC OF SCIENCE, AND
PHILOSOPHY OF SCIENCE

The rise of psychology as an empirical science in the last decades of the nineteenth century inspired philosophers and scientists to advance theories *about* logic within the conceptual framework of a psychology of association, often combined with biological concepts of adjustment and achievement. These quite legitimate inquiries were, however, often marred by excursions into formal logical and methodological domains—an invasion that met little organized resistance before Frege and Husserl because of the lamentably low level of active logical research in those times. When this situation changed, reaction against "psychologism" set in with such tremendous force that not only were psychological conceptions swept out of logic, but a kind of witchhunt was carried far into the domain of general philosophy of science, a field where many approaches are needed, and in which that of nonformal, nonnormative study must be fundamental in any delimitation of actual objects or processes studied. Thus, authors using terms which admit both of logical and nonlogical interpretations were criticized as if they *intended* to talk within the domain of logic, even if they did not. It is a stroke of irony that the anti-empirical attitude has been strongest among philosophers who, in a broad way, belong to the empirical traditions in philosophy, whereas the philosophers more influenced by Neo-Thomist, Marxist, phenomenological, or existentialist philosophy encourage systematic study of nonformal and nonlogical aspects of science.

The impact of symbolic logic and the renewed interest in logical problems quite generally, together with the perennially strong inclination of philosophers to rely on pure thinking rather than on masses of empirical material, has worked in the direction of identifying philosophy of science with "logic" of science. The term "logic" is used in more or less broad senses, the main emphasis, however, being on the philosophical irrelevance of actual happenings, for instance, the way a term happens to be applied. A nonfactual program is explicitly stated by Karl Popper.

The deep effects of trying to take up a consistently logical rather than factual point of view is seen, for example, in Popper's (1959) account of the empirical basis of science in his book on logic of science. A theory is (by definition) tested by basic statements. Certain stipulated logical or "formal" requirements for testing can be satisfied only by singular existential sentences. Therefore, theories are tested by singular existential sentences. Consequently, theories are, by definition and stipulation, such that we can derive the (admirable) falsifiability doctrine of Popper. What goes on is practically at all times *logic* of science—as we are justified in expecting from the title of the book. The question of observability is treated rather lightly, as are other "material" (Popper's word) problems of immense nonlogical importance, which emerge when we ask, What *kinds* of singular existential sentences are to be classed as basic? Which are the kinds that have, *in fact,* been thus classed until now?

Popper complains—rightly, I think—of traditional confusion of logical with nonlogical aspects of problems, deploring the ill effects for logic of science. I myself regret the bad effects for the material, or nonlogical, aspects. It is, incidentally, to be expected that explicit, consistent treatment of the nonlogical aspects will make it easier for the logician to eliminate them. The recent history of the logic of science has shown how difficult is this elimination. Today there is a tendency to derive material conclusions from formal investigations just because modern logic has furnished explicit and scientific ways of handling formal problems, whereas material problems are largely dealt with intuitively or implicitly in the absence of any established nonlogical science of science.

REFERENCES

ALLPORT, G. W. *Theories of perception and the concept of structure.* New York: Wiley, 1955.

BRIDGMAN, P. W. *The logic of modern physics.* New York: Macmillan, 1948.

BRIDGMAN, P. W. Einstein's theories and the operational point of view. In P. A. Schilpp (Ed.), *Albert Einstein: Philosopher-scientist.* Evanston: The Library of Living Philosophers, 1949. Pp. 333-55.

BRUNER, J. S., GOODNOW, J. J. & AUSTIN, G. A. *A study of thinking.* New York: Wiley, 1956.

BURNS, H. W. Pragmatism and the science of behavior. *Phil.,* 1960, **27,** 57-74.

CAMPBELL, D. T. Methodological suggestions from a comparative psychology of knowledge. *Inquiry,* 1959, **2,** 152-183.

EINSTEIN A. On the electrodynamics of moving bodies. In *The principle of relativity.* New York: Dover Publications 1923.

EINSTEIN, A. On methods of theoretical physics. In *The World as I see it.* New York: Covici Friede, 1934. Pp. 30 ff.

EINSTEIN, A. Remarks to essays appearing in this collected volume. In P. A. Schilpp (Ed.), *Albert Einstein: philosopher-scientist.* Evanston: The Library of Living Philosophers, 1949. Pp. 663-88.

GEACH, P. *Mental acts.* London: Routledge & Kegan Paul, 1957.

GUTHRIE, E. R. Association by contiguity. In S. Koch (Ed.) *Psychology: a study of science.* New York: McGraw-Hill, 1959. Vol. 2, pp. 158-195.

GUTHRIE, E. R. *The psychology of learning.* New York: Harper, 1935.

JAMES, W. Does consciousness exist? *Journal of Philosophy, Psychology and Scientific Method,* 1904, **1,** 477-91.

KAILA, E. *Det Kongelige Universitets Arsberetning 1938-1939.* Oslo: Bröggers, 1941.

KOCH, S. (Ed.) *Psychology: a study of a science.* New York: McGraw-Hill, 1959.

KUHN, T. S. The structure of scientific revolutions. In O. Neurath (Ed.), *International encyclopedia of unified science.* Univ. Chicago Press, 1962. Vol. 2.

LEWIN, K. *Field theory in social science.* London: Tavistock Publications, 1952.

NAESS, A. *Erkenntnis und wissenschaftliches Verhalten.* Oslo: I Kommisjon hos Dybwad, 1936.

NAGEL, E. *The structure of science.* New York: Harcourt, Brace & World, 1961.

OAKSHOTT, M. *Political education.* Cambridge: Bowes and Bowes, 1951.

PARSONS, T. *The structure of social action.* Glencoe: Free Press, 1949.

POLANYI, M. *Personal knowledge.* Univ. of Chicago Press, 1958.

PETERS, R. Observationism in psychology. *Mind,* 1951, **60,** 43-61.

POPPER, K. *The open society and its enemies.* London: Routledge & Kegan Paul, 1945.

POPPER, K. *The poverty of historicism.* London: Routledge & Kegan Paul, 1957.

POPPER, K. *The logic of scientific discovery.* New York: Basic Books, 1959.

RYLE, G. *The concept of mind.* London: William Brendon, 1949.

SKINNER, B. F. *Science and human behavior.* New York: Macmillan, 1953.

STEVENS, S. S. Psychology and the science of science. Reprinted in P. W. Wiener (Ed.), *Readings in philosophy of science.* New York: Scribner, 1953. Pp. 158-181.

STEWARD, J. P. Hull's system of behavior: an evaluation. *Psych. Rev.,* 1954, **61,** 145-159.

TOLMAN, E. C. *Purposive behavior in animals and men.* New York: Appleton-Century, 1932.

WEBER, M. *Gesammelte Aufsätze zur Wissenschaftslehre.* Tübingen: Verlag J. C. Mohr, 1951.

WINCH, P. *The idea of a social science.* London: Routledge & Kegan Paul, 1958.

6 ANATOL RAPOPORT

THE USES OF MATHEMATICS
IN PSYCHOLOGY

WHEN PSYCHOLOGY BECAME an experimental science about a century ago, it became inevitable that mathematical methods would eventually find application in psychological research. To see why this is so, let us examine the general role of mathematics in any experimental science.

THE DESCRIPTIVE ROLE OF MATHEMATICS

An experiment is a procedure which allows observation under controlled conditions. The results of an experiment are the recorded observations together with the description of the conditions under which the observations were made. Obviously, not all the conditions can be described. Only what is thought to be relevant to the results is mentioned. When an experiment involving some relatively unexplored events is planned, it is generally not known in advance what is relevant and what is not; but there is a way of making reasonable guesses. These guesses are put to a test by replicating the experiment. A replication is a repetition of the experiment while the conditions thought to be relevant are kept the same. If the results of the experiment are also the same, the conjecture is corroborated that other conditions, which had not been deliberately held constant (controlled) were indeed irrelevant. A stronger test could be made if some conditions thought to be irrelevant were deliberately changed. If no changes were observed in the results, this would be a stronger indication that the conditions were indeed irrelevant.

Such is the highly idealized paradigm of a controlled experiment. Ideally, we know all the conditions relevant to the results; in order to observe the results under another set of conditions, we can alter the relevant conditions at will; for a given set of relevant conditions, we always observe the same results.

We can specify the results of each experiment in this form: If so, and so, and so . . . (listing all the relevant conditions), then so (stating the

68

result). The more different ways the relevant conditions can be combined, the more statements of this sort we can make.

Suppose now there are n relevant conditions, and each condition can be realized in m ways. Then there will be m^n potential results. With even moderate values of m and n, this can be a prodigious number. If there are, say, five conditions, and each can be realized in ten ways, we can record 100,000 results! Obviously, by this process it would take too much work to record the accumulated knowledge and to make it available when needed. One of the functions of mathematical description is to remove this difficulty.

To simplify matters, suppose there is only one relevant condition, but that it can be realized in very many ways. This is the case if the condition is described by a numerical value. As an example, consider an experiment to determine the pressure exerted by a gas upon the walls of the container in which the gas is confined. Suppose all conditions but one are either irrelevant or controlled (kept constant), the only relevant variable condition being the volume of the cylindrical container, which one can vary at will by moving a piston up and down. The number of ways this condition can be realized, that is, the number of different possible volumes, is potentially infinite, and so an indefinitely large number of statements can be made concerning the pressure exerted by the gas (one for each volume). It turns out, however (if the temperature of the gas is not too low and the pressure not too high, and within certain limits of accuracy), that, although both the pressure and the volume change, the *product* of the two numbers specifying, respectively, the volume and the associated pressure remains constant. All our results can then be recorded in a single mathematical statement,

$$PV = C$$

where P denotes the pressure measured in some appropriate units, V the volume, also in appropriate units, and C is a constant, that is, a number which depends only on those units.

Such a statement as $PV = C$, into which many observations have been "packed," is called a *law*. Mathematical equations are admirably suited to express such laws; that is, they express many separate observations in a single statement.

Two questions immediately arise in connection with the statement of the law. The first question is whether the law really includes all the statements that could have been made under the conditions of the experiment. Suppose one hundred readings in the range of pressures from 0.1 atmosphere to 2 atmospheres satisfy our law. But we could have taken readings at pressures and volumes between the recorded ones. Does the product PV have the same value C at those intermediate points? To answer this question, we can take further readings. The ultimate question, whether the law holds *everywhere* in the range, will not be answered by this procedure, because there is a limit on how many separate readings we can make. However, experience with laws of this kind gives us a certain degree of confidence in the belief that the law we have established holds within the range, and we keep this belief unless it is controverted by evidence.

The second question concerns other possibly relevant conditions. Recall that we have kept the temperature constant. Let us now hold the volume constant, denoting it by V_0 to remind us of its constancy, and change the temperature, say by supplying heat to the container, which we assume to be of conducting material, so that the gas is always in thermal equilibrium with its environment. We will discover another law, namely,

$$PV_0 = C_v T$$

where C_v is now another constant. That is to say, the pressure will vary proportionately to the temperature, provided the temperature is measured appropriately.[1] Holding the pressure constant (for example, placing a weight on the movable top wall of the cylinder in which the gas is confined), and changing the temperature, we establish still another law, namely,

$$P_0 V = C_p T$$

where C_v is now another constant. All these laws can be combined into a single one, namely,

$$PV = RT$$

where R is a definite numerical constant associated with one mole of the gas. Now all three quantities, P, V, and T, can be varied at will, but however they vary, the quantity PV/T will remain constant (R) *provided the gas is in thermal equilibrium with its environment*. We have thus combined three laws into one and so have described many experimental results with great economy.

THE DEDUCTIVE ROLE OF MATHEMATICS

However, the power of mathematics as a language of science is not confined to its efficiency in describing the results of experiments. Besides a descriptive aspect, mathematics has also a deductive aspect which enables the scientist who commands this language not only to describe experiments already performed and to anticipate further results of *similar* experiments but also to anticipate results of *different* experiments, sometimes seemingly unrelated to the preceding ones. To see this, let us pursue

---

[1] The temperature T must be measured from absolute zero, about $-491°$ F.

the investigation of our gas by varying its pressure under somewhat different conditions.

So far, we had supposed that the gas was kept in thermal equilibrium
with its surroundings by having the walls of the cylinder made of conducting
material. In particular, we had supposed that volume and pressure changed
under constant temperature. Such a process is called *isothermal*. Let us now
suppose, on the contrary, that the walls are made of *insulating* material.
(Such a process is called *adiabatic*.) If we were to vary the volume of the
gas under these new conditions, we would find that the relation $PV = C$ no
longer held. By studying the relation between the values of P and those of
V, we might (if we were fortunate) determine another relation, namely
$PV^\gamma = C$, where γ is not 1, as in the previous case, but greater than 1. If
mathematics were confined to its descriptive role, this new relation would
be simply added to our catalogue of "laws." If we went on in this way, the
catalogue of laws would become very long, just as our catalogue of facts
would become unmanageably long if we listed all the results of a single experiment without attempting to combine them into a single law. When, however, mathematics is used in its *deductive* capacity, we can combine laws to
deduce other laws. When this happens, the laws fit into a *theory*. In particular, the relation $PV^\gamma = C$, which accounts for the experimental results observed in the adiabatic expansion of a gas, can be deduced from our previous
relation $PV = C$ (for the isothermal process) and from two other laws
established in thermodynamics. These laws are:

(1) If heat is added or subtracted from a certain mass of gas, the volume
being kept constant, the temperature of the gas changes by an amount proportional to the amount of heat.

(2) If the gas does work, it loses an amount of heat proportional to
the amount of work done.

We have now all the information to deduce the new relation $PV^\gamma = C$.
However, the deduction cannot be made unless the laws are stated in the
language of mathematics. Only then can the deductive "machinery" be applied. The mathematical form of these two laws looks like this:

(1) $dQ = C_v\,dT$. Change in heat is proportional to change in temperature.)

(2) $Q = JW$. (Amount of heat is proportional to amount of work.)

By appropriate choice of units, we can make $J = 1$, so that $Q = W$.

Now when the gas expands adiabatically, it does work at the expense of
heat loss (since, being insulated, it cannot receive heat from its surroundings). For each small change in volume dV, the amount of work done is
$P\,dV$ (pressure times the small change in volume). This must be compensated by an equivalent amount of heat change, namely dQ (from our law 2
above). Therefore we write

$$C_v dT + P dV = 0$$

If dV is positive, dT is negative, and vice versa. We had established previously that, for one mole of gas, $PV/R = T$. To calculate the equivalent of a small change in T, we take the differential of both sides (a procedure established in the differential calculus) and find

$$\frac{PdV + VdP}{R} = dT$$

Substituting this value of dT in the previous equation, we get

$$\frac{C_v}{R}(PdV + VdP) + PdV = 0$$

or, re-arranging terms,

$$(C_v + R)PdV + C_vV\,dP = 0$$

Now, C_v and R are both constants. Therefore the expression $(C_v + R)/C_v$ is also a constant. If we call this constant γ and re-arrange terms again, we get, finally,

$$dP/P + \gamma dV/V = 0$$

We now perform integration (a procedure established in the integral calculus) to obtain the relation PV^γ = constant. We have thus *predicted* the relation between the pressure and the volume of a gas in an adiabatic process. Naturally, the truth of this new law will have to be established by putting our prediction to experimental tests. If the results are as predicted, we have corroborated the underlying *theory,* which connects the facts established in thermodynamics with those established in experiments with gases. Thus we have done more than discover a new law. We have fitted several laws into one scheme in which the various facts are connected by *logical* relations. These relations are uncovered through the deductive use of mathematics.[2]

Several fields of science have gone through a progressive "mathematization," that is, a transition from a nonquantitative stage to a quantitative stage, in which mathematics was used descriptively, to a mathematico-deductive stage, in which mathematical reasoning became the predominant theoretical tool. Several of these fields are known collectively as physics. But the unity implied in the name reflects the unity of the theoretical method rather than the similarity of content. Mechanics, sound, light, electricity, magnetism, radioactivity—all of these deal with events which seem widely disparate. In spite of this apparent disparity, physics is now an essentially unified science by virtue of the fact that the laws governing one set of phenomena can be derived from laws governing another set.

---

[2] From the same theory, we can deduce $R = C_p - C_v$ and $\gamma = C_p/C_v$ and thus predict the numerical value of γ and R from the observed values of C_p and C_v.

The laws of thermodynamics and of sound propagation can be derived from those of mechanics; the laws of light propagation from those of elec-tromagnetism; and so on. In the last century, chemistry has been firmly welded to physics, physiology to chemistry, genetics to physiology, popula-tion dynamics to genetics. The links were cemented by theory developed on mathematical foundations.

The subject of the present discussion is the extension of this process to psychology. Here the same transition can be traced from qualitative to quantitative description, from descriptive to deductive uses of mathe-matics. Accordingly, we can distinguish between quantitative psychology, where mathematics is used mostly as a descriptive language, and mathe-matical psychology, where the emphasis is on deductive use of mathe-matics.

THE USE OF DESCRIPTIVE MATHEMATICS IN PSYCHOLOGY

Naturally, mathematical description becomes possible only after quanti-ties have been identified which stand in some sort of relation to each other. To use once more our example from physics, it was known for a long time that gases have the property of "elasticity." When we press on a confined gas, it "presses back." The statement "Air is elastic" is a qualitatively descriptive statement. We progress to a quantitative description when we have isolated two measurable quantities, such as pressure and volume, and have related these quantities by an equation, for example, $PV = C$.

To effect a similar transition in psychology, we must find appropriate quantities to relate to each other. When psychology was primarily a branch of philosophy concerned with the "properties of the mind" or "the nature of consciousness," or with the classification of "emotions," it was difficult to see how quantities relevant to these matters could be identified. To be sure, it seemed that the semiquantitative concepts of "more" or "less" could be applied to some psychological categories. For example, in the realm of sensations (supposedly relevant to "the nature of consciousness") one un-derstood the meaning of "brighter," "louder," or "sharper." One had some vague notion of degrees of intelligence (supposedly related to "mind"), levels of anger ("emotion"), and the like. But it is a big step from these intuitive perceptions of graduations to the formulation of meaningful measures and a still bigger step to the discovery of relations among the measures formulated.

Three circumstances give evidence that quantification of psychological categories may, after all, be feasible. First, categories previously thought to be intrinsically qualitative turned out, on closer examination, to have a strictly quantitative basis. Second, some introspectively perceived psychic states were found to manifest themselves in physically measurable overt changes. Third, categories previously thought to be only "weakly" quantifiable later turned out to be more "strongly" quantifiable. We shall soon say more precisely what we mean by weak and strong quantification.

A well-known example of a category believed to be distinctly qualitative but eventually quantified is color. Before the physical nature of light was discovered, it seemed inconceivable that the difference between red and green could be expressed by a number. But it can. What we perceive as "red" is the effect on our retina of certain electromagnetic vibrations, whose frequency is about 5.88×10^{15} cycles per second. Therefore, in a certain real sense, the difference between red and green is a difference of 3.7×10^{14} cycles per second of electromagnetic vibrations.

In sound, corresponding differences of frequencies of mechanical vibrations are already directly perceived as quantitative differences (we are aware of a scale of "pitch"). But differences of timbre are not so perceived. Nevertheless, differences in timbre have been found to be due to differences in relative amplitudes of overtones. These differences account for the variations of "tone color" in the sounds produced by different instruments and even in the sounds produced on the same instrument by different players.

An example of physically manifested psychic states is found in the psychogalvanic skin response associated with anxiety and similar emotional states. This reaction is utilized in the well-known "lie detector."

Finally, let us examine the different "degrees of quantification," which we distinguished as "weak" and "strong." We feel that differences of, say, length or weight are expressible more exactly than differences of, say, preference. Although we can say without hesitation that we prefer oranges to pears, and pears to bananas, we may be at a loss to say whether our preference for oranges over pears is larger than our preference of pears over bananas. Without a thermometer, we are in a somewhat similar situation with regard to temperature. We can easily arrange several bodies in order from the warmest to the coolest; but we perceive only vaguely the sizes of the *differences* between their degrees of warmth. The thermometer, however, measures these differences as well.

It seems, then, there is a distinction between magnitude scales (like the scales of preference), on which only relative magnitudes of pairs of "quantities" are recorded, and numerical scales (like those of length or of temperature), on which differences of magnitudes can also be distinguished.

When we examine the matter still more closely, we find that numerical scales are also of different "strength." Consider the scale of length and that of temperature. We know what we mean when we say that one stick is twice as long as another. But we can say with equal assurance that one body is twice as warm as another? It might seem that we could say that a spring day (60° F) is twice as warm as a winter day (30° F). Consider, however, the meaning of 30° F and 60° F. These are degrees above zero on the Fahrenheit scale, that is, above the temperature of melting ice mixed with salt. But there is nothing special about this "zero." The temperature of melting ice without salt (32° F) could equally well be chosen as "zero." Then what we called 30° F would be −2°, and what we called 60° would be 28°. Now, the ratio of 28 to −2 is certainly not 2! It is not even positive.

The fundamental difference between a temperature scale such as the Fahrenheit and the length scale is that in the latter the "zero" is fixed naturally, while in the former it is chosen arbitrarily. Zero length is indeed a zero magnitude. Zero temperature on commonly used scales is not. There is, to be sure, a zero temperature, which is naturally fixed, namely the absolute zero derived in thermodynamics.[3] When temperatures are measured from that zero, it does make sense to say that one temperature is twice as large as another. For example, this ratio will be manifested in the corresponding volumes of a gas under the same pressure, according to the equation $P_0V = C_pT$ discussed above. But this zero has no intuitive meaning for us (unlike, say, zero length). It was derived *theoretically*. In short, the quantification of temperature was "strengthened" by a mathematical theory.

To summarize, we have distinguished between three kinds of quantification:

(1) The *ordinal* scale, which allows comparison of magnitudes but not of their differences.

(2) The *interval* scale, which allows comparison of magnitudes and of their differences but not of their ratios.

(3) The *ratio* scale, which allows comparison of magnitudes, differences, and ratios.

For the sake of completeness, we should mention two other scales, the *nominal* scale (which is weaker than all the rest) and the *absolute* scale, which is stronger than all the rest. On the nominal scale, numbers can be assigned to things without regard for their relative magnitudes, as, for example, numbers are assigned to football players or to social security cards. On the absolute scale, numbers have *already* been ascribed to all the magnitudes. Such are the ratios themselves on the ratio scale; also, the results of counting objects, events, and the like. An important example of quantities measured on the absolute scale are probabilities. Probabilities are absolute numbers, because they are not measured in special units. In contrast, length, weight, and money magnitudes (all measured on ratio scales) have units. Unlike absolute quantities, the numerical values of quantities measured on a ratio scale depend on the units used (1 dollar equals 100 cents).

The mathematization of psychology has been intimately interwoven with the nature of these various scales and of the corresponding appropriate uses to which mathematics can be put. Obviously, the stronger the

---

[3] The temperature T must be measured from absolute zero, about −491° F.

scale, the greater is the range of mathematical operations which can be performed on the corresponding quantities. The tendency, therefore, has been to justify sharpening the scales on which psychological quantities can be measured.

In particular, the sharpening of ordinal scales to interval scales has been a major preoccupation of quantitative psychology. A standard method utilizes the so-called JND (just noticeable difference). Suppose we wish to establish the "subjective scale" for brightness. As we gradually increase the brightness of a visual stimulus, we may be able to establish pairs of stimuli whose brightness is barely distinguishable. Then the difference between the brightness of any two stimuli can be taken as the number of such steps (JNDs) between them.

In some modalities of sensation, intervals can be directly (intuitively) compared, as, for example, lengths. An interesting example is in the perception of pitch differences. A moderately musical person recognizes musical intervals as equal regardless of the reference tone. This is attested by the recognition and reproduction of tunes in different keys. Now different "intervals," as perceived by the ear, correspond to equal ratios of frequencies. This correspondence establishes a mathematical relation between the "objective" scale of pitches (frequencies) and the "subjective" scale. In fact, the latter are linear functions in the *logarithms* of the former.

One of the earliest investigations of quantitative psychology was concerned with establishing relations of this sort. The well-known Weber-Fechner law states that the relationship between subjective and objective scales is generally logarithmic. Recently, serious doubts appeared on theoretical grounds concerning the validity of this law, but these doubts do not detract from its historical importance.

As soon as a stable relationship is discovered among two or more variables, the stage is set for at least a descriptive mathematical formulation. Early quantitative psychology was understandably concerned with those areas where scales could be established of the sort that allow quantities to be related mathematically. The aim of the investigations was to establish quantitative "laws." Frequently, when two variables were associated, one was related to some stimulus magnitude, the other to a response magnitude. We have already mentioned the equation relating physical and "perceived" magnitudes. Even more straightforward relations could be established between magnitudes of stimuli and objectively measured magnitudes of *overt* responses. Examples are quantitative studies of reaction times as functions of stimulus intensity (which can itself be defined in various ways) and as functions of the number of stimuli in the set from which the stimuli are serially chosen at random ("choice reaction times").

The linking of physiology and psychology in Pavlov's work on conditioned responses opened the way to a mighty extension of quantitative psychology. Pavlov's physiological approach was transplanted to the

United States at the time when behaviorist psychology was in a period of exuberant growth. American psychologists concentrated on the study of *behavioral* variables in conditioning and learning experiments. This field offered a wealth of quantifiable data. Learning was conceived primarily as the sum total of progressive changes in the response patterns. These changes could be readily quantified: frequency of "successful" responses, latencies of response, persistence of response after cessation of reinforcement, and so on. The independent variables (controlled by the experimenter) offered an equally large selection: magnitudes, frequencies and spacing of reinforcements, complexities of the task, states of deprivation (supposedly related to learning motivation), and so forth. Lack of a priori knowledge of which conditions were relevant to the learning process made the list of possible independent variables (to be controlled or deliberately varied) practically inexhaustible.

Because of this wide range of alternative paths of investigation and the relative ease of quantifying the variables, and because the experiments could be performed on a wide variety of laboratory animals, including human beings (allowing quantitative comparison of the behavior of species), conditioning and learning experiments have for a long time dominated quantitative psychology.

THE ROLE OF STATISTICS

Here we must mention a peculiarity of behavioral data, which has put a characteristic stamp on the methods of quantitative psychology and, as we shall see below, also on those of mathematical psychology. Behavioral data are generally much more subject to fluctuation than physical data. Individuals, of the same species, vary much more widely among themselves than, say, different samples of the same gas. To be sure, individuals can be lumped into classes. But no class of individuals shows the constancy of behavior exhibited by, say, the class of all objects of a given mass (where mass is the variable of interest) or by a sample of a given compound (where the chemical properties of the compound are of interest). It is true that, viewed as physical or chemical objects, living individuals also obey the laws of physics and chemistry. But viewed as "psychological objects," as behaving organisms, they do not exhibit nearly so much regularity. Indeed, the very variability of individuals is of central interest in psychology.

Even a single individual shows variability in practically any trait: in his perception of stimulus differences, reaction times, rates of learning, preferences, attitudes, patterns of responses. Faced with this problem, psychologists who wished to pursue quantitative methods turned to the *statistical* description of data. A statistical description refers not to a single measurement but to a whole set of measurements, involving a whole "population." Frequently the population is a group of individuals, but it can equally well be a group of responses of a single individual or of a population of individuals.

The key concept of statistical description is the *distribution*. Suppose, for example, that each individual in a population is characterized by some numerical score. A plot showing how many or what fraction of individuals in the population are characterized by a score in a given range reveals the distribution of the scores in the population. A distribution, then, is a *correspondence* between score intervals and the associated numbers (or population fractions) of people.

The concept of distribution allows the psychologist to compare groups of individuals as well as individuals and so to establish classifications of groups. For example, the psychologist may be interested in comparing performances of two age groups on some task. He will be comparing two distributions. In general, he will not be able to test every member of both groups. At his disposal will be only samples from both populations. His task, then, is to infer the properties of the distribution of scores, in the whole populations comprising each age group, from the corresponding distribution in the samples. He will be comparing directly some quantities which characterize the sample distributions, say their means (averages). He will want to know whether the observed difference of the means really represents a difference in the means of the whole populations. It may have happened, after all, that the scores of the individuals in one sample came predominantly from the higher end of their population distribution, whereas those in the other sample came from the lower end. Statistical methods enable the psychologist to estimate the *degree of confidence* with which he can generalize his observations in the groups tested to the populations they are supposed to represent. To put it in another way, statistics provides a measure of the extent to which generalizations based on less than absolutely reliable observations need to be qualified.

The need to qualify "facts" implies *a fortiori* the need to qualify "laws." Where the physicist can speak with confidence of a mathematical function which relates one variable to another, the psychologist, dealing at each step with a distribution of the dependent variable associated with a fixed value of an independent variable, speaks only of a correlation of the two variables.

Correlations, like mathematical functions, are related to the notion of causality. We say that Y may be a cause of X if X occurs when and only when Y occurs. We have more confidence in our conjecture if we can make X occur (or cease) at will and if, when we do so, Y also invariably occurs or ceases.

Suppose now that X and Y are functionally related by the equation $y = f(x)$, meaning that, whenever X assumes a given numerical value x, Y assumes a certain corresponding numerical value y. Again we may con-

jecture that Y is the cause of X, and again we can do so with some confidence only if we can impose at will different values to X, observing, as
we do so, that Y follows suit, as determined by the relation $y = f(x)$. For
example, having observed for many days that the direction of the sun in the
sky is an exact mathematical function of the time of day, as shown on our
watch, we cannot conclude that the relation is a causal one. Indeed, we can
show that it is not by moving the hands of the watch without any per-
ceptible effect on the sun. In short, a mathematical function represents
a sort of weakened causality. The existence of strict causality implies
the existence of a mathematical function, but not vice versa.

What has been said of mathematical function applies to correlation. However, correlation offers weaker evidence for causality than a mathematical
function, for a correlation does not pinpoint a value of the dependent variable for each value of the independent variable. Instead, a correlation
associates to each value of the independent variable a *range* of values
of the dependent variable between which we can be reasonably sure the
latter may fluctuate. The narrower this range, the stronger is the correlation. If the range reduces to a point, we have a mathematical function,
the limiting case of a correlation.

The degree to which a relation between two variables x and y approaches a linear function $y = ax + b$ is represented by a number known
as the correlation coefficient. Thus number, as appears from our discussion, indicates a "degree of causality" (if causality is indeed behind the
correlation) connecting the variables. If there are several causal factors associated with a given phenomenon, correlation measures indicate the extent to whch each of the partial causes contributes to the total effect. There
are many statistical techniques designed to analyze this pattern of possible
causal contributions. A well-known one is known as *analysis of variance*.

Techniques such as the analysis of variance have been introduced into
psychology to meet the crucial difficulty of applying exact quantitative
methods in that field. An essential difference between an experiment in
physics and one in psychology is that in the former all but the variables
studied can usually be kept effectively constant, so that the relationships
studied are truly those among the variables observed. In psychological experiments, this is not the case. Extraneous, uncontrolled variables force
themselves constantly into the picture or exert a covert influence on the
results. Consequently, exact mathematical functions can rarely be established. Correlations, on the other hand, persist even if the basic causal
relations are masked by multiple and variable factors. It is the object of
many statistical techniques to "tease out" the contributions of various
factors to the range of variation of the results. In this way, mathematics
is put to use to deal with the complexity of causal relations which characterize psychological data.

One of these techniques, in particular, growing out of the analysis of variance, has found a wide range of applications, namely *factor analysis*. The original task of factor analysis was to reveal the independent (mutually uncorrelated) "factors," in terms of which a performance of a subject on some task can be described. These factors become the coordinate axes of a multidimensional space, in which the performance scores become points. The coordinates of the points represent the magnitudes of the distinct "abilities" contributing to the total score.

In search of these abilities, we could subdivide the task into subtasks and record the corresponding subscores. However, we would not know without further analysis whether these subtasks tap independent abilities. Conceivably, only one ability may be relevant to the total task. If this is so, the subscores recorded for a population of subjects will be strongly correlated: individuals ranking low (high) in one subscore will tend to rank low (high) on all of them. If there are two such underlying abilities (say in arithmetic and in space perception), it may happen that one group of subtasks taps one of them and another group taps the other. If so, then the subscores within the corresponding groups of subtasks will be correlated, but not subscores between the groups. It may happen, however, that both abilities are involved in all of the subtasks in varying degrees. Then this neat split of correlations will not be observed. A factor analysis, on the other hand, will reveal the two abilities even if they are mixed in the subtasks.

The same technique applies in principle to the quantitative study of personality. Such studies usually make use of questionnaires in which the subjects' attitudes or reported behavior patterns are recorded on ordinal scales. Attitudes which "go together" will be strongly correlated in a population of subjects (for instance, ethnic prejudices and right-wing political sympathies). From these correlations, a factor structure of personality can be established.

More generally, factor analysis serves to reveal the smallest number of *unrelated* factors (*orthogonal* factors, as they are called), which together account for the entire variance observed in a set of data. This method illustrates the use of mathematics in disentangling complex networks of causality.

Closely related to factor analysis are "unfolding techniques" used to establish a preference or perception space with respect to a set of stimuli. Suppose it is possible in some way to establish a subjective "distance" between each pair of a large set of stimuli. The problem is to determine the number of dimensions required to "imbed" the stimuli as points, such that all the distance relations are satisfied. Naturally, if they are to be imbedded into a single dimension (like beads on a string) a very drastic condition must be satisfied: of the three distances associated with each triple of stimuli, one distance must be the sum of the other two. As the allowed number of dimensions increases, restrictions are relaxed. The minimum number of dimensions required reveals the structure of the stimulus space and so the components of the stimuli.

THE USE OF DEDUCTIVE MATHEMATICS IN PSYCHOLOGY

So far, we have confined our account to the descriptive uses of mathematics in psychology, where the aims are to summarize observations into relationships described by formulas, to estimate the degree of determination of a variable by others, and to discover the "structure" of interrelated effects. In every case, data are the starting point of the analysis. Another set of data provides another starting point. If this process goes on, the descriptions may multiply into a vast, chaotic collection. Knowledge so accumulated would be, to say the least, hard to get at when needed. We have already seen how the deductive function of mathematics counteracts this tendency. Without thermodynamic theory, the behavior of gases seems to follow different laws under isothermal and under adiabatic conditions. In the light of thermodynamic theory, both phenomena are instances of more general, deeper laws. There is no question, therefore, that it is highly desirable to use the deductive power of mathematics in any science. The only question relates to the feasibility of the procedure.

The feasibility of deductive mathematics in physical science stems from an early discovery of extremely general laws governing physical phenomena (for example, the laws of conservation of matter and energy) and from the possibility of checking these laws under strictly controlled conditions. We have seen how statistical methods have to some extent obviated the necessity for strict control (with a view to isolating a single variable) in gathering psychological data. However, the use of deductive mathematics in psychology is made difficult by the paucity of general psychological laws comparable to those governing the behavior of matter and energy as such.

This latter difficulty is somewhat circumvented in psychology by the use of *mathematical models*. A mathematical model differs from an established law in that the validity of the model does not come into question at the time it is formulated. The model is postulated as a starting point of a theoretical investigation.

Suppose we are confronted with data obtained from a learning experiment. An animal in a maze chooses one of several turns, of which some are "rewarded" and others "punished." As learning progresses, the "correct" turns become more frequent at the expense of the "wrong" ones. We could record the data by plotting the cumulated number of errors against the total number of trials. Since the total of errors is cumulative, the resulting curve will be a rising one, tapering off to a constant value as errors become rare.

The task of descriptive mathematics is to choose an equation relating w, the total number of errors, to t, the total number of trials, so as to fit the observed curve as closely as possible. Such an equation $w = f(t)$ will then represent the "law of learning." This approach would lead to an economical description of what was observed but would have little theoretical leverage. Confronted with another set of data, we would have to start over again. Conceivably, this time an equation of an altogether different type would give the best fit, even though the two curves were similar in appearance. We would be at a loss to find a unifying principle even if such a principle did underlie both laws.

The function of a mathematical model is not so much to describe the data accurately as to describe them *rationally*, that is, as consequences from certain reasonable assumptions. We might start with the following assumption related to our learning data.

"At any given trial, the animal has a certain propensity for making a wrong response. We assume that this propensity suffers a constant decrement after each wrong response (because of the punishment)."

Translated into mathematics, this reads

$$dw/dt = A - kw$$

The derivative dw/dt, being the rate of change of errors with respect to trials, represents the probability of error (the mathematical interpretation of "propensity.") The constant A is the initial probability of wrong response, and kw the total decrement suffered after t trials.

The solution of this equation (assuming no accumulated errors at the start) is

$$w = \frac{A}{k} (1 - e^{-kt})$$

Having thus *derived* the equation of the learning curve from our assumption, we can try to find values of A and k which give the best fit of the curve to the observed values of w. But our task is by no means finished even if we succeed in fitting the data. We can draw *further* inferences from the mathematical model, which we could not do if we had fitted the data with a purely descriptive equation. Recall that the constants A and k (called the *parameters* of the equation) can be interpreted in terms of our model. The parameter k represents a learning rate and A represents the initial probability of error. If we put $t = \infty$, we get $w = A/k$, the total number of errors expected. Now, k is supposedly characteristic of the animal, while A is subject to experimental control, since we can suppose that the initial probability of error is the ratio of the possible wrong responses to the total number of responses. Suppose we take the same animal (or a litter mate), to justify assuming the same or nearly the same value of k, and deliberately change A by changing the ratio of wrong turns to total turns in the maze. We are then in the position to *predict* the total number of errors in the new experiment.

We can thus put the deductive aspects of mathematics to use as it is in physical science.

The mathematical model has, as it were, both "forward" and "backward" logical connections. We have just explored the "forward" connection, that is, traced the consequences (predictions) deduced from a model. To trace the model backward means to deduce the model itself from prior considerations. In the case of our learning model, this could be done as follows. We may suppose that simple learning, especially in nonhumans, is to some extent a result of ordinary conditioning processes. Next, we know that the nervous system is composed of very great numbers of elements of various complexity—neurons, chains of neurons, nuclei, tracts, and others. Without for the moment specifying the nature of the elements involved in conditioning, let us see how we can interpret the learning model just discussed.

If, at the start of learning, the elements are haphazardly conditioned to each of the possible responses, we may suppose that each trial involves a "sampling" of the elements, and the probability of wrong response corresponds to the fraction of "wrongly" conditioned elements in the sample. Our model implies that the fraction of wrongly conditioned elements changes after each trial at a rate proportional to their own concentration. This would be the case if, for example, a constant fraction of the wrongly conditioned elements in each sample were correctly conditioned following the trial.

Note that the validity of the assumption is not the issue here. The purpose of the mathematical model is to investigate the *consequences* of the assumption. If the predictions of the model are disconfirmed or if the assumptions seem unreasonable on a priori grounds, we have a choice of an indefinite number of alternative models. We could suppose, for example, that the correctly conditioned neural elements facilitate the conditioning of other elements. This would imply that the rate of change of the fraction of correctly conditioned elements is proportional to the fraction already so conditioned and also the fraction not yet so conditioned. This leads to the equation

$$dp/dt = kp(1 - p)$$

where p, the probability of correct response, equals $1 - dw/dt$. The solution of this equation for w as a function of t leads to

$$w = \frac{1}{k} \log \frac{1}{A(e^{-kt} - 1) + 1}$$

where A is the initial probability of wrong response and k is a learning rate.

This model is, of course, different from the preceding one. It predicts the total number of wrong responses as $1/k \log (1/1 - A)$ instead of A/k. We have now two models to compare with the data and with each other for the respective degrees of agreement with observations. But we also have the possibility of interpreting the parameters and so to put the models to *further* tests in different experimental conditions or with different subjects (assigning different values to the parameters). Thus investigations can proceed more systematically, and their results can be fitted into larger theoretical schemes than when mathematics is confined to its descriptive capacity.

STOCHASTIC PROCESSES

The use of mathematical models in psychology is beset by the same difficulties as is the use of descriptive mathematics, namely, the variability of the data. Statistical considerations, therefore, play an important part in evaluating the results of testing a model. The mathematical theory of probability, which underlies statistical methods, enters the more recent mathematical models in psychology in still another way. We have already seen that probabilities of events are important variables in mathematical psychology. If it is possible to take very large samples of events, probabilities become directly observable as frequencies. But if the probability of, say, a given response of a given individual *itself* changes during the process investigated, then obviously a large sample of responses will furnish information only about the average probabilities in the sample, not about the systematic changes from response to response. A branch of probability theory which deals with sequences of events whose probabilities are constantly changing is called the theory of *stochastic processes*. This theory is now one of the principal tools of the mathematical psychologist.

A stochastic process involves so-called random variables, that is, variables which can assume any of a range of values, each with a certain probability. Essentially, as in statistics then, the objects of investigation in a stochastic process are distributions. In addition, however, a given stochastic process represents a mathematical model, derived from assumptions about the relations among the probabilities. Probabilities are represented by numbers on an absolute scale, and operations on them present no conceptual difficulties. However, admitting a "probability" as a numerical variable opens the door for higher-order probabilities. For example, in the stochastic theory of learning one speaks of "the probability that a given probability of response has a certain value." Thus, the elements of a stochastic model can become quite abstruse. Moreover, since probabilities cannot be directly observed, to say nothing of "probabilities of probabilities," estimation by statistical techniques plays a vital role in work with stochastic models. In this way, the application of the theory of stochastic processes provides an important link between statistical and mathematical psychology.

NEW AREAS OF PSYCHOLOGICAL RESEARCH
SUGGESTED BY MATHEMATICAL METHODS

We have briefly surveyed the various mathematical methods used in psychology. We have also mentioned a few content areas where mathematical methods have been successfully applied, namely, psychophysics (in which, for the most part, the relations between the physical aspects of stimuli and responses are studied) and elementary learning theory (in which changes in response patterns under reinforcement are studied.) In the last two decades, the psychologist's mathematical tool kit has been enriched by the development of two new areas of applied mathematics, information theory and decision theory. Both have been applied to psychophysics. But they have also opened up additional content areas of psychology to colonization by mathematicians.

Information theory provides a precise measure (on a ratio scale) of the "amount of information" in a stimulus, provided we can specify a repertoire from which the stimuli are chosen. For instance, if we expect to receive any one of n stimuli, each with respective probability p_i ($i = 1, 2, \ldots, n$), then the average information per stimulus received is calculated to be

$$- \sum_{i=1}^{n} p_i \log p_i$$

The application of this measure in psychophysics has to do largely with calculating rates of "processing" information. Stimuli impinge on the subject at a certain rate in information units per second. If the subject must react with appropriate responses (for example, in typing or in reading music at sight), he acts as a channel over which the information flows. It turns out that in several instances the characteristics of this channel can be inferred for example, its capacity, its ability to utilize redundancy in the signals, its noise characteristics, and others. Results of such investigations have been applied in the design of man-machine systems, in which human beings and mechanisms are linked in the processing of information.

Information theory has been developed as an adjunct to cybernetics, the mathematical theory of automata and automatic control devices. It has been suggested that the concepts of cybernetics be applied to a theory of the nervous system, particularly of the brain, whose primary function is unquestionably the processing and storage of information.

A partial linking of psychology and physiology occurred when the mechanisms of sensory perception and of elementary neural processes (for instance, reflexes) became understood. The slender channel connecting the two disciplines would be greatly widened if the more complex nervous activity residing in the brain were more fully understood. The enormously complex structure of the brain makes it very difficult to study this activity directly. Some mathematically inclined psychologists and psychologically inclined mathematicians hope to gain a better understanding of the physiology of mental processes by studying the characteristics of automata, which *simulate* mental activity. Besides the devices used in technology, there now exist cybernetic devices specially constructed for research purposes. Mathematical theories relevant to the working of these devices treat of parameters and functions interpreted as "memory," "learning rates," "efficiency of pattern recognition," and "algorithms of reasoning," all suggestive of mental processes. It goes without saying that direct inferences from the working of automata to the working of the brain are foolhardy. The value of the cybernetic approach is rather in suggesting hypotheses to be tested by physiological and psychological experiments.

Decision theory concerns rational behavior under risk or uncertainty or in conflict situations. A simple paradigm involving decision under risk is a gamble: should one accept or reject it? When opportunity exists for repeating the gamble many times, one can assume that the expected gain of the gamble will be the actual average gain per play. In this case, acceptance of gambles with positive expected gain seems to be a good rule. However, if the gamble cannot be repeated, it does not always seem reasonable to accept "long shots" even if the very large probability of losing a moderate amount is more than offset by the tiny probability of winning a very large amount. The seeming inapplicability of the expected-gain rule in such cases led to the formulation of *utility theory,* which assumed that decisions under risk are guided by expected utility of gains (in general not proportional to the overt gains) rather than by the expected gains themselves.

The problem of determining a person's utility function in different contexts has become another widely discussed problem of mathematical psychology. The situation is complicated by the fact that the probabilities of events, which are taken into account in "calculated risk," may be those estimated by the subjects rather than those objectively given. This leads to a theory of "subjective probability," concerned with the way people estimate probabilities of events on the basis of experience. A particularly interesting question is whether utilities of events influence their subjective probabilities and vice versa.

Mathematical decision theory has been applied to psychophysics on the assumption that the nervous system of a subject evaluating barely distinguishable or barely recognizable stimuli is faced with a decision problem under uncertainty in which different kinds of errors are assigned different (dis)utilities.

Another branch of mathematical decision theory of possible pertinence to psychology is the theory of games. A game is essentially a situation in which outcomes of alternative courses of action are determined not by a single decision-maker but by two or more, whose interests are wholly or partially opposed. The mathematical theory of games, coupled with appropriate experiments, offers an extension of mathematical psychology into areas where conflict situations and the concomitant psychological processes are of primary interest.

SUMMARY

In summary, the mathematization of psychology is currently progressing not only in areas narrowly circumscribed by physical measurements (as in psychophysics) but also in areas with which psychologists have been traitionally concerned—gross behavior and aspects of mental and emotional life. The use of mathematical methods has been at times facilitated by established correspondences between psychic and physical events (such as modalities of sensation, psychogalvanic skin responses as indicators of emotion, and so on). At other times, attempts to quantify psychological categories facilitated their definitions in terms of overtly observable events or in terms of theoretical constructs assumed to underlie the events (utility, subjective probability, information capacity, position on a personality scale). The only universal measure of gross behavioral data is the frequency of an event or of an observation. Accordingly, the frequency of an observed event became of importance in psychology comparable to that of the measured magnitude in physical science. The intimate connection between frequency and probability and the need to deal with the variability inherent in behavioral data have made mathematical statistics an integral and vital component of both quantitative and mathematical psychology.

7 WILLIAM BEVAN

ON THE APPROACH OF THE
EXPERIMENTAL PSYCHOLOGIST *

THERE ARE A NUMBER OF WAYS in which the several activities collectively identified as performing experiments may be figuratively characterized. One is as a game in which the goal of the experimenter-player is to confirm anticipated relationships in as expeditious, economical, and aesthetically satisfying a fashion as possible. The basic rules are rather simple and easy to learn; the techniques vary in complexity, depending on the phenomena under consideration. The intuitive strategies that separate the highly original, creative investigation from others come only after deep immersion in a problem area, but otherwise defy understanding. Two criteria are predominant: all solutions must be empirically grounded, and all operations, both procedural and conceptual, must be logically coherent. It is usually expected that those two requirements will complement each other. However, if they come into conflict, the experimenter, when he has satisfied himself that his procedures are appropriate, is committed to granting precedence to the empirical criterion and denying certain of the assumptions which gave rise to his investigation.

This chapter is an attempt on the part of a workaday experimental psychologist to describe the psychology of doing experimental studies of behavior. It is not a treatise on the philosophy of science, although much that is dealt with comes under the scrutiny of this separate discipline. My concern with certain philosophical issues is motivated by practical considerations related to getting a research job done. Issues of a purely systematic nature, often subtle beyond my comprehension, I leave to the philosophers. Neither is this paper a set of instructions on how to perform experiments. This task is left to the writers of laboratory manuals and the design statisticians. Rather, it is my purpose to identify the assumptions and attitudes

* This chapter originated as part of a series on perceptual frames of reference supported by the Physiological Psychology Branch, Office of Naval Research [Contract Nonr 3634(01) between Kansas State University and the Office of Naval Research, William Bevan and Harry Helson, co-principal investigators].

that I find present to guide my own work, and which I believe I hold in common with other experimental psychologists. The chapter consists of four major divisions: a delineation of the outlook and assumptions shared by behavior scientists, a description of their materials, some underlying properties of method, and a discussion of the art of doing experiments in psychology.

THE POINT OF VIEW OF THE EXPERIMENTAL PSYCHOLOGIST

Each experimenter takes certain things for granted when he undertakes to perform experiments; some of his assumptions are explicit, others are implicit. They deal with the conceptual orientation (which the psychologist calls his theory, although in terms of the criteria provided for theory-making by the systematists it may be poorly constructed theory, indeed) that he finds useful, the general nature of the phenomena he studies (these are superordinate to any particular assumptions dictated by his theory and thus would be held in common by experimental psychologists regardless of theoretical persuasion), and the nature of data and the properties of his method. Assumptions of the first sort will more than likely be explicitly stated. Many relating to the latter two categories go unrecognized, and one of the most important exercises any investigator, behavioral or otherwise, may engage in involves "teasing out" for scrutiny those that lie hidden in his thinking.

This chapter does not concern itself with assumptions relating to the content of specific theories. Rather, it deals with the experimental psychologist's broader biases concerning the material he wishes to study and the most fruitful way of going about this activity. The three propositions which subdivide this section represent the nature of his bias concerning his subject matter.

Behavioral Phenomena Are Physical Phenomena Almost without exception, present-day experimental psychologists agree on the correctness of this statement. That they all agree on what is meant by it is another matter.

One very influential interpretation of physical phenomena is identified with early behaviorism. From Watson to the present, many psychologists have insisted that behavioral events are in principle definable in terms of the substantive concepts that characterize the physical sciences. To such persons, for example, conditioning is thought of as electrochemical change at the synapse (Johnson, 1927), memory as involving the elaboration of molecular lattices in the brain tissue (Katz & Halstead, 1960), and emotion as the disruption of cortical organization (Hebb, 1949). Though concern for physiological mechanisms almost disappeared from the intel-

lectual currency of psychologists in the thirties, forties, and early fifties—
due primarily to the vigor and impressiveness of such persons as Tolman,
Spence, and Skinner—the return, in the 1950s, to an interest in physiological psychology and the explosive increase of this interest is testimony
to the depth of this conviction.

At the same time, there has been a persistent uneasiness about this interpretation. Originally, it stemmed from the problem of the status of introspective observations. Watson had equated the observable with the physiological and had declared that only the observable was a proper subject
of scientific inquiry. The existence of subjective events was even denied.
While there has been much parochial concern among the methodologists
of behavioral science concerning the status of introspective data, the concern of the working experimenter has been motivated by a more practical
consideration: accepting the criterion of intersubjectivity at face value
makes certain important areas of interest inadmissible to scientific inquiry.
Allport (1947) summed up this problem in his charge that psychology's ad-
diction to the machine model and its attendant preoccupation with
lower animals as ideal subjects have resulted in an inability on the part of
systematic psychology to adequately accommodate the most important aspects of human behavior—moral nature and social skills. This sentiment
has been expressed more recently by Koch (1961), who insists that major
psychological problems require that degree of sensitivity to the subtleties
of individual experience identified with the humanities. The physicalistic
orientation of psychologists also has been accompanied by a preoccupation
on their part with situational variables and an ignoring of value properties
intrinsic in behavior itself. Hebb (1952) has admitted that present-day
psychological theorizing is inadequate, but he argues that this does not
result from the use of the physiological idiom, but rather from the use of
an already-dated set of physiological concepts. In his view, the central
problem of psychology is the problem of thought, and the peripheralistically
oriented physiology of the 1920s prevalent among many present-day psychologists is not conceptually adequate to handle the matter of behavioral
processes identified with higher brain centers.

The central concept identified with the methodological approach of
behavioral science is that of intersubjectivity, that is, the requirement that
all observations be capable of confirmation by more than one observer.
This has meant to most psychologists of the past several decades that their
proper subject matter is circumscribed by the operations that yield dispositional concepts and those that constitute empirical-logical links between the hypothetical and the dispositional levels. That is to say, one
may deal only with events of a public character or processes directly linked
to them. Zener (1958) meanwhile has suggested that the criterion be
broadened from one of intersubjective agreement to one of replicability

of obtained correlations between sets of conditions and experiential report. This is not far from what logical positivists themselves are now saying. Carnap (1956) for example, comments: "Although many of the alleged results of introspection were indeed questionable, a person's awareness of his own state of imagining, feeling, etc., must be recognized as a kind of observation in principle not differing from external observation and therefore as a legitimate source of knowledge, though limited by its subjective character" (pp. 70-71). If the admissibility of intrapersonal observation as objective observation is recognized, then the methodological problem becomes one of technical competence, not logical constraint, and the experimentalist in psychology faces the need to enhance each observer's range of sensitivity to his own reactions and his precision and reliability in transforming these into data.

It is apparent that the public–private dichotomy present in the original behavioristic criterion for defining the admissibility of data results from some confusion between the nature of observations and the nature of data. Observations, whether they be of one's own dreams or involve the pointer readings so frequently mentioned by the operationists, are always, in the final analysis, subjective and private. Data, on the other hand, whether they describe dreams or pointer readings, are always public in nature, for they are human conventions devised for the communication of information derived from observations. The matter, therefore, is not one of public versus private realms of observation. Rather, it is a matter of the efficiency—that is, the completeness, precision, and reliability—with which observations are transformed into data.

This all suggests that behavioral phenomena are physical phenomena in quite another sense—that is, they have the same formal properties that the phenomena of physical science have. They yield data which are objective and replicable, and they are accounted for in terms of general principles, which, like physical laws, are assumed to be invariate for all situations to which they apply. Thus, as Adams (1954) has put it, "A sentiment or a physical system or a superego is just as physical a notion as a cell assembly, an engram, a reflex arc, or even an atom" (p. 66).

The problem of generality has a special reference for the psychologist, for he is faced with extrapolating from one phyletic level to another. A study of the interpretative activities of the experimental psychologist suggests that in these activities he takes recourse to analogy. To the extent that he can assume that the actions, past history, and biological nature of another organism in a particular situation resemble what he concludes his own would be in that situation, he will identify behavior in terms of his own behavior and experience. The confidence that he attributes to these interpretations will vary directly with the degree of judged similarity between himself and the organism observed.

Behavioral Phenomena Are Complex   It has become increasingly clear in the last decade that even the simplest behavioral phenomenon represents a complex of determining processes. This recognition is seen in many quarters: in Hebb's plea (1952) for an enlightened use of physiological models, in his identification (1949) of thought as the central problem of psychology, and in his theoretical interpretation (1949) of the course of perceptual learning; and in Koch's criticism (1961) of extant theories of motivation and his conviction that an understanding of the major problems of psychology requires levels of experiential sensitivity identified with the humanities. The current interest in perception also typifies this awareness of complexity. Classical introspectionism concentrated its attention on the sensory processes, which it viewed as the simple building blocks of perception. Its studies of these phenomena were limited exclusively to the identification of their physical stimulus correlates. In contrast to this approach, since the late 1940s widespread interest in perception has involved two aspects: a consideration of its motivational determinants, and the effects of both specific practice and generalized learning on it. Other interest in perception has involved early experience, social factors, personality organization, unusual environments (for example, those involving marked enhancement or reduction in level of stimulation as well as imbalances in the atmosphere and extremes of temperature), the influence of damage to the central nervous system, and the subtle and diffuse effects identified with drugs and changes in endocrine status. Traditional psychophysical theory, in both its Fechnerian and modern version, assumes that judgmental magnitudes are adequately specified by reference to corresponding physical stimulus magnitudes (Guilford, 1954; Stevens, 1957). In contrast, adaptation-level theory (e.g., Helson, 1959) formally recognizes three classes of determining variables: (1) the focal stimulus of traditional psychophysics, (2) the immediate background, of major concern to Gestalt psychology, and (3) residual stimulation, which includes a wide range of determinants, both identified and nonidentified, but which, it may reasonably be assumed, are predominantly of central origin.

The awareness of complexity on the part of the present-day experimental psychologist is seen in certain broad attitudes and approaches. He has of late shown more reticence about extrapolating experimental results across species and situations. In his animal experiments he has, to an increasing degree, chosen species closer to man on the evolutionary scale than the white rat, and in his theoretical exercises he no longer views the rat as a simpler version of the human machine. After many years of relative neglect, Brunswik's notions (1956) of representative design and ecological validity have caught hold, and more serious attempts to simulate in the laboratory the situation to which the experimenter wishes to generalize his results are in evidence—most frequently, this means "the situations of everyday life." He shows greater concern for the effect on his data of procedural variables such as order-effects, instructions, individual differences in the experimenter's technique, personality characteristics of both experimenter and subject, sex differences, and incidental situational factors.

Still, the profound influence of the experimenter on experimental data is only partially given formal recognition (McGuigan, 1963). At the same time, use of complex experimental designs to control incidental variables as well as to identify subtle behavioral determinants has been widely adopted by all but the most committed of the students of operant conditioning. These latter are more inclined to confine themselves to situational variables and, at least in prototype, eschew the goal of general predictability (Skinner, 1938). Even when interest is confined to the role of the focal stimulus in behavior, this now tends to be marked by a greater sensitivity to subtle relations in the stimulus array—as in Gibson's analysis (1950) of the stimulus determinants of impressions of form in depth—than has heretofore been the case.

However, the recognition of complexity at the empirical level should not be confused with the goal of conceptual simplicity which the experimental psychologist shares with other scientists. It would appear that even the most empirically minded scientist is not content with the production of data alone. Observations must be fitted together into an explanatory scheme that is logically adequate to the domain into which the data fall and which at the same time is neat, deft in contrast to clumsy, and pleasing. Why the conceptual scheme must be simple and aesthetically satisfying are profound psychological problems that we do not purport to answer here. Suffice it to say that aesthetic satisfaction appears to be the goal of all creative work and that this aspect of the problem is extra-logical. At the same time, the task of identifying what shall constitute a conceptually simple explanation involves certain logical considerations. Many of the theories of the past several decades lead readily to the suspicion that the common practice has been to begin with a point of view and then to work to preserve its integrity by the reclassification and exclusion of data that it fails to accommodate, by the introduction of auxiliary hypotheses, or both. Popper (1959) has made much of the subtlety of the epistemological problem of simplicity.

How knowledgeable the working scientist must become in the logician's analyses is a matter of practical concern. At present, he regards as most simple the theory that adequately accommodates, with the smallest number of assumptions, the largest number of phenomena within its domain. Furthermore, the assumptions are expected to be general and a priori rather than special and *ad hoc*.

Behavioral Data May Be Scaled or Otherwise Subjected to Quantification
The physical science ideal and the goal of scaled data are synonymous.

Adopting the approach of the physical sciences as a methodological model is tantamount to a commitment to quantification and to measurement as the physical sciences achieve them. In its most efficient form, this means identifying observations as numbered positions, along a single dimension, which may be summarized by the operations of arithmetic.

For the experimental psychologist, it is not so much a matter of whether or not he can quantify. The outcome is ultimately a matter of the convention he will use to describe his observations; at least in some respects, it will be arbitrary once his measurement model is selected. Rather, it is a matter of what level of quantification is most efficient with the phenomena he has under study; that is to say, what form of quantification communicates the maximum amount of information without distortion.

What levels are possible with behavioral data can be understood at least in part by reviewing the kinds of operations the experimental psychologist performs when he collects data. The great diversity of data that characterizes behavioral science can be identified in terms of two kinds of quantification: (1) counting and (2) measures of intensity. The rational processes involved in the formalization of data are either discriminational or judgmental, although, in the case of any particular datum, which is involved may be unclear. In the case of the discriminational, the experimenter need only identify the occurrence or nonoccurrence of an event (the event may itself be the occurrence or nonoccurrence of a difference among events). In contrast, the judgmental requires the assessment of degree of magnitude or the identification of scalar position relative to some criterion dimension.

The ultimate form that data take is not perfectly correlated with the nature of the collection process. Some counting data presuppose judgmental evaluation of several individual occurrences before discriminations can be made. On the other hand, some measures of intensity are derived from counting data and from certain assumptions about the relationship of the frequency distribution of these data to an underlying intensive continuum. For example, if one is interested in quantifying the preponderance of cigarette smoking in a particular group, he will undoubtedly count the number of smokers involved. But first he must set criteria for the identification of smokers and classify each case before a count can be made. Meanwhile, if one wishes to estimate the maximum height an individual can jump, one has him scale a bar, beginning at a height he can successfully negotiate on 100 per cent of the trials allowed. This procedure is then repeated with the bar a fixed increment higher on successive trials, until his 100 per cent success is transformed into 100 per cent failure. The scale value corresponding to this frequency count then becomes a reasonable estimate of the magnitude sought.

The complementarity of counting and intensive measures relates to the fact that, almost without exception, scientific data are representational. This is the case regardless of whether the conventions the scientist uses to describe the data come from his own experience or are acquired from physics. Rate of bar-pressing in the white rat may, depending on the circumstances, indicate sensory discrimination, strength of drive, or level of learning. The only instance in which behavioral data constitute direct quantification is when the psychologist is interested in performance phenomena per se, and here the nomenclature is the same as that of molar physics: latency, duration, speed, magnitude of output, efficiency, and the like. Even in the case of performance phenomena, none of the measures involved are fundamental in the same sense that certain physical dimensions like distance, mass, and time are fundamental, that is, independent of other measures for their specification (Campbell, 1928).

The experimental psychologist was committed to quantification over one hundred years ago by Herbart, by Weber, and by Fechner. In his *Psychologie als Wissenschaft,* Herbart argued that psychology was a mathematical science. Herbart's mathematics, however, was not measurement mathematics but the elaboration of rational equations in the service of a particular metaphysics, and it has not survived. But, along with Weber's empirical principle linking the difference threshold to stimulus magnitude, it did provide the basis for Fechnerian psychophysics, the prototype of measurement in psychology.

A metaphysician and mystic as well as a physical scientist, Fechner believed that if the psychophysical relationship could be quantified, the mind-body problem could be resolved. The solution he proposed he referred to as Weber's law. This he deduced from several assumptions: that for every physical magnitude within the sensible range there exists a corresponding sensory magnitude; that the origin of sensory dimensions coincides with the absolute threshold; and that from the Weber ratio it may be properly inferred that the difference limen (or any small increment in the stimulus) corresponds to a constant distance on the sensory dimension. Since differential sensitivity is proportional to stimulus magnitude, the psychophysical relationship is inferred to be a logarithmic one:

$$\text{Judgment} = C(\log \text{Judged Stimulus} - \log \text{Absolute Threshold Stimulus})$$

The construction of a psychophysical function then would involve basically two measures: a determination of the absolute threshold and the JND, and the cumulation of JNDs from the origin over the sensible range.

Fechner denied the possibility that sensations could be measured directly. All one could do was to count the frequency with which sensations (or sensory differences) were present or absent. This is equivalent to constructing a set of conditional probabilities relating a series of stimuli to a criterion response. Thurstone (1927a, 1927b) turned this reasoning around. The true judgmental magnitude corresponding to any stimulus magnitude is held to be the mode of a distribution of responses given to that magnitude. Assuming that the response dispersion for any stimulus is normal, the discrimination of this stimulus from any other reflects the degree of overlap of the two dispersions involved. When overlap is small, the two stimuli are easily discriminated; when it is great, they are readily confused. Since the degree of dispersion may be expressed in terms of any common measure of variability, the specification of sense distance becomes possible. This is formally stated as the law of comparative judgment:

$$\text{Judgment}_1 - \text{Judgment}_2 = Z_{12} \sqrt{\sigma^2_1 + \sigma^2_2 - 2r\sigma_1\sigma_2}$$

where Z is the proportion of times one stimulus is judged higher than the other, and σ^2_1 and σ^2_2 are the variances of the perceived values produced by the two stimuli.

The solution of this equation thus replaces the JND as Thurstone's measure of distance. Its presumed advantage is that it allows for the construction of psychological continua regardless of the nature of the stimulus scale—indeed, even in cases (such as, attitudes, beliefs, and so forth) where a physical continuum evades ready identification or logically does not exist.

Of late, both Fechner's and Thurstone's approaches to scaling have come in for serious criticism. For some time, the Weber fraction has been known not to be constant throughout the sensible range of the several sensory continua, and recently Stevens (1957, 1958b) has presented data suggesting that JNDs are not equal in size. Luce and Edwards (1958), meanwhile, have pointed up certain weaknesses in Fechner's mathematical reasoning. The most serious challenge, however, resides in Stevens' argument (1961) that it is not only empirically unjustified but logically untenable to generate scales from measures of confusion. "Starting from scales," he states (1961), "we can determine error distributions, but starting from assumed error distributions we cannot establish scales" (p. 37). To replace the Weber-Fechner law and the law of comparative judgment, he presents the power law.

Using direct estimation methods in which the subject is required to identify his judgment in terms of a numerical scale referenced to an arbitrary value assigned some reference stimulus (such as, the effective threshold), Stevens (1960) has assembled data on more than twenty sensory dimensions from which he has constructed rectilinear log-log psychophysical functions with slopes varying between .3 and 3.5. These experiments identify the power relationship in the power law:

$$\text{Judgment} = C(\text{Judged Stimulus} - \text{Effective Threshold})^n$$

where C is a constant having to do with the magnitude of the numbers used in the response scale and n is the exponent of the power function.

Stevens has concluded that the power law allows the construction of ratio scales. However, this conclusion, as Rosner points out (1962), needs qualification. On physical ratio scales, both intervals and ratios are defined. In addition, intervals and ratios are linearly related. If Stevens' scales are true ratio scales, interval judgments would be a linear function of ratio judgment. But, as Stevens himself has shown (Stevens & Galanter, 1957), category scales are concave downward when plotted against magnitude estimation scales. Furthermore, recent data (Bevan & Pritchard, 1963; Black & Bevan, 1960) which demonstrate that subliminal stimulation may induce shifts in category scale values raise doubt concerning the absolute magnitude of Stevens' reference values.

Garner, Hake, and Eriksen (1956) have recently suggested that, in direct-magnitude estimations, the subject is actually matching the perceived stimulus magnitude with subjective impressions of number, and that, if the psychophysical function for number were taken into account, the difference between equal-interval (psychophysical category scales are generally treated as equal-interval scales) and direct-magnitude scales would be resolved. If one considers the dimensions of sensory intensity and subjective number both to be special cases of a general scale of subjective magnitude, then a subjective number becomes the reference stimulus against which the judgments of magnitude are scaled. Subjective values for numbers are, we know, not fixed, but depend on the number context in which they occur. Viewed in this light, the number reference value becomes a part of the judgmental background specified by adaptation-level theory.

According to this latter point of view (e.g., Helson, 1959), the judgmental reference value is the product of both first-order (stimulus) and second-order (contextual) independent variables, as Rosner refers to them. Formally defined, it is as follows:

$$AL = \bar{S}^p, B^q, R^r$$

where AL is the reference value, $\bar{S}$ is an average of the stimuli being judged, B is the present background stimulation against which judgment occurs, and R is residual stimulation, that is, those aspects of context contributed by past experience and other variables not formally identified in the psychophysical experiment. In many psychophysical experiments, the experimental situation is such that the residual is effectively zero. For such instances, the expression may be written: $AL = \bar{S}^p B^q$. Since individual judgments are referenced to adaptation level, they may be described as follows:

$$\text{Judgment} = S_i - AL$$

where S_i is the magnitude of the stimulation processes associated with the stimulus being judged.

If it is assumed that there is some general constant (n) that defines the relationship between the physical and the subjective scales involved,

$$\text{Judgment} = (S_i - AL)^n$$

When the power law is written as the general case, it is as follows:

$$\text{Judgment} = S_i^n$$

When it is recognized that scalar magnitude is referenced to the effective threshold, it becomes

$$\text{Judgment} = (S_i - S_0)^n$$

Now, if the effective threshold is identified with the subjective neutral point, rather than the absolute threshold, and thus rendered equivalent to *AL,* the expression becomes

$$\text{Judgment} = (S_i - AL)^n$$

and the power law is seen to be a special case of the adaptation-level principle, derived from situations in which contribution of B and R variables is usually relatively small.

The approaches to quantification reviewed here have all involved the same measurement model, the single linear dimension of classical physics. There is currently much concern with the fact that, in many judgmental situations, stimuli to be judged vary simultaneously on several dimensions. This has led to two kinds of work: (1) empirical studies in which a limited number of dimensions are systematically covaried and the effect of this on judgment ascertained (Bevan & Turner, 1962; Turner & Bevan, 1962) and (2) the elaboration of scaling theory to accommodate sets of stimuli which vary on an unknown number of dimensions. In this latter instance, stimuli are represented as points in Euclidean space, the similarity of any two being indicated by the distance between them in this space (e.g., Messick, 1956; Torgerson, 1958).

THE MATERIALS OF THE EXPERIMENTAL PSYCHOLOGIST

The goal of the experimental psychologist is to establish scientific facts. These differ from other kinds of facts—legal, theological, and so on—in that they result from the application of methods which differ in certain important ways from those used in the nonscientific disciplines. But most, if not all, facts have this in common: they are derived, on the one hand, from concepts and, on the other, from data. "All that is factual," Goethe is said to have observed, "is already theory." Facts take shape against a conceptual background. At the same time, new concepts grow out of already established fact (Bevan, 1953).

The Use of Models   The conceptual framework of the experimental psychologist is many-faceted. Certain assumptions, as already noted, are related to the general nature of psychological phenomena. Others are related to the nature of psychology as an intellectual discipline and the methods appropriate to its pursuit. On these is overlaid the particular theoretical bias of the investigator. Inspection of the activities of the experimental worker as he formulates a problem prior to conducting an experiment and as he prepares to interpret his data after the experiment is completed reveals a frequent preoccupation with analogical reasoning. This helps him to see the nature of the relationships he anticipates among his data before they are collected and to tie them to other data after being collected. Much has been written in recent years about the place of models in the logic of science. Braithwaite (1953), for example, has commented at length on the relationships of the model to the corpus of a theory. Von Bertalanffy (1952) has classified models into contrasting types according to whether they are static or dynamic, molecular or molar, and material or formal. And in addition, Lachman (1960) has differentiated four types of modular function: as a mode of representation, as rules of inference, as interpretations of the calculi of theories, and as pictorial representations.

In addition, distinction must be made between the logician's concern for the formal properties of models and the practicing experimenter's use of models as instruments of science making. The latter typically will not (nor need he) give any more attention to the logical properties of the model than he will to the internal workings of a piece of equipment that he uses in data collection. Of course, he must discover when it is appropriate to use the model, and when a disanalogy exists: that is, when the model differs in some important respect from the empirical relationships obtaining among the variables of his experiment. But this last is a matter of common sense, experience, intuitive skill, conceptual artistry —things which are not the necessary consequences of preoccupation with logical form and structure. Indeed, it seems highly probable that the practicing experimenter's use of models is, in principle, more simple and direct than logical analysis might lead one to expect. Models must be simple and direct to be effective, and subtlety exists not in their structure but, as Oppenheimer puts it (1956), in finding the disanalogy that will enable the scientist to preserve what is right about his analogy. Each of the laws of Newtonian mechanics may be extended to atomic mechanics if it is assumed that the momentum and the coordinate are not numbers but objects such that the product of the momentum and the coordinate is not the same as the product of the coordinate and the momentum, and that the difference between these two products is an imaginary, universal, atomic constant (Oppenheimer, 1956).

It is vital that the importance of common sense to the activity of model-making be given recognition. Although it is true that the instruments of a science make possible concepts and data that transcend the realm of ordinary experience, it does not follow that what we learn of nature from ordinary experience lies outside our science. Oppenheimer (1956) describes a number of ideas identified with common sense that have been incorporated into modern physics after three hundred years of rejection from physical doctrine: the physical world is not completely determinate; there is a limit to what can be objectified without reference to the actual operations of observations; the phenomena being studied are inseparably linked to the methods of study in the evolution of data; events are indivisible, individual, and, in their essentials, not reproducible.

Finally, it is also important to recognize that success in the formalization of a science depends on its level of development. Regardless of the methodological sophistication of its adherents, one cannot expect the same degree of conceptual articulation in a field with few firmly established facts or general principles as one finds in a more advanced field. Certainly, to transpose a model from one science to another when the relationships between the two sciences are not clearly understood is an exercise of indeterminate merit. The fact that most discussions of the problems of theory construction and other matters in the philosophy of science which are written by psychologists draw heavily on physics for illustrative material, rather than on psychology itself, prompts the suspicion that a preoccupation with issues of so highly systematic a nature may be somewhat premature.

The Nature of Data   As was noted earlier, there is an important difference between observations and data. Data are statements that describe observational events. They may be expressed in many forms—in the natural language of everyday speech, in the technical language of some particular intellectual discipline, in graphic form, and in terms of one or another form of mathematics. However, regardless of their form of expression, all data have one thing in common: they symbolically represent—they do not reproduce—observations. Different forms of data communicate information from observations with different degrees of efficiency. Although the nontechnical verbal forms of everyday life provide the richest vocabulary for the description of experience, they are at the same time the most imprecise. In contrast, although its range of expression may be comparatively limited, the formal language of a mathematical system will convey information with a minimum of excess meaning. None will completely describe an observation which the observer regards as important or otherwise relevant. This is further complicated by the apparent fact that observers differ in the sensitivity and the comprehensiveness of their observations.

Psychological data fall into two broad classes: those having to do with the behaving *organism* and those having to do with the *situation* in which behavior occurs. Situational data, in turn, are of two general types: stimulus data, related to events impinging on the organism, and response data, describing the organism's reaction to stimuli. The traditionally defined experimental psychologist has directed his attention for the most part to situational variables (perhaps because the classical psychophysicist has for so long viewed the psychophysical problem as one of quantifying the correspondence between physically defined stimuli and sensation and perhaps because the classical behaviorist for so long insisted on equating objectivity with the language of physical science). Relatively little interest over the years has been displayed in laboratory studies of behavioral development, of individual differences, of behavioral genetics, and of similar aspects. By the same token, little formal concern in experimental design has been evidenced for variables like pretest experience and differences in temperament. Meanwhile, it is becoming increasingly clear to the experimental psychologist that it is possible to perform perfectly good experiments without being committed to the classical S-R epistemology, that the biggest difference in the laboratory work of the physicalist and the phenomenalist may be one of precision, and that quantification is not limited to the dimensions of physics. Thus, one may, in principle, investigate curiosity as readily as hunger and measure attractiveness as easily as brightness.

Indeed, if one examines the laboratory practice, rather than the metaphysics, of the experimental psychologist, one will soon discover that purely physical knowledge has never been adequate to the identification of stimuli and responses. To begin with, stimuli are identified by their capacity to evoke particular kinds of responses; the experimenter, in designing an experiment, falls back on his own experience as an observer in the selection of S-R variables to investigate. This is so whether the subjects are human or subhuman. I strongly suspect that even the most hardheaded behavioristic purist selects, as reinforcement for his rats in the lever-pressing or T-maze situation, objects which he believes are meaningful to them, though he could never admit this in his theory. But this last is exactly what is necessary. Theoretical exercise must be made consistent with laboratory practice, and if the identification of S and R reflects, to use Koch's phrase (1959), "the perceptual sensitivities of human observers," this property must be incorporated into their definition within the corpus of a theory.

Converging Operations Two broad metholodogical problems are faced in the definition of stimuli and responses: validity and reliability. In the case of the former, the concern is that the measures or other operations that the experimenter devises to represent a variable under consideration be truly representative. In the latter, interest is in the consistency resident in the measure. For the past thirty years, psychologists have been enthusiastic advocates of the doctrine of operationism, and in this time the literature reveals many instances of its uncritical application.

Investigators appear to proceed to their experiments with the assumption that, if they can invent an operation to measure a concept, it will be adequate to doing so. Thus, it may be taken for granted that if a rat is deprived of food for a certain period of time he will be motivated to run through a maze to obtain a pellet of food in the goal box, or that if a human subject is given a short time interval to complete an experimental task he will be working under stress. Recently, many American pharmaceutical houses set up operant-conditioning laboratories for the screening of compounds without, I am sure, any clear notion of the significance of such screening data.

Whether or not a concept as measured by different sets of operations is one and the same (that is, whether length measured by a meter stick is the same as length measured by triangulation) is a matter to be settled by the philosophers of science. Meanwhile, Garner, Hake, and Eriksen (1956) point out that Bridgman, in his formulation of the principle of operational definition, was talking about *sets* of operations, and they propose that confidence in the validity of definition may be enhanced by the planning of sets of interrelated experiments which provide complementary data on variables under consideration. These they call *converging operations*. Their discussion of perceptual defense is instructive. If, for example, recognition times obtained for vulgar and neutral words are longer for the former than the latter, the difference may be attributed to perceptual defense. But it may also be due to response suppression. In order to discriminate between these two hypotheses, an experimenter might add a condition to his experiment such that vulgar stimuli were used to evoke nonvulgar responses, and vice versa. Not all multiple-operation experiments are converging. Garner, Hake, and Eriksen (1956) indicate two types which are not. (1) *Repeat* operations may enhance the reliability of the original finding but they do not clarify its nature. (2) Similarly, *transform* operations in which one set of conditions is simply substituted for the original (for example, synonyms used in place of the original vulgar and nonvulgar words) can do no more than reinforce the original conclusion. An impressive illustration of the value of converging operations is seen in Meunzinger's series of experiments on the nature of punishment, to be referred to later.

The problem of reliability is more competently understood by the experimental psychologist and requires little discussion here. The experimenter has a variety of devices available to aid in achieving maximum reliability. He may use pointer readings rather than verbal descriptions; he may use more refined equipment; he may employ a variety of procedural controls, such as counterbalancing, to reduce systematic effects associated with incidental variables; and he may use statistical procedures to segregate the incidental sources of variance once these get into his data. Both validity and reliability are important concerns, but the former must take precedence over the latter. Nothing is gained by niceties of measurement if we are not quite sure of what we are measuring or whether or not it is, in fact, worth measuring.

THE METHODS OF THE EXPERIMENTAL PSYCHOLOGIST

There are at least two ways in which a short section on the methodology of experimental psychology can be written: one may provide a compendium of procedures, or one may attempt to identify the attitudes and assumptions the experimental psychologist holds concerning his methods. I prefer the latter.

Unlike many other young sciences, psychology, from its earliest period, has emphasized the role of experimentation as the basic method for carrying on its affairs. Unlike biology, with which it is often identified, it has had in its history no taxonomy and no periods of natural history. With perhaps the exception of the nosological systems of the early abnormal psychology, there has been no preoccupation with classification of behavioral phenomena, and, perhaps with the exception of certain recent publications in human engineering, there have been few if any handbooks of the sort identified with physical science and engineering. The emphasis on the formal experiment appears to be tied to the persistent demand for quantification. It is interesting to note that, in his *Handbook of Human Physiology,* Johannes Müller proclaimed that the speed of the nerve impulse defied measurement, and his treatment of sensory processes and the mind was largely metaphysical and speculative. In little more than a decade after Müller's pronouncement, Helmholtz had measured the speed of the nerve impulse and had found it, indeed, to be rather slow. Still a few years later, Fechner had proposed his solution to the mind-body problem and had provided the methods by which to attain solution.

Orienting Attitudes One implicit attitude concerning the significance of experiments is particularly widespread among experimental psychologists. They are prone to think of their results in extremely general terms. This generality involves both species and situations. Except as he is, from time to time, caught short in his application of experimental data, the experimental psychologist is inclined to view his findings as valid without regard to the readily apparent differences between his laboratory situations and those obtaining outside the laboratory. Indeed, he is likely not to keep in mind the great dependence that behavioral data have on the particular methods used in securing them. One need only read the usual textbook treatment of specific behavioral phenomena to verify this practice. The same state of affairs holds for species. In the development of particular theoretical issues, data from a variety of sources are brought together in the supporting evidence, and one senses an equation of the white rat with the human observer. That is, there appears to be the assumption that the white rat is substitutive for the human observer in the explanation of behavior in the general case. From this point it is an easily taken step to the attitude that a white rat *is* a human observer, albeit a rather simple one, in some laboratory situation under consideration.

In recent years, Brunswik (1956) has made an eloquent statement of the principle that experiments must be representative in design: that is, that they must be so designed that they will yield data which will correlate positively with data from the situations to which one intends to generalize his experimental data. Representative experiments are identified by two criteria: (1) they have *ecological validity*, that is, they sample a range of situations that are typical for the type of subject being observed; and (2) they are *functional* in intent, that is, they sample independent–dependent variable relationships over a typical range of magnitudes. It is paradoxical that attention in psychological experiments, outside of psychophysics, has been directed more to the identification of independent variables, less to the determination of S-R functions. Even with an increased use, in the past several decades, of complex designs which facilitate the determination of such functions, greater attention persists toward the identification of variables and their interactions.

Psychological experiments also have been concerned more often with situational, in contrast to intraorganismic, determinants of behavior. This, perhaps, is because the former are more accessible, more easily identified, and more readily controlled.

Psychological experiments generally are simple in conceptualization. Though complex design procedures have been introduced, most variables are present in, at most, one or two degrees of magnitude, and interactions above the first order are difficult to interpret. A major virtue of complex designs, of course, is that they allow for reduction in the size of error terms and thus the demonstration of effects with smaller samples of subjects. Moreover, the indices that constitute data in psychological experiments are simple ones. Generally, the response operations required of the subject are simple acts like saying "yes" and "no," pressing a key, or tracking a particular signal. Performance is scored for the frequency with which responses or response errors occur, their latency, duration, or both, and only relatively infrequently involves direct estimates of magnitude. When physiological measures are used as indices of behavior, these are, more frequently than not, simple measures.

Error, in the experimental psychologist's mind, is something to be eliminated. His greatest concern is with variable error and its effect on the precision of his data. He will repeat observations to reduce error; he will use counterbalancing and other design procedures to reduce its bias; and he will employ complex designs to remove the influence of known variables and their interactions from the assessment of the effects in which he is primarily interested. The constant errors typically have held little interest for him, and the specialty of individual differences has never been a major area of psychological investigation.

Levels of Measurement There are basically four levels of measurement (Stevens, 1958a). That is, the numerals assigned to represent observations will differ in the information they convey, and these differences may be ordered into four categories. In the simplest type, they identify the observational event or class of events. Or they may indicate position in a linear array of events. Examples of these two levels are the seat numbers assigned to students in a class and the ranking of scores on an essay quiz. Evaluative criteria are often complex, and it is not possible, as Coombs (1953) has pointed out, to achieve a pure case of rank-ordering. Then one must be content with a partially ordered metric. For example, if the answers on an essay test are evaluated for both factual accuracy and original thought, test paper A may be clearly superior to test paper B on both and the two may be ordered so that A is higher than B. Meanwhile, test paper C may be factually less accurate than B but display more originality. Thus, it is not clear whether B is higher than C or C is higher than B. Unless some a priori rule has been made about the relative weight of the two factors or a decision to score the tests independently on the two criteria, the strongest form of scale that can be achieved is the partially ordered scale.

Most frequently, the data of the experimental psychologist are of the ordered type, and the number of analytical operations he can perform legitimately upon them is limited to three: the computation of medians, percentiles, and rank-order correlations. Meanwhile, his goal in measurement is to attain strong scales. These are of two types: interval, which identifies position on a linear dimension (provided that information about scalar distance between magnitudes may be scaled); and ratio, which allows the precise estimate of relative magnitude. Examples of interval and ratio measures are the numerical scores on a standardized achievement test and the time scores on tests of manual dexterity. Stevens (1958a) has maintained that certain sensory scales like the sone and the bril scales are ratio scales. However, a true ratio scale must have a true zero. Stevens has identified this as the absolute threshold (more recently, he has used the rather vague term, effective threshold). However, recent work demonstrating the predominant influence of contextual factors, particularly subliminal stimulus inputs (Black and Bevan, 1960), brings into question the assertion of sensory ratio scales.

The interval scale is perhaps the most useful all around and the experimenter will do all that he can to achieve it, often by the simple expedient of making certain heuristic assumptions and intuitively treating his scale as one of equal-appearing intervals. However, often it is not possible to even assume a pure interval scale, at which time the ordered-metric scale may be appropriate. In this form of scale, information on relative distance between items at different parts of the scale is available although none is provided on the size of the scale unit of measure. Coombs (1950) provides a method for the construction of the partially ordered metric in his unfolding technique.

Psychophysical Methods   Psychophysics is, as we noted earlier, the prototype of strong scaling. The psychophysical methods may be described as being either indirect- or direct-scaling methods.

The indirect methods are identified with Fechner and Thurstone and are based on the assumption that sensations may not be measured directly. Fechner's expedient was to assume that the absolute threshold constituted the limiting value on a sensory dimension and that JNDs were equal. He thus constructed psychophysical functions by means of the operation of cumulating JNDs. Similarly, Thurstone proposed to infer psychological magnitude from a knowledge of the proportions of times each stimulus is judged greater or less than every other item with which it is compared.

In contrast, Stevens has assumed an isomorphism between the operations of response and the sensory magnitudes underlying responses. He thus has proceeded to construct scales directly from the experimental operations of bisection, fractionation, and, most recently, magnitude estimation.

Reference has already been made to the shortcomings of Fechner's procedure of cumulating JNDs, and at present, no convincing experimental evidence for the validity of the law of comparative judgment exists. Nor is the record of the direct-scaling methods any better. Garner, Hake, and Eriksen (1956), in their discussion of converging operations, comment that there is no evidence that sensory magnitude scales are true reflections of a sensory process. Stevens' scale for the direct estimation of loudness (1956) is identified for special comment. When a subject is required to communicate his impressions of loudness in terms of a numerical scale, he may be matching his impressions of loudness with his impressions of numerical size rather than reflecting a metric property of the perceptual system.

Another way of classifying the psychophysical methods has been proposed recently by Rosner (1962), based on the type of computational devices used in arriving at numerical values. There are what Rosner calls S statistics and R statistics. The methods that employ S statistics are the methods used in threshold determination and the adjustment methods. These are the indirect methods just described. The computational routines associated with the S methods describe the distribution of a particular response with reference to the sample of stimuli that aroused it. The psychophysical function is constructed by plotting the corresponding conditional probabilities or median adjustments against the scaled stimulus values. The R methods involve summarizing the distribution of responses to particular stimuli. Scale values derive either from the conditional probabilities or the average magnitudes assigned to the several stimuli. Thurstone's and Stevens' scaling methods are both examples of the R methods, as is the use of reaction-time data (Kellogg, 1931) in scaling.

The methods of multidimensional scaling developed within the last decade provide for the scaling of similarity among stimuli, when the dimensions of similarity are unknown, in terms of distance between points in a Euclidean space of least dimensionality. They are, therefore, R methods. Another approach to the problem of multidimensionality is worth exploring. This involves the application of category scaling to situations in which the independent variables are some limited and specified number manipulated in fully prescribed ways. For example, in a recent experiment Bevan and Turner (1964) obtained judgments of size when the variable of lightness was allowed to covary with size in a perfectly positive, negative, or random fashion. From these data, three psychophysical functions were constructed. Using the condition of random correlation as the basis for comparison, it was found that the judgment of size was augmented in the condition of positive correlation and that the opposite held true for the case of negative correlation. Next, by fitting equations to these three functions and deriving a numerical estimate of their slopes, it was possible to construct a higher-order function from which to predict a psychophysical function for size estimation when, everything else being equal, any degree of relationship existed between this variable and stimulus lightness.

Psychology has taken its quantitative models primarily from the physical sciences. An approach worth examining is that of the similarity and dimensional methods used during the last thirty or more years for the purpose of comparing empirical functions with simple quantitative models of biological systems. In a recent review article, Stahl (1962) identifies a dozen physiological constants deducible from the allometric equation of Huxley. Von Békésy's work with models of the inner ear (1960) provides an example of interest to experimental psychologists.

THE ART OF EXPERIMENTAL PSYCHOLOGY

The skillful experimental psychologist is a person who possesses a thorough knowledge of the experimental literature, particularly that segment related to his area of special interest; who is well trained in the techniques of apparatus construction, maintenance, and use; who is well versed in the methods of experimental design, observational procedure, and statistical analysis; and who is informed about the logic of modern science.

But he must be more. He must be thoroughly conversant with the lore of experimental psychology. He must possess a creative imagination that will allow him to translate hypotheses into effective experiments and enable him to detect at the earliest possible time the unexpected in his data and capitalize upon it for further lines of investigation. Being familiar with the lore of a field involves knowing the myriad little things that contribute to effective experiments. This is knowledge that is not taught in formal classes or presented in textbooks and handbooks. It is largely omitted from experimental reports. It is acquired through conversations and collaboration with other investigators and through doing experiments oneself. It consists of a knowledge of endless detail that makes the difference between a successful and an unsuccessful experiment: what type of design is best for a particular problem; what sorts of and how many subjects are needed; what instructions are best and how these are best given; what incidental factors in the situation may be ignored and what must be controlled; what responses need be observed and recorded; what sorts of data are best.

What lies behind creative imagination we cannot at present specify with confidence. But we do know that there are persons who can do exceedingly clever experiments that cut to the heart of an issue whereas others, just as intelligent and well trained in the facts and methods of psychology, seem to lack the knack. Guthrie (1959), in a discussion of the orienting attitudes of the experimental investigator of learning, points out that patterns of stimuli and patterns of attendant responses have a psychological significance that must be dealt with. "It is not enough," he says, "that they be available in the physical situation nor is it enough that the organism's attention orients sense organs to receive them; it is further necessary that they have meaning for the responding organism" (p. 165). Psychologists who plan conditioning experiments undoubtedly choose their stimuli in the light of their past experience that these do get responded to by the subject. I would go a step further and suggest that the skillful experimenter has the capacity of placing himself in the role of subject and viewing the experimental situation from this vantage point. In performing this exercise, he will know not only whether or not his chosen signals will evoke the response he is interested in, but he also may gain some insight into the subtleties of the situation as the subject perceives it and, therefore, some comprehension of the behavior that he will observe in his experiment.

An Experimenter at Work   I should like to conclude this discussion by describing a series of experiments by Muenzinger and his colleagues on the properties of punishment and the validity of the law of effect. They are reported in a set of nine papers, entitled "Motivation in Learning," that appeared between 1931 and 1941 and were summarized by Muenzinger in the 1945 Annual Research Lecture presented at the University of Colorado (1946). I have chosen this series, not because I have any special interest in the problem it was devised to resolve or because I find Muenzinger's theoretical orientation particularly appealing. Rather, I have selected this program of studies because the experiments are simple in conceptualization and because they illustrate very nicely the mind of an experimenter at work. They demonstrate that no experiment, no matter how comprehensive in design, fully resolves a theoretical issue or establishes an experimental hypothesis. What each does achieve, if it is well executed, is added clarity and an increased articulation of the question that gave rise to the study in the first place.

Muenzinger's goal was to clarify the relationship of punishment to performance efficiency. In all of his experiments, his vehicle was the single-unit T maze; the subject's task was that of choosing a lighted alley leading to food in the goal box. Albino rats can reach errorless performance in this task in an average of about 100 trials. If shock is added for incorrect choices, the same level of accomplishment will be reached in about 40 trials. Thorndike's law of effect would account for such facilitation by stating that the annoying consequences of entering the incorrect alley produced a weakening of the S-R bonds that linked the stimulus cues provided by the alley to the entering response, whereas the satisfying consequence of entering the correct alley strengthened this S-R connection.

But, as Muenzinger realized, the law of effect describes only one of several possible reinforcement patterns. Therefore, his first concern was with the effect upon performance of shock for correct responses. He predicted that if the correct response were both rewarded and punished, performance would be generally poor, since the strengthening effects of the former would be counteracted by the latter. In his basic experiment, he ran three groups of rats: (1) those which received only food on the correct trials; and (3) those which received both food and shock for the correct response. The results were quite surprising. The group receiving food alone reached criterion (two consecutive days of 10 errorless trials each) in 114 trials as expected. The group rewarded for correct and punished on incorrect trials took 39 trials as expected. But the group both rewarded and punished on the correct trials averaged only 49 trials and were not significantly poorer than group 2.

In attempting to account for the facilitating effect produced by punishing the correct response, Muenzinger reasoned that punishment might influence performance efficiency not by weakening incorrect S-R bonds but by making the animal more alert to the problem's critical cues. Therefore two more groups of animals were tested: (4) those which received shock both for the correct and incorrect alleys; and (5) those which were shocked in the starting alley prior to reaching the choice-point. The group which was shocked for both correct and incorrect responses reached the criterion in an average of 40 trials, equaling the performance of groups 2 and 3. In contrast, the group shocked in the starting alley took 118 trials to reach criterion, indicating that shock under these conditions had no facilitating effect at all. In order to further check on the possibility that punishment exerted its influence through general arousal, a sixth group received shock in the starting alley and in both correct and incorrect alleys and met criterion in 49 trials, a level of performance not significantly different from that of groups 2, 3, and 4.

Muenzinger's conclusion at this point was that punishment increased performance efficiency by sensitizing the subject to the cues critical to solution of the task. He further hypothesized that reward and punishment are complementary states related to the attainment or frustration of goals. Thus, securing food and escaping shock both may be rewarding, while not securing food and receiving shock both may be punishing. To check the possibility that escape from shock is rewarding, group 7 received shock from start box to goal box with no food in the goal box. Its mean criterion performance was 52 trials, not significantly different from 2, 3, 4, and 6 and clearly better than group 1, the food-alone group.

Muenzinger next turned to examine another aspect of the law of effect. This hypothesized not only that punishment produced its effect by weakening S-R bonds but that this resulted from the annoyance associated with it. If, as Meunzinger had concluded, punishment was effective because it alerted the subject to important cues, then it was necessary to ask if this alertness resulted from annoyance or from some other cause. This meant replacing shock at the choice-point with some other type of reinforcement. Group 8 received a buzzer in the correct alley; group 9 received it in the incorrect alley. For group 10, the grids were removed from both alleys and the animal was faced with jumping a gap to reach the goal box. For group 11, the gap was located in the starting alley prior to the choice-point. The substitution of the buzzer for the shock in groups 8 and 9 produced no facilitation of performance. In contrast, the group with the gap in both alleys averaged 49 trials to criterion; its control, group 11, 110 trials. Delay at the choice-point was as effective as shock at the choice-point in facilitating learning. In order to get some clearer notion of why this was so, Muenzinger next examined other data he had available on all his groups. In groups with scores above 100, the average amount of V.T.E. behavior (head-turning at the choice-point) was only about one half that observed in the groups performing at a level of 40-50 trials to criterion. He, therefore, concluded that any condition, including punishment, that will cause the subject to pause at the choice-point and indulge in V.T.E. behavior will facilitate performance.

This last hypothesis was tested by observing a group (12) in which the subject was simply restrained in the alley of its choice for 3-5 seconds on each trial by the lowering of transparent doors and then allowed to continue to the goal box. These rats reached criterion in 68 trials, and were considerably better than the food-alone group (1).

Muenzinger's interpretation of the role of punishment in learning, based on the performance of these twelve groups of rats in the T maze, is that it facilitates performance because it prompts the subject to pause at the choice-point, and that this pause increases the probability that he will detect the cues that must be discriminated for successful solution of the experimental task.

REFERENCES

ADAMS, D. K. Learning and explanation. In *The Kentucky symposium: Learning theory, personality theory, and clinical research.* New York: Wiley, 1954. Pp. 68-80.

ALLPORT, G. W. Scientific models and human morals. *Psychol. Rev.,* 1947, **54,** 182-192.

BEVAN, W., JR. Modern psychologists: scientific woozle hunters? *Nordisk Psychol. Monografiserie,* 1953, No. 4.

BEVAN, W., & PRITCHARD, JOAN F. The effect of subliminal tones upon the judgment of loudness. *J. exp. Psychol.,* 1963, **66,** 23-29.

BEVAN, W., & TURNER, E. D. The influence of lightness upon the judgment of size. *Amer. J. Psychol.,* 1964.

BLACK, R. W. & BEVAN, W. The effect of subliminal shock upon the judged intensity of weak shock. *Amer. J. Psychol.,* 1960, **73,** 262-267.

BRAITHEWAITE, R. B. *Scientific explanation.* Cambridge: Cambridge Univ. Press, 1953.

BRUNSWIK, E. *Perception and the representative design of psychological experiments.* Berkeley: Univ. California Press, 1956.

CAMPBELL, N. R. *An account of the principles of measurement and calculation.* London: Longmans, 1928.

CARNAP, R. The methodological character of theoretical concepts. In H. Feigl and M. Scriven (Eds.), *Minnesota studies in the philosophy of science.* Vol. 1. Minneapolis: Univ. Minnesota Press, 1956. Pp. 38-76.

COOMBS, C. H. Psychological scaling without a unit of measurement. *Psychol. Rev.,* 1950, **57,** 145-158.

COOMBS, C. H. The theory and methods of social measurement. In L. Festinger and D. Katz. (Eds.), *Research methods in the behavioral sciences.* New York: Dryden Press, 1953. Pp. 471-535.

GARNER, W. R., HAKE, H. W., & ERIKSEN, C. W. Operationism and the concept of perception. *Psychol. Rev.,* 1956, **63,** 149-159.

GIBSON, J. J. *The perception of the visual world.* New York: Houghton Mifflin, 1950.

GUILFORD, J. P. *Psychometric methods.* (2nd ed.) New York: McGraw-Hill, 1954.

GUTHRIE, E. R. Association by contiguity. In S. Koch (Ed.), *Psychology: a study of a science.* Vol. 2. New York: McGraw-Hill, 1959, Pp. 158-195.

HEBB, D. O. *The organization of behavior.* New York: Wiley, 1949.

HEBB, D. O. The role of neurological ideas in psychology. In D. Krech and G. S. Klein (Eds.), *Theoretical models and personality theory.* Durham, N.C.: Duke Univ. Press, 1952, Pp. 39-55.

HELSON, H. Adaptation level theory. In S. Koch (Ed.), *Psychology: a study of a science.* Vol. 1. New York: McGraw-Hill, 1959. Pp. 565-621.

JOHNSON, H. M. A simpler principle of explanation of imaginative and ideational behavior and of learning. *J. comp. Psychol.,* 1927, **7,** 187-235.

KATZ, J. J., & HALSTEAD, W. Protein organization and mental function. In W. Halstead (Ed.), Brain and behavior. *Comp. Psychol. Monogr.,* 1950, **20,** 1-39.

KELLOGG, W. N. The time of judgment in psychometric measures. *Amer. J. Psychol.,* 1931, **46,** 65-86.

KOCH, S. Toward an indigenous methodology. Address to Eastern Psychol. Assn., Atlantic City, April 1959.

KOCH, S. Psychological science versus the science-humanism antinomy: Intimations of a significant science of man. *Amer. Psychologist,* 1961, **16,** 629-639.

LACHMAN, R. The model in theory construction. *Psychol. Rev.,* 1960, **67,** 113-129.

LUCE, R. D., & EDWARDS, W. The derivation of subjective scales of just noticeable differences. *Psychol. Rev.,* 1958, **65,** 222-237.

McGUIGAN, J. The experimenter—a neglected stimulus object. *Psychol. Bull.,* 1963, **60,** 421-428.

MESSICK, S. J. Some recent theoretical developments in multidimensional scaling. *Educ. psychol. Measmt.,* 1956, **16,** 82-100.

MUENZINGER, K. F. Reward and punishment. *Univ. Colo. Stud., Gen. Ser. A,* 1946, **27** (4), 1-16.

OPPENHEIMER, R. Analogy in science. *Amer. Psychologist,* 1956, **11,** 127-135.

POPPER, K. R. *The logic of scientific discovery.* New York: Basic Books, 1959.

ROSNER, B. S. Psychophysics and neurophysiology. In S. Koch (Ed.), *Psychology: a study of a science.* Vol. 4. New York: McGraw-Hill, 1962. Pp. 280-333.

SKINNER, B. F. *The behavior of organisms.* New York: Appleton-Century-Crofts, 1938.

STAHL, W. R. Similarity and dimensional methods in biology. *Science,* 1962, **137,** 205-212.

STEVENS, S. S. The direct estimation of sensory magnitudes—loudness. *Amer. J. Psychol.,* 1956, **69,** 1-25.

STEVENS, S. S. On the psychophysical law. *Psychol. Rev.,* 1957, **64,** 153-181.

STEVENS, S. S. Measurement and man. *Science,* 1958, **127,** 383-389. (a)

STEVENS, S. S. Problems and methods of psychophysics. *Psychol. Bull.,* 1958, **54,** 177-196. (b)

STEVENS, S. S. The psychophysics of sensory function. *Amer. Scientist,* 1960, **48,** 226-253.

STEVENS, S. S. Toward a resolution of the Fechner-Thurstone legacy. *Psychometrika,* 1961, **26,** 35-47.

STEVENS, S. S., & GALANTER, E. H. Ratio scales and category scales for a dozen perceptual continua. *J. exp. Psychol.*, 1957, **54**, 377-411.

THURSTONE, L. L. Psychophysical analysis. *Amer. J. Psychol.*, 1927, **38**, 368-389. (a)

THURSTONE, L. L. A law of comparative judgment. *Psychol. Rev.*, 1927, **34**, 273-286. (b)

TORGERSON, W. S. *Theory and method of scaling.* New York: Wiley, 1958.

TURNER, E. D., & BEVAN, W. The simultaneous induction of multiple anchor effects in the judgment of form. *J. exp. Psychol.*, 1962, **64**, 589-592.

VON BÉKÉSY, G. *Experiments in hearing.* New York: McGraw-Hill, 1960.

VON BERTALANFFY, L. Theoretical models in biology and psychology. In D. Krech and G. S. Klein (Eds.), *Theoretical models and personality theory.* Durham, N.C.: Duke Univ. Press, 1952. Pp. 24-38.

ZENER, K. The significance of experience of the individual for the science of psychology. In H. Feigl, M. Scriven, and G. Maxwell (Eds.), *Minnesota studies in the philosophy of science.* Vol. 2. Minneapolis: Univ. Minnesota Press, 1958. Pp. 354-369.

8 OTTO KLINEBERG

SOME PHILOSOPHICAL AND METHODOLOGICAL PROBLEMS IN SOCIAL PSYCHOLOGY

THE FIRST REACTION of the writer to the invitation to prepare this chapter was one of mild surprise and scepticism. The divorce (or emancipation) of psychology from philosophy has been accomplished, although not quite everywhere as yet, with relatively friendly feelings on both sides. Since social psychology represents a recent development in psychology, with the aid of contributions from sociology and cultural anthropology, the emancipation would seem to be all the more complete and the lines of connection with philosophy even more tenuous. It required only a little reflection, however, to realize how many of the classical problems of philosophy, as well as a few more modern ones, are of concern to the social psychologist and how little we can afford to ignore our philosophical origins. The laws of social learning are not so far removed from the utilitarian principle of the pursuit of pleasure and the avoidance of pain. The study of humor leans heavily on the theories of Schopenhauer, Bergson, and Herbert Spencer; the instinct theory goes back at least to Hobbes; the concept of empathy was suggested by Lipps. Kurt Lewin, in the development of field theory, started with Aristotle, even if only to criticize his classificatory approach. The list of social psychological problems first enunciated by philosophers could be continued almost indefinitely.

The nonphilosophical (or antiphilosophical) social psychologist might retort that these are merely examples of an historical connection, irrelevant to the contemporary state of our discipline. Gardner Murphy (1939) states that Thomas Hobbes was the first social psychologist; Gordon Allport (1954) gives the credit to Auguste Comte; in neither case, it may be argued, does it follow that Hobbes or Comte have anything to say to us today. The fact is, however, that many of the problems with which social psychologists are *now* concerned, whether they realize it or not, are philosophical problems, not only in the sense that they were first stated and studied by philosophers, but also because they are still resistant to a purely scientific approach. It is to these problems that we now turn, with the understanding that what follows can make no claim to completeness, but is presented rather as a sampling of what may be included under this heading.

THE NATURE OF MAN

The problem of human nature in its broadest sense, which has concerned all the great names in the history of philosophy, continues to preoccupy the contemporary representatives of all, or almost all, the social sciences, including social psychology. A sociologist has entitled one of his books *The Nature of Human Nature* (Faris, 1937). An anthropologist speaks of "the core of all investigations of cultures: can we arrive at any satisfactory knowledge of what constitutes human nature?" (Radin, 1933). For the social psychologist, who deals with the processes of human interaction, with the influence of human beings on one another, the concern with human nature has moved in at least three interrelated directions.

The first of these is the classical problem of human motivation, the springs of action. Granting with Aristotle that man is a social animal, what makes him one? What are the impulses or drives that move man in his contacts with his fellow men? We have many theories of motivation but no agreement as to what the essential motives are, where they come from, the nature and limitations of their effects, their relative strength, or their degree of dependability.

A second aspect of this problem relates to the nature of man apart from society, man without culture, anterior to and independent of the process of socialization. No answer can be found (in spite of behaviorists like John B. Watson) by examining the newborn; the data are inadequate, and socialization begins too early in life, to a certain extent even before the child is born. Nor can the answer be found in the descriptions of feral man; the cases are anecdotal and limited in number, and the conditions of isolation too uncertain and uncontrolled. To the extent that they can be accepted, they do suggest that man without culture shows little that is "human," but they leave many questions unanswered. A more fruitful approach has been to borrow from the anthropologists, and search for the common-human across the tremendous variations in the cultures that have been described. The argument continues, however, as to just how much of human behavior must be ascribed to cultural relativity, and how much can be explained by what has been called "the psychic unity of mankind." According to Redfield (1957), Robert E. Park admired Sumner's *Folkways* and used to quote Sumner's statement that "The mores can make anything right"; then he would add: "But they have a harder time making some things right than others." The argument continues, also, as to what these "others" are that are most easily accepted. Some psychologists have tried to cut the Gordian knot by stating that human behavior is never *either* biological *or* social, but always *biosocial*. This is an advance indeed, but it leaves open the question as to how the interpenetration is to be interpreted, as well as the relative importance of the two components.

A third aspect of the problem of human nature of major concern to social psychologists has overtones of an ethical character. Is human nature, if left to itself, essentially good or bad? It is customary in this context to contrast Rousseau and Hobbes, the "noble savage" versus the "war of all against all." Less well known, perhaps, is the fact that the same opposition occurs in Chinese philosophy; Mencius is in this respect similar to Rousseau, and Hsün Tsu to Hobbes. This issue comes close to the continuing concern with the extent to which hostility or aggressiveness is native to man, or whether he can as easily reflect altruistic and cooperative tendencies. Here the usual position is to assume that both hostility and altruism are "native" in the sense that both occur, but the question as to which is more likely, and under what conditions, largely remains unanswered. The practical implications of this issue in a world which constantly gets smaller and more dangerous can hardly be overestimated.

THE INDIVIDUAL IN THE GROUP

The classical philosophical problem of the relation of part to whole, and more specifically of the whole as more than the sum of its parts, has its counterpart in social psychology. When Herbert Spencer spoke of the "group mind" and Gustave LeBon of a "crowd mentality," the usual reaction of psychologists was one of violent criticism, partly on the ground that a mind required a nervous system, and therefore by definition could be ascribed only to individuals. With the advent of a Gestalt approach to social behavior, and particularly with the development of group dynamics, the pendulum moved part of the way back. The group was not assigned a mind, but it did have "characteristics" which accompanied a form of behavior which distinguished it from that of the individuals of which it was composed. Cartwright (1950) speaks of laws of group behavior that "could be established independently of the purposes or the specific activities of the group." It is not being suggested that we are back to a group mind, but we are left with a problem almost as complex. If there are laws of group behavior irrespective of the nature of the group, then do the individuals who constitute the group count for nothing? Is the whole, in this case, not only more than or different from the sum of its parts, but independent of its parts, the individual human beings of which it is composed? Or are there laws which apply to all groups in some of their aspects, with room left for other laws, or no laws, for those aspects in which groups differ because they are made up differently? Progress is certainly being made in the direction of answers to these questions, but we are far from having reached a position acceptable to all social psychologists.

PERCEPTION OF THE EXTERNAL WORLD

At first glance, it may seem a far cry from the "New Look" in the study of perception to the age-long controversy between realists and idealists in epistemology, but the connection is not difficult to establish. In both cases, we are dealing with the question of the degree of correspondence between what we perceive and what is "out there," the Kantian opposition between phenomenon and thing-in-itself. Recent developments in the social psychology of perception have emphasized the importance of *functional* factors, supplied by the perceiver because of his personal qualities, his values, fears, and expectations, as contrasted with the *structural* factors which are due to the nature of the external stimuli and the characteristics of the receptors. This is not quite the same problem as the Kantian one, but it is related; it raises the same kind of query as to the extent to which our perceptions faithfully mirror external reality.

The present position among social psychologists may be summarized in the statement that all agree that functional factors play a part; the difference arises with regard to how great a part. The earlier studies by Stern and Muensterberg had focused attention on the extent to which testimony varied according to the attitudes and background of witnesses to the same event, and the observations of many anthropologists showed how even such simple acts as the matching of colors might be affected by culturally determined classifications. The more recent experiments by social psychologists have rightly attracted considerable attention, but, unfortunately many of the results have not stood up under replication. Work continues actively in this field, but the problem remains: how much, in what ways, and under what conditions, do functional factors affect perception so as to cause deviations from the faithful representation of *real* events?

An attempt to bridge the gap between perception and reality is made by those psychologists who have applied a phenomenological approach to social psychology. Basing his views partly on those of Husserl, for example, MacLeod (1951) insists that the phenomenal world is not a private world. "The bulk of the phenomena are not mine at all . . . for each of us there are some phenomena of a private or subjective nature but together we live in a public world . . ." The problem is not thereby resolved, however. What is private, what public? What happens to create discrepancies between the two worlds? How decide between them in such cases? One is reminded of Pascal's famous phrase, *Vérité en deça des Pyrénées; erreur au delà.*

LANGUAGE AND THOUGHT

Cultural variations in color classification, to which reference was made above, appear to be related to differences in nomenclature, in the way in which colors are named. This opens up the more general problem of the manner and extent of linguistic influences on our thought processes, also a classical philosophical problem. It has in fact been suggested that the very nature of philosophical systems themselves may have been determined, at least in part, by the language spoken by their creators. Aristotle, for example, has been described as absolutely dependent, in his logic, on the characteristics of the Greek language. "If Aristotle had spoken Chinese or Dacotan, he would have had to adopt an entirely different logic, or at any rate an entirely different theory of categories" (F. Mauthner, quoted by Rank, 1932).

This problem has entered the field of social psychology from two different directions. The first of these is by way of general semantics; even though the claims of some of its proponents that the proper use of words would restore sanity to the world and remove the causes of conflict and misunderstanding have usually been considered greatly exaggerated, much research has been stimulated by the concepts and theories involved. The second direction is connected with the name of Whorf (1949), who, more than anyone else, has been responsible for the theory that thought processes are relative to the language used. This so-called Whorfian hypothesis has also been responsible for experimental research by social psychologists, with the result that doubt has been thrown on the extent of the linguistic relativity involved. With regard to both general semantics and the views of Whorf, the consensus nevertheless seems to be that language is important in the ways suggested. The problem remains: how important? What are the limits to linguistic influence? Are there still universals in the thought processes after due allowance has been made for the linguistic factors involved?

ROLE THEORY

In a recent book on the place of the role concept in social psychology (Rocheblave-Spenlé, 1962), one of the precursors of role theory is said to be the philosopher Josiah Royce, who was one of the first to insist that we learn about ourselves through the reactions of others, rather than learning about others through analogy with ourselves. Another precursor was John Dewey, whose use of the term "habit" is regarded as very close to the current use of the term "role." Martin Buber also is credited with moving from a view of man as *essence* to man as a system of *relations*. Although the role concept entered social psychology by way of sociologists like G. H. Mead and Cooley and anthropologists like Linton, its philosophical origins are by no means unimportant.

Although there is no complete agreement as to the definition of role, a widely held view would equate it with the acts expected of an individual because of his position in his society. This, one of the simplest of the many definitions given, leaves a great many questions unanswered. Acts expected *by whom?* By the society as a whole, our own subculture, our friends and our family, our reference groups, ourselves? When these expectations conflict, which ones predominate? What happens to the others?

There was at least one important "philosophy" which apparently took care of this problem reasonably well, namely, that ascribed to Confucius. In his social and ethical system, roles were definite and expectations clear. The reciprocal roles of parents and children, husband and wife, elder and younger brother, governor and governed, were free of any uncertainty, although deviations did occur in practice. The differential effects of varying degrees of definiteness in role prescriptions have not been fully explored.

Another problem which persists in this area refers to the relation between personality and the various roles which the individual is called on to perform. Is personality defined, and fully defined, by such roles, or is there something else which cannot be explained by or subsumed under role? If the latter, what is that "something else"? Can what is individual and idiosyncratic still be explained by role theory?

THE ETHICS OF EXPERIMENTATION

The reference to ethics in the Confucian system leads us to a more specifically ethical problem in social psychology, which is at the same time a methodological problem. Even a cursory glance at journals and textbooks in this field reveals an astonishingly large number of studies which involve some form of deception of the subjects. In one sense this is nothing new, since research on suggestion, with which experimental social psychology may be said to have started, could not have been conducted if the subject had known the purpose of the experiment. Today, however, deception has been raised to the level of a fine art, and the ingenuity expended on discovering new ways to deceive induces in the reader a mixture of admiration and worry.

A mild degree of deception is undoubtedly necessary in many social psychological experiments, and probably harmless. If one is studying the effects of two forms of communication on attitude change, the influence of contact on intergroup relations, or the efficiency of problem-solving in the individual or group situation, advance information about the purpose of the experiment would wreck it completely. Even a one-way screen is an instrument of deception, but probably no one would deny its value or wish to see it disappear completely.

The problem becomes more serious when deception is accompanied by some form of manipulation, when the subject is made angry or fearful or is led to question his own judgment or capacity. In such cases, the threat to the ego may be a serious one, and the need to undo the damage—if indeed there has been damage—becomes imperative. When a serious psychologist of recognized scientific stature conducts such an experiment, we can usually rely on him to take the proper safeguards. What happens, however, when dozens of young hopefuls in as many different laboratories replicate, modify, and extend the original technique without the necessary experience and understanding? There is a real dilemma here: deception cannot be avoided if social psychological research is to continue; deception must be kept in bounds so that no one is harmed by it. Social psychology in this connection needs its own code of ethics so as to harmonize scientific progress with concern for the individuals who have agreed to serve as our subjects.

Deception and manipulation are often regarded as essential characteristics of propaganda, with which many social psychologists have concerned themselves. This view undoubtedly contains some exaggeration, since propaganda may be honest, and directed toward an honorable goal. At the same time, it is true that a great deal of research in the field of propaganda is relatively indifferent to truth or honesty and concerned exclusively with the discovery of techniques for "making up the other man's mind." This has led to the criticism that social psychology is contributing to the discovery of diabolic psychological weapons which may be used by some future Goebbels for the enslavement of masses of unsuspecting people. If this is truly a criticism, it is one which we share with all other scientific disciplines. The discoveries of the physicist or the bacteriologist can be used to build or to destroy; so, although to a much more limited extent, can those of the social psychologist. He shares with others the scientific duty to extend the boundaries of knowledge. How this knowledge will be used is another matter, one which touches the fundamental problem of the place of values in social psychology.

VALUES

Social psychologists have always been concerned with values, but mainly as an object of research. Values have been studied, measured; people have been classified on the basis of their dominant values; the influence of values on perception and memory, and their relation to attitudes, have been extensively investigated. At the same time it has been argued that scientists as such should be indifferent to values, although as human beings they have every right to them.

Such a dichotomy is difficult to maintain, however, perhaps particularly so in the case of the social psychologist. This does not mean that other disciplines have not had to face the same problem. Atomic scientists have by no means been indifferent to the uses to which their discoveries have been, and may be, applied. The anthropologist Nadel (1951) concludes that values cannot be eliminated from the study of society. He quotes Morris Cohen to the effect that we are constantly passing value judgments, when we speak of people or behavior as being normal or abnormal, for example. Social psychologists have in large numbers committed themselves to an organization (The Society for the Psychological Study of Social Issues) which has taken definite stands against ethnic discrimination, war, and all forms of exploitation. The dilemma arises when we raise the question of the coexistence of such values with objective research on the issues involved. The most constructive approach, in the opinion of this writer, would be to recognize the existence of our values, to be aware of their nature, to avow them explicitly, and to take them into account when interpreting the results of our own investigations.

This may occasionally represent a complicated and difficult procedure. It has been known for a long time that, in public opinion studies, there tends to be some degree of correspondence between the views of the interviewer and those of the respondents, and steps have to be taken to eliminate or "cancel" the effects of interviewer bias. Recently, however, the conviction has grown that even in experimental situations of a certain type, the values (for example, degree of authoritarianism) of the people involved, experimenter and subjects alike, may exert an influence on the results obtained. This creates a serious methodological problem which requires careful and extensive investigation in order to determine the limits of the "experimenter bias" effect. The influence of this factor seems to be especially marked when the experiment involves observation and rating of other persons, but is apparently not limited to such cases.

SOCIAL PSYCHOLOGY AND POLITICAL SYSTEMS

Value systems may not only affect specific observations and experiments; they may pervade the very core and substance of a discipline. Gordon Allport (1954) regards the current interest in social psychology as characteristically an American phenomenon, related to the pragmatic tradition, the need to preserve the values of freedom and individual rights, and the strength of humanitarian motives. At the same time, there has been considerable development in France, the United Kingdom, Canada, Australia, and other countries in the Western tradition. What about the Soviet Union? Obviously the concepts of "freedom" and "individual rights" would have a different meaning to Soviet scholars. Social psychology as a separate discipline does not exist there, although many Soviet psychologists would regard their studies in education, the characteristics of collectives, industrial cooperation and similar fields as falling within the social psychological framework. It is difficult to determine exactly how much of Soviet psychology is imbued with Marxist philosophy, but it is probably safe to say that, to the extent that it is social, the identification is very nearly complete. With regard to the neighboring discipline of sociology, a recent article (Mshvenieradze and Osipov, 1962) indicates that the influence of Marxism is pervasive. "The main task confronting Soviet sociologists at present is scientifically to substantiate the concrete modes of communist construction, to study the laws governing the transition from socialism to communism, the formation of communist social relations, communist culture and 'way of life.' " Can there be any communication, any meeting of minds, between Soviet sociologists (or social psychologists) and those of the West? What degree of overlap is there in areas of research interest? What agreement, if any, underlies the differences in terminology and definition? Is there a universal social psychology, or are there many variations depending on the political background and training of the investigator? This is perhaps the major methodological problem which we now face.

REFERENCES

ALLPORT, G. W. The historical background of modern social psychology. In G. Lindzey (Ed.), *Handbook of Social Psychology*. Cambridge, Mass.: Addison-Wesley, 1954. Pp. 3-56.

CARTWRIGHT, D. *The research center for group dynamics*. Michigan: Univ. Michigan Press, 1950.

FARIS, E., *The nature of human nature*. New York: McGraw-Hill, 1937.

MACLEOD, R. B. The phenomenological approach to social psychology. *Psychol. Rev.*, 1947, **54**, 193-210.

MSHVENIERADZE, V. V., & OSIPOV, G. V. Sociology in the U.S.S.R. *Journal Soc. Sci. Information*, 1962, **1** (n.s.), 49-73.

MURPHY, G. *Historical introduction to modern psychology*. (Rev. ed.) New York: Harcourt, Brace, 1949.

NADEL, S. F. *The foundations of social anthropology*. London: Cohen & West, 1951.

RADIN, P. *The method and theory of ethnology*. New York: McGraw-Hill, 1933.

RANK, O. *Art and the artist*. New York: Knopf, 1932.

REDFIELD, R. The universally human and the culturally variable. *J. Gen. Educ.*, 1957, **10**, 150-160.

ROCHEBLAVE-SPENLÉ, A. M. *La notion de rôle en psychologie sociale.* Paris: Presses Universitaires, 1962.

WHORF, B. L. *Language, thought, and reality.* Cambridge: Technology Press, 1956.

PART II SYSTEMS

9 W. HORSLEY GANTT

PAVLOV'S SYSTEM

PAVLOV

Although in 1920, when I graduated in medicine, I had never heard of the conditional reflex, and of Pavlov only as the physiologist of digestion, his name is now known to every educated person throughout the world. The prediction of H. G. Wells in 1927, (Pavlov, 1928, p. 39) that Pavlov would be better known one hundred years after his death than during his lifetime, is being realized. "You ring a bell and the dog secretes saliva" is how most people think of the conditional reflex. Despite such vulgarization, the conditional reflex is now a psychological axiom with which even the schoolboy is acquainted. Pavlov's name has become connected with the conditional reflex almost as intimately as Einstein's with relativity.

In spite of Pavlov's fame and wide use of general method in psychology, there is today (particularly in the West) little more knowledge of the details of his work, the laws he enunciated, and their significance than during his lifetime. In 1926, when Pavlov's first book, summarizing his research on the conditional reflexes, was published, one of his oldest pupils and collaborators (his biographer Savich) told me that he doubted whether six people, including those who worked with Pavlov, understood his book. Nor was this attributable to obscurity or lack of clarity in Pavlov's style. Erwin Straus, the author of a scholarly, detailed, and constructive criticism (1937) of Pavlov's system says: "Among the large number of Pavlovian supporters, there are only a few who have verified his experiments, or what is more important, who have read what he wrote."

The evaluation of the Pavlovian school, including that of his successors, such as Skinner, the electrophysiologists, and others, fluctuates from the extreme optimism that "the behaviorists are the people who have got to save the world; they may win the race with total destruction" (Gilder) to the more cautious statement (1960) of Grey Walter: "At the present time there is still not one single principle of mental physiology that can claim the status of a natural law, in the sense that it receives universal acceptance and permits deductive prediction or extrapolation."

Objective methods had to some extent been used to record "mental" events, but it was Pavlov who first devised a strictly quantitative physiological measurement for these events. In perspective, Pavlov's work may be viewed as an end of the "adolescence" of science, the period beginning with Francis Bacon and ending with the advent of the atomic age, characterized by the scientist's optimistic belief that a complete scientific accounting of the universe would resolve the chief human ills and usher in a utopian epoch. This point of view will be amplified later.

EVOLUTION OF PAVLOV'S WORK

The facts of the formulation of the conditional reflex by Pavlov may be said to date back to Descartes. This earlier genius compared the living organism, in its reactivity to the external environment, to a machine. Descartes introduced into the behavior of the organism the concept of determinism, a concept not only basic to science up to a generation ago, but specifically related to Pavlov's attack on the science of the "mind." [1]

Pavlov (1941b) says:

It is universally accepted that the notion of the reflex originated with Descartes. But what was known about the detailed structure of the central nervous system, especially in connexion with its activity, in the time of Descartes? For the physiologico-anatomical distinction between sensory and motor nerves was not made until the beginning of the 19th century. It is evident that for Descartes the idea of determinism alone formed the essence of the notion of a reflex and from it issued Descartes' conception of the animal organism as a machine. In this sense all later physiologists interpreted the reflex, tying the individual action of the organism up with the individual stimuli, at the same time gradually bringing to light the elements of nervous structure in the form of different afferent and efferent nerves and in the form of special paths and points (centres) of the central nervous system, until they finally gathered together the characteristic features of the functions of the latter system (p. 133).

In common with most modern biologists, Pavlov emphatically disagreed with Descartes' dualism.

The next figure on whom Pavlov drew consciously was Sechenov, the "father of Russian physiology." The thesis of his work, *Reflexes of the Brain* (1863), was that all behavior, all our mental life, is based on the physiological reflex.

Sechenov's ideas were mainly theoretical. He considered that thinking re-

---

[1] "Mind" would not generally be used by Pavlov; he employed the phrase "higher nervous activity." The term "mind," however, is better suited for a general discussion, since Pavlov intended higher nervous activity to be the scientific aspect of mind ("psychical phenomena").

sulted from the inhibition of reflex action. This concept undoubtedly arose from Sechenov's physiological experiments on central inhibition. He showed that sodium chloride placed on the optic thalami of the de-cerebrated frog prevented the reflex withdrawal of the leg from an acid solution. Pavlov's idea of external inhibition was equivalent to Goltz's so-called *Quakversuch* (inhibition of croaking by stimulation of another point on the body during the elicitation of the croaking by tactile stimulation on the back).

PAVLOV'S GASTROINTESTINAL WORK

The conditional reflex concept, did not, however, arise from this historical evolution. Its source was Pavlov's own study of the physiology of the digestive system, for which he won the Nobel Prize in 1904, the first given in physiology. It is important to note that although Pavlov borrowed terms from current neurophysiology, particularly from Sherrington, his concepts were based directly on the facts of the physiological experiments on secretion of the gastrointestinal tract. Because of the importance of this physiology in the derivation of the conditional reflex, I shall summarize his work on digestion (Pavlov, 1910).

Except for some experiments on the cardiovascular system, Pavlov devoted the first half of his professional career to the study of the gastrointestinal secretions. While working with Heidenhain in Breslau, Germany, Pavlov devised an operation which was largely responsible for the discovery of the conditional reflex. Heidenhain had introduced the "chronic" experiment, in which gastric juice was collected from the isolated gastric pouch of the dog—but in this pouch, the vagal nerves were severed. Pavlov improved this operation by ingeniously preserving the vagal nerve connections to the pouch. Thus he obtained a true reflection, in the isolated pouch, of the secretion in the main part of the stomach. Pavlov also used pancreatic and salivary fistulae for the study of secretion in the intact animal. The salivary fistulae had been devised two hundred years previously by the Dutch physiologist, DeGraaf.

In the study of the gastrointestinal secretions in the dog over a long period, that is, in the chronic experiment, it was possible to make observations which were the basis for the formulation of the conditional reflex. When food was introduced into the mouth or into the stomach there began within a few minutes salivary, gastric, and pancreatic secretions in the externalized fistulae. This was the well-understood physiological reflex, later called the unconditional reflex by Pavlov. Such secretions were characterized by a constant relationship between the amount of a given food and the quantity of secretion, generally a linear relationship. But Pavlov observed many irregularities in and interferences with this constant relationship. These occurred when the dog saw the *Diener* who was accustomed to bring the food, or when he heard his footsteps. Pavlov recognized these anomalies as due to "psychical" causes. But how could he study them?

For two years he debated this question. Would they be law-obeying, deterministic? To embark upon this investigation meant devising new experimental methods, entering an entirely new field, so far not investigated by physiologists and spoken of chiefly subjectively. Psychologists, as well as others, were at that time accustomed to explain these secretions by such subjective representations as "The dog is hungry and wants food."

Although it was generally recognized that the mouth waters at the thought of food, there was no conceptual basis for representing the thought or the symbols of food by a quantitative, physiological measure. Pavlov (1941a) says,

> Where is that knowledge, where is the understanding that might enable us to know correctly the state of our fellow man? In our psychical experiments on the salivary glands (we shall provisionally use the word psychical), at first we honestly endeavored to explain our results by fancying the subjective condition of the animal. But nothing came of it except unsuccessful controversies and individual, personal, uncoordinated opinions. We had no alternative but to place the investigation on a *purely objective* basis (p. 50).

To Pavlov, it became apparent that the salivary secretion was the measure par excellence for the subjective counterpart of the signal for the physiological event of food in the mouth.

In making this transition, Pavlov remained within the domain of the physiology of digestion. He was dealing with a physiological stimulus (food) and a physiological secretion, both of which could be measured, quantitatively and precisely. To adapt this method to a study of "psychical" phenomena required the addition only of another stimulus, the conditional stimulus, namely, visual, auditory, olfactory, or tactile signals for the food.

Thus the paradigm for the new type of experiment was purely physiological. Pavlov began with signals naturally connected with the food, natural conditional stimuli in the appearance of meat or of bread. Later he substituted for these artificial signals, such as bells or lights. The use of artificial stimuli enabled him to introduce *quantification* by regulating their intensities.

Using the healthy animal over a long period of its life (the chronic experiment) was also a great advance in the new study.

Now, a half century after these discoveries, it is hardly necessary to do more than mention the terms and the concepts which Pavlov erected on the basis of his experiments.

Subsequently, Pavlov devised experiments largely on the patterns of the physiological ones he had previously made, always reducing his observations and experimental results to physiological terms. These terms were derived not only from his own physiology of digestion but also from current neurophysiology, many of which came from Sherrington, the great contemporary physiologist of the segmental nervous system (positive and negative induction, irradiation and reciprocal inhibition).

Pavlov attempted to follow the sound scientific principle of reducing the experiment to its simplest basis, operating with as few variable elements as possible. In this way, and through the use of careful controls, he was able to find out the relationship between two specific things at one time, the rest of the matrix being kept constant.[2]

By virtue of his method, the reactions of the organism fell naturally into positive and negative categories, that is, excitatory and inhibitory conditional reflexes and their interactions. The method determines what we measure; it was his method which reduced the activity of the living structure into excitatory and inhibitory responses.

Inhibition is perhaps an unfortunate word for the process opposite to the excitatory conditional reflex because this word has been used for a variety of phenomena: (1) Certain nerves carry impulses which diminish an activity already in progress, for example, the nerve in the mussel which relaxes the tonic closure of its shell and the vagus which slows the heart in higher animals. (2) Central inhibition was discovered by Sechenov, the father of Russian physiology, who, in the middle of the last century, found that sodium chloride placed on the optic thalami of the frog inhibited its movements. Reciprocal inhibition of the extensor and flexor muscles, as in walking, is a familiar case. (3) Pavlov divided inhibition on the suprasegmental level into two kinds, external and internal. The former is what might be called in ordinary parlance "distraction"; it is what we see in the inhibition of the conditional reflex when someone opens the door, or the inhibition caused by a distended bladder. (4) Internal inhibition is a learned, acquired function *developed* from the excitatory conditional reflex. Pavlov called it internal because he considered that its locus was the same as that of the positive conditional reflex from which it was elaborated, whereas external inhibition occurs outside of this locus. Another form of inhibition is the Freudian phenomenon of inhibition, too well known in psychiatry to require description here.

Pavlov's concept of inhibition was somewhat new, and specific to his concept of the conditional reflex. Ordinary inhibition played a minor role in his experiments. The new function was a learned, acquired one related to and dependent on the acquired conditional reflex. Since salivation cannot be measured by a negative quantity, inhibition could be estimated only by its effects on other functions, but not by direct, quantitative

---

[2] The difficulty in dealing with a complex living organism is not that of maintaining a constant external environment, but rather the correct evaluation of the continually shifting internal environment.

methods. Here was a serious deficiency of the method, especially as inhibition was a cornerstone for the structure. Nevertheless, Pavlov devised many an ingenious experiment illustrating the conversion of excitation into inhibition, and vice versa, or their interactions.

The internal inhibition which Pavlov produced from the excitatory conditional reflex was not a neutral, passive state but an active one. Although it was not expressed by either movement or salivation, its effects could be seen in various ways: through disinhibition, inhibition became the positive excitatory conditional reflex; the summation of inhibitory states produced sleep; "collision" between excitation and inhibition resulted in disturbed behavior or "neurosis."

After obtaining facts from the procedures planned to produce inhibition, one of which was the production of a drowsy state and even sleep, Pavlov conceptualized that normal sleep resulted from a summation or extension over the cortex of inhibitory states. He obtained in his dogs many degrees of partial sleep or limited inhibition which he described as hypnotic phases—equivalent, paradoxical, and ultraparadoxical. When he saw inhibition affecting the motor system and not the salivary, he considered such a state comparable to the catalepsy seen in certain psychoses.

Induction, positive and negative, refers to augmentation or diminution of one process by the other, owing to a time sequence. Thus, the excitatory conditional reflex is larger when preceded by inhibition; and excitatory conditional reflexes which follow one another without the interposition of the inhibitory ones tend to become gradually weaker.

Pavlov made a great deal of what he called irradiation and concentration. This had to do with the slow spread of the conditional excitation, as Pavlov thought, first over the cortex, later into the subcortex and its subsequent concentration about the original point of stimulation. Although these experiments have been questioned as to their statistical validity, as well as for the slow spread of the nervous process (requiring as long as minutes to move through the brain), recent electrophysiology has provided some confirmation of Pavlov's theory.

Pavlov discovered and described the orienting reflex (investigatory, focusing response) as a reaction to a novel environment. This is not the same as the startle reflex. It is probably basic to learning. As I have shown experimentally in both dogs and in humans (Gantt, 1943), the absence of the orienting response means diminished alertness and decreased intelligence, whereas an exaggerated orienting response is associated with hyperreactivity and anxiety. Robinson and I demonstrated in 1943 that there is a definite cardiac component (in cardiac heart rate) of the orienting response (Robinson & Gantt, 1947). As shown by Pavlov's alternate term "investigatory," he thought that this was at the basis of the investigative function, culminating in the research ability of the human being (Pavlov, 1928).

While studying the interplay of conditional excitatory and inhibitory processes, Pavlov found that certain dogs became markedly and chronically disturbed when the excitatory conditional stimulus closely resembled the inhibitory in physical character. Thus, when a dog was confronted with a certain tone which meant food (excitation) and another tone of nearly the same pitch which meant no food (inhibition), many dogs became so disturbed that they no longer gave their regular reactions. Pavlov first recognized this conflict in the dog in 1911, but not until 1923, when he repeated similar experiments, did he characterize the situation as one of "experimental neurosis." This term was generally used to cover all chronic behavioral disturbances, regardless of their severity and of their character. Clinically, some of these would be classified as similar to anxiety, psychosomatic disorders, depressions, mania, catatonic states, and so on.

After two decades, as Pavlov's study progressed, he noted that dogs varied in their reactivity and susceptibility to nervous breakdown. Thus Pavlov saw that there were factors other than the *external* environment which determined both the resistance to breakdown and the character of the symptoms. This constitutional factor Pavlov described as *temperament,* basing his groups on the Hippocratic classification: two normal groups, the sanguine and the phlegmatic, and two extreme pathological groups, the melancholic and the manic.[3]

Although what Pavlov chiefly measured quantitatively were the external events, strength of stimuli (both conditional and unconditional), and amplitudes of responses, he freely postulated as to what went on in the nervous system. Thus, he put forward many hypotheses concerning the location of the excitation within the cortex and the subcortex. He considered that the "analyzer" included the peripheral sense organ with all its internal pathways and connections. Pavlov performed a number of cerebral extirpations which led him to the conclusion there was no central locus for the conditional reflex function, but that each analyzer had a centralized ending in the cortex, from which center this function was diffusely spread over the whole cortex. Thus, the visual conditional reflex function was mainly concentrated in the area striata, but the function was also represented in adjacent parts of the occipital lobes and even thinly distributed over the whole cortex. It followed that, in order to abolish auditory or visual conditional reflexes, it was necessary to extirpate the entire cortex.

It is important to note that, in making these deductions, Pavlov dealt chiefly with the dog, using mainly the salivary conditional reflex as the

---

[3] In a personal communication, Dr. John E. Peters says: "I have felt for some while that limiting the mention of temperamental types to the Hippocratic ones, though colorful and interesting, is an injustice to the richness of Pavlov's work on the subject, and may be a conceptual dead end."

measure. Naturally, he would not extend this conclusion to lower animals in which the cortex is absent or poorly developed.

Lashley's extirpation experiments performed on rats indicated substantially what Pavlov had found except that the dog in Pavlov's experiments showed a higher degree of localization and specificity.

Although Pavlov was an extraordinarily skillful surgeon, at the time he performed his extirpations the methods of anatomical post mortem examination were not so accurately carried out as in the best laboratories today. Relatively little attention was paid to the location of the motor conditional reflex. Even during Pavlov's lifetime, there was some dispute in his own laboratory as to whether the conditional reflex could persist in decorticated dogs. The argument concerned chiefly the interpretation of the residual reaction after decortication—whether it was general or specific.

The choice of the salivary secretion as a measure for the new conditional reflex, although unfortunate for medicine, was apt for Pavlov's purpose. Pavlov consciously selected the salivary gland because of its few connections with functions other than the ingestion of food and, furthermore, because its secretion could be quantitatively estimated. This function was also one which Pavlov had previously used in his study of the physiology of digestion. The salivary fistula caused very little disturbance to the dog, much less than did the gastric pouch,[4] and the secretion could be rapidly collected and easily registered outside the experimental room. Thus, the experimenter was separated from the dog.

The cardiovascular system evidently suggested itself to Pavlov as a measure for the conditional reflex, but he rejected it because of its manifold connections with other functions. In his early physiological work, Pavlov had studied blood pressure and heart rate in the dog. Besides the complexity of the cardiovascular system, at that time to record blood pressure and heart rate automatically, from another room, was no simple task.

PAVLOV AND PSYCHIATRY

In the last decade of his life, at about the age of seventy-eight, Pavlov visited the psychiatric clinic regularly and began the application of his concepts to the clinic.

Previously, two of Pavlov's pupils, Krasnogorsky and Ivanov-Smolensky, had carried on extensive experimentation with the human being. Since 1907, Krasnogorsky had been using the salivary conditional reflex principally in children, through the application of a salivary disc on the inside of the cheek over the foramen of the parotid duct. This anticipated by some

---

[4] However, Pavlov's dogs were so well cared for, and the operations so skillfully performed, that even those animals with gastric pouches and pancreatic fistulae lived a normal life. While in Pavlov's laboratory, I saw a fourteen-year-old dog who had had a gastric pouch for twelve years and was still in good health.

years the work of Lashley and Mateer in the United States. Using this method, he found many abnormalities in the conditional reflexes of retarded and pathological children, such as epileptics. Ivanov-Smolensky, although a pupil of Pavlov's, used the motor method of Bekhterev. Whereas Krasnogorsky adhered closely to the pattern of Pavlov's experiments on dogs, using food as the unconditional stimulus and measuring the drops of saliva recorded automatically outside the room, Ivanov-Smolensky's method deviated considerably from this pattern by giving commands and verbal stimuli to his subjects. He also showed pictures to elicit the orienting reflex. Though his stimuli were far removed from the simple unconditional physiological stimuli of Pavlov and Krasnogorsky, Ivanov-Smolensky attempted to explain his results on the basis of Pavlovian concepts, specifically, induction, irradiation, and concentration.

In recent years, after 1950, Krasnogorsky began extremely interesting experiments related to the development of language in the child, both the motor and conceptual aspects. Thus, words for numbers were found to have a quantitative relationship to the salivary conditional reflex.

Luria, Sokolov, Ayrapetyants, Novikova, and others have added considerably to the earlier work of Krasnogorsky and Ivanov-Smolensky, especially with retarded children and on the orienting reflex.

Ayrapetyants formed a conditional reflex to the distention of the bladder, using as a signal the pressure recorded on a scale visible to the patient. After the conditional reflex was elaborated, the patient felt the discomfort when the high-pressure figure on the scale was shown, though no liquid had entered the bladder (Ayrapetyants, 1956).

In spite of the tremendous volume of factual data which had been obtained through the experiments and through the testing of humans in Russia by the conditional reflex method, Pavlov's interest remained, on the other hand, conceptual. He tried to draw analogies between what he found in neurotic dogs and the clinical psychoses. In doing this, he erred in considering psychiatric classification, such as schizophrenia and paranoia, as vigorously, scientifically founded, whereas every psychiatrist knows that these diagnoses are only provisional. Pavlov sought to explain neuroses and psychoses as analogous to his temperaments and to human categories.

An example of his chemical application to the clinic was the imperturbability of the conditional reflexes in castrated dogs, which he considered comparable to the rigidity of thinking in the paranoiac (Pavlov, 1941b, pp. 113, 162).

Another application of Pavlovian theory which has been extensively used in Russia since his death is his idea of *protective inhibition*. This was based on the fact that when conditional stimuli exceed a certain strength, the resulting conditional reflexes no longer increase correspondingly but pass over into inhibition. Pavlov considered this a mechanism protecting the organism from overstimulation, with consequent destruction of nervous function or tissue. This principle has been widely used in Russia in the "sleep" therapy applied to psychiatric patients—however, without striking results.

The lack of success with sleep therapy is probably due to the fact that in psychiatric disorders the main cause is not overstimulation but a disturbed social relationship—what I call *effect of person* (Gantt, 1953, 1956, 1958, 1961; Gantt, Newton, & Royer, 1961; Royer, Newton, & Gantt, 1962).

Another explanation is given in a personal communication by Peters:

> *Effect of person* can conceivably just as well lead to transmarginal inhibition due to exhaustion of nervous processes. Hence transmarginal inhibition may not be relevant as to why sleep therapy has not been so successful.

Rokhlin (1962) summarizes Pavlov's contributions to psychiatry as (1) a consistent theory of the pathophysiology of schizophrenia, (2) an explanation of the symptoms, and (3) a rational basis for therapy. He adds that many of Pavlov's opinions are not "firmly established scientific propositions or conclusions of finished scientific research, but are rather bold scientific conjectures, preliminary scientific hypotheses, thoughts and ideas on some particular question" (pp. 454-504).

Pavlov (1941b, p. 150) divided human beings into two main groups, artists and thinkers, depending upon relationships based upon language —his *second signaling* system. These two main groups can involve Pavlov's other groupings into temperaments.

Pavlov's chief contribution to the understanding of the human being probably was his formulation of human function inherent in language. He recognized that the function of speech, appearing for the first time in nature in the human being, was a definite advance over all subhuman higher nervous system developments. Language is important not only as a means of communication, but as representative of the ability for wide generalizations and elaborations and consequent semantic conflicts, as well as for the grandiose achievements of the human.

In the animal, Pavlov saw the possibility of forming conditional reflexes to direct signals, the conditional stimuli—the primary conditional reflex. But in the human being, there exists the function of representation of both concrete and abstract things through words. These language symbols constitute Pavlov's second signaling system. Inherent in this function is the prodigious extension of the elaboration and representations erected around the primary signalizations, a function which may or may not spill over into words.

LANGUAGE

The concept of the second signaling system, or language function, should not be confined to speech, either spoken or written. Words, the peripheral expression of language, are to the intrinsic function of language what movements are to the total conditional reflex; the essential activity is *within* the central nervous system.

The activity inherent in language occurs independently of the external peripheral expression (the motor activity of the vocal cords, or of the hands in writing) just as in other motor acts the conditional reflex excitation is present whether the executor muscles are paralyzed or not. Thus, the dog can form the motor conditional reflex during the period of muscular paralysis, caused by crushing the anterior nerve roots or under curare, as quickly as he can without paralysis (Royer, Newton, & Gantt, 1962). Because the language function is central, a Helen Keller can form all the internal elaborations peculiar to language, although she may not utter a word, has never heard speech, and may not write. On the other hand, an aphasiac with all the peripheral structures intact is unable to communicate because there is damage *within* the central nervous system.

It is quite possible that the function represented by language extends even to what in the subhumans would be considered the primary conditional reflexes, namely, the first signaling system. Through his ability for generalization and elaboration, man *may* be able to elaborate other signals, such as gestures, as if they were words, that is, to treat the elements of the first signaling system as if they were in the second signaling system. The gesticulatory language of deaf-mutes may be an instance of primary signals (gestures) operating in the second signaling system because these gestures have been elaborated on the basis of language. It is quite possible, moreover, that what we consider stimuli in the first signaling system in humans may partake of the quality of the second signaling system because of the extensive capacity for elaboration and generalization—what we see expressed in pure language—inherent in man. This question, however, remains hypothetical.

In Pavlov's formulation of this main difference between the animal and the human being, expressed in conditional reflex terms, we see his extraordinary capability for an insight derived from physiological experiments and concepts.

Perhaps the great accumulation of experiments in Russia on humans with the Pavlovian method has not been more productive, either in the application or in opening up new fields for study, because Pavlov's successors have tended to equate too closely the complex situation in the human experiments with the simpler one in the dog. By virtue of the function expressed in the second signaling system, much more is involved in dealing with the human being, because of his capability for elaboration. The elements of the experiment constitute for the human being a far greater complex of interwoven factors than is present in the animal experiment.

An example of the need for the concept of the second signaling system, is cited—not, however, to illustrate precisely this—by Skinner (1957, p. 457). He mentions that in conversation in 1934 with Whitehead, the philosopher-mathematician, Whitehead was baffled by the inability of the Pavlovian conditional reflex to explain the mechanism of this statement: "No black scorpion is falling upon this table." From the point of view of Pavlov's concept of language as a complex elaboration of secondary signals, it is apparent that such a sentence cannot be fitted into the same pattern as that of the simple primary conditional reflexes of the dog (Pavlov, 1941b, pp. 113, 162). Skinner points out that, in language, the words represent different signals for the speaker and for the listener.[5]

Skinner does not agree with those (such as John Lilly) who think subhumans (porpoises, chimpanzees) possess the function of language.[6] There is an analogy, however, with the conditional reflex of the dog when we use a simple and strong physiological unconditional reflex such as faradic shock. As this demands an immediate reflex withdrawal, its results are comparable to the animal experiment. On this basis, I have developed a simple conditional reflex test to estimate the neurological integrity of the individual or the status quo of the psychiatric patient (Gantt, 1950, pp. 163-68).

In the field of heredity, Pavlov has been misinterpreted on both sides of the Atlantic. In 1924, he stated in the course of a speech in Edinburgh that it seemed that the ease of forming conditional reflexes could be inherited (Razran, 1958). Later, he made no further written reference to this, although he told me personally that this was one of the biggest scientific errors of his life (Gantt, 1960, pp. 219-239).

GROWTH AND EXTENSION OF PAVLOV'S WORK

In Russia, Pavlov has been the Aristotle of Russian science, affecting nearly all branches of biological research. After the last war and before the death of Stalin, there was political pressure to make Pavlov the patron saint of science from whom it was unwise to differ. I have dealt with this phase of Soviet science (Gantt, 1951) and shall not repeat it here. Fortunately, this era is past. Russian scientists have told me that it is now possible to incorporate Freud into their discussions and articles. The extent of the Russian work in the wake of Pavlov is evidenced by the fact that, in 1958, the second largest research institute in Russia, that of

---

[5] Personal communication.
[6] Personal conversation, February 1963.

Bykov at the Academy of Science in Leningrad, had a staff of seven hundred, including two hundred scientists. This institute is now headed by Professor V. N. Chernigovsky.

In Russia, Pavlov's work has been extended into many fields, notably neuroanatomy (Sarkissov, Asratyan), biochemistry (Vladimirova), psychiatry (Popov, Rokhlin, Snezhnovsky), psychology (Luria, Sokolov). Surprisingly enough, except for the clinical applications of Traugott (1958) and Lichkov and Balonov (1959) there has been very little systematic investigation of the cardiac conditional reflexes. To this discipline several laboratories abroad, however, are devoting their efforts, among them those in Prague (Horvath, Ehrlick, Fronkova), in Amsterdam (Visser, Huetner), the laboratory of Arthur Paterson in West London Hospital, and in this country, the Pavlovian Laboratory of the Johns Hopkins University, the Veterans Administration Psychophysiologic Laboratory at Perry Point, the Veterans Administration Laboratory at North Little Rock (Murphree) and, at the University of Arkansas Medical Center (Reese, Dykman), the laboratory of Liddell at Ithaca.[7]

Bykov and his collaborators in Russia worked extensively on the inclusion of the autonomic nervous system, Rusinov in Russia, and others in this country on the extension to the EEG phenomena (Bykov, 1957; Razran, 1961).

Outside of Russia, probably the most productive European school in neuroanatomy has been that of Konorski in Poland.

The American work which is most closely allied to that of Pavlov is represented by the school of behaviorism and the studies of such psychologists as Thorndike, Watson, Lashley, Solomon, and Skinner, not to mention those who have worked definitely in the Pavlovian tradition, as Liddell and Gantt. Until quite recently, there has been little systematic use of the classical Pavlovian method other than by the two latter groups.

Behaviorism, from the time of Thorndike to Skinner, has been an American development. In fact, it is to Thorndike that Pavlov gives the credit for the discovery of the conditional reflex! In 1921 he wrote:

Some years after the beginning of the work with our new method I learned that somewhat similar experiments on animals had been performed in America, and indeed not by physiologists but by psychologists. Thereupon I studied in more detail the American publications, and now I must acknowledge that the honour of having made the first steps along this path belongs to E. L. Thorndike. By two or three years his experiments preceded ours, and his book must be considered as a classic, both for its bold outlook on an immense task and for the accuracy of its results. Since the time of Thorndike the American work (Yerkes, Parker, Watson, *et al.*) on our subject has grown.

---

[7] Howard Liddell was one of the first pioneers in the United States to use the Pavlovian type of conditioning. He employed sheep, dogs, goats, and hogs. He died in October 1962.

It is purely American in every sense—in collaborators, equipment, laboratories, and publications (1928, p. 40).

Skinner and others have added a new and useful application in "operant," or "instrumental," conditioning. Though the underlying mechanisms may be identical, the emphasis is different: operant conditioning is concerned primarily with the control of behavior and its external relations, whereas Pavlov's conditioning deals mainly with internal relations, known or hypothetical. There are areas where this distinction breaks down, as in the placing of electrodes in the brain.

The statement of Pavlov concerning this difference, although made forty years ago, has validity today:

> The Americans, judged by the book of Thorndike, set out on this new path of investigation in quite a different manner from us. From a passage in Thorndike one may conjecture that the practical American mind applied to everyday life found that it is more important to be acquainted with the exact outward behaviour of man than with guesses about his internal states with all their combinations and changes. With these considerations concerning man, the American psychologists proceeded to their laboratory experiments on animals. From the character of the investigations, up to the present, one feels that both the methods and the problems are derived from human interests.
>
> I and my co-workers hold another position. As all our work developed out of physiology, so it has continued directly in that path. The methods and the conditions of our experimentation, as well as the scheme of the separate problems, the working up of the results, and finally their systematisation—all this has remained in the realm of the facts, conceptions and terminology of the central nervous system. This approach to our subject from both the psychological and the physiological sides enlarges the sphere of the phenomena under investigation (1928, p. 40).

Work with the cardiac conditional reflex in my laboratories has revealed two principles of nervous activity not previously formulated, autokinesis and schizokinesis.

Autokinesis is the term I have given to designate the function and capacity of an organism to change *from within*. This involves the forming of an apparently new relationship between centers in the central nervous system, based on past experiences but developing in the absence of the repetition of the original experience, and without re-enforcement from the *external* environment. Thus in Nick (the dog described in my *Experimental Basis for Neurotic Behavior*), there appeared a whole train of neurotic symptoms related to the original stress, but developing and becoming worse during three years when the animal was removed from the laboratory environment. Even more striking manifestations were observed in the dog "V3," whose symptoms were characterized as similar to those of a catatonic patient by a number of eminent psychiatrists.

My laboratory studies have been chiefly directed to abnormal behavior, and hence, to the pathologic aspect of autokinesis. There is, however, positive, as well as negative, autokinesis. In the normal animal, autokinesis can be seen in the elaboration of new relationships among the original excitatory foci, modifying or completely changing the relationship between the conditional reflexes. Besides examples from my laboratory, there is a host of examples from the laboratories of other workers, as well as from ordinary life. Embryology itself is a phenomenon of development from within, change depending on the internal structure rather than the external environment. Although such autonomic functioning has long been observed, my laboratories have provided a unique opportunity to obtain quantitative measurements for comparison of the past and present responses.

Schizokinesis refers to a dysfunction observable between the visceral and the motor responses to stimuli. This is antithetical to the function of perfect adaptation and balance described by Claude Bernard as maintenance of a constant *milieu intérieur* and by Cannon as homeostasis.

Our research has shown that the cardiac conditional reflex appears more quickly than either the motor or secretory component, often being formed after a single experience, whereas the leg movement or appearance of the secretion to the bell may require 30 to 100 reinforcements. Paradoxically, its disappearance is slower. The cardiovascular conditional reflex is not only not lost by the passage of time, but *it may not be possible to extinguish it,* as can be done with the other conditional reflexes by repeating the conditional stimulus without the unconditional stimulus, for instance, the bell without food. In some dogs, the acquired heart rate conditional reflexes have lasted for eight or more years after the other components have dropped out.

The phenomenon of schizokinesis suggests an innate lack of adaptability in the organism. This rigidity of the cardiovascular system (and to some extent, of the respiratory system) may be responsible for the persistence of blood pressure changes to the traces of old emotional stimuli and situations long after their occurrence and even when they are forgotten. Externally, the body may appear calm and unperturbed, although internally, as seen in the blood pressure and heart rate, there may be violent agitation.

Pascal stated a physiological, as well as poetic, truth when he wrote, "The heart has reasons that reason knows not of." The heart remembers and reacts in the absence of movements or even conscious memory.

Several observations of the fact, but not the principle, of schizokinesis have been noted in the Russian literature. Pavlov (1927) reported a case where the dog became "cataleptic," gave a copious salivary conditional reflex to food but stood motionless and did not eat. Rokhlin states that Ivanov-Smolensky found that in schizophrenic patients there was a "dissocation of conditioned reflex activity. While conditioned motor reactions did not form at all, vegetative reactions (two-phase respiratory, cardiovascular) formed well" (1962, pp. 454-504).

Autokinesis will perhaps direct our attention away from the strictly mechanistic, external aspects of the conditional reflex to the changing world within us. There has been too much preoccupation with the repetitive reflex character of the response and its relation to the external environment—the analogy of the Cartesian machine—and too little with the ontogenetic evolution within the individual.

In making this plea for a profitable extension of the investigation, I would like to acknowledge my indebtedness to Pavlov for his methods, which have made possible the concept of autokinesis.

EVALUATION OF PAVLOV

Several serious treatises have been devoted to the evaluation of Pavlov's work, among them those of Konorski (1949), Straus (1937), Wells (1956-1960), Kubie (1952), Skinner (1957).

Konorski's book on Sherrington and Pavlov is a classic written by one familiar with the teachings of both of these scientists. In spite of his thoroughly scientific approach, the failure in making a successful synthesis may well be due to the complexity of the subject and the fragmentary nature of both Sherrington's and Pavlov's science when compared with the complexity of the nervous system, spinal cord, and brain.

Erwin Straus's book considers Pavlov from the point of view of a philosopher. Straus accepts the experimental facts reported by Pavlov, but he objects to Pavlov's deductions. And he points out certain inconsistencies. Straus (1937) admits that, in spite of these errors, Pavlov, like Columbus, discovered a new world of science.

The relation of Pavlov's teaching to psychoanalysis has been dealt with by French and Alexander (1941), Kubie (1952), and Harry Wells (1956, 1960). French and Alexander have attempted to apply psychoanalytic concepts to some psychosomatic disorders, such as asthma, while Kubie points out the inadequacies of Pavlov's ideas of inhibition for psychoanalytic theory. Wells, in a two-volume treatise on Pavlov and Freud, espouses the work of Pavlov as a thorough, "materialist" scientist versus Freud as a nonscientific "idealist." In spite of the partisan nature of this book (others are perhaps equally partisan on another side), Wells's treatise is worth reading for the scholarly thoroughness with which he writes on both Pavlov and Freud. His bias, however, is not disguised. He divides all his characters, scientists and biologists, into sheep and goats, the monist-materialists and the dualist-idealists. Practically all are lily-white or coal-black, except for an occasional one like Descartes who cannot be categorized.

The prevalence of the Freudian philosophy in America (Dos Passos, 1961, pp. 24-30) was brought forcibly home to me in 1959 in a discussion with a small group of students at a southwestern university far removed from the eastern metropolitan centers. In spite of the fact that the teaching there is not considered to be pre-eminently psychoanalytic (on the contrary, there is a laboratory in this medical school for the study of Pavlovian conditioning) a medical student, in response to some of my critical statements about Freud, replied: "Doctor, this disturbs me. If you do not believe in Freud, what else is there to believe in?"

Freud was largely, as Dos Passos (1961, pp. 24-30) pointed out in a letter to the late Howard Liddell, a poet and philosopher. Freud used the deductive logical method: he set up dogmas from his early observations (not controlled experiments) from which he reached conclusions.

Pavlov, on the other hand, employed the inductive method of collecting facts through controlled laboratory experiments. Most of his life and thinking was within the walls of the laboratory.

Though they may espouse monism, most scientists will recognize that for the subjective phenomena of our life there are no objective representations. A simple test is to try to communicate to anyone the sensation of the color "blue." No matter what you say about its wave length or other measurable physical properties, these do not even approach the subjective feeling. They are of a different order—and never the twain shall meet.

Pavlov says science must be satisfied with its practical achievements— its ability to give us the measurable relationships in physical, objective items. Perhaps the monist should heed the counsel of Planck, not to ask of science questions it cannot answer.

PAVLOV: THE END AND THE BEGINNING
OF AN ERA

Scientists have been motivated by an insatiable curiosity, a hunger to know the truth. Although this urge in itself is amoral, there is generally the conviction that out of this truth will come an immense benefit to the human in his struggle with the forces of nature and evil. Many scientists would not subscribe consciously to any purpose that smacked of conventional morality, although they are usually themselves strongly moralistic. Until the discovery of atomic energy and its military application, the scientist has been justified in his beliefs. He has seen as a result of his discoveries the eradication of most diseases, the subjugation of nature, and the utilization of energy for human use and happiness.

Pavlov was a master experimenter. He developed the physiological experiment to its highest level, using hypothesis, skillful well-designed operations, the normal animal over its life span (the chronic experiment), careful controls, and the established method of Cartesian coordinates in finding the relations between two factors. Furthermore, observation, emphasized by Locke, was a prime method of Pavlov. Engraved above his new laboratory at Koltushi are the words "Observation and Observation."

But since the death of Pavlov, a multitude of new instruments have been thrust into the scientist's hands. He is confounded by a welter of probabilities, uncertainty principles, statistics, computers. He must call in a host of specialists, many of whom are only mechanical and electronic engineers—more interested in the instrument than in the experiment for which the instrument was designed.

Pavlov considered himself a monist. By this he meant he did not deny anything of the spirit—only the appropriateness of its intrusion into the objective, scientific experiment (1941, p. 80).

EVALUATION WORK

Until the time of Pavlov, physiology had used the method of the acute experiment for many reasons. Before anesthesia, experiments had been conducted on cold-blooded animals such as the pithed frog, and indeed the frog is now a favorite object for many experiments. It was with the frog that Sechenov had discovered his "central inhibition." After the introduction of anesthesia in the mid-nineteenth century, the acute experiment of physiology was enormously expanded on mammals—rabbit, cat, dog, anthropoids. The acute experiment is the chief method of present physiology. What may be obtained can be seen from the monumental contributions of Sherrington, described in his *Integrative Action of the Nervous System,* to the understanding of reflexes.

However, the acute experiment reduced the animal to the operation of only the more basic and primitive living forces. It is actually a dying structure, with all the more highly elaborated, finer mechanisms and those dependent on the more delicate structures, such as the cerebral cortex, eliminated. The physiologist is working with a pathologic instead of a physiologic specimen. In most such experiments, the animal does not recover from the effects of the procedure and cannot be observed subsequently.

Much knowledge has been gained from the acute experiment. It has its specific advantages. The external environment except for those stimuli which the experimenter wants to introduce, is minimized. In this way the number of factors is diminished so that one may see the obvious relations between two or three prepotent forces. Also, one is relieved of the responsibility of caring for animals following experimentation.

Because the acute experiment concerns only a part of the living structure, it is obviously not suited to explore the more complex functions responsible for behavior. And even in the study of the lower structures, it often is in error because in life other forces in the organism come into play which may completely alter the function studied.

From his earliest work, Pavlov began to use the chronic experiment in preference to the acute. The methods he designed were for this purpose. The salivary fistula, the pancreatic fistula, the miniature stomach, the choledochus fistula, and the Thiry-Vella fistula, enabled him to study the animal in its normal situation, to study the digestive juices in the course of the dog's healthy life. These specific methods were either designed or adapted by Pavlov for that end.

But even when the chronic experiment was not implied by the method, Pavlov observed the rules of the chronic experiment. Thus in his study of blood pressure, he trained dogs to undergo the procedure without anesthesia. He repeated the experiments from day to day, accustoming the dog to stand quietly on the table while he inserted a cannula into its artery to measure accurately the blood pressure. This was in the 1880s, when little such work was done—still true today.

The chronic experiment has three specific advantages: (1) All the forces of the living structure are capable of acting together as they do in life. One is working with the total organism instead of the part. (2) The animal is a normal, healthy one—not a pathological, dying specimen. (3) The animal can be studied over its life span. In Pavlov's laboratory I have seen a dog twelve years after the performance of a Pavlov pouch still alive and "working," and in my own laboratory we have studied many animals over their entire life, especially the neurotic dogs, Nick and V3, both of whom lived in the laboratory to fourteen years.

This long-term study enables one to use controls on the same dog, and to see the results of what was done previously. From such accumulated effects arose the facts on which were based the concept of the neuroses. In the history of medicine, we also have the famous and enormous contribution to the physiology of digestion, made by Beaumont over a hundred years ago in his study of the patient Alexis St. Martin with a gunshot wound of the stomach.

Physiology has shied away from the chronic experiment for a number of reasons. Among these are: tradition—a very strong factor in all of science; the practical difficulty of caring for animals throughout their lives; and the greater caution necessary in making the observations, owing to the variability of behavior and multiplicity of symptoms, compared to the acute experiment. The difficulty and complexity of the chronic experiment in the investigation of the higher nervous activity, the difficulty of handling the large number of factors, was what concerned Pavlov over the two years when he was deliberating whether to undertake this new research.

The hazards inherent in the chronic experiment are based on the same factors that provide the advantages. As there are so many phenomena that one may observe in the chronic experiment, the inferences drawn depend greatly upon the wisdom of the experimenter in deciding on the items significant to the investigation. To cite but one example, in the experimental neurosis, which is the important factor: the closeness of discrimination between the conditional stimuli; the role of the experimenter and his relation to the dog; the deprivation of companionship; the discomfort, or if faradic shock is used, the pain? In the acute experiment, the number of choices the experimenter has to make are greatly reduced.

In fact, some modern experimenters conduct the chronic experiment without availing themselves of its benefits. Thus, rats are often run through automatic procedures with the mechanical registration of only one or two items and with no observation involving the intuition of the experimenter. Everything is left to the ingenuity of the machine. The gain in accuracy of measurement is at the expense of all those direct, technically unaided observations by the experimenter which furnish the basis for the construction of new concepts, new theories, and new experiments. Without such opportunity for observation, the experimentation is likely to become too mechanical and to mark the sterile end product, the absolute zero of investigative science.

The chronic experiment gave Pavlov the possibility of making the observations from which have arisen the concept of the experimental neurosis, the classification of differences or variability in the dogs according to Hippocratic types or temperaments, and the acknowledgment of the role of the person, that is, the social factor.

Inherent in the method of Pavlov is the intensive study of a small number of dogs, during which the individual is exhaustively observed over a long period of its life. Many phenomena of behavior are recorded which, because of their novelty and lack of standardization, cannot be registered on a machine, for example, the orienting reflex, or response to a new element of the environment. Such observations are, however, subject to the liability of anthropomorphic interpretation—a hazard to be constantly recognized, even though it cannot be avoided.

At the opposite pole to Pavlov's intensive study of a few individuals is the statistical record of large numbers of animals, particularly in experiments with rats. By taking only the averages, nice mathematical relations can be elaborated, everything can be fitted into a formula, and while the results indicate what happens to whole populations, the individual is neglected. Thus the results of an effect in two opposite types may not be seen because statistically they cancel each other out. If one were to average the color of an equal number of blacks and whites, the results would be gray, although not a single individual had this color (Bernard, 1865). Is it not time to inquire whether psychology has gone too far in its enthusiasm for statistical values, for standard deviations, and may now be in danger of the lot of the dog in the fable who drops the meat for the shadow? Should we not preferably differentiate between instances where the statistical method is the one to employ, and those where only direct observation of the intelligent observer is the paramount quality for the advancement of a particular investigation?

Pavlov's method of the chronic experiment is unattractive to physiology for several important reasons. Only a few animals can be studied, and they must be carefully observed by an observer who is not only intelligent and trained but also fitted by temperament to do this work. Furthermore, the observer must depend less on statistical methodology than on his powers of observation. And he has the hazardous task of steering between the rocks of statistics on the one side, and on the other, the whirlpool of anthropomorphism.

Lastly, the Pavlovian viewpoint differs from the American in several ways. American behaviorism and its allied schools are characterized by their emphasis on the practical. By tradition, they are related to psychological concepts rather than to physiology, although many of their adherents now have excellent physiological training. Measurement and statistical methods are used more in the United States, individual observation less, than in the Pavlovian school.

Again, the dog, the prima donna of the Pavlovian laboratory, is replaced by the rat in American psychology. Whereas Pavlov concerned himself intently with what went on inside the organism and constructed many theories on the basis of his laboratory experiments, many American psychologists, for instance, Skinner and his collaborators, feel that more is achieved by concentrating their attention on accurate measurement of the external phenomena, the stimuli and the responses, and treating the brain as the "black box" of Ashby (1960). This emphasis of Skinner on what is observable rather than on theory is a needed balance to the prevalence of the Freudian point of view in the United States which has just the reverse tendency—the devotion of the chief effort to theories as to what goes on inside and the neglect of external measurements. The achievements of Skinner and his school is *ipso facto* evidence for the success of his method and teaching.

Finally, Pavlov, as well as every student of the nervous system, owes much to Descartes' concept of reflex. Pavlov and Sherrington adhered to this concept either implicity or explicity in their epochal researches. The difference between them is that whereas Sherrington did not think that his laboratory methods could give him the ultimate answers to the riddle of our mental life, Pavlov (1941) had the adolescent hope that at some future time "the omnipotent scientific method will deliver man from his present gloom, and will purge him from his contemporary shame in the sphere of interhuman relations" (p. 41).

REFERENCES

AYRAPETYANTS, E. S. *Die höhere Nerventätigkeit und die Rezeptoren der innerin Organe.* Berlin: 1956.

ASHBY, W. Ross. *Design for a brain.* New York: Wiley, 1960.

BALONOV, L. Y. Conditional reflex regulation of cardiac activity in the human (in Russian). *Akad. Nauk SSSR,* 1959.

BERNARD, CLAUDE. *Introduction of l'étude de la médicine expérimentale.* Paris: 1865.

BYKOV, K. M. *The cerebral cortex and the internal organs.* W. Horsley Gantt (Ed. & tr.). New York: Chemical Publishing Co., 1957.

DOS PASSOS, JOHN. *Midcentury,* Boston: Houghton Mifflin, 1961.

FRENCH, T., & ALEXANDER, F. Psychogenic problems in bronchial asthma. *Psychosom. Med. Monog.,* 1941, **2** (1,2).

GANTT, W. H. Measures of susceptibility to nervous breakdown. *Amer. J. Psychiat.,* 1943, **99** (6), 839-849.

GANTT, W. H. The conditional reflex function as an aid in the study of the psychiatric patient. In P. H. Hoch & J. Zubin (Eds.), *Relations of psychological tests to psychiatry.* New York: Grune & Stratton, 1950. Pp. 163-168.

GANTT, W. H. Russian physiology and pathology. *Soviet Science,* 1952, **2,** 8-39.

GANTT, W. H. Principles of nervous breakdown—schizokinesis and autokinesis. *Annals of New York Academy of Sciences,* 1953, **56** (2), 143-163.

GANTT, W. H. What the laboratory can teach us about nervous breakdown. In I. Galdston (Ed.), *Medicine in a changing society.* New York: International Univ. Press, 1956. Pp. 72-110.

GANTT, W. H. Recent Contributions to Objective Psychiatry. In *Proc. 6th Annual Psychiatric Institute.* Princeton: 1958. Pp. 72-73.

GANTT, W. H., PAVLOV & DARWIN. *Evolution after Darwin.* Vol. 2. Univ. Chicago Press, 1960. Pp. 219-239.

GANTT, W. H. Factors involved in the development of pathological behavior: schizokinesis and autokinesis. *Perspectives in Biology and Medicine,* 1962, **5** (4).

GANTT, W. H. & DYKMAN, R. A. Experimental psychogenic tachycardia. In P. H. Hoch & J. Zubin (Eds.), *Experimental psychopathology.* New York: Grune & Stratton, 1957. Pp. 12-19.

GANTT, W. H. NEWTON, J. E. O., & ROYER, F. L. Development of the experimental neurosis: mechanism and factors. In *Proc. Third World Congress of Psychiatry,* Vol. 2. Montreal: Third International Congress in Psychiatry, 1961. (a)

GANTT, W. H., NEWTON, J. E. O., & ROYER, F. L. Principles of nervous breakdown. In *Proc. Third World Congress of Psychiatry,* Montreal: Third International Congress in Psychiatry, 1961. (b)

KONORSKI, J. *Conditioned reflexes and neuron organization.* London: Oxford, 1949.

KUBIE, L. K. Problems and techniques of psychoanalytic validation and progress. In E. Pumpian-Mindlen (Ed.), *Psychoanalysis as science*. New York: Basic Books, 1952. Pp. 46-124.

PAVLOV, I. P. *Conditional reflexes*. London: Oxford, 1927.

PAVLOV, I. P. *Lectures on conditioned reflexes*. New York: International Publishers, 1928.

PAVLOV, I. P. *The work of the digestive glands*. Philadelphia: Lippincott, 1910.

PAVLOV, I. P. *Lectures on conditioned reflexes*. New York: International Publishers, 1941. (a)

PAVLOV, I. P. *Conditional reflex and psychiatry*. New York: International Publishers, 1941. (b)

RAZRAN, G. Pavlov and Lamarck. *Science*, 1958, **128,** pp. 758-760.

RAZRAN, G. Interoceptive conditioning. *Psychol. Rev.* 1961, **68** (2), pp. 81-147.

ROBINSON, J., & GANTT, W. H. The orienting reflex (questioning reaction): cardiac, respiratory, salivary, and motor components. *Bull. Johns Hopkins Hosp.*, 1947, **80** (5), 231-253.

ROKHLIN, L. L. Pavlovian concept of schizophrenia in Pavlov. *Selected works*. Moscow: Foreign Languages Publishing Co., 1962.

ROYER, FRED L., NEWTON, J. E. O., & GANTT, W. H. CNS excitation versus peripheral activity in cardiac conditional reflexes. *Trans. Amer. Neurol. Ass.*, 1962, **87,** 258-259.

SECHENOV, I. M. *Reflexes of the brain*. St. Petersburg: 1863.

SKINNER, B. F. *Science and human behavior*. New York: Macmillan, 1953.

SKINNER, B. F. *Verbal behavior*. New York: Appleton-Century-Crofts, 1957.

STRAUS, ERWIN. *Vom Sinn der Sinne*. Berlin: 1937.

TRAUGOTT, N. N. Evolution of physiological functions. *Akad. Nauk. SSSR*, 1958.

WALTER, W. GREY. Where vital things happen. *Amer. J. Psychiat.*, 1960, **116** (8), 674.

WELLS, H. K. *Pavlov and Freud*. Vols. 1 and 2. New York: International Publishers, 1956 and 1960.

10 BENBOW F. RITCHIE

CONCERNING AN INCURABLE VAGUENESS
IN PSYCHOLOGICAL THEORIES *

> Work and pray, live on hay,
> You'll get pie in the sky,
> When you die—
> It's a lie!
> —*Song of the I. W. W.*

If the reader wonders how it is that so many acute minds have accepted the Berkeleyan argument, let him remember how infrequently men say, "This argument would prove the truth of my contention but it is invalid all the same."—M. R. Cohen, *Reason and Nature.*

Ye that do not wish well to the proceedings of adulterers, it is worth your while to hear how they are hampered on all sides.—Horace, *Satires.*

As a psychologist, cursed with an unshakable conviction that we should understand what we believe, I have for a long time been troubled with questions about the logical and semantical well-being of psychological theories built over, or around, a set of so-called "operational, empirical, coordinating, or functional behavioral definitions." I hope in this chapter to make the troublesome character of these questions so apparent that some ambitious young psychologist, philosopher, logician, or semanticist will be goaded into showing us how they are to be answered. Perhaps they can be answered without throwing out the baby (operationism) with the bath, but I strongly doubt it; and as I have no stomach for washing such a messy baby, I shall confine my efforts to catching the little rascal and popping him in the tub. After that, it is up to his parents or his guardians to discover a way of cleaning him without killing him.

If we begin by thinking of learning as a process in which some set of associations is changed by training, we can then distinguish two kinds of

---

* For discussion, criticism, and advice I want to thank David Krech and Leo Postman, neither of whom can be held responsible for my conclusions.

150

learning theories by calling attention to two different ways (1) of conceiving of these associations, and (2) of conceiving of how these associations are changed by training. One kind of learning theory (for example Hull's) regards the associations as conditioned responses and presumes that training in which reward follows the response is both necessary and sufficient to increase the strength of such habits. The other kind of theory (for example Tolman's) regards the associations as habits of expecting one sort of stimulus pattern (S_2) to occur after a certain response (R) to a certain other stimulus (S_1). This kind of theory also presumes that training in which this S_1-R-S_2 triad regularly occurs is both necessary and sufficient to increase the associative strength of such cognitive habits. Most contemporary textbooks on the psychology of learning distinguish the S-R reward theories from the S-R-S cognitive theories in some such way, and many of them, after contrasting the two kinds of theory, conclude that, because the ideas of S-R habit and reward are less vague than the idea of expectancy, the S-R reward theories are to be preferred. As Kendler (1959) puts it, "S-R psychology dominates the psychology of learning. The success of S-R psychology is partly due to the fact that it forces its user to think in terms of manipulable experimental variables and observable responses. . . . Cognitive theory," on the other hand, says Kendler, "is either asleep or dying." There is, of course, no more effective soporific than vagueness, and the troubles I have in understanding theories built from operational definitions have led me to doubt whether either sort of theory is awake to the world of fact it purports to explain.

Among learning theorists, the most important controversies appear to be those that inspire the greatest amount of indecisive experimentation. Most of these controversies arise from disputes about whether reward is either necessary or sufficient to increase the associative strength of an S-R pair. Postman (1962) and Estes (1960), both S-R psychologists, have recently argued about whether such associations are strengthened little by little with each rewarded trial, or whether they are instantly and completely formed on some fortuitous trial. This dispute, as we shall see, ultimately comes down to this question: Is reward sufficient to increase associative strength? Thorndike, Hull, Spence, Miller, and their students have argued for thirty years with Tolman and his students about the correct interpretation of the latent-learning experiments. This apparently endless dispute ultimately comes down to this question: Is reward necessary to increase associative strength?

Those who believe that reward is either necessary, or sufficient, or both, appear to have a strong case, and they find it hard to understand why Tolman and his students are not persuaded by it. Their case is simply stated. Although hundreds of well-controlled experiments have investigated the effects of rewards on associative strength, not one of them has decisively refuted the belief that reward is both necessary and sufficient. From this they conclude that, because these two hypotheses are probably not false (else they would have been disproved), they are probably true. Why then are Tolman and his students not persuaded? The answer is simple. Although there is no evidence that refutes these hypotheses, the reason for this may lie not in the fact that the hypotheses are true, but in the fact that they are so vague at critical points they cannot be shown to be false. When we think about the kinds of evidence we need to test these hypotheses, and about the kinds of definitions we have for the terms "reward" and "$_sH_r$," (an abbreviation for the associative strength of an S-R pair), we may begin to understand why some psychologists suspect that neither of these hypotheses is testable.

"An operational definition of a term," says Deese (1958, p. 5), "is a description of the operations performed by an experimenter or observer and the changes in behavior that result." If two experiments investigating the effects of stimulus intensity on reaction time yield contradictory outcomes, the first question to ask is whether "stimulus intensity" and "reaction time" have the same meaning for the two experiments. The most precise way of deciding this is to ask each experimenter what operations he uses to measure various stimulus intensities and reaction times. The description of the operations provide us with operational definitions of these two key terms. By emphasizing such questions about our terms, the thesis of operationism has helped to keep our ideas tied to concrete laboratory facts and to prevent them from floating off into abstract speculations that are not readily laid open to experimental treatment.

"Desire, reward, motives, etc.," Deese goes on to say, "can all be given surprisingly precise definitions if described in this way. A hungry rat, according to the operational definition agreed on by psychologists, is one that has been deprived of food for a period of time after having been on an accustomed feeding schedule." In this passage as well as in the one that follows, Deese states the widely held, uncontested, orthodox view of the one correct method for defining or explicating the meanings of all the concepts in all contemporary learning theories. In the following passage, Deese gives a formal definition of reinforcement (a more ceremonious word for "reward") and his explanation of what is meant by strength of response, or $_sH_r$.

A reinforcement is any stimulus event that will increase or maintain the strength of a response or a stimulus-response connection associated with it. . . . Strength of response is properly an intervening variable, something that cannot be directly observed. Rather we infer the strength of a response from some aspect of the response we can measure. . . . The most important indicator of strength of response is a measure ordinarily called probability of response. This is the likelihood that a response will occur in a given unit of time when a particular stimulus is presented. . . . Some investigators prefer to limit the measurement of strength of response to probability, and still other investigators try to reduce all other possible indicators of strength of response to some form of probability of occurrence. In practice, however, many other indicators are used. Two of these are reaction time or latency, and amplitude or magnitude of response. (p. 16)

For our present discussion we need a precise operational definition for each of two expressions: (1) "x is an S-R pair with an $_sH_r$ greater than zero"; and (2) "x is an event that rewards some S-R pair." Following the ideas in Deese's discussion, we propose a pair of operational definitions for these expressions.

DEFINITION 1. If x is an S-R pair, and S now evokes its paired R, then x *is an S-R pair with an $_sH_r$ greater than zero*. Thus, to be an S-R pair with an $_sH_r$ greater than zero is to be a pair in which S *can* evoke its paired R.

DEFINITION 2. If x is an event that follows an S-R pair, and increases the $_sH_r$ of that pair, then x *is an event that rewards some S-R pair*. Thus, to be a reward is to be an event that *can* strengthen some S-R pair.

Such are the sorts of operational definitions or rules that we psychologists use to explain what we mean by "$_sH_r$" and "reward." Although it is difficult to estimate from our behavioral indices the exact $_sH_r$ of any S-R pair, if the S evokes its paired R, we must, by this rule, conclude that the $_sH_r$ is greater than zero. Similarly, although we cannot exactly estimate the rewarding power of any stimulus, if this stimulus increases the $_sH_r$ of any S-R pair, we must, by this rule, conclude that it is a reward. One may, of course, ask how, with *this* definition of reward, we can sensibly ask for *evidence* that rewards increase $_sH_r$. Meehl (1950) considered this problem some years ago and suggested what has now become the orthodox solution. Meehl argued that with this definition we can identify instances of events (for instance, food, water, and so on) that increase the $_sH_r$ of particular S-R pairs, and then search for *evidence* that such events will increase the $_sH_r$ of any S-R pair. As Kimble (1961, pp. 206-207) puts it, "No one worries about it any more," now that we know that a reward "in one situation will function as such in another. This transituational character of reinforcement breaks the circle." Let us for the present, while we can, be guided by Kimble's reassuring comments. Later, we shall see.

Now that we have a clear understanding of what is operationally meant by "$_sH_r$" and "reward," we may consider what we need to do to test the belief that reward is either necessary or sufficient to increase $_sH_r$. Before we turn directly to this question, however, it will help to consider a simpler case where the meanings of the key terms are not only easier to grasp but also easier to retain. Here we can focus our attention upon the logical differences between these two kinds of hypotheses. An understanding of these differences is essential to an understanding of what we need to do to test these two hypotheses. Once these points are clear, we can return to an analysis of our hypotheses about reward and $_sH_r$. Consider, then, what we must do to test each of the following illustrative hypotheses: (1) three or more packs of cigarettes per day for forty years is *sufficient* to produce lung cancer; and (2) three or more packs of cigarettes per day for forty years is *necessary* to produce lung cancer.

To believe that this cigarette diet is *sufficient* to produce lung cancer in forty years is to believe the following general proposition:

HYPOTHESIS 1. For all *x,* if *x* has had three or more daily packs for forty years, then *x* has lung cancer.

How, now, do we test this proposition? and what kind of evidence must we get to confirm it? To test it we must search high and wide for one person who has smoked three or more daily packs for forty years, and who *does not have* lung cancer. Should we find such a person this hypothesis is false: this cigarette diet is not sufficient to produce lung cancer. However, if we fail to find such a person no matter how widely we search among persons of different ages, occupations, and climates, it becomes more and more reasonable to suppose that the hypothesis is true rather than false. Such evidence *confirms* the hypothesis to the degree that the search has varied over a wide range of conditions and has failed to find a negative instance. Thus, the key to testing and to confirming such an hypothesis is to search everywhere for a smoker on this diet who *does not have* lung cancer.

Now consider the hypothesis that this cigarette diet is a *necessary* condition for producing lung cancer. To believe this is to believe the following:

HYPOTHESIS 2. For all *x,* if *x* has lung cancer, then *x* has had three or more daily packs for forty years.

To test and to confirm this hypothesis we must search everywhere for one person with lung cancer who *has not had* three or more daily packs for forty years. If we fail to find one such person, no matter how widely we search, it becomes more and more reasonable to suppose that the hypothesis is true.

So far, we have presumed that the meanings of our key terms "3-pack diet" and "lung cancer" were free from vagueness, that is, that we would never be in doubt about whether or not a certain person had been on this diet for forty years, or about whether or not a certain person had lung cancer. If we are wrong in this presumption, then our power to confirm either hypothesis will be limited precisely by the amount of vagueness in these two terms. As long as there are some cases in which we have no doubts about the person's diet and health we can test those hypotheses with these cases, but as long as there are other cases where we cannot remove our doubts, we must recognize that the failure to find negative instances, no matter how wide our search, may be the result of our inability to identify such instances when they occur. Thus, such hypotheses as these only become highly confirmed when the key terms are free from vagueness, the factual search has been wide and deep, and no negative instances have been found.

If this explanation of what must be done to test and to confirm such hypotheses is correctly and clearly stated, there should be no difficulty in understanding what we must do to test and confirm the two hypotheses that concern us.

HYPOTHESIS 3. For all x, if x is an S-R pair and x has been rewarded, then x has an $_sH_r$ greater than zero.

HYPOTHESIS 4. For all x, if x is an S-R pair and x has an $_sH_r$ greater than zero, then x has been rewarded.

To test the hypothesis that reward is *sufficient* (hypothesis 3) we must search for: One rewarded S-R pair that has an $_sH_r$ *not* greater than zero.

To test the hypothesis that reward is *necessary* (hypothesis 4) we must search for: One S-R pair with an $_sH_r$ greater than zero that has not been rewarded.

To say that either hypothesis is confirmed (that is, it is unreasonable *not* to suppose it true) is to say: (1) that the key terms in the hypothesis are free of vagueness; (2) that we have searched widely for negative cases; and (3) that we have failed to find one.

We have already conceded that despite the vast number of experiments that have studied the effects of rewards on learning, we have as yet found no evidence that proves that either of these hypotheses is false. Such evidence would serve to confirm these hypotheses, but only if our operationally defined concepts of "$_sH_r$" and "reward" were sufficiently free of vagueness to enable us to detect most negative instances should they occur. If, however, these concepts are too vague to detect them, then it is impossible to test or to confirm these hypotheses. From an examination of several of the controversies current among those of us who are learning theorists, I have come to wonder whether such operationally defined concepts are not so vague that no theory of learning built from them can be tested or confirmed. To illustrate how I was led to this disturbing doubt, let us consider the current controversy between Postman (1962) and Estes (1960) about how the associative strength ($_sH_r$) of a paired associate changes with practice.

Imagine a learning curve for a group of subjects in a paired-associate experiment. Each trial presents the subjects with a list of paired associates. Each subject has two seconds after the first member of each pair appears to respond with the second member. At the end of training, the experimenter calculates the mean number of correct responses (that is, those meeting his criteria of speed and accuracy) on each of the trials. From these means, he plots his learning curve to show how often the group responded correctly to the items in the list. In all such curves, the correct responses increase gradually with practice.

Most psychologists believe that these gradual increases in the learning curve reflect gradual increases in the associative strengths of each of the S-R pairs for all of the subjects. Each trial, according to this view, increases the associative strength of each of the S-R habits. As the strengths of these habits accumulate, the frequency with which subjects make correct responses increases.

Some psychologists, however, do not accept this interpretation of the learning curve and ask us to examine, instead, the changes in response to a particular item in a particular subject. Here we observe that, although the subject may fail for several trials to give a correct response to this item, once he does give one, he rarely misses it again. This suggests, say these psychologists, that each of the S-R habits may be acquired once and for all on some single trial. Thus, according to this view, the learning curve merely records the gradual accumulation by the group of such one-trial, once-and-for-all associations. This has been called "the one-trial hypothesis," in contrast to the more orthodox "incremental hypothesis."

Estes (1960) has recently published some paired-associate experiments that appear to contradict the incremental hypothesis, but not the one-trial hypothesis. Postman (1962) has published a reply to Estes' papers that appears to contradict the one-trial hypothesis and show that Estes' experimental evidence does not contradict the incremental hypothesis. Let us begin with Postman's criticisms of the one-trial hypothesis.

Postman argues that this hypothesis implies the following four consequences, each of which is contradicted by experimental fact: (1) that no learning of an S-R pair occurs in the trials before the first correct response; (2) that overtraining will not increase the retention of such S-R pairs; (3) that there can be no competition in recall between alternative responses to the same stimulus; and (4) that, if an S fails to evoke its paired R on the first test trial, it will not evoke this R on later test trials. If these four propositions are implied by the one-trial hypothesis, as Postman says, then Postman's facts and arguments are devastating.

However, these consequences are derivable from the one-trial hypothesis only if one assumes, as Postman thinks this hypothesis must, that the strength of an S-R association remains "at zero as long as the subject continues to make errors" and that "an item failed on the first test trial must be assumed to have zero strength, and hence should not occur as a correct response on subsequent test trials." In short, Postman's criticisms presume that the one-trial hypothesis contains the following definition, or operational rule:

DEFINITION 1A. If x is an S-R pair, and S does *not* now evoke its paired R, then x is *not* an associated pair.

But this rule must be rejected by the one-trial hypothesis because it implies that an S-R pair is *not* associated whenever R fails to be evoked by S for whatever reason (for example, change in instructions, a change in contextual stimulation, and so forth). Both Guthrie and Estes, the main advocates of the one-trial hypothesis, have always maintained that the probability of a formerly rewarded response depends not only on whether this response has been associated with certain stimuli, but also on how similar the present total pattern of stimulation is to the pattern that was presented when the association was formed.[1] This proviso logically excludes rule 1A, and provides the rationale for answers to each of Postman's four criticisms.

Although, as Postman's evidence shows, some learning of a paired associate occurs before the subject's first correct response, the one-trial hypothesis assumes that this early learning is masked by hidden intertrial variations in stimulation. The correct response will not be evoked until a trial occurs that first presents an associated stimulus pattern. The more intertrial variation, the greater the delay before the first correct response.

When overtraining increases retention, the one-trial hypothesis assumes that the added trials increase the variety of stimulus patterns associated with the correct responses and thus increases retention by reducing the probability that an unassociated pattern will occur in the retention test.

When response-competition occurs in recall, the one-trail hypothesis assumes that the intratrial variation in stimulation, occurring during two-second exposure of each stimulus item, results in an alternation between competing responses associated with the different patterns that appear within that period.

When a response that was missed on the first test appears on a later test trial, the one-trial hypothesis assumes that the intertrial variation in stimulation reduced the probability that an associated pattern would appear until a later test.

So much for Postman's criticisms of the one-trial hypothesis. Without rule 1A (no response implies no association) Postman's facts and argu-

---

[1] Although the attacks Estes made on the incremental hypothesis were accompanied by important changes in his own hypothesis (from what he calls a "linear model" to a "one-element model"), the key transfer axiom, *that the probability of a test response depends, in part, on the amount of difference between the test S and the S to which this R has been associated,* was not changed. Because, in his later one-element model, Estes emphasized the one-trial, all-or-none character of associative change, some of his critics mistakenly thought that Estes had given up this axiom. However, no hypothesis that proposes to describe how training with one S influences the response to a later test S can do without some form of this transfer axiom. What distinguishes Estes' later analyses of paired-associate learning from his earlier analyses is that in the later ones he assumes (with no evidence whatsoever) that the differences between training and testing stimulation are negligible. This gratuitous assumption allows him to infer that "the strength of an S-R association remains at zero as long as the subject continues to make errors." This inference is, of course, the keystone of Estes' attack on the incremental hypothesis, and because Estes did not make the logical grounds for this inference clear, his critics mistakenly concluded that Estes had given up the key transfer axiom, and had adopted in its place the operational rule in Definition 1A.

ments come to nothing, and the one-trial hypothesis flatly rejects rule 1A.

By this time it should be clear that the dispute between the one-trial and the incremental hypotheses comes ultimately down to a dispute about whether or not reward is *sufficient* to increase $_sH_r$. The incremental hypothesis, by assuming that the $_sH_r$ of each S-R pair is increased on each trial, is committed to the premise that reward is sufficient. The one-trial hypothesis, on the other hand, denies this premise in its assumption that there may be no increase in the $_sH_r$ of some S-R pairs until after the first trial.

Estes' experiments are simply and beautifully designed to find rewarded S-R pairs in which the $_sH_r$ is *not* greater than zero. His subjects were given one trial in which both members of a list of eight paired associates were exposed. This, he and Postman agree, was a rewarded trial for all S-R pairs. Following this, each subject was tested with the stimulus member of each pair. This, he and Postman agree, was an unrewarded test trial. In this test, 49 per cent of the responses were correct. If reward is a sufficient condition for increasing $_sH_r$, as the incremental hypothesis presumes, this outcome implies that one rewarded trial increased the $_sH_r$ of all pairs to the point where the probability in each pair of evoking a correct response was .49. If this be granted, then, Estes argues, the proportion of correct responses in a second test must be approximately the same for those S-R pairs that were missed on the first test as for those pairs that were not. Estes' evidence contradicts this conclusion: 71 per cent of the stimuli that evoked correct responses on the first test did so again on the second test, whereas only 9 per cent of the stimuli that failed to evoke correct responses on the first test succeeded in evoking them on the second test. Estes concludes from this that the $_sH_r$ of the twice-missed pairs was *not* greater than zero. Such a conclusion contradicts the incremental hypothesis by showing that reward is not sufficient to increase the $_sH_r$ of all S-R pairs.

However, this conclusion can be drawn from the evidence only if we presume, as Estes does, that the incremental hypothesis implies that the $_sH_r$ of an S-R pair is *not* greater than zero when the S fails to evoke its paired R on two or more test trials. In brief, Estes' criticism of Postman, like Postman's criticism of Estes, is based on forcing the following kind of definition or operational rule upon his opponent:

DEFINITION 1B. If x is an S-R pair, and S does *not* now evoke its paired R, then x has an $_sH_r$ *not* greater than zero.

In practice, Estes requires two tests before he concludes that the $_sH_r$ is *not* greater than zero, but the idea is the same whether he requires one or a thousand tests—if the response is not evoked then the $_sH_r$ is not greater than zero. This rule is, however, no more acceptable to Postman than it is to Estes, and Postman rejects it by asserting that the probability of a response depends not only on whether $_sH_r$ is greater than zero, but also on the magnitude of the response-evocation threshold of the S-R pair, as well as on many other conditions such as motivation, stimulus context, and so on. "No observable response will occur," says Postman, "until habit strength has reached the value required for the attainment of the reaction threshold." Thus, Postman argues, although every S-R pair received the same incremental $_sH_r$ from the one rewarded trial, some S-R pairs have low and some have high reaction thresholds. The twice-missed pairs in Estes' experiment were those pairs with higher thresholds than those that were not missed twice. Although Estes claims that the pairs missed on the first test were no more difficult to learn when a second reward was given, such evidence tells us nothing about the assumed differences in reaction thresholds. Thus Postman saves the incremental hypothesis by rejecting the operational rule 1B, just as Estes saves the one-trial hypothesis by rejecting operational rule 1A.

One could at this point ponder the merits of two hypotheses that account for apparently contrary evidence, one by appealing to assumed hidden intertrial variations in stimulation, and the other by appealing to assumed hidden differences in reaction thresholds. This however would distract us from our primary goal—the discovery of a way of testing the hypothesis that reward is sufficient to increase $_sH_r$. As we have taken pains to make clear, to test this hypothesis, we must be able to detect all instances of *rewarded but unassociated S-R pairs*. Both Estes and Postman have rejected the operational rules for detecting such pairs suggested by their critics. Can we now devise new rules acceptable to either Estes or Postman that would let us test the hypothesis?

Consider the following Estesian rule for "x is a rewarded but unassociated S-R pair":

DEFINITION 2A. If x is an S-R pair, and if x has been rewarded at least once, and if the present S is identical to an S that was present when R was rewarded, and if the present S does *not* evoke this R, then x is a rewarded but unassociated S-R pair.

Rule 2A. takes account of each of Estes' objections to rule 1A., and as a result should express what Estes means by this concept. But now consider the practical difficulties that arise when we try to use this rule to detect rewarded but unassociated S-R pairs. We must know (1) what exact S pattern was present whenever the response was rewarded, and (2) what exact S pattern is present in the test. Only if we know that the S pattern in the test is identical to one of the S patterns present when the response was rewarded, can we conclude from no response that the S-R pair was rewarded but not associated. However, our knowledge of what S patterns are present during training and testing is never exact. On the contrary, it is usually extremely vague, and this vagueness so contaminates our search for evidence that there is little ground for hoping that we can, with such a rule, test the hypothesis that reward is sufficient to increase $_sH_r$.

Consider then instead the following Postmanian rule for "x is a rewarded S-R pair with an $_sH_r$ *not* greater than zero."

DEFINITION 2B. If x is an S-R pair, and if x has been rewarded at least once, and if $\Delta_s H_r$ (when it occurs) is greater than the reaction-threshold of this S-R pair, and if the present S does *not* now evoke this R, then x is a rewarded S-R pair with an $_s H_r$ *not* greater than zero.

To the extent that this rule takes account of Postman's objections to rule 1B., it should express what Postman means by this concept. Obviously, if with each reward $\Delta_s H_r$ is greater than zero (as Postman believes), then the class of rewarded pairs with an $_s H_r$ not greater than zero will be empty. If, however, the class is not empty, then Postman's belief, that reward is sufficient to increase $_s H_r$, is false. But now consider the practical difficulties in using this rule to test that hypothesis. We must know (1) the exact value of $\Delta_s H_r$ for this S-R pair; (2) the exact number of times this pair has been rewarded, and (3) the exact magnitude of the reaction threshold for this pair. Our task is further complicated, as Postman points out, by individual differences among subjects. Not only do different pairs have thresholds of different magnitudes, but also the magnitude of the threshold of any one S-R pair may be different for different subjects. Thus nothing could be vaguer than this rule.

Postman rejects Estes' inference that the $_s H_r$ of twice-missed items is zero, because, according to Postman, this inference is valid only if the frequency of correct responses on test 2 "can be shown to be independent of the number of prior reinforcements." Perhaps, if we can make clear what is meant by "independent of prior reinforcements," this idea will give us a practical operational rule. Postman describes an experiment in which the frequency of correct responses on test 2 was greater when the subjects had six prior rewarded trials than when they had only one or two such trials. This evidence makes clear what is meant by saying that the frequency is *dependent* on prior reinforcement, but it does not make clear what evidence would be needed to say the frequency was *independent* of prior reinforcement; and *this* is the concept we need. Suppose Postman ran another experiment and in this case found no evidence that the frequency of correct responses was greater after six reinforcements than after one. Would this force him to conclude that, in this case, the frequency was independent of prior reinforcement, and that therefore the $_s H_r$ was not greater than zero? Obviously not. Only if there were no change in the frequency after *"almost endless"* reinforcements would he be logically forced to conclude that the frequency was independent of prior reinforcements. Such an interpretation of the operational rule, however, makes it as vague and useless as those we have already considered and rejected.

This logical criticism of the last suggested rule may seem too abstract and removed from matters of experimental fact to be taken seriously. If this logical criticism were the only objection to this rule we might try to circumvent this objection by adopting some arbitrary criterion of how many reinforcements are enough to conclude that the frequency of response is independent of prior reinforcements. Consider the following rule:

DEFINITION 3B. If x is an S-R pair, and if x has been rewarded N times (where N is greater than one), and if S does *not* now evoke R, then x is a rewarded S-R pair with an $_sH_r$ *not* greater than zero.

Such an operational rule is exact enough to let us detect every S-R pair with an $_sH_r$ *not* greater than zero, provided that pair has been rewarded N times. But what about the pairs that have been rewarded less than N times? When they fail to evoke a response, what can we say about the $_sH_r$ of such pairs? Obviously, we can say nothing, and because we can say nothing, this rule is no less vague than each of the rules we have already examined and rejected.

One cannot view these operational attempts to define the idea of an unassociated S-R pair, without beginning to wonder how much vagueness of this sort dilutes every other psychological theory. Consider the following hypotheses, each a cornerstone of some theory of learning.

HYPOTHESIS 1. Rewarding an S-R pair is *necessary* to increase the $_sH_r$ of that pair.

HYPOTHESIS 2. Not rewarding a formerly rewarded S-R pair is *sufficient* to decrease the frequency with which this S will evoke its paired response.

HYPOTHESIS 3. Pairing a reward N or more times with any S is *sufficient* to make that S become a reward.

HYPOTHESIS 4. Drive x (say, fear) is *necessary* for the evocation of some behavior (say, exploration).

HYPOTHESIS 5. The selection of the relevant cues is *necessary* for learning to discriminate between two stimulus patterns. To test and confirm these hypotheses (that is, to make it more reasonable to suppose them true than to suppose them false) we must search high and wide for negative instances and fail to find one. Thus, the *only* evidence that will confirm these hypotheses is evidence that shows how widely and intensively we have searched without finding a negative instance. Consider then the sorts of *negative instances* for which each of these hypotheses sends us searching.

INSTANCE 1. An S-R pair that has *not been rewarded,* although the $_sH_r$ of this pair is greater than zero.

INSTANCE 2. An S-R pair in which the S continues to evoke its paired R at the former frequency, although this pair is *no longer rewarded.*

HYPOTHESIS 3. An S that has *not become a reward,* although this S has been paired N or more times with a reward.

HYPOTHESIS 4. An animal that does *not have drive x* (for instance, fear), although it is now exploring.

HYPOTHESIS 5. An animal that has learned to discriminate between two stimulus patterns, although it has *never selected the relevant cues.*

Now, it is pointless to search for such negative instances unless we have an exact operational rule (or some other precise meaning) for each of the underlined phrases. If it is pointless to search for negative instances, then there *can* be no grounds for supposing these hypotheses to be either true or false, and if there can be no grounds for supposing them to be either true or false, then these hypotheses have no testable meaning.

Kimble (1961), a psychologist who believes, as we saw earlier, that "no one worries any more" about the circularity of the law of effect, expressed another widely held view when, after reviewing the various latent-learning studies, he said that "it is impossible to rule out the possibility that reward was present in some form in any experiment on latent learning." Psychologists, like Neal Miller (1951), J. S. Brown (1953), and O. H. Mowrer (1960), who have exploited the vagueness in the concept of the fear drive, have made it equally clear that we can never rule out the possibility that fear, in some form, is motivating the animal's behavior. Finally, the long controversy over the noncontinuity hypothesis (our hypothesis 5) has made it quite evident that we can never rule out the possibility that the animal has somehow managed to select the relevant cues.

All this is most puzzling when we remember, as Kimble (1961) reminds us, that the latent-learning experiments "were conducted by some of psychology's finest craftsmen in the art of experimental design." Why, then, were these fine craftsmen unable to make sure that the animals were *not* rewarded after the response? And if they could not make sure of this, what led them to do these pointless experiments? The answer must be that, because they had an exact operational rule for *"x* is a reward," they mistakenly thought that this was sufficient to allow them to test the hypothesis that reward is necessary to increase $_sH_r$. However, as we have seen, not even the finest of craftsmen can test this hypothesis unless, in addition to his knowledge of the mathematical and experimental tools of psychology, he has an exact meaning for *"x* is *not* a reward." This they did not have, and as a consequence their experiments could not rule out the possibility that the animal's response may have been rewarded.

It is embarrassing to admit that we have sent our finest craftsmen out to test meaningless hypotheses and to recall the years we have spent in vain efforts to understand the results of their pointless experiments, but embarrassing as these admissions are, they seem less shocking than our failure to draw the proper conclusion from our final recognition that these hypotheses have no testable meaning. Like Osgood (1953), who concedes that the principle of reinforcement is "currently untestable," most of us have concluded from this that "there is not sufficient evidence here to force us to abandon the reinforcement principle." Osgood, in speaking of the principle as *"currently* untestable," appears to temper his criticism by suggesting that it could be tested if only we were clever enough to find the relevant evidence, but such a suggestion is seriously misleading. The virtue we need is not cleverness, but courage—the courage to give an exact meaning to expressions like *"x* is *not* a reward." Such a decision takes courage because, once we have given exact meanings to such expressions, our most cherished beliefs are directly open to empirical refutation. No one takes kindly to such refutation, and yet the courage to take this risk is an essential ingredient in scientific inquiry. Thus, the only proper conclusion to our final recognition that these hypotheses have no testable meaning is the candid confession that we know nothing about the effects of reward upon increasing associative strength and that we can never learn anything about any of these matters until we become courageous enough to make these hypotheses testable.

The title of this chapter speaks of an incurable vagueness in psychological theories. I have tried to show how this vagueness springs from faults in our ways of operationally defining our terms, and how this vagueness spreads to every hypothesis that depends for its meaning on such definitions. It remains for me to explain why I believe that this vagueness is incurable.

Anyone who hopes to cure this vagueness must recognize at the start that few, if any, of his patients will admit that they are sick. We psychologists have good reason to be proud of our laboratories, our growing experimental literature, and the wide range of problems that we have begun to attack. We are also proud, though I doubt that we have good reason to be, of our theoretical sophistication. As Kimble (1961) puts it in the preface to his book, "Knowledge of the philosophy of science, considered esoteric in the 1930's, is now commonplace." Whoever is reckless enough to tell us that we have no theories of learning, and indeed that we have no grounds for any of our most cherished beliefs, must expect neither a sympathetic nor an understanding audience. I shall close this essay with some quotations taken from various psychologists. In these passages we explain to the world why our theories are immune to empirical refutation. I hope these quotations will explain why I think that the vagueness of our psychological theories is an inherent and incurable part of these theories.

After reviewing some objections to various untestable hypotheses, Mowrer (1960, p. 211) says, "At this point, Conant's famous dictum comes to mind, that a theory is never overthrown by the facts, only by *another* (*better*) *theory!* . . . It takes a theory to 'kill' a theory, and as of the moment there seems to be no other theory which, in comprehensiveness and power, is comparable to the one here espoused." In another place but on the same point Logan (1959, p. 331) says, "Our theories are not sufficiently explicit nor our laws sufficiently certain to support conclusive disproofs. For that matter Conant has correctly observed that theories are overthrown by better theories, but not by contrary evidence." In the conclusion to his paper criticizing Estes' one-trial learning hypothesis, Postman (1962) says, "The incremental position which is part of the warp and woof of much contemporary learning theory takes too many forms to be testable by a single paradigm. Theories die hard, and crucial experiments are rarely successful in psychology."

In each of these quotations I find a curious sort of professional pride in the fact that some of our most important ideas are so "theoretical" that they are exempt from empirical refutation. This tendency to rationalize our vagueness finds its most complete expression in the following passage which, taken out of context, sounds rather more ironic than, I suspect, Irion (1959, p. 539) intended it to sound.

> It is well known, of course, that there is a logic of science. It is, perhaps, less well understood that there is also a psychology of science and that psychologists, no less than other scientists, are subject to its laws. Such a psychology of science concerns itself with the ways in which scientists behave in their scientific endeavors, and we should not be surprised to find that their behavior does not always conform to the rules of the scientific game, that is, to the logic of science. For example, according to the logic of science, no theory can be maintained in the face of one single, well-established, contradictory fact. Conant and others, however, have pointed out that scientists do not often reject a theory, particularly one that is well established, on this basis. Instead theories tend to persist until more adequate ones are presented and, indeed, even under these circumstances, scientists have often seemed loath to discard some of their theoretical beliefs.

Let me end my discussion of the incurable vagueness in psychological theories by suggesting two axioms for Irion's psychology of psychology.

(1) If a psychologist cherishes some hypothesis H (because of its rhetoric, its appearance, or for some other reason), and if H has no testable meaning, then this psychologist will call H a "theory" and his belief in H will be directly proportionate to his cherishing of H. [This is the Law of Affect.]

(2) If a psychologist discovers a fact that contradicts some cherished hypothesis, H, then the psychologist will not discard H as false, but instead will revise H so that H becomes an untestable "theory." [This is the Law of Semantic Homeostasis.]

REFERENCES

BROWN, J. S. Problems presented by the concept of acquired drives. In M. R. Jones (Ed.), *Current theory and research in motivation, a symposium.* Lincoln: Univ. Nebraska Press, 1953.

DEESE, J. *The psychology of learning.* New York: McGraw-Hill, 1958.

ESTES, W. K. Learning theory and the new "mental chemistry." *Psychol. Rev.* 1960, **67,** 207-223.

IRION, A. L. Rote learning. In S. Koch (Ed.), *Psychology: a study of a science.* Vol. 2. New York: McGraw-Hill, 1959. Pp. 538-560.

KENDLER, H. H. Learning. In *Annual review of psychology.* Stanford, Calif.: Annual Reviews, Inc., 1959, Pp. 43-88.

KIMBLE, G. A. *Hilgard and Marquis' conditioning and learning.* New York: Appleton-Century-Crofts, 1961.

LOGAN, F. A. The Hull-Spence approach. In S. Koch (Ed.), *Psychology: a study of a science.* Vol. 2. New York: McGraw-Hill, 1959.

MEEHL, P. E. On the circularity of the law of effect. *Psychol. Bull.,* 1950, **47,** 52-75.

MILLER, N. E. Learnable drives and rewards. In S. S. Stevens (Ed.), *Handbook of experimental psychology.* New York: Wiley, 1951.

MOWRER, O. H. *Learning theory and behavior.* New York: Wiley, 1960.

OSGOOD, C. E. *Method and theory in experimental psychology.* New York: Oxford, 1953.

POSTMAN, L. J. One-trial learning. In C. N. Cofer & Barbara S. Musgrave (Eds.), *Verbal behavior and learning: problems and processes.* New York: McGraw-Hill, 1963. Pp. 295-321.

11 JOHN P. SEWARD

CHOICE-POINTS IN BEHAVIOR RESEARCH

AT SOME TIME, an experimenter does well to stand back and look at himself to see where he is going. A collaboration of psychologists and philosophers of science would seem to be a fitting occasion for such an exercise. Its aim is not, or should not be, to justify one's own way of doing things at the expense of others. It is rather to consider remote goals and to evaluate, as objectively as possible, alternative means of achieving them. One result should be to make the researcher more keenly aware of the strengths and weaknesses of his own viewpoint.

In a small way, I should like to attempt such an appraisal. Since bias is unavoidable, let me start by stating my position. I consider myself a somewhat tender-minded behaviorist, that is, an S-R psychologist primarily concerned with what goes on *between* S and R. For our present purpose, however, let us take a purely imaginary case: an undergraduate psychology major, uncommitted to any doctrine, who wants to study animal behavior and wonders how to go about it. Our first step as his advisers will be to make a brief, abstract survey of the possibilities before him. Then, to be more realistic, we shall assume that our protégé becomes absorbed in a specific problem, obliging us to go into its history and current status. As a result, we may find ourselves in a better position to settle some of the original issues.

GENERAL ORIENTATION

First to be faced is the question: What do I seek? Since our novice knows something about rats and mazes, it will be helpful to use an analogy. He is to think of himself in the start box with a sign over the exit: "Laws of Behavior." He goes through and soon finds himself at a choice-point between two paths. One is marked "Empty Organism," the other, "Black Box." As our subject vacillates, helpless as a rat, we add a few verbal cues. To choose "E.O." is to join the ranks of the psychological positivists, who are concerned solely with establishing orderly relations

166

between overt responses and external conditions. Led by B. F. Skinner, these "radical empiricists" insist on reducing behavior to its simplest terms, omitting explicit reference to anything between input and output. To choose "B.B.," on the other hand, is to focus on the O between S and R; the black boxers confess curiosity about the hidden mechanisms of behavior and keep looking for some way to pry off the lid.

At this point, our student interrupts: "Does it really matter which path I take? How do I know they won't arrive at the same place in the end?" Several comments come to mind:

Most car owners are content to know what will happen when they shift a gear or press a pedal—and to call their auto club if it doesn't happen. Others, who may also be club members, have to know what goes on under the hood. On the whole, advocates of "E.O." seem more concerned with predicting and controlling behavior than with understanding it, while the opposite seems true of the "B.B." school. But if this is a rule, it probably has many exceptions on both sides; there is nothing to prevent a pragmatist from being curious, or vice versa. Indeed, a survey might show that the two groups differed not so much in ultimate goals as in what they held to be the better method of reaching it.

Until recently, at least, the interior of the "B.B." has been hardly accessible, and psychologists must still use hypothetical constructs to guess how it works. This means, as operationists have long pointed out, that we need S-R correlations in order to infer constructs and to test their validity. But that does not quite close the issue. Even an avowed technologist might find an empirical law less useful as an end in itself than as a basis for a more finely structured theory. For the theorist, the choice is obvious.

A case in point is the pig described by Breland and Breland (1961), Skinner's former associates, in their interesting paper on the exigencies of training animals. This pig—and his behavior was typical—was rewarded with food for carrying wooden coins and depositing them in a bank. Instead, he "rooted" the coins more and more persistently as training continued, until he failed to earn an adequate daily ration. "The examples listed [covering a wide range of species] we feel represent a clear and utter failure of conditioning theory" (p. 683), a failure attributed by the authors to neglect of the animals' instinctive patterns of behavior. To assume that the organism was empty simply did not work. It should be added that, in spite of this restriction, the Brelands' conditioning methods were frequently successful.

If our young disciple chooses the path of positivism, no barrier remains between him and his first experiment (except, perhaps, the want of a hypothesis). But if he insists on meddling with mechanisms, he will have to face some more choices. The number is arbitrary, depending on how the alternatives are classified. Since we are free to build our own "cognitive map" of psychology, we introduce a choice-point with five divergent paths (not counting the approach), each path standing for one way of conceptualizing the mechanics of behavior. Let us consider them in turn.

Subjective Experience The most "natural" explanation of the behavior of another organism, human or animal, is in terms of the observer's own experience. A dog salivates "because he expects food" and stops salivating "when he no longer expects it." He jumps over the barrier "in order to avoid the shock."

Criticisms of this approach have been familiar since Watson declared war on the mind: (1) It "begs the question" by using as explanatory tools the very events we are trying to understand. (2) It violates Lloyd Morgan's version of the law of parsimony by appealing to processes at a higher level than necessary to explain the event. (3) It provides at best a partial account of behavior, since it ignores the part played by unconscious processes. (4) It relies on a method—introspection—notorious for its unreliability.

In view of these admitted shortcomings, a hard-headed investigator of animal behavior purges himself, publicly at least, of any recourse to anthropomorphism. Much more of it, I suspect, goes on in his private thoughts than ever appears in print. This is natural, even inescapable. Beginners in French are sometimes urged not to interpolate the English synonym between a French word and its "meaning." This may or may not be a good thing, but it is practically impossible. It can also be argued that familiar verbal mediators serve a useful purpose in learning a language until they drop out as no longer necessary.

If the foregoing argument is labeled trite and the analogy remote, I shall not be too disturbed, since I do not believe that mentalistic theories should live very long. Sooner or later, all terms referring to private experience must be critically examined and either eliminated or translated into constructs of unequivocal meaning. It is only early in the search for possible mechanisms, when the need is for ingenuity and variety of ideas, that the psychologist should free himself of behavioristic Thou-shalt-nots. With this qualification, I subscribe wholeheartedly to the warnings of the objectivists.

Neuropsychology Next to subjective experience, the shortest route to the mechanisms of behavior would seem to be through the nervous system. Lashley (1951), discounting the value of cybernetics, remarked that "we are more likely to find out how the brain works by studying the brain itself and the phenomena of behavior than by indulging in farfetched physical analogies" (p. 35). After thirty years of investigation yielding "a good bit of information about what and where the memory trace is not" (1950, p. 477), Lashley was obviously not indulging in easy optimism. His work stands as a warning that anyone thinking of opening the black box should first ponder Pandora.

Let us take his dare, at least long enough to consider the consequences. We need not start at the beginning. The structure and functions of the nervous system have been under investigation longer than the scientific study of behavior. Neuroanatomists have mapped in some detail the tracts, nuclei, and distribution of neurons in various species; as methods improve, the maps become increasingly precise. Neurophysiologists working at the "organ level" have compiled hoards of data on the effects of ablating various parts and of stimulating or recording at specific points. At a still more molecular level, biochemists and biophysicists explore the secrets of neural transmission.

Psychologists are entitled to feel nothing but respect for their achievements. Nevertheless, it is doubtful that a piecemeal attack will ever deliver an adequate physiological explanation of behavior. As Gregory (1961) points out, we need some knowledge of how a machine works before we can learn more by judicious meddling. For this purpose a "block diagram" of boxes, functions, and flow lines is more useful than a map of the wiring. If he is right, psychologists have a contribution to make at the strategic level: a tentative theory of behavior.

Take the method of ablation, for example. It is true that Lashley started his search from the standpoint of reflex-arc or switchboard theory, with its implied S-R connectionism, and that the body of his findings can be considered a refutation of both views. But Diamond and Chow (1962), asserting that later studies derive their impetus from earlier ones rather than from neural models, make a good case for an empirical approach. Let us therefore take an example from their paper: the role of the temporal lobe in monkeys.

Evidence was first presented from a variety of ablations and tasks that "learned visual discriminations are uniquely affected by lesions of the temporal neocortex, and that the deficit from this lesion is specific to visual habits" (p. 211). The next step was to establish, by further lesions, the path from visual to temporal cortex. A final problem was the nature of the deficit. Attempts to answer this question were summarized as follows:

> Results from these studies show that the visual defect following the removal of temporal cortex in monkeys cannot be attributed to a sensory change. Further, it is not the result of the animal's failure to comprehend the testing procedure. Nor can the loss be attributed to a complete disappearance of specific memory traces corresponding to specific visual habits. What actually happens to the monkey's visually guided behavior after surgery remains a challenging question (p. 214).

It is just here, it seems to me, though I cannot prove it by producing one, that a theory of visual discrimination might "break the code" and point the way to a decisive experiment. A more convincing example of how a behavior theory can integrate the results of ablation studies is to be found in Pribram's work on the amygdala (1962).

My thesis, far from new, is not beyond dispute. I simply agree with Milner (1961) that "functional neuroanatomy" will not by itself meet the neuropsychologist's need. Borrowing further from Milner and Gregory, I propose the following subgoals for a long-range strategy: (1) an idea, the more explicit the better, of how behavior is regulated in terms of interaction between organism and environment; (2) an abstract model, conforming to the structure and functions of a generalized nervous system as known or conjectured, and regulating behavior in the manner described. Physiological tactics—ablation, stimulation, and electrical recording— could then be used to test predictions from the model. In short, what is called for is a theory of a theory. It seems a long detour; whether a short-cut can be discovered remains to be seen.

Mechanical Analogies   One possible shortcut—the one that failed to impress Lashley—is to find a mechanism, less intricate than the mammalian nervous system, that will duplicate its functions, at least in part. Such devices—servomechanisms, analogue and digital computers—may be borrowed from industry; others may be invented for the purpose. The first step in the analogical, as in the physiological, approach is to strip down the desired behavior to its essentials; the second, to consider the possible types of system called for. At this point the two approaches diverge: the neuropsychologist tries to stay within the limits set by current neurology; the mechanical model builder gives himself more freedom, and therein lies the hope of saving labor.

Sometimes the distinction is readily made. Lorenz' (1950, p. 256) hydraulic system for picturing the dynamics of instinct does not claim the remotest relation to anatomy—or to physiology—except in principle. Neither does Walter's (1953) *Machina speculatrix* or Ashby's (1960) *Homeostat*. But in other cases the dividing line is hard to draw. Milner's "learning network" (1961, p. 123) looks like the flow chart of a control system but is meant to represent "*a* brain even if not *the* brain" (p. 132). Milner actually meshed the two strategies when he suggested testing the system "by translating it into mathematical form and employing high-speed computers to simulate the operation of the circuits" (p. 131).

Deutsch's (1960) model, less influenced by neurology, provides a clearer example of the analogical approach. To represent the central nervous system he proposes two classes of "links," primary and secondary. Primary links take care of bodily needs; each is excited by some chemical change and depressed by stimulation of an "analyzer." The thirst link, for example, is excited by dehydration and depressed by receptors in the mouth and throat. Secondary links serve an instrumental function; each is supplied with an analyzer and a motor output. Series of links are either inborn or learned through successive activation. Once formed, they act like chains of switches, transmitting excitation in reverse order: that is, the flow is from drive to consummatory response and so on from the end toward the start of the behavioral sequence. But when an analyzer is fired it "throws the switch," cutting off excitation from preceding links; its link then proves to be a servomechanism and regulates the motor output so as to maximize its own stimulation. Deutsch shows that if, for example, such a machine were a thirsty rat in a maze, it would eliminate blind alleys and take shortcuts but fail on detour problems.

This brief sketch cannot do more than give the flavor of Deutsch's provocative theory, and no detailed critique will be attempted here. But two comments are pertinent. First, a basic assumption of the system—that excitation is transmitted backward through a series of links—is without a known counterpart in neurology. This need not disturb Deutsch, to be sure, since he does not care how closely his model resembles the nervous system but only how well it predicts behavior. And it must be said that in his hands the theory has scored some remarkable successes.

The second comment, a more general one, is a by-product of my own attempts to assimilate Deutsch's theory. It occurred to me that along with the accepted criteria of a good scientific theory—economy, logical rigor, verifiability, agreement with data—another might be included that is generally overlooked. Perhaps it is omitted because it is essentially subjective. I refer to the *usefulness* of a model. To be useful in the sense here intended, a theory should fit the user's way of thinking. Some models, like old shoes, are comfortable to wear; others refuse to be "broken in." Unfortunately the comfort of models, as of shoes, is seldom enough to ensure respectability.

Stimulus-Response Mediational Theory   Whether one chooses to travel by way of "brain waves" or computer programs, there is still need for what Kendler (1961) would call a *pretheoretical model* at the behavioral level. Its concepts may come from phenomenology, Gestalt theory, information theory, or neobehaviorism. But instead of coordinating them with neural or mechanical events, one may prefer to elaborate a set of intervening processes drawn from the original level. Notwithstanding the fresh movements now emerging, the viewpoint most characteristic of American psychology is still an extension of S-R doctrine.

Mediation theory stems from the same root as the neo-Watsonian positivism we left at the first choice-point. "Mediators," however, would object to the term "hyphen psychologists" suggested by Miller (1959, p. 242). They would rather adopt the S-O-R formula from Dashiell and Woodworth and fill the O with such constructs as may be inferred from observed behavior. In view of the hazards involved, it is not surprising that this has proved to be a highly controversial enterprise. Followers of Hull and Tolman have had to fight a running battle with Skinner's left-wing co-horts—or right-wing, depending on one's point of view. The movement has also enjoyed plenty of bombardment from without and dissension within. I say "enjoyed," since on the whole its vitality seems unimpaired.

As the most fully developed position, Hull's system has borne the brunt of attack. It will serve our purpose to consider a few of the major criticisms. We shall want to see how well these alleged shortcomings have been removed either by changes within Hull's system or by new forms of mediational theory.

Hull's System: Content   We may start with the content of the Hullian postulates. Due in part to their origin in learning theory, they have been found most deficient in their treatment of motivation and perception. Here are some typical comments:

Hull recognized only two classes of motive: (1) homeostatic needs producing drives and drive stimuli such as those of hunger and thirst; (2) tissue injury with its drives of escape and fear. A great deal of behavior, as Woodworth (1958) pointed out, was simply ignored: response to novel stimuli, play, exercise of capacities, seeking and maintaining specific kinds of stimulation, and social behavior other than reproductive. But other S-R theorists have taken steps to remedy the defect. Berlyne's (1960) work on exploratory behavior comes quickly to mind, while Brown and Farber (1951) and Amsel (1962) have handled the concept of frustration in a systematic manner. Admittedly, these efforts are only a beginning.

Closely related to Hull's drive theory of motivation was his drive-reduction theory of reinforcement, long but mistakenly considered the keystone of the system. Thorndike's law of effect had already set the stage for the latent-learning controversey; as the successor to "effect," Hull's reinforcement principle continued to goad experimenters. To the evidence from Tolman's laboratory was added that of sensory conditioning and of learning reinforced by saccharin, nonnutritive but tasty. The cumulative effect was more convincing than any single experiment. One by one, leading Hullians relinquished the drive-reduction postulate. Mowrer (1960), after dropping it from fear-conditioning, found he did not need it for problem-solving either. Spence (1956), who was never much concerned with the nature of reinforcement anyhow, has tentatively dropped it as a factor in instrumental, appetitional learning. Miller (1959) retains the hypothesis not because he believes it but because it still suggests interesting experiments. Hull himself, it is not always realized, was characteristically open-minded on the issue (see 1952, p. 153). Obviously, S-R theory does not stand or fall with any specific notion of the nature of reinforcement.

Hull's handling of perception was probably the weakest part of his system. It seems almost inevitable that a strong emphasis on the input and output of behavior should soft-pedal the problems of sensory integration. Kendler (1961), however, defends S-R analysis not as a way of avoiding perception but as the soundest approach to it.

Steps in this direction have been slow but sure. The prevailing strategy has been to admit any form of sensory organization—stimulus-patterning, response to ratios, selective attention—only when forced to do so by experimental evidence. Hull introduced the principle of afferent interaction, but it is customary to dismiss it as an ineffectual gesture. Spence refused to accept transposition as evidence for relational response in animals, but did not include verbal subjects, for whom his hypothesis of summated gradients broke down (1952a, p. 160). Similarly, he conceded stimulus-patterning to nonarticulate organisms if no component cues were differentially reinforced (1952b).

Another step was taken when Wyckoff (1952) introduced "observing responses" and Spence (1940, 1960) admitted "orienting responses" into discrimination theory. Both terms referred primarily to overt receptor adjustments, but Wyckoff was willing to include the focusing of the eye. And although they are not assigned a specific anatomical location, Lawrence's (1949) mediating process, Kendler's (1961) mediating event, and Berlyne's (1951) attention are surely not limited to observable behavior.

Implicit in these criticisms—and sometimes explicit (Broadbent, 1961) —is the preconception that Hull's is an "open-chain" system, starting with S and going straight through to R, whereas the fine modulations of behavior demand the "closed-loop" type of system familiar to engineers. It is true that in his best-known exposition (1943) Hull left his system (except for mediated stimulus generalization) essentially open. But he had earlier proposed a general form of feedback, the "pure-stimulus act" (1930), and a specific form, the "fractional anticipatory goal reaction" (r_G) (1931), and shown how they could be derived from the conditioning of overt responses and how they might direct sequences of behavior. In his final work (1952), Hull again made r_G crucial to a number of derivations.

In other S-R formulations, it is fair to say, feedback plays an important role. Spence (1956) provides a good example, with his classically conditioned r_g-s_g generalizing back to motivate instrumental sequences. Miller (1959) reminds us that, years ago, he and Dollard (1941) proposed a cybernetic explanation of copying. Actually, Miller's use of "response-produced drive induction" goes back to his well-known reply to Tolman (1935). And what of Tolman himself, whose expectancy theory was essentially a closed-loop model? Critics who would read Tolman out of the

S-R group would have to do so on some other ground. In Mowrer's (1960) system, the effects of reward and punishment on a response depend on two stages of feedback, one consisting of proprioceptive or other cues produced by the response itself, the other consisting of changes in drive conditioned to these cues. Finally, in Osgood's extension of S-R theory to language, the meaning of a sign is "part of the very behavior produced by the significate" (1957, p. 356).

Hull's System: Form   Hull's formula for scientific method is well known and widely accepted. It includes three steps: (1) statement of a set of explicit postulates with all terms operationally defined; (2) logical deduction of theorems referring to the phenomena in question; (3) comparison of theorems with the results of experiment, leading to confirmation or revision of the system.

For some time, my attitude toward Hull's theory was to reject its content as essentially wrong but to accept his method as essentially sound. Recently, two critical commentaries on Hull's theorizing, both by British psychologists, have forced me to reconsider his method. With one I am inclined to agree; with the other, to take issue. Let us start with the latter.

Deutsch (1960) started by distinguishing two types of theory, generalizing and structural. The first type "explains" the eating behavior of a particular rat by the empirical rule that food-deprived rats are likely to eat. The second type proposes a set of principles referring to events occurring at some other level and from them deduces eating behavior. Deutsch's clear preference for structural theory contrasts sharply with Skinner's defense of empirical laws. But Deutsch went on to put Hull's system in the generalizing class. This is interesting when we recall that Hull also distinguished this kind of reasoning from deductive theory in the first chapter of his *Principles of Behavior* (1943).

Deutsch argued that such "hypothetical constructs" as drive stimulus and r_G were hypothetical only in the trivial sense that they were unobserved. More to the point, they were drawn by analogy from the stimuli and responses of overt behavior and were assigned the same properties. Hull's system was thereby reduced to a set of empirical generalizations.

It could be questioned whether all of Hull's intervening variables (for instance, drive, habit strength, reactive inhibition, oscillatory potential) fit Deutsch's classification. Aside from that, it is possible that constructs from a more remote source might yield deductions covering a wider range. Scope is, after all, the great virtue of a high-level theory. But the significant question is: Can a system conceivably generate new regularities, heretofore unobserved, or can it handle only particular instances of those already known?

Hull's method was to seek the essentials of behavior in simple situations and use them to predict outcomes under more complicated conditions. A striking example was his successful derivation of the orders of reaction latencies in response-chaining by rats (1952). His system may not be structural by Deutsch's definition, but it surely has the power to do more than generalize.

The second critic, Broadbent (1961), recognizing Hull's stature as a theoretician, asked why his hypothetico-deductive method had recently fallen from favor. Broadbent was probably right in suggesting that the reason may lie deeper than content. Since the method is self-correcting, sooner or later any major error should be eliminated. For some reason, it appeared, the checks were not being applied. Broadbent's diagnosis was that Hull's system was too intricate and formalized for its own healthy growth. Let us see how such a condition might arise. With so many hypothetical variables intervening between S and R, deductions became uncertain. The more precisely Hull quantified his postulates, the less likely it became that they would be confirmed in detail. Cotton (1955) showed how difficult it could be to derive a measurable function from Hull's principles. In his own derivations, such as the latencies of response-chains noted above, Hull resorted to drastically simplifying assumptions. In terms of the program at the opening of this section, so much effort was devoted to step 1 that steps 2 and 3 could no longer be strictly applied.

What is the remedy? Simply to test a theory at a less precise level is not enough, since the test may be too coarse to weed out competing theories. Unfortunately, Hull was so occupied with his own system that he paid little attention to other views. What is needed, according to Broadbent, is a time-honored tool almost forgotten in the current rush to empiricism: the crucial experiment. As in the old game of Twenty Questions recently made scientifically respectable by information theory, the first hypothesis tested should be broad enough to split contending theories roughly in half; the next should do the same for the survivors, and so on. As the process continues the successful theories must be stated—and tested—with increasing precision. Eventually, some future system may reach the level of quantification at which Hull began.

Mathematical Models   A theory can be quantified without becoming an independent approach. All the approaches so far considered, if seriously pursued, must inevitably turn to mathematics: the subjective, in order to scale judgments; the physiological, to handle EEG tracings; the mechanical, to use digital computers; even the empirical, to fit learning curves. Such procedures presuppose data already gathered or a qualitative theory taking shape.

Separate treatment is needed only when the model in question has been developed with relatively little basis in the facts or theories of behavior. Information theory, game theory, and mathematical biophysics provide clear examples, and stochastic learning models (Bush and Mosteller, 1955) should also be included.

A formal theory has distinct advantages over an informal one. Some of its implications may emerge as properties of the model employed, and experimental tests are less equivocal. On the other hand, as we saw in the last section, a price must be paid for these benefits. A model may prove to be strictly miniature; that is, it may apply only within narrow limits—to a simple situation or a special area or particular experimental conditions. Where it fails to fit, its meager foundation is probably of little help in suggesting improvement, so changes must be largely *ad hoc*.

These objections may be surmounted, and Estes (1959) seems to have made a good start. His statistical model is grounded in a stimulus-sampling theory that leads quite directly to response probability, a variable much easier to measure than Hull's reaction potential. By keeping his theory close to the laboratory, Estes has shown it to be an instrument of power and scope.

This path, therefore, can be recommended with reservation. Besides mathematical training, the investigator who chooses it needs to be alert to its dangers. As in other approaches, the chief risk lies in using the model as a substitute for, rather than a supplement to, the study of behavior.

A SPECIFIC PROBLEM

"How does a dog learn to shake hands?"

It is our captive auditor, the young student, speaking; he evidently stopped listening some time ago to pursue his own train of thought. I find the interruption quite refreshing, since I must confess to a growing dissatisfaction, possibly shared by the reader. Any abstract classification smells of the dissecting room, whereas scientific research is no corpse but a living organism defiant of pigeonholes.

Well how *does* a dog learn to shake hands? Almost every dog owner has tried to teach his pet this simple trick—and probably succeeded. If asked how, he would probably say, "I showed Jocko a biscuit, told him to shake, grabbed his paw, shook it, and gave him the biscuit. After a few times Jock lifted his paw at sight of the biscuit in my hand." On further questioning the most likely explanation would be, "He wanted the biscuit" (subjective experience).

Miller and Konorski (1928) were apparently the first to study this bit of behavior systematically. In a typical experiment they placed a dog in a Pavlov frame, raised one leg by pulling a cord attached to its ankle, and then presented food. Before long, the dog was spontaneously raising its leg. This type II conditioned reflex (CRII)—so called to distinguish it from Pavlov's type I—proved to have several variants, and the study of its properties has occupied Konorski and his colleagues ever since.

In this country, the corresponding event was Skinner's (1938) publication of his epoch-making experiments on lever-pressing in rats. Common ground was clarified by a preliminary exchange with Konorski and Miller. Both sides agreed on the distinction between two types of conditioning, and Skinner made it sharper by imbedding one type in *operant* and the other in *respondent* behavior. Their common problem, in Skinner's terms, was operant conditioning. Beyond that, however, their paths diverged. The Warsaw group has sought the inner mechanics of the two types of conditioning and their interactions. Skinner's laboratory has concentrated on measuring the susceptibility of response rate to changes in the conditions of reinforcement. Reinforcers, in turn, are defined merely by their capacity to increase the probability of the recorded response. No attempt is made to determine how this subtle influence is mediated. Until the survey is complete, the organism must remain empty.

Physiological Hypotheses   Leaving the first choice-point without further "vicarious trial-and-error" behavior, we are ready to look into the black box. Shortly after Miller and Konorski's early papers, Pavlov (1932) reported the following incident in a salivary conditioning experiment:

> The valve did not work very well and when the tube was shaken some of the powder would fall into the plate. The dog quickly learned to make use of this. . . . And such shaking occurred almost constantly whenever the dog, while eating its portion of food, brushed against the tube. This, of course, is exactly what takes place when the dog is being trained to give the paw. . . . In the latter case the words "paw," "give," the tactile and kinesthetic stimulation which arises when the dog lifts its paw, etc., are linked up with feeding. Here the noise of the shaking tube, the tactile and kinesthetic stimulation from knocking against the tube, all were likewise connected with the act of eating, with excitation of the alimentary center.
>
> Two additional physiological facts are clearly manifested. First, the definite kinesthetic stimulation is connected with performing the movement that originated it. Secondly, when two nervous centers are connected or joined together, the nervous processes move from one to the other in both directions. . . . When the lifting of the paw is followed by the presentation of food, the excitation undoubtedly proceeds from the kinesthetic point to the alimentary center. But when the connection is established and the dog, being in a state of alimentary excitation, gives the paw itself, the excitation obviously runs in the opposite direction.
>
> I cannot interpret this fact in any other way (pp. 123-24).

Pavlov seems never to have tried to explain this phenomenon more formally, that is, to state the general conditions under which excitation would "run in the opposite direction." The reason may be that he failed to distinguish clearly between classical and instrumental conditioning, to use the convenient terminology of Hilgard and Marquis (1940). This is strange, since if paw-lifting could be considered a simple case of backward conditioning Pavlov would have been the first to recognize it.

Loucks (1935) also resorted to backward association to "explain" the results of his well-known study. He had paired a buzzer with a brief and evidently nonpainful shock applied directly to the right hind-leg area of the motor cortex; 600 trials to each of three dogs had failed to condition flexion to the buzzer. Two other dogs, given food after each pair of stimuli, developed stable CRs. It was not simply that these dogs were different, since one of them extinguished and failed to relearn the response when food was omitted. Loucks concluded that the reward, although it followed the flexion, was responsible for its conditioning. But how could this be?

> It is evident that the movement of the limb at cortical shock results in . . . proprioceptive impulses. . . . When this proprioceptive stimulation is followed by food . . . there is an opportunity for a backward association to be set up between the sensory experience and the eating of food (p. 17).

Loucks's study implied that responses of skeletal muscles may not be subject to classical conditioning, in which an inadequate stimulus is paired with an adequate stimulus, but only to the instrumental type, in which a reward is paired with the response. Several later experiments using similar methods have questioned this conclusion. Conditioned motor responses have been established by pairing external stimuli with direct stimulation of the cerebellum (Brogden & Gantt, 1942) and motor cortex (Nikolayeva, 1959), and by pairing two cortical stimuli (Doty & Giurgea, 1961). The crucial factors are obscure. But even if reward proves to be not indispensable to motor conditioning, its value is well established, not only by Loucks, but by countless experiments on rats, pigeons, and other species. This is the effect we are trying to understand.

Until recently, Konorski, too, stressed the role of kinesthetic feedback. In his original theory of type II conditioning, proprioceptive stimulation from the induced response became part of the CS to a type I alimentary CR. Arousal of this CR I before food was given produced inhibition of the eating center with "exaltation of the motor cortex," resulting in flexion.

Konorski's theory was apparently challenged by Woodbury's (1942) negative finding. Woodbury repeated Konorski's procedure on a single dog, with a soft shoe substituted for Konorski's ankle-strap to ensure passive movement, and obtained no conditioned flexion in 350 trials. It is not clear what Konorski would have predicted here, since he nowhere stated explicitly that purely passive movement was enough. But the question remained whether the stimulation produced by active movement was necessary for instrumental learning.

Recent evidence, most of it from Konorski's own laboratory, suggests a

negative answer. Knapp, Taub, and Berman (1958) had successfully recon-
ditioned an avoidance response in three monkeys after complete deafferentation of the responding forelimb. Could the same thing be done using
a food-rewarded response? Jankowska (1959) "instrumentalized" a
scratch reflex by tickling the ear and pairing the response with food. Cats
and rats had one or both hind limbs deafferented by section of the dorsal
roots. Animals rhizotomized after training retained a recognizable copy
of the conditioned movement. Others—and this seems to me more significant—rhizotomized *before* training acquired the response within normal
limits. On the basis of this and similar evidence (Gorska & Jankowska, 1961;
Gorska, Jankowska, & Kozak, 1961) Konorski now believes that instrumental conditioning does not depend on proprioceptive impulses.

He and his associates are still looking for a better theory. One attractive
hypothesis—that CR II might be represented by feedback loops between
cortex and brainstem or cerebellum—has lost ground before the stubborn
persistence of learned responses after a variety of severe ablations. At
present, the theory most favored in Warsaw[1] emphasizes two factors in operant conditioning: (1) arousal of the motor area by a drive emanating
from the eating center; (2) termination of the motor excitation by food.
This permits the last response to be consolidated (possibly by reverberating
circuits) without retroactive interference. It is intriguing to watch the convergence of Konorski's physiological account with the behavioral concepts of
Guthrie and Hull, to which we now turn.

Stimulus-Response Theories: Reinforcement Hypotheses Since our
goal is explanatory rather than descriptive, we are limited to theories that
attempt a noncircular definition of reinforcement. Guthrie's view, often
identified with the contiguity principle, is included because it states a general, though negative, condition of reinforcement, namely, absence of retroactive interference. A response is reinforced when it is followed immediately by removal of stimuli that would otherwise be conditioned to
competing responses. The diagram below may epitomize the process.

$$S_C\text{———}S_C\text{———}S_C\text{———}S_C$$

$$R_1 \qquad R_2 \qquad R_3$$

The diagram shows a sequence of three incompatible responses to a situation (S_C). Each R dissociates the preceding one until R_3 terminates S_C,
thereby saving its own connection.

In Hull's system, reinforcing events take either of two forms: diminution
of a drive stimulus (primary reinforcement), or a stimulus associated di-

[1] This theory was presented in a lecture at the Brain Research Institute, University
of California, Los Angeles, July 25, 1962.

rectly or indirectly with such diminution (secondary reinforcement). A second diagram shows the course of events.

$$S_C\text{------}S_C\text{------}S_C$$
$$R_1 \qquad R_2 \qquad R_3$$
$$S_D\text{------}S_D\text{------}S_D\text{------}\cancel{S_D}\text{ or } S^r$$

Here, successive responses occur in the presence of external cues (S_C) and an internal motivating stimulus (S_D). One response (R_3) acquires an increment of habit strength to S_C and S_D if it terminates or reduces S_D or produces a stimulus (S^r) associated with S_D reduction.

Note that in one case Guthrie's diagram coincides, in effect, with Hull's; namely, when S_C consists largely of S_D. The clearest example would be learning to escape from punishment; by introducing an internal-conditioned S_D (fear), we can include avoidance. Reward training, however, cannot be completely explained by this type of reinforcement, since S_D removal sometimes occurs only after considerable delay, if at all. Hull—but not Guthrie— can fall back on S^r, but only to face the troublesome question: How can a stimulus coming after a response increase its strength?

Stimulus-Response Theories: Incentive Hypothesis The incentive hypothesis attempts to answer this question as follows: When an operant response is rewarded, its sensory feedback becomes classically conditioned to the consummatory response (R_G). When the operant is later started, its proprioceptive cue arouses a fraction of R_G with *its* proprioceptive cue. The two response-reproduced cue-fractions combine to evoke the complete operant.

Implied in this account are two assumptions: (1) Proprioceptive feedback is connected, either innately or through exercise, with its "proper" response, but its partial arousal is usually too weak to cross the motor threshold unaided. (2) Partial arousal of R_G has the capacity (perhaps by feeding back into regenerating circuits?) to augment other ongoing activity as well as itself. Secondary reinforcement is here seen as the facilitation of an incipient instrumental response by an incipient goal response.

A mediational mechanism of reinforcement requires two diagrams to represent behavior before and after learning.

For clarity, the rectangle that represents the organism before learning is left empty—but not for long. Diagram (*a*) shows a constant situation (S_C) in which a sequence of three operants was followed by a consummatory response (R_G), each R being accompanied by its proprioceptive stimulus (S_P). Diagram (*b*) shows the occurrence of the rewarded R after learning, with the mediating processes supposed to give it priority over its competitors. Unrewarded R's are short-circuited by fractional feedback until that of the successful R arouses added excitation from r_G-s_G and breaks over the threshold of overt movement.

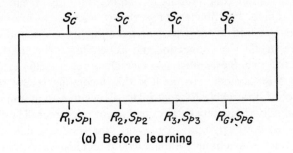

(a) Before learning

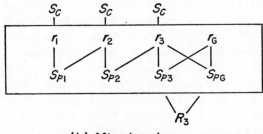

(b) After learning

The incentive hypothesis is not original. It resembles Konorski's earlier view in assuming classical conditioning of R_G to proprioceptive stimuli. It shares with Anokhin's (1959) theory of "reverse afferentiation" the idea that reinforcement involves conditioned excitation of the unconditioned center. Spence's (1956) theory of instrumental learning postulates conditioning of R_G to R-correlated stimuli, including proprioceptive ones, and attributes to s_G a nonassociative, or motivational, as well as an associative function; so does the present hypothesis. It would be essentially identical with Mowrer's (1960) latest theory of secondary reinforcement, based on conditioning of "hope" to R-correlated cues, if it did not differ in one significant respect: it considers s_G an accelerator, while Mowrer's "hope" is coupled with drive decrement. In this respect, my notion is closer to Sheffield's concept of reinforcement as drive induction through partial arousal of R_G (Sheffield, Roby, & Campbell, 1954). Its affiliation with Tolman's (1959) and Woodworth's (1958) cognitive theories is also clear.

The hypothesis is open to a number of serious criticisms. With Mowrer, I assume that a rewarded response reinforces itself by positive feedback; once aroused, therefore, it is more likely to be made. But neither theory as so far developed predicts that it will ever be more readily aroused. What initiates the response (Ishihara, 1962)?

It is doubtful that Mowrer can meet this objection without admitting a factor of direct motor conditioning, or "habit," into his system. Spence has provided for it in the cue-function of s_G; that is, once s_G has moved backward through generalization to form part of the stimulus-compound evoking R, it can acquire an effective connection and so help to get R started.

The incentive hypothesis must also face Deutsch's (1956) critique of the use of r_G by S-R theorists. His point is that mediating rs and ss are given the properties of observable Rs and Ss; it follows that their connections are strengthened indiscriminately by any concurrent reinforcer. The S-R theorist tacitly assumes, however, that an r_G—say, for food—is not strengthened by an S_G of water; else a hungry animal would find his r_G conditioned to cues leading to water and would take the wrong path. But this is contrary to fact (Kendler, 1946).

It seems to me that Deutsch's argument is based on a confusion, not always prevented in S-R theory, between classical and instrumental conditioning. With Spence and Mowrer, I assume that r_G is classically conditioned and therefore dependent for reinforcement on the occurrence of the specific US adequate to arouse it. Instrumental conditioning is what we are trying to explain. It would not be helpful to do so by invoking a factor that is itself dependent on the process in question (see also Ritchie, 1959).

The most urgent threat to the incentive hypothesis is the evidence already cited from Konorski's laboratory that proprioception is unnecessary to appetitive instrumental conditioning. Only one loophole is apparent: although all afferent impulses from the hind limb itself were presumably eliminated, those from accessory movements of postural adjustment were not. Conceivably, these concomitant cues, as part of the total ear-scratching pattern, could have assumed the mediating role of the missing components; that is, they could have become conditioned to the eating responses on the one hand and to the motor output of flexion on the other. In view of the drastic surgery involved, there is a question whether this possibility is real enough to justify an attempt to eliminate *all* proprioceptive accompaniments. Perhaps, with increased precision of electrode placement, the key to response representation that we have sought in the periphery may be found in the sensorimotor cortex.

REORIENTATION

We have had our moment of reflection. We have used it, first, to evaluate the approaches open to psychologists; secondly, to make a brief excursion into learning theory. We are now ready to reconsider our choice of method.

Two conclusions emerge: (1) There are many paths to scientific knowledge of behavior, all legitimate and all useful, perhaps even necessary.

Radical positivism has proved a fruitful movement in psychology, but its program—the systematic description of observable behavior—is too limited for the science as a whole. In terms of our example, Skinner's doctrine may establish the technology of dog training on a solid empirical basis but it will never reveal the inner mechanics of a dog's handshake. (2) Our analogy of a choice-point, though a convenient classificatory device, is not to be taken literally. It suggests that methods of research, like divergent paths, are mutually exclusive, and we have found that this is not necessarily true. Looking into the problem of conditioned flexion in the dog, we found a physiologist, Konorski, using techniques of ablation and stimulation to test hypotheses hard to distinguish from those of psychologists like Guthrie and Mowrer.

The possible relations among methods may be stated more precisely. On closer inspection, they arrange themselves in two dimensions. A vertical dimension distributes levels of investigation, such as *molar* and *molecular;* here the case for mutual interdependence is fairly self-evident. A horizontal dimension appears in that there may be more than one approach at the same level; for example, neurological and mechanical, or Gestalt and S-R. Here the problem of choice is more complicated.

Consider the behavioral level. To interpret a body of related facts by constructs drawn from different frames of reference would add little but confusion. But there is an alternative to eclecticism. Behavior is diverse enough to accommodate a variety of approaches for some time to come. There are problems of perceptual capacity that lend themselves readily to the syntax of information theory (Attneave, 1960), learning problems tailor-made for S-R analysis, and problems of decision-making for which stochastic models are considered mandatory. This situation may go on a long time. It is not likely to last forever. Inevitably, schools of thought will push their frontiers into one another's territory. This has happened before (as in discrimination learning and conflict), is happening now (as information theory and S-R mediation theory apply their own tools to problem-solving), and will happen again. Occasionally, two models may turn out opposing predictions that set the stage for a crucial test, and these touchstones should be diligently sought. More often, a decision between systems must rest on less tangible criteria: fruitfulness, economy, verifiability, and the like; to which may be added a less familiar candidate—ease of translation to other levels. When such choice-points are reached, the dependence of psychologists on a philosophy of scientific method will become acute.

REFERENCES

AMSEL, A. Frustrative nonreward in partial reinforcement and discriminative learning: some recent history and a theoretical extension. *Psychol. Rev.*, 1962, **69,** 306-328.

ANOKHIN, P. K. Characteristics of the afferent apparatus of a conditioned reflex and its importance for psychology. In *The central nervous system and human behavior*. Nat. Inst. Health Russian Scientific Translation Program, 1959. Pp. 241-272.

ASHBY, W. R. *Design for a brain: the origin of adaptive behaviour*. (2nd ed.) New York: Wiley, 1960.

ATTNEAVE, F. *Applications of information theory to psychology*. New York: Holt, 1959.

BERLYNE, D. E. Attention, perception, and behavior theory. *Psychol. Rev.*, 1951, **58,** 137-146.

BERLYNE, D. E. *Conflict, arousal, and curiosity*. New York: McGraw-Hill, 1960.

BRELAND, K., & BRELAND, M. The misbehavior of organisms. *Amer. Psychologist*, 1961, **16,** 681-684.

BROADBENT, D. E. *Behaviour*. New York: Basic Books, 1961.

BROGDEN, W. J., & GANTT, W. H. Intraneural conditioning: cerebellar conditioned reflexes. *Arch. Neurol. Psychiat.*, 1942, **48,** 437-455.

BROWN, J. S., & FARBER, I. E. Emotions conceptualized as intervening variables —with suggestions toward a theory of frustration. *Psychol. Bull.*, 1951, **48,** 465-495.

BUSH, R. R., & MOSTELLER, F. *Stochastic models for learning*. New York: Wiley, 1955.

COTTON, J. W. On making predictions from Hull's theory. *Psychol. Rev.*, 1955, **62,** 303-314.

DEUTSCH, J. A. The inadequacy of the Hullian derivations of reasoning and latent learning. *Psychol. Rev.*, 1956, **63,** 389-399.

DEUTSCH, J. A. *The structural basis of behavior*. Univ. Chicago Press, 1960.

DIAMOND, I. T., & CHOW, K. L. Biological psychology. In S. Koch (Ed.), *Psychology: a study of a science*. Vol. 4. New York: McGraw-Hill, 1962. Pp. 158-241.

DOTY, R. W., & GIURGEA, C. Conditioned reflexes established by coupling electrical excitation of two cortical areas. In J. F. Delafresnaye (Ed.), *Brain mechanisms and learning*. Springfield, Ill.: Charles C Thomas, 1961. Pp. 133-151.

ESTES, W. K. The statistical approach to learning theory. In S. Koch (Ed.), *Psychology: a study of a science*. Vol. 2. New York: McGraw-Hill, 1959. Pp. 380-491.

GORSKA, T., & JANKOWSKA, E. The effect of deafferentation on instrumental (Type II) conditioned reflexes in dogs. *Acta Biol. Exp.*, 1961, **21,** 219-234.

GORSKA, T., JANKOWSKA, E., & KOZAK, W. The effect of deafferenation on instrumental (Type II) cleaning reflexes in cats. *Acta Biol. Exp.* 1961, **21,** 207-217.

GREGORY, R. L. The brain as an engineering problem. In W. H. Thorpe and

O. L. Zangwill (Eds.), *Current problems in animal behaviour.* Cambridge: Cambridge Univ. Press, 1961. Pp. 307-330.

HILGARD, E. R., & MARQUIS, D. G. *Conditioning and learning.* New York: Appleton-Century-Crofts, 1940.

HULL, C. L. Knowledge and purpose as habit mechanisms. *Psychol. Rev.,* 1930, **37,** 511-525.

HULL, C. L. Goal attraction and directing ideas conceived as habit phenomena. *Psychol. Rev.,* 1931, **38,** 487-506.

HULL, C. L. *Principles of behavior.* New York: Appleton-Century, 1943.

HULL, C. L. *A behavior system.* New Haven: Yale Univ. Press, 1952.

ISHIHARA, I. Comment on Prof. Mowrer's two-factor learning theory. *Psychologia,* 1962, **5,** 41-48.

JANKOWSKA, E. Instrumental scratch reflex of the deafferentated limb in cats and rats. *Acta Biol. Exp.,* 1959, **19,** 233-247.

KENDLER, H. H. The influence of simultaneous hunger and thirst drives upon the learning of two opposed spatial responses of the white rat. *J. exp. Psychol.,* 1946, **36,** 212-220.

KENDLER, H. H. Problems in problem-solving research. In R. A. Patton (Ed.), *Current trends in psychological theory.* Univ. Pittsburgh Press, 1961. Pp. 180-207.

KNAPP, H. D., TAUB, E., & BERMAN, A. J. Effect of deafferentation on a conditioned avoidance response. *Science,* 1958, **128,** 842-843.

LASHLEY, K. S. In search of the engram. *Sympos. Soc. exp. Biol.,* 1950, **4,** 454-482.

LASHLEY, K. S. Discussion. Symposium on the brain and the mind. *Trans. Amer. Neurol. Ass.,* 1951, **76,** 34-36.

LAWRENCE, D. H. Acquired distinctiveness of cues: I. Transfer between discriminations on the basis of familiarity with the stimulus. *J. exp. Psychol.,* 1949, **39,** 770-784.

LORENZ, K. Z. The comparative method in studying innate behaviour patterns. *Sympos. Soc. exp. Biol.,* 1950, **4,** 221-268.

LOUCKS, R. B. The delimitation of neural structures essential for learning: the attempt to condition striped muscle responses with faradization of the sigmoid gyri. *J. Psychol.,* 1935, **1,** 5-44.

MILLER, N. E. A reply to "sign-gestalt or conditioned reflex?" *Psychol. Rev.,* 1935, **42,** 280-292.

MILLER, N. E. Liberalization of basic S-R concepts: extensions to conflict behavior, motivation and social learning. In S. Koch (Ed.), *Psychology: a study of a science.* Vol. 2. New York: McGraw-Hill, 1959. Pp. 196-292.

MILLER, N. E., & DOLLARD, J. *Social learning and imitation.* New Haven: Yale Univ. Press, 1941.

MILLER, S., & KONORSKI, J. Sur une forme particulière des réflexes conditionels. *C.R. Soc. Biol.,* 1928, **99,** 1155-1157.

MILNER, P. M. The application of physiology to learning theory. In R. A. Patton (Ed.), *Current trends in psychological theory.* Univ. Pittsburgh Press, 1961. Pp. 111-133.

MOWRER, O. H. *Learning theory and behavior.* New York: Wiley, 1960.

NIKOLAYEVA, N. Y. Changes in the excitability of various regions of the cerebral cortex in the presence of the formation of motor conditioned reflexes. In *The central nervous system and human behavior*. Nat. Inst. of Health Russian Scientific Translation Program, 1959. Pp. 333-342.

OSGOOD, C. E. Motivational dynamics of language behavior. In M. R. Jones (Ed.), *Nebraska symposium on motivation—1957*. Lincoln, Neb.: Univ. Nebraska Press, 1957. Pp. 348-424.

PAVLOV, I. P. Reply of a physiologist to psychologists. *Psychol. Rev.*, 1932, **39**, 91-127.

PRIBRAM, K. Interrelations of psychology and the neurological disciplines. In S. Koch (Ed.), *Psychology: a study of a science*. Vol. 4. New York: McGraw-Hill, 1962. Pp. 119-157.

RITCHIE, B. F. Explanatory powers of the fractional antedating response mechanism. *Brit. J. Psychol.*, 1959, **50** (1), 1-15.

SHEFFIELD, F. D., ROBY, T. B., & CAMPBELL, B. A. Drive reduction versus consummatory behavior as determinants of reinforcement. *J. comp. physiol. Psychol.*, 1954, **47**, 349-354.

SKINNER, B. F. *The behavior of organisms*. New York: Appleton-Century, 1938.

SPENCE, K. W. Continuous versus non-continuous interpretations of discrimination. *Psychol. Rev.*, 1940, **47**, 271-288.

SPENCE, K. W. Mathematical formulations of learning phenomena. *Psychol. Rev.*, 1952, **59**, 152-160. (a)

SPENCE, K. W. The nature of the response in discrimination learning. *Psychol. Rev.*, 1952, **59**, 89-93. (b)

SPENCE, K. W. *Behavior theory and conditioning*. New Haven: Yale Univ. Press, 1956.

SPENCE, K. W. Conceptual models of spatial and non-spatial selective learning. *In Behavior theory and learning: Selected papers*. Englewood Cliffs, N.J.: Prentice-Hall, 1960. Pp. 366-392.

TOLMAN, E. C. Principles of purposive behavior. In S. Koch (Ed.), *Psychology: a study of a science*. Vol. 2. New York: McGraw-Hill, 1959. Pp. 92-157.

WALTER, W. G. *The living brain*. New York: Norton, 1953.

WOODBURY, C. B. A note on "passive" conditioning. *J. gen. Psychol.*, 1942, **27**, 359-361.

WOODWORTH, R. S. *Dynamics of behavior*. New York: Holt, 1958.

WYCKOFF, L. B., JR. The role of observing responses in discrimination learning. Part I. *Psychol. Rev.*, 1952, **59**, 431-442.

12 ABRAM AMSEL

ON INDUCTIVE VERSUS DEDUCTIVE
APPROACHES AND NEO-HULLIAN
BEHAVIORISM *

THIS CHAPTER EXAMINES the distinction between inductive and deductive approaches to the scientific study of behavior, with particular reference to the theories of Clark L. Hull and Kenneth W. Spence, which have often been characterized as deductive. I will suggest that much of the current neo-Hullian thinking is closer to the kind of theorizing contained in the writings of Hull, Spence, Miller, and others in the thirties than it is to the 1943 (*Principles of Behavior*) Hull and its revisions; that it (current neo-Hullian theory) is both inductive and deductive in the sense that all theoretical models built with empirical constructs are inductive and deductive; and that in certain of its deductive aspects it begins with conditioning concepts that are employed as a basis for deriving particulars of instrumental behavior.

Although the Hullian system is not and never was *only* the statements contained in the *Principles,* certainly Hull's more formal ventures into behavior theory were very important, mainly because of their specificity, their resultant susceptibility to experimental test, and their vulnerability to change. If Hull's theory of 1943 had remained substantially unchanged by 1963, it would have proven a failure. No behavior theory at this stage of the game *should* survive twenty years of experimental testing; and Hull's theory has been tested more vigorously than any psychological theory in history. Its overriding value was that it served as a stimulant for organized experimental attacks on small problem areas within a larger conceptual framework. Both Hull's supporters and his opponents did what Hull, himself, has been criticized for not doing in the *Principles:* they sought ". . . additional deductive symptoms . . . to enlarge the empirical reference of the (Hullian) theoretical variables" (Koch, 1954). Sometimes they found them

* This chapter was prepared while the author held a research grant from the National Science Foundation.

and sometimes they did not. The theory of 1943 was deductive in the sense that it lent itself to the derivation of experimental implications—it suggested what experiments might profitably be performed. However, it was not a deductive approach in the sense of a body of theorems derived from a set of postulates relating undefined terms—an axiomatic system. This point was brought out very clearly twenty years ago by Bergmann and Spence (1941). They attempted to correct the erroneous impression, which Hull himself was largely responsible for, that the theory started with purely formal terms, rather than with empirical constructs.

INDUCTIVE VERSUS DEDUCTIVE APPROACHES

Perhaps it is time that working behavioral scientists left the lofty realm of methodological distinctions to others as, for the most part, physical scientists do. I remember something Bergmann said to some graduate students at Iowa about fifteen years ago. It was to the effect that, perhaps, in the end—after we had taken his courses in history and systems of psychology, and philosophy of science, and had been led through the methodological elegancies of the distinctions which were possible at a philosophical level between various theoretical approaches to the study of behavior—perhaps, after all of this, we should go into our laboratories as philosophically naïve as possible, and leave the philosophy of science to the philosophers. He was saying, as I recollect, that ours was a scientific job that might better be approached with an attitude of doing what comes naturally to the well-trained scientist: accepting the reality of the natural phenomena with which he begins and being more concerned with what he can discover and understand than with what form the discovery must take.

It is in this naïve spirit that I offer the opinion that the distinction between inductive and deductive approaches to learning theory has been overdone—too finely drawn from the viewpoint of the scientist. Obviously, nobody's theory is all inductive or all deductive, and, although differences in emphasis exist, these boil down to differences in the strategy of finding relationships, to differences in the degree to which unifying concepts are sought, and to differences in the temperament of the theorist.

I have used in the classroom an example which expresses this naïve scientific approach to such a difference in emphasis. Recall the children's puzzle in which numbered points are joined to form the outline of an object or animal ("find what is hidden by joining the dots"). To see that the hidden thing is a chicken, one joins the dots in numerical order and an outline of the bird emerges. All you have to know to solve this puzzle is (1) the rules of numerical order, and (2) how to draw lines from one point to another. For our purposes, let "point" be an experimental (or other) datum, and let "chicken" be a *pattern* of related experimental (or other) data: a higher-order relationship, an integration of knowledge, a theory. The question is:

What set of tactics should be followed in the discovery of the chicken? The answer, in the case of the example we have given, is quite simple. Join the points and see what it gets you. The rules are clear and unambiguous; the animal is there to be uncovered; the only thing to hold you up is finding the next numeral.

Now let us change the game a bit. The page is now, not a scattering of isolated dots with numerals next to them, but a page almost black with dots. Only some of these dots outline the hidden pattern, and there are no numerals at all to guide the joining of these critical points. But you still have to find the hidden animal, by joining dots. You don't know how many dots to join, or where they are on the page. Your task is complicated by the fact that in order to outline the hidden animal you must first find those points which, out of the total complex of points, are relevant (have a number) and then find the number of each point.

It is in this kind of game that the difference between an inductive and a deductive approach might have some meaning for the scientist. The difference is in the strategy of finding the relevant points, as well as in discovering how each relevant point fits into the pattern, that is, what number it has. If every point on the page black with dots represents a possible experiment to determine if that point is relevant to the outline, one can proceed systematically, for example from left to right and top to bottom, as in reading, to test whether points have numbers or not. If an experiment uncovers a relevant variable, the point achieves some identity; if it does not, the point remains numberless and contributes nothing to the outline one seeks. This is playing the game inductively. However, even with such an inductive approach there comes a time when enough numbers are evident so that the locations of others are suggested. At this stage, the procedure becomes deductive. The player is now reasoning: "If this pattern is in fact the profile of a chicken, as it appears, the other points ought to be about here, and here, and there." This, for example, is what Hull (1943) did in some instances, most notably, perhaps, in his theorizing about the form of the learning function from the Perin-Williams data.

The relatively deductive strategy in psychological theory is only a matter of guessing earlier in the game and of adopting procedures for testing these guesses. The deductively oriented player is trying to avoid the necessity of testing every point (or most of them) on the page. He is trying to find the outline of the hidden animal by doing a hundred experiments rather than perhaps ten thousand. He reasons that, although he may end up having to do just as many as his "inductive-minded" friend, it is unlikely he will have to do any more and, if he is lucky, he may get away doing far fewer. An example of a very early guess at the form of a relationship in Hull (1943) is his formula for generalized drive strength (D) as determined by the drive strengths contributed by the existing relevant and irrelevant needs.

Perhaps a little repetition here to make the point will be excused. The postulates of Hull's theory (1943) were not meant as axioms. In his monograph on rote learning with Hovland and others (1940), Hull apparently felt he was engaged in formal, axiomatic-deductive theorizing. But Bergmann and Spence (1941) very plainly pointed out the error in this approach:

> Hull does not begin with a set of purely formal terms, having no other meaning than that imparted to them by a set of implicit definitions, from which are then derived new terms and theorems made testable by means of co-ordinating definitions. Instead he begins with terms directly operationally defined.

By 1943, Hull acknowledged that his theory was of the intervening-variable type. Further, as I recall, Hull's foremost "disciple," teaching at Iowa, had a favorite manner of referring to Hull's postulates, as "guessed-at laws" relating empirical constructs. Hull was, perhaps, too highly selective and restrictive in the experiments he chose as a basis for these guessed-at laws; however, if one overlooks Hull's obvious infatuation with scientific formality and looks at what he actually did, even at his most formal, one sees inductive activity which takes the form of guessing early about generalities and deductive activity which takes the form of deriving implications for future research. Hull was evidently in a hurry. He wanted to try to get away with doing the 100 experiments in a given area instead of the 10,000.

At any point in time, the major difference between inductive and deductive approaches to theory-building is the manner of deciding what to look at next, the strategy for deciding which experiment to try. In the terms of our puzzle analogy, the difference is in how to go about finding the relatively few points out of the many which are numbered and which, systematically joined, will yield a meaningful pattern.

Apparently, when Skinner (1950) questioned whether theories of learning were necessary, many readers substituted for "theory" the words "axiomatic-deductive system" and substituted for "necessary" a word such as "desirable." Axiomatic theories are certainly not necessary and perhaps not even very fertile in psychology at present. The kind of theorizing exemplified by Hull and Spence is not of this sort, but rather of an empirical-construct variety. Though the mathematical-model treatment of learning theory had as its predecessor the mathematical approach to the intervening-variable theory of Hull and Spence, it seems clear that developments out of the original work of Estes (1950) and of Bush and Mosteller (1951) more closely approximate the formal axiomatic procedure.

Even empirical-construct theories are not necessary, in the sense that one cannot in principle get along without them in the business of ordering natural phenomena. As far as I am aware, nobody ever said that theories were "necessary." However, the fact that they are unnecessary does not make them undesirable or infertile, and their use remains a matter of scientific taste and temperament. It is interesting to note, without necessarily taking it too seriously, that a recent survey of systematic psychologists rates Skinner the foremost living *theorist* in the decade 1950–1960, a rating enjoyed by Hull in the previous two decades in the same study (Coan & Zagona, 1962).

HULLIAN AND NEO-HULLIAN BEHAVIORISM

I have already claimed that for the past twenty years Hullian theory has been under closer and more penetrating examination than any other behavior theory. This scrutiny has been by psychologists, as well as by philosophers of science, logicians, and mathematicians. The examination has been both experimental, applying empirical tests for the accuracy of the theorems (the references here would be in the hundreds and perhaps thousands), and methodological, dealing with the formal or systematic structure of the theory (e.g., Koch, 1954). Logan (1959) has recently written on the Hull-Spence approach in a way which adds to the experimental and methodological a historical dimension. What I have to say in this section will not have the persuasiveness of an experimental test, nor the elegance of a methodological analysis, nor the scholarly sweep of historical perspective. Nor will I be concerned primarily with evaluating what Hull has done; the necrology written by Spence (1952) remains the authoritative, in-the-family statement of Hull's achievements and influence. I will offer an opinion on a subject on which opinions abound: the present status and the future of neo-Hullian behaviorism. I would emphasize the "one-man's-opinion" nature of these comments because, certainly, there can be no spokesman for the aspirations and expectations of a group so large and with interests so diverse as those who would class themselves neo-Hullians, mainly because of a common conceptual language and a set of similar attitudes toward the role of theory—and to a lesser extent, the form of theory—in the science of behavior.

So far as I can see, Hullian theory is already many kinds of things, each to some degree influenced by Hull's *Principles of Behavior* (1943) and later systematic developments (Hull, 1950, 1951); but influenced to an even greater degree by the very important theoretical and experimental writings in the thirties and early forties of Hull and people whose views were then close to his (most notably N. E. Miller, Mowrer, and Spence, but also others such as J. S. Brown, Dollard, Hovland, and Sears, to mention a few.) Hull's 1943 theory and the 1949 revision were relatively unified treatments of simple, nonintentional learning (classical conditioning and simple, instrumental learning) and are still among the most completely integrated theories we have. However, even in Hull's own late work, particularly in his book, *A Behavior System* (1952), completed just before his death, there is an indication that he was returning to some of the interests, evident in his earlier papers, which he had shelved temporarily to concentrate on a rigorous analysis of classical and instrumental conditioning. As Spence (1952) has pointed out, he regarded such an analysis of conditioning as basic to an understanding of more complex behavior and had gone through a period of being greatly influenced by formal considerations. In many respects, Hull's theorizing in the thirties, which employed a conditioning-model approach to more complex instrumental behavior, is more like Hullian theory today than is his 1943 theory.

Spence's *Behavior Theory and Conditioning* (1956) combined some of the features of Hullian theorizing, as exemplified by the *Principles,* with older as well as newer ideas. This treatment shows Spence more concerned with data than Hull was; somewhat less prone than Hull was to earlier guesses based on small amounts of data; in this respect, somewhere between Hull and Skinner in temperament.

There is evidence in these Silliman lectures of Spence's, as there was before and has been since, of two levels of theorizing. The first is the more formal and tends to be of the mathematical, intervening-variable variety. Here, Spence's departures from earlier Hullian theory include these innovations: an abandonment of the two-factor theory of extinction in favor of a response-competition position based on nonreinforcement; a new two-factor treatment which tentatively makes reinforcement necessary for classical aversive conditioning but not for instrumental reward learning; and changes in Hull's equation for E, which involve (1) the postulation of one incentive motivational factor, K, instead of two, J and K, and (2) adding this K factor to D instead of multiplying K and D. A detailed account of these and other departures by Spence from Hull's 1943 theory and its revisions can be found in Logan (1959).

Although the major revisions of the formal Hullian system as it stood in 1952 have been due to Spence, the past decade has witnessed many separate theoretical developments of the broader Hullian psychology. These have to do with the second level of theorizing evident in Spence (1956) and are, in general, attempts to extend the S-R language and the concepts of a conditioning model to areas not covered in the *Principles.* One example is the treatment of nonreward as an active factor in motivation, partial-reinforcement acquisition, and extinction, and in discrimination learning by Amsel (1951, 1958, 1962) and by Spence (1960). Berlyne's (1964) treatment of knowledge in terms of the stimulus-response language of Hullian theory is a second example. Another example is Logan's (1956, 1960) micromolar model of the response and companion treatment of correlated reinforcement. Yet another example is Spence's theory of the emotional variable (r_e) in conditioning and paired-associate learning (1958). These and other departures from Hull's theory by Hullians have in common a disposition to be led by the data. They are not only more data-oriented theoretical ventures than that from which they depart; they are also less formal, and more in the nature of conditioning models of instrumental behavior.

The movement away from excessive preoccupation with form in neo-Hullian work may be at least partly responsible for the absence, since Hull's death, of quantification studies. While some have said that Hull's work in this area was overambitious and premature, and others, that the Hullian procedure of deriving quantification out of a single experimental situation was meaningless, and still others, that waning interest in quantification studies reflects mainly the difficulty of the task, my own feeling is that failure to follow up on the quantification work represents a movement away from the formalism of Hullian psychology in the forties. The quantification work had more form than substance; and neo-Hullians seem, with exceptions, to be more concerned with the substance than the form of the theory.

CHARACTERISTICS OF NEO-HULLIAN BEHAVIORISM

I would like now to describe what I feel are some of the characteristics of neo-Hullianism. In attempting this, I would hope to be reflecting the attitudes of a group of people, but I do not pretend to be the spokesman for any group. The description will consist of answers to five questions: (1) Is the theory more or less unified than it was? (2) Is it more applicable to some kinds of behavioral phenomena than others? (3) Will the $H \times D$ type of formulation continue to be important? (4) Will recent developments in neurophysiology and neuropsychology have much impact on the theory? (5) Will S-R versus cognitive arguments persist?

Is the Theory More or Less Unified than It Was?   It seems rather obvious that Hullian theory is less unified than it was ten years ago, and that it was less unified then than it was in 1943. This is not surprising: the 1943 treatment dealt, after all, mainly with classical and instrumental conditioning. The current Hull-Spence approach, on the other hand, is a collection of separate but related treatments of various behavioral phenomena, having descriptive language and the more basic conceptions in common. The beginnings of this return to interests in a wider range of phenomena were already apparent in Hull's last book (1952). Here, the separate chapters, each representing a behavioral problem area, could not be derived in a strict fashion from the set of postulates at the beginning and what was said or implied in one chapter might be contradicted in another. (For example, in Chapter 5, on the antedating goal response [Hull, 1952, p. 128] there is, in the treatment of delay of reinforcement, an apparent return to $H = f(w)$, which had been abandoned earlier.)

As the Hullian type of approach is applied to an ever-wider range of phenomena the theoretical forays will be more restricted than Hull's, but based on more specific evidence. The relatively broad coverage of behavior envisioned by Hull in the last chapter of *Behavior System* is likely to be reduced to experimental operations in small pieces; and tighter, more data-bound generalizations will emerge, on the order of Spence's recent theorizing. When this kind of theoretical activity has organized separate problem areas and has gained reasonable predictive control over them, there will be a movement toward integration and greater theoretical unity. This, at least, is the present writer's guess.

An example of the difficulty of maintaining theoretical unity is the following: Too often, one finds experiments employing two or more of the Hullian dependent variables (latency, amplitude, frequency or probability, and resistance to extinction) in which an independent experimental variable produces a significant effect as measured by one response indicant but not as measured by another (e.g., Campbell & Kraeling, 1954; Heyman, 1957; Kobrick, 1956).

The trend which this suggests is toward fragmentation of the Hullian system into separate theoretical treatments—and perhaps very different ones—of the various response attributes. One move in this direction is already well under way in the Yale laboratory, where Logan (1956, 1960) has put to use Hull's (1952) distinction between macromolar and micromolar approaches to the treatment of the dependent variable, particularly for vigor or amplitude measures of response strength. The macromolar treatment assumes that quantitatively different behaviors are different strengths of the same response, whereas the micromolar treatment assumes that different speeds, latencies, and amplitudes (vigors) of behavior (for instance, running) are different responses. Within the framework of the micromolar-macromoloar distinction, Logan has developed the interesting distinction between correlated and noncorrelated reinforcement, which shows great promise as a theoretical strategy for handling changes in response magnitude as a function of changes in magnitude and delay of reward. And, certainly, the resistance to extinction measure, one of four dependent variables in Hull's early theorizing, has been handled by neo-Hullians in a manner which amounts to a separate conditioning model (Amsel, 1958, 1962; Spence, 1960). This last example, the treatment of resistance to extinction and its relation to partial reinforcement, necessitated a fairly radical change in Hullian thinking about goal factors, particularly in the conceptualization of the role of nonreinforcement (nonreward). It is interesting to note, however, that this change in thinking about nonreward, from a nonactive to an active factor in behavior, is actually a return to an earlier position, most explicit in Spence's treatment of discrimination learning in the thirties (Spence, 1936, 1937), in which nonreward is regarded as an active factor determining inhibitory tendencies.

· · ·

As I have indicated, the return to this earlier position has proven particularly useful in dealing with partial-reinforcement acquistion and extinction phenomena and discrimination learning. This type of theory, which Lachman (1960) has termed conditioning-model theory, and which represents a major characteristic of neo-Hullian theorizing, emphasizes the role of classically conditioned implicit responses, particularly in instrumental learning under nonaversional motivation. (Lachman's paper should be consulted for a description of the characteristics of such theory.) In this approach, the major function of the goal stimulus (S_G) is to serve as the unconditioned stimulus to a goal response (R_G), and hence provide for classical conditioning of cues antedating the goal (S_A) to portions of the R_G, that is, conditioning of r_G. When S_G is not present at the termination of the behavior sequence in the presence of cues (secondary reinforcing stimuli) usually signaling its presence, r_G is not reduced and R_F (frustration) results. The response R_F is conceptualized as having aversive motivational properties (these motivational properties have been demonstrated in several experiments on the so-called *frustration effect*—increased vigor following nonreward). When the organism is removed from a nonrewarding situation, there is R_F reduction, and my guess (Amsel, 1961) is that this is at least part of the so-called "secondary reinforcement effect." With continued nonrewards, R_F ultimately becomes conditioned to S_A and yields r_F-s_F which is a competing ("inhibitory") mechanism in instrumental learning.

Is the Hull-Spence Kind of Theorizing More Applicable to Some Kinds of Behavioral Phenomena than Others?   As indicated elsewhere (Amsel, 1961) the answer to this question is yes, in my opinion. The Hull-Spence approach to theory has been and will continue to be more suitable for integrating the phenomena of nonintentional, goal-oriented learning. To quote from the earlier discussion:

> Interests in current learning theory can be divided into two classes: those which deal with the acquisition of knowledges (information), skills, and games ("human learning"), and those which have to do with more general motive-incentive oriented (instrumental) learning. The former class involves instructions, induced sets, and verbal mediation; the latter, a kind of learning which, in addition to being more general (observable in a variety of organisms), is usually "nonintentional" and nonarticulate. Theorists, like Hull and Spence, most often criticized as "mechanistic," have been dealing almost exclusively with goal-oriented behavior of nonarticulate organisms and with the behavior of humans operating at prearticulate and subarticulate levels. In man, as well as in animals, this kind of learning involves mainly conditioning and its derivatives, stimulus-selective learning and response-selective learning, determining the strengthening and weakening of approach and avoidance tendencies, broadly conceived. When one considers such learning, the topog-

raphy of the criterion experimental response is usually of very little importance per se. It is at this level of learning that hypotheses derived from animal studies have been applied most profitably to the understanding of man's adjustment to his environment (i.e., to the development of "personality"). If you doubt this assertion, ponder for a moment on where in the *learning* literature you would go to find hypotheses applicable to the explanation of a child's tantrums, or an adolescent's conflicts, or an adult's alcoholism (p. 34).

With respect to response topography, we might compare the relative indifference of Hull-Spence theory to the specific instrumental response form (running, bar-pressing, panel-pushing, jumping, and so forth) with which it deals in deriving its generalities to some current interests in the Skinnerian system in response "shaping," ranging from the training of complex sequences of behavior in pigeons to teaching of knowledge through the use of self-instructional devices (Ferster & Skinner, 1957; Skinner, 1953; Skinner, 1954). To me, these represent opposites with respect to interest in specific response topography in current behavior-theory strategies. I would venture that Skinnerians will have much to say in the next ten years about acquisition of complex, chained patterns of behavior, for example, acquisition of knowledge and skills. Perhaps, in this area, a nontheoretical approach will be fruitful, because so much of what is needed is better description.

To carry this argument further, in the case of perceptual-motor skills, it is instructive that Hullians by training and, I think, attitude toward theory have found very little direct use for Hullian conceptualizations in their recent work, outside of the area of response decrement where, interestingly enough, the work-related inhibition concepts of Hull, which Spence has not emphasized in his treatment of selective learning, continue to have relevance. Without attempting here to document the assertion, the recent work of investigators like Adams, Ammons, and Bilodeau, to mention a few, seems to me testimony that skills research will not, in the near future, find its important explanatory constructs and principles in the postulates of Hull-Spence neobehaviorism, wherever else they may not find them.

In the areas traditionally called verbal learning, problem-solving, and concept-formation, the basic structure of Hull-Spence theory is also little evident, even in the S-R analyses by students of Spence who, when they deal with conditioning or selective learning, are closer to the Hullian persuasion (e.g., Goss, Irion, Kendler, Underwood). However, one exception to this is Maltzman, whose recent paper on the role of motivation in thinking (Maltzman, 1962) shows evidence, as did an earlier one (Maltzman, 1955), of his continuing use of Hullian ideas in the S-R analysis of higher mental processes. Hull's own venture into theorizing in the area of verbal learning (Hull *et al.*, 1940) bears little formal resemblance to his theorizing in the areas of conditioning and nonverbal learning which began in the early thirties. The work in verbal learning—and I use this designation in its broadest sense—remains largely in the non-theoretical, motivationless, strict-associationist tradition, and takes its explanatory conceptions almost entirely from the language of transfer, and more recently from the language of information theory and the computer. Irion's revision of McGeoch's *Psychology of Human Learning* (McGeoch & Irion, 1952) shows little evidence of being influenced by Hullian theorizing in the sections which deal with traditional verbal learning paradigms, and overlaps the Hullian theorizing mainly where it refers to conditioning or selective learning. Underwood (1961) reviewing ten years of work on distribution of practice, finds no occasion to refer to either Hull or Spence, or to constructs important in their theorizing.

Recent theoretical treatments of concept-formation (Goss, 1961) and problem-solving (Kendler & Kendler, 1962) depend little if at all on anything uniquely Hullian, although these writers have, in other contexts, expressed their ideas in terms of a Hullian approach. In these instances, S-R models are developed to describe mediating processes in concept-formation and problem-solving. However, the S-R schemes are neutral with respect to particular systematic flavor. The Kendlers are explicit on this score. They adopt an S-R learning pretheoretical model, recognizing that the model "ignores many of the points of disagreement among S-R learning theories." They point out, rightly I think, that many of the systematic differences among S-R theorists like Hull, Guthrie, Spence, and Skinner "become attenuated and some even disappear when viewed from the distance of problem solving behavior" (p. 3).

Human (verbal) learning has been essentially a motivationless and incentiveless psychology, while the core of Hull-Spence theory has been the $H \times D$—more recently, the $H \times (D + K)$—formulation. The work at Iowa and elsewhere with the Manifest Anxiety Scale (MAS) has involved a few experiments in which the drive concept is introduced into verbal learning situations. However, in these experiments, which are in the Hull-Spence framework, the interest is not primarily in the laws of verbal learning, but in the use of the paired-associate and serial learning techniques as complex learning situations for humans as contrasted to eyelid conditioning, a simple learning situation.

Clearly, Hull was fascinated by the whole question of automatic adaptive and adjustive mechanisms. His early writings contained several references to his feeling that the homeostatic concept was central to the whole problem of learning. Hull's emphasis on survival (1934) and defense reactions (1929) and automatic adjustment mechanisms (1943, 1952) remained part of his central concern. It is only reasonable to suppose that one so concerned with such mechanisms would develop a system of constructs more relevant to understanding the learning of personality than the acquisition of knowledge. It seems to me that such interests still carry over into neo-Hullian theorizing, particularly to that portion of it which has a conditioning model at its core.

Will the H × D Formulation Continue to Be Important, or Will D Become Unnecessary, as Some Have Suggested?   Central to all Hullian theoretical endeavors has been the distinction between habit strength (H), on the one hand, and drive and incentive strength (D and K), on the other. The continuing problem of maintaining the independence of these major constructs has been discussed in many connections.

The separation of the learning (H) and motivational (D and K) variables will be particularly important in some of the recent Hullian formulations which have underlined the importance of the fractional anticipatory goal construct (r_G-s_G, r_F-s_F) in the learning and performance of instrumental behavior. In the case of these explanatory constructs, which have the status of classically conditioned response processes, producing characteristic interoceptive stimulation, we are theorizing about the habit strength ($_sH_{r_G}$) of external stimulus cues to evoke such responses; the incentive-producing properties ($r_G{\rightarrow}K$) of these hypothetical responses; and the habit strength ($_{s_G}H_R$) of the internal, conditioned-response-produced stimuli to evoke instrumental responses. All of these factors will affect the instrumental behavior in question. The difficulty is that we are making inferences about the habit strengths $_sH_{r_G}$ and $_{s_G}H_R$ and the contribution of r_G to generalized motivation through K from the same overt response. Separating these learning and motivational properties of antedating goal responses is not very difficult theoretically, but extremely difficult experimentally. Possibly, some of the newer psychophysiological research techniques will provide measurement operations for the independent evaluation of H and D effects which will correlate highly with evaluations from behavioral techniques.

Setting aside these considerations, Hullian theory has been a healthy influence on motivational psychology, and this may turn out to be one of its major long-term contributions. It has taken the complexity out of the drive mechanism and put it into behavior tendencies (E) through habit strength (H). In this way it has given teeth to the important distinction between learning and performance, and has done so in an experimentally testable fashion. Certainly, Hullians have on several occasions (Brown, 1953; Farber, 1954) offered a rule of procedure which I would restate as follows: *If the motivational theory is as complex as the behavior for which it accounts it affords no explanatory advantage.* Otherwise there is the tendency to return to a situation not unlike the heyday of instinct psychology—a motive for every (human) behavior because, as Brown (1953) has pointed out, a want or desire can be demonstrated, *at a verbal level,* for any goal-oriented activity.

It is always possible that some successful behavior theory of the future will take the Hullian dictum on motivation (simplicity in motivation, complexity in behavior) so to heart that it will simplfy the motivation concept out of existence. This seems, in fact, to be the direction Estes (1958) has taken when, in his neo-Guthrian associationism, he puts the entire burden of the motivation system into the drive stimulus (S_D) and its associative connections, denying the necessity for postulating an energizing factor in behavior. With Estes this is a matter of harsh theoretical necessity: the properties of D, or anything resembling it, simply do not fit the current statistical theorizing, which requires an associationistic point of view much stricter and less yielding than even the associationism of Guthrie from which it springs.

Even if it is possible to build a behavioral theory without D or any other motivational energizer, there can still be considerable argument about the desirability and fruitfulness of such a course of action. The argument of parsimony will be persuasive only when associationistic but driveless behavior theories can organize and explain a range of phenomena far greater than they can at present.

The degree of explanatory necessity for the drive concept would seem to depend upon the breadth of phenomena which a theory "bites off to chew." In relatively general theories of behavior, we can expect some kind of motivation concept to be around for a long time. Such an assertion is supported by recent descriptions of nonspecific, drivelike facilitation from stimulation of the ascending reticular activating system and the currency of terms such as "activation" and "arousal." But, I do believe that neobehavioristic theory of the future will make further strides toward taking complexity out of motivation theory. My own preference in this, as indicated elsewhere (Amsel, 1958), is to work backward from classes of goal events, distinguishing three classes only, reward, punishment, and frustration, and relating primary, secondary, and also incentive motivation to these classes of goals. This type of generalization would, I am convinced, take in at least most of the motivating conditions which are under experimental control.

Will Developments in Physiology and Neurology Affect the Formulation?
Both Skinner (1950) and Spence (1956) have argued that for each division of natural science there can and should exist integration in terms of abstractions derived from observations at that level. Skinner's position is the more unyielding of the two. Spence has indicated in various places that whatever help we can get from physiology in stating behavioral laws is not unwelcome, but that it is such *behavioral* laws that psychologists uniquely seek. N. E. Miller has taken the more neutral position that "the most profitable level of analysis will vary with the specific phenomena being stud-

ied" (1959, p. 199). Interestingly enough, Hebb's recent statements on these matters seem to place him closer to Spence than to Miller. Hebb, regarded by many as an arch reductionist, has put it this way:

> It was said above that a phase sequence is a psychological construct, not a physiological one. The statement, which applies also to the cell assembly, needs explanation. Not only are these hypothetical processes too complex to be recorded physiologically; they also relate primarily to the behavior of the whole intact animal, and exist as constructs whose necessity is found only in the attempt to explain such behavior. It is the evidence of behavior that led Pavlov and Hull to the stimulus trace, not physiology; the physiological evidence, by itself, and for traces with time period of 10 or 15 secs, almost rules this out. It is behavior alone that justifies the conception of expectancy. When behavior indicates the existence of such forms of ideation or mediating process, we reconsider the evidence of anatomy and physiology and, with hindsight, see how the constructs may, conceivably, be made compatible with what we know of brain function; but this does not change the fact that they originated as *behavioral* constructs, nor the fact that the knowledge we have of their properties is still derived mostly from behavior (1959, p. 631).

Knowledge of physiological mechanisms may be valuable to the neobehaviorist in several ways. They may suggest variables relevant to important behavior phenomena which have been overlooked by behaviorists; but this is not very likely, because the study of the mediating mechanism presupposes some knowledge of its external stimulus and response counterpart. For example, the pioneer work of Delgado, Roberts, and Miller (1954) and Olds and Milner (1954), showing that learning of instrumental responses can be "motivated" and "reinforced" by direct stimulation of selected portions of the brain is an example of how behavioristic concepts and techniques are affecting neurophysiological research, rather than vice versa. I feel there is little in this kind of work that will have much effect on neobehavioristic *theory* since it is primarily an attempt to show similarity in effects produced by exteroceptive stimulation or deprivation, on the one hand, and by brain stimulation, on the other. This is important work, whose significance is not minimized, but whose contribution, at this stage, is mainly to brain localization (Olds, 1955, 1956), comparable to earlier work on localization of sensory and motor functions. But what was thought to be a fairly complete knowledge of motor functions of the cortex has not helped much in our *psychological* definition of a response; nor has the extensive exploration of the sensory projection and association areas of the cortex given us any substantial boost in defining the stimulus of our conceptual systems. These still remain problems which behavior theory must solve at its own level, no at a more molecular level; and I believe the same will be true of the kinds of conceptual problems presented by such terms as *motivation* and *reinforcement*.

However, it is already clear that developments in neurophysiology can be helpful in certain behavioral experiments and in the statement of behavioral laws. As Spence (1952) has suggested, ". . . It is conceivable that physiological connotations can and will be developed for (Hull's) intervening variables. . . ." If they can, that is, if stable and standardized physiological measuring techniques can be developed which can be shown to be related to behavioral measurements and to known environmental antecedents, this might permit such advances in experimental technique as continuous measurement of drive level throughout an experimental session and detection of changes in motivational level from day to day in cases where subjects are required to report on several different occasions. Malmo (1958) has stressed the potential importance of such procedures in learning experiments, making specific reference to work with the MAS where inferences about drive level are made from answers to questions. As Malmo points out, a subject, for example a low-anxiety subject as measured by the scale, ". . . could have a highly 'arousing' (drive-increasing) experience . . . immediately prior to the experiment." Certainly, such a thing would be immensely useful in behavioral experiments, and also in theorizing to the extent it provided a further basis for independent evaluation of D, and conceivably also for the separation of H and D and K effects.

I expect that physiological information will continue to play some part in the invention of significant behavioral constructs. For example, constructs like *drive stimulus* (S_D) and *fractional anticipatory goal response* $(r_G$-$s_G)$ are obviously not independent of any knowledge of physiology, even though their definition need include no specific physiological designation or referent. Likewise, behavior-inferred constructs will continue to be important in providing research leads for physiological psychologists and physiologists.

Will S-R versus Cognitive Arguments Persist? It seems fairly clear, when one examines recent experiments reporting animal behavior, that references to Tolman have all but disappeared. Insofar as Tolman represented cognitive psychology as it was applied to explanations of simpler behavioral processes, such as selective learning in animals and conditioning in humans, it now seems safe to say that cognitive psychology of that kind is no longer an important factor in the explanation of behavior. The major overlap of interests between cognitive theorists and S-R theorists of the Hullian inclination has been in "expectancy" as a mediating mechanism. This boils down to a difference between a *conditioning-expectancy* and a *cognitive-expectancy* model. Stimulus-response conditioning-expectancy theory is r_G theory, and the advantage of this kind of theory over the cognitive-expectancy variety is that the conditioning model has definite rules and limits of operation established by the findings of conditioning experiments. The use of such a model restricts the theorist to properties of the mediating mechanism characteristic of conditioned responses, which have been studied and identified in a variety of conditioning experiments (Lachman, 1960). On the other hand, the cognitive-expectancy language has been a language of common sense. Such a language is difficult enough to apply profitably to humans operating at a language level; it is much more difficult to apply rigidly to lower anmials operating in simple situations or to humans operating at prearticulate or subarticulate levels. The result has been that the cognitive theorists, generally speaking, have left the lower-level learning phenomena to the stimulus-response psychologists and have moved on to tackle more complex human behavior, usually involving language—a level of behavior for which their kind of theorizing was always more appropriate.

Thus, what may appear as a rapprochement between S-R and cognitive points of view really does not amount to a rapprochement at all. It is simply that cognitive psychologists have, for the most part, moved into an area more appropriate to the meaning of the word *cognitive:* the study of the acquisition of knowledge by humans. Adherents to the older cognitive psychology of Tolman, applied to lower-level learning phenomena, seem to be scarce. The new cognitive psychology is a different animal: it is an attempt to describe cognitive processes in the language of the computer and information theory. It speaks not of demands, appetites, expectancies, and readinesses but rather of inputs, outputs, and channel capacities. "Plans" have replaced cognitive maps, but the plan seems a more exclusively human phenomenon. In place of means-ends-readinesses, and sign-Gestalt-expectations, there are bits and chunks of information to be "processed" by the organism. The new cognitivists and structuralists are questioning the vitality of stimulus-response psychology in much the same way that the Gestaltists and older cognitivists did twenty years ago. There are, however, at least two important differences: (1) The current challenge is, at least, at a level more appropriate to the language of the challenger; the earlier challenges were not. (2) The new cognitivists carry with them a more powerful, analytical language than did the old, and many of them are, for psychologists at any rate, "hard-headed" mathematicians.

It remains to be seen whether the new cognitive approach will do what the old one did, which was mainly to serve as a loyal opposition, to force a sharpening of the stimulus-response language and theory, and to make the S-R psychologists pay attention to things they might otherwise have overlooked. There is a feeling among psychologists I talk to that this will not be the case because the meeting ground is much more restricted than it was. There also seems to be a feeling that arguments between conflicting systematic viewpoints will decline even more sharply than they already have, as different theoretical strategies are invented to cope with restricted problem areas. This would be in line with a more or less general feeling that the day of the system in psychology has all but given way to the day of the tighter, more data-bound theory and, within a theory, the even tighter model (Amsel, 1961).

Psychologists will certainly continue to argue their preferences, even if these preferences reflect only the language they use. I have suggested that these arguments are not very likely to be about the simpler phenomena; for these phenomena, some form of stimulus-response analysis seems to be adequate and appropriate. The question of a powerful and suitable theoretical language for the study of "higher mental processes"—concept-formation, problem solving, thinking and the acquisition of knowledge—is what will be at issue. The Kendlers have already opted for a stimulus-response language, although they are not ready to choose one particular theoretical form of this language over any other. Nevertheless, they want to talk about knowledge and problem solving in terms of associations, and in terms of mediating mechanisms couched in the language of stimulus and response. The information processers are going to talk about inputs and outputs and about "coding" rather than stimulus-response mediation. Mandler (1962) has recently suggested that when we go from the simple to the complex, from the lower to the higher animal forms, from lower to higher levels of human functioning, we may very well be going from associations to structures. Here is a suggestion that we do not really need to choose between stimulus-response and cognitive approaches to the study of behavior, but that each is a more appropriate description for some particular level of observation.

Where do the neo-Hullians fit into all of this? While Hull's theory of 1943, or its 1949 revision, or even the more recent revisions by Spence of the theory, cannot be expected to handle phenomena they were never intended to handle, we certainly can expect extensions of these ideas to more complex phenomena. Some of these were already in existence in the thirties, when Hull and others were applying a stimulus-response analysis to more complex phenomena and to terms such as "purpose" and "directing ideas." Spence (1952) indicates that Hull had himself planned to return to his original interests in higher-level phenomena after he had brought some organization into the study of simpler ones. I would venture a guess that Hullians and other S-R psychologists will continue to prefer to see how far they can go with their conceptions, and will continue to invite other psychologists, using other conceptions, to prove that they can go as far, or farther, and do it as well, or better.

REFERENCES

AMSEL, A. A three factor theory of inhibition: An addition to Hull's two factor theory. Paper read at meeting of Southern Society for Philosophy and Psychology, 1951.

AMSEL, A. The role of frustrative nonreward in noncontinuous reward situations. *Psychol. Bull.*, 1958, **55**, 102-119.

AMSEL, A. Hope comes to learning theory. *Contemp. Psychol.*, 1961, **6**, 33-36.

AMSEL, A. Frustrative nonreward in partial reinforcement and discrimination learning: Some recent history and a theoretical extension. *Psychol. Rev.*, 1962, **69**, 306-328.

BERGMAN, G., & SPENCE, K. W. Operationism and theory in psychology. *Psychol. Rev.*, 1941, **48**, 1-14.

BERLYNE, D. E. Knowledge and stimulus-response psychology. *Psychol. Rev.*, 1954, **61**, 245-254.

BROWN, J. S. Problems presented by the concept of acquired drive. In M. R. Jones (Ed.), *Current theory and research in motivation*. Lincoln: Univ. Nebraska Press, 1953. Pp. 1-21.

BUSH, R. R., & MOSTELLER, F. A mathematical model for simple learning. *Psychol. Rev.* 1951, **58**, 313-323.

CAMPBELL, A., & KRAELING, D. Response strength as a function of drive level during training and extinction. *J. comp. physiol. Psychol.*, 1954, **47**, 101-103.

COAN, R. W., & ZAGONA, S. V. Contemporary ratings of psychological theorists *Psychol. Rec.*, 1962, **12**, 315-322.

DELGADO, J. M. R., ROBERTS, W. W., & MILLER, N. E. Learning motivated by electrical stimulation of the brain. *Amer. J. Physiol.*, 1954, **179**, 587-593.

ESTES, W. K. Toward a statistical theory of learning. *Psychol. Rev.*, 1950, **57**, 94-107.

ESTES, W. K. Stimulus response theory of drive. In M. R. Jones (Ed.), *Nebraska symposium on motivation*. Lincoln: Univ. Nebraska Press, 1958. Pp. 35-69.

FARBER, I. E. Anxiety as a drive state. In M. R. Jones (Ed.), *Nebraska symposium on motivation*. Lincoln: Univ. Nebraska Press, 1954. Pp. 1-46.

FERSTER, C. B. & SKINNER, B. F. *Schedules of reinforcement*. New York: Appleton-Century-Crofts, 1957.

GOSS, A. E. Verbal mediating responses and concept formation. *Psychol. Rev.*, 1961, **68**, 248-274.

HEBB, D. O. *A neuropsychological theory*. In E. Koch (Ed.), *Psychology: a study of science*. New York: McGraw-Hill, 1959. Vol. I, pp. 622-643.

HEYMAN, W. Certain relationships between stimulus intensity and stimulus generalization. *J. exp. Psychol.*, 1957, **53**, 239-248.

HULL, C. L. A functional interpretation of the conditioned reflex. *Psychol. Rev.*, 1929, **36**, 498-511.

HULL, C. L. Learning: II. The factor of the conditioned reflex. In C. Murchison (Ed.), *Handbook of general experimental psychology*. Worcester, Mass.: Clark Univ. Press, 1934. Pp. 382-455.

HULL, C. L. *Principles of behavior.* New York: Appleton-Century, 1943.

HULL, C. L. Behavior postulates and corollaries—1949. *Psychol. Rev.*, 1950, **57**, 173-180.

HULL, C. L. *Essentials of behavior.* New Haven: Yale Univ. Press, 1951.

HULL, C. L. *A behavior system.* New Haven: Yale Univ. Press, 1952.

HULL, C. L., HOVLAND, C. I., ROSS, R. T., HALL, M., PERKINS, D. T., & FITCH, F. B. *Mathematics—deductive theory of rote learning.* New Haven: Yale Univ. Press, 1940.

KENDLER, H. H., & KENDLER, T. S. Vertical and horizontal processes in problem solving. *Psychol. Rev.*, 1962, **69**, 1-16.

KOBRICK, J. L. The relationships among three measures of response strength as a function of the numbers of reinforcements. *J. comp. physiol. Psychol.*, 1956, **49**, 582-585.

KOCH, S. Clark L. Hull. In S. Koch (Ed.), *Modern learning theory.* New York: Appleton-Century-Crofts, 1954. Pp. 1-176.

LACHMAN, R. The model in theory construction. *Psychol. Rev.*, 1960, **67**, 113-129.

LOGAN, F. A. A micromolar approach to behavior theory. *Psychol. Rev.*, 1956, **63**, 63-73.

LOGAN, F. A. The Hull-Spence approach. In S. Koch (Ed.), *Psychology: a study of science.* New York: McGraw-Hill, 1959. Vol. II. Pp. 293-358.

LOGAN, F. A. *Incentive.* New Haven: Yale Univ. Press, 1960.

McGEOCH, J. A., & IRION, A. L. *Psychology of human learning.* New York: Longmans, 1952.

MALMO, R. B. Measurement of drive: An unsolved problem in psychology. In M. R. Jones (Ed.), *Nebraska symposium on motivation.* Lincoln: Univ. Nebraska Press, 1958. Pp. 229-265.

MALTZMAN, I. Thinking from a behavioristic point of view. *Psychol. Rev.*, 1955, **62**, 275-286.

MALTZMAN, I. Motivation and the direction of thinking. *Psychol. Bull.*, 1962, **59**, 457-467.

MANDLER, G. From association to structure. *Psychol. Rev.*, 1962, **69**, 415-427.

MILLER, N. E. Liberalization of basic S-R concepts: Extensions to conflict behavior, motivation, and social learning. In S. Koch (Ed.), *Psychology: a study of science.* New York: McGraw-Hill, 1959. Vol. 2, pp. 196-292.

OLDS, J. Physiological mechanisms of reward. In M. R. Jones (Ed.), *Nebraska symposium on motivation.* Lincoln: Univ. Nebraska Press, 1955. Pp. 73-139.

OLDS, J. A preliminary mapping of electrical reinforcing effects in the rat brain. *J. comp. physiol. Psychol.*, 1956, **49**, 281-285.

OLDS, J., & MILNER, P. Positive reinforcement produced by electrical stimulation of septal area or other regions of the rat brain. *J. comp. physiol. Psychol.*, 1954, **47**, 419-427.

SKINNER, B. F. Are theories of learning necessary? *Psychol. Rev.*, 1950, **57**, 193-216.

SKINNER, B. F. *Science and human behavior.* New York: Macmillan, 1953.

SKINNER, B. F. The science of learning and the art of teaching. In *Current trends in psychology and the behavioral sciences.* Univ. Pittsburgh Press, 1954.

SPENCE, K. W. The nature of discrimination learning in animals. *Psychol. Rev.,* 1936, **43,** 427-449.

SPENCE, K. W. Analysis of the formation of visual discrimination habits in the chimpanzee. *J. comp. Psychol.,* 1937, **23,** 77-100.

SPENCE, K. W. Clark Leonard Hull: 1884-1952. *Amer. J. Psychol.,* 1952, **65,** 639-646.

SPENCE, K. W. *Behavior theory and conditioning.* New Haven: Yale Univ. Press, 1956.

SPENCE, K. W. A theory of emotionally based drive (D) and its relation to performance in simple learning situations. *Amer. Psychologist,* 1958, **13,** 131-141.

SPENCE, K. W. *Behavior theory and learning.* Englewood Cliffs, N.J.: Prentice-Hall, 1960.

UNDERWOOD, B. J. Ten years of massed practice on distributed practice. *Psychol. Rev.* 1961, **68,** 229-247.

13 GREGORY RAZRAN

EVOLUTIONARY PSYCHOLOGY: LEVELS OF LEARNING—AND PERCEPTION AND THINKING *

HISTORICALLY, THE DOCTRINE OF EVOLUTION was, as is well known, a prime stimulus to the rise of American functional psychology. It is, of course, also true that Western studies of animal learning were in all respects Darwin-inspired. George Romanes (*Animal Intelligence,* 1881; *Mental Evolution in Animals,* 1883), father of comparative psychology; C. Lloyd Morgan, father of experimental comparative psychology (*Introduction to Comparative Psychology,* 1894) and of the guiding principle of its interpretation (the "Lloyd Morgan Canon"); and Leonard Hobhouse, originator of many techniques for testing animal intelligence and learning (*Mind in Evolution,* 1901), were all avowed evolutionists. So were the founder of the *American Journal of Psychology* (1887) and first president of the American Psychological Association (1892), G. Stanley Hall, and the author of America's compendious *Dictionary of Philosophy and Psychology* (1901-1902), J. Mark Baldwin.

In present-day behavioral American psychology, the voice of evolution is, however, quite feeble. With few exceptions, systematizers of both the conditioning-and-learning and the perception-and-thinking varieties seem to largely ignore evolution as a framework of research and thought. Pragmatic convenience—evolutionary differences are hard to fit into fixed systems, general laws must first be fully utilized (cf. Titchener's "generalized mind")—and paucity of thoroughgoing, full-scale, experimental phyletic and ontogenetic comparisons of modifiable behavior are inter-

---

* Based on an address delivered before the Moscow Section of the All-Union Pavlov Society of Physiologists, July 11, 1961, and before the Prague Section of the Czechoslovakian Societies of Higher Nervous Activity and of Psychology, July 30, 1961.

Research done under Grant M-4455 of the National Institute of Mental Health, National Institutes of Health, Public Health Service, United States Department of Health, Education, and Welfare.

207

208 GREGORY RAZRAN

twined in producing "no-evolution" approaches and views. Still, the voice of evolution has really not been altogether mute in our land, and there is indeed evidence that, in the wake of considerable rapprochements between and some denouements of conventional systems in more recent years, it is gaining new strength and appeal (Beach, 1950; Bitterman, 1960; Nissen, 1951; Schneirla, 1952).

Evolution has fared considerably better in Pavlov's system of higher nervous activity. Although reflexes and conditioning may well appear to favor views of phyletic and animal-human equalization and have indeed greatly contributed to such views in this country, Pavlov's own system does not seem to have thereby lost evolutionary emphasis. His steadfast refusal to regard human language as a mere conditioned vocal reaction (Pavlov, 1927, 1932, 1933) was no doubt in itself a bulwark of evolutionary distinctness and of scientific and philosophic prescience.[1] Likewise, Beritov, who originally interpreted all modifiable behavior in terms of individually acquired (conditioned) reflexes (Beritov, 1927), has for some time now adopted an evolutionary two-level system (1947, 1961)—individual reflexes at lower levels and individual reflexes plus what he calls psychonervous image-direction at higher levels—while the late L. A. Orbeli, Pavlov's immediate successor in the U.S.S.R. Academy of Sciences and in the Koltushi Institute, was long a champion of evolutionary physiology (Orbeli, 1947) and founded a special institute for it. Significant evolutionary commitments are also quite evident in the research and thought of Anokhin (1949, 1958), Asratyan (1953), Ayrapetyants (1960), Biryukov (1959), Karamyan (1956), Slonim (1961), Voronin (1957), and a number of other current Soviet leaders in the study of the physiology of higher nervous activity. Above all, Russian laboratories have to date yielded a vast amount of experimental data—approximately five hundred experiments —on comparative conditioning in phylogeny and ontogeny, with special emphasis on compound-stimulus conditioning in animals and language acquisition or verbal conditioning in young children.

Yet the Russians, too, have so far not developed a modern evolutionary system of higher nervous activity or learning[2]—have not delincated

---

[1] Cp. Magoun, Darling, and Prost (1960): "Animal studies suggest that vocalization in emotional expression is managed by a neural mechanism in the middle brain stem, and data from clincial neurology support the presence of such a subcortical emotional mechanism in man as well. No functional relationship is known between this deeplying mesencephalic system for emotional vocalization, widely present through the animal kingdom, and the topographically distant cortical areas for symbolic speech, which exist only in the associational cortex of the human brain" (pp. 43-44).

[2] Differences between Pavlov's higher nervous activity and American behavioral psychology as reflected in "learning" or "learning theory" pertain only to interpretations and not to the scope of the field. Pavlov equated "higher nervous activity" with "behavior" in the title of his first book on conditioning (Pavlov, 1923). He obviously meant "learned behavior" which is exactly the meaning of "learning" in current Amer-

specific levels, not integrated concepts with all available empirical evidence, and not related level to level through common and special functional laws or generalizations. And this is exactly what the present writer intends to do. A generous grant from the National Institutes of Health has permitted him to examine at first hand, in the last five years, almost all Russian, and a good deal of Czech and Polish, experimental data on higher nervous activity as well as to visit Russian, Polish, and Czech laboratories in the summers of 1961, 1963, and in the spring of 1964. Moreover, the writer's own work and views have always had strong evolutionary predilections. In 1935, summarizing his first series of experiments on salivary conditioning in human subjects and surveying the then-available evidence in the entire field, he wrote:

> It would really be a curious freak or organismic evolution the outstanding feature of which is the evolution of the brain and that special modifiability, called learning capacity, if the laws of this modifiability remained fixed and did not evolve (Razran, 1935, p. 7).

In 1955, he stated:

> The view that learning existing on this planet for hundreds of millions of years has continued in one quantitative continuum without evolving any new qualitatively distinct level seems very unlikely and discouraging (Razran, 1955, p. 93).

The main thesis of the present article will thus be the advocacy of a view of evolutionary levels of learning—specifically, a contention that an empirical and logical analysis of the evidential basis of the learning in both West and East (that is, primarily the United States and Russia) strongly suggests the existence of a hierarchy of four levels of learning, with the likelihood of four additional levels which, for the time being, will be accorded the status of sublevels. The analysis, it will further be argued, suggests also that perception and thinking be regarded as special evolutionary-higher levels of learning; that each level of learning is mediated by its own type of neural action, specific with respect to locus or pattern or both; and that the formal properties of the hierarchy of levels are somewhat as follows: (1) Each higher level of learning evolved from a lower level as an antecedent and thereat evolved some functional laws specific to itself and not derivable from its antecedent. (2) Lower levels normally coexist with higher levels so that, typically, learning manifests itself in the operation of all four levels, the first three levels, the first two levels, or only the first level. (3) Specific learning effects differ at different levels, thus pro-

---

ican usage, and it is of course also true that the term "behavior" in the titles of the books by Tolman, Hull, Skinner, and Spence refers to learned behavior. Or, to put it somewhat differently: "higher nervous activity" is defined in current Russian textbooks as "the study of conditioned reflexes," which, in a broad sense (and surely in the Russian sense), means exactly what we mean by "learning."

ducing level conflict in some cases and level cooperation in others. Normally, higher-level effects dominate lower-level ones because of the former's greater efficiency, yet under certain circumstances lower-level ones dominate because of greater universality.

An analytic definition and classification of learning will precede the identification of the levels and the expansion and defense of the thesis.

GENERAL DEFINITION AND
CLASSIFICATION OF LEARNING

Traditionally, learning has often been defined as simply "profit through experience." If we replace the word "profit" by the less assuming and less evaluative "modification" and replace "experience" by "reaction" or "reacting," we arrive at: "Learning is a modification of a reaction [or, 'reacting' if the stress is on the process] through reacting." The term "modification" must admittedly be qualified as "more or less permanent" to exclude transient changes due to fatigue and to general oscillations in organismic reactivity (known as attention, motivation, interest, and the like in higher animals and men). Moreover, it should be made clear that, in essence, reaction-modification results not from mere repetition of reacting but from interaction with other reactions: there surely would be little learning if an organism's reactions were insulated from each other. Therefore: "Learning is a more or less permanent modification of a reaction (or reactions) through interaction with other reactions and through reacting."

It seems convenient—and essential—to be catholic in the use of the term "reaction" and to specify, at the outset, five types: neural, visceral, somatic, verbal, and cognitive. The restrictive trend of admitting within the framework of learning (and psychology in general) only the middle three, the macrobehavioral, types of reactions is palpably on the downgrade. Neural reactions are rapidly gaining overriding significance, not only in their old role of inferable, behind-the-scene explanatory models, but also in the striking new role of direct participants in the very arena of learning manifestations: as reactions modifying learning (Delgado, Roberts & Miller, 1954; Olds, 1960; Olds & Milner, 1954; and others[3]) and as reactions modified by learning (Galambos & Morgan, 1960; Jasper & Smirnov, 1960; John, 1961; Livanov & Polyakov, 1945; Morrell, 1961; Rusinov, 1959; and others). Likewise, few students of the field would argue now for a total eschewing of cognitive variables. Although the value of postulating arrays of complex cognitive constructs at levels at which direct behavioral observables are amply available may surely be questioned, the need for according operational reality to common sense reports of imagery, meaning, pain, and

---

[3] Space precludes full documentation of the empirical evidence of this chapter. A 946-item bibliography will be sent to readers on a first-come-first-served basis upon request to the author.

pleasure is just as surely becoming more and more exigent. Private and subjective as these reports are, they undeniably point to public and objective
(neurobehavioral) correlates and hence should not be left out of science, at
least not until the correlates gain their own operational status as direct observables. To put it differently, verbal reports are not mere verbal events.

The omission of the term "stimulus" in the definition of learning calls
for another brief clarification. On the face of it, the reason seems simple:
a stimulus does not exist for an organism until the stimulus evokes some
reaction in the organism. The uses to which the term has been put by theorists and students of the field—such as S-S (stimulus-stimulus) theories of
learning, S type of conditioning, reinforcing S, pure S act—are confusing in
their seeming implication that stimuli are directly and fully apprehended or
that perception requires no reaction on the part of the organism. To give but
one example: If a considerable amount of learning may be effected in
wholly curarized and paralyzed animals (Solomon & Turner, 1962), it
would surely, in our present state of knowledge, be more heuristic to say
that the results tend to support an intraneural (or neural-cognitive, if one
cares to push cognition so far downward; the writer regards this as fortuitous) view of learning than to state that the results tend to support an S-S
theory. Admittedly, this taxonomic S habit has come down from the era of
traditional behaviorism when only effector reactions were allowed exalted
R status and interneural reactions were shackled in limbo, a position which
even then the perceptive Lashley strongly contested and which now is hardly
tenable. This is of course not to say that effector reactions do not attain a
quale such as proprioceptive and interoceptive feedback and environmental
contact which may well be of special significance in learning, but only that
noneffector interneural reactions are also Rs of considerable value—that,
indeed, persistent thinking in denuded S categories may obscure scientific
inquiry into the *sine qua non* of learning.

Classification of the evidence of learning in terms of interactions of
reactions suggests a division into two broad categories: *modificatory* and
integrative. Modificatory learning is best thought of as a binary or two-
reaction interaction in which one reaction is modifying and the other is
modified. The modifying reaction will be designated here by capital
letter *G* (the last letter of *modifying*) and the modified reaction by
small letter *d* (the last letter of *modified*), the difference in size of letters
meaning to imply that the modifying reaction is, in sum-total, invariably
more potent or dominant than the modified reaction—a view the evidence
for which could hardly be contested. In terms of outcomes of interactions,
the modificatory category of learning needs to be further divided into two
subcategories: one subcategory in which the modifying reaction, *G,* imparts some of its characteristics to the modified reaction, *d* (or the modified
reaction assumes some of the characteristics of the modifying one), so that
d + *G* becomes *dG;* another subcategory in which the modifying reaction

strengthens or weakens the modified reaction so that $d + G$ becomes $dD(G)$ or $dd(G)$. There is reason to believe that only the $dD(G)$ variety of the second subcategory forms an unmistakably distinct class or level of its own, the $dd(G)$ variety being a form of dG learning in which the G is clearly inhibitory and imparts its inhibitory—or decremental— characteristics to its antecedent d. Moreover, as it will be reasoned in a later section, this inhibitory dG learning seems to be related to a more general and primitive sublevel of dG learning in which the d and G are biologically (and physically) antagonistic to each other.

The integrative category of learning refers to integrations of several (typically, more than two) reactions into one unitary reaction conceived as learning resulting from the interactions of *afferent* reactions: $a + b + c + \cdots n$ becoming $(abc \cdots n)$. Most objectively and directly, this learning is exemplified in Russian studies of compound-stimulus conditioning in which, in the course of training the conditioning, at first each component stimulus, but eventually only the total compound, is effective in evoking the conditioned reaction (Asratyan, 1938; Babkin, 1910; Beritov, 1932; Bregadze, 1930; Krakulis, 1960; Lukov, 1944; Zeliony, 1907; Zevald, 1941; and many others). However, evidence for *inferring* the operation of a like mechanism may also be found in several American experiments on the effects of overlearning on transfer and habit reversal (Harlow, 1949, 1959; Mandler, 1962). Some years ago, the writer named this integrative learning, *configural conditioning* (Razran, 1939c, 1939d, 1939e); but it seems obvious now that it would be better classed as *afferent configuring,* the conditioning being merely an efferent manifestation of its afferent existence and emergence. The mechanism of the configuring is, it may be noted, identical with Hebb's (1949) postulation of superordinate t in perception; and is also not unrelated to Harlow's "learning sets" and Mandler's "analogic structures," on the one hand, and to *Aktualgenese* or microgenetic approaches to perception (Undeutsch, 1942), on the other. Moreover, it should be added that results of a considerable number of recent Russian experiments are quite definite in demonstrating that this afferent configuring does not manifest itself in lower animals but increases continually in scope and effectiveness in vertebrate and mamalian evolution (Baru *et al.,* 1959; Beritov, 1959; Voronin, 1957; and others), which, interestingly, is again similar to several indications of American findings on the phylogenesis of learning-set and habit-reversal capacity (Boycott & Young, 1958; Koronakos & Arnold, 1957; Warren, Brookshire, Ball, & Reynolds, 1960).[4]

---

[4] Compare also a recent statement by Konorski and Lawicka (1959, pp. 195-196). "There is much evidence collected both by Pavlov's school and in our laboratory showing that the cortical representation of the compound of conditioned stimuli cannot be simply considered as composed from the particular centres representing each element of the compound. First, the possibility of differentiation in which the compound plays

Finally, evidence will be adduced to suggest the need of postulating: (1) a nonconfigured variety of afferent integration in which component reactions are merely modified in relation to each other—$a + b + c + \cdots n$ becoming $a \leftrightarrow B \leftrightarrow c \leftrightarrow \cdots n;$ (2) a subcategory of a special level of configuring involving words and best described as symbolization— $A + B + C + \cdots N + W$ becoming $Sy(ABC \cdots N)$; and (3) an advanced variety of symbol interaction producing true predication or semanticization—$Sy_a + Sy_b$ becoming Sy_{ab}.

The category of integrative learning differs radically from the modificatory one in what might for a lack of a better name be called creativity or productivity. For, unlike the learning of the first category, integrative learning is not just a process of modifying old reactions—through strengthening them as in $dD(G)$ learning or through expanding the ways (realms of stimuli) of eliciting them as in dG learning—but it is a special process-product mechanism of bringing into being varieties of altogether new reactive units which take their assigned posts along the old units and indeed normally come to dominate and control the old units. Configuring, symbolization, and semanticization almost force one to postulate resultant existence of enduring cortical—and perhaps also subcortical—action units designated as "configures" (percepts?), symbols (syntheses of words and sets of configures), and "sememes" (unit-patterns of symbols). Indeed, in view of some recent neuromorphological evidence (Kukuyev, 1955; Polyakov, 1959; Zhukova, 1953), one is inclined to hypothesize further and say that configures are in essence compressed proprioceptive integrations (*Gestaltungen*) of orienting reflexes of components of compound-stimulus conditioning that come to be specially represented in the motor and premotor areas of the brain—represented in a manner similar to the projection of symbols and sememes in the associational human cortex, long claimed by clinical neurologists. Symbols and sememes are by definition exclusive products of human evolution, whereas configures are here, as indicated, thought to be existent also in higher animals. Imagery as a subjective correlate of configures is a tempting assumption, particularly in light of the experiments of Beritov, the eminent Soviet academician and neurophysiologist.

Enlargement and defense of what has so far been said—ambitious and difficult as it may appear—will now follow in the form of a full discussion

---

a role of the positive conditioned stimulus while its elements are inhibitory speaks in favour of this conclusion. If the respresentation of this compound were nothing else than the sum of the centres of its elements such a differentiation would be of course impossible, because the sum of two inhibitory reflexes cannot result in the excitatory reflex. . . . All these data go to show that the compound stimulus must be considered as a stimulus different from its component stimuli. Of course it may be, and most often it is, similar to its elements, as judged by the high level of generalization between them. But it can be differentiated from its elements in exactly the same way as are differentiated simple stimuli when they are similar to one another."

of the known basic properties of each of the postulated four main levels of
learning modifiability: dG, $dD(G)$, $(abc \cdots n)$, and $Sy(ABC \cdots N)$.

dG LEARNING: IDENTIFICATION AND
BASIC MECHANISMS AND ATTRIBUTES

Learning at the dG level will readily be recognized as embracing Pavlovian or classical conditioning, which alone has yielded, as is well known, a
host of "laws" that, at least in some ways, may be prototypic of all learning.
For historical and some pragmatic reasons, it will henceforth be named dG
conditioning. Describing it as substitutive in character would in general
seem tenable, even if the substitution is not (there is no reason why it
should be) complete—that is, dG differs from G—and is furthermore far
from definitive with respect to essence and mechanism involved. Its two essential general attributes, however, are no doubt phyletic antiquity and universality. It was noted earlier that objective evidence indicates that the integrative category of learning becomes operative only in higher animals.
It is now necessary to add that, while $dG(G)$ learning surely extends further downward in the evolutionary scale, it, too, is by all tokens not a
wholly primitive and universal level of learning modifiability (difficult to
obtain with visceral reactions,[5] restricted to special classes of Gs, disrupt-
able by cortical ablations, lacking sufficient evidence of existence in lowest
animals, and several other considerations to be detailed in a following section). Not so dG conditioning. Experiments clearly show that in some
greater or lesser degree dG conditioning is demonstrable in animals which
have been curarized (Solomon & Turner, 1962), decorticated (Galambos
& Morgan, 1960), midpons transsected (Affani, Marchcafava, & Zernicki,
1962), and perhaps even in spinal animals (Dykman & Shurrager, 1956),
in coelenterates (Zubkov & Polikarpov, 1951) and infusoria (Plavilstchikov, 1928; Tchakotine, 1938), in the rat (Caldwell & Werboff, 1962;
Gunin, 1960), guinea pig (Klyavina, 1961), rabbit (Malakhovskaya,
1961), and human neonates (Papousek, 1960), and even in chick embryos (Blinkova, 1961; Hunt, 1949) and human fetuses (Spelt, 1948);
that almost all its basic laws are fully manifest in interoceptively produced
visceral and somatic reactions (Ayrapetyants, 1952; Bykov, 1943; Makarov, 1959; Razran, 1961), of which human subjects are, by their own reports, wholly unaware (Makarov, 1959); that some of its basic laws are
evident in interactions of electroencephalographic reactions (Galambos &
Morgan, 1960; John, 1961; Rusinov, 1959); and that in simple form,

---

[5] Evidence on $dD(G)$ conditioning of some visceral reactions in human subjects has
been reported by Lisina (1958) and Fowler and Kimmel (1962). However, even if
we disregard the likelihood of cognitive complications—obvious and recognized by
Lisina, relatively controlled by Fowler and Kimmel—the evidence surely shows that
the $dD(G)$ conditioning of these reactions is, compared with dG conditioning, difficult.

nonverbal idiots do as well with it as normal adults (Grings, Lockhart & Dameron, 1962). On the other hand, it is, at the same time, quite true that the laws of dG conditioning operate also in some fashion in man's most complex and cognitive reactions: changes in perceptions (Solley & Murphy, 1960; Razran, unpublished a) and meanings (Staats & Staats, 1957; DiVesta, 1961), in acquisitions and modifications of aesthetic tastes and of social attitudes and political and scientific convictions (Razran, unpublished a; Staats & Staats, 1958), and even in efficacy of problem solving (Razran, 1954). In the last-mentioned experiment, subjects' speeds of unscrambling scrambled food-related words such as *bhurrmaeg, ledmat,* and *theocecal* were significantly increased at the sight of specific photographs and sound of specific short musical selections which were presented to the subjects several times during eating: that is, the G of eating imparted some of its characteristics to the d of observing the photographs or listening to the music.

As might be suspected, however, the universality of dG conditioning does not mean equal effectiveness throughout phylogeny, ontogeny, and all states and reaction systems of animal and human functioning. All empirical evidence points, on the one hand, to the generalization that the laws of dG conditioning manifest themselves fully only in lower animals, in very young children, in adult human subjects when reactions or reaction relations are uncognized—and, in all cases, not fully with all types of reaction interactions. Or, to put it differently, the laws of dG conditioning manifest themselves fully only when other levels are not operative. When other levels are operative, dG conditioning becomes dominated by the evolved functional laws of the other levels, the domination being the greater, the higher the level of the learning, and the specific effects of the domination being incremental when dG-other learning relations are synergic, and decremental when these relations are antagonistic. On the other hand, there is also sufficient evidence to suggest strongly that under the impact of higher levels the effects of dG conditioning are merely suppressed and may well reassert themselves and dominate higher-level effects when the organism is malfunctioning—drugs, fatigue, emotion, physical and mental disturbances, or, simply, inattention and preoccupation.

Only a few specific laboratory examples will be cited in support of what has been said. (1) When lifting a dog's paw is followed by feeding, early manifestation of dG conditioning such as turning the head towards the food, mouth opening, licking, and the like, are soon superseded by $dD(G)$ learning effects of strengthening the lifting (readier and quicker lifting, less aid from experimenter, and finally lifting when merely placed on stand), while the head turning and other eating-accompanying reactions are no longer evident. Yet, when he is excited, the dog will remanifest his dG conditioning and temporarily fail his $dD(G)$ learning (Gambaryan, 1962; Konorski, 1936, 1948). (2) In human subjects, semantic verbal dG conditioning quickly comes to dominate the phonetic variety (Luria & Vinogradova, 1959; Razran, 1939b, 1949a, 1949b, 1949c, 1949d, 1952; Shvarts, 1954, 1960), which, among other things, correlates negatively with age (Riess, 1946) and intelligence (Luria & Vinogradova, 1959). But fatigued and drugged (sedated) subjects revert their semantic conditioning to phonetic (Luria and Vinogradova, 1959; Shvarts, 1954, 1960), and it has also been proven that the verbal conditioning of schizophrenics is significantly more phonetic than that of normal adults (Peastral, 1961). (3) Cognitive attitudes (conceived here as combinations of configures, symbols, and sememes) affect very significantly dG conditioning of even partly cognized human reactions (Hilgard, 1938; Norris & Grant, 1948; Razran, 1935). In a recent well-controlled Russian experiment (Pratusevich, 1960), for instance, seven- and thirteen-year-old children almost completely inhibited their well-established conditioned salivary reflexes to such conventional stimuli as the sound of a bell or the flash of a light, when the experimenter accompanied the administration of the stimuli by respective statements of "No bell is sounded" and "No light is flashed," or even by mere "Nyet" (other verbal expressions had no effect). And in the same experiment, it was also clearly demonstrated (what had been known for some time) that subjects conditioned to sensory stimuli transfer completely their conditioning to the names of stimuli (that is, from sound of a bell to word "bell" pronounced or seen) which, too, hardly follows laws of simple dG conditioning. Still, the writer has shown many times that (1) when human subjects are preoccupied or do not know that they are being conditioned, their laboratory results are fully dG in nature, and (2) that cognitive attitudes do not completely abolish simple dG conditioning. Similar results, that dG eyelid conditioning is not entirely annulled in face of contrary instructions, were obtained by Hilgard (1938) and others in this country, and by Avakyan (1960) in the Soviet Union.

Digressing for a while into clinical considerations, it might be noted that, interestingly, the laboratory-discovered dynamics of dG conditioning are, at least formally, not unlike the clinically-arrived-at dynamics of the "unconscious." It should be made clear, however, that the "unconscious" of dG conditioning is that of unconscious habit, rather than of Freudian goal-directed striving, laden with pleasure and aggression, for which the learning analogue, if any is wanted, would seem to be $dD(G)$ conditioning. Robot, Frankenstein, and golem, rather than Eros and Thanatos, are the analogues of dG conditioning in the realm of metaphors, while incidental learning is a limited parallel of it in the field of experimentation (limited in the sense that its subject matter has been primarily verbal material and not visceral and somatic reactions).

A further digression into the field of literature brings to mind a strikingly perceptive statement, bearing on the present analysis, made by John Ruskin over one hundred years ago in relation to the then-prevailing arguments about the role of association in the perception of beauty. Wrote Ruskin in 1846:

> Association is of two kinds, Rational and Accidental. . . . To say that Rational Association causes beauty is a mere confusion of terms; it is no theory to be confuted, but a misuse of language to be set aside. . . .
>
> Yet, "Accidental Association" is commonly involuntary and oftentimes so vague that no distinct image is suggested . . . undestroyable by any reasoning, a part thence-forward of our constitution, destroyable only by the same arbitrary process of association by which it was created. Reason has no effect upon it whatsoever. And there is probably no one opinion which is formed by any one of us, in matters of taste, which is not in some degree influenced by unconscious associations of this kind.

Another general characteristic of *dG* conditioning which needs some new discussion is the relation of such conditioning to so-called adaptive behavior. Much has been made by different writers of the signal value of the conditioned stimulus in preparing the organism to avoid danger and to anticipate fulfillment of basic needs. But it is quite obvious that the same conditioned stimulus may give rise to maladaptive behavior in the form of unneeded avoidances and approaches, which extinction, complicated by spontaneous recovery, could only partly remedy; and that, among other characteristics, the highly nondifferentiated (generalized) nature of *dG* conditioning in early stages of development, paralleling most life situations, is surely not conducive to specific adaptations. Moreover—and more importantly—contrary to the views of some theorists, existing evidence is quite definite in showing that *dG* conditioning need not be related to central needs and need reductions of the organism and may well be a partitive organismic event. To cite but two of many possible examples: (1) There are no differences between the generalizations derived from the hundreds of Russian experiments on salivary conditioning in dogs with food as the unconditioned stimulus and generalizations derived from hundreds of corresponding experiments with acid as the unconditioned stimulus, even though the needs and need reductions are admittedly distinct, if not opposite, in the two cases; (2) *dG* conditioning may manifest itself in electroencephalographic reactions of paired sensory stimuli where need reductions are hardly assumable, and it may indeed manifest itself before any overt reactions occur (Jasper & Shagass, 1941; Iwama & Abe, 1953; Schastny, 1956; T'su, 1960).

The most plausible general neural hypothesis of the formation of *dG* conditioning would seem to be one based on a synthesis of Pavlov's view of "strong brain centers attracting weak ones" with Ukhtomsky's dominance doctrine (Ukhtomsky, 1923, 1949-1954). The writer suggested such a synthesis in 1930, and elaborated it in 1957; it was independently developed by Anokhin and Strezh in 1932 and is now quite common among Russian students of higher nervous activity and has recently been supported by John (1961) (cf. also recent American consummatory and prepotent accounts of reinforcement in $dD(G)$ conditioning—Premack, 1959; Sheffield, Roby, & Campbell, 1954). For our present purposes, the hypothesis need merely be stated as follows: (1) for dG conditioning to occur, two foci of neural action must be activated simultaneously or in close succession; and one focus, the G in our equation, must be considerably dominant over the other, the d; (2) the locus of the activated foci may be anywhere in the cortex, subcortex, and perhaps even spinal cord; and (3) within limits, the extent of the activation may vary widely. That is to say, dG conditioning is in itself quite an arbitrary and we might say a mechanical level of learning with respect to total organismic action and needs: depending on methodological arrangements in the laboratory and chance coincidence in life situations, it may or may not involve such needs and action (think of food, fright, and cardiac dG conditioning, on the one hand, and of patellar, plantar, eyeblink, and GSR, on the other). The aforementioned analogue of robot, Frankenstein, or golem would seem to fit this level of learning.

A primitive sublevel of dG conditioning in which the d and G are antagonistic to each other was assumed in the introductory section of this article. The assumption stems from the consideration that in typical dG conditioning the modified d is a sensory reaction or, more objectively, a reaction involving what Pavlov called an orienting reflex (or reflexes) which by its very nature is neutral to the abience (avoidance-aversion) and adience (approach-appetition) of the dominant G reaction that modifies it. But no such special system of neutral sensory-orienting reactions appears to exist in lowest animals or in lowest reaction-groups of higher animals. In both, all reactions seem to be arranged in antagonistic abience-adience pairs, and learning, the elimination of one reaction in a pair, is in a way a "must" when both reactions are repeatedly combined. This logical analysis seems, however, to be paralleled by empirical evidence only regarding the inhibitory variety of this learning—adient reactions inhibited by abient ones— which by all tokens is quite universal among lower animals: a paramecium coming to reject nonnutritious carmine (Losina-Losinsky, 1931), a sea-anemone to reject pieces of filter paper (Fleure & Walton, 1907), a flatworm inhibiting locomotion in response to light which innately facilitates or initiates it (Hovey, 1929), a cockroach no longer running to a dark chamber under similar circumstances (Turner, 1912), and the like. Evidence of replacement of true abient reactions by adient ones is meager and so far has been reported only for a few dogs (Yerofeyeva, 1912, 1921) and children (Slutskaya, 1928). The adjective "true" is used here to distinguish between abient stimulation and abient reactions or, more specifically, to indicate that mild abient stimulation may well not produce true abient reactions. As Sokolov (1958, pp. 62-66) has proven, such stimulation, notably mild shock stimulation, evokes, at least in the first few trials, sensory-orienting reactions which thus become conditioned to subsequent Gs in regular dG fashion.

The relative ease of manifestation of this decremental-inhibitory learning-type modification of adient reactions by abient ones in primitive organisms in which sensory-orienting reactions are little, if at all, involved, suggests that this modification may well be the phyletically oldest variety of learning interaction. Or, in other words, punishment learning as such— designated as $dd(G-)$ learning, the weakening or inhibition of a modified d reaction through interaction with a modifying abient $G-$ reaction—may well antedate, in evolution, both first-level substitutive dG and second-level strengthening $dD(G)$ learning, even if superficially this learning resembles —more strictly, contrasts with—second-level learning. However, there is the important consideration that, with continuing evolution of sensory-orienting reactions in animals' reaction-systems, abient punishment reactions become subject also to typical substitutive dG learning, thus giving rise to a conflict of far-reaching import. For then, the abient reactions become classically conditioned to be elicited by the stimuli of the sensory-orienting reactions although, at the same time, the classically elicited *conditioned* abient reactions become weakened or inhibited through interaction with their own *unconditioned* abient reactions. This conflict or dilemma of abient or aversive conditioning has long, and at times ingeniously (Solomon and Wynne, 1954), been debated by experimenters and theoreticians in the field. Still, the writer believes that the implications of the conflict have not as yet been fully realized, and he is tempted to make use of them in support of a rather radical view that *all* abient learning—except for the proposition that the cessation of an abient reaction is adient in nature (Skinner's negative reinforcement)—could be accounted for in terms of only classical dG and punishment $dd(G-)$ conditioning, without recourse to a special category of so-called avoidance learning which now has for some decades engulfed a large portion of American thought in the area.

More specifically, yet very briefly, the writer's tentative "revisionist" view rests upon three considerations. First, there is the large body of empirical evidence to show that throughout the animal kingdom substitutive dG abient conditioning is highly efficacious with respect to quick acquisition, slow extinction, and ready involvement of second-order classical conditioning. Hence, there is the likelihood that, except for complications by cognitive factors which are not under discussion here, trials of avoidance learning are primarily series of trials of slow extinction and concomitant involvement of second-order classical conditioning to general experimental settings and dG-produced proprioceptive and interoceptive stimuli. Second, comes the obvious fact that avoidable abient learning is free from decremental punishment $dd(G)$ conditioning. Hence, its superiority over unavoidable abient learning is merely negative, that is, due, not to positive learning through avoidance, but to the absence of unlearning through pun-ishment (or presence of unlearning in "unavoidance"). Third, the conven-tional view of the mechanism of avoidance learning as escape-reinforced through removel of acquired fear is hard to reconcile with the wide prev-alence of such learning in cases in which fully developed fear reactions cannot be readily assumed (animals low in phyletic scale, ablated and drugged animals).

Another case of primitive decremental learning is that of habituation, to which all living things and all types of reactions are admittedly subject in some degrees (Bulygin, 1951; Harris, 1943; Hinde, 1954; Mysyashchikova, 1952). Variation in degree of habituation is, however, so extreme—if one compares, for instance, the thousands of trials needed to habituate even partially one's patellar reflex with the several trials to fully habituate one's galvanic skin reflex—that the heuristic value of regarding all habituations as manifestations of one underlying dd mechanism might well, at least for the time being, be doubted. Elsewhere (Razran, unpublished b), the writer brought forth evidence to show that the order of the rate of habitua-tion, from slower to faster rate, is that of viscerovisceral, somatosomatic, viscerosomatic, and somatovisceral reflexes.

The reverse of habituation, incrementation through reacting or dD mod-ification, sometimes called sensitization, is of course also known but seems to be even more variable than habituation. Space prevents discussing in detail here the mechanisms of either habituation or sensitization, except to say that both no doubt involve varying degrees of interaction with feedback reactions which may well account for the variability of outcome, and that by its very nature sensitization eventually turns into habituation. Canaliza-tion or concentration may be an appropriate term for sensitization when the initial reaction to some stimulus is diffuse, that is, involves a complex of strong and weak reactions and the strong reactions become stronger as the weak reactions become elminated in accordance with Ukhtomsky's dominance doctrine. Or, in other words, repetition may set up a dominant focus yet, empirical evidence indicates that only some reactions may thus become dominant.

IDENTIFICATION AND BASIC ATTRIBUTES OF $dD(G)$ LEARNING

As might be suspected, $dD(G)$ learning refers to a class or level of learn-ing variously known as reward learning (Thorndike, 1898), type II condi-tioning (Miller & Konorski, 1928), conditioned conditioning (Ivanov-Smolensky, 1928), operant conditioning (Skinner, 1938), success learning (Schlosberg, 1937), heterodynamic conditioning (Zeliony, 1937), instru-mental conditioning (Hilgard & Marquis, 1940), and reverse neural con-nections (Beritov, 1960). The outcome of this learning, the $dD(G)$

strengthening of one reaction by another, is admittedly not under dispute, but only the type of reaction that is so strengthened: the d—operant, instrumental, adaptive, previously conditioned—and the type of the reaction that is doing the strengthening, the G (primarily its specific qualitative effects such as contingency of occurrence, positive affect, need or drive reduction, and arousal of special neural center, but sometimes also its total quantitative dimension such as dominance or prepotency or extent of reverse neural connections). And here the debate has indeed been, and continues to be, profuse and entangled. A brief clarification of the main issue is thus in order, particularly since the writer's view is much at variance with conventional formulations. Stripped of nonessential confusions, the main issue no doubt is: When does pairing of d and G produce dG learning modification and when a $dD(G)$ one?

To begin with, the type or qualitative nature of the G cannot obviously be the dG–$dD(G)$ determinant, for the simple reason that the same G— let us say, a food reaction—gives rise to dG in one case and to $dD(G)$ in another. (That is not to say that the class of Gs is equal in both cases—on the contrary, there is good reason to believe that the Gs of $dD(G)$ are a limited group while the Gs of dG are universal with respect to type and limited only by quantitative dominance dimensions—but only that since dG and $dD(G)$ share a common group of Gs, the Gs alone cannot be the differential determinants of the two.) Again, there is sufficient evidence to question the contention that $dD(G)$ learning—which for historical reasons might henceforth be designated as $dD(G)$ *conditioning*—is confined to d reactions that Skinner classed as operant. Not only the many experiments in Konorski's laboratory (*Acta Biologica Experimentalis,* 1940–1960), which long have shown that the attributes of $dD(G)$ conditioning of animals' movements are wholly independent of the manner of the production of the movement (for example, whether paw-lifting of a dog is produced by shock, mechanically by means of a pulley, or simply by waiting until the dog lifts it by himself), but also the more recent and just as numerous Russian studies on $dD(G)$ conditioning of some orienting reactions (Sokolov, 1958; Vinogradova, 1961; Voronin, 1959), the special studies of $dD(G)$ conditioning in the laboratories of Asratyan (1953, 1960), Gambaryan (1962), Skipin (1959), and Voronin (1960), Grindley's (1929) experiment on such conditioning of the investigatory reactions of guinea pigs to the sound of a metronome, and Gerd's (1957) scientific report on the Durov school of animal training—all militate against attributing the specific essence of $dD(G)$ conditioning solely to the operant nature of the d reaction. To quote Woodworth and Schlosberg (1954): "This difference [between the d reaction in a Pavlov- and a Skinner-type of conditioning] may not be important; it merely arises from the different exploratory movements aroused by the bell and by the lever —looking and listening in one case, manipulation in the other" (p. 549).

However, while Woodworth and Schlosberg do not consider the operant nature of the modified reaction the determinant of $dD(G)$ conditioning, they, like a number of other students of the field, nonetheless equate $dD(G)$ conditioning with the instrumental or *contingency relation* of d to G. Just what is this d-G contingency that is allegedly specific to $dD(G)$ conditioning and not found in the dG variety? At one time, it apparently meant that in $dD(G)$ conditioning, unlike in that of the dG variety, the d literally produces the G (more exactly, the stimulus of the G)—the organism, so to speak, produces its own payoff in the exact manner of the rat in a Skinner box. Later, presumably because of some extra thought and evidence of comparable $dD(G)$ conditioning in paw-lifting and neck-stretching in which there is no literal instrumental production of G by d, the conception of the d-G contingency was modified. To quote Skinner (1953, p. 85): "So far as the organism is concerned, the only property of the contingency is temporal. The reinforcer simply *follows* the response" (italics in original; read: always follows). That is to say, in $dD(G)$ conditioning, G always follows d.

If so, one may ask whether it is not likewise true that, in practice, the same temporal contingency obtains in dG conditioning, in which, as is known, the typical methodological arrangement of conditioned stimulus-unconditioned stimulus intervals is such that permits pre-G occurrence of not only the investigatory-orienting reflex, the pre-modified d reaction which alone is the correct homologue of lever-pressing and paw-lifting in $dD(G)$ conditioning (Razran, 1939 a; Woodworth & Schlosberg, 1954), but also of the conditioned or modified d reaction. Indeed, in Russian experiments, the d-G contingency of orienting reflex-unconditioned reflex is so regularly observed (and in recent years also carefully measured) that the Russians are beginning to suggest that the essence of conditioning consists of linking two unconditioned reflexes, the orienting reflex and the unconditioned reflex proper (Asratyan, 1955). Moreover, even if we agree —incorrectly, the writer posits—to compare the pre-G appearance of the conditioned or modified d reaction in dG and $dD(G)$ conditioning, one may further ask, what special significance is there in the appearance being that of an overt or effector reaction? Is not there unmistakable evidence that conditioning may well be executed interneurally and indeed may *thus* manifest itself prior to any overt or effector appearance of it (*supra*)? Or, in other words, there is surely reason to assume that in typical dG conditioning, as in $dD(G)$ conditioning, the unconditioned G reaction always follows some d reaction which in the course of training becomes a following of a conditioned d reaction, even if this reaction is not always overt or effector in nature.

In short, it is the writer's contention that past formulations have failed to demonstrate adequate reaction-interaction differentials (d, G, and d-G) to account for the differences between dG and $dD(G)$ conditioning, and that, without such a demonstration, postulated differences in underlying mechanisms such as contiguity versus drive reduction are premature and in a large way meaningless. A complete account should, to be sure, include both—a demonstration of adequate reaction and reaction-interaction differentials, and a plausible hypothesis of underlying mechanism differences —but by all logic the first should precede the second, which is what the writer will attempt in the forthcoming paragraph.

The chief suggestion of a presumed adequate, previously undiscussed, reaction and reaction-interaction differential between dG and $dD(G)$ conditioning comes from many recent Russian studies of the role of orienting d reactions in typical dG conditioning—that is, conditioning in which the d stimulus is purely sensory and the measurable d reactions are a variety of somatic, visceral, and electroencephalographic reactions. The total evidence of these studies is quite clear in disclosing that: (1) although dG conditioning is initially facilitated by discernible orienting d reactions, its continuing and final success is highly correlated with the organism's habituation to these reactions; (2) periods of failure of dG conditioning—so common in its developmental dynamics—correlate not merely with insufficient habituation to the orienting reactions but with the appearance of $dD(G)$ conditioning, that is, when such failure is evident, the orienting reactions become strengthened, rather than weakened, by the modifying G reactions; and (3) $dD(G)$ conditioning of orienting reactions is particularly manifest when the sensory d stimuli are of fairly high intensity and produce considerable increases in the absolute and relative amounts of somatic reactions of the total orienting reaction pattern. Or, in other words, the evidence points to the existence of what might be called a quantitative dominance-stability differential between d reactions of the dG and $dD(G)$ conditioning or, more specifically, to a view that *dD(G) conditioning comes into being only when the d reaction of the d-G equation is considerable in scope, primarily somatic in arrangement, and presumably possessive of a certain degree of organismic dominance, in the sense of not being readily reversible (habituable) and replaceable by the modifying G reaction.*

Thus, the problem of the behavioral dichotomy of the two categories (subcategories in the classification of the present article) of conditioning may indeed be on the verge of a new solution. All that would be necessary is to consider two related suppositions: one, that sensory stimuli of higher intensity produce other than orienting d reactions; another—and more essential one—that the locomotor and manipulatory and vocal d reactions of typical $dD(G)$ conditioning are by their very nature more dominant and stable than the orienting and visceral reactions of the dG variety. Both suppositions appear to the writer to be reasonable: the first, in considering common sense and such a simple controlled observation as that of Biryukov (1958) that bats will just turn their heads (orient) to sounds of 22 cy but will fly (locomote) when the sound is 40 cy; the second, in considering comparatively the evolutionary and biological status of each type of *d* reactions. The second consideration brings to mind such contrasting adjectives for the two reaction-classes as these: preparatory versus consummatory, pre-adaptive versus adaptive, generalized versus specific, orienting versus operant (if by operant is meant a mode of a reaction and not of type of stimulation), and the writer's suggestion elsewhere of "preparatory mobilizing-the-organism reactions" versus "preparatory managing-the-stimulus reactions." Even if these classifications offer only prolegomena to the solution, there need be no confusion as long as we merely keep in mind that one class of reactions is sensory-orienting-visceral and the other is locomotor-manipulative-vocal. Eventually, the solution and true classification will no doubt come from obtained knowledge of the brain, that is, information on a differential between the two classes of reactions in terms of projected loci and patterns of total-neural action in each case. As yet, of course, we have no such information.

For the present, the most plausible hypothesis of a neural differential between dG and $dD(G)$ conditioning would seem to be one based upon the views of Beritov. According to Beritov, conditioning always involves a two-way transformation of neural connections: one forward or direct, from the neural center governing the *d* reaction to that of the *G* reaction, $d \rightarrow G$; and one, backward or reverse, from the neural center of the *G* reaction to that of the *d* reaction, $G \rightarrow d$. In classical or what we call dG conditioning, the argument goes, the neural direction is primarily forward, whereas in operant or what we call the $dD(G)$ level, the direction is reversed. *The less dominant d in dG conditioning is, so to speak, drawn into the G orbit, whereas the more dominant d in dD(G) conditioning draws the orbit to itself.* The Beritov hypothesis is really not devoid of some direct empirical evidence. There are known cases of dG conditioning in which the *G* stimulus produces a *d* reaction along with the *d* stimulus producing a *G* reaction (Bernstein, 1934; Dzhavrishvili, 1956), and there are also records which show that dG conditioning brings about electroencephalographic changes in both the *d* and *G* brain centers (Rabinovich, 1961). An alternate neural hypothesis of $dD(G)$ conditioning would no doubt be one that would postulate that in some way this conditioning brings into action special reaction-strengthening brain centers such as the limbic system in the pioneer experiments of Olds and Milner (1954), which have since been multiply duplicated and extended (*supra*). The difficulty here is apparently the need of accounting for the lack of such strengthening when the *d* reactions are of the sensory-orienting-visceral category. Perhaps, however, the projection areas of locomotor-manipulative-vocal reactions are in some way more closely connected with the special brain centers than those of other reactions.

Space permits only a very brief summary discussion of three remaining aspects of $dD(G)$ conditioning: specifics of acquisition and extinction, seriation, and the role of cognition. All that will be said about the first aspect is that there is by now no doubt that, at least as far as food Gs are concerned, $dD(G)$ conditioning is much quicker in formation and much more irreversible (unextinguishable) in retention than is dG conditioning (Razran, 1955b). Skinner and his many followers have certainly proven that (Ferster & Skinner, 1957; Skinner, 1938, 1953), and thereby added, in the writer's opinion, another significant body of evidence to one of the main theses of the present article that $dD(G)$ conditioning is a higher, evolutionarily more efficacious form of learning than is dG conditioning. Seriation as used here refers to efferent compounding of single conditioned reactions, the theory of which was originally discussed very comprehensively by Watson (1924) and later by Skinner (1938, 1953) under the term of chaining, and skillful and complex laboratory examples of which were recently demonstrated by Voronin and Napalkov (1959). The formula of this compounding is simply $d_1 + d_2 + d_3 \cdots d_n + G = d_1 \rightarrow d_2 \rightarrow d_3 \rightarrow \cdots d_n$, $dG_1 + dG_2 + dG_3 + \cdots dG_n = dG_1 \rightarrow dG_2 \rightarrow dG_3 \rightarrow \cdots dG_n$, $dD(G)_1 + dD(G)_2 + dD(G)_3 + \cdots dD(G)_n = dD(G)_1 \rightarrow dD(G)_2 \rightarrow dD(G)_3 \rightarrow \cdots dD(G)_n$, and its linkage mechanism is admittedly dG in type, primarily proprioceptive dG. There is of course no doubt that an analysis of such compounding is most significant in extending the ontology of learning to a good portion of its pragmatics, serial motor and verbal and even visceral habits. However, it appears also to be clear that by its very nature efferent compounding, unlike afferent, involves no extra level of learning and hence will no longer be considered here.

Experimental delimitation of the role of cognition in $dD(G)$ conditioning is admittedly more difficult than it is in dG conditioning. The reason is simple. The d reactions in $dD(G)$ conditioning are in human subjects largely cognized and are in general not too fixedly related to antecedent stimuli, whereas at the dG level some d reactions are wholly uncognized (visceral, interoceptively produced) and some could readily be made so through manipulation of fixed stimuli. Yet, this very fact points, obviously, also to the consideration that $dD(G)$ conditioning occurs in contexts in which cognition is more available and thus, according to most philosophies, more utilized. Few indeed would presumably question the role of cognition (its neuroverbal correlate, to be sure) in $dD(G)$ conditioning—the premise that affects, configures (percepts), symbols (not to mention words), and sememes operate in it, both as modified d and modifying (reinforcing) G reactions and as factors influencing the modification of other somatic and, possibly, even visceral reactions. One supposes that it would be quite feasible to equate all $dD(G)$ conditioning or learning with either a Freudian type, psychic yet unconscious, pleasure-seeking and pain-avoiding affect learning, or even with cognition as such by saying, for instance, that the "law of effect" is a "law of knowledge." To do this, however, one must patently ignore the existence of fully developed $dD(G)$ conditioning in fish, its manifestations in uncognized settings and reactions (Hefferline, Keenan & Hartford, 1956) and, more than that, the heuristic fragility and vacuity of subjective generalizations divorced from man's biology, neurology, and animal ascent in the evolutionary scale. At the beginning of this chapter, the writer stated that he is opposed to the "postulation of complex cognitive constructs when behavioral generalization are amply available"; $dD(G)$ conditioning is a case in point.

$(abc \cdots n)$ LEARNING OR AFFERENT CONFIGURING: BASIC MECHANISMS AND ATTRIBUTES

Afferent configuring was defined earlier in the article as a nonverbal form or level of learning, related to perception. The quale of the postulated perception-learning relation, it should be made clear at the outset, inheres not in the acknowledged claim that percepts as existents modify learning and are modified by it, nor in the unrecognized-by-the-writer supposition that learning is primarily perception, but in the view that perception, defined as afferent configuring attained through special integration of afferent reactions, is as such a special higher form or level of learning. Perception, so conceived, evolved, it is held, out of learning somewhere in the phyletic scale (lowest animals learn but do not perceive, and lowest reactions of higher animals and men may enter learning but not perceptual relationships). And thereby, it is thought, it possesses a common enough hierarchical base with learning to be subsumed under it, yet also sufficient specific fundamental characteristics and mechanisms to be regarded as learning's most distinctive level. What is common to learning and perception stems from the fact that both learning and perception come into being as a result of modifications of reactions through interaction with other reactions. What is particularly distinctive about perception which is learning is the shift to afferent–afferent interaction and the dominative, interproprioccptive, and suprasummative modes of its reactions interactions.

It will be convenient to discuss first the specifics of afferent configuring or perception-learning: the dominative, interoproprioceptive, and suprasummative modes of its integration. Dominative integration relates to what was called earlier in the chapter non-configured afferent integration and designated specifically as $a \leftrightarrow B \leftrightarrow c \leftrightarrow \cdots n$. As reflected in empirical results of Russian experiments on compound-stimulus conditioning, it refers to an early stage in the conditioning in which the animals have not yet come to develop true configured conditioning and react to both compounds and components, but in which there has already occurred a radical reorganization of the reactions to the components: the weak components become weaker and eventually totally ineffective while the strong components become stronger. It will be noted that this mode of integration is formally identical with what experimenters in Gestalt psychology have described as leveling and sharpening, and that, on close examination, it is essentially different from the two levels of learning as such, where weak reactions become either strengthened as in $dD(G)$ level or replaced by stronger reactions as in a dG one. That is to say, in learning as such there is always a gain in information, whereas in the dominative mode of afferent integration there is a loss of information, the weak reaction is altogether lost. The only superficial learning parallel in which information is completely lost is habituation to unconditioned reactions (extinction is in essence not such a parallel, since it is merely a reversal and a loss of acquired information, and may, furthermore, be compensated by a gain of some reactions), from which dominative integration differs, of course, in that its loss occurs despite G or reinforcement reactions and that it involves afferent and learned rather than efferent and innate reactions.

Both interoproprioceptive and suprasummative integrations bear on full-fledged afferent configuring. That is, to use again examples of compound-stimulus conditioning, when animals come to react to a compound but not to its individual components in cases in which the component-stimuli are administered simultaneously (simultaneous compound), and to react only to a particular temporal sequence of a compound when the stimuli are applied in close succession (successive compound). Interoproprioceptive integration refers to the general finding that, as compound-stimulus configuring becomes complete, component conditioned stimuli may be replaced by largely unrelated stimuli without disrupting the conditioned reaction of the total compound. Presumably, it is postulated here, this effect is due to a developing conditioning dominance of the interoproprioceptive or feedback portion of the original conditioned stimulus or rather of its orienting reaction (movement-produced stimuli), a portion which by its very nature is quite unspecific and thus readily replaceable (Ayrapetyants, 1960). The effect might indeed be likened to the Gestalt concept of closure and normalization. For, even though the likeness is incomplete in the sense that in compound-stimulus conditioning some substitutive stimulus is needed to continue the configuring, one might argue that in closure, too, some substitutive stimulus producing some kind of substitutive interoproprioceptive reaction becomes operative. At any rate, the discovered findings surely appear to shed light on the dynamics of configuring as a process of internalization, wresting control from external fixed stimulation. And, it might be added, views that interoproprioceptive action is at the base of long-discovered wide perceptual generalization in animals are not new (Hebb, 1949).

Suprasummative integration goes of course to the very heart of afferent configuring: its rise, as was stated earlier, as a process-product bringing into action new reactive units that normally come to dominate and control old units.[6] Whereas dG and $dD(G)$ conditioning and non-configured afferent learning are engaged in transforming and fastening old neural pathways and old neural centers, afferent configuring molds and occupies new neural centers. The word is "emergence," which, however, is not meant here to be a merely inferred general functional event without specific identification with respect to locus and pattern. There is all the logic and some empirical evidence for assuming that the feedback interoproprioceptive reactions of the orienting reactions to sensory stimuli, whose preliminary substitutive role in configuring was mentioned in the preceding paragraph, are also the final mediators and executors of the configuring (Anokhin, 1958; Polezhayev, 1958). Consider that these interoproprioceptive reactions: (1) are in their very existence second-relay systems (or we might say, second-signal systems) recoding first-relay information of incoming environment-organism events; (2) are relatively non-specific in character and thus particularly suited to compress and generalize this information; (3) are closely related to each other and hence able to impart to the total pattern of first-relay primary sensory information such formal properties as sequence, number, ratios of duration and intensity, rhythm, proximity, similarity, continuity, and the like; (4) are wholly new products of the organism's ontogenetic reaction history which by all tokens should seek *sui generis* representation in the organism's brain; (5) are indeed found to be so represented in the motor and premotor areas of the brain, the development and differentiation of which correlate, according to best recent information, most highly with mammalian evolution (*supra*)—and the entire view of the mechanism of configuring becomes, the writer thinks, pointedly tenable and even cogent and, what is equally significant, testable and verifiable in all its parts.

A further basic attribute of configuring that well merits mention here is that, while configuring no doubt expands immensely the realm of an organism's reactions through numerous new combinations and permutations of available afferent reactions and surely raises greatly the organism's efficiency to cope with the environment through the acquisition of larger units of action and interaction, it is, nonetheless, true that therewith a great deal of information is lost, the organism becoming no longer capable of re-

---

[6] Sensory preconditioning (Brogden, 1939; Wickens & Briggs, 1951) does not appear to be a case of afferent integration, only of afferent interaction between orienting reactions in simple substitutive manner of dG conditioning. Scores of Russian experiments disclose that repeated paired administrations of a light and a sound may result in a dog or a monkey turning to the source of the sound when the light is flashed or to the source of the light when the sound is administered. The Russians call sensory preconditioning association-formation or associative conditioning, either of which seems to the writer to be an appropriate term for the phenomenon in the sense that it denotes humanlike dG learning without overt activation of a biologically potent reaction, a learning, which, incidentally, does not manifest itself in lower animals.

acting significantly to individual components of total environmental stimulus-patterns. Such high synthesis of reactivity, on the one hand, and loss, on the other, is strikingly similar to what philosophers or philosophically-minded scientists often consider is the relation of subjective experience to external reality; specifically, the relation to or reflection of, physical and behavioral reality in imagery. Beritov, a pioneer in the study of compound-stimulus conditioning, has in more recent years postulated image-direction in higher animals as a level of modifiable behavior, higher than that of simple conditioning (*supra*). His views and their pertinence to the present article will be considered in following section on symbolization.

The specifics of configured and non-configured afferent integration have not obscured, it is hoped, the hierarchical relation of this integration (or perception) to dG and $dD(G)$ conditioning—the fact that both integration-perception and conditioning are results of modifications of reactions through interaction with other reactions, and hence must share, and indeed do share, such common determinants as the absolute and relative attributes of participating reactions, repetition, passage of time; such a common basic manifestation as transfer to unmodified reactions (generalization-differentiation); as well as highly correlated effects with respect to action of various physical, chemical, and biological agents and factors. All that might be said is that in conditioning the end-result of the modifications is primarily efferent while in integration-perception it is primarily afferent (the mechanism-process effecting and controlling the modifications may well be, when available, largely central-internuncial in both cases, more so, most likely, in the second than in the first case) and also that in conditioning the interaction is primarily binary, between two reactions, while in integration it is primarily multiple, among many reactions. Yet it is quite obvious that the factor of dominance-subordination is basic to all the modifications discussed so far: dG—dominance of G; $dD(G)$—greater dominance of d; $a \leftrightarrow B \leftrightarrow c \leftrightarrow \cdots n$—dominative non-configured integration; and $(abc \cdots n)$—dominance of configures over components. And it is equally true that internalizations through substitutive interoproprioception is operative—in varying degrees, to be sure—in all the modifications. Likewise, while Russian conditioning experiments show that afferent configuring becomes in the course of repetition, or practice, relatively independent of its original G or reinforcer (another significant index of its being a higher level), their own and all American studies of perception are of course in unison in demonstrating that repetition, or practice, is in itself a highly important determinant of this configuring or preception as it is of modificatory learning. Moreover, there is the mass of evidence that configuring-perception may be radically changed through mechanisms of dG and $dD(G)$ learning or conditioning.

The last two statements obviously confront directly the present analysis with the studies of perceptual learning by Murphy and his associates—

notably, Solley and Murphy (1960); with the Gibson and Gibson-Postman (1955) controversy on specificity and differentiation versus enrichment and association of perception; and, indeed, with a large portion of all research and thought in the field. For instance, in the light of the analysis, the Solley-Murphy studies have dealt only with what might be called ARP and not IIC perceptual learning; that is, with the extrinsic modifications of the products of perception through associations, rewards, and punishments and not with the intrinsic modifications of the very process of its coming into being through internal integration and configuring of interacting reactions. What Solley and Murphy have found and formulated fits fully the writer's view that the first two levels of learning coexist with the third. Yet their statement that "Learning does not and cannot bring something out of nothing" (1960) must be answered by the writer as: "Yes it can and it does," if you examine carefully the slow-motion results of some five hundred Russian experiments on compound-stimulus conditioning and are willing to accept the thesis that basically, both as a mechanism and a product, perception is an individual achievement of afferent learning rather than merely an ancestral bequest of some categorical existent. Likewise, the writer would argue that IIC perceptual learning may account for Gibson's doctrine of specificity or differentiation, answer Postman's question of what is the mechanism of this specificity or differentiation, and in fact point to how specificity and differentiation may be combined with enrichment and integration. And it was already shown, it will be remembered, that functional generalizations of compound-stimulus conditioning are, at least in form, much like those derived from Gestalt studies. Previously unpublished —indeed, never written-up—results of a long series of experiments done by the writer some years ago in a complex area far removed from that of simple conditioning, which at the time of experimentation was differently conceptualized, will now, it is hoped, clarify somewhat what has just been said and contribute toward a synthesis of *von unten herauf* with *von oben herab* psychologies.

In these experiments, 420 adult Americans, mostly college students, characterized 24 colored slides of paintings, ranging from fifteenth century Bellinis to modern Légers, and 24 short (45 to 60 seconds) musical selections—classical, romantic, modern, oriental, folk—by checking adjectives on a modified Kate Nevner octagon of 80 adjectives, 10 in each category: happy . . . jubilant; sad . . . somber; stirring . . . dramatic; soothing . . . dreamy; humorous . . . playful; serious . . . dignified; spiritual . . . philosophical; and romantic . . . sensual (the subjects also rated the items on an affect scale of 5). The octagon is reproduced in Table 13-1. The main experimental variables were: (1) the effects of repetition, checking the adjectives by matched groups on 1st, 5th, 9th and 13th presentation, and (2) the effects of association or conditioning, presenting the items 1 to 6 times during free luncheons and during relative states of hunger, and testing for resulting conditioned or associated changes. As may be seen in the table, the octagon also offered opportunities to study the effects of spatial proximity and symmetry.

The mass of data collected in the series of experiments cannot of course be detailed and documented here. Yet the general results were quite clear

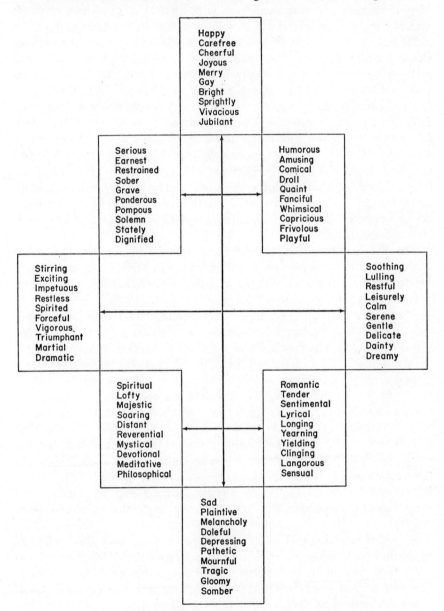

Table 13-1. A modified Kate Nevner octagon of 80 adjectives.

in showing that (1) repetition alone produced far-reaching changes in the adjectival characterizations of the music and art items; that (2) by and large, the changes moved in the direction of greater correspondence with expert opinion (professional musicians and artists) and with group norms; that (3) the changes correlated highly with a leveling-and-sharpening kind of specificity, that is, with a contraction in number of categories checked; that (4) the changes correlated to a large extent also with what might be called enrichment of content, that is, with increases in number of adjectives checked within the categories; and that, (5) spatial proximity and symmetry were minor, but not wholly insignificant, factors in the repetition-produced changes. On the other hand, the main results were also definite in demonstrating that, although association or conditioning with hunger or food shifted significantly the characterizations to what might be called food-related adjectives and categories, and increased the total number of adjectives checked, these factors as such (apart from repetition) lessened correspondence with expert opinion and with group norms, lessened specificity, and almost wholly annulled the role of the factors of spatial proximity and symmetry. (There was also evidence that an excessive number of repetitions—number depending on item-complexity—disrupted correspondence and specificity.)

The five generalizations of the cited experiment suggest, the writer thinks, three, even more general, statements: (1) "Good" veridical learning development of perceptions (or judgments) is essentially a matter of an autochthonous configural dynamics, a self-propelled intrinsic integration or reorganization through sheer repeated exposure, rather than an extrinsic modification through accrued association or conditioning in the conventional sense. (2) The specificity of acquired perception may well be primarily a function of permuted integrations, that is, of differentiations among arising integrations, N stimuli generating theoretically $N!$ integrations and $N - 1!$ differentiations. (3) Both the specificity and the veridicality of acquired perceptions are typically paralleled by enrichment in content. Or: "Elaboration of new qualities," (Postman, p. 444), "responding to variables of physical stimulation not previously responded to," "*greater* correspondence with stimulation," (italics in original), and, above all, "perception gets richer in differential responses, not *images*" (writer's italics; Gibson & Gibson, p. 34) are in general accord with the principle and properties of perception as afferent configuring, as developed in the present article.

A further assertion that in learning or perception association and reorganization are in essence complementary concepts, that is, that there is no association without reorganization and no reorganization without association, also follows from the writer's analysis, except that he would prefer to relinquish both these terms and adopt the more neutral and descriptive, yet dynamic, one of interaction. Finally, it should be noted that perception conceived as an observable process and level of learning need not deny the possible existence of innate ready-made perceptual products. Orienting reflexes behave functionally like conditioned reflexes, yet are admittedly innate. The odor of meat elicits, according to recent studies, unconditioned reflexes in carnivores in varying degrees: salivation in tiger and lion cubs (Slonim, 1961); general excitement in puppies (Kupalov, 1962). Phyletic learning does of course not mean the inheritance of acquired characteristics.[7]

$sy(abc \cdots n)$ LEARNING OR SYMBOLIZATION: MECHANISMS AND ATTRIBUTES

It seems appropriate to begin the discussion of symbolization as a higher (highest) level of learning, related hierarchically to simple conditioning, with quotations from Pavlov. In 1927, Pavlov stated:

> Of course, a word is for man as much a real conditioned stimulus as are other stimuli common to men and animals, yet at the same time it is so all-comprehensive that in this respect it allows no quantitative or qualitative comparisons with conditioned stimuli of animals. Because of the whole preceding life of adult man, words are connected up with all external and internal stimuli reaching the cortex, signalling all of them and replacing all of them, and thus are able to evoke all those reactions of the organism which otherwise are determined by the actual stimuli themselves (p. 429).

The formulation became much more specific in 1933, when Pavlov wrote:

> In man there comes to be . . . another system of signalization, a signalization of the first system—speech, its basis or basal components being kinesthetic stimulations of the speech organs. Thereby a new principle of neural action is introduced—an abstraction and at the same time a generalization of the numerous signals of the preceding system that in their turn become further analyzed and synthesized by the new generalized signals. It is a principle that affords limitless orientation in the surrounding world and brings into being man's highest adaptation—science in its common-to-all-men empiricism as well as in its special form. This second-signal system and its organs, the latest attainment in evolution, must be particularly fragile . . . (1933, p. 292).

And, again, at the 14th Physiological Congress in Rome, in 1932, Pavlov said:

---

[7] Elsewhere (Razran, 1961), the writer called attention to the vast significance of ecological factors in species specificness of the dynamics and efficacy of specific types of conditioning reactions. Anokhin's (1947, 1949) "functional system"—which, for lack of space, cannot, unfortunately, be discussed here—is a comprehensive account of the problem. The writer expects to expound Anokhin's view in a forthcoming publication.

. . . speech, especially and first of all its kinesthetic stimuli, going from the speech organs to the cortex are second signals, signals of signals [of many signals]. These signals are in essence abstractions of reality and means of generalization, constituting our extra, *uniquely human, higher thought* (italics in original; 1932, p. 1154).

Clearly, the Pavlov concept of the relation of speech or language or words to conditioning is quite complex and not as simple as that of either Watsonian behaviorism or neobehaviorism (cf. Skinner, 1957; Mowrer, 1960). Presumably, words as units of true language, must possess, in Pavlov's view, at least three extra and higher-than-simple conditioning's attributes: (1) they must be compounded of a number of stimuli or rather reactions, (2) the reactions or stimuli must be previously conditioned, and (3) the conditioning must comprise a large amount of kinesthesis. On the other hand, it is quite obvious that Pavlov knew and indeed considered the fact that words as patterns of sounds could be simply conditioned, without the aforementioned attributes, as in conditioning a higher animal to respond to its name, an infant or an ape to point to its nose at command, a child to salivate at the sound of an unknown word (in one experiment, in Krasnogorsky's laboratory reported by Shastin in 1932, children were even conditioned to salivate at the sound of the Russian word *"nel'zya"* ("don't"). Or, in other words, Pavlov distinguished true words from what might be called vocal CRs (vocal conditioned reflexes) which, incidentally are, in the writer's opinion, still only vocal CRs even if they are of the $dD(G)$ variety, such as increasing the rate of a dog's barking when the barking is followed by feeding, and even when the barking becomes discriminated with respect to a particular stimulus (Lawicka, 1957). Again, it must be understood—and it is hoped will become clearer in later paragraphs—that the generalization attribute which Pavlov ascribes to words is not of the same kind and level as that of his stimulus or response generalization in the conditioning in animals.

Now, Kol'tsova (1958), the present Head of the Division of Higher Nervous Activity of Children in the Pavlov Institute of Physiology, performed a series of experiments with children, one to two years of age, in the light of Pavlov's view of the special nature of language acquisition. Her main objective in the series to be cited was to discover optimum experimental conditions for the children's ability to: (1) select a doll or a book irrespective of particular size, shape, and color from among a number of different objects at the sound of "Give me the doll" or "Give me the book"; (2) point to and name correctly four objects of a toy cardboard aquarium (walls, fish, fishing pole, pail); and (3) differentiate between two classes of a number of toy objects, one of which was combined with the word *object* and the other of which was either not combined with the word or was combined with another word. With respect to the doll and book, the experimental conditions were varied by presenting to the children either only one kind, or many kinds of each object, and by combining the presentations with either only one, or with many reactions, to words such as "Give me the doll," "Pick up the doll," "Put away the doll," "Give me the book," "Pick up the book," "Open the book," and the like. With respect to the toy aquarium, the variations consisted of letting the children handle the toy objects, or just letting them look at them, when the experimenter pronounced their names; while in the case of the differentiation between the two classes of toy objects, a mild air puff delivered to the children's eye was combined with the presentation of both classes of objects to one group of children, but with only the class of objects named by the experimenter, to the other group. At any rate, in all cases the Kol'tsova results were clear in demonstrating that the more varied were the attributes of the presented objects and, particularly, the more varied the children's reactions to them, the more successful was the final performance of generalizing to related objects and differentiating from unrelated ones, and of correct naming and pointing to them. Presenting one particular book twenty times but having the child react to it in twenty different ways was more successful in imparting a stable word-concept of book than presenting twenty different books with one reaction, and both types of varying presentations were much more successful than presenting only one book and instilling only one reaction, twenty times.

Compared with experiments on compound-stimulus conditioning, Kol'tsova's studies point to significant differences, some obvious and some in need of disclosure. It is obvious, for instance, that far-reaching new learning occurred in the children without any overt biological G or reinforcer. It was indicated earlier that even afferent configuring becomes in course of time and training importantly independent of its G and that this independence is a sign of its higher evolutionary status: dG conditioning, except for the abient variety, is very much dependent on its G; $dD(G)$ conditioning, as Skinner has shown, is less dependent; afferent configuring is dependent only to a limited degree; and, now, acquisition of true language or symbolization is hardly at all dependent. Perception-minded reinforcement psychologists (Solley & Murphy, 1960; Woodworth, 1947) would no doubt say that perception and symbolization carry their own reinforcement, a statement with the general verisimilitude of which the writer has no quarrel. However, since reinforcement itself is a term in need of interpretation with respect to its nature, he prefers to use dominance (which is indeed used by some current students of the field to explain reinforcement) acquired by configuring and symbolization in the course of their formation as processes and retained by them after they are formed as products.

Another—and, broadly, more systematic—difference between Kol'tosova's experiments and those of compound-stimulus conditioning inheres in the fact that the component-elements in the children's acquisition of language were not reactions to sensory *stimuli* such as sounds of metronomes, flashes of lights, or scratchings of skin, but reactions to definite *objects* which, most likely, had evolved in the children configures or percepts either prior to the experiment or in the course of the experimentation. That is to say, the resultant compound reaction was not a configure of reactions, but a configure of configures, and what is even more important, it was not merely an afferent configure of configures but was bridged over by words, by what might be called verbal efferentation.

This verbal efferentation, clearly the specialty of configuring in symbolization, is postulated here as the most important attribute of this configuring imparting to it a new higher evolutionary dimension of efficiency and potency which mere afferent configuring has failed to achieve. A digression into (1) subjective psychology by assuming that configures or percepts are correlated, at least in their origin and on occasions, by subjective experience of imagery, and (2) the neurophysiology of Beritov who, as was already indicated, assumes imagery and image-direction in some higher behavior of higher animals, will, it is hoped, clarify the argument of the postulation. It is well known from subjective psychology that imagery by itself cannot become a source of detailed cognitive information. Try as you may to read off details from an image of your breakfast table, or to answer from an image what kind of a six you have on your watch, or whether there is a *q* on your telephone dial, and you will not succeed no matter how many times the table, the watch, or the dial was seen by you in the past. Yet it will no doubt suffice for someone to tell you once, or for you to check and note (say to yourself in words or symbols) once, that there is no *q* on the dial, or that there is no six on your watch or that the six is in Arabic numbers, and you will remember the fact for a long time. Likewise, Beritov, who assumes that imagery in animals is produced in the course of firing of special short-axon star cells in the cortex, points out that the neuroanatomy of the cells is such that while their firing is in itself efficient and full of its own feedback, it can produce efferent action only through the mediation of lying-below pyramidal and internuncial neurons. Like some potentates, the short-axon star cells or images are unable to communicate with one another. The rise of words and language and of correlated speech areas in the cortex provides thus, in the writer's view, this means of communication between configure and configure and between configure and ready efferent reactions. Without verbal efferentation and mediation, afferent configuring may well be only a lyric cry in the wilderness rather than a part of normal business.

Space permits no further discussion of symbolization and word-symbols as verbally efferented configures of configures, except for two short statements: one, that word-symbols become themselves arranged in hierarchical order in correspondence with the individual's reactions to the nature of objects and events; another, that words as physical stimuli or vocal CRs constantly interact with words as finished configured symbols. With respect to the first statement, the writer believes that he proved the existence of such word-symbol hierarchies as *animal-dog-terrier, week-day-night,* and *mineral-copper-water* in his studies of salivary semantic conditioning in adult human subjects who were misinformed about the purpose of the study (Razran, 1949a, 1949b, 1949c, pp. 291-293). The specific quantitative relationship of the writer's verbal hierarchies, in terms of milligrams of conditioned saliva, was strikingly confirmed recently by Whitmarsh and Bousefield (1961) who used the same words but a relationship in terms of communality of associations, while Fedorov and Volkova demonstrated the existence of similar hierarchies in the salivary conditioning of children in Krasnogorsky's laboratory (Krasnogorsky, 1954, pp. 308, 481). Volkova's results merit special mention. When a child was conditioned positively to the word *crow* and negatively to the word *daisy,* his salivary secretions, to sixteen randomly tested words, *beak, feathers, wings, birds, fly, sing, chirp, peck, living thing, nails, flowers, plants, bloom, leaves, stem,* and *root,* were respectively: 26, 21, 18, 16, 13, 13, 13, 12, 11, 11, 1, 1, 1, 0, 0, 0 drops of saliva. With respect to the second statement, the writer showed in 1939 the coexistence of phonetic and semantic conditioning in the salivary conditioning of college students who, conditioned to a word like *surf,* with similar results for words *style:fashion-stile; urn:vase-earn;* and *freeze:chill-frieze.* This finding was fully duplicated and confirmed with conditioning of the galvanic skin reflex in 1940 by Riess who, further, showed a positive correlation of semantic conditioning with age (1946), while Luria and Vinogradova (1959) in the Soviet Union reported that semantic conditioning correlates positively with intelligence and negatively with fatigue. The reports of Shvarts (1954, 1960) in the Soviet Union that phonetic vasoconstrictive conditioning reappeared when subjects were administered chloral hydrate, and of Peastral in (1961) in this country that the conditioning of schizophrenics is significantly more phonetic than that of normal subjects, are particularly interesting.

The sublevel of symbolization designated as *predication* or *semanticization* will likewise, for lack of space, be allowed here only very brief discussion. The sublevel was postulated in the light of: (1) the assertion of semanticists that only full sentences or propositions or judgments bear *meaning,* single words carrying only *sense;* (2) Penfield's (1952) confirmation of such assertions by apparent demonstration that, judged by subjects' reports of the effects of direct brain stimulation, there are in the cortex separate loci for "sensory" and "concept" experiences; (3) related general clinical evidence; and (4) the writer's (1949, 1952) studies of sentential versus propositional transfer of salivary conditioning in adult human subjects. When the writer's subjects were conditioned to a sentence like "Poverty is degrading," they transferred their conditioning to variations and single-word replacements of the sentence as follows: "Wealth is uplifting"—58 per cent, "Wealth is not degrading"—52 per cent, "Poverty is not uplifting"—45 per cent, "Wealth is degrading"—36 per cent, "Poverty is not degrading"—33 per cent, "Poverty is uplifting"—33 per cent, and "Wealth is not uplifting"—25 per cent. It is quite obvious that the amount of transfer was much more a function of the logical propositional equivalence of the generalization sentence to the conditioned sentences than of their sentential single word-similarity, the latter being presumably only a small contributing factor (cf. 58 per cent transfer to "Wealth is uplifting" with that of 33 per cent to "Poverty is not degrading" for propositional equivalence, and the 33 per cent to "Poverty is not degrading" with that of 25 per cent to "Wealth is not uplifting" for word similarity). Hence, the writer has for some time accorded true enduring existence and *sui generis* cortical representation to semantic units corresponding to propositions or judgments. He has assumed that these units arise in suprasummative fashion as a process of configured learning through interaction of single word-symbols, and has designated the process of its formation as *predication* or *semanticization* and the formed enduring units as *sememes*. Word symbols continually interact, the writer thinks, to form sememes which, it may be further posited, are the true units of true human thought.

A TRIPARTITE DIVISION AND PROBLEMS OF ADJUSTMENT AND PHILOSOPHY

There is good reason and some evidence to believe that, in the normal adult human being, the two upper levels of learning in practice often combine to form one cognitive level. If one examines, for instance, the extraconditioning controlling factors or attitudes of the conditioning of wholly or partly cognized reactions in adult subjects, one finds the presence of: (1) what might presumably be called percepts such as perceiving, or catching on to the purpose of the experiment, or perceiving and thus becoming influenced by the nature of the experimental setting and the personality of the experimenter, or the like; as well as (2) the presence of such judgmental or symbolic-semantic content as "He will not fool me" or "If I don't cooperate, he will not use me again," and the like. On the other hand, it must be obvious that symbols-sememes differ from percepts in that the latter are largely stimulus-bound, absorbing the "past" into the "present," whereas the former become, by their very nature, more and more independent of present stimulation and acquire a true historical dimension, assimilating the "present" into the "past" (and, one might add, the "future" which is the "past"). Moreover, it also seems true that symbols-sememes are by their very nature less influenced by the individual's needs and affects than are percepts, both because needs and affects confront first formation of percepts and only later the formation of symbols and sememes, and because symbols-sememes interact and check each other in a way that percepts cannot. Now, if we only assume, as we might, that needs and affects interfere with veridicality and impart irrationality to human learning and action, we seemingly arrive at the conclusion that the fourth level of learning is not only more historical but also more rational than the third level and that in practice there is integral interaction between the third and second levels. Finally, there is dG conditioning which, as discussed all along, was argued to be noncognitive and neutral to needs and affects and thus, indeed, also to reason. (For the present purpose, reason or rationality may as well be defined as correspondence with physical or social reality, or both.)

In fine, in terms of pragmatic effects rather than of evolutionary origin and ontological content, a tripartite and somewhat different division of levels of human learning and action ensues—specifically: (1) a historical cognitive-rational level; (2) a contemporaneous, partly rational and partly irrational (irrational in sense of opposed to rationality) affective-organismic level; and (3) an historical, noncognitive, "anaffective" (neutral toward affects), and "arational" (neutral toward rationality) segmental level. The formal properties of the three pragmatic levels are thought to be the same as those of the four evolutionary levels; that is, lower levels coexist with higher levels, higher levels normally dominate and control lower levels, but lower levels may come to dominate and control higher levels in conditions of organismic malfunctioning.

Thus conceived, a number of basic divergencies between the present account of man, his conflicts and achievements, and other more conventional, notably depth psychology, accounts are obvious. For one thing, it is held here that conflict exists among different levels of learning and not just between the innate and learned nature of man. The same event such as an automobile accident or an unexpected amatory conquest may well produce, in accordance with the different levels of learning, widely differing and highly conflicting learning effects with respect to the individual's future state and action and decisions of action. For another thing, it is affirmed here that the historical-cognitive-rational human level will normally by itself forge ahead and control the other levels; that by and large evolution moves toward a gain in reason; and that, other things being equal, even the simplest learning of repeated exposure to the environment is improving or adjusting. Thirdly, and perhaps most importantly, it is posited here that reason-reality continually conflicts not only with the unreason of affects but also, and perhaps more so, with the unreason of unreason. To be effective and happy, man must learn to dominate and control not only the Eros and Thanatos (or any other related formulation) but also, and perhaps more so, the golem or robot within him, his unknown-to-him mechanical-biological habits unheeding his affects and "unminding" his reason.

Fourthly and finally, conflict, in general, is presumed as a multiple hierarchical event occurring and effecting changes at all levels and surely at both cognitive and noncognitive ones.

The optimistic view of the power of the historical-cognitive level of human learning and action should, however, as a final word, be qualified. For, obviously, this level is a later ontogenetic achievement, arising after the other levels have wrought in their own deep-reaching learning effects on the individual, and is thus mostly concerned, at least as far as the basic pattern of the individual's needs and need-satisfaction goes, with modifying and managing *fait accompli* old learning rather than with new learning. Moreover, a good portion of learning can simply not be effected through mere cognition or what we called reason, and another portion seems to require prior learning at another level for cognition to elicit effects. No one, one supposes, has learned to control his sphincter muscles through mere cognition and reason, and one may well doubt that it can be learned so. Likewise, while it is surely easy to teach an adult human subject through word-produced cognition to lift his finger at the flash of a red light or to know that a red light means "stop" without serial pairings of red light with finger-lifting or with stepping on the brakes, the subject will obviously not learn through mere instruction or thoughts to contract the pupil of his eye or to wiggle his ears or to stop excessive heartbeat at the sight of a lover or an enemy or, for that matter, to swim or play polo. Knowledge and information alone may not, and often of course do not, spell control and action. Yet, without cognition, control and action are not only of little value in advancing human progress but also are very limited in scope —only tether the golem within us. And what we want is golem with Eros, and Minerva with them.

SUMMARY

An empirical and logical analysis of all fundamental data on conditioning and learning (from both Russian and American laboratories), in terms of phyletic antiquity and functional universality and efficiency, strongly supports a view of the existence of an evolutionary hierarchy of four levels of learning. The analysis also suggests the existence of four sublevels of learning and a view that lower levels or sublevels do not cease to operate when higher levels or sublevels evolve but coexist with them, higher levels normally dominating lower levels, but lower levels manifesting themselves when higher levels are for some reason not functioning with full efficacy.

Specifically, the following levels and sublevels of learning were indicated in the analysis: (1) sublevel *Oa*—habituation, or *dd* learning, decrement of a reaction through reacting, manifested in varying degrees by all organisms and all types of reactions, and its opposite, sensitization, or *dD* learning, increment through reacting; (2) sublevel Ob—punishment, or $dd(G\,-)$ learning, inhibitory decrement of an adient reaction through interaction with an antagonistic abient one; (3) level I—classical dG conditioning in which, through paired interaction, a less dominant reaction assumes some characteristics of a more dominant reaction (typically, but not exclusively, the less dominant reaction is sensory-orienting or visceral in nature); (4) level II—reinforcement (or reward or operant) $dD(G)$ conditioning in which a locomotor or manipulatory or vocal reaction d becomes incremented through interaction with either the initiation of an adient reaction G or the cessation of an abient reaction $G\,-$ (G and $G\,-$ need not be specified in the resultant reaction); (5) sublevel IIIa—dominative nonconfigured afferent integration, or $a \leftrightarrow B \leftrightarrow c \leftrightarrow \cdots n$ learning, in which, through interaction, weak afferent components of an afferent compound reaction become weaker and strong components become stronger (leveling and sharpening in Gestalt terminology); (6) level III—afferent configuring, or $(abc \cdots n)$ learning, in which interaction of afferent components of a compound reaction gives rise to a new suprasummative configured reaction or configure (percept in phenomenological terms); (7) level IV—symbolization or $Sy(ABC \cdots N)$ learning, in which configures become integrated and efferented through words to form symbols or word-symbols; and (8) sublevel IVa—predication or semanticization, or $Sy_a + Sy_b = Sy_{ab}$ learning, in which symbols interact to form meaning-units or sememes.

There is sufficient empirical evidence to indicate that (1) learning of sublevels Oa and Ob and level I becomes operative almost at the very dawn of life, in infusoria; that (2) level II learning appears somewhere in higher invertebrates but is already fully manifest in fish; that (3) level III learning exists in fish and turtles in only very inchoate form but is quite evident in birds; and, of course, that (4) level IV is the exclusive attainment of man. There is also reason to postulate that the neural bases of levels I and II differ with respect to pattern and perhaps also locus, and that levels III and IV are no doubt mediated by their own specific areas and patterns.

A graphic summary of the main thesis of the present article is given in figures 13-1, 13-2, and 13-3. Figure 13-1 diagrams the argument that the phyletic antiquity of each level and sublevel of learning correlates negatively with the efficiency of the learning and positively with its universality; figures 13-2 and 13-3 attempt to demonstrate, in some detail, that, along with phyletic status, levels of learning are functions of the types of reactions involved in the reaction-interaction which produces the learning. Five types of unlearned interacting reactions are recognized: consummatory abient, consummatory adient, sensory-orienting, visceral, and locomotor-manipulatory-vocal. The locomotor-manipulatory-vocal reactions are considered as one type of "preparatory managing reactions" while the visceral and the sensory-orienting reactions are regarded as two separate types of "preparatory mobilizing reactions" since they behave similarly

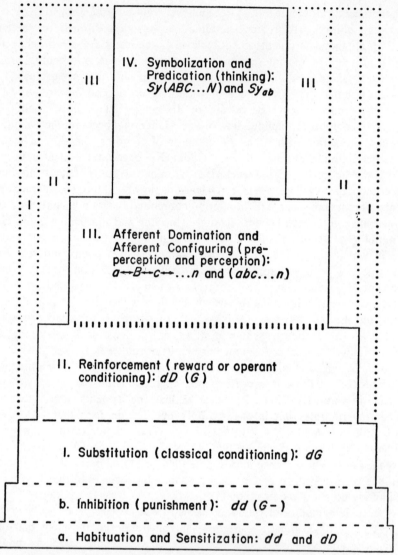

Figure 13-1. Levels of learning. The universality of each level is represented by the width of its parallelogram; its functional efficiency, by the height of the parallelogram; and its total efficiency (functional efficiency × universality), by the area of the parallelogram. The phyletic antiquity of each level is indicated by its vertical position in the diagram. The dotted lines indicate the coexistence of lower and higher levels.

with respect to conditioning but not to configuring, that is, only sensory-orienting reactions become configured. The resultant learned reactions are of six types: punished, classically conditioned (substituted or transformed),

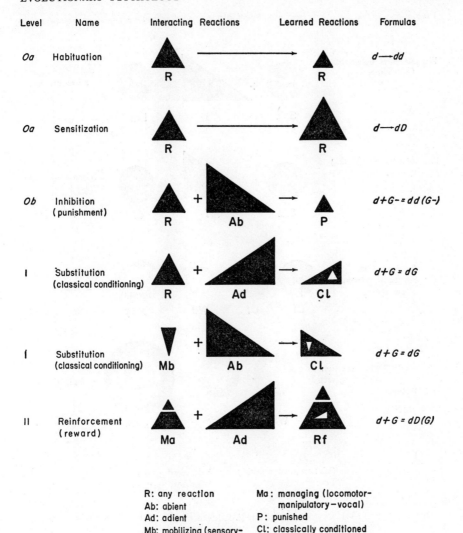

Level	Name	Interacting Reactions	Learned Reactions	Formulas

Figure 13-2. Levels and sublevels of learning: *Oa, Ob,* I, and II.

reinforced (rewarded), configured (perceived, in traditional terminology), symbolized-verbalized, and semanticized-predicated—also, habituated and sensitized. (Locomotor-manipulatory-vocal reactions may comprise some learning before they are fully manifest, while it is not unlikely that some configures are unlearned.)

There is also some reason to divide learning into three levels—disregarding sublevels and combining the third with the second level—when adult human action and pragmatic effects rather than evolutionary origin

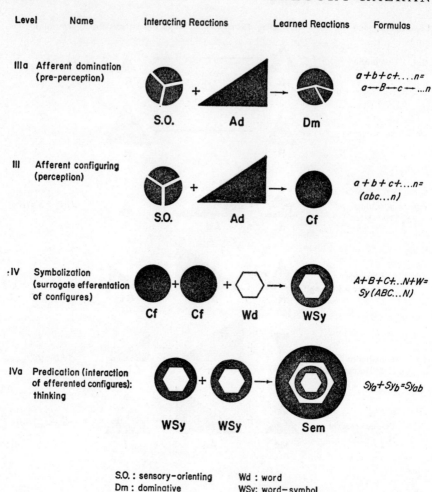

Level	Name	Interacting Reactions	Learned Reactions	Formulas

IIIa   Afferent domination
       (pre-perception)

S.O.   Ad   Dm

$$a+b+c+....n=$$
$$a \leftarrow B \leftarrow c \leftarrow ...n$$

III   Afferent configuring
       (perception)

S.O.   Ad   Cf

$$a+b+c+....n=$$
$$(abc...n)$$

:IV   Symbolization
       (surrogate efferentation
       of configures)

Cf   Cf   Wd   WSy

$$A+B+C+..N+W=$$
$$Sy(ABC...N)$$

IVa   Predication (interaction
       of efferented configures):
       thinking

WSy   WSy   Sem

$$Sy_a + Sy_b = Sy_{ab}$$

S.O. : sensory-orienting   Wd : word
Dm : dominative   WSy: word-symbol
Cf : configured   Sem: sememe

Figure 13-3. Levels and sublevels of learning: IIIa, III, IV, and IVa.

are the basis of the division. Such levels might best be designated as: (1) a historical level of symbols and sememes, least influenced by present organismic needs and affects and most imbued with what might be called judgment or rational cognition; (2) a contemporaneous level of percepts, needs, and affects, in which antagonistic interaction of reality-percepts and need-affects, of cognition and uncognition, and of what might be called rational perceptual cognition and irrational affective cognition continually occur; and (3) a mechanical, though highly dynamic, level in which problems of cognition, affects, and needs as such do not exist. Robot, Eros, and Minerva appear to be appropriate metaphorical analogues for the three levels of human learning and action. The third, the robot-mechanical level of human action and learning has, in the writer's opinion, been woefully neglected in the last few decades in Western research and thought—negelected by both experimentalists, preoccupied with roles of needs and motives, and philosophers and clinicians, under the spell of affects and libidos. The "unconscious" mind may well largely be beyond, more correctly, below the realm of needs and motives and pains and pleasures and preferred directions.

REFERENCES

Acta Biol. Exp., 1928–1960. Vols. 1-21. Warsaw, Poland.

AFFANI, J., MARCHCAFAVA, P. L., & ZERNICKI, B. Higher nervous activity in cats with midpontine pretrigeminal transsections. *Science,* 1962, **137,** 126-217.

ANOKHIN, P. K. Key problems in the study of higher nervous activity. In P. K. Anokhin (Ed.), *Problems of higher nervous activity.* Moscow: Akad. Med. Nauk, 1949. Pp. 9-128.

ANOKHIN, P. K. *Internal inhibition as a problem in physiology.* Moscow: Medgiz, 1958.

ANOKHIN, P. K. The role of the orienting-investigatory reaction in the formation of the conditioned reflex. In L. G. Voronin, A. N. Leont'yev, A. R. Luria, Ye. N. Sokolov and O. S. Vinogradova (Eds.), *The orienting reflex and orienting-investigatory activity.* Moscow: Akad. Pedag. Nauk RSFSR, 1959. Pp. 9-20.

ANOKHIN, P. K., & STREZH, E. Study of the dynamics of higher nervous activity. II. Differentiation of two positive conditioned stimuli. *Nizhegor. med. Zh.,* 1932, Nos. 7-8, 53-77.

ASRATYAN, E. A. Systemacity in the functioning of the cerebral cortex. *Trud. fiziol. Lab. Pavlova,* 1938, **8,** 1-15.

ASRATYAN, E. A. *Physiology of the central nervous system.* Moscow: Akad. Med. Nauk, 1953.

ASRATYAN, E. A. A new formulation of conditioned and unconditioned reflexes. *Zh. vyssh. nervn. Deyatel.,* 1955, **5,** 480-491.

ASRATYAN, E. A. (Ed.) *Central and peripheral mechanisms of motor activity of animals.* Moscow: Akad. Nauk, 1960.

AVAKYAN, R. V. Studies of auditory analyzer through conditioned eyelid reflexes. *Zh. vyssh. nervn. Deyatel.,* 1960, **10,** 23-31.

AYRAPETYANTS, E. Sh. *Higher nervous function and the receptors of internal organs.* Moscow: Akad. Nauk SSSR, 1952.

AYRAPETYANTS, E. Sh. Comparative study of the principle of replacement and inter-analyzer integration. In E. Sh. Ayrapetyants (Ed.), *Problems of comparative physiology of analyzers.* Leningrad Univ., 1960. Pp. 9-40.

BABKIN, B. P. Contributions to the study of the acoustic analyzer. *Trud. O-va Russ. Vrach. St. Petersburg,* 1910, **77,** 197-230.

BALDWIN, J. M. (Ed.). *Dictionary of philosophy and psychology.* New York: Macmillan, 1901-1905.

BARU, A. V., BOLOTINA, O. P., KRASASKAYA, N. A., LUKINA, E. V., PAVLOV, B. V., PRAZDNIKOVA, N. V., SAFYANTS, V. I., & CHEBYKIN, D. A. Study of the dynamics of conditioned-reflex activity of representative classes of vertebrates. *Trud. Instit. fiziol. Pavlova*, 1959, **8**, 99-106.

BEACH, F. A. The snark was a boojum. *Amer. Psychologist*, 1950, **5**, 115-124.

BERITOV, I. S. Uber die individuell-erworbene Tätigkeit des Zentralnervensystems. *J. Psychol. Neurol.*, 1927, **33**, 113-335.

BERITOV, I. S. *Individually acquired activity of the central nervous system*. Tiflis: GIZ, 1932.

BERITOV, I. S. *Basic forms of nervous and psychonervous activity*. Moscow: Akad. Nauk SSSR, 1947.

BERITOV, I. S. *Neural mechanisms of spatial orientation of higher vertebrates*. Tbilisi: GSSR, 1959.

BERITOV, I. S. *Gagry Colloquium: III: Mechanisms of development of temporary nervous connections*. Tbilisi: GSSR Akad. Nauk, 1960.

BERITOV, I. S. *Neural mechanisms of the behavior of higher vertebrates*. Moscow: Akad. Nauk, 1961.

BERNSTEIN, A. L. Temporal factors in the formation of conditioned eyelid reactions in human subjects. *J. gen. Psychol.*, 1934, **10**, 173-197.

BIRYUKOV, D. A. The nature of the orienting reaction. In L. G. Voronin, A. N. Leont'yev, A. R. Luria, E. N. Sokolov, & O. S. Vinogradova (Eds.), *The orienting reflex and orienting-investigatory activity*. Moscow: Akad. Pedag. Nauk RSFSR, 1958.

BIRYUKOV, D. A. Basic problems of evolutionary physiology of nervous activity. In D. A. Biryukov (Ed.), *Research on evolution of nervous activity*. Leningrad: Akad. Med. Nauk, 1959. Pp. 5-9.

BITTERMAN, M. E. Toward a comparative psychology of learning. *Amer. Psychologist*, 1960, **15**, 704-712.

BLINKOVA, T. P. Characteristics of unconditioned- and conditioned-reflex reactions in chick embryos. In the *Third Scientific Conferences on Evolutionary Physiology dedicated to the memory of Academician L. A. Orbeli*. Leningrad: 1961.

BOYCOTT, B. B., & YOUNG, J. Z. Reversal of responses in *Octopus vulgaris* Lamarck. *Anim. Behav.*, 1958, **6**, 45-52.

BREGADZE, A. Physiology of behavior to complex stimuli: Food-motor behavior to a complex visual figure. *Med. biol. Zh.*, 1930, **6**, 483-494.

BROGDEN, W. J. Sensory preconditioning. *J. exp. Psychol.*, 1939, **25**, 323-332.

BULYGIN, I. A. Some data on the comparative characteristics of viscero-motor and dermo-muscular reflexes. *Dokl. Akad. Nauk SSSR*, 1951, **80**, 493-496.

BYKOV, K. M. *The cerebral cortex and the internal organs*. Moscow: VMMA, 1943: Medgiz, 1944, 1947, 1954. (Translated into Chinese, Czech, English, French, German, Japanese, and Polish.)

CALDWELL, D. F., & WERBOFF, J. Classical conditioning of new born rats. *Science*, 1962, **136**, 1118-1119.

DELGADO, J. M. R., ROBERTS, W. W., & MILLER, N. E. Learning motivated by electrical stimulation of the brain. *Amer. J. Physiol.*, 1954, **179**, 587-593.

DI VESTA, F. J. Contrast effects in the verbal conditioning of meaning. *J. exp. Psychol.*, 1961, **62**, 535-544.

DYKMAN, R. A., & SHURRAGER, P. S. Successive and maintained conditioning in spinal carnivores. *J. Comp. physiol. Psychol.*, 1956, **49**, 27-35.

DZHAVRISHVILI, T. D. The problem of two-way temporary connections. *Trud. Instit. fiziol. Beritashvili*, 1956, **10**, 163-187.

FERSTER, C. B., & SKINNER, B. F., *Schedules of reinforcement.* New York: Appleton-Century-Crofts, 1957.

FLEURE, H. J., & WALTON, C. Notes on the habits of some sea anemones. *Zool. Anz.*, 1907, **31**, 212-220.

FOWLER, R. L., & KIMMEL, H. D. Operant conditioning of the GSR. *J. exp. Psychol.*, 1962, **6**, 563-567.

GALAMBOS, R., & MORGAN, C. T. The neural basis of learning. In J. Field, H. W. Magoun, and V. E. Hall (Eds.), *Handbook of physiology.* Vol. 3. Baltimore: Waverly Press, 1960. Pp. 1471-1499.

GAMBARYAN, L. S. *Problems of the physiology of the motor analyzers.* Moscow: GIZ, 1962.

GERD, M. A. An analysis of the training process. In *Materials of conference on psychology.* Moscow: Akad. Pedag. Nauk, 1957. Pp. 683-689.

GIBSON, J. J., & GIBSON, ELEANOR J. Perceptual learning: Differentiation or enrichment? *Psychol. Rev.*, 1955, **62**, 33-40.

GRINDLEY, G. C. Experiments on the influence of the amount of reward on learning in young chickens. *Brit. J. Psychol.*, 1929, **20**, 173-180.

GRINGS, W. W., LOCKHART, R. A., & DAMERON, L. F. Conditioning autonomic responses of mentally subnormal individuals. *Psychol. Monogr.*, 1962, **76**, 39 (whole no. 558).

GUNIN, V. I. Changes in higher nervous activity of albino rats upon extirpation of the cortical ends of the visual analyzer in early life. *Zh. vyssh. nerv. Deyatel.*, 1960, **10**, 456-463.

HARLOW, H. F. The formation of learning sets. *Psychol. Rev.*, 1949, **56**, 51-65.

HARLOW, H. F. Learning set and error factor theory. In S. Koch (Ed.), *Psychology: a study of a science.* Vol. 2. New York: McGraw-Hill, 1959. Pp. 492-537.

HARRIS, J. D. Habituatory response decrement in the intact organism. *Psychol. Bull.*, 1943, **40**, 385-422.

HEBB, D. O. *The organization of behavior.* New York: Wiley, 1949.

HEFFERLINE, R. F., KEENAN, B., & HARTFORD, R. A. Escape and avoidance conditioning in human subjects without their observation of the response, *Science*, 1959, 130, 1338-1339.

HILGARD, E. R. An algebraic analysis of conditioned discrimination in man. *Psychol. Rev.*, 1938, **45**, 472-496.

HILGARD, E. R., & MARQUIS, D. G. *Conditioning and learning.* New York: Appleton-Century-Crofts, 1940.

HINDE, R. A. Changes in responsiveness to a constant stimulus. *Brit. J. Animal Behavior*, 1954, **2**, 41-45.

HOBHOUSE, L. *Mind in evolution.* London: Macmillan, 1901.

HOVEY, H. B. Associative hysteresis in marine flatworms. *Physiol. Zool.*, 1929, **2**, 322-333.

HUNT, E. L. Establishment of conditioned responses in chick embryos. *J. comp. physiol. Psychol.*, 1949, **42**, 107-117.

IVANOV-SMOLENSKY, A. G. Basic forms of conditioned- and unconditioned-reflex activity of man and their anatomical substrate. *Zh. Nevropat. Psikhiat. Korsakova*, 1928, **21**, 229-245.

IWAMA, K., & ABE, M. Conditioned galvanic skin reflex and electroencephalogram. *Tohoku J. Exp. Med.*, 1953, **57**, 327-335.

JASPER, H., & SHAGASS, G. Conscious time judgments related to conditioned time intervals and voluntary control of the alpha rhythm. *J. exp. Psychol.*, 1941, **28**, 503-508.

JASPER, H., & SMIRNOV, G. D. (Eds.) The Moscow Colloquium on electro-encephalography of higher nervous activity. *EEG and clinical neuro-physiology*, 1960, **13**. Suppl. 13, no. 1.

JOHN, E. R. High nervous function: Brain function and learning. *Ann. Rev. Physiol.*, 1961, **23**, 451-484.

KARAMYAN, A. I. The evolution of cortico-cerebellar interrelations. *Zh. vyssh. nervn. Deyatel.*, 1959, **9**, 436-443.

KIMBLE, G. A., MANN, LUCIE I., & DUFORT, R. H. Classical and instrumental eyelid conditioning. *J. exp. Psychol.*, 1955, **49**, 407-417.

KLYAVINA, M. P. Conditioned-reflex generalization in animal embryos, neonates and early postnatal periods. In *Third Scientific Conference on Evolutionary Physiology dedicated to the memory of Academician L. A. Orbeli*. Leningrad, 1961. Pp. 93-94.

KOL'TSOVA, M. M. *The formation of higher nervous activity of the child.* Moscow: Medgiz, 1958.

KONORSKI, J. *Conditioned reflexes and neuron organization.* New York: Cambridge Univ. Press, 1948.

KONORSKI, J., & LAWICKA, W. Physiological mechanism of delayed reactions. I. The analysis and classification of delayed reactions. *Acta Biol. Exp.*, 1959, **19**, 175-196. Appendix 3, pp. 195-196.

KONORSKI, J., & MILLER, S. Conditioned reflexes of the motor analyzer. *Trud. fiziol. Lab. Pavlova*, 1936, **6** (1), 119-288.

KORONAKOS, C., & ARNOLD, W. J. The formation of learning sets in rats. *J. comp. physiol. Psychol.*, 1957, **50**, 11-14.

KRAKULIS, A. A. *Conditioned-reflex regulation of nervous activity.* Riga: LSSR, 1960.

KUKUYEV, L. A. Evolution of the nucleus of the motor analyzer and subcortical ganglia. *Zh. vyssh. nervn. Deyatel.*, 1953, **3**, 765-773.

LAWICKA, W. The effects of prefrontal lobectomy on the vocal conditioned reflexes in dogs. *Acta Biol. Exp.*, 1957, **17**, 317-325.

LISINA, M. I. The role of orientation in the transformation of involuntary into voluntary reactions. In L. G. Voronin, A. N. Leont'yev, A. R. Luria, E. N. Sokolov, and O. S. Vinogradova (Eds.), *The orienting reflex and orienting-investigatory activity*. Moscow: Akad. Pedag. Nauk RSFSR, 1958. Pp. 339-344.

LIVANOV, M. N., & POLYAKOV, K. L. Electrical processes in rabbits' cortex during the formation of a conditioned defense reflex to a rhythmic stimulus. *Izv. Akad. Nauk SSSR, Biol. Otdel.*, 1945 (3), 286-290.

LOGAN, F. A. A comparison of avoidance and non-avoidance eyelid conditioning. *J. exp. Psychol.*, 1951, **42**, 390-393.

LOSINA-LOSINSKY, L. K. Zur Ernährungs-physiologie der Infusorien. Untersuchungen uber die Nahrungsauswahl und Vermehrung bei *Paramecium Caudatum. Arch. Protistenk.*, 1931, **74**, 18-120.

LUKOV, B. N. The summation of short-lasting conditioned stimuli. *Trud. fiziol. Lab. Pavlova*, 1944, **11**, 109-116.

LURIA, A. R., & VINOGRADOVA, I. S. An objective investigation of the dynamics of semantic systems. *Brit. J. Psychol.*, 1959, **50**, 89-105.

MAGOUN, H. W., DARLING, L., & PROST, J. The evolution of man's brain. In M. A. B. Brazier (Ed.), *The central nervous system and behavior*. New York: Josiah Macy Jr. Foundation, 1960. Pp. 33-126.

MALAKHOVSKAYA, D. B. Development of specialized movements in postnatal periods in rabbits. In *Third Scientific Conference on Evolutionary Physiology dedicated to the memory of Academician L. A. Orbeli*. Leningrad, 1961. Pp. 126-127.

MAKAROV, P. O. *The neurodynamics of man*. Leningrad: Medgiz, 1959.

MANDLER, G. From association to cognition. *Psychol. Rev.*, 1962, **69**, 415-427.

MILLER, S., & KONORSKI, J. Sur une forme particulière des réflexes conditionnels. *C.R. Soc. Biol., Paris*, 1928, **99**, 1155. (b)

MORGAN, C. L. *Introduction to comparative psychology*. New York: Scribner, 1894.

MORRELL, F. Electrophysiological contributions to the neural basis of learning. *Physiol. Rev.*, 1961, **41**, 443-494.

MOWRER, O. H. *Learning theory and symbolic behavior*. New York: Wiley, 1960.

MYSYASHCHIKOVA, S. S. The extinction of vegetative reactions upon the stimulation of the peripheral apparatus of various analyzers. In K. M. Bykov (Ed.), *Voprosy fiziologii interotseptsii*. Moscow: Akad. Nauk SSSR, 1952. Pp. 411-427.

NISSEN, H. W. Phylogenetic comparison. In S. S. Stevens (Ed.), *Handbook of experimental psychology*. New York: Wiley, 1951. Pp. 347-386.

NORRIS, EUGENIA B., & GRANT, D. A. Eyelid conditioning as affected by verbally induced inhibitory set and counter-reinforcement. *Amer. J. Psychol.*, 1948, **61**, 37-49.

OLDS, J. Differentiation of reward systems in the brain by self-stimulation technics. In E. R. Ramey and D. S. Doherty (Eds.), *Electrical studies on the unanesthetized brain*. New York: Hoeber, 1960. Pp. 17-51.

OLDS, J., & MILNER, P. Positive reinforcement produced by electrical stimulation of septal area and other regions of rat brain. *J. comp. physiol. Psychol.*, 1954, **47**, 419-427.

ORBELI, L. A. *Problems of higher nervous activity*. Moscow: Akad. Nauk, 1949.

PAPOUSEK, H. Podmíněné motorické potravové reflexy u kojencu. III. Experimentální podmíněné rotăcni hlavu. (Conditioned food-motor reflexes in infants. III. Conditioned head-turning reflexes.) *Ceskoslov. Pediat.*, 1960, **15**, 1057-1066.

PAVLOV, I. P. *Lectures on the functions of the cerebral hemispheres*. Leningrad: Biomedgiz, 1927.

PAVLOV, I. P. Physiology of higher nervous activity. *Priroda*, 1932 (Nos. 11-12), 1139-1156.

PAVLOV, I. P. Essai d'une interpretation physiologique de l'hysterie. *L'Encephale,* 1933, **28,** 288-295.

PAVLOV, I. P. *Complete works.* Moscow-Leningrad: Akad. Nauk SSSR, 1949. 5 vols.

PEASTRAL, A. Studies in efficiency: Semantic generalization in schizophrenia. Ph.D. thesis, Univ. Pennsylvania, Philadelphia, 1961.

PENFIELD, W. Memory mechanisms. *Arch. Neurol. & Psychiat.,* 1952, **67,** 178-191.

PLAVILSTCHIKOV, N. N. Observations sur l'excitabilité des infusoires. *Russ. Arkh. Protist.,* 1928, **7,** 1-24.

POLEZHAYEV, E. F. The role of the orienting reflex in the coordination of the activity of the cerebral cortex. In L. G. Voronin, A. N. Leont'yev, A. R. Luria, E. N. Sokolov & O. S. Vinogradova (Eds.), *The orienting reflex and orienting-investigatory activity.* Moscow: Akad. Pedag. Nauk RSFSR, 1958. Pp. 97-111.

POLYAKOV, G. I. Progressive differentiation of cortical neurones in human ontogeny. In S. A. Sarkisov and N. S. Preobrazhenskaya (Eds.), *The development of the central nervous system.* Moscow: Medgiz, 1959. Pp. 11-26.

POSTMAN, L. Association theory and perceptual learning. *Psychol. Rev.,* 1955, **62,** 438-446.

PRATUSEVICH, YU. M. *Verbal stimuli in children.* Moscow: GIZ, 1960.

PREMACK, D. Toward empirical behavior laws: I. Positive reinforcement. *Psychol. Rev.,* 1959, **66,** 219-233.

RABINOVICH, M. YA. Electrophysiological analysis of the activity of different layers of the cortex during the formation of a conditioned reflex. *Zh. vyssh. nervn. Deyatel.,* 1961, **11,** 463-473.

RAZRAN, G. Theory of conditioning and related phenomena. *Psychol. Rev.,* 1930, **37,** 25-43.

RAZRAN, G. Conditioned responses: an experimental study and a theoretical analysis. *Arch. Psychol.,* 1935, **28** (Whole No. 191).

RAZRAN, G. The law of effect or the law of qualitative conditioning. *Psychol. Rev.,* 1939, **46,** 445-463. (a)

RAZRAN, G. A quantitative study of meaning by a conditioned salivary technique (semantic conditioning). *Science,* 1939, **90,** 89-91. (b)

RAZRAN, G. Studies in configural conditioning: I. Historical and preliminary experimentation. *J. gen. Psychol.,* 1939, **21,** 307-330. (c)

RAZRAN, G. Studies in configural conditioning: III. The factors of similarity, proximity, and continuity in configural conditioning. *J. exp. Psychol.,* 1939, **24,** 202-210. (d)

RAZRAN, G. Studies in configural conditioning. VI. Comparative extinction and forgetting of pattern and of single-stimulus conditioning. *J. exp. Psychol.,* 1939, **24,** 432-438. (e)

RAZRAN, G. Attitudinal determinants of conditioning and of generalization of conditioning. *J. exp. Psychol.,* 1949, **39,** 820-829. (a)

RAZRAN, G. Semantic and phonetographic generalizations of salivary conditioning to verbal stimuli. *J. exp. Psychol.,* 1949, **39,** 642-652. (b)

RAZRAN, G. Some psychological factors in the generalization of salivary conditioning to verbal stimuli. *Amer. J. Psychol.,* 1949, **62,** 247-256. (c)

RAZRAN, G. Sentential and propositional generalizations of salivary conditioning to verbal stimuli. *Science*, 1949, **109**, 447-448. (d)

RAZRAN, G. Experimental semantics. *Trans. NY Acad. Sci.*, 1952, **14**, 171-177.

RAZRAN, G. The conditioned evocation of attitudes (cognitive conditioning?). *J. exp. Psychol.*, 1954, **48**, 278-282.

RAZRAN, G. Conditioning and perception. *Psychol. Rev.*, 1955, **62**, 83-95. (a)

RAZRAN, G. Operant versus classical conditioning. *Amer. J. Psychol.*, 1955, **68**, 489-490. (b)

RAZRAN, G. The dominance-contiguity theory of the acquisition of classical conditioning. *Psychol. Bull.*, 1957, **54**, 1-46.

RAZRAN, G. The observable unconscious and inferable conscious in current Soviet psychophysiology: interoceptive conditioning, semantic conditioning, and the orienting reflex. *Psychol. Rev.*, 1961, **68**, 81-147.

RAZRAN, G. Conditioning and attitudes: tastes, judgments, and beliefs. Unpublished. (a)

RAZRAN, G. Interoceptive conditioning. Unpublished. (b)

RIESS, B. F. Semantic conditioning involving the galvanic skin reflex. *J. exp. Psychol.*, 1940, **26**, 238-240.

RIESS, B. F. Genetic changes in semantic conditioning. *J. exp. Psychol.*, 1946, **36**, 143-152.

ROMANES, G. J. *Animal intelligence.* London: Kegan Paul, 1881.

ROMANES, G. J. *Mental evolution in animals.* London: Kegan Paul, 1883.

RUSINOV, V. S. Electroencephalographic studies in conditioned reflex formation in man. In M. A. B. Brazier (Ed.), *The central nervous system and behavior.* New York: Josiah Macy Jr. Foundation, 1959. Pp. 33-126.

RUSKIN, J. *Modern painters.* Vol. II. London: Allen, 1903. Pp. 71-72.

SCHASTNY, A. I. Bioelectric changes in the muscles of dogs' limbs during the formation of conditioned defensive reflex. *Dokl. Akad. Nauk SSSR*, 1956, **107**, 350-351.

SCHLOSBERG, H. The relationship between success and the laws of conditioning. *Psychol. Rev.*, 1937, **44**, 379-394.

SCHNEIRLA, T. C. A consideration of some conceptual trends in comparative psychology. *Psychol. Bull.*, 1952, **49**, 559-597.

SHEFFIELD, F. D., ROBY, T. B., & CAMPBELL, B. A. Drive reduction versus consummatory behavior as determinants of reinforcement. *J. comp. physiol. Psychol.*, 1954, **47**, 349-354.

SHVARTS, L. A. The problem of words as conditioned stimuli. *Byul. eksp. Biol. Med.*, 1954, **38** (12), 15-18.

SHVARTS, L. A. Conditioned reflexes to verbal stimuli. *Vopr. Psikhol.*, 1960, **6** (1), 86-98.

SKINNER, B. F. *The behavior of organisms; an experimental analysis.* New York: Appleton-Century, 1938.

SKINNER, B. F. *Science and human behavior.* New York: Macmillan, 1953.

SKINNER, B. F. *Verbal behavior.* New York: Appleton-Century-Crofts, 1957.

SKIPIN, G. V. The interrelation of various forms of conditioned motor-defense reflexes in animals. *Zh. vyssh. nervn. Deyatel.*, 1959, **9**, 429-435.

SLONIM, A. D. *Fundamentals of general ecological physiology of mammals.* Moscow: Akad. Nauk SSSR, 1961.

SLUTSKAYA, M. M. Converting defensive into food reflexes in oligophrenics and in normal children. *Zh. Nevropat. Psikhiat.*, 1928, **21**, 195-210.

SOKOLOV, E. N. *Perception and conditioned reflex.* Moscow Univ., 1958.

SOKOLOV, E. N. (Ed.), *The orienting reflex and problems of higher nervous activity.* Moscow: Akad. Pedag. Nauk, RSFSR, 1959.

SOLLEY, C. M., & MURPHY, G. *Development of the perceptual world.* New York: Basic Books, 1960.

SOLOMON, R. L., & TURNER, L. H. Discriminative classical conditioning paralyzed by curare can later control discriminative avoidance responses in normal state. *Psychol. Rev.*, 1962, **69**, 202-219.

SOLOMON, R. L., & WYNNE, L. C. Traumatic avoidance learning: The principle of anxiety conservation and partial irreversibility. *Psychol. Rev.*, 1954, **61**, 353-385.

SPELT, D. K. The conditioning of the human fetus in utero. *J. exp. Psychol.*, 1948, **38**, 338-346.

STAATS, A. W., & STAATS, C. K. Meaning established by classical conditioning. *J. exp. Psychol.*, 1957, **54**, 74-80.

STAATS, A. W., & STAATS, C. K. Attitudes established by classical conditioning. *J. abnorm. Soc. Psychol.*, 1958, **57**, 37-40.

TCHAKHOTINE, S. Réactions conditionnés par micropuncture ultraviolette dans le comportement d'une cellule isolée (*Paramecium caudatum*). *Arch. Instit. Prophyl.*, 1938, **10**, 119-133.

THORNDIKE, E. L. Animal intelligence: an experimental study of the associative processes in animals. *Psychol. Monogr.*, 1898, **2**, No. 8.

T'SU, C. General and local changes in EEG during the formation of conditioned motor reflexes in man. *Bull. exp. Biol. Med.*, 1960, **49**, 110-114.

TURNER, C. H. An experimental investigation of an apparent reversal of the responses to light of the roach (*Periplaneta orientalis* L.). *Biol. Bull.*, 1912, **23**, 371-386.

UKHTOMSKY, A. A. Dominance as a working principle of neural centers. *Russ. Fiziol. Zh.*, 1923, **6** (1-3), 31-45.

UKHTOMSKY, A. A. *Collected works.* Leningrad Univ., 1950-1954. 5 vols.

UNDEUTSCH, U. Die Aktualgenese in ihrer allgemeinpsychologischen und ihrer characterlogischen Bedeutung. *Scientia*, 1942, **72**, 37-42.

VINOGRADOVA, O. S. *The orienting reflex and its neurophysiological mechanism.* Moscow: Akad. Pedag. Nauk, 1961.

VORONIN, L. G. *Comparative physiology of higher nervous activity.* Moscow Univ., 1957.

VORONIN, L. G. Mechanism of chained conditioned reflexes. In P. S. Kupalov (Ed.), *Problems of physiology and pathology of higher nervous activity.* Leningrad: Medgiz, 1960. Pp. 184-195.

VORONIN, L. G., & NAPALKOV, A. V. Methodological techniques for the formation of complex systems of conditioned motor reflexes in animals. *Zh. vyssh. nervn. Deyatel.*, 1959, **9**, 126-134.

WARREN, J. M., BROOKSHIRE, K. H., BALL, G. G., & REYNOLDS, D. V. Reversal learning by white leghorn chicks. *J. comp. physiol. Psychol.*, 1960, **53**, 371-375.

WATSON, J. B. The place of kinesthetic, visceral, and laryngeal organization in thinking. *Psychol. Rev.*, 1924, **31**, 339-348.

WHITMARSH, C. A., & BOUSEFIELD, W. A. Use of free associational norms for the prediction of generalization of salivary conditioning to verbal stimuli. *Psychol. Rep.*, 1961, **8**, 91-95.

WICKENS, D. D., & BRIGGS, G. E. Mediated stimulus generalization as a factor in sensory preconditioning. *J. exp. Psychol.*, 1951, **42**, 197-200.

WOODWORTH, R. S. Reinforcement of perception. *Amer. J. Psychol.*, 1947, **60**, 119-124.

WOODWORTH, R. S., & SCHLOSBERG, H. *Experimental psychology.* New York: Holt, 1954.

YEROFEYEVA, M. N. *Electrical stimulation of the skin of the dog as a conditioned salivary stimulus.* Thesis. St. Petersburg, 1912.

YEROFEYEVA, M. N. Additional data on nocuous conditioned reflexes. *Izv. Instit. Lesgafta*, 1921, **3**, 69-73.

ZEVALD, L. O. Materials on the problem of systematicity. *Trud. fiziol. Lab. Pavlov*, 1941, **10**, 324-331.

ZELIONY, G. P. *The reactions of dogs to auditory stimuli.* Thesis. St. Petersburg, 1907.

ZELIONY, G. P., VYSOTSKY, N., DOBROTINA, G., IRZHANSKAYA, K., MEDYAKOV, F., NAUMOV, S., POLTYREV, S., & TUNTSOVA, E. Forms and means of forming associated reflexes. In *Transactions of 6th All-Union Congress of Physiologists, Biochemists, and Pharmacologists*, Tbilisi, 1937. Pp. 165-171.

ZHUKOVA, G. P. Development of cortical end of motor analyzer. *Arkh. Anat. Gistol. Embriol.*, 1953, **30**, 32-38.

ZUBKOV, A. A., & POLIKARPOV, G. G. Conditioned reflexes in coelenterates. *Usp. sovr. Biol.*, 1951, **32** (5), 301-302.

14 RICHARD C. ATKINSON
ROBERT C. CALFEE

MATHEMATICAL LEARNING THEORY *

MATHEMATICAL LEARNING THEORY probably began in 1885 when Hermann Ebbinghaus attempted to fit some data from an experiment on recall with a simple logarithmic function. However, the term has come to be associated closely with a number of recent developments in psychology, and it is these developments and their immediate historical antecedents that we will consider in this paper. In particular, we will discuss the role of mathematical models in contemporary learning theory, with special reference to the influence of such models on research and theory. A number of points that we wish to make clear will then be illustrated by a detailed consideration of a specific experiment. In this example, we will show how the design and analysis of experiments are related to a mathematical approach to learning.

Prior to 1950, the most significant attempt to formulate a mathematical theory of learning was that of Clark L. Hull. His theoretical system and variations of it (Hull, 1943; Logan, 1959; Spence, 1956) were based on the postulation of a set of unobservable intervening variables, psychological constructs such as habit and drive. These intervening variables were related to the observable dependent and independent variables by certain functions that were to be empirically determined. Within the Hullian framework, behavior basically was a deterministic process, though a probabilistic overlay was added. All response measures were functions of a single underlying factor, reaction potential, and it was usually assumed that, since all response measures should be correlated, the experimenter was free to choose the measure that he thought most appropriate.

In general, experiments designed to test theories in the pre-1950 period were of two types: the comparative experiment and the factorial experiment. (For a historical account of this period, see Hilgard, 1956.) In a comparative experiment, a situation was arranged in which opposing predictions could be made by different theories. Few of the experiments

* The preparation of this chapter was supported by the National Institute of Health (Grant M-5184) and by the National Science Foundation (Grant 24264).

proved to be as crucial as they were designed to be, since the protagonists were quite skillful at finding an interpretation of the theory that accounted for the results, and the theories themselves were quite resilient.
The consequence of this experimentation was that it shortly became difficult to distinguish one theoretical system from another (Seward, 1956).

As an example of the factorial experiment, we may mention the efforts
to determine whether drive and incentive combine additively or multi-
plicatively. If the latter condition holds, one would expect a significant interaction term when a factorial design is analyzed by the analysis-of-
variance technique. (A factorial design is one in which several levels of
each variable are represented in all possible combinations.) A non-
significant interaction would be interpreted as evidence for the additive
hypothesis. Clearly, the outcome depended on numerous conditions other
than the assumption being tested, such as the choice of levels of the variables, the degree of experimental control, and probably the response
measure chosen. In particular, to the extent that experimental control was
poor, the additive hypothesis would be favored.

NEW DEVELOPMENTS

In the late 1940s and early 1950s, there appeared a group of new developments that have come to be called mathematical learning theory.
Let us at the outset state that we cannot hope to do justice to all the investigators whose work properly falls within this category. And we can only
mention in passing that, in addition to developing a number of new learning situations for their own purposes, experimenters have applied mathematical theories of one type or another to a wide variety of standard
learning paradigms, such as classical conditioning, avoidance conditioning, discrimination learning, stimulus generalization, paired-associate learning, memory processes, and concept-formation. (For recent reviews, see
Bush, 1960; Estes, 1959; Restle, 1959.)

The movement has been characterized by a number of features. Behavior is seen as an essentially probabilistic phenomenon. The primary
behavioral measure is taken to be the probability of occurrence of a
member of some response class. Theories are stated in a way that has
made mathematical development feasible. There has been a tendency to
interpret behavioral phenomena, not by reference to underlying molecular processes, but by specification of the *rules of operation* (Estes, 1962).
These rules are simple mathematical laws whose implications describe the
overt response character of a behavioral system, much as Newton's laws
describe the activity of the solar system.

In a sense, mathematical learning theory is a misnomer. One should
not imagine that mathematical learning theory represents a position that
is opposed to other learning theories. What is actually being expressed is

an increased dependence on the use of mathematics in the formulation of learning theory irrespective of whether the theory is oriented toward stimulus-response notions, cognitive constructs, expectancies, or some other approach. As we shall see, issues that in the past have crucially differentiated opposing theoretical systems, when formulated in a precise mathematical fashion, can live together quite comfortably within a single system. The use of mathematics has allowed the psychologist to analyze more adequately the content of his statements, and to determine whether a particular set of data are consistent with these statements.

Two main lines of development in mathematical learning theory, which appeared almost simultaneously, are those associated with Bush and Mosteller (1951, 1955) and Estes (1950, 1959). Bush and Mosteller began with what Restle (1959) has called an abstract theory. For reasons of mathematical simplicity, they assumed that the probability of a given response on a trial could always be expressed as a linear function of the probabilty of the same response on the preceding trial. The form of the linear operator (that is, the parameter values of the function) depended on the type of reinforcement even that intervened. Though the theory was abstract, Bush and Mosteller showed that derivations and parameter estimation problems could be greatly simplified if certain restraints based on extratheoretical considerations were imposed on the models. These considerations were of a sort that made sense psychologically. An example is the "equal alpha" condition, where for certain two-choice problems, (for example, a T maze) the symmetry of the situation permits the assumption that the learning-rate parameters associated with the two responses are equal.

Estes' theoretical formulation, which has come to be known as stimulus sampling theory, was of an entirely different form. The environment was represented by a large population of discrete, mutually exclusive conceptual entities which he called stimulus elements. Each element was conditioned to one and only one response class. The organism took a sample from the set of elements, and the probability of occurrence of any response class was simply the proportion of elements in the sample which were conditioned to that class. The reinforcement event acted on the conditioning relations of the sample of elements in some specified fashion (for example, all elements in the sample became conditioned to the response class which was designated as correct) and the sample was then returned to the population for resampling at a later time. In Estes' initial development of these notions, the function describing changes in response probability was a linear function similar to the Bush-Mosteller model.

Let us now mention a number of ways in which these systems represented advances over earlier formulations. A feature of psychological theories from Freud through Hull has been the postulation of multiple unobservable processes that may interact in some complicated fashion to either complement or oppose one another. At a qualitative level of analysis, by a suitable post facto weighing of such processes, one may account for virtually any experimental result. Mathematical models have allowed theorists to introduce and evaluate such notions in an unambiguous manner. One may assume more than one underlying process, and then determine the contribution of each process unequivocally.

Another advance brought about by mathematical developments in learning theory concerns changes in the organization and analysis of data. In this regard, perhaps the most important role of mathematical models has been to provide a framework within which the detailed trial-by-trial aspects of behavior can be scrutinized (Anderson, 1959). An experiment designed only to establish the existence of a gross relation between two variables, such as response speed and reward magnitude, ignores the many sequential properties of psychological phenomena. Examination of these properties is a significant step forward in that it provides a source of behavioral information that cannot be obtained from an analysis of average-performance curves. Theories stated only in qualitative terms do not provide an adequate means for analyzing and interpreting such complex sequential phenomena.

In this connection, we may note Estes' distinction (1959) between three levels of prediction from a mathematical model: extrapolation, overdetermination, and situational invariance. Extrapolation refers to the ability of a model to account for those statistics from which parameters are estimated. (This requirement is not as simple as it may seem. For example, no choice of parameters for a linear equation will give a satisfactory fit to the typical learning curve.) Overdetermination refers to prediction, within the same body of data, of statistics that are independent of those yielding the parameter estimates. Finally, situational invariance is the degree to which parameter estimates made in one experimental situation can account for data collected in other experiments. The mixed record of successes and failures of mathematical models shows that these requirements are not trivial. For example, in numerous studies (Anderson, 1960; Atkinson and Estes, 1963; Suppes and Atkinson, 1960) the learning-rate parameters that satisfy the mean learning curve requirements have proven inadequate in accounting for asymptotic sequential dependency statistics.

Among recent trends within the area of stimulus-sampling theory, we may mention the introduction of models where the number of stimulus elements in the population is severely limited, leading in the limit to the one-element model. In many learning situations, it is reasonable to suppose that the subject does not sample randomly from a large population of different cues, but restricts his attention to a few homogeneous aspects of the environment. In particular, the subject may distinguish between stimulus events which consist of the same "elements," but that have different patterns. For example, in a paired-associate task, one can assume that each stimulus word is represented by a single pattern that is sampled with probability 1 when the stimulus word is displayed. In analyzing such tasks, there has been a shift from linear-operator models to Markov models. In the latter models, the description of the organism on a particular trial is phrased in terms of the momentary state of each stimulus element; taken together, these descriptions constitute the state of the organism. It is usually assumed that the change in response probabilities from trial n to trial $n + 1$ of an experiment is dependent only on the state of the organism on trial n and on a transition matrix that specifies the change in states associated with each reinforcement event. This assumption, plus the restriction on the number of elements in the population, has served to reduce the number of states in the Markov process to a manageable number. The resulting models have proven mathematically tractable, and have given an excellent account of a wide array of data.

In addition to the specification on the stimulus side of the exact cues that are being sampled, there has been a relaxation of the original stimulus-sampling assumption that each element is conditioned in an all-or-none fashion to some response class. For example, one may postulate neutral states where, if an element is sampled, the subject simply responds at random from among the available response alternatives (LaBerge, 1959). An element may be "strongly" conditioned to a response, in which case, for example, at least two negative reinforcements must occur before the element changes conditioning to another response class, versus a "weak" state, where a single error may produce a change in conditioning (Atkinson & Estes, 1963).

As an example of the effect of the use of models on experimental design, we may mention the Bower paired-associate experiments (1961, 1962). In these experiments, an attempt was made to evaluate a one-element stimulus-sampling model in which the learning is assumed to occur abruptly, in an all-or-none fashion; the ability of such a model to account for paired-associate data has been extremely good. It is important to note several features of Bower's experiments that are relevant to the effects of a mathematical approach on research techniques. First, the experiments were designed explicitly to test a particular model. In the classical paired-associate task, both stimuli and responses frequently were verbal items such as nonsense syllables or familiar words. It seemed to Bower that at least two processes were taking place in the traditional situation —learning of the response set and the association of responses with the appropriate stimuli. The one-element model was designed to account only for the latter process. Hence, response items were chosen that one could assume would already be part of the subject's response repertoire. Further, in terms of the model, it was desirable to treat each subject's protocol as though the several stimulus-response pairs were learned independently.

Consequently, stimuli were chosen that, in other situations, showed minimum interference with each other. Thus, the theory as interpreted in the model dictated the criteria for the selection of stimulus and response items that would be appropriate to test Bower's ideas about the associative phase of paired-associate learning. The criticism sometimes made that such experiments are contrived and artificial fails to recognize the goal of laboratory research, which is to restrict the introduction of extraneous variables that are not relevant to the hypothesis being considered.

MODELS IN PSYCHOLOGICAL RESEARCH

In the remaining part of this paper, we shall try to give some concrete illustrations of the role of models in psychological research. In order to do this, it will be necessary to describe a typical experimental problem, outline several alternative models, and then indicate some of the strategies and tactics involved in making a comparison among the models. The task we select is a highly special case of paired-associate learning. The reason for selecting this experimental problem is that it illustrates many of the problems in psychological theorizing without introducing too much mathematical complexity.

The experiment involves a list of 18 different paired-associate items. The stimulus member of each pair is a single Greek letter and the response is the number 1 or 2. The subjects are told the response alternatives available to them, and each number occurs equally as often as the to-be-learned response. Hence the probability of a correct response by guessing is $\frac{1}{2}$.

Two types of trials are defined. On a study trial, the eighteen letter-number pairs are exhibited singly in a random order. The subject is instructed simply to associate each letter with the appropriate number and is not required to make a response. On a test trial, the letters alone are presented singly in a new random order and the subject attempts to give the correct number to each letter. The subject is required to respond to each letter on a test trial (even if he is uncertain and must guess), but he is not told whether his response is correct.

In the experiment we shall examine, two study trials were given followed by four test trials; the standard notation for this type of experiment is simply $R_1R_2T_1T_2T_3T_4$ (Jones, 1962). If we represent a correct response by c and an error by e, then the response protocol for an individual stimulus item (that is, a particular Greek letter) over the four test trials will consist of an ordered four-tuple of cs and es. For example, the protocol $e_1c_2e_3e_4$ would indicate a correct response on T_2 and incorrect responses on T_1, T_3, and T_4. The role of theory in this situation is to predict the types of sequences that will occur and their relative frequencies.

One feature of our experimental situation that has been established by several studies is that if we run enough test trials in sequence, then in time the subject will become consistent in his response to each stimulus. For some stimuli the stereotyped response is the correct one; for other stimuli it is incorrect.

The models that we shall examine are imbedded in the controversy regarding all-or-none learning versus incremental learning. Of late, there have been some particularly important studies dealing with this issue, but we will not attempt to review them here. Rather, for illustrative purposes, we will take a naïve approach and outline one model that might be viewed as characterizing the incremental position and another that typifies the all-or-none viewpoint.

The incremental model is in the spirit of Hullian theory and is very similar to the early work of Bush and Mosteller (1951, 1955). We assume that at the start of a trial there is a fixed number p associated with each stimulus item that specifies the probability that a correct response will be made to that item. The effect of a study trial is to increment that probability by a constant proportion θ of the total possible change. Specifically, if p is the probability before a study trial, then after a single study trial the new probability will be $p + \theta (1 - p)$. That is, the new probability is the old one plus a constant θ of the possible increase. In mathematical terminology, we say that the effect of a study trial is to apply an operator Q to the operand p to yield a new quantity $Q(p)$; that is, $Q(p) = p + \theta (1 - p)$. As will be evident later, it will be more convenient to write this reinforcement operator in the following form:

$$Q(p) = (1 - \theta)p + \theta \tag{1}$$

To obtain the new probability after two successive study trials we apply the operator Q twice, namely,

$$Q^2(p) = Q[Q(p)] = (1 - \theta)^2 p + (1 - \theta) \theta + \theta$$
$$= 1 - (1 - p)(1 - \theta)^2$$

By induction one can show that, after n successive study trials,

$$Q^n(p) = 1 - (1 - p)(1 - \theta)^n$$

For our experimental situation, the initial probability of guessing correctly is ½ and hence we would set $p = \frac{1}{2}$. Thus, for this model the probability of a correct response on the first test trial following n successive study trials will be

$$\Pr(c_1) = 1 - \frac{1}{2}(1 - \theta)^n \tag{2}$$

The all-or-none learning process that we shall consider is one that has been actively investigated by Estes (1960, 1961), Bower (1961, 1962),

Restle (1963), Suppes and Ginsberg (1963), and others. For this model, we assume that each stimulus item is in one of two conditioning states: $\underline{\underline{C}}$ or $\underline{\underline{G}}$. In state $\underline{\underline{C}}$, the stimulus is conditioned to the correct response and on a test trial will elicit that response with probability 1. In state $\underline{\underline{G}}$, the stimulus is not conditioned to any response, and in this state the probability of a correct response is ½; that is, a correct response will occur at the chance level. All items at the start of the experiment are in state $\underline{\underline{G}}$, but on each study trial there exists a probability θ that conditioning will occur. Thus, the probability that a particular stimulus item is in state $\underline{\underline{C}}$ after one study trial is θ, after two study trials $\theta + (1 - \theta)\theta$, after three study trials $\theta + \theta(1 - \theta) + \theta(1 - \theta)^2$, and so on. More generally, the probability of being in state $\underline{\underline{C}}$ after n successive study trials is

$$\Pr(\underline{\underline{C}}_n) = 1 - (1 - \theta)^n \tag{3}$$

For this model, the expected probability of a correct response on test trial T_1 after n successive study trials would be

$$\Pr(c_1) = 1 - (1 - \theta)^n + \frac{1}{2}(1 - \theta)^n$$

$$= 1 - \frac{1}{2}(1 - \theta)^n \tag{4}$$

That is, the probability of being in state $\underline{\underline{C}}$ plus ½ times the probability of being in state $\underline{\underline{G}}$. The all-or-none character of this model is represented by the fact that for the underlying states the probability of a correct response can take on only two values; either ½ if the subject is in state $\underline{\underline{G}}$, or 1 if the subject is in state $\underline{\underline{C}}$. Further, the transition from $\underline{\underline{G}}$ to $\underline{\underline{C}}$ occurs in an all-or-none fashion on a single trial.

To summarize to this point, for the incremental model two study trials generate a fixed number associated with each stimulus item that specifies the probability of a correct response on the first trial. We shall call this number ϕ, and it is given by equation 2 when $n = 2$; that is,

$$\phi = \frac{1}{2}(1 - \theta)^2 + \theta(1 - \theta) + \theta \tag{5}$$

For the all-or-none model, each stimulus item will be in either state $\underline{\underline{C}}$ or state $\underline{\underline{G}}$. If the item is in state $\underline{\underline{C}}$, a correct response occurs on a test trial; if the item is in state $\underline{\underline{G}}$, a correct response occurs with probability ½. The probability of being in state $\underline{\underline{C}}$ after two study trials will be called x and is given by equation 3; that is,

$$x = \theta + (1 - \theta)\theta \tag{6}$$

The next question is with regard to the events that occur on a test trial. As noted earlier, it is known that behavior eventually becomes stereotyped if sufficiently long series of test trials are run, and this observation suggests that systematic changes may be occurring over test trials. A plausible assumption that accounts for the changes is that in the absence of an experimenter-determined reinforcing event (that is, the experimenter telling the subject which response was correct) the emitted response is the response reinforced. This last phrase characterizes much of the theoretical work of contiguity theorists such as Guthrie (1935): the last response to take place in the presence of a stimulus will remain associated with it and will tend to reoccur when the stimulus is presented again.

The assumption that the emitted response is the one reinforced on a test trial delimits a class of qualitative theories that can be experimentally investigated. But this class of theories is large and difficult to characterize; also, too frequently new experimental findings can somehow be made to agree with almost any of the theoretical positions. Thus, much is to be gained by taking a qualitative assumption concerning test trial effects and examining the consequences of stating it mathematically. To illustrate, assume that a qualitative theory predicts a difference between two experimental groups; an experiment is run to test for the difference and none is obtained. What conclusion can be drawn? Either that no difference exists or that if it exists it is too small to be detected by the experimental procedures utilized. In contrast, with a quantitative theory we know not only the direction of the predicted difference but also the exact magnitude. Consequently, the equipment and experimental procedure can be designed so that they are sufficiently sensitive to detect the difference if it is present. Then if no difference is found, there can be no alibi that the effect might be too small to be detected. Experiments that find no differences are ambiguous in evaluating qualitative predictions; for quantitative theories such results have an exact interpretation.

For the incremental model, we shall assume the same reinforcing operator on test trials as on study trials. Specifically, if p is the probability of a correct response and that response occurs on a test trial, then the new probability will be $Q(p) = (1 - a)p + a$ where a is the parameter describing learning under self reinforcement. If an incorrect response occurs (which has probability $q = 1 - p$), then that response will be reinforced, which means that Q will be applied to q; that is, $Q(q) = (1 - a)q + a$. By inspection of the last expression, we see that reinforcing an incorrect response is equivalent to applying the operator $Q'(p) = (1 - a)p$. Stating our ideas exactly, if p is the probability of a correct response on a test trial, then p^* (the value at the end of the test trial) will be

$$p^* = \begin{cases} Q(p) = (1 - a)p + a & \text{if the correct response occurs} \\ Q'(p) = (1 - a)p & \text{if the incorrect response occurs} \end{cases} \tag{7}$$

From these equations, it can be shown that the probability of a correct response will approach 1 or 0 as the run of test trials becomes large. Thus, asymptotically some items will absorb on the correct response and others on an incorrect response. If ϕ denotes the probability of a correct response to a specific stimulus item at the start of the test sequence, then the probability that this item absorbs on the correct response will be ϕ.

Our assumption that on a test trial the emitted response is reinforced also has a natural interpretation in terms of the all-or-none model. As before, we assume that reinforcement of a response conditions the stimulus to that response with some probability, say β. If the stimulus is conditioned to the correct response on a test trial (that is, is in state $\underline{\underline{C}}$), then that response occurs and by reinforcing it we guarantee that it remains in state $\underline{\underline{C}}$. If the stimulus item is in state $\underline{\underline{G}}$, then with probability ½ the correct response occurs, and by assumption this is reinforcing on a test trial; hence with probability β, the item moves to state $\underline{\underline{C}}$. Now, it is obvious that we must also allow for the occurrence of an incorrect response; if an item is in state $\underline{\underline{G}}$ and an incorrect response occurs, then the item will become conditioned with probability β to the incorrect response. Therefore, in addition to states $\underline{\underline{C}}$ and $\underline{\underline{G}}$ which characterize study trials, we also need a state $\underline{\underline{E}}$ to denote conditioning to an incorrect response. These notions are embodied in the following transition matrix:

$$
\begin{array}{c}
\\
\underline{\underline{C}}\\
\underline{\underline{G}}\\
\underline{\underline{E}}
\end{array}
\begin{array}{ccc}
\underline{\underline{C}} & \underline{\underline{G}} & \underline{\underline{E}}\\
\left[\begin{array}{ccc}
1 & 0 & 0\\
\frac{1}{2}\beta & 1-\beta & \frac{1}{2}\beta\\
0 & 0 & 1
\end{array}\right]
\end{array}
\qquad (8)
$$

The rows indicate the state at the start of a test trial and the columns the state at the end of the trial. Each entry denotes the probability of a transition from one state to another. In state $\underline{\underline{C}}$ (or $\underline{\underline{E}}$), no change can occur on a test trial. In state $\underline{\underline{G}}$, the item may become conditioned to the correct response if it occurs (with probability ½) and conditioning is effective (with probability β); similarly in state $\underline{\underline{G}}$ the item may become conditioned to the incorrect response if it occurs and conditioning is effective. As in the case of the linear model, each stimulus item eventually absorbs in either state $\underline{\underline{C}}$ or $\underline{\underline{E}}$. Thus, after a long run of test trials, a given stimulus item will eventually elicit either a correct or an incorrect response consistently.

These, then, are the two models we shall examine. From a qualitative viewpoint each represents the same psychological process; that is, they both assume that a reinforcement tends to increase the likelihood of the reinforced response and they both assume the same subject-determined reinforcement schedules. However, the exact nature of the change that occurs following reinforcement is quite different for the two models. This is illustrated by the fact that the probability of a correct response in the incremental model may take on any value from 0 to 1, whereas for the all-or-none model it can take on only the values 0, ½, or 1. This fact alone indicates that there are substantial differences between the two models and it becomes important to determine which interpretation of the reinforcing event best approximates the actual learning process.

In order to compare these models, we need to derive some predictions. Consider first the incremental model and the possible outcomes for a given stimulus item on trials T_1 and T_2. What is the probability of two correct responses? Well, a correct response will occur on T_1 with probability ϕ (see equation 5) and, since the correct response occurred on T_1, the probability of a correct response on T_2 will be $(1 - a)\phi + a$ (see equation 7). The probability of two correct responses is simply the product of these two probabilities. Similarly, the probability of an incorrect followed by a correct is $(1 - \phi)$ times $(1 - a)\phi$; that is, the probability of an incorrect response on T_1 times the probability of a correct response on T_2 given that the preceding trial was incorrect. In this way we obtain the following expressions.

$$\Pr(c_1 c_2) = \phi[(1 - a)\phi + a]$$
$$\Pr(c_1 e_2) = \phi[1 - \{(1 - a)\phi + a\}] \qquad (9)$$
$$\Pr(e_1 c_2) = (1 - \phi)[(1 - a)\phi]$$
$$\Pr(e_1 e_2) = (1 - \phi)[1 - (1 - a)\phi]$$

By similar methods, expressions can be obtained for the probability of any sequence of responses over the four test trials. We display a few of these equations to indicate that even for a simple model of this sort the elaboration of the theory leads to predictions whose consequences are too complicated to be understood without the tools of mathematical analysis:

$$\Pr(c_1 c_2 c_3 c_4) = \phi\,[(1 - a)\,\phi + a]\,[(1 - a)^2\,\phi + (1 - a)a + a]$$
$$[(1 - a)^3\,\phi + (1 - a)^2\,a + (1 - a)a + a]$$
$$\Pr(c_1 c_2 c_3 c_4) = \phi\,[(1 - a)\phi + a]\,[(1 - a)^2\,\phi + (1 - a)a + a]$$
$$[1 - (1 - a)^3\,\phi - (1 - a)^2\,a - (1 - a)a - a] \qquad (10)$$
$$\vdots$$
$$\Pr(e_1 e_2 e_3 e_4) = (1 - \phi)[1 - (1 - a)\phi]\,[1 - (1 - a)^2\,\phi]$$
$$[1 - (1 - a)^3\,\phi]$$

Predictions for the same quantities can be obtained for the all-or-none model. Consider first the possible outcomes for a given stimulus item on trial T_1 and T_2. The probability of two correct responses in a row is $x + (1 - x)\frac{1}{2}[\beta + (1 - \beta)\frac{1}{2}]$. That is, with probability x the stimulus item is in state $\underset{=}{C}$ before the first test trial and hence will generate correct responses on all subsequent trials; with probability 1-x, the stimulus item starts in state $\underline{G}$ and a correct response occurs on T_1 with probability ½. Further, a correct response can occur on T_2 if (1) conditioning was effective on T_1 (that is, with probability β) or (2) if conditioning was not effective and by chance the subject again guessed correctly on the next trial. Proceeding in this way, we obtain the following expression:

$$\Pr(c_1c_2) = x + \frac{1}{2}(1-x)[\beta + (1-\beta)\frac{1}{2}]$$

$$\Pr(c_1e_2) = \frac{1}{4}(1-x)(1-\beta) \qquad (11)$$

$$\Pr(e_1c_2) = \frac{1}{4}(1-x)(1-\beta)$$

$$\Pr(e_1e_2) = \frac{1}{2}(1-x)[\beta + (1-\beta)\frac{1}{2}]$$

Using the same methods, one can obtain expressions for the sequence of events over the four test trials. For example,

$$\Pr(c_1c_2c_3c_4) = x + \frac{1}{2}(1-x)[\beta + \frac{1}{2}\beta(1-\beta)$$

$$+ \frac{1}{4}(1-\beta)^2\{\beta + (1-\beta)\frac{1}{2}\}]$$

$$\Pr(c_1c_2c_3e_4) = \frac{1}{16}(1-x)(1-\beta)^3$$

$$\vdots \qquad (12)$$

$$\Pr(e_1e_2e_3e_4) = \frac{1}{2}(1-x)[\beta + \frac{1}{2}\beta(1-\beta)$$

$$+ \frac{1}{4}(1-\beta)^2\{\beta + (1-\beta)\frac{1}{2}\}]$$

Armed with these equations, we now face the task of deciding which model provides the best account of our data. Table 14-1 presents observed frequencies for two identical experiments, one using sixty college students at Stanford University and the other sixty fourth-grade children from the Oakland city schools.[1] As indicated earlier, each subject was run on 18 paired associates, so that over a group of subjects we have information on $18 \times 60 = 1080$ test-trial sequences. The table gives the frequency with

---

[1] This study was conducted by Duncan Hansen of Stanford University.

which each sequence occurred in the two groups. In subsequent analyses, we assume that the items in the list are of equal difficulty and that all subjects in a group learn at the same rate; that is, we postulate that the values of the various parameters are the same for all subjects in the college group and for all subjects in the grade school group. Of course, this assumption is suspect, but for purposes of this paper it seems justified since it greatly simplifies subsequent analyses. For, with this assumption, the response sequence associated with any given stimulus item can be viewed as a sample of size one from a population of sequences all generated by the same underlying process. A discussion of the problems involved in treating individual data and group data is given in Suppes and Atkinson (1960).

TABLE 14-1. Observed frequencies for response sequences.

SEQUENCE CODE	T_1	T_2	T_3	T_4	COLLEGE GROUP	GRADE SCHOOL GROUP
1	c	c	c	c	633	474
2	c	c	c	e	22	51
3	c	c	e	c	19	39
4	c	c	e	e	28	38
5	c	e	c	c	16	30
6	c	e	c	e	19	27
7	c	e	e	c	23	20
8	c	e	e	e	54	71
9	e	c	c	c	43	40
10	e	c	c	e	6	15
11	e	c	e	c	11	24
12	e	c	e	e	10	33
13	e	e	c	c	26	23
14	e	e	c	e	11	19
15	e	e	e	c	14	15
16	e	e	e	e	145	161

In order to make predictions for the data displayed in Table 14-1 we need estimates of the parameters ϕ and a for the incremental model and x and β for the all-or-none model. There are many ways of making these estimates, but for the present problem a simple method is to select the pair of parameter values that minimizes the χ^2 function.[2] To illustrate the method, let $p_i(a, \phi)$ denote theoretical expressions for the four-response probabilities given in Equation 10, where the subscript i refers to code numbers assigned in Table 14-1. Further, let O_i ($i = 1$ to 16) denote the observed frequencies for one

---

[2] For a review of some of these statistical methods as they apply to learning models, see Chapter 2 in Suppes and Atkinson (1960).

of the groups in Table 14-1 and let $T = O_1 + O_2 + \ldots + O_{16}$. Then we define the function

$$\chi^2(a,\phi) = \sum_{i=1}^{16} \frac{[Tp_i(a, \phi) - O_i]^2}{Tp_i(a,\phi)} \tag{13}$$

and select our estimates of a and ϕ so that they jointly minimize the χ^2 function. Under the null hypothesis, this minimum χ^2 has the usual limiting distribution with 16–3 degrees of freedom. (If n parameters are estimated, then there are $16-n-1$ degrees of freedom.)

Using this method, we obtain parameter estimates for the incremental model with the following minimum χ^2 values:

	COLLEGE	GRADE SCHOOL
a	.383	.331
ϕ	.705	.636
minimum χ^2	256.3	192.7

Using the same minimum χ^2 method for the all-or-none model, we obtain the following parameter estimates:

	COLLEGE	GRADE SCHOOL
β	.291	.191
x	.409	.297
minimum χ^2	40.4	67.0

The foregoing parameter estimates generate the predictions presented in Table 14-2. For both the college and the grade school groups, the all-or-none model provides the closest correspondence between predicted and observed proportions on the four-response data. The superiority of the all-or-none model is also reflected in the obtained minimum χ^2s. For the college group, the χ^2 for the incremental model is more than six times that for the all-or-none model; whereas for the grade school group, the ratio is almost three to one in favor of the all-or-none model. Since all the χ^2s are based on the same number of degrees of freedom, it seems reasonable to conclude that the all-or-none model provides the best account of these data. Further, independent of any comparative analysis of the models, the correspondence between the all-or-none predictions and these data is reasonably good in terms of the degree of accuracy that psychologists have come to expect in research of this sort. See Atkinson and Estes (1963) for a discussion of this point.

268 RICHARD C. ATKINSON & ROBERT C. CALFEE

TABLE 14-2. Observed proportions and predictions for the incremental model and the all-or-none model.

SEQUENCE	COLLEGE			GRADE SCHOOL		
CODE		*Incremental*	*All-or-None*		*Incremental*	*All-or-None*
	Observed	*Predictions*	*Predictions*	*Observed*	*Predictions*	*Predictions*
1	.586	.476	.549	.439	.359	.426
2	.020	.035	.013	.047	.044	.023
3	.018	.060	.013	.036	.070	.023
4	.026	.004	.024	.035	.009	.034
5	.015	.045	.024	.028	.052	.034
6	.018	.020	.013	.025	.026	.023
7	.021	.020	.013	.019	.026	.023
8	.050	.044	.054	.066	.051	.061
9	.040	.066	.054	.037	.071	.061
10	.006	.018	.013	.014	.025	.023
11	.010	.018	.013	.022	.025	.023
12	.009	.027	.024	.031	.035	.034
13	.024	.025	.024	.021	.031	.034
14	.010	.020	.013	.018	.028	.023
15	.013	.020	.013	.014	.028	.023
16	.134	.102	.140	.149	.121	.129
χ^2		256.3	40.4		192.7	67.0

Finally, we should note that the parameter estimates for both the all-or-none model and the incremental model have the expected properties. For the all-or-none model, the estimate of x is larger for the college group than for the grade school group, reflecting the fact that more learning occurred for the former group on the study trials. Also, the parameter β characterizing the conditioning rate on test trials is larger for the college group, indicating that the postulated self-reinforcing event had more effect for the college students. Similarly, for the incremental model the estimates of both ϕ and a are greater for the college group than for the grade school group.

What conclusions can be drawn from our analysis of these two models? Should readers not familiar with psychology conclude that incremental models are clearly less satisfactory than all-or-none models and that subsequent theory construction should be along all-or-none lines of development? This might be one conclusion, but few psychologists inclined toward incremental theories of learning would be in agreement. They, of course, would want to see many more comparisons between the two models on a variety of experimental data. Further, they probably would argue that the incremental model presented here was too simple and that a more sophisticated interpretation of incremental theory would lead to much better results.

On this last point, psychologists favoring an all-or-none position would agree, but they, in turn, would point out that similar improvements easily could be made for the all-or-none model. Further, they would emphasize that both models estimated the same number of parameters and are of similar mathematical difficulty and that these facts are important when one evaluates the clear superiority of the all-or-none process.

It is not necessary to pursue such arguments to realize that a single comparison of this sort is unlikely to change anyone's theoretical disposition. Only as more evidence accumulates and more variations of each model are investigated will it become clear which approach is more parisimonious. Certainly since the time of Henri Poincaré we have known that no theory is correct in an absolute sense. Rather, some theories tend to be more useful than others in accomplishing the goals of the scientific enterprise if they (1) lead to natural and unambiguous interpretations of phenomena, (2) have a tractable logical structure, and (3) suggest new experimental dimensions. The success of the relativity theory was not due to the fact that the new concepts of space and time were in any sense more *true* than the old ones. For any of the phenomena that could be explained by the new theory also could be explained on the basis of absolute dimensions of space and time. But such explanations became extremely cumbersome and artificial when contrasted to the explanations offered by relativity theory.

If we accept the notion that a single comparison of the sort offered in this paper cannot be regarded as crucial in selecting between models, then what is the next step? As indicated earlier, one obvious requirement is to extend the application of the two models to many other types of experiments. As more experimental comparisons are made a better understanding of the properties of each model will be obtained which will give us a measure of their relative power. However, in addition to extending the range of application it also is important to take each experiment and, by inspection of the discrepancies between theory and observation, obtain some clues for modifications that will lead to a better model. This part of the scientific enterprise is extremely challenging. In effect the theorist, by scrutinizing unexpected perturbations in the data, attempts to come up with either a modification of the basic assumptions or a new interpretation of how the assumptions can be applied. We doubt if such revisions follow any clear or systematic pattern; more often than not the theorist tries many new schemes and then reports the one that seems most promising. From the viewpoint of understanding the scientific process, it is unfortunate that the trial and error stage between successive revisions of a model is not occasionally recorded. Looking at the end product tends to give the misleading impression that theory develops in a neat and orderly fashion.

In this next section, we shall try to give the reader some idea of the way the psychologist may use a set of experimental results to suggest changes in the theory. We could present examples for either the incremental or the all-

or-none model since both have natural extensions suggested by our data. However, it would be too lengthy to attempt both in this paper; consequently, we will examine only possible revisions of the all-or-none theory. We select this model because the modifications to be considered are tractable and will not introduce any new mathematical techniques. The modifications illustrate two types of revisions that can occur in a theory: one modification represents a reinterpretation of how the axioms can be applied and the other, a basic change in the axioms.

Inspection of the correspondence between predictions for the all-or-none model and our data indicates two striking discrepancies. First, the theory predicts that the probability of a correct response on T_1 followed by an incorrect response on T_2 is the same as the probability of an incorrect response on T_1 followed by a correct response on T_2; that is, $\Pr(c_1e_2) = \Pr(e_1c_2)$. However, the data clearly contradicts this prediction, as indicated below:

	COLLEGE	GRADE SCHOOL
$\Pr(c_1e_2)$	.104	.137
$\Pr(e_1c_2)$	.065	.104

These quantities are obtained directly from Table 14-2; that is, $\Pr(c_1e_2) = p_5 + p_6 + p_7 + p_8$ and $\Pr(e_1c_2) = p_9 + p_{10} + p_{11} + p_{12}$. For both groups $\Pr(c_1e_2)$ is larger than $\Pr(e_1c_2)$.

Another discrepancy between theory and data is with regard to the probability of a correct response on test trial n. The theory predicts that this quantity, averaged over items, should be a constant; that is, $\Pr(c_n) = x + (1 - x)\frac{1}{2}$. The appropriate statistics are given below.

	COLLEGE	GRADE SCHOOL
$\Pr(c_1)$	.754	.694
$\Pr(c_2)$	.715	.661
$\Pr(c_3)$	.719	.629
$\Pr(c_4)$	.727	.616

In both groups, there is a tendency for the probability of a correct response to decrease over test trials. Parenthetically, the incremental model makes the same predictions; that is, $\Pr(c_1e_2) = \Pr(e_2c_1)$ and $\Pr(c_n) =$ constant.

Both of these observations suggest the need for a process in the model that will produce an increase in the error rate over test trials. One way of doing this is to assume that the conditioning parameter associated with a correct response is different from that associated with an incorrect response. Specifically, we can assume that when an item is in state G on a test trial, then (1) if a correct response is made it becomes conditioned with probability μ and

(2) if an incorrect response is made it becomes conditioned with probability δ. The transition matrix given in equation 8 would now be rewritten as follows:

$$
\begin{array}{c}
& \underline{\underline{C}} \qquad\qquad \underline{\underline{G}} \qquad\qquad \underline{\underline{E}} \\
\begin{array}{c} \underline{\underline{C}} \\[1em] \underline{\underline{G}} \\[1em] \underline{\underline{E}} \end{array}
\left[
\begin{array}{ccc}
1 & 0 & 0 \\[1em]
\frac{1}{2}\mu & 1 - \frac{1}{2}(\mu + \delta) & \frac{1}{2}\delta \\[1em]
0 & 0 & 1
\end{array}
\right]
\end{array}
\qquad (14)
$$

At a qualitative level of analysis, this change provides for the discrepancies noted above. It can be shown that

$$
\Pr(c_1 e_2) = \frac{1}{4}(1 - \mu)(1 - x)
$$

$$(15)$$

$$
\Pr(e_1 c_2) = \frac{1}{4}(1 - \delta)(1 - x)
$$

which implies that $\Pr(c_1 e_2) > \Pr(e_1 c_2)$ when $\delta > \mu$. Similarly, it can be shown that the probability of a correct response on test trial n is

$$
\Pr(c_n) = x + \frac{(1 - x)}{2}[1 - \frac{1}{2}(\mu + \delta)]^{n-1}
$$

$$
+ \frac{(1 - x)\mu}{\mu + \delta}[1 - \{1 - \frac{1}{2}(\mu + \delta)\}^{n-1}] \qquad (16)
$$

When $\delta > \mu$ this equation describes a function decreasing over test trials that approaches $x + \dfrac{(1 - x)\mu}{(\mu + \delta)}$ in the limit.

What psychological rationale can be offered for postulating that $\delta > \mu$? There are several, but we shall mention one that assumes differences in learning rates for various paired-associate items. Let us suppose that some stimulus-response connections are easier to learn than others; for instance, for some subjects the Greek letter ω may be easier to associate with response 1 than 2. If response 2 is assigned as the to-be-learned response, then this item should be learned more slowly and consequently would have a higher probability than other items of being in state $\underline{\underline{G}}$ after two study trials. If the item still is in state $\underline{\underline{G}}$ after the study trials then, since response 1 is the more compatible response, the item will be more likely to become conditioned to an error response over the series of test trials. In essence, the assumption is that stimulus items not conditioned to a correct response after a series of study trials will tend to favor association with an error response on test trials.

The proposed modification that assumes differential conditioning parameters may be regarded as a revision of the basic axioms of the model. The next modification we offer simply requires a reinterpretation of how the model might be applied. Originally, it was assumed that after a series of study trials each stimulus item was either in state $\underline{\underline{C}}$ (with probability x) or state $\underline{\underline{G}}$ (with probability $1 - x$). A natural extension of these ideas is to permit the possibility that the item also may be in state $\underline{\underline{E}}$ at the end of a study trial. That is, it seems reasonable to assume that at the start of T_1 there is a probability x' that the item will be in state $\underline{\underline{C}}$, a probability y' that the item will be in state $\underline{\underline{E}}$, and a probability $1 - x' - y'$ that it will still be in state $\underline{\underline{G}}$.

Introducing these two modifications yields a model that has four parameters to be estimated from the data (namely, μ, δ, x', and y') as compared with two in the original all-or-none model. The question is whether the addition of two parameters yields a substantial improvement in the fit of the model.

The four parameters were estimated separately for each set of data by selecting that parameter vector (μ, δ, x', y') that minimized χ^2. The obtained estimates were as follows.

	COLLEGE	GRADE SCHOOL
μ	.207	.041
δ	.289	.270
x'	.478	.379
y'	0	0

The predictions for the revised model based on the above estimates are given in Table 14-3. The table also presents the associated minimum χ^2s. It is evident, by comparing these predictions and χ^2 values with those given in Table 14-2, that the revised model does a better job. The improvement is not very large for the college data but is dramatic in the case of the grade school data.[3] However, it is evident that the improvement in prediction is due entirely to but one of the two modifications. The change that permitted an item to be in state $\underline{\underline{E}}$ at the end of a study trial did not yield an improvement in prediction, because in both the college and the grade school groups the estimated value of y' was 0. Thus, the revision that postulated differential conditioning parameters for correct and incorrect responses accounts entirely for the improvement in the fit of the modified all-or-none model.

---

[3] Statistical tests to evaluate these comparisons are available and are discussed in reference to learning models by Suppes and Atkinson (1960).

TABLE 14-3. Observed proportions and predictions for the revised version of the all-or-none model.

SEQUENCE	COLLEGE		GRADE SCHOOL	
CODE	Observed	Predicted	Observed	Predicted
1	.586	.578	.439	.435
2	.020	.016	.047	.034
3	.018	.015	.036	.026
4	.026	.026	.035	.045
5	.015	.022	.028	.028
6	.018	.015	.025	.026
7	.021	.013	.019	.020
8	.050	.054	.066	.075
9	.040	.041	.037	.033
10	.006	.015	.014	.026
11	.010	.013	.022	.020
12	.009	.024	.031	.035
13	.024	.020	.021	.022
14	.010	.013	.018	.020
15	.013	.012	.014	.015
16	.134	.123	.149	.141
χ^2	30.2		21.7	

Without pursuing this example further, we hope that the reader has a fairly clear picture of our view of the theoretical enterprise in psychology. However, there is one last point. If we scan the χ^2s given in this paper and select the one associated with the best fit (the modified all-or-none model applied to the grade school data), a value of 21.7 is obtained with 11 degrees of freedom. This value of χ^2 is significant at the .05 level, and therefore on the basis of statistical considerations we would reject the model. The sensible retort to this statement is the point we have tried to emphasize throughout the paper. We always assume that any model can be rejected on statistical grounds if enough observations are made. The goal is not to reject or accept a given model at some predetermined level of significance, but rather to make comparisons among models and ask how well a model performs relative to other models. Simply stated, a model will not be rejected on purely statistical grounds, but will be rejected only when there are other models that consistently do a better job of prediction.

In conclusion, we view the use of mathematical models as virtually synonymous with the construction of a quantitative theory of behavior. From a mathematical standpoint it is logically possible to have a theory of behavior that leads only to qualitative predictions. However, it is difficult to find in the history of science, let alone in the history of psychology, theories of this sort that have had sustained empirical significance. From the systematic standpoint, a theory or model based only on qualitative distinctions leads to a small number of testable predictions. Aristotle's physics and Lewin's topological field theory (1936) are good examples. The absence of precise systematization leads usually to pseudo-derivations from the theory. By pseudo-derivation we mean the derivation of prediction that requires many additional assumptions that are not part of the original theory. Further, as the set of phenomena that we study expands in complexity so also does the reasoning necessary for the design of experiments and the formulation of hypotheses. Ordinary logic becomes inadequate and the elaboration of the theory requires the powerful tool of mathematical analysis.

Finally, we remark that we have avoided a discussion of the general nature of models and theories. The words "model" and "mathematical model" are used in a variety of related senses by behavioral scientists and philosophers. Often the most reasonable interpretation is that the model is the set of mathematically formulated postulates that express in precise form the intuitive notions of the relevant psychological theory. Despite the dominance of this usage in the literature of the behaviorial sciences, we prefer to use the more precise concept of model that has been adopted by mathematical logicians. Roughly speaking, a model is an abstract object that satisfies a theory. A theory given in axiomatic form can, if one chooses, be identified with its set of axioms. It is not to the point to enter into technical details here. What is important in our opinion is that models have a role to play whenever theory is constructed. From our standpoint, if a theory has systematic content and is not simply a vague collection of heuristic ideas, then there exist models that satisfy the theory, and it is up to the experimenter to determine whether these models provide an adequate analysis of behavioral phenomena. We believe that the role of mathematical models in psychology is not really separate from the role of systematic theorizing.

REFERENCES

ANDERSON, H. H. An analysis of sequential dependencies. In R. R. Bush and W. K. Estes (Eds.), *Studies in mathematical learning theory*. Stanford, Calif.: Stanford Univ. Press, 1959. Pp. 248-264.

ANDERSON, H. H. Effect of first-order conditional probability in a two choice learning situation. *J. exp. Psychol.*, 1960, **59**, 71-93.

ATKINSON, R. C. & ESTES, W. K. *Stimulus sampling theory*. In R. D. Luce, R. R. Bush, and E. Galanter (Eds.), *Handbook of mathematical psychology*. Vol. 2. New York: Wiley, 1963. Pp. 121-268.

BOWER, G. H. Applications of a model to paired-associate learning. *Psychometrika*, 1961, **26**, 255-280.

BOWER, G. H. A model for response and training variables in paired-associate learning. *Psychol. Rev.,* 1962, **69**, 34-53.

BUSH, R. R. A survey of mathematical learning theory. In R. Duncan Luce (Ed.), *Developments in mathematical psychology.* Glencoe, Ill.: Free Press, 1960.

BUSH, R. R., & MOSTELLER, F. A mathematical model for simple learning. *Psychol. Rev.,* 1951, **58**, 313-323.

BUSH, R. R., & MOSTELLER, F. *Stochastic models for learning.* New York: Wiley, 1955.

ESTES, W. K. Toward a statistical theory of learning. *Psychol. Rev.,* 1950, **57**, 94-107.

ESTES, W. K. The statistical approach to learning theory. In S. Koch (Ed.), *Psychology: a study of a science.* Vol. 2. New York: McGraw-Hill, 1959. Pp. 380-491.

ESTES, W. K. Learning theory and the new mental chemistry. *Psychol. Rev.,* 1960, **67**, 207-223.

ESTES, W. K. New developments in statistical behavior theory: differential tests of axioms for associative learning. *Psychometrika,* 1961, **26**, 73-84.

ESTES, W. K. Learning theory. *Annu. Rev. Psychol.,* 1962, **13**, 107-144.

GUTHRIE, E. R. *The psychology of learning.* New York: Harper, 1935.

HILGARD, E. R. *Theories of Learning.* (Rev. ed.). New York: Appleton-Century-Crofts, 1956.

HULL, C. L. *Principles of behavior: an introduction to behavior theory.* New York: Appleton-Century-Crofts, 1943.

JONES, J. E. All-or-none versus incremental learning. *Psychol. Rev.,* 1962, **69**, 156-160.

LABERGE, D. A model with neutral elements. In R. R. Bush and W. K. Estes (Eds.), *Studies in mathematical learning theory.* Stanford, Calif.: Stanford Univ. Press, 1959. Pp. 53-64.

LEWIN, K. *Principles of topological psychology.* New York: McGraw-Hill, 1936.

LOGAN, F. A. The Hull-Spence approach. In S. Koch (Ed.), *Psychology: a study of a science.* Vol. 2. New York: McGraw-Hill, 1959. Pp. 293-358.

LUCE, R. D. *Individual choice behavior: a theoretical analysis.* New York: Wiley, 1959.

RESTLE, F. A survey and classification of learning models. In R. R. Bush and W. K. Estes (Eds.), *Studies in mathematical learning theory.* Stanford, Calif.: Stanford Univ. Press, 1959, 415-428.

RESTLE, F. Sources of difficulty in learning paired associates. In R. C. Atkinson (Ed.), *Studies in mathematical psychology.* Stanford, Calif.: Stanford Univ. Press, 1964. Pp. 116-172.

SEWARD, J. P. Reinforcement and expectancy: Two theories in search of a controversy. *Psychol. Rev.,* 1956, **63**, 105-113.

SPENCE, K. W. *Behavior theory and conditioning.* New Haven: Yale Univ. Press, 1956.

SUPPES, P., & ATKINSON, R. C. *Markov learning models for multiperson interactions.* Stanford, Calif.: Stanford Univ. Press, 1960.

SUPPES, P., & GINSBERG, R. A fundamental property of all-or-none models. *Psychol. Rev.,* 1963, **70**, 139-161.

15 MARY HENLE

ON GESTALT PSYCHOLOGY

THIS CHAPTER WILL BE concerned with some problems of the present status and uses of Gestalt theory. Although the relations of Gestalt psychology to other approaches cannot be dealt with within the limits of this discussion, one aspect of this problem will be considered. The practice of translating the concepts of one theory into those of another seems to be gaining in popularity. Some recent attempts to translate Gestalt conceptions in this way will be examined. The relation of Kurt Lewin's topological and vector psychology to Gestalt psychology will also be considered in part. Next, the attempt will be made to correct certain misunderstandings of Gestalt theory. The chapter will conclude with the writer's assessment of the present status of this approach and of some of the tasks ahead.

ATTEMPTS TO TRANSLATE GESTALT CONCEPTS INTO THE TERMS OF OTHER THEORIES

Implicit in the attempt to translate the concepts of one approach into those of another is the assumption that no essential differences exist between them. The issues become ones of terminology only. If such attempts are successful, they would have far-reaching consequences for theoretical controversy in psychology. An examination of such translations is thus important for an evaluation of the status of each approach.

Since, traditionally, controversy in many problem areas has been between Gestalt theory and the S-R psychologies, emphasis in the present discussion will be on efforts to translate the former into terms of the latter.

Hull (1952, p. 267) sees a correspondence between his concept of reaction potential and Lewin's concepts of valence and field force. In a more recent analysis, Campbell (1963)[1] likewise suggests:

Life space functions as the explanatory and predictive equivalent of D, K, and $_sH_R$. D and tension system are easily equated. . . . The newly prominent

---

[1] I choose Prof. Campbell's discussion for detailed analysis because of its clarity and explicitness.

concept K . . . is in striking convergence with Lewin's concept of valence. . . . Hull's $_sE_R$ and Lewin's force vector converge, both being products of tensions, valences, and mediational knowledge. The directional feature of the force vector is equivalent to the specification of the response involved, the length of the vector to the strength of the response tendency. To complete the equivalences, the structured pathways to the goal region are here interpreted as analogues of $_sH_R$, which for this purpose is translated as knowledge of means (with K as knowledge of ends), or as familiarity with the responses to make if you want to make them (p. 119).

Examining these suggested correspondences more closely, we may agree that it is not hard to find a rough equivalence between Hull's D and Lewin's tension system. It must be noted, however, that the former concept lacks the specific properties that Lewin (1938, p. 98) ascribed to tension: the tendency of the tension of a system to become equal to that of surrounding systems and the existence of forces at the boundary of a system in tension. That these are important properties is indicated by the fact that from them Lewin derives the tendency to resumption of interrupted tasks, substitute value in the case of communicating tension systems, diffuse resolution of tension in time, and others—all of which he describes as more or less proved (1938, pp. 99-100). Furthermore, given these properties, "the tension in a system S has to be determined always relative to the tension of its neighboring systems" (p. 98). No such relational determination seems to be necessary in the case of the drives of Hull's theory.

Incentive or K in Hull's view is, as Campbell points out, similar to Lewin's concept of valence. But Campbell himself (1963) suggests an interesting difference:

> The K of Hullian theory seems more economical in that in the performance formula, it is independent of contemporaneous drive, whereas Lewinian valence is a part function of the momentary state of the tension system (p. 119).

Whatever the respective merits of the two concepts in this regard—and these, it seems to me, need to be decided by reference to the facts, not primarily by standards of parsimony—it would appear that they play different roles in the two theories and thus cannot be regarded as equivalent.

With regard to a possible convergence between $_sE_R$ and psychological force, Köhler (1959) has already pointed out that Hull's main concepts "were obviously meant to be scalars" (p. 733), not vectors; that is, they possess magnitude but not direction. Habit strength and thus reaction potential are S-R conjunctions, tendencies for a given stimulus to evoke a given response (e.g., Hull, 1951, p. 20). "It is the *connection* of the stimuli to the responses which is new and results from the reinforcement" (Hull, 1951), p. 19).[2] Thus $_sE_R$ lacks a directional aspect; it does not

---

[2] If $_sH_R$ and $_sE_R$, viewed as connections or associations, lack the properties of vectors, they also lack those of tension systems. Cf. Lewin, 1938, p. 99.

refer to an incentive or valent region in the life space. To specify the "responses involved" is not to introduce such a reference, for by response Hull clearly means muscular, glandular, or electrical response (1943, p. 406). That response refers to movement rather than being a relation to an object is seen, for example, in Hull's characterization as defeatist the attitude that "what is called goal or purposive behavior is of such a nature, that it cannot be derived from any conceivable set of postulates involving mere stimuli and mere movement" (1943, p. 26). Hull defines "strictly purposive behavior" as "an organism's cognition of its own acts" (1952, p. 152). "We often know what we are about to do before we perform an act, sometimes long before." Again the emphasis on response is apparent. Even the concept of fractional antedating goal reactions (r_G) which, Hull considers, "constitutes on the part of the organism a molar foresight or foreknowledge of the not-here and the not-now" (1952, p. 151) refers to anticipatory *responses,* not to incentive objects, such reactions as "sniffing, salivating, smacking the lips and swallowing" (Brown, 1961, p. 177) in case food is the goal object.

Finally, to equate habit strength to Lewin's "structured pathways to the goal region" seems to me either to extend the meaning of $_sH_R$ beyond that intended by Hull, or else to impoverish the conception of the cognitive structure of the psychological environment. Such an equation would require the specific demonstration that $_sH_R$ can account for these Lewinian concepts: the structuring of the life space into regions that are qualitatively different from one another, separated by boundaries (which themselves possess particular properties), some connected with others; the relative structuredness or unstructuredness of the regions; the position of the person inside or outside a region and the changes in his position, his space of free movement, and so on. Since no such demonstration has been provided, the statement must be regarded as unproved.

A single example will be used to suggest that specific comparison would yield important differences between the treatment of the same problem by Hull and Lewin. In his discussion of behavior in space, Hull (1952, Ch. 8) considers adience and abience, approach and withdrawal in relation to objects. Implicit in the discussion is a conception of direction toward and direction away from, a conception that appears to coincide with direction in physical space. Lewin carefully distinguishes between psychological and physical directions (1938, pp. 21-22); for example, he defines direction toward in terms of distinguished path (p. 26), a concept lacking in Hull. The distinguished path, Lewin points out, is probably the one for which the positive valence of the means is maximal (p. 27). Hull offers as a theorem (1952, Theorem 61, p. 227) that "Adience in free space, within the limits of the oscillation function ($_sO_R$) will tend to a straight line toward the adient object." Lewin, employing hodological rather than Euclidean space, points out that "since topology does not know differences of size, one cannot use shortness as a general principle" for the selection of a path that will determine direction (1938, p. 25). A continuation of this analysis would only serve to multiply differences.

Important as are the differences between specific concepts of Hull and Lewin, the real divergences between the two can be seen only if one views these concepts as parts of whole bodies of theory. Again, only a few points of comparison are needed since they show the fruitlessness of detailed analysis of this kind. Lewin employs vectorial concepts, following the pattern of field physics, which, Köhler points out (1959, p. 733), played no decisive part in Hull's theorizing.[3] Hull's is essentially a learning theory; he is concerned with the conditions under which S-R connections are reinforced and particular responses evoked. His whole set of postulates may be regarded as an attempt to anchor the pivotal concept of effective reaction potential to observable antecedent and consequent conditions (1943, p. 342). Lewin, on the other hand, is primarily concerned with the interaction of contemporaneous events in the life space. Although he by no means regards experience as unimportant (cf. Lewin, 1935, p. 269), he has little to say about habit-formation. Lewin is much concerned with the cognitive structure of the psychological environment, while Hull leaves undetermined the question of whether the capacity of human beings "of speech, symbolic behavior, with its accompanying advantages to the higher mental processes" (1952, p. 4) introduces any primary behavioral laws. "What the philosophers have called *cognition*" is made a matter of fractional antedating goal reactions (1952, p. 150), and a subjective aspect or equivalent of sE_R is assumed (p. 342). However, Hull shows no interest in "subjective" experience. As Heider points out (1959): "In contrast to Lewin's concern with the life space, psychology today often considers input and output as the primary object of study" (p. 5).

We conclude from this discussion that the theoretical convergence of Hull and Lewin has not been demonstrated.

Hull (1943, pp. 48 f.; 1951, p. 93) believes that his concept of afferent neural interaction (later afferent stimulus interaction) is substantially equivalent to a principle employed by Gestalt psychologists, most explicitly by Köhler. This postulate states in part that "all afferent impulses (ss) active

---

3 Hull refers to "behavioral vectors" in connection with his prediction of the behavior of a "naïve organism placed midway between two duplicate abient objects in free space" (1952, Theorem 82, p. 243), and adds: "It is tempting to assume the physical vector analogy in this situation, but such an assumption is extremely risky unless supported by convincing empirical evidence. However striking the analogy, it must never be forgotten that *molar behavior theory is not molar physics*." However, no vectorial concepts have been introduced; Hull relies here, as elsewhere, on the concept of reaction potential.

In another place (1952, p. 269) he states that the theory of adient and abient behavior "involves examples of *bona fide* field theory," but he adds that it differs from physical field theories "in most respects."

at any given instant, mutually interact converting each other into $\check{s}$s which differ qualitatively from the original ss . . ." (1952, p. 11). The result of the interaction is a generalization fall from $_{\check{s}}E_R$ to $_{\check{s}}E_R$, and thus a difference in strength of reaction potential. The principle of Köhler's which Hull sees as comparable is quoted as follows (from Köhler, 1940, p. 55): ". . . a theory of perception must be a *field theory*. By this we mean that the neural functions and processes with which the perceptual facts are associated in each case are located in a continuous medium; and that the events in one part of this medium influence the events in other regions in a way that depends directly on the properties of both in their relation to each other."

Two points will suffice to call into question the supposed equivalence of the two concepts. First, the only property of the interacting events that Hull considers relevant is the quantitative difference between the reaction potentials in question; and the only effect of the interaction is a generalization fall, a diminution of reaction potential. Köhler applies his principle to the mutual attraction of objects presented simultaneously or successively in several sensory departments, to stroboscopic movement, perceptual organization which depends on similarity, and the like. Second, Hull's principle, unlike Köhler's, views interaction as occurring piecemeal. Thus the afferent impulses s_1 and s_2 are simply regarded as transformed into $\check{s}_1$ and $\check{s}_2$, and from that point on they are treated additively. Afferent stimulus interaction alters the quantitative value of the elements, which are then summated. (For an example, cf. Hull, 1943, p. 218.)

Burwen and Campbell (1957) undertook a study of the generality of attitudes toward authority figures, starting from the hypothesis that "attitudes towards parental authority originating in the family situation . . . generalize and manifest themselves as attitudes toward superiors in later social situations" (p. 24). Although the results were negative, the authors regard their original predictions as "consistent with the principle of stimulus generalization in conditioning theory" as well as with Gestalt principles of "generalization based upon configurational similarity from one authority situation to another" (p. 30) and also with expectations based on psychoanalytic theory. Of interest for present purposes is the implied equivalence between stimulus generalization of S-R theory and configurational similarity.

Stimulus generalization, for Hull (1952, p. 64) and others, "is based on a continuous series of potential stimuli, . . . a stimulus continuum," for example, a series of pitches, colors, light intensities, and so on. While Gestalt psychologists have not gone far in the investigation of configurational similarity, it is clear that their conception is not limited to quantitative differences along a stimulus continuum. Thus Goldmeier (1937) describes whole properties, retention of which preserves figural similarity despite other changes in a form; and he distinguishes functions of different importance for the preservation of similarity. The difference is not merely one of a "semantic barrier" (Campbell, 1963), of stating the same problem in S-R or cognitive terms, but one of conceptions of similarity. Mere translation would consist in the shift from wave lengths to colors or from frequencies of vibrations to tones (actually, Hull uses both terminologies).[4]

In like manner, other instances of supposed similarities between central concepts of S-R or associationist psychologies and Gestalt psychology could be analyzed; for example: Hull's (1952) claim of a correspondence between requiredness and subjective aspects of $_sE_R$ (p. 342); his assertion that the restructuring of the field, as used by Lewin, "corresponds in effect to the results of experimental extinction upon the preferred members of the spatial habit-family hierarchy" (p. 267); Campbell's "translation" of perception of causality as conditioned response (1963); the relating of Thorndike's concept of belongingness to Gestalt concepts (cf. Hilgard, 1956, p. 28; also Mowrer, 1950, pp. 215-216). In all these cases, we would find that the claimed similarities overlook essential differences. It has been pointed out elsewhere that "reconciliations can be reached in psychology only by focusing on the existing differences, examining them, and carrying on research to settle issues" (Henle, 1957, p. 303). Until the issues have been resolved, little seems to be gained by translating the concepts of Gestalt psychology into those of other approaches.

Of course, this is not to say that no progress has been made in settling the issues. Thus Prentice (1959) points out:

> The most impressive example of the weight of the experimental evidence that supports the gestalt conception in perception is the cessation of controversy about matters of theory in the study of form and grouping (p. 447).

Boring, likewise, sees "a radical change in emphasis" in the psychology of perceived form, "from the discussion of patterns of elements to the formulation of the dynamic structure of perceptual fields," a change he considers to have been "wrought entirely by Gestalt psychology" (1942, p. 256). As another example, Asch (1960) has recently investigated certain problems of the formation of associations from the point of view of Gestalt psychology. His approach led him to break out of the paradigm of the association experiment. The result was not a reconciliation with association theory, but a new body of data (and problems) that any theory of the formation of associations must henceforth take into account. The point

---

[4] Incidentally, it is hard to see specifically how the authors' predictions are consistent with either conception of similarity. Thus, attitude toward father and attitude toward boss are not points on a stimulus continuum; for what are the stimuli? Nor has any attempt been made to state whole qualities or functional relations which the two attitudes share; to say that both are concerned with authority does not go beyond the given and is certainly no theory of similarity.

in scientific investigation is not to reconcile divergent points of view, but to contribute to the clarification of problems.

Nor is the present analysis intended to deny similarities between concepts developed by Gestalt psychologists and those of psychologists of other orientations. Relevant comparisons could indeed be made.[5] It must be remembered, however, that the comparison of bodies of thought is a Gestalt problem. A given concept plays its role in a system of ideas, and both its function and its content may be changed by abstracting it from its context. Lewin (1938) points out: "Laws and definitions are a network of statements which only as a whole can be viewed as right or wrong" (p. 16). This circumstance does not mean that comparisons are impossible, but that they must be made with care.

HAS LEWIN DEVELOPED A GESTALT PSYCHOLOGY OF PERSONALITY?

A number of recent writers (Cartwright, 1959; Deutsch, 1954; Heider, 1959; Henle, 1957) have applied the term "metatheory" to some of Lewin's work. Heider derives Lewin's "principle of the autonomy of psychological concepts" (1959, p. 3) from his metatheory; and Deutsch (1954, pp. 182 ff.) characterizes as metatheoretical also his emphasis on the total situation, on systematic rather than historical concepts of causation, his dynamic approach, and other aspects. This part of Lewin's work is distinguished from his efforts to develop a "specifically psychological theory" (p. 189). In this category Deutsch includes such concepts as life space, tension, force, valence, and so on.

It is the hypothesis of the present writer that the latter concepts, too, are mainly metatheoretical. If we compare Lewin's account of personality with most others, the most striking difference is his apparent lack of interest in the more permanent aspects of the personality. His examples are of the following type: a man has lost his job and finds his possibilities of ac-

---

[5] In view of Professor Welch's charge (1948, p. 175) that "At times it would seem that some Gestalt psychologists are determined to deny similarities between their school and any other," a couple of rather astonishing relationships will be indicated. Although Gestalt psychology is usually regarded as a cognitive approach, there is nothing in it that is incompatible with the assumption of unconscious processes made by most personality psychologists. (The specific nature of these assumptions is another matter, one that would require detailed examination.) Koffka (1935, p. 51) points to forces that determine behavior but are outside of awareness as one line of evidence that "the psychological field cannot be identical with the behavioural environment." Likewise Köhler (1938, Ch. 4) describes experiences that refer to transphenomenal realities.

As another example, I have the impression that specific analysis would show important similarities (as well as certain differences) between the Gestalt principle of isomorphism and Jung's principle of synchronicity (1955).

tion much changed; a child must do an unpleasant task or be punished; a baby tries to reach a rattle a little distance away; a person wants to complete a task he has undertaken. There is very little interest in the more permanent motives underlying such momentary actions. Conflict is discussed, for example, in the situations of reward and punishment, or in the choice between two activities, but not in relation to unaccepted needs or excessive standards; level of aspiration is discussed apart from the Achievement of the individual; and the child's efforts to sit on a chair or to retrieve a toy are unrelated, say, to effectance motivation. For many purposes, Lewin represents the individual as an undifferentiated region within the life space. If he indicates differentiations within the person, for example, a system under tension, this is usually for the sake of the momentary example rather than to describe the properties of the particular individual. Freud, by contrast, wrestled with such problems as the nature of the fundamental motives underlying behavior, the specific satisfactions and frustrations encountered at various stages of development, the fears and major conflicts that typically confront an individual, the specific dynamic bases of symptoms.

How are we to understand this curious contrast? More specifically, how can Lewin's strange neglect of the content of the personality be understood? It seems to me that Lewin was not, on the whole, attempting to construct a theory of personality—that his title, *A Dynamic Theory of Personality,* is a misnomer; but that he was engaged mainly in developing a metatheory, in setting forth the formal characteristics of a theory of motivation.

As a single example, we may consider the conception of force in Lewinian theory. Lewin was not concerned with enumerating the principal motives that drive and direct behavior, as were such writers as Freud, McDougall, Murray, and others. Rather, he attempted to describe the properties of force that are presupposed by *any* theory of motivation based on this concept. Force possesses the property of direction, which cannot be determined in topology, the mathematics Lewin used at first. Thus he was led to develop the concepts of hodological space (Lewin, 1938). Within this framework, direction is defined. Distance becomes important not only for the determination of strength of forces, but also for the definition of "direction away from"; thus difference of distance has to be given a meaning in hodological geometry. Likewise, many other problems in the conceptualization of force were worked out. The important point is that these solutions are relevant to any theory that is concerned with the content of motivation.

Since the distinction between theory and metatheory is, in practice, not clear, this view of Lewin must remain a hypothesis in the absence of specific test. A test would consist in attempting to fit various theories of personality to Lewin's concepts. That such tests would yield at least some positive results is suggested by the numerous parallels that have been pointed out between Lewin's concepts and those of writers who would, strictly speaking, be called theorists of personality.[6] Thus Heider (1960) remarks:

> One is struck by the similarities between psychoanalysis and Lewin's theory. Lewin uses the concept of tension in his person model much as the concept of energy is used in psychoanalysis. Dr. Rapaport says about energy that it is "a scalar, a directionless entity and thus displaceable." The same could be said about tension. . . . The difference between the two theories consists mainly in that Freud talks about instinctual drives while Lewin talks about quasi-needs. . . . There are also similarities between the concept "object of an instinct" and Lewin's concept of "region with valence" . . . (pp. 253-254).

Again, Deutsch characterizes Lewin's theoretical approach as a motivational or dynamic psychology, like Freud's or McDougall's (1954, p. 188). Lewin himself (1938) prefaces his discussion of the *Conceptual Representation and the Measurement of Psychological Forces* with the remark: "This monograph contains very little psychological theory which is not accepted by most psychologists and psychological schools" (p. 18). These parallels, it is suggested, are largely correspondences between Lewin's metatheory and various theoretical accounts of personality and motivation. Lewin describes (1938) as gratifying "the finding that the various schools of psychology show a surprisingly high degree of agreement if one forgets differences in terminology and tries to represent nothing else than the interrelation of facts: in other words, tries to use a mathematical language" (pp. 3-4). But is not this the level of metatheory?

The above analysis of the proposed convergence between Hull and Lewin can now be seen as a demonstration that the theory of the former does not correspond to the metatheory of the latter.[7]

It must now be added that it would be an error to regard Lewin as only a metatheorist. Theory about theory cannot be tested experimentally, only theory; and Lewin was extraordinarily resourceful in opening up the field of human motivation to experimental study. Some of the experimental work tests hypotheses derived from theoretical propositions of such a high order of generality that they, like the metatheory, might fit a number of diverse theories of personality (for example, statements about consequences of unresolved need tension), while others are more specifically Lewinian theory (for example, statements about level of aspiration).

In any case, since Lewin was so largely concerned with developing a

---

[6] Or prototheorists, to borrow a term from Bruner (1956).

[7] Cf. Henle (1957, pp. 298-299) for a discussion of two other attempts to reconcile the ideas of Freud and Lewin.

metatheory,[8] it is here suggested that he has not developed a Gestalt theory of personality.[9] This task remains for the future.

SOME PERSISTENT MISUNDERSTANDINGS OF GESTALT PSYCHOLOGY

This section will deal briefly with certain misunderstandings of Gestalt psychology, chosen for their importance as well as their longevity.

Nativism Boring (1942, p. 33) remarks that "it would seem that the Gestalt psychologists have a good chance of being the modern nativists." [10] Tolman, too, contrasts his view of "acquired sign-gestalten" with a view he attributes to Gestalt psychology, of "innately ready, pure perceptual ge-stalten" (1959, p. 95). Allport (1955, p. 139) speaks of the "nativistically-oriented ideas of gestalt." [11]

That Gestalt psychology is not a nativistic theory was already indicated by Koffka in the 1920s (1928, e.g. p. 80). More recently, the matter has been made altogether clear by Köhler (1950) who has pointed to processes that are neither inherited nor learned, natural processes that do not depend upon the chromosomic equipment of the organism—thus are not products of evolution—nor upon the particular life experience of any individual. These considerations, which he derives from the principle of invariance in evolution, apply to concepts concerned with action, as contrasted with constraints which develop in the course of evolution.

The cortical action underlying perception or other psychological processes is modified, of course, by constraints, the inherited histological structures of the nervous system. "But, *qua* action, it can never be understood

---

[8] It is clear that it is no criticism of Lewin to call him a metatheorist. It is no easier, and no less important, a task to seek clarity about the kind of theory needed than to attempt to develop a theory of personality.

[9] The question of whether there would have been specific theoretical disagreements between Lewin and other Gestalt psychologists can unfortunately not be answered. Köhler (1959, p. 733) prefaces a discussion of motivation with the remark: "I do not know up to what point Lewin would have accepted what I am now going to say."

[10] Boring sees nativism as turning into phenomenology, and apparently regards phenomenology as opposed to explanation and perhaps also as anti-analytical (1942, pp. 32-33). That phenomenological observation is regarded by Gestalt psychologists as only a starting point for scientific investigation is clear not only from their theoretical writings but also from their research reports. The issue of analysis—the opposition of Gestalt psychologists to a particular kind of analysis, but not to analysis as such—has recently been discussed again by Prentice (1959, pp. 432-433) and need not be considered here.

[11] Not all authors make the error of regarding Gestalt psychology as a nativistic theory. Thus Hilgard (1956, p. 229 n.) points out that Koffka's anti-empiricism "did not make him a nativist." Hochberg (1957, p. 74) also comments: "The Gestalt theorists were *not* nativists in the traditional sense."

only in such terms. For all action is also a matter of processes which evolution has not affected" (Köhler, 1950, p. 293), processes which are independent of the chromosomes of the species, forms of action which the organism shares with all of nature. Thus it is incorrect to speak of "innately ready, pure perceptual gestalten." While such processes are not learned, they are not inherited either. The same argument applies, of course, to thinking, motivation, and all other psychological processes.

The Role of Past Experience   Partly because of the misunderstanding about nativism, but mainly because of its explicitly anti-empiristic position, Gestalt psychology has been viewed as underestimating the influence of past experience on contemporary psychological processes. Prentice (1959) finds that "Gestalt theory suffers from a kind of confusion engendered by its interest in the phenomena of learning and memory on the one hand and its antiempiristic bias on the other" (p. 454). Campbell (1963) refers to the neglect of past experience and sees "classical gestalt psychology" as focused on "pure perceptual problems . . . uncontaminated by filtration through the residues of past experience" (p. 133).

Why this view persists is hard to understand in the light of discussions by Köhler (e.g., 1947, especially Ch. 5) and Koffka (1935) which make it clear that their criticisms are directed against a particular use of past experience on perceptual and other psychological events. Koffka (1935, p. 639 n.) states that "an anti-empiristic attitude does not mean the denial of the enormous value of experience. Not *that* it makes use of experience causes our objection to empiricism, but *how* it makes use of it." Specifically, Gestalt psychologists have objected to the use of empiristic hypotheses to bolster up the constancy hypothesis (cf. also Hochberg, 1957, p. 74). They have objected to the position that previous experience, out of nothing, itself produces organized precepts and cognitions. This is an issue that Köhler and Wallach have reintroduced in connection with their work on figural aftereffects (1944, p. 316). They conclude: "It seems no longer possible to interpret the existence of visual things, figures, or other particular entities in visual fields as a result of learning processes." They specifically distinguish this issue from that of the influence of familiar figures on the perception of other patterns.

It is true that Gestalt psychology (like other psychologies) has not as yet carried very far the investigation of this second problem, the ways in which previous (organized) experiences influence a present organization. Still, some beginnings exist, for example, the investigation of Krolik (1934), along with some theoretical discussions (e.g., Wallach, 1949).

The same problem has arisen in the psychology of thinking, where the concern of Gestalt psychologists has again been with *how* previous experience influences the thinking process, not *that* it does so. In Wertheimer's words (1959):

In short, the role of past experience is of high importance, but what matters is *what* one has gained from experience—blind, understood connections, or insight into structural inner relatedness. What matters is how and what one recalls, how one applies what is recalled, whether blindly, in a piecemeal way, or in accordance with the structural requirements of the situation (p. 62).

The Influence of Motivation and Attitudes on Perception Although Wertheimer (1938) included objective set (along with past experience) among the factors of organization, the influence of motivational processes on perception has been considered to be troublesome to Gestalt theory.

Prentice (1959, p. 449) suggests, in connection with such "nonstimulus influences" that certain empirical issues need to be settled before the reported effects can be considered evidence against Gestalt theory, specifically the question of whether the reported changes are truly perceptual rather than changes in subjects' responses. He also points to the importance for perceptual theory of the fact that these effects have almost always been demonstrated under conditions of reduced stimulation. He concludes that "to the extent that these influences stem from 'needs,' 'attitudes,' 'attention,' and the like, . . . present [Gestalt] theory cannot yet incorporate them" (pp. 449-450).

Allport (1955) is of the opinion that perceptual set

does not seem to have been well integrated into the theory. The prevailing state of the subject, and its atypical and individualized effect upon perception, have not seemed important in the framework of the universal, formal, and nativistically oriented ideas of gestalt. . . . The omission of motivational factors has been severely criticized by some of the other perceptual theorists (p. 139).

Similarly, Witkin and his co-workers (1954) consider that

the finding that people do have characteristic ways of perceiving makes it necessary to modify the Gestalt concept of perception. Because of the operation of these personal "sets" there is greater possibility for individual variation in manner of organizing perceptual experiences than could be expected on the basis of the Gestalt emphasis on field determinants (p. 496).

Three points need to be taken into account in evaluating these criticisms of Gestalt theory.

The effects under consideration are not at present well understood; even their limits are not known, as Prentice indicates. This means that no theory can incorporate them in detail. Attention is the only one of these influences whose nature has begun to be understood. In an elegant research, Köhler and Adams (1958) bring it into the same universe of discourse as perceptual processes themselves. These authors conclude: "Attention intensifies the process which underlies the perception of an object. Under such circumstances, satiation is accelerated, and corresponding figural after-effects are enhanced" (p. 503). It cannot be said that attention, insofar as it has been investigated, presents any particular difficulties for Gestalt theory as opposed to other psychological theories. It would seem wise, therefore, to postpone judgment about other "nonstimulus influences" until they are better understood.

There is no reason, from the point of view of Gestalt psychology, why complex data should not be organized in alternative ways *when the material permits*. Some of Wertheimer's early demonstrations were of such effects, as also Rubin's work with ambiguous figures. More recently, the present writer (1955) has suggested a number of ways in which motivational and attitudinal processes may influence perception and cognition in accordance with the organization on which they act—that is, influences that do not violate the presented structure. There is at present no reason to hold that motivational processes are incompatible with organizational ones.

There is, furthermore, nothing in Gestalt theory to suggest that influences from the person do not affect other parts of the psychophysical field.[12] Koffka, introducing the ego as the "hero of the play" (1935, p. 319), made it quite clear that it is a highly important part of this field, and this same point may be found in the writings of Wertheimer (1959), Asch (1952), and others. For example, although denying that the ego always acts as exclusive framework for our orientation in space, Asch adds: "There are conditions in which the ego-system functions as part of the field, subject to the laws governing the latter" (p. 295).

In sum, the criticism that Gestalt psychology leaves no room for motivational, attitudinal, and attentional influences on perception and other cognitive processes seems to be based on misunderstanding. Of course, further research into the manner of operation of these influences—by Gestalt psychologists and others—is badly needed.

---

[12] That some of these differences are reliable and related to other enduring characteristics of individuals is the interesting contribution of Witkin and his co-workers. One conclusion they draw from these findings is hard for the present writer to understand: "In his perception, and in other areas of his psychological functioning, the individual is not 'subservient' to the field to the extent conceived in Gestalt theory; he is not a passive, mirrorlike recorder upon whom the field impresses itself, but an active agent who contributes to the progress and outcome of the act of perceiving" (1954, pp. 496-497). To deal only with the main point, we may ask why the cerebral processes that underlie form and color perception—themselves a "contribution" of the individual —are any less active than the (entirely unknown) cerebral processes that underlie motives and other personal dispositions.

ON GESTALT PSYCHOLOGY   289

PRESENT STATUS AND TASKS AHEAD

Koch has recently expressed the view that psychology "has constructed a language which renders virtually impossible a differentiated exploration of the content of man" (1961, p. 631). He continues: "What has hardly been in the picture except by innuendo so far, has been the world outside the cloisters" (p. 639).

For the Gestalt psychologist, the experience is one of *déjà-vu*. Gestalt psychology arose, it will be recalled, out of the "crisis of science" (cf. also Koffka, 1935, Ch. 1; Köhler, 1938, Ch. 1; Wertheimer, 1944). In the beginning of the present century—as today, if Koch is right—scientific psychology was flourishing; it was developing explanatory principles, but they had no relevance to the most important human problems. Indeed, these were regarded by many as beyond the scope of scientific psychology, the domain of *Geisteswissenschaftliche Psychologie*. The solution of the Gestalt psychologists was different. They held that scientific psychology had failed to be relevant to human life, not because the scientific method cannot deal with it, but because of the atomistic assumptions regarded as self-evident by psychologists using this method. Gestalt psychology is to be understood as an attempt to develop a scientific psychology along non-atomistic lines.

If we are again today in a crisis of science, has this attempt failed? Or has Gestalt psychology made its contribution and, as Boring suggests (1950, p. 600) is it "now dying of its success by being absorbed into what is Psychology"? It seems to me that neither possibility is correct. With regard to the latter, the analysis in the first part of this paper has indicated real differences between Gestalt theory and other theoretical currents in psychology. And the paragraphs to follow will suggest that there is no reason to suppose that the contributions of Gestalt psychology are finished.

There remains to be considered the possibility that the current "crisis of science" suggests that the solution offered by Gestalt psychology in the early part of the century was inadequate to deal with it. I would like, on the contrary, to present the view that scientific psychology remains unable to deal with so many significant human concerns precisely because it has not yet sufficiently discarded atomistic and additive assumptions, precisely because the Gestalt approach has not yet been sufficiently widely applied. For example, the great bulk of the research in the field of learning, largely under the influence of associationist, behaviorist, and neobehaviorist conceptions, has been concerned with rote learning, conditioning, and the learning of lower animals and human beings in other highly constricted situations. The learning that human beings do most of their lives is largely of a more meaningful kind. Gestalt psychology has studied meaningful learning, problem-solving, productive thinking. Why do we not understand more of everyday human learning? Possibly because the Gestalt approach has not yet been widely enough applied.

Of course, the most urgent human problems are not exclusively, or even primarily, cognitive ones. Where does Gestalt psychology stand with regard to problems of value, human relations, personality? Again, at least in the first two of these areas, the beginnings that exist suggest that a widespread application of the Gestalt theoretical approach would indeed bring scientific psychology closer to problems of major human concern. With regard to value, Köhler's important analysis of value and its relation to science (1938), Wertheimer's discussions of ethics (1935), freedom (1940), and truth (1934), Duncker's treatment of ethical relativity (1939), Arnheim's work on aesthetics (e.g., 1957)—all open up problems for psychological investigation. Asch's contributions to social psychology (e.g., 1952) likewise open up new problems and point in new directions.

In the field of personality it must be said that, while Gestalt psychology has come near to some of its problems, it has not yet specifically dealt with them. (Lewin's work has been described above as largely metatheoretical rather than theoretical.) And yet this seems to be an area to which Gestalt theory could make significant contributions. For example, Asch's work on forming impressions of personality (1946) has shown these impressions to be organized structures, containing central and peripheral parts and exhibiting other properties of organization. It would be strange indeed if these impressions were not in some respects veridical—if personality itself did not exhibit organization. Many writers, it is true, have pointed to the organized nature of personality but none, so far as I know, has developed specific organizational concepts for the personality. This might be an area in which Gestalt theory, one of whose central concepts is organization, might make important contributions.[13]

How will the work required to carry out the program of Gestalt psychology be accomplished? I can do no better than repeat Köhler's recent invitation to the behaviorists (1959):

Why should we fight? Many experiments done by Behaviorists seem to me to be very good experiments. May I now ask the Behaviorists to regard the use of some phenomenal facts, and also of field physics, as perfectly permissible? If we were to agree on these points, we could, I am sure, do excellent work together. It would be an extraordinary experience—and good for psychology (p. 734).

---

[13] In addition, the predilection of Gestalt psychologists for phenomenological observation suggests an important and neglected approach to many problems of personality and motivation (cf. Henle, 1962).

REFERENCES

ALLPORT, F. H. *Theories of perception and the concept of structure*. New York: Wiley, 1955.

ARNHEIM, R. *Art and visual perception*. Berkeley and Los Angeles: Univ. California Press, 1957.

ASCH, S. E. Forming impressions of personality. *J. abnorm. soc. Psychol.,* 1946, **41,** 258-290.

ASCH, S. E. *Social psychology*. New York: Prentice-Hall, 1952.

ASCH, S. E., CERASO, J., & HEIMER, W. Perceptual conditions of association. *Psychol. Monogr.,* 1960, **74,** No. 3. Whole No. 490.

BORING, E. G. *Sensation and perception in the history of experimental psychology*. New York: Appleton-Century, 1942.

BORING, E. G. *A history of experimental psychology*. (2nd ed.) New York: Appleton-Century-Crofts, 1950.

BROWN, J. S. *The motivation of behavior*. New York: McGraw-Hill, 1961.

BRUNER, J. S. Freud and the image of man. *Amer. Psychologist,* 1956, **11,** 463-466.

BURWEN, L. S., & CAMPBELL, D. T. The generality of attitudes toward authority and nonauthority figures. *J. abnorm. soc. Psychol.,* 1957, **54,** 24-31.

CAMPBELL, D. T. Social attitudes and other acquired behavioral dispositions. In S. Koch (*Ed.*), *Psychology: a study of a science*. Vol. 6. New York: McGraw-Hill, 1963. Pp. 94-172.

CARTWRIGHT, D. Lewinian theory as a contemporary systematic framework. In S. Koch (Ed.), *Psychology: a study of a science*. Vol. 2. New York: McGraw-Hill, 1959. Pp. 7-91.

DEUTSCH, M. Field theory in social psychology. In G. Lindzey (Ed.), *Handbook of social psychology*. Vol. 1. Cambridge, Mass.: Addison-Wesley, 1954.

DUNCKER, K. Ethical relativity?: an enquiry into the psychology of ethics. *Mind,* 1939, **48,** 39-57.

GOLDMEIER, E. Über Ähnlichkeit bei gesehenen Figuren. *Psychol. Forsch.,* 1937, **21,** 146-208.

HEIDER, F. On Lewin's methods and theory. *J. soc. Issues,* suppl. ser., 1959, No. 13. Pp. 1-13.

HEIDER, F. Comments on Dr. Rapaport's paper. In M. R. Jones (Ed.), *Nebraska symposium on motivation, 1960*. Lincoln: Univ. Nebraska Press, 1960. Pp. 253-257.

HENLE, MARY. Some effects of motivational processes on cognition. *Psychol. Rev.,* 1955, **62,** 423-432.

HENLE, MARY. Some problems of eclecticism. *Psychol. Rev.,* 1957, **64,** 296-305.

HENLE, MARY. Some aspects of the phenomenology of the personality. *Psychol. Beiträge,* 1962, **6,** 395-404.

HILGARD, E. R. *Theories of learning*. (2nd ed.) New York: Appleton-Century-Crofts, 1956.

HOCHBERG, J. E. Effects of the Gestalt revolution: the Cornell symposium on perception. *Psychol. Rev.,* 1957, **64,** 73-84.

HULL, C. L. *Principles of behavior*. New York: Appleton-Century, 1943.

HULL, C. L. *Essentials of behavior.* New Haven: Yale Univ. Press, 1951.

HULL, C. L. *A behavior system.* New Haven: Yale Univ. Press, 1952.

JUNG, C. G. Synchronicity: an acausal connecting principle. In C. G. Jung and W. Pauli, *The interpretation of nature and the psyche.* New York: Pantheon Books, 1955. Pp. 1-146.

KOCH, S. Psychological science versus the science-humanism antinomy: intimations of a significant science of man. *Amer. Psychol.,* 1961, **16,** 629-639.

KOFFKA, K. *Growth of the mind.* (2nd ed.) New York: Harcourt, Brace, 1928.

KOFFKA, K. *Principles of Gestalt psychology.* New York: Harcourt, Brace, 1935.

KÖHLER, W. *The place of value in a world of facts.* New York: Liveright, 1938.

KÖHLER, W. *Dynamics in psychology.* New York: Liveright, 1940.

KÖHLER, W. *Gestalt psychology.* (Rev. ed.) New York: Liveright, 1947.

KÖHLER, W. Psychology and evolution. *Acta Psychologica,* 1950, **7,** 288-297.

KÖHLER, W. Gestalt psychology today. *Amer. Psychol.,* 1959, **14,** 727-734.

KÖHLER, W., & ADAMS, PAULINE, A. Perception and attention. *Amer. J. Psychol.,* 1958, **71,** 489-503.

KÖHLER, W. & WALLACH, H. Figural after-effects. *Proc. Amer. philos. Soc.,* 1944, **88,** 269-357.

KROLIK, W. Über Erfahrungswirkungen beim Bewegungssehen. *Psychol. Forsch.,* 1935, **20,** 47-101.

LEWIN, K. *A dynamic theory of personality.* New York: McGraw-Hill, 1935.

LEWIN, K. *The conceptual representation and the measurement of psychological forces.* Durham, N. C.: Duke Univ. Press, 1938.

MOWRER, O. H. *Learning theory and personality dynamics.* New York: Ronald Press, 1950.

PRENTICE, W. C. H. The systematic psychology of Wolfgang Köhler. In S. Koch (Ed.), *Psychology: a study of a science.* Vol. 1. New York: McGraw-Hill, 1959.

TOLMAN, E. C. Principles of purposive behavior. In S. Koch (Ed.), *Psychology: a study of a science.* Vol. 2. New York: McGraw-Hill, 1959. Pp. 92-157.

WALLACH, H. Some considerations concerning the relation between perception and cognition. *J. Pers.,* 1949, **18,** 6-13.

WELCH, L. An integration of some fundamental principles of modern behaviorism and Gestalt psychology. *J. gen. Psychol.,* 1948, **39,** 175-190.

WERTHEIMER, M. On truth. *Soc. Res.,* 1934, **1,** 135-146.

WERTHEIMER, M. Some problems in the theory of ethics. *Soc. Res.,* 1935, **2,** 353-367.

WERTHEIMER, M. Laws of organization in perceptual forms. In W. D. Ellis (Ed.), *A source book of Gestalt psychology.* New York: Harcourt, Brace, 1938. Pp. 555-569.

WERTHEIMER, M. A story of three days. In Ruth N. Anshen (Ed.), *Freedom: its meaning.* New York: Harcourt, Brace, 1940.

WERTHEIMER, M. Gestalt theory. *Soc. Res.,* 1944, **11,** 81-99.

WERTHEIMER, M. *Productive thinking.* (Enl. ed.) New York: Harper, 1959.

WITKIN, H. A., LEWIS, H. B., HERTZMAN, M., MACHOVER, K., MEISSNER, P. & WAPNER, S. *Personality through perception.* New York: Harper, 1954.

16 PETER A. BERTOCCI

FOUNDATIONS OF PERSONALISTIC PSYCHOLOGY

> All books on the psychology of personality are at the same time books on the philosophy of the person.
> —(G. W. Allport, 1962, p. xi.)

PERSONALISTIC thought is unified in metaphysics, in theology, in ethics, and in psychology by one methodological principle, and by one conviction. The principle is: The human being as he experiences himself, as *erlebt,* provides data that all theorizing about him and the world must not disregard or explain away. The conviction is: the human being is a unique unity, to be described, to be interpreted, but not to be dissolved into some other kind of being. This unity cannot be proved if by proof one means that this contention is based on some more fundamental premise. There is no more fundamental fact than the unity of being that constitutes the reasoner himself.

In the attempt to expound and defend this central theme, personalistic philosophers have developed theories of mind, mind–body, and personality that would be relevant to the different facets of human experience: cognition (in all of its ranges), feeling, conation, willing, and moral, aesthetic, and religious sensitivity. Thus the psychological *trend* that we are calling "personalistic" has always been a part of personalistic philosophy.

Recent personalistic psychology has been searching for a *modus vivendi* that will keep it alive both to more speculative philosophical concerns and to scientific data relevant to a balanced understanding of the dimensions of personality. In what follows, we shall outline and consider some of the philosophical and psychological developments that have led to and influenced the personalistic perspective in the study of personality.

METHODOLOGICAL CONSIDERATIONS

Plato argued in the *Phaedo* and elsewhere that the human soul could never be understood as an additive collection of parts. It is self-moving, irreducible to physiological events, and can fulfill itself only by realizing a structure of values that gives it purpose. A broad stream of successors— Aristotle, Augustine, Aquinas, Descartes, Locke, Berkeley, Leibniz, Kant, Fichte, Lotze, C. Renouvier, R. Eucken, J. McTaggart, G. Howison, J. Ward, F. R. Tennant, W. Temple, B. P. Bowne, W. James, M. W. Calkins, W. McDougall, W. Stern, A. C. Knudson, D. C. Macintosh, R. Niebuhr, J. Maritain, E. Gilson, A. C. Garnett, H. Bergson, P. Weiss, C. Hartshorne, J. Wild, C. A. Campbell, J. Macmurray, A. Castell—whatever their differences, joined in battle on three fronts.

First, they defended the individuality, relative autonomy, and unity of the finite mind against absorption into one Absolute by either rational or mystical means. These thinkers are theists, near-theists, and pluralists.

Second, they defended the intrinsic unity, individuality, and continuity of self-existence against atomization by associationist psychology and sensationistic empiricism, without neglecting the influence of learning on individual development.

Third, they resisted the reduction of mental to spatial or material being. Self-consciousness, logical or rational cognition, and moral, aesthetic, or religious sensitivity, cannot, they held, be explained without residue in spatial terms.

In a word, personalists have been so impressed by the active, creative responsiveness and moral autonomy of the human being that they could not envision him as a "pulse-beat of the Absolute," or a concatenation of ideas, feeling, impressions, or brain-events, or a "mirror of culture."

There are methodological issues involved in this personalistic approach. The "variety of *human* experience," to adapt James' phrase, has kept personalists problem-centered and not method-centered; at every turn, they have resisted *methodological imperialism* whether in philosophy or psychology. The touchstones of personalistic investigation—the unity in variety, the continuity despite discontinuity, the uniqueness despite similarity, the purposiveness in the orderly and predictable, the distinctive rational-moral-aesthetic-religious dimensions in the matrix of the alogical, nonmoral, brute factors in man—defy any one approach to human nature.

Furthermore, the personalist keeps reminding himself that every perspective a person takes *is taken by a person,* that, in other words, a philosophical and psychological theory must make the activities of the investigator intelligible. The very possibility of a scientific experiment depends on a knower who can survive the time-consuming process, who, having set the experiment up for a purpose, remembers the beginning, middle, and ending of the experiment (Brightman, 1958). Indeed, anything about the experiment is logically dubitable and deniable except the existence of a time-binding observer and his purpose.

Nor can this methodological concern, that theoretical conclusions about human nature be consistent with the presupposition of experiment and theorizing, be left here. Any theory about human beings must not only pay attention to conscious experience and its givens; it must be confirmable by, or consistent with, what is present in consciousness. Theories about the body, or about the unconscious, about any environment, physical, social, or divine, are unacceptable if they distort, slight, or contradict what is phenomenally given in consciousness. The intellectual journey from consciousness starts with data in consciousness, and however far it travels from this home base, it must return to it and be examined for its capacity to illuminate conscious experience.

For example, there is no denying that "red" is a datum in consciousness. The explanations of this experience by reference to processes in the physical world, cones in the eye, occipital processes, and so on are all to the good. But it would be another thing to hold that the "red" as experienced is "in" the occipital lobe. The personalist extends the warning against the stimulus error to the caution: All processes and entities resulting from theorizing—philosophical, scientific, theological—shall not be substituted for the conscious data themselves.

Finally, personalists may disagree with one another about the interpretation of what is immediately given in consciousness. But they agree in principle that *no one type, or aspect of, "given" conscious experience be allowed to dictate arbitrarily the nature of another,* that the aesthetic experience, for example, be not allowed arbitrarily to determine the nature of interpretation of religious or moral experience. Radical empiricism, synoptic examination as well as analysis—this is the methodology that alone can provide hypotheses which, however far they range, will not lose their anchorage in what is phenomenally given.

We turn now from general methodology to analysis of a basic cleavage among personalists that will serve to throw light on problems being encountered by contemporary psychologies of the "self." There is no cleavage about the issue. A person changes. However paradoxical, to say that change takes place, rather than substitution, is to say that change is impossible without permanence. To say that change can be known is to assert at least that a knower exists at the beginning of succession in change and at the end, and knows them as beginning and end. A succession of experiences is not an experience of succession (Bowne, 1897). There can be no series known as a series if the knower is only one member in the series.

To use C. A. Campbell's illustration: When Big Ben strikes the tenth stroke it can be known as tenth only by a knower who exists from stroke one to stroke ten. The kind of unity and continuity that personal experience exhibits simply cannot be an artifact; and it is unintelligible as a collection, or as a series, without that which makes "collection" and "series" possible. So urge both philosophical and psychological personalists. The Gestalt contention that the whole is greater than the sum of its parts is nothing new in the history of personalistic thought, for, as Leibniz showed, the kind of unity that psychic activity displays is original or intrinsic and never built up bit by bit.

THE SELF

But how is the unity to be conceived? Is there a unified entity that persists through change, binding changes together but itself unchanging? [1] Personalistic thinkers have been haunted by this difficult notion of a self unifying its activities, and yet not to be identified with these changing activities. They have had no little trouble in conceiving such permanence and change together, and have sometimes emphasized one at the expense of the other. The struggle in Borden P. Bowne (1910) is instructive, as Franquiz (1942) shows. But C. A. Campbell's recent statement (1957) is an especially revealing example of the psycho-logic of substantive soul psychology.

When I hear the second stroke of Big Ben, *as* the second stroke, Campbell argues, I must not only remember the first but remember *that* I heard it. I am not only a self-identical subject, but conscious of it. All cognition, he concludes, forces us "to posit a self which is 'over and above' its particular experiences; something that *has*, rather than is, its experiences, since its experiences are all different, while *it* somehow remains the same" (Campbell, 1957, p. 77). Yet Campbell does not wish to identify his substantival self with John Locke's *je-ne-sais-quoi* or unknowable substratum

---

[1] Yes, say the soul-psychologists, or substantialists. What we may call the Platonic wing of personalism in this respect—Plato, Augustine, Descartes, Locke, Leibniz, Kant, Bowne—agree in defining this unchanging unity as nonphysiological, and nonspatial. The Aristotelian-Thomistic wing, however, has sought to overcome the chasm between mind and body thus created by Platonic soul-psychologists by conceiving of the soul as the principle or form of life that is not reducible to body. Arnold (1954), for example, has recently sponsored such an Aristotelian-Thomistic view in her argument that man is an irreducible "compound unity" of hierarchical levels, physical, biological, and psychological (rational-volitional). William McDougall (1920) came close to this when he recognized a relation of mind to body so intimate that "psychological interaction may be, for all we know, a necessary condition of all consciousness." But he insisted, nevertheless, that the soul is a "psychic being," and added that it must not be conceived of as "a core or substratum underlying and distinct from all attributes of a thing," nor as incapable of growth and change.

William Stern (1924, 1938), to state a third alternative, held that the person is "psycho-physically neutral." But he distinguished a person from a thing because, despite the plurality of its parts, it "constitutes a real, unique, and intrinsically valuable unity, and, as such . . . achieves a unitary, purposive self-activity."

In this sample of differences we note a common concern: to maintain that the mind or self, whatever its relation to body, is actively engaged in all its activities and yet not to be identified with any one of them.

or with Kant's "characterless" ego. His contention is that "to deny that the self is *reducible* to its experience is by no means to deny that the self manifests its real character (in whole or in part) *in and through experiences*" (p. 82).

But is it intelligible to say that the *I* is the same and yet changes? The "how" of self-unity in change, Campbell argues, is logically unintelligible. Nevertheless, what is given in experience is an *I* that in thinking is aware of its identity with the *I* that feels B and desires C, and has other conscious experiences. Can logical demands be allowed to explain away a nonlogical given? Self-psychologists will agree with Campbell that demands for a logically intelligible "how" must not be allowed to dictate what experience must be. But, as we shall see, Brightman, for example, will urge that we can conceive of this psychic unity in more radically empirical terms.

Before leaving Campbell and soul psychology, it will be well to make a distinction he makes that is basic to the way in which both soul and self psychology conceive the difference between unity of self or soul and unity of personality.

We must not confuse, says Campbell, the identity of the self, the *I* (that has, but is not, its activities) with the personal identity that it develops. The personal identity, that is, the character ("personality" would be the American term), is acquired by the self in the course of its experiences. It is "a set of relatively stable dispositions to feel, think, and behave in more or less marked ways" (1957, p. 86). A self, in other words, comes to conceive of itself, or to identify itself, with these acquired, salient features. When a person says, "I was not myself when I did that," he is referring to this character.

We might restate this distinction by speaking of the originative *I,* soul, or self, which remembers these stable dispositions as its own, as the *ontic self* or *agent.* In order to develop, sustain, and identify these dispositions, it has to be self-identical. Its character and personality tell the story of the particular course the ontic self has taken. In other words, the agent-self always exists in two dimensions—as unlearned, sustaining, immanent unity, and as learned unity expressing the nature of interaction between itself and environment. But: "The self may function when the person[ality] does not, but the person[ality] cannot function when the self does not" (p. 88). That is, the ontic self can and does function beyond the boundaries of any set of stable dispositions.

The question we shall soon be asking is this: Does psychology of personality require such a self? Whatever the answer may be, the fact is that philosophers like Campbell are concerned lest psychology of personality neglect this distinction between a self-identical self and the personality which it acquires and to which *it* gives unity. Furthermore, they would welcome Campbell's exposition as he shows how this distinction can help us to understand both the unity of personality when it does exist and the development of subsystems that are not harmonious with one another.

For example, let us, with Campbell, assume a self, an original psychic unity present in, but not exhausted by, its activities. It starts on its career with native affective-conative tendencies and capacities closely related to a particular body. In interaction with the social and physical environment, it develops its person[ality]. In such interaction, the self's energies are not, as it were, "poured without remainder into its functioning as a person[ality]." This makes it possible for self-identity to be retained both when personality identity is being developed and also when it is interrupted either through bodily disrepair or through psychological dissociation.

In other words, the same self can develop different subsystems to serve different functions. In normality, the self moves with ease from one to another. But abnormality occurs when conflict between subsystems is so great that dissociation seems the best way out. However, were the self not identical there could be no felt conflict. And were it not identical and persistent despite the conflicts of the subsystems into which it had not poured itself completely there could be no healing. Two personalities, if they belonged to two independent spiritual entities, could never be integrated again.

In such a view, we can see how a substantive soul psychology (or a personalistic soul-psychology), developed to care for certain fundamental epistemic and metaphysical problems, can also throw light on how complex personality developments, dissociations, and reintegration are possible. In Campbell's view we see a very subtle rendering of the substantive view of selfhood, a dogged determination to avoid "pure" egos, on the one hand, and "bundle" views of self, on the other. F. R. Tennant (1928) would fall in line with this general account of ontic self and personality, but he would deny that the ontic self can be experienced.

Nevertheless, whether one holds with Campbell that the ontic self only reveals itself in part in its activities, or with Tennant that the pure ego is never an object of consciousness, all such substantive or near-substantive views have called forth dissent from personalistic self-psychologists on methodological grounds mainly. They have argued that any "has-but-is-not" view of the self and its activities opens the door to uneconomical multiplication of entities and to possible obscurantism. The only check we have on anything beyond experience is in experience. But what is more, why go beyond experience for unity when it is there in self-experience? Such is the main thesis of philosophical self-psychologists.

To bring the problem into clear focus: The main problem of the *soul*-psychologists is to give an account of the self-identical soul that will be faithful to change and plurality. The problem of the *self*-psychologists is to be faithful to the need for unity. The agonizing of William James with this tension in different stages of his development is fascinating but cannot here be traced in detail. It is Capek's well-defended contention (1953), that despite appearances and disappearances of the "I" in James' thought, his final view, most adequately expressed in *A Pluralistic Universe,* confirms the passage in the *Principles:*

> The universal conscious fact is not "feelings and thoughts exist" but "I think" and "I feel." . . . It could only be a blunder if the notion of personality meant something essentially different from anything to be found in the mental procession. But if that procession be itself the very "original" of the notion of personality, to personify it cannot possibly be wrong. It is already personified (Vol. 1, pp. 226-227).

This line of reasoning is developed by the best recent proponent of self-psychology, E. S. Brightman (1932, 1958), a more thorough-going empiricist than his teacher, B. P. Bowne, the founder of personalistic idealism in America. The undeniable data for all theorizing are to be found in the undeniable existent, the conscious datum-self. This datum-self is not a substantive soul, but a complex unity of conscious experience; it is not a mathematical point, but a "saddle-back" (James' term), a *durée,* a temporal span with its own complex unity. It is not a unity *in* but a unity *of* interpenetrating or fused sensing, remembering, reasoning, emoting, wanting, willing, feeling and their modes or "states," such as sensations, images, ideas, loves, hates, hopes, intentions, and volitions. It is this complex, *erlebt* present that is the undeniable *I.* It is this psychic unity that is the only certain model we have of being—a throbbing, temporal, changing, yet self-identical and acting unity of psychic givens. Theorizing starts in *this* reasoning-wanting unity, as it brings its built-in norms of reason to bear in understanding the occurrence, the changes, the sequences, in its present states.

This personal self, this I, is not Stern's neutral *unitas multiplex* (1924, 1938), nor Campbell's unity that *has* but not *is* its activities. The experiencing self is this temporal, changing, yet self-identical kind of being, and no logic must be allowed to explain it away. An adequate psychology must describe its nature and development, and metaphysics must give the most coherent account possible of its relation to other forms of being. There simply is no experiential evidence, Brightman urges, for an unchanging unity.

However, in my given *I* (or datum-self), there are data that need further explanation. Reasoning about such data leads us to develop theories about the conditions for their being what they are, theories about body, about the unconscious, or, in a word, about *the whole self or person.* We come to realize, for example, that the datum-self is a specious present continuous with its past and moving into a future. But what is important methodologically for Brightman is that no theory of the "sources of the conscious"—be it Freud's, Jung's, or that of an absolute idealist, theistic

dualist, materialist or naturalist—is acceptable if, in the end, it is incoherent with the existence, and complex qualitative nature of, the undeniable datum-self.

We need not linger here, except to note that this account of the personal self, if it were substituted for Campbell's, could account equally well
for the acquired dispositions and subsystem unities that are needed in describing personality. The unity of the knowing-wanting self (to telescope
functions) is not poured without residue into particular habits, sentiments,
attitudes, traits, or "personalities" that stabilize the particular "adjustments" that particular self has made.

SELF-EXPERIENCE

As we turn to the early decades of the twentieth century, to a period of
more explicit conflict between philosophical personalistic psychology and
general scientific psychology we are impressed by the synoptic style, the
radical empiricism that persists in the personalistic demand that scientific hypotheses be adequate to the data of consciousness. William James
aside, there is no better defender of self-psychology on the scientific level
than Mary W. Calkins (1914, 1915).

Calkins was caught with James, Bowne, McDougall, and others in the
advance of psychological movements that were to model the science of
psychology on patterns exemplified in the physical sciences. In *A First Book
in Psychology,* a text that appeared as a fourth revision in 1914, she argued
that "psychology is a science of self," and the next year she reviewed specific
psychological evidence relevant to her thesis that the self cannot be "bowed
out of psychology on the ground that scientific introspection has failed to
discover it" (1915).

The self, as Calkins saw it, is self-identical, unique, related to its social
and physical environment, but not "beyond or beside" the experience it
has. When the psychologist tries to define the self by making it a member
of some broader class, or to isolate it experimentally, it must perforce escape him. For the self is in a class by itself; it is ubiquitous and cannot
be isolated as it might be if it were only a part of experience. It cannot
yield itself to experimentation for it is doing the experimenting; but it can
be described by "controlled introspection."

Calkins is equally resistant to near-self-psychologists who hold that the
self is directly experienced in some experience but not in others (such
as perception). A full self-psychology must hold that "all consciousness is
consciousness of self and that the psychologist, therefore, willy-nilly studies
the self." Desirable as it is to know the physiological and physical conditions of introspective phenomena, what is in consciousness must be
described for what it is.

Considerations related to Calkin's basic concern that psychological science make proper allowances for the possible distinctiveness of human self-experience appear in many places. Magda Arnold (Arnold & Gasson, 1954), for example, points to an anomaly: the willingness of psychologists to disregard data relevant to human behavior and that only human beings can provide, namely, introspective data—especially since they can only finally justify disregard of it by trusting introspection!

Furthermore, she warns, the psychologist ought at least to be aware that he is often presupposing philosophical conclusions, including his philosophy of science, in approaching what is given in personal experience. Thus, to assume a lawful universe that presumably has no place for freedom and purpose in it, or that aesthetic, religious, and moral experience can give no possible evidence about its nature, is to operate *from* a philosophical position and not from observation of what is given in human experience itself. Her stricture is scientifically important because hidden philosophical assumptions have a way not only of restricting one's "sense of the problem" but also of determining how observed data are interpreted.

Finally, what is given in experience as a whole must be kept before us and not be sacrificed to the conveniences of method. Procedures for studying man must be fitted to the problem, not the problem to the Procrustean bed of method. Accordingly, as Allport observes (1947), the psychologist who uses a machine model must be aware that it is drawn not from clinical or social psychology, but from the physical sciences. Again, he who uses animal or infantile models should be aware that they "lack the long range orientation that is the essence of morality."

A. Maslow joins Allport in concern lest the higher ranges of human experience be treated on the premature assumption that the higher is simply an extension of the lower. Maslow (1954, 1962) in particular urges that self-actualizing persons and "peak experiences" be seen not as deviations from the "the normal" but as fulfillments without which "the average" and "the lower" may be seriously understood.

Such methodological cautions are developments of the broader philosophical method we have seen to characterize personalistic philosophy. Thus, speaking methodologically, we can summarize: Personalistic psychology is problem-centered and not model- or method-centered, whether the model or method be drawn from "successes" in physics, biology, logic, or theology. Models can help if we do not forget that we are using them, but neither man the sinner nor man the robot or feedback idol can be given arbitrary priority. The psychologist of personality cannot afford to disregard continuity or discontinuity with the subhuman, cannot de-emphasize similarity for the sake of uniqueness, the lower for the sake of the higher, or be unaware of philosophies and theologies relevant to the interpretation of man. Facts—from every source, ticketed with the method by which they were obtained—and values, individual or universal, high or low, labeled so that they may be observed in experience—are grist for the personalistic psychologist's intent to understand relationships among the varieties of human experience.

THE ORGANIZATION OF SELF

The evolution of Gordon W. Allport's probing and theorizing is not only guided by such basic methodological considerations as we have reviewed, but it is also a revealing commentary on the movements and problems that we have outlined. We center attention on Allport's psychology of personality because it is the most systematic psychological account of human experience that reflects a personalistic frame of mind.

If James, like Calkins and Ward, lived in the adolescent stage of psychology's rejection of its philosophical parent, Allport lived in the young adulthood that fathered behaviorism, objective psychology, Gestalt and depth psychologies, and tests and other statistical techniques for describing personality. If "objective" psychologies waged war on consciousness and introspection and sought "positive" laws of behavior, depth psychologies, less firmly rooted in physiology, set the conscious personality uncertainly on generic unconscious energies—with the common result that no account was given of the uniqueness that characterizes personality. Allport found support in Gestalt psychology against atomism and overreliance on unconscious mechanisms, and in favor of a phenomenalistic approach to conscious phenomena.

But there is one point at which Allport stands alongside all other academic psychologies, namely, against philosophical interpretations—such as that of personalistic idealism and absolute idealism—that seems to favor the conscious at the expense of the unconscious and question the bodily integumentation of the person (Allport, 1953). Allport sets out, therefore, as a psychologist not with a substantive soul or a self-psychology, but with descriptive, naturalistic presuppositions. This is to say that his naturalism is not doctrinaire. He sees the human being as a biological creature, whose personality is "a unique creation of the forces of nature" (1961, p. 4), whose development can be conceived in terms "neither exclusively mental nor exclusively neural (physical)" (1961, p. 28).

The newborn babe lacks "the characteristic organization of psychological systems," has "a *potential* personality" that develops "within the skin." The givens of personality are an idiographic complex of physique, temperament, and intelligence, motivated in infancy by essentially biological and nutritional drives. As the infant matures and interacts with the social and physical environment, he develops a personality. Once beyond the infantile stage, this personality cannot be understood in terms of biological motives alone. It is the postinfantile development, with its transformation of beginnings and its growing individual pattern that captivates Allport's attention and finally brings him to focus attention not on self-psychology but on psychology of "self."

Before considering the factors in Allport's own thought that call for a "self," it will be well to take note of a trend in the investigation of personality that resulted in the reappearance of terms like "self," "ego," "self-actualization"—a development that Allport has influenced and by which he in turn was influenced. The contributors to this trend are many —such investigators as M. Arnold, H. Ansbacher, R. Assagioli, N. Brown, C. Buhler, H. Cantril, A. Combs, M. C. D'Arcy, F. Deutsch, E. Erikson, V. Frankl, H. Hartmann, K. Goldstein, S. Jourard, P. Lecky, K. Horney, E. Fromm, C. Moustakas, O. Mowrer, G. Murphy, H. Murray, C. Rogers, P. M. Symonds, A. L. Van Kaam, R. White, and C. Wilson—but despite their variety, A. H. Maslow (1962) suggests that they might constitute a kind of "third force" in contemporary psychology. What impresses us is that there emerges from members of this group, who, like Allport, have set aside souls, selves, and mind–body problems, observations and reflections that refocus attention on problems in psychology of personality similar to those faced by philosophical personalists when they confronted the variety and unity, the continuity and discontinuity of human experience. A thumbnail sketch of the reappearance of what might be called the *psychological* self or ego must suffice.

Freud, having hypothesized the unconscious because of resistance in consciousness exhibited by his patients, developed, in turn, a theory of the conscious ego and then of a largely unconscious superego to explain the specific directions of individual personality formations. In the thought of Jung and Adler, persistent and unique organizations of response, at once influencing and expressing the conscious and unconscious givens of life in their interaction with the environment, were distinguished as the *persona* and "style of life" respectively. And when individual development was seen in the context of mental health (the fulfillment of potential or self-actualization), as in the thought of Karen Horney (1950), Erich Fromm (1951), and A. Maslow (1954, 1962), the "self" reappears as the "authentic" or "real" being. The intrinsic needs of the self, such psychologists urge, must find adequate expression throughout the different phases of life if the individual is to escape mediocrity and illness.

On these views, so far as the writer can tell, the self is a kind of being whose qualitative demands, for responsible freedom, for authentic individuality, for self-actualization, will be felt as a kind of inner guide to preferences. As Fromm and Maslow put it, "one *ought* to become what he *is*" (1951). No created image of the divine, no introjected demands of a culture, are envisaged in this portrait of man; he is an existent-potential self that cannot be lastingly frustrated without illness. What seems to have happened is that among these psychologists the description of personality has moved from "public" physiological categories to hypotheses of at least nonlocalizable capacities and functions related "somehow" to the physiological—and called by terms—*ego, self, style of life*—terms intended to emphasize the individuality of needs, responsiveness, and creative direction.

The *psychological* self was also to emerge from another area of investigation, in learning and theory of perception especially, and once again as a dynamic influence in what was selected and retained. Thus, Gestaltists pointed out that the psychological or behavioral environment, the inner space of the individual, however stimulated by the geographical environment, reflected the nature of the holistic tendencies in the perceiver. Phenomenologists like Combs and Snygg (1959) emphasized that the world of the individual could not be understood without understanding his frame of reference. Transactional psychologists, like Hadley Cantril (1950, 1959), observed that what the individual perceives has no one-to-one correspondence with the external world but reflects a transaction responsive to the individual's own organization as well as the "objective" state of affairs.

The basic conclusions emerging from these investigations is that what a person knows and perceives will be a function of the degree and nature of his self-involvement, of his conception of himself. Theories of learning that make repetition, reinforcement, and tension reduction central fail to explain the selectivity and the permanence of learning that seem clearly to be not a function of repetition, reinforcement and tension reduction. The human learner and perceiver respond to an immediate stimulus situation not simply in the light of the past but in the light of long-range goals, persistent frames of reference, or concept of self. Nor can the emphasis be placed on the underlying, universal needs or motives; it must be shifted to contemporary ego structure.

It is dangerous to ascribe too much unity in what are mainly trends away from emphasis on the objective past or the objective present. We are more concerned here to point to the ferment which is part of the "environment" in which Allport's system is a constructive, sensitive response. And since we are talking about the reappearance of the self, we must note the kinds of cautions and disclaimers that often accompany talk about the self.

First, although Cantril claims, "it is only through the life-setting and participation that meaning and continuity are given to the self," he warns against the mistake of "positing an abstract self" or "ego" that can "somehow be isolated, pointed to, analyzed, or experienced apart from any social contact" (1959, p. 133).

Second, Carl Rogers points out that the reorganization of the self is late in coming, that it resists change unless it is nondirectively encouraged. He acknowledges that his thinking about the self is close to G. H. Mead's "I" and "me," and associates himself with Lewin, Angyal, and Allport with the remark that the self is "an organizer of experience and to some extent an architect of self" (1959, p. 7).

The integrative function of the self as it arises from, and transforms, the social matrix is emphasized by both Cantril and Rogers (and others). But the question must arise: Is the self that organizes experience, that is said to be an architect of "self," identical with the initiating self? Is the organizing self itself a product of a confluent environment? If so, do the "environmental influences" simply fall into a unity or is a unified selective "architect" being assumed unwittingly? Social theories of self, we suggest, seem to make the self a "crossroads" of interacting factors, and thus provoke two questions: Why should the result not be a collective "omnibus" self rather than an architect? And why, in view of new arrivals at the crossroads, does unity and pattern survive, especially since there is no selective traffic officer present, presumably? These are the concerns that come to mind as one also reads Hilgard's recent Presidential Address (1949). But the interchange between Snygg and Combs (1959) and M. Brewster Smith (1959) is unusually relevant to this whole problem of the ambiguous status or double role of the self.

Snygg contends that "the fundamental need in a phenomenological system appears to be the preservation of the organization and integrity of the phenomenological field and especially of that part of the field which is the phenomenal self, whence our tendency to remain unaware of, or to reject with emotion, data inconsistent with our own beliefs" (1959, p. 13). He explains in a footnote that "the self we are trying to preserve is the phenomenal self, that is to say, our own picture of ourselves." On this view, what is meant by "preservation" is the preservation of this phenomenal self, the self that stands for self-respect, self-esteem, status, and cognate concepts. And we ask: What develops and preserves this phenomenal self?

Hence we concur when M. Brewster Smith wonders whether one term, "self," is not being asked to perform two tasks. For the self, hypothesized as a phenomenal entity to account for perceptual organization and the self-identity involved in the phenomenological field, can hardly be the same as the developer of the self, and the self-concept. "Can a phenomenal self consider perceptions and reintegrate itself [see Rogers above]; can a threatened phenomenal self deny perceptions; or is this rather double-talk resulting from the attempt to make one good concept do the work of two?" If he is to be coherent, the phenomenologist must smuggle in "a hidden second concept," or "organizing, selective processes in the personality which are somehow guided by the nature and status of the self (among other things) and somehow, in turn, have an influence in its nature and status" (1959, p. 261).

What does Snygg reply to this? His answer is methodological. The assumption of "a hidden organizer is . . . neither necessary nor helpful";

at best it is a "second order construct" set up to explain . . . a mystery by a greater mystery" (1959, p. 276). He urges rather: "When organization is found it does not need to be explained in order to be used in prediction" (1959, p. 226).

The issue seems fairly clear. Snygg hesitates to go to "a hidden organizer" because he is interested in prediction. Now, no philosopher or psychologist would hold that so ubiquitous an agency as the (organizing) self has specific predictive value—except that it is important to know whether the organizing agency at age seven can be banked on to be using the same logical principles and making similar basic demands at fifteen and twenty-five.

But what seems clearly to be dodged here is this issue: Shall the psychologist, in the name of predictability, and what *may be* mystery from the point of view of predictability, allow himself to be unaware of his presuppositions, and to double-talk? Can we remain content when a phenomenological psychologist says: "The essential characteristic of any organized field is its tendency to maintain its organization in the face of intruding forces" (Snygg, 1959, p. 276)? Or do the data show that the organization maintained can so radically change, and yet remain self-identical, that we should wonder how the organized field can maintain its organization in the face of intruding forces. We fear that the double-talk persists.

DYNAMIC CONTINUITY OF PERSONALITY

We return to Allport, then, with the problem of the critical factors in the organization of personality uppermost, and ask: Why does the problem of the self become important for him? In what sense is a doctrine of self "fruitful" or "a greater mystery"? What are his concerns about such a doctrine?

The Allportian challenge to psychological science and to psychology of personality in particular is that it confront and develop the techniques and theory for understanding individuality. With Bergsonian fervor, Allport keeps hammering away at the ineptitude of generic concepts for growing uniqueness in personality organization. There is pattern, there is growth, there is order in both pattern and growth, and these invite the construction of theoretical concepts that will not allow the idiographic to escape. No preconceived notion of what science "must be" keeps him from trying to understand the individual order of change.

To come closer, for Allport personality is a living system, a system from which, to use Hegelian language, we can abstract different dimensions—but should not forget that we abstracted them! The true personality is the whole, "a total functioning structure," albeit "an incomplete system, manifesting varying degrees of order and disorder" (1961, p. 566). Allport's faith, if you will, is that if we view the personality as an open-ended system, interacting with, but not a function of, society or environment, there is hope that, without losing track of strands that can up to a point be nomothetically described, we can see them as they are, the interwoven aspects of a dynamic organic system.

It is hard to label Allport's system neatly for this very reason. Gough has recently (1962) urged that the term "psychomorphology" might do more justice to the "dynamics and morphogenesis of structure" in Allport's emphasis on the unified complexity of personality. It is our contention that not only does his system actually fall more clearly into the personalistic framework of self-psychology, but that without an adequate articulation of self-psychology the actual system he expounds leaves unanswered questions and faces unnecessary difficulties. Let us see why.

Allport, we have said, wishes to draw "special attention to those laws and principles that tell how uniqueness comes about" (1962, p. 572). Uniqueness in motivation is simply inexplicable if we start with any one generic drive (like the id), with propensities (as proposed by McDougall) or even with the very flexible instinctoid needs of Maslow. Psychologists should give up what has been a fruitless, agelong struggle to substantiate any list of universal drives, and realize that such commonness as there is in motivation can be accounted for on the basis of learning in similar environments (1940). In any case, no list of inborn needs, however channelized and directed, can actually account for the "qualitative differences between infant and adult (such as the emergent motives of social responsibility), and also for the extraordinary diversity of adult motives unique in each particular personality" (1962, p. 203). Furthermore, while the fact is that "human beings are busy living their lives into the future," such theories of motivation are "busy tracing these lives backward into the past (1962, p. 206); and they treat the person as a reactive agent rather than the progressive, proactive being that he feels himself to be.

Allport accordingly advances his well-known doctrine of the functional autonomy of motives to explain the undeniable data: "Adult motives are infinitely varied, self-sustaining, *contemporary* systems. They are not fossils" (1961, p. 211). Whatever their historical connection with past motives may be—and it is one thing to say that they are reducible to "underlying" unchanging drives and another to prove it—the present "go" of motivation is autonomous. For example, the motives after twenty-five years of marriage are a transformation of the motives that led to marriage in the first place; and they are self-sustaining.

There are many important empirical and theoretical issues at stake here (Bertocci, 1940), but we focus on a critical one. Instinctive and drive theories, for all their difficulties, did manage to account for continuity in change. The more flexible the universal motives were held to be, the more did they seem to allow, in view of differences in ability and environment, for diversity between persons and for differences within a life history as well as for continuity.

If Allport gives up the continuity in striving that doctrines of persisting motives provide, if he substitutes a doctrine of motives that stresses the discontinuity of present motivational structures with the past, he is faced with the formidable problem of accounting for the inner, long-range, complex variety and continuity of personality. At a deeper metaphysical level, Allport's doctrine of functional autonomy of motives, is a doctrine of emergence (nutritional needs aside). But metaphysical theories of emergence explain variety, novelty, and plurality always at the possible expense of systematic unity, so, if the discussion is pushed to a deeper level, the same problem of accounting for unity despite discontinuity needs to be faced.

However, staying at the psychological level, what is to hold a personality (not its bodily aspect alone) together if motives, being functionally autonomous, have no continuous inner bonds with each other or with pervasive motives? On the face of it, there is no ground for assuming either continuity or unity of aim if functional autonomy, the emergence of new motives, the supplanting of old, is taken seriously. Yet it is the complex unity of the unique system that Allport makes the obstinate empirical datum of personality theory.

In *Becoming* (1955), and more elaborately in *Pattern and Growth in Personality* (1961), Allport develops his conception of the *proprium* or *propriate* striving, in order to describe the dynamic continuity discoverable in personality after the infantile stage. For as partially formed interest systems develop, we can distinguish the "central" and "warm" portion of personality from portions that are on the rim of one's being. The child is developing a sense of "self" and his interests fit into the "self-system" (1961, p. 107). In other words, in some learning activities he is more ego-involved than in others. "Whatever is ego-relevant is absorbed and retained" (1961, p. 107).

The facts of growth and patterning in personality demand that we "allow adequately for coherence and self-relevance" in a way not possible on quasimechanical and intellectualistic theories of learning. Propriate striving gives us the kind of concept we need if we are to understand the "evolving sense of self."

Allport outlines several aspects of this "evolving sense," each involving a dimension of the complex unity: the movement from unorganized sensorimotor experiences at birth to the fixing of recurrent bodily sensations into a "bodily me" which, "while not the whole of one's self," continues to be "a lifelong anchor for our self-awareness" (1962, p. 114); the achievement of continuous self-identity made possible especially by language and one's own name; the self-esteem that reflects others' evaluation of him; the extension of self and of his self-image as the growing individual tries to discover his place among others, as well as his vocation and his life goal. What is crucial is that as the individual develops into adolescence and adulthood, "long-range purposes and distant goals add a new dimension to the sense of selfhood" (1960, p. 126). Since each of these dimensions involves "matters of importance to the organized emotional life of the individual," they are best united or fused under "a fresher and broader label," *proprium* (1961, p. 127).

This *proprium,* then, is Allport's suggestion for fusing "selves" and "egos" as advanced by other psychologists, and it serves to provide the continuity in organization that is so vital for understanding his theory of personality and its uniqueness. This propriate self we also learn is *"the self 'as object' of knowledge and feeling"* (1961, p. 127), (italics added). It is this self "of which we are immediately aware" and of which we think as "the warm, central region of life." Furthermore, as such a warm, central region, "it plays a crucial part in our consciousness (a concept broader than self), in our personality (a concept broader than consciousness), and in our organism (a concept broader than personality). Thus it is some kind of core in our being. And yet [he hastens to add] it is not a constant core," for it sometimes takes command "of all our behavior and consciousness" and sometimes seems to go completely offstage, leaving us with no awareness whatsoever of self" (1961, p. 110).

In epistemic terms, Allport is obviously talking about the empirical, the phenomenal and phenomenological self, of which "each of us has an acute awareness" (1961, p. 111). It is this self which the "presumably conscious infant," who "lacks self-consciousness completely," gradually distinguishes from the world and becomes "the pivot of later life" (1961, p. 111). And it is this self, the growing long-range dynamic forward-thinking motivational core, which is the matrix of contemporaneous motives. In a word, although contemporary motives are functionally autonomous of antecedent motives, they are never functionally autonomous of the *proprium* that is developing and expressing in these different ways the relatively systematic "go" of personality, "sometimes consciously, but often unconsciously" (1961, p. 129).

One can readily see why Allport believes that he has solved the problem of continuity and discontinuity in motivation. And the case is all the more plausible when Allport develops the distinction that his theory of the propriate self as the "object known" forces upon him. Thus Allport purposely asks: "Who is the I who knows the bodily me, who has an image of myself and sense of identity over time, who knows that I have propriate strivings? I know all these things, and what is more, I know that I know them" (1961, p. 128). Some knowing subject or self is required, Allport now contends, as a continuant "somehow" from infancy to death.

But when it comes to determining "the nature of" the knowing "I"

Allport has serious qualms, and of the sort we have already encountered in the case of the self-psychologist against the soul psychologist, and of the sort we have seen Snygg advance against Smith.

THE APPROPRIATED SELF

We conclude our study, therefore, by noting Allport's hesitations against self-psychology in particular, and asking whether a self-psychology is not actually what will give greater coherence to his theory of the propriate self and the development of personality.

In favor of self-psychology, Allport grants that to hold that the self as a knowing, striving, willing agency in personality would indeed properly focus, as he has, "on the unity and coherence that mark the propriate functions of personality" (1961, p. 129). But "from the scientific point of view," he suggests: "If we admit the self as a separate agent that knows, wills, wants, and so on, are we not in danger of creating a personality within a personality? We seem to be postulating 'a little man within the breast' " (1961, p. 129). And, furthermore, we keep on begging the question, or "passing the buck" to such a "little man," if we say "the self does this or that" and so forth.

Allport accordingly concludes: "It is my position that in the structure of *personality,* if rightly understood—including, of course, the propriate structure—we shall find the explanations we seek. It is unwise to assign our problems to an inner agent who pulls the strings." And he urges that whatever philosophical purposes might justify our regarding the self as a continuing entity, in psychology we do well to avoid the sharp separation of the self "as agent" from the functioning of the propriate systems within the personality (1961, p. 130).

Allport later returns to the same problem from another angle. In actual life, he says "a fusion of the propriate states is the rule." But behind these experienced stages of selfhood, he adds, "you catch indirect glimpses of yourself as 'knower.' " And he asks: "Who is the self that knows these self-functions?" The question is especially important because "we are not only aware of what is peculiarly ours, but we are also aware that we are aware" (1961, pp. 137, 138).

Further, Allport rejects not only the postulation of a transcendent knower, but also a combined knower-wanter-striver-willer. Why? Because it sets up "a master coordinating agent within the personality" that pulls the strings. Where, then, does this leave him? A knower he needs—and accepts—a knower each of us presumably catches a glimpse of, but he cannot allow it to be conceived as something beyond the stream of patterned experience. But the creative-volitional nature gets different treatment! "It seems on the whole sounder to regard the propriate function of wanting, striving, willing as interlocked within the total personality structure" (1961, p. 138).

To readers of this chapter it will be clear that Allport's objections to some unempirical, hidden homunculus are grounded in the same radical empiricism that inspired self-psychology in its rejection of soul psychology. Allport's strictures against an agent pulling the strings, but not revealed, in conscious experience or in personality, cannot be ignored by any philosophy, let alone psychology, that would ground logically intelligible hypotheses without remainder in terms of experience. Indeed, this is the very reason for Brightman's beginning with the unity *in* and *of* conscious experience as given and for his building hypotheses about the whole self, including the body and the unconscious, on evidence provided by conscious experience. Any personalist must tread cautiously where experiential data (in the broader sense or as confined to consciousness) are scanty. What remains to be shown is that the logic or psychologic of personalistic theory must take us beyond, not "the scientific viewpoint," but the very quandary in which Allport seems to leave us.

To be specific, if the "self" or *proprium* of personality is acquired, and as a part of the personality that is also acquired, then a continuant that begins the learning, moves from one learned solution to another as it recognizes and responds to new problems, must be involved to play the "integrative" role in behavior. There is a self-identity of the knower without which to talk of personality as a learned system is meaningless. No system, especially if it is a growing structure, is without a systematizer. Nor need the systematizer be an homunculus. At every stage from birth to death it is engaged in the differentiations and interpretations that makes *this* as opposed to another possible personality actual. It is never disengaged from any actual phase in the growth of personality or *proprium*.

In other words, what experience seems to tell us at every stage is that the knowing being, active at one moment *in* perceiving and thinking about the road ahead as he drives, is nevertheless not exhausted in these specific modal activities, for he can turn his attention to other matters, thus using other activities, and then come back to these. What we must do is to begin also with the *kind* of being who is actively knowing and involved in the ways he expresses his needs at a given stage in his development, and a given environment. This kind of being is not a puller of strings but pulling, pushing, and aiming in response to problems in a given way now; he is *now becoming* the pulling-pushing-aiming-self-in-personality. Nevertheless, this self cannot be identified, or interlocked exclusively with any particular stage in development of personality, for its activities are potentially broader than any one personality in which its activities are being expressed. Were this not so, were it completely exhausted in any one personality, it could not guide the changes that take place in personality.

There is no analogy for the kind of relation between any unified, active, changing, knowing self and *its* personality; we must try to grasp this dynamic relation without giving in to substantive modes of thought. The self is not an agency that might invest itself, as a person might invest his capital in different banks, but remain unchanged and uninvolved in directing the changes that take place. *The personal self cannot delegate powers to his personality!* At any moment, a personality is the knowing self's relatively variable way of dealing with the external-internal pressures; it will never be exactly the same self again because of this experience. But it will continue to function as a knower, wanter, willer, fertilized by its past and present and now giving birth to a new future. This self is indeed "interlocked" with its total personality structure, but not exhausted in its basic activity potential by the personality it has developed in a given environment. I am the personality that my self, given its needs and capacities, has been able to acquire in America. Had I been born and brought up in China, my knowing, wanting, willing, feeling (agent-knower) would have taken different forms, but they would not be different capacities.

Does not what Allport says about propriate striving and the *proprium* fit neatly into this scheme? All the more neatly, we suggest, for now we have a discriminating agent-knower forging its empirical self-identity, a self-identity that affects its further acting-knowing, but sensible to keep it from varying the content of its *proprium* (within limits).

In relation to the *appropriated* self, or *proprium,* indeed, contemporary motives may be autonomous. But a question that would take us further into motivation theory than we can go here would still need to be asked. Granted that the *proprium* is acquired but relatively enduring, the fact is that it too is subject to change. Must not the knower from the very beginning to the end of its existence also be a wanter, with enduring though flexible needs? Any propriate self is the solution *thus far* to the individual wanter's struggle for autonomy and identity in a given growth-environmental situation. The fact that the *proprium* can be changed, that what is now propriate may become peripheral, and vice versa, calls for both wanting and knowing in a unified continuant.

If our reasoning is correct, then, a self, understood as the unity of its intrinsic activities, is engaged in discovering and realizing its own potential in a challenging, nurturant environment. In seeking to fulfill itself, in learning to trans-act successive *proprium*-personality systems, it is always engaged in the selective process of taking and giving. It is always discriminating and developing what we might call the warmer and colder aspects of adjustment in accordance with unrealized potential that is making itself felt. The self is never without *some* personality, but *which* personality is a byproduct of its interaction with the environment in the light of the maturation-learning processes and activities that define its being at any one time.

If our reasoning is correct, we cannot accept Allport's suggestion and interlock the propriate functions of wanting, striving, and willing within the personality structure while the knower remains disengaged from the *proprium.* Indeed, how shall we understand the statement that propriate functions are "felt as self-relevant" if there is no want or need for whose gratification they are relevant? If, as we assume, there is no knowing without interest (of various sorts), the knowing self must also be a knowing-wanting unity (or a *unitas multiplex* of knowing-feeling-wanting-willing-oughting-activities, as we would propose). Knowing in all of its dimensions—from sensory perception to logical, aesthetic, moral, and religious valuation and action—takes place as one phase of a unified matrix that is also feeling and wanting (at least).

To be sure, a theory of motivation must indeed meet Allport's strictures against unchanging needs and unchanging souls or selves. But, once more, if the agent-self is conceived as a concrete original unity of activities (a unity in which different activities may be discriminated but not abstracted out, and if among these activities may be discerned generic dynamic tendencies that demand expression and gratification but can be expressed and gratified in different ways), one can keep the dynamism and the future-orientation Allport rightly wants as integral to the very being of a unified self (see Bertocci & Millard, 1963). At the same time, one can explain why some sets of propriate strivings, why some habits, attitudes, sentiments, traits, intentions, and even styles of life do in fact give way to others. For while these are developed as part of, or along with, propriate strivings, they must ultimately meet the requirements of the active-potential self's knowing-wanting nature. It should be clear that on this view there are not generic goals first, and then channelizing into specific motives. There is only a continuant knowing-wanting unity that is a "fighter for ends," seeking satisfaction for its maturing and challenged potential, seeking to sustain itself from moment to moment in the light of the transactions it undergoes and of its conception of itself and the total environment.

Thus, unique and unified to begin with, living in environments its own given nature and life history makes eligible for it, the self acquires its own characteristic more or less systematic mode of adjustment (personality); it continues to live from the vantage point and achievement of that personality until further change is forced on it or selected, or both. But as it grows and learns, it is this knowing-wanting self that discriminates the near and the far, the possible and the impossible, the convenient and the necessary. In this process, the valuable and the disvaluable *to it,* the *proprium* or warm center of its adjustment, is acquired, enhanced, and sustained against attack, until it proves to be so inadequate that new adjustments are made. The self that was Saul becomes Paul, and Paul, no doubt, was the Paul that Saul *could* develop in view of Saul's past. But it could not become Paul without giving expression and direction to unused and un-realized potential.

Perhaps enough has been said to indicate that Allport's qualms about self-psychology can be met, and at the same time bring greater coherence into the interpretation of the growth and pattern in personality. Although such a self-psychology would lead to no specific prediction, it does provide greater theoretical foundation for the order in uniqueness without which prediction is hard to explain.

Personalistic philosophy and psychology can move, if you will, at different levels of description and interpretation, with full awareness of the interpenetration of the two. But the personalist, of all philosophers and psychologists, does not stop being a philosopher and start being a psychologist, or vice versa, especially when the understanding of personal development is at stake. As he tries to understand the nature of the person, his personality and his *proprium,* he uses every means of penetrating the unknown. Above all, he insists that the person be not lost in the artificial battle of disciplines; for he realizes that there are in the last analysis different ways which persons have developed in order to understand themselves and the world in which they live.

REFERENCES

ALLPORT, G. W. Motivation in personality: reply to Mr. Bertocci. *Psychol. Rev.* 1940, **47,** 533-554.

ALLPORT, G. W. The ego in contemporary psychology. *Psychol. Rev.,* 1943, **50,** 451-478.

ALLPORT, G. W. Scientific models and human morals. *Psychol. Rev.,* 1947, Reprinted in G. W. Allport, *Personality and social encounter: selected essays.* Boston: Beacon Press, 1960.

ALLPORT, G. W. The psychological nature of personality. *The Personalist,* 1953, Reprinted in *Personality and social encounter: Selected essays.* Boston: Beacon Press, 1960.

ALLPORT, G. W. *Becoming,* New Haven: Yale Univ. Press, 1955.

ALLPORT, G. W. *Pattern and growth in personality,* New York: Holt, Rinehart & Winston, 1961.

ARNOLD, MAGDA, & GASSON, J. A. *Human person.* New York: Ronald Press, 1954.

BERTOCCI, P. A. A critique of G. W. Allport's theory of motivation. *Psychol. Rev.,* 1940, **47,** 501-532.

BERTOCCI, P. A. *An introduction to philosophy of religion.* New York: Prentice-Hall, 1952.

BERTOCCI, P. A., & MILLARD, R. M. *Personality and the good: psychological and ethical perspectives.* New York: David McKay.

BOWNE, B. P. *Theory of thought and knowledge.* New York: Harper, 1897.

BOWNE, B. P. *Metaphysics.* New York: American Book Co., 1910.

BRIGHTMAN, E. S. The Finite Self. In C. I. Barrett (Ed.), *Contemporary Realism in America.* New York: Macmillan, 1932.

BRIGHTMAN, E. S. *Person and reality* (an introduction to metaphysics). (P. A. Bertocci et al., Eds.) New York: Ronald Press, 1958.

CALKINS, MARY W. *A first book in psychology*. (4th rev.) New York: Macmillan, 1914.

CALKINS, MARY W. The self in scientific psychology, *Amer. J. Psychol.* 1915, **26,** 455-524; 495.

CAMPBELL, C. A. *On selfhood and godhood*. New York: Macmillan, 1957.

CANTRIL, H. *The "why" of man's experience*. New York: Macmillan, 1950.

CANTRIL, H. Perception and Interpersonal Relations. In A. E. Kuenzli (Ed.), *The phenomenological problem*. New York: Harper, 1959. Pp. 182-199.

CAPEK, M. The reappearance of the self in James. *Phil. Rev.*, 1953, **42,** 533.

COMBS, A., & SNYGG, D. *Individual behavior*. Harper, 1959.

FRANQUIZ, J. A. *Borden Parker Bowne's treatment of the problem of change and identity*. Rio Piedras: Univ. of Puerto Rico, 1942.

FROMM, E. *The sane society*. New York: Rinehart, 1955.

GOUGH, H. G. Review of G. W. Allport's *pattern and growth in personality*. *Contemp. Psychol.*, 1962, **7,** 313-315.

HILGARD, E. R. Human motives and the concept of the self. *Amer. Psychol.*, 1949, **4,** 374-382.

MCDOUGALL, W. *Body and mind*. New York: Macmillan, 1920.

MASLOW, A. H. *Motivation and personality*. New York: Harper, 1954.

MASLOW, A. H. *Toward a psychology of being*. New York: Van Nostrand, 1962.

ROGERS, C. Some observations on the organization of personality. In A. E. Kuenzli (Ed.), *The phenomenological problem*. New York: Harper, 1959. Pp. 49-76.

SMITH, M. B. The phenomenological approach in personality theory: some critical remarks. In A. C. Kuenzli (Ed.), *The phenomenological problem*. New York: Harper, 1959. Pp. 253-268.

SNYGG, D. The need for a phenomenological system of psychology. In A. E. Kuenzli (Ed.), *The phenomenological problem*. New York: Harper, 1959.

STERN, W. *Person und Sache*. Vol. 1., 1924, p. 16 (as quoted in A. C. Knudson, *Philosophy of personalism*. New York: Abingdon Press, 1927).

STERN, W. *General psychology from the personalistic standpoint*. New York: Macmillan, 1938.

TENNANT, F. R. *Philosophical theology*. Vol. 1. London: Cambridge Univ. Press, 1928.

17 LAWRENCE S. KUBIE

THE SCIENTIFIC PROBLEMS
OF PSYCHOANALYSIS *

THE PLACE OF PSYCHOANALYSIS among the sciences is a crucial issue. An objective assay must recognize both its present limitations and its future potentials for growth and for research. This focuses our attention on psychoanalysis as a process of exploration and not on its superstructure of theories or their varied forms; nor will we be concerned with psychoanalysis as a therapeutic instrument. All attempts which have been made to compare the therapeutic efficacy of the psychotherapies have been premature and culpably naïve. The technical problems which must be solved before such studies can be meaningful have been discussed repeatedly in papers to which the interested reader will be referred.[1]

It was regrettable, although unavoidable, that psychoanalysis had to begin as a therapeutic technique. Its development would have been sounder had it been possible for it to be at first an instrument and object of basic research, unbiased by therapeutic urgencies. This is not the first time in medical history that new agents and new procedures have been applied prematurely to therapeutic purposes, and then in some measure have been misused even by their discoverers and proponents. Nor is it the first time that this has given rise to misinterpretations and misunderstandings. This has been true of many drugs, of many biological agents such as sera and antibiotics, and of many physical agents such as heat, cold, electrical

---

* This chapter is based on a revision of an article by the author on "Psychoanalysis and Scientific Method" which appeared in the *Journal of Nervous and Mental Disease*, Vol. 131, No. 6, December 1960, pp. 495-512.

[1] In 1930, the Berlin Institute published its honest but overconfident report on the apparent therapeutic fruits of the first ten years of its existence. Psychoanalysts have since then devoted much thought to the problems involved in the evaluation of therapy. For reasons explained in publications cited below, none of these evaluative studies has yielded significant data. Those who fail to appreciate the complex difficulties of such studies and the even greater difficulty of comparative evaluations of different psychotherapies blunder seriously in their efforts. Indeed, most studies of this problem bear the imprints both of naïveté and of bias.

316

stimulation, the X ray, and other forms of radiant energy. Such errors are always corrected gradually.

It is misleading to assume, as some do, that mercenary reasons account for the early use of psychoanalysis for therapeutic purposes. The deeper reason was that at the outset only those who were in dire need and to whom existing therapies had brought no relief would subject themselves to this new, untried, and arduous regimen. Without this vast pool of uncured and largely untreated neuroses, there could have been no psychoanalytic Odyssey. Moreover, urgent appeals for help still draw the humane investigator away from his researches into therapeutic involvement, unless the institution for which he works were not only to forbid him to assume therapeutic responsibilities, but also provided a pool of therapists to whom he could refer those whose needs become apparent to him in the course of his studies (Kubie, 1956b). Yet there are no full-time research institutes which have so far-sighted and humane a program as this.

As a science, psychoanalysis has paid a price for the fact that its origin and development was made possible only by its immediate commitment to the service of human needs. The price has been high; but it will not be too high in the long view of history, if we now set out on the process of correcting the consequent errors. It was inevitable that analysis should be tossed into the therapeutic arena prematurely, but this does not justify a continued tolerance of this today, when men and women are eager to undergo analysis for training purposes, as part of research projects, and out of philosophical and intellectual curiosity. This fact points to a healthy change in the temper of our culture: a lessened defensiveness, a willingness to accept the complexity and the motley color of human personality, and a greater humility about the role of conscious processes in personality. This change is itself a result of the cultural impact of psychoanalysis and has occurred in spite of its many scientific deficiencies.

An obvious error in logic resulted from the fact that human beings subjected themselves to analysis only when driven to it by the failure of other forms of therapy and because they had heard that somehow in the course of analysis a certain undetermined number seemed to reach a resolution of some of their difficulties. Hope and their own needs led them quite naturally to assume that, in those cases in which therapeutic results had attended or followed analysis, the analytic experience had played a major role in these improvements. This was *post hoc* reasoning. In many instances it was true; but it remained unproven. For us as scientists, such a sequence of events provides only a challenging working hypothesis, the testing of which is necessary in spite of the difficulties of testing. Yet one may wonder whether analysts would have had the courage to push ahead on their ever-lengthening and more arduous analytic voyages without some measure of innocent and optimistic lapses in logic. For this, too, we should in retrospect have tolerance and sympathy as we now try to apply

318 LAWRENCE S. KUBIE

more exacting criteria. In short, as we look back historically and with the detachment which is supposed to be an attribute of the philosophic mind, the fact that analysis began as a therapeutic instrument should lead us to conclude that insofar as this made possible the birth of psychoanalysis it was in balance good, even if it clouded many scientific issues. Now, however, we have reached a point at which we must use analysis both as an object of basic research and also as one instrument among many for the study of the analytic process itself. In many centers this is starting already, gropingly, grumblingly, but with dedicated purpose. I do not doubt that the outcome will be many important changes in technique, and in the superstructure of concept, terminology, and theory.

In his article in the *Encyclopaedia Britannica,* Freud (1926) predicted that, in historical retrospect, the cultural significance of psychoanalysis would be measured in terms of its value as a method of psychological investigation and as a theory of human psychology, rather than as a technique of therapy. Moreover, he warned repeatedly against the biases which are introduced into analytic theorizing by an overemphasis on therapeutic needs. Yet conscientious exhortations and self-criticism cannot eliminate all the distortions which flow from the therapeutic applications of psychoanalysis. This can be done only by subjecting the analytic process to direct investigation *outside* therapeutic settings. This obviously will create new technical problems and new fallacies. Much has been written about the differences that the absence of a therapeutic need and motive will introduce; but there are as yet no objective studies of these hypothetical if reasonable assumptions. To explore them will be one of the first essential steps in systematic research into psychoanalysis.

This is not all that can be said about the problems of research into the psychotherapeutic and psychonoxious leverage of psychoanalysis; but it may be enough to indicate both some of its complexities as well as why I choose not to become involved in them until we can first survey the position of psychoanalysis in science from a nontherapeutic point of view.[2]

[2] The many extrinsic variables which must be taken into account in any effort to compare the results of various organic and psychological methods of treating psychiatric conditions were discussed in several symposia. One of these (Oberndorf et al., 1948) was held in Boston in the late forties and was published in the *International Journal of Psychoanalysis.* Two others (Brenman et al., 1948; Bronner et al. 1949) were published in the *American Journal of Orthopsychiatry.* A statistical study of variations in psychoanalytic practice (Kubie, 1950a) was published in *Psychiatry.* The Hixon Fund Lectures, delivered at the California Institute of Technology and published by the Stanford University Press (Kubie, 1952) considered the special problems of validation and prediction and the peculiar difficulties of setting up control groups in the psychotherapies. An article on some unsolved problems of psychoanalytic psychotherapy (Kubie, 1956c) appeared in the volume called *Progress in Psychotherapy,* edited by Frieda Fromm-Reichmann. This paper considered various other factors which make such comparative studies premature at this time and outlined the specific conditions which must be met before such studies can have any value. A description

Therefore, I will now consider in sequence (1) some of the limitations inherent in psychoanalytic methods, (2) the essence of psychoanalysis as a process, (3) how this process fits into the framework of scientific methodology, and (4) finally, what we might call the philosophy underlying the concept of psychodynamics in general.

LIMITATIONS

This will not be an exhaustive list of limitations. Nor will it be organized systematically. It is instead a representative sample of some of the limits within which psychoanalysis has operated in the past, and beyond which it is now trying to reach.

Among the scientific disciplines and methodologies, psychoanalysis has had to struggle with unique difficulties which result from the fact that it has been dependent largely upon auditory data, with only minor visual additions. Because of the dominant importance and speed of the spoken word as an instrument of communication, because of the slower pace of writing, and because of the limited range of variation, and consequent relative stereotype, in gesture and expression as methods of communication, the ear has had to be the major source of psychoanalytic data. To an even greater extent than visual data, auditory data are vulnerable to distortion both in the moment of perception and in recall. As Abraham Kaplan pointed out, science has been forced to abandon the doctrine of immaculate perception (Kubie, 1956d).

Recent studies of subliminal and preconscious perceptions (most of which, unfortunately, have been restricted to tachistoscopic studies of visual input) have shown that the incessant bombardment of the individual by preconscious afferents plays a more important role than could have been appreciated in Freud's day. Indeed, there is abundant evidence from daily experience that subliminal afferents from auditory, olfactory, tactile, kinesthetic, proprioceptive, and enteroceptive modalities play a major role in everything which goes on in the central nervous system (Fisher, 1956; Klein, Smith, & Spence, 1959; Marsh & Worden, 1956). Yet, even to this day, their implications for psychoanalysis have not been explored. Future research will have to include investigations of the processes of preconscious perception via every sensory modality, and also of the processes of preconscious response. The purpose of this will be not only to free the psychoanalytic interview from its too exclusive dependence upon conscious

---

of the structure of a multidisciplinary institute for basic research in psychiatry (Kubie, 1956b) was published in the *Bulletin of the Menninger Clinic* in 1956. A paper on the neurotic process as the focus of physiological and psychoanalytic research (Kubie, 1958b) brought together still more of these factors. Finally, the difficulty of attaining the quality of technical, clinical, and personal maturity which such research necessitates has been explored in still other studies (Kubie, 1953a, 1958b, 1958c, 1962).

auditory input, but also to include in its theoretical structure and in its exploratory and therapeutic techniques considerations of the role of preconscious (subliminal) input from all modalities, preconscious central processing, and preconscious responses on autonomic and somatomuscular levels.

Distortions of auditory data occur in a quite specific way during the very process of perception. As we listen to words, we alter what we hear. We do this "preconsciously," that is, automatically and without being aware of it. In fact, this is essential both for successful cognitive communication and for empathic communication as well. We "correct" what we hear in our effort to understand what anyone says to us and how anyone feels in our presence. We do this as we listen to patients and again as we try to reconstruct from memory both what was said and how. To demonstrate this preconscious "correcting" of experience, one need only record a sample of one's own free speech, and then listen to the recording while reading a transcript made by an expert secretary (Kubie, 1958c). One discovers that in transcribing from the machine, the conscientious secretary will have "corrected" what the tape said. Moreover, unless specially schooled not to do this, the better the secretary, the greater will be the effort to have the tape "make sense," and the greater are the "corrective" distortions in the transcript of the recording. We can hardly escape concluding that until it became feasible to introduce techniques of precise recording and reproducing, the raw data from analytic interviews rested on the insecure grounds of man's fallible memory of his distorted percepts. Nor was it possible to subject linguistic, paralinguistic, or kinesic responses to formal or statistical analysis, until the techniques of recording and screening became generally available (Kubie, 1958c).

New distortions are produced by the introduction of mechanical contrivances into any human relationship. There are comparable problems, however, in every science. The microscope and the stethoscope introduced distortions. Blood drawn from the vein is changed in transfer to a test tube for chemical analysis. If science advances in spite of these technical flaws, it is by learning to recognize the changes that are introduced by the refined instruments of observation, of recording, and of measurement, by learning how to limit these changes and how to maintain their approximate constancy, how to allow for them, and finally, how to correct for them. This must be done before it is safe to derive new theories from the data which new methods provide. Psychoanalysis is following a sound precedent, as it prepares for the first time to make more precise records of the raw data of analytic communications.

Nor is it an accident that Freud's most basic research into dream psychology, which consisted primarily of his studies of his own dreams, were dependent not on anyone's memory of spoken word, but on his own *written* records both of his own dreams and of his own free associations to them. This should have alerted analysts to the importance of the permanent record for the advance of their discipline.

The fact that every moment of behavior is transitory forces us to depend upon memory, with its inevitable retrospective distortions. Moreover, because the transient moment leaves a permanent change in the observed and the observer, it can never be re-enacted unchanged. Consequently, until there were ways to record the material of psychiatric and psychoanalytic interviews, it was impossible for the observer to study them repeatedly, or to subject them to scrutiny by other observers.

Another major limitation has been the difficulty of setting up precise controls. This is a complex subject, which has been discussed in several of the publications to which I have already referred (Kubie, 1956c). The only point to make here is that the use of groups of supposedly similar ailments to balance against hypothetical normals is so fallacious as to make a mockery of the principle of control. We are forced to use a more cumbersome and less precise method of control, in which each individual is studied in minute detail before any generalization is carried over from one to another. This method introduces other sources of error. The answer will ultimately be found in developing methods of pooling the experience of many observers on many patients, each of which is recorded meticulously for parallel interpretation and statistical analysis. (A limited start toward this has been made by the Central Fact Gathering Committee of the American Psychoanalytic Association.)

The superficial study of large numbers has certain values; but it loses much of this value unless, out of the larger group, an unweighted and statistically adequate sample of representative individuals can be subjected to microscopic scrutiny, by methods which are derived from formal analytic techniques. These steps introduce new errors, but have at the same time their special values. Whether the values counterbalance the errors will require detailed testing.

There are limitations in our techniques of *validation*. In the first place, although we speak of "an" interpretation, the determinants of human behavior are always multiple. As a result, the word "interpretation" actually covers a group of interrelated interpretations. It has often been pointed out that it is not difficult to prove that certain interpretations of the meanings of behavior are possible (Hilgard, 1952; Sears, 1943, 1944). Nor is it difficult to take a step beyond that, and to show that in many instances an interpretation is plausible or even probable. What is difficult is the critical final step, to prove that in any specific instance any one interpretation is adequate and unique, and therefore constitutes the one necessary hypothesis. Psychoanalysis has rarely been able to present data which meet these ultimate criteria; yet this type of evidence is essential for the validation of analytic procedure and techniques. Until we reach this point, any interpretation must be presented as one likely hypothesis among several, never as *the* interpretation.

Conclusive validation of a specific interpretation in a specific situation has been possible chiefly with the material from uninformed children, naïve psychotic patients, and subjects under hypnosis (Kubie, 1952). The literature is full of examples drawn from these three sources, where the patient, child, psychotic, primitive, or hypnotic subject, sounds as though he had written the textbooks. These data carry the validity of precise experimentation (Kubie, 1953b, 1958b).

In the past, validation has been approximated by applying several criteria: the emotional responses to an interpretation; the changes which occur in the patient's subsequent communications (that is, changes both in form and content); concomitant changes in his stream of free associations; the sudden accessibility of hitherto inaccessible material (memories, feelings, conflicts, ancient fears, and shames); still other changes which seem to follow on the increased accessibility of such data. Although these are by no means to be dismissed as meaningless, they are peculiarly liable to the *post hoc–propter hoc* fallacy. We must not forget that in presenting an interpretation one frequently must talk about some tabooed topic. This in and of itself can free the patient to talk about this or related tabooed topics, whether the specific interpretation was correct or incorrect. Therefore, a subsequent increase of "freedom" is not conclusive evidence for the validity of the specific interpretation. Changes in the material after an interpretation are circumstantial and inferential evidence rather than conclusive. The only conclusive evidence of the validity of an interpretation would be if through it one achieved greater precision of predictions; and before this can be estimated, a vast amount of precise quantitative and qualitative work must be done to establish the degree of precision of predictions and the relative incidence of correct and incorrect predictions in settings which are free from the pressing demands either of therapy or of teaching.

A great deal has been claimed for the importance of *prediction* in the validation of interpretations. There is no doubt that in the daily practice of analysis, and particularly in the supervision of students, accurate predictions are occasionally made as to what is about to occur in the life of a patient—the kind of material that he is going to produce, the kind of dream which he is going to have, the kind of feelings that he is going to generate. Sometimes such predictions are quite startlingly correct. Yet no study has been made of the frequency with which such predictions are incorrect, nor of the ratio of correct to incorrect predictions. Nor has anyone studied how frequently no predictions are made; yet this would be essential in a statistical survey. It is possible that the analyst becomes sufficiently confident to venture a prediction only under special circumstances. He may not venture a prediction out of a preconscious fear of being incorrect. As a result of his withholding of predictions, such predictions as he ventures cannot constitute a random or representative sample. Not to include the withheld predictions would unfairly weight any sample of correct predictions in the favor of analysis.

Equally significant is the fact that no one has tested the effects of any change in technique or in the techniques of interpretation on the ratio of correct to incorrect predictions. Therefore, although we cannot dismiss as meaningless the occurrences of correct predictions, we must be cautious about basing any claims on such sporadic successes. These considerations underscore still further the importance of rigorous statistical analyses of analytic methodology and of analytic validation.

To avoid any misconceptions, it should be understood than an interpretation is not a prophecy. It is an hypothesis about the meanings of past events and about the confluent forces which have produced some pattern of behavior, thought, and feeling. Predictive implications are latent in any interpretation; but these are not expressed. The implication is that if the hypothesis is correct, and if any of the forces which constitute the described constellation should change, then the behavior will change. The analyst does *not* make any such prophecy to the patient. At most the analyst may ruminate about these future events: either silently to himself or under certain special circumstances to a student, but never in the hearing of the patient and not to the patient.

If such implicit predictions were made to the analysand, then the fact that the analyst had ventured to make the prediction would introduce into the stream of the analytic process an element which would exert an influence on the subsequent chain of events, quite apart from the influence of the interpretation itself. Such a prediction would constitute what is called a "self-fulfilling prophecy." But since the prediction is never made to the patient, the self-fulfilling prophesy is not a complicating problem which must be considered here.

It is almost impossible to speak about dynamic processes without using quantitative figures of speech, that is, some kind of "more" and "less." Yet our right to assume that quantitative differences actually exist is not unlimited (Kubie, 1947; Pumpian-Mindlin, 1958).[3] Furthermore, it is wholly invalid to assume that quantitative changes are the only variables that can account for differences in activity, in personality, and in illness. Today this whole area is being subjected to critical scrutiny by a number of analysts and critics, who are concerned with the changes in psychoanalytic theory which the development of cybernetics, information theory, communications engineering, and electronic computers is forcing on us. Relevant here is the work, among others, of Pumpian-Mindlin (1958), McCulloch and Pitts

---

[3] A personal communication from W. S. McCulloch also bears on this point.

(1943), Colby (1955), Ruff (1956), Miller (1955, 1960), Gerard (1958), Ashby (1956, 1958, 1960), Grey-Walter (1953), and Chassan (1956).

Two other grave deficiencies in our current conceptual equipment are closely related to the problem of quantitative differences. These are the lack of basic criteria of change (Kubie, 1956a, 1956c), and the tendency of all systems of psychology to develop the illusion that a new description (which may be a more precise description or merely new terminology for an old description) has greater *explanatory* value than the old. The distinction between description and explanation is of critical importance; yet theoretical formulas in psychoanalysis are usually mixtures of the two.

This leads to a consideration of certain instrumental deficiencies. I have already mentioned one, namely, that which derives from the fact that we depend predominantly on the ear. This is, however, a lack which is being overcome. The use of infrared motion photography will carry us forward another step by making it possible to study activity in the dark as in the light. Yet we still lack techniques by which to validate assumptions about quantitative changes. Thus, we lack instruments with which to assay the relative roles played concurrently by conscious, preconscious, and unconscious processes and the changes in their relative roles which may occur during an analysis. Paradoxical though it may seem, it is easier for us to study the impact of unconscious processes on conscious and preconscious activity than the impact of conscious communications on what goes on behind the iron curtain in the system of unconscious processes (Hilgard, 1952). Here, again, we need new instruments.

As a result of these procedural deficiencies, we find ourselves with certain conceptual limitations. We are not yet clear as to what constitute (1) the internally cohesive clinical syndromes which have a common origin, a common history, and a common fate; (2) the conglomerate drives which operate as conflicting or cooperating units in the personality; or (3) the basic personality units whose variations must be first described and then explained. These have been formulated and reformulated in many ways; from time to time, analysts have agreed on them briefly, but never for long. Dissatisfaction with each formulation leads to fresh formulations, about which new disagreements arise. This is not unnatural; but it means that we have not yet completed the primary descriptive steps, which are essential in the development of any natural science, and which must be accurately done and tested before etiological hypotheses can be seriously considered. We cannot set out to explain something before we can agree on a description of the nature of what it is we are attempting to explain. (4) Nor is it clear how best to formulate the nature of the energetic processes, their original sources, the derivative forms which such energetic processes can assume, or the role which hypothetical differences in energy may play in psychological affairs. We have not been able to eliminate from our thinking the figurative language of the physics of the 1880s and 1890s: the physics of mechanics and of hydraulic engineering, or the concept of electricity as a weightless fluid flowing through solid tubes. These images still dominate analytic speech and theoretical conceptions. Thus, in many directions a process of conceptual clarification is only starting. Only a few psychoanalysts have given up the primitive concepts that the activity of the central nervous system requires the transfer of matter, or the transfer, increase, or decrease of energy, or the transmutation of one form of energy into other forms, to replace these with concepts of the transmission of bits of information as a more appropriate conceptual model. A full discussion of these issues would necessitate a recapitulation and a thorough re-examination of the theory of instincts, of instinct derivatives, and of their transformations under the impact of symbolic processes in man (Kubie, 1956a).[4]

Having listed some analytic deficiencies, let me turn to what I consider the essential virtues of psychoanalysis as an exploratory process, and why in spite of its deficiencies I consider analysis to be of basic importance to all of science.

PSYCHOANALYSIS AS A SCIENTIFIC PROCESS

It is possible to divide psychoanalysis into components in many ways. Those which I will use have no special virtue, except insofar as they are helpful for the consideration of our problem.

The ultimate goal of analysis includes changes in basic components of personality, such as changes in the definition of personality boundaries, changes in identifications, changes in all conscience functions, reduction and realignment of areas of conflict, the reconciliation of irreconcilable goals, and the like. In its effort to move toward such long-run objectives, the immediate and initial goal of analytic exploration is to illuminate the concurrent roles of conscious, preconscious, and unconscious processes in human thought, feeling, purpose, behavior, and relationships. As a ther-

---

[4] Freud's "economic" principle made the explicit assumption that it is impossible to explain either normal or abnormal psychology without assuming that they are based on differences in quantities of energy. This point of view reflected the concepts of the times, when physics thought only in terms of transmissions of mass or of energy and the various transmutations of one form of energy into another. Even the transmutation of energy into mass and vice versa, which is a commonplace today, was only dimly perceived then. Today we are more concerned with the transmission and processing of bits of information in the nervous system, which occurs and varies with minimal investments or variations in energy consumption or output, just as it occurs in electronic computers. This simple fact is forcing a careful if somewhat reluctant revision of a great deal of psychoanalytic theory, terminology, and concept. Miller (1959, 1960) points out that it gives us actually a new fourth dimension: "density," the number of bits of information transmitted and processed per unit time.

apy, psychoanalysis attempts to redistribute their roles and to shrink the areas in which unconscious processes have a controlling influence. All of this, however, is outside the range of this chapter, which is concerned with psychoanalysis as an exploratory technique. Therefore I will consider only the following elements of psychoanalysis as a process (Kubie, 1956c): the constancy of the setting; the constancy of attitudes; the analytic incognito; the role of interpretations as working hypotheses; the role of transference and countertransference in interpretations and identifications; the crucial significance of free association.

In the struggle to explore the inner space of human psychology and human personality, the basic challenge is the clarification of the respective roles of three "levels" or systems of concurrent processes, the interplay among them, and their individual or summated effects on behavior, thought, purpose, and feeling in human life. I will say at once that there is abundant evidence, largely overlooked, that among these processes the most pervasive and continuous is neither conscious nor unconscious, but what we call preconscious. This seems to consist of a continuous and remarkably rapid stream of afferent, integrative, creative, and efferent human mentation, mediated by coded cues and signals, but without fully developed symbolic representation: what the Würzburg school used to call "imageless thought." In the waking state, through the use of symbols, our conscious processes provide a relatively slow, limited, and weighted sample of this continuous preconscious stream. Our *unconscious* processes constitute in turn an even more fragmentary and distorted symbolic sample of the conscious samples of the underlying preconscious stream.[5]

In sleep, preconscious processing constitutes a variable but apparently continuous preconscious dream flow. Of this "the dream," as we ordinarily know it, is only a condensed fragment, a weighted sample expressed predominantly through visual imagery. The result is a cluster of visual hieroglyphics with multiple simultaneous conscious, preconscious, and unconscious implications. No matter how we structure the personality or organize it, no matter how we use such conceptual metaphors as id, ego, and superego, or regression, defense, identification, incorporation, denial, reversal, and so on, since each and every one of these operates on all three of these levels concurrently, the critical problem remains the same: can we determine the relative roles of these three concurrent systems of processing and sampling, and their interplay? To determine this will require the development of techniques by which to isolate the influence of each of the three systems of mental activities as they operate concurrently in human affairs. At present, faulty though it is, psychoanalysis is the only instrument

---

[5] Note that in the unconscious system it is never the symbol or the symbolic act which is unconscious, but its relation to that which it is supposed to represent, but masks instead.

which even approximates this goal. Out of it more precise instruments will evolve: but these will be rooted in the pioneer work of Freud.

I have stated this position without indicating in detail wherein this thesis is an extrapolation from the position which Freud took many years ago, and which he then allowed to fall virtually into disuse, but without ever disowning it. His scientific imagination seemed merely to be drawn in another structural direction. One might think of this period in his life as a tide which drew him to an earlier anatomical rather than a physiological shore, paralleling perhaps his earlier neuroanatomical interests. Because of this shift in the emphasis of Freud's theoretical structure, the description given here is an extrapolation from Freud's earlier position, but varies in certain important ways from his later "structural" metaphors and from the current fashions in psychoanalytic theory which derive from his structural concepts. This seems to me to be one of the virtues of my own point of view; the structural metaphors seem to me to have long since proved their sterility. Yet the reader should be warned that there are other experienced and thoughtful analysts whose thinking conforms more closely to Freud's later schema and who do not agree with me.

What troubles me far more is the difficulty of giving adequate operational descriptions of how to differentiate among conscious, preconscious, and unconscious processes. It is easy to characterize their consequences. This I have done in many previous articles, pointing out the easily recognizable characteristics of behavior in which conscious processes dominate the fields of force (Kubie, 1954), and also the characteristics of behavior in which preconscious processing flows freely, dominating the psychic stream and furnishing a continuous supply of processed experience for conscious symbolic sampling (Kubie 1958a, 1958b). Nor has it been difficult to describe the special qualities of that behavior which is dominated by processes in which the link between the conscious symbols and their unconscious roots has been severed or distorted, which is what occurs when unconscious processes are dominant. Unhappily, however, to separate out three types or levels or systems of psychological process through their characteristic effects on behavior is not the same as recognizing, isolating, characterizing, and, ultimately, measuring the role which each is playing in a stream of events and processes in which the three are intermingled. We can state with considerable confidence that human experience can be perceived, processed, represented (and also misrepresented), and responded to, in three ways. We can recognize these three ways from their results. But this is an indirect process of identification. An operational definition in terms of the techniques by which each can be isolated and measured is not yet within our grasp. Clinical psychologists and neurophysiologists and electroencephalographers must set themselves to the task of devising test instruments which will provide methods by which to sharpen our identifications of these three

concurrent methods of dealing with experience, tests which might appraise
the relative role of each in any one moment of behavior, and which might
even give us an indication of those areas in life in which conscious and preconscious processes dominate as opposed to those areas in which unconscious processing holds the upper hand. This differentiation is difficult
since none of these processes ever operates alone, and all three always operate concurrently.

This then is a basic challenge. We recognize its importance fully; but we
cannot yet cope with it adequately.

Let me summarize by indicating again that I characterize the primary
exploratory goal of the analytic process as an attempt to clarify the continuous interplay of concurrent conscious, preconscious, and unconscious processes in every moment of life, whether awake or asleep, and in every aspect of human personality and behavior. Their interaction enters into every
creative act in science, art, music, or literature, and into all neurotic and
psychotic processes as well, with or without organic substrate. Therefore,
this interaction is at the core of our understanding of all human psychology,
sick or well. Implicit here is a concept of the relationship between neurosis
and health which involves the essential nature of the neurotic processes,
its genesis, and the role of conflicts on all three levels. It is not my purpose
to discuss this here. Instead, I will refer to previous studies of the question
(Kubie, 1954, 1958a). But with this premise in mind, we can now consider
in what analysis as a process consists.

The framework of the analytic interview maintains to a unique degree a
relative constancy of external variables, making it possible to repeat observations and to collect data day after day under relatively unchanged external circumstances. The situation is sufficiently standardized to enable us
to make comparable observations on one person at different times, and also
on different people.

The formality of this framework cannot eliminate the fluctuating state of
the *observer* (to wit, the analyst); but it limits the impact of these fluctuations on the interaction between analyst and analysand and, therefore, on
the process of observation. Thus the analyst's "incognito," his formal aloof-
ness, his avoidance of any extra-analytic role or contact, all help to minimize and to render constant the distortions which would otherwise be inter-
posed by the analyst's unconscious processes, helping him to approximate
the role of a relatively passive and inert observer and recorder of his own
percepts of the patient's productions.

A situation results in which the majority of the spontaneous variables
which are introduced into the stream of material arise out of the subject of
the investigation—the analysand. This makes it approximately possible to
study the mind of another without distortions and interference from that of
the observer.

The analyst makes his own conscious samples and conscious summaries of his conscious and preconscious responses to the subject's productions; from time to time he shares these with the patient in the form of "interpretations" (the term the analyst uses for his working hypotheses).

This requires further explanation. By remaining as ill-defined as is humanly possible, by masking his own emotional reactions, his aesthetic tastes, his political and religious views, his family ties, the details of his personal life, and his feelings about the patient and the patient's communications, the analyst attempts to remain a cipher about whom the patient can imagine anything he feels and feel anything he must. The analyst's goal thus is to be a blank human screen, on whom the patient can project his concurrent conscious, preconscious, and unconscious feelings and fantasies. As long as the analyst as a real person remains essentially unknown to the patient, the patient's thoughts, feelings, and fantasies about the analyst will not be earth-bound to reality. Instead, they will be products of the patient's imaginative and creative psychological potentials. To the extent to which the analyst remains unknown, he will be a sample of humanity drawn from a grab bag; and on this relatively blank image of the analyst the patient can then drape his fantasies, as one might drape a costume on a dummy in a store window (Kubie, 1950b).

The study of this process in the analysis gives the patient insight into the hidden and subtle ways in which similar projections can distort any and all of his daily human relationships—his response to the stranger he passes on the street, to the acquaintance who greets him, to a boss, to an associate, to a child. Gradually, the fact becomes inescapable to him that these are all projections of his own unconscious needs, conflicts, and fantasies, many of them transplanted from the remote past. In short, the analytic incognito makes it possible for the patient to use the analyst as though he were an animated, mobile, more-or-less symmetrical stimulus card in a Rorschach or a Thematic Apperception Test; an animate object on which to project his feelings and fantasies. The study of the distortions of reality which such projections produce illuminates for the subject the distortions which can enter into all of his personal relationships. This is part of what is meant by the study and clarification and analysis of transference processes.

Conversely, if the analyst allows himself to become known to the patient, he will perforce anchor the patient to reality, thus obscuring the role of the patient's unconscious needs and feelings.

Note that I have not said that any of this *eliminates* countertransference processes. We are justified only in saying that the conscientious maintenance of the analytic incognito lessens the impact of countertransference processes on all three levels and significantly reduces the distortions which they can otherwise introduce. These considerations have been more fully explained in other available studies (Kubie, 1950b).

The question is often raised whether the analytic incognito is a fiction or a fact. Is it not inevitable that even if the analyst is unknown at the start of the analysis, he must lose some part of this incognito each day, each time he greets a patient or says goodby, each time he speaks, each time he offers an interpretation? Over the course of an analysis, does not the analyst's incognito suffer gradual decrements through the cumulative effects of minute cues, both subliminal and conscious? There are the daily differences in expression, posture, gesture, intonation, dress. Do not all of these betray to the analysand much about the analyst as a person, his moods and his convictions, his allegiances and his vulnerabilities? Of course this is true. Unless he wore a mask and gown, or analyzed from behind a screen, and made all of his comments and interpretations by typewritten notes, or had them transmitted in some stereotyped fashion and in a voice not his own, the patient must gradually accumulate clues about him. Yet such clues are faint and ambiguous; and into the analysand's interpretation of them he will project his own fantasies. Consequently, as long as the analyst keeps his distance and holds in check his own exhibitionistic impulses, the analytic value of the patient's fantasies about him will not be lost merely because the patient gradually picks up uncertain clues as to the real nature of the man behind the analytic mask.

For certain investigations, it might well be important to eliminate even such faint clues as these. The analyst's presence might be represented by something as impersonal as a typed card, or by a voice electronically altered in transmission so that its modulations would be obscured. For ordinary purposes, one stops short of experimental perfection, and in therapeutic or training analyses the analytic incognito is relative and not absolute.

Nevertheless, the more intact is the incognito, the greater is its value for translating transference forces and also for evaluating the validity and the impact of any interpretation. This is because when an interpretation is made from behind the screen of an intact analytic incognito it constitutes a single variable introduced into a *relatively* constant analytic interaction. Without the incognito, the same interpretation would drop into a turbulent sea of complex waves of transference and countertransference, in which so many variables would be interacting that the interpretation of the role of any one of them would be almost impossible. Consequently, the effort to maintain as strict an incognito as is possible conforms to an elementary principle of scientific research, namely, to aim always to introduce one variable at a time.

Furthermore, if the psychoanalyst is scrupulous about not establishing any extra-analytic contacts with his patients, the analyst will avoid an array of additional sources of dangerous confusion. Once an analyst establishes a social relationship with his patient, he begins to make demands on the relationship which serve his needs rather than the patient's. Thereafter, the analyst's unconscious conflicts will play an increasing role among the processes which shape his interpretations. Self-serving purposes become confusingly interwoven with his efforts to be patient-serving. Therefore, both for scientific and for therapeutic purposes, it is essential for the analyst to eschew extra-analytic contacts with his patients. There can be no compromise about this principle.

In small communities, the fact that everyone knows everyone else creates a serious obstacle to the analytic incognito. In such centers there are only a few analysts, and the people who seek to be analyzed, whether for educational, cultural or therapeutic purposes, inevitably come from a small in-group. Everyone who has worked in small university towns, in research institutes, or psychiatric hospitals which are remote from large centers knows how difficult this situation is and how it tends to contaminate the analytic process. Here, as in so many activities in life, practical exigencies force realistic compromises; but this does not alter the scientific principle. A surgeon who is operating in a jungle may have to operate without benefit of sterile instruments. He may have to accept the risks involved and do the best he can. Surgery in a sterile field with clean hands and clean instruments is better surgery than surgery with unsterile hands in a dirty field. Similarly, analysts who work under unfavorable circumstances may have to make comparable compromises. For the scientific investigation of the analytic process itself and in the use of analysis for psychological exploration, the incognito is essential. Although this is not our concern here, there is every reason to emphasize its importance in therapy as well. Therefore to conduct an analysis in an uncontaminated field, that is, under circumstances in which the analytic incognito will not be continually invaded and penetrated, is essential for its scientific use and exploration.

Finally, I would emphasize the fact that transference and countertransference are not peculiar to psychoanalysis. They operate in every human relationship. But in analysis they are studied as in no other procedure. At this point, I must again remind the reader that I am not considering therapeutic leverage, but only the scientific and exploratory value, first, of something which is called the analytic incognito, and second, of the analysis of transference and countertransference processes. These devices are essential for protecting the material which the analyst is observing by limiting the distortions through contamination by the observer.

FREE ASSOCIATIONS AND THE ANALYSIS OF TRANSFERENCE PROCESSES

Significance of Free Associations It is strange that the challenge of free associations has been neglected even by analysts. This failure is evidenced by the absence of critical investigations into variations in the patterns of free associations in response to variations in neurophysiological and psychophysiological conditions. This lack has been one of the major obstacles to the steady growth of psychoanalysis as a science. It is fair to add, however, that such studies have become possible only since automatic recording has been readily available. I have already indicated that it is impossible to listen to ordinary speech without distorting our perceptions of it. It is even less possible to take in, imprint, and recall a string of free associations. We distort them first at the time of perception, and again, to an even greater degree, in retrospect: this is true no matter how phonographic the mind of the listener. We can remember an entire sentence as a unit; but if we break up that sentence into syllables and scramble them, it becomes impossible to remember the same number of "nonsense" syllables. Yet free associations, when they are truly free in the technical analytic sense, approximate strings of ideas and words or even fragments of words and ideas without apparent relevance or pattern. Consequently, the task of perceiving, imprinting, and recalling free associations becomes so difficult that only a recording device can provide the raw data of analytic observations for critical qualitative and quantitative analysis as to content, meaning and form (Kubie, 1958c).

Free associations are important for many reasons. They constitute a mirror image of the conditioned reflex, as I first pointed out (Kubie, 1934). Their deeper importance arises out of the fact that this is our only approximation to a technique by which to secure relatively unweighted and therefore representative samples of *all* that is going on in the mind at any one time (Kubie, 1952, 1956d). Any conversation which is goal-directed, any effort to talk about a chosen topic, involves an automatic, preconscious process of selection and rejection. When I am talking about baseball, I cannot at the same time talk about football; and if I talk about football, I cannot talk about science or philosophy. From the conscious election of a topic to talk about flows a preconscious process of screening, selecting, and rejecting. This goes on all the time at extraordinary but still unmeasured and uncalculated speeds (Kubie, 1958b). Yet it is what makes human speech possible. Under these circumstances, the spoken word is only a selected and weighted fragment of all that is going on in the speaker's head at any moment. Clearly, then, when we need a more representative cross section of another's mental process, we must conduct an approximation of a Gallup poll. This we can do only if the speaker talks without electing to focus on any topic, or to exclude anything which comes to his mind, so providing the raw material of free associations. By not excluding or selecting anything *deliberately,* free associations become free of conscious choice, selection, or rejection; and by the same token, automatic preconscious selection and rejection are at least minimized. What is unmasked thereby is the influence of *unconscious* processes on the preconscious linkages among feelings, ideas, actions, and purposes, which are themselves the products of conditioning (Kubie, 1934, 1958a). It is this which gives the technique of free association its unique significance as a method for unmasking the concurrent influence of conscious, preconscious and unconscious processes in mental activity. Glover said long ago that as long as free associations are flowing, an analysis is moving.

Dependence of Free Association on the Analysis of Transference Processes The analytic incognito assists in the clarification of those special projections which constitute transference processes. This in turn helps the patient to use the critical exploratory tool of analysis, the technique of free association. Obviously, if free associations are to be studied, they must be communicated. Therefore, it is essential to minimize all factors which impede their *communication*. Among such factors, unacknowledged and unconscious transference attitudes play a dominant role; and their resolution through interpretation is essential. No other experimental or observational situation has as yet been designed which, for this specific purpose, is comparable to the analytic situation. Every element in formal analysis contributes to the eliciting of free associations, to wit, the analytic incognito, the constancy of external variables, the noninterference by the analyst, the interpretation which is introduced as a deliberate and variable working hypothesis, and the watchful eye on transference and countertransference pressures and the tracing of such attitudes to their sources. All of these facilitate both the production and the communication of free associations. They do not facilitate the easier gratifications of conventional conversation. On the contrary, they rigorously reduce the opportunity for such gratifications.

This is not an oversimplification: it is the core of the matter. As stated, it may sound easy; but, in practice, it is difficult and elusive. Few individuals, whether as patients or as participants in experiments, can produce free associations in this sense for more than intermittent bursts, scattered among hours of automatic organized defense against it. The potentially facilitating influence of drugs or of other physiological variables has not yet been adequately explored.

How then do we know that associations are *free?* We must reply: that we do not *know* in any ultimate sense; that of this we have only approximate knowledge; and that we will not have conclusive indications of how truly free "free associations" are until, through the use of recording devices and their meticulous quantitative and qualitative study (including timing), we secure more precise data than has yet been available as to the nature of such material. When this type of research is carried out, we may find that there is a continuous spectrum, or else a spectrum with bands of clustered characteristics, stretching from the bound associations of goal-determined speech to the freer aspects of the products of free associations.

Furthermore, in all such investigations the rigorous application of the techniques and principles of the developing disciplines of linguistics and paralinguistics will play an important contributory role.

Further Areas for Research Implicit in this formulation are the differences between the coded signals which mediate preconscious processing, the symbolic process which mediates conscious sampling, and the distorted symbolic process of "unconscious" sampling (Kubie, 1952, 1958b). A full discussion of these issues would take us far afield. Here I would emphasize only the fact that the symbolic process has implications for the concept of the human mental apparatus as a communicative machine.

It is through the interposition of coded signals and symbols that the human system can anticipate any thrusting needs from within or any thrusting impulse from without; and because of these anticipatory warnings it becomes possible for the human machine to make needed corrections *before* the responsive deviation occurs. Indeed, this is the essential distinction between instinctual processes in the human animal and in other animal forms, insofar as they have been studied (Kubie, 1956a). This again is an area of psychoanalytic thought which must be reformulated by analysts in their search for clarification of the analytic concept of instincts, as a basis for interdisciplinary work in this field.

Analysts must also turn their attention to the role of all preconscious activities: the incessant bombardment by subliminal stimuli in all afferant modalities internal and external; the subsymbolic processing which occurs within the human machine to implement all preconscious activity and which corresponds to the coded signal of the communications engineer. These processes and their variations from one man to another and in different states of illness have not yet been made the object of specific study.

This leads directly to still another area for basic research, which derives from the newer knowledge of feedback and cybernetics and their relationship to psychological functions in general and to psychoanalysis in particular. A tendency is inherent in all feedback mechanisms to minimize any stimulus-response deviation. This is implicit in the concept of reciprocal innervation of Sherrington, and in the Freudian concept that pleasure is characterized by a reduction of tension. Yet psychoanalysis derived its verbal model from the pre-existing concepts of physics, which are wholly inappropriate. Not only our language but also our thinking about the dynamics of change in mental phenomena must be wholly recast. Without going further into these questions, it may be predicted that in the long run the application of principles based on models derived from modern electronic engineering, information theory, communications engineering, mathematical machinery, digital and analogic computers and electronic devices in general, will clarify much that at present is confused in psychoanalytic theory, concepts, and terminology. Eventually, these will furnish analysis with further techniques for critical self-examination. Instead of transfers of material or of energy or its transmutation, analysts will find themselves concerned with the reception, storage, processing, transmission, and reproduction of individual or clustered bits of information.

The Philosophic Position It is necessary, finally, to discuss briefly the philosophical assumption that underlies the analytic assumption that dynamic interactions can occur among psychological events. This issue was spelled out more fully in a paper which appeared relatively recently (Kubie, 1957). There is much in the body of that paper that I would change, if I were writing it today; but with only a few essential changes for the sake of clarity and accuracy, the philosophical statement stands up fairly well and will be condensed here.

Any consideration of dynamic interactions on the level of psychological experience stirs a venerable philosophical conundrum out of its Rip Van Winkle slumbers. Fortunately, although the problem is ancient, I have the temerity to believe that it can be resolved simply. The idea that sequences of psychological events can exert dynamic influences on one another seems, at first thought, to do violence to the scientific spirit and to the laws governing the conservation of mass and energy. Yet this need not worry us. There is no difficulty in understanding in physical terms how perceptual stimuli which arise from *immediate* occurrences initiate sequences in the central nervous system, both chain reactions and reverberating circuits, and thereby influence the behavioral and symbolic (that is, psychological) expressions of central activity. Such units of input initiate coded signals which transmit further processes and give rise to new chains of coded signals and, finally, to their symbolic sampling, which constitutes the conscious level.

Furthermore, because of the low level of energy interchange in reverberating circuits within the nervous system, once these processes are launched they can continue in transmutable forms even for years. In this sense they are "stored." Thereafter, any symbol which represents past or spatially distant events, or events which are anticipated in that abstraction which we call "the future," can serve as new coded signals for some nervous apparatus in the here and now; and those new coded signals in turn trigger or redirect or redistribute further processes. We are, therefore, merely using verbal shorthand when we talk of cause and effect on the psychological level. To say that one state of mind causes another, whether in myself or in someone else, is a legitimate semantic elision. We do not need each time to go through the cumbersome and pedestrian steps of saying that in my mind preconscious coded signals and their conscious symbols of one moment touch off a chain of preconscious coded signals and conscious symbols, either in my own mind again or in the mind of someone else to whom I have communicated these symbolic samples by word or gesture. The shorter statement does no violence to our basic concepts of the physical world, provided that in our theoretical constructions and in our experimental work we do not forget that in this process, within one person, the effective stimuli to each successive step are the coded signals for internal communications, whereas from one person to another the effective stimuli are the symbolic cues which are communicated from man to man.

From this, we may generalize further to say that it is the preconscious coded signal through its conscious symbolic counterpart which enables one psychological state to influence another. It may seem strange that we even stop to explain this, since its occurrence is an elementary fact of human experience. If it did not happen, our past could never influence our present or future, nor could there be any communication on the level of psychological interaction. No mere event could then have a lasting influence on anyone. Yet we know that the thoughts and feelings of today are integral with those of tomorrow, and that words, expressions, gestures and events "communicate with one another," in this manner of speaking. We also know that my symbolic activities, acting through perceivable symbolic or subliminal signals, are incorporated into the psychological processes and ultimately into the personalities of other human beings, whose symbolic and preconscious responses in turn and in the same way become incorporated into mine. In short, in all goal-directed animal behavior, superimposed on the preconscious devices for coded signaling within the machine, are the devices for symbolic sampling, processing and communicating. Comparable sequences are thereby initiated within each of us.

Moreover, once my own symbolic cues have been activated, they become events to me which are quite as potent as are the symbolic attitudes, expressions, gestures, and acts of a friend or stranger. It is this which stamps the human race with its uniqueness, the extraordinary development of which distinguishes man from even the highest primate. *Preconscious coded signaling* is the instrument by which experience is processed within us on the psychological level and can be translated into somatic changes or, conversely, somatic experience into psychological change. The *symbolic process* is the instrument for self-criticism and rumination and for deliberately communicating signals, information, and interactions. Together these are the instruments of our greatest creative power, but also of our greatest vulnerability (Kubie, 1954, 1958a). Furthermore, although both systems are vulnerable, of these two (the mechanisms of conscious symbolic sampling and of preconscious coded signals), the conscious symbolic process is patently the more vulnerable to distortions which are of organic or psychogenic origin.

Evidently, then, the coded signal and the symbol are the two psychophysiological implements, an understanding of which is essential for an explanation both of normal and of pathological human psychological function. This is the key concept in psychodynamics and psychogenesis, whether of normal or sick activity. That from earliest childhood the symbolic process can go off its rails is perhaps the greatest challenge that medicine faces today; because if this did not happen, there could be neither the neurosis nor the psychosis as we know it in the human being.[6]

---

[6] This is far from being all there is to the psychopathological process; but this is the aspect of it which is most relevant to our philosophical dilemma.

At the same time, the symbolic representation of remote events binds widely separated times and far places into one immediate interacting psychological continuum. This is one of its several essential functions; and whereas on conscious and also on preconscious levels we can sharply distinguish the past from the present and the near from the far, on the obscure levels of dynamic unconscious processes, near and far, past, present, and future fuse into a continuum so complete that differentiation among them is lost. This process was first described clinically by Freud (1957). More recently, it was demonstrated experimentally (Kubie, 1953c; Penfield, 1952).

We can summarize this brief salute to an ancient philosophical dilemma by stating that, in the study of dynamic interrelations on the level of psychological experience, no assumptions which violate basic scientific concepts of the world are needed since, by means of symbols (whether these are conscious or whether they function as preconscious coded signals), effective and sustained interactions can occur among sequences of psychological experiences. The symbol turns abstraction into a concrete stimulus.

REFERENCES

ASHBY, W. R. Cybernetics. *Recent Progr. Psychiat.*, 1958, **3**, 94-117.

ASHBY, W. R. *Design for a brain*. (2nd ed.) Wiley, New York, 1960.

ASHBY, W. R. The effect of experience on a determinate dynamic system. *Behavioral Sci.*, 1956, **1**, 35-42.

BRENMAN, M., and others. Research in psychotherapy. Round Table, 1947. *Amer. J. Orthopsychiat.*, 1948, **28**, 92-118.

BRONNER, A. F., and Others. The objective evaluation of psychotherapy. Round Table, 1948. *Amer. J. Orthopsychiat.*, 1949, **29**, 463-491.

CHASSAN, J. B. On probability theory and psychoanalytic research. *Psychiat.*, 1956, **19**, 55-61.

COLBY, K. M. *Energy and structure in psychoanalysis*. Ronald Press, New York, 1955.

FISHER, C. Dreams and perception. *J. Amer. Psychoanal. Assn.*, 1954, **2**, 389-445.

FISHER, C. Dreams, images, and perceptions. *J. Amer. Psychoanal. Assn.*, 1956, **4**, 5-48.

FREUD, S. Psychoanalysis. In *Encyclopaedia Brittanica*, Vol. 31. (13th ed.) 1926. Pp. 253-255.

FREUD, S. The unconscious (1915). In *Collected Papers*. Vol. IV. New York: Basic Books, 1959, Pp. 98-136.

GERARD, R. W. (Ed.). Concepts of biology: a symposium. *Behavioral Sci.*, 1958, **3**, 88-215.

GREY-WALTER, W. *The living brain*. New York: Norton, 1953.

HILGARD, E. R. Experimental approaches to psychoanalysis. In E. Pumpian-

338 LAWRENCE S. KUBIE

Mindlin (Ed.), *Psychoanalysis as science*, Stanford, Calif.: Stanford Univ. Press, 1952. Pp. 3-45.

KLEIN, G. S., SMITH, G. J. W., & SPENCE, D. P. Subliminal effects of verbal stimuli. *J. abnorm. soc. Psychol.*, 1959, 59, 167-176.

KUBIE, L. S. The relation of the conditioned reflex to psychoanalytic technique. *Arch. Neurol. Psychiat.*, 1934, 32, 1137-1142.

KUBIE, L. S. The fallacious use of quantitative concepts in dynamic psychology. *Psychiat. Quart.*, 1947, 16, 507-518.

KUBIE, L. S. A pilot study of psychoanalytic practice in the U.S. with suggestions for future studies. *Psychiat.*, 1950, 13, 227-245. (a)

KUBIE, L. S. *Practical and theoretical aspects of psychoanalysis.* New York: International Univ. Press, 1950. (b)

KUBIE, L. S. Problems and techniques of psychoanalytic validation and progress. In E. Pumpian-Mindlin (Ed.), *Psychoanalysis as science.* Stanford, Calif.: Stanford Univ. Press, 1952. Pp. 46-124.

KUBIE, L. S. The problem of maturity in psychiatric research. *J. Med. Educ.*, 1953, 28 (10, Pt. 1), 11-27. (a)

KUBIE, L. S. Psychoanalysis as a basic science. In F. Alexander (Ed.), *Twenty years of psychoanalysis.* New York: Norton, 1953. Pp. 120-145. (b)

KUBIE, L. S. Some implications for psychoanalysis of modern concepts of the organization of the brain. *Psychoanal. Quart.*, 1953, 22, 21-68. (c)

KUBIE, L. S. The fundamental nature of the distinction between normality and neurosis. *Psychoanal. Quart.*, 1954, 23, 167-204.

KUBIE, L. S. Influence of symbolic processes on the role of instincts in human behavior. *Psychosom. Med.*, 1956, 28, 189-208. (a)

KUBIE, L. S. An institute for basic research in psychiatry. *Bull. Menninger Clin.*, 1956, 20, 281-287. (b)

KUBIE, L. S. Some unsolved problems of psychoanalytic psychotherapy. *Progr. Psychother.*, 1956, 1, 87-102. (c)

KUBIE, L. S. The use of psychoanalysis as a research tool. *Psychiat. Res. Rep. Amer. Psychiat. Ass.*, 1956, 6, 112-136. (d)

KUBIE, L. S. The psychodynamic position on etiology. In New York Academy of Medicine, Committee on Public Health, *Integrating the approaches to mental disease.* New York: Hoeber, 1957.

KUBIE, L. S. *The neurotic distortion of the creative process.* Lawrence: Univ. Kansas Press, 1958. (a)

KUBIE, L. S. The neurotic process as the focus of physiological and psychoanalytic research. *J. Ment. Sci.*, 1958, 104, 518-536. (b)

KUBIE, L. S. Research into the process of supervision in psychoanalysis. *Psychoanal. Quart.*, 1958, 27, 226-236. (c)

KUBIE, L. S. The maturation of psychiatrists or the time that changes take. *J. Nerv. Mental Dis.*, 1962, 135, 286-288.

MCCULLOCH, W. S., AND PITTS, W. A logical calculus of the ideas immanent in nervous activity. *Math Biophys.*, 1943, 5, 115-137.

MARSH, J. D., & WORDEN, F. G. Perceptual approaches to personality. *Psychiat. Res. Rep. Amer. Psychiat. Assn.*, 1956, 6, 171-176.

MILLER, J. G. Toward a general theory for the behavior sciences. *Amer. Psychologist*, 1955, 10, 513-531.

MILLER, J. G. Psychoanalysis and systems theory. In Academy of Psychoanalysis, *Science and psychoanalysis.* New York: Grune & Stratton, 1958. Pp. 109-125.

MILLER, J. G. Information input overload. Presidential address, Amer. Psychol. Ass., Div. Clin. Psychol., Sept. 4, 1959.

MILLER, J. G. Information input overload and psychopathology. *Amer. J. Psychiat.,* 1960, **116,** 695-704.

OBENDORF, C. P., and others. Symposium on the evaluation of therapeutic results. *Int. J. Psychoanal.,* 1948, **29,** 7-20.

PENFIELD, W. Memory mechanisms. *A.M.A. Arch. Neurol. Psychiat.,* 1952, **67,** 178-198.

PUMPIAN-MINDLIN, E. Propositions concerning energetic-economic aspects of the libido theory. Read before the Conference on Conceptual and Methodological Problems in Psychoanalysis. New York Academy of Science, March 4-5, 1958.

RUFF, G. E. Critique of Colby. *Behavioral Sci.,* 1956, **1,** 143-154.

SEARS, R. R. Experimental analysis of psychoanalytic phenomena. In J. M. Hunt (Ed.), *Personality and behavior disorders.* Vol. 1. Ronald Press, New York, 1944. Pp. 306-332.

SEARS, R. R. Survey of objective studies of psychoanalytic concepts. New York: Social Science Research Council, Committee on Social Adjustment, 1943. Bulletin 51.

18 HEINZ L. ANSBACHER

THE STRUCTURE OF

INDIVIDUAL PSYCHOLOGY

ADLER'S THEORIES of personality, mental disorder, and psychotherapy, which he termed "individual psychology," are relatively simple, direct conceptualizations which may be summarized in the following series of axioms and postulates.

(1) Life in all its forms is characterized by movement.

(2) This movement has a direction which is toward overcoming difficulties, toward growth, expansion.

(3) In man, who is capable of taking an attitude toward himself, the general biological movement is extended into a striving which may be described as a striving from a felt minus situation to a plus situation, from a feeling of inferiority to superiority; a striving for perfection or totality, for success.

(4) This striving receives its specific form and direction from the individual's unique, subjectively conceived goal of success, or self ideal.

(5) The goal of success is influenced by objective biological and social factors, but is ultimately the subjective creation of the individual. Because it is an ideal, it is a fiction.

(6) The goal is only partly in the individual's awareness. To the extent that it is not, it is the psychologist's hypothetical construct. The content of the unconscious is a construction of the psychologist.

(7) The human individual is a self-consistent organization, like all organisms, and it is unique.

(8) The self-consistency is reflected in the individual's style of life, formed in accordance with his self ideal.

(9) All part-functions are subordinated to the life style. This includes biological as well as psychological functions.

(10) The life style, or personality structure including the goal, may be inferred inductively by viewing the individual's past and present situations and all his expressions and actions in their coherence.

340

(11) The individual is endowed with creative power.

(12) The individual's uniqueness ultimately rests in this creative power.

(13) Objective biological and social conditions, past and present, provide probabilities, opportunities, and limitations. They are not directly causal factors in the individual.

(14) Individual causality is derived from the individual's goal-directed life style, which uses the objective conditions provided by heredity and environment, but was originally and ultimately the individual's creation. Thus the individual is in the last analysis self-determined.

(15) The goal-directed life style influences particularly the individual's perceptions, providing him with an apperceptive schema.

(16) As an aspect of the life style including his apperceptive schema, the individual forms an opinion of himself and the world.

(17) Actions are determined by the opinion of oneself and the world as well as by the goal.

(18) The goal becomes the final cause, the ultimate independent variable. To the extent that it provides the key for understanding the individual, it is a working hypothesis of the psychologist.

(19) The individual cannot be considered apart from society. He is inextricably embedded in it. His very thinking, using language as a main tool, is socially determined, since language is a social product and is socially acquired.

(20) All important life problems of the individual, including certain "drive" satisfactions, are social problems, namely, problems of general human relations, occupation, and love.

(21) The logic which follows from human interrelatedness is the closest approximation to an "absolute truth."

(22) Man has an innate capacity for understanding his social embeddedness, a social feeling. When this capacity has been developed into social skills of cooperation and fellowmanship, it acquires secondary dynamic attributes in the form of social interest. Thus socialization is a matter of development, not of repression.

(23) Because the main problems which man faces in life are of a social nature, he cannot solve them successfully without a sufficiently developed social interest.

(24) Mental health is characterized by a goal of success which is formed under the influence of social interest, is self-transcending, and is on the socially useful side. Social interest is the criterion of mental health.

(25) Mental disorder is characterized by underdeveloped social interest, increased inferiority feelings, and an exaggerated compensatory goal of personal superiority over others. It means actual failure in life when the individual becomes confronted with the problems of life.

(26) Psychotherapy is based on providing encouragement through a

good human relationship. Thereby the patient's social interest is strengthened. Beyond this, the patient is given an understanding of his erroneous life style so that he may adopt a better method of living.

A full statement of individual psychology, with all essential references, is to be found in the systematic, edited presentation of the writings of Adler (1956).

The purpose of the present paper is to examine individual psychology with regard to basic logical assumptions, basic methodology, the logic of key terms, clinical method, and therapy.

BASIC LOGICAL ASSUMPTIONS: ORGANICISM

Individual psychology stands on the basis of organismic biology. It shares the view that, in contrast to mechanical events, "vital processes have a *prima facie* purposive character; organisms are capable of self-regulation, self-maintenance, and self-reproduction, and their activities seem to be directed toward the attainment of goals that lie in the future. . . . Moreover, living things are organic wholes, not 'additive systems' of independent parts" (Nagel, 1961, pp. 400-401).

Holism and Gestalt Theory   Probably the most fundamental principle of organicism is that the whole is more than the sum of its parts. The whole is a new emergence; if one attempts to reduce it to its parts, one will lose exactly what one has attempted to study. When Smuts (1926) coined the term "holism" and proposed a fundamental factor operative in the universe "towards the making or creation of wholes" (p. 98), Adler responded to it with enthusiasm (Ansbacher, 1961).

We need not be surprised, then, that Klopfer (1925) considered individual psychology "the most vigorous and consistent application of the Gestalt theory of Wertheimer and Koehler," and that one of the leading Gestalt psychologists today, Solomon Asch (1952), still shows very strongly this basic theoretical kinship with individual psychology (Langman, 1960), although this is not recognized by Asch himself.

Social-Science Orientation   Among the organismic theorists Adler most clearly emphasized that in accordance with such theory the individual must not only be considered an integrated whole but must be understood in his setting, as part of a larger organization. "For good reasons Individual Psychology avoids studying the human being in isolation. It sees him always only in the cosmic and social context" (p. 95).[1]

---

[1] Where quotations from Adler are identified only by page references these pertain to Adler (1956).

Since the most significant human behaviors are those of social interaction, the social context assumed the greatest importance in Adler's thinking. "In addition to regarding an individual's life as a unity, we must also take it together with its context of social relations. . . . The child has interlocking relations with the mother and family which could never be understood if we confined our analysis to the periphery of the child's physical being in space. The individuality of the child cuts across his physical individuality, it involves a whole context of social relations" (p. 127).

It is for such considerations that Adler is today grouped with the social psychological theorists such as Fromm, Horney, and Sullivan (Hall & Lindzey, 1957). Gardner Murphy (1949, p. 341) found that "Adler's was the first psychological system in the history of psychology that was developed in what we should today call a social-science direction."

Teleological Explanation and Hierarchical Organization Organicism ascribes a dominant place to teleological explanation (see Sinnott, 1957). We are in fact dealing with teleological (or functional) statements whenever we find "such typical locutions as 'the function of,' 'the purpose of,' 'for the sake of,' 'in order that,' and the like—more generally, the occurrence of expressions signifying a means-ends nexus" (Nagel, 1961, p. 403). In these instances, mechanistic explanations are considered inadequate. This is exactly Adler's position: "That mysterious creative power of life which expresses itself in the desire to develop, to strive, to achieve, and even to compensate for defeats in one direction by striving for success in another . . . is *teleological*" (p. 92).

In contrast, Freud acknowledged as early as 1908 that he focused on the means, rather than on the means-ends nexus, in stating: "Our interest is focused on the way [in which something comes about, develops], not on the final goal" as he found Adler doing (Nunberg & Federn, 1962, p. 321).

Again according to Nagel (1961), organismic biologists stress the hierarchical organization of living bodies and processes. They deny "that the processes found at higher levels of a hierarchy are 'caused' by, or are fully explicable in terms of, lower-level properties" (pp. 432-433). They regard them "as conditioned by, but irreducible to, the modes of action of lower unities" (Russell, 1930, p. 187). Considerations of this kind are implicit in Adler's protest against reducing human dynamics to animal drives. He also recognized that the emergence of higher levels is in certain ways conditioned by the satisfaction of lower needs. "Only great deprivations are capable of making organ satisfaction the goal" (p. 124) and, "Nothing stands more in the way of the development of social interest than an increased inferiority feeling" (p. 124). Thus the well-known hierarchy of motives of Maslow (1954, pp. 80-106) is in line with Adler's (pp. 123-125) thinking and can be considered a further development of it.

Emergent Evolution and Humanism Consistent with the foregoing, "Individual Psychology stands firmly on the ground of evolution and, in the light of it, regards all human striving as a striving for perfection" (Adler, 1933a, pp. 36-37). Adler's implied understanding of human evolution is in accord with that of G. G. Simpson (1951): "In man a new form of evolution [societal evolution] begins, overlying and largely dominating the old, organic evolution. . . . Its possibility arises from man's intelligence and associated flexibility of response. . . . Plan, purpose, goal . . . enter with the coming of man . . . With them comes the need for criteria of choice. Good and evil, right and wrong . . . become real and pressing features of the whole cosmos as viewed by man" (p. 179). Sharing the anthropocentric, humanistic point of view which Simpson (1951, p. 139) declares as valid, Adler would "consider unessential the question whether man is the center of the world. Our intention would be to make him the center. In this way mankind attains a task and a goal which, although unattainable, points the way and the direction" (p. 461).

All this is in accordance with the general idea of human progress and perfectibility, an admittedly optimistic view, which Adler (1937a) propounded emphatically. Thus Adler would have considered of great importance the examination of man's becoming (Allport, 1955) and of human potentialities (Murphy, 1958).

Open System and Creativity Freud (1957), in assuming "the principle of constancy of psychical energy" (pp. 10, 138), accepted for psychology the first law of thermodynamics. He also accepted the second law of thermodynamics—that of entropy, or of the degradation of energy, according to which a quantity of energy, while remaining constant, tends to decrease in quality, ultimately reaching equilibrium—in the form of the death instinct, "the urge of animate matter to return to an inanimate state" (1950, p. 350), and the related nirvana principle, "the tendency of the mental apparatus to reduce its tension to zero" (1957, p. 138). But both laws are applicable only to inanimate, closed, physical systems, whereas living organisms are more or less open systems (von Bertalanffy, 1952).

Adler can be counted among the open system theorists by his denial of both laws. Regarding the first he noted, "The question of conservation or loss of psychological energy loses all meaning" (p. 285, see also p. 91); regarding the second, "This equilibrium which life seeks is not death . . . but a harmony of the body which strives toward evolution" (1933b, p. 70).

What places individual psychology positively among the open system theories is Adler's concept of the free creative power of the individual. Collier (1962) has shown that independence or freedom from the environment is one of the implications of open systems, that it increases as we ascend in phylogenetic and ontogenetic development, and that the maximally open system provides for such a concept as creativity. Expressing the same thought Anderson (1957) said:

> The continuum in the theory of probability extends from the virtual "dead certainty" at the state of relatively complete degradation of matter, equilibrium, at the one extreme, to the relatively improbable prediction of the emergence of an original at the highest theoretical integration or organization of matter, at infinity (one chance in infinity), in the "open system." . . . Personality growth . . . requires a concept of negative entropy [or the enhancement of energy], and . . . a theory of improbability with the ultimate prediction of one chance in infinity: creativity (pp. 152 & 154).

In line with these considerations, Allport (1960) concludes that the concept of a truly open, rather than a semiclosed system is required for a personality theory which attempts to do justice to the phenomena of individual change, becoming, growth, and creativity.

From the conception of creativity Adler derived the uniqueness of the individual. He conceded that the individual is unique by heredity alone and that he lives necessarily in an environment which in the last analysis is unique. Uniqueness derived from these factors would, however, still be causalistic, or deterministic. In Adler's conception, the individual is an active agent who *uses* his hereditary and environmental equipment. He uses it in the pursuit of his goal of success which he creates in response to these objective factors. "This response is not simply a passive reaction but a manifestation of creative activity on the part of the individual" (p. 177).

In Adler's sense, everyone is creative. Mental disorder is also a creation, but on the useless side and for private purposes. What is generally regarded as creativity, in a limited use of the term, is for Adler that particular form which proves of value to others as well.

BASIC METHODOLOGY: PHENOMENOLOGICAL OPERATIONALISM

The methodology of individual psychology is certainly that of phenomenology. "More important than disposition, objective experience and environment is the [individual's] subjective evaluation of these. Furthermore, this evaluation stands in a certain, often strange relation to reality" (p. 93). Therefore, in the words of Koffka (1935, p. 73), it is necessary "to look naïvely, without bias, at the fact of direct experience. . . . We call this kind of observation 'phenomenology,' . . . as naïve and full a description of direct experience as possible." Adler was convinced "that a person's behavior springs from his opinion. We should not be surprised at this, because our senses do not receive actual facts, but merely a subjective image of them, a reflection of the external world" (p. 182). Thus, "Individual Psychology examines the attitudes of an individual" (p. 185).

There are today numerous theories of psychology which together with individual psychology are considered by Maslow (1962, p. vi) to form a third force, opposing the Freudian and the experimental-positivistic-behavioristic theories of human nature. This group, of which individual psychology is certainly the oldest, could be characterized by essentially sharing the preceding basic assumptions and especially the phenomenological approach, or as it is often called, the cognitive approach.

One of the most distinguishing characteristics of individual psychology among the third-force theories is, however, that it consistently combines the phenomenological approach with the stipulation that data so obtained must be operationally verifiable. Thus individual psychology is similar to behaviorism in methodology, although not at all in substantive theory, a differentiation clearly made by Nagel (1961, p. 480).

Operationalism has been defined as "the doctrine that terms, propositions, concepts, constructs, and theories . . . have no other meaning than is yielded by the procedures or operations by which the things or processes to which they refer are known" (English & English, 1958, p. 358). The method of behaviorism is "nothing more than a thoroughgoing operational analysis of traditional mentalistic concepts" (Skinner, 1953, p. 586). Similarly, individual psychology is in methodology pragmatic, which term "means only the rule of referring all thinking, all reflective considerations, to consequences for final meaning and test" (Dewey, 1959, p. 105).

In contrast to other subjectivistic and to psychoanalytic writings, there is no "predilection for terms that avoid the embarrassing question of the spatial dimensions, physical or otherwise, of terms at the primary level" (Skinner, 1956, p. 86). One will not find in Adlerian literature terms such as real self, inner self, primary processes, inner forces, latent homosexuality, archetype; nor any reference to inner conflict, or aggressive or emotional "needs" which the individual "handles" in one way or another. Quite to the contrary, any behavior or process is seen as part of a movement with regard to some point outside. For the interpretation of a symptom Adler's advice was to look for the opponent. "The opponent is never absent" (p. 388).

In this sense Adler's methodology can be called one of *phenomenological operationalism*. This derives from his conception of life as movement and of human life as movement toward a subjectively conceived goal of success. Thereby the entire subject matter receives a dimension in space and becomes transactional and open to inspection. "The raw material with which the Individual Psychologist works is the relationship of the individual to the problems of the outside world" (p. 205).

This position is not far removed from Tolman's (1932) "purposive behaviorism" and what Miller, Galanter, and Pribram (1960) have called "subjective behaviorism." Adler's position is philosophically based on Vaihinger's (1921) "idealistic positivism" by which Adler was greatly influenced at the time of his first major book (1912).

Seeking the Context, Not "Depth" Adler did not look for any forces behind or underneath the symptom other than the whole individual's unique way of striving for success, his style of life. The meaning of a specific form of behavior is by nature ambiguous, but it can be determined by regarding it in its larger context of which the individual himself is not aware. Thus individual psychology cannot be considered a depth psychology which implies that something substantive can be found lurking within the individual, if you only dig deeply enough. "Individual Psychology is far removed from any theory of shallow 'depth psychology' " (Adler, 1927).[2]

An illustration of how Adler applied the principle of operational context in treatment is the following incident. A middle-aged man who had been in psychoanalytic treatment before he came to Adler explained that he suffered from an unresolved Oedipus complex. Adler's reply was: "Look here, what do you want of the old lady?" [3] This humorous remark demonstrates how the operational orientation does away with a non-operational redundancy by illuminating the matter in its operational context. Similarly, Adler (1928) asked various interpreters of Hamlet, "would they more easily decide to murder their uncle, than Hamlet did" (p. 211 n.).

Actions Speak Louder than Words This axiom of common-sense operationalism was applied by Adler consistently in evaluating introspective data. He expressed this principle through Martin Luther's admonition, "not to watch a person's mouth but his fists" (p. 18), or through the quotation from the Bible, "By their fruits ye shall know them" (1934, p. 5).

One example of the application of this principle would be Adler's interpretation of guilt feelings. A patient may express a sense of guilt, yet at the same time go on with "guilty" behavior without exercising "active contrition" (p. 307). Adler would consider such guilt feelings but a device for eating one's cake and having it too, permitting one to feel virtuous while continuing with unvirtuous behavior. In this sense he referred to Nietzsche's aphorism, "Conscience pangs are indecent" (p. 272). As for "unconscious guilt feelings," these did not exist for Adler, since unconscious feelings are non-operational.

Pragmatic Limitation There is certainly an aspect of transcendentalism in individual psychology (p. 142). Else the entire idea of human

---

[2] Here the present writer must admit that in an earlier study he committed the mistake of designating individual psychology as depth psychology (Ansbacher & Ansbacher, 1956).

[3] Personal communication of Dr. Alexandra Adler.

progress, the concepts of striving for a goal, and of an ideal community, as well as the acceptance of man's seeking perfection, truth, and meaning in life would not be possible. Yet Adler remained on operational grounds at the same time, by applying consistently the pragmatic limitation that "we must work with what we have" (Feigl, 1956, p. 32). Thus, on the one hand, he did not dismiss as meaningless the transcendental questions which quite regularly emerge in human beings, and, on the other hand, was able to avoid an endless search for the meaning of life or the ultimate truth, which may lead away from reality and is often found in mental disorder. This he did by providing, where at all possible, an operational pragmatic answer to these "unanswerable" questions.

The answers were transcendental in leading beyond the individual, from self-centeredness to self-transcendence, but they remained operational by leading no further than the widest conceptually operational limits we can set, namely our fellowmen, all of mankind, and the future of mankind. Thus Adler gave these problems a concrete dimension, from oneself to others. The fact of man's living in society was regarded as an "absolute truth" (p. 128). The meaning of life was defined pragmatically: "Life means—to contribute to the whole" (1931, p. 9).

In this way also God was understood, as concretization of the idea of perfection; and religion, as a sanctification of human relations (pp. 460-462). All transcendental questions are answered in a manner in which their understanding would feed back into actual living.

Similarly, Adler gave a limiting operational definition also of mental health: it is striving for success on the socially useful side of life, whereas mental disorder is a striving on the socially useless side (pp. 158, 254-255). The criterion of mental health became social interest (p. 154).

LOGICAL ANALYSIS OF TERMS

All terms of individual psychology correspond to Adler's holistic, social, and operational orientation, and were kept on the lowest possible level of abstraction. For example, *distance* behavior is used instead of what is often called alienation (Ansbacher, 1956). The *getting type* replaces the oral character (Mosak, 1959). *Depreciation tendency* would be used instead of oral aggression, *selectivity* of perception and memory instead of repression. Adler was greatly concerned lest a term become reified and it be forgotten that what the term intends to designate is not an essence he had "discovered," but an ongoing movement which he was describing. The explanatory aspect of a term did generally refer to a goal rather than an antecedent condition. Often a term was in the nature of a heuristic fiction in the sense of Vaihinger (1911). Adler considered his concepts only as devices for ordering observed phenomena for a special purpose. The following is an examination of some of his key terms.

The Unconscious Since individual psychology is still often misnamed a form of psychoanalysis or depth psychology, instead of being called a theory of personality and psychotherapy, let us first see what Adler had to say about the unconscious: "It is nothing other than that which we have been unable to formulate in clear concepts. It is . . . parts of our consciousness, the significance of which we have not fully understood" (pp. 232-233). He acknowledged the similarity to the behavioristic view by referring to Watson. Designating, at one time, unconscious processes as having remained pre-psychological, he added: "These preliminary processes did not become condensed into a conscious judgment or words (Watson)" (1930, p. 88).

During his later years, Adler stressed the aspect of the unconscious as a heuristic fiction or working hypothesis of the psychologist. We quote from lecture notes, taken by the present writer, dated March 20, 1936: "Nothing is in the unconscious. E.g., all the meaning of a dream is invented by the interpreter; it was not there before. Where formerly there was simply lack of understanding, interpretations are given; or new interpretations are given to old notions. To be able to do this, one must look for everything very carefully like a detective. This is difficult work. The inferiority complex is only an idea given by us to the patient. He behaves 'as if' he had an inferiority complex. After we tell him that, he has a new concept to work with." The next year a similar statement by Adler appeared in print:

> I, myself, as the inventor of the "inferiority complex" have never thought of it as of a spirit, knowing that it has never been in the consciousness or unconsciousness of the patient but only in my own consciousness, and have used it rather for illumination so that the patient could see his attitude in the right coherence (1937b, p. 776).

Style of Life What we can observe in an individual either through his introspections or his overt behavior are always ongoing processes which are partial functions of the totality of the living, moving, goal-directed individual and imbued with the specific characteristics of this totality. This totality of the ongoing process Adler eventually named style of life, and it corresponds to what other theories may call in a less dynamic way personality, ego, self, or personality structure, radix, or unity thema, and so forth. The following may serve as a definition by Adler, including, as it does, the various aspects which are subsumed under style of life: "Styles of life are the proper subject-matter of psychology; . . . we are considering the psyche itself, the unified mind; we are examining the meaning which individuals give to the world and to themselves, their goal, the direction of their strivings, and the approaches they make to the problems of life" (1931, p. 48).

Not until 1926 did Adler arrive at this term. It replaced such previous terms as psychological main axis, guiding idea, schema of life, *modus vivendi,* or life plan, the last of which had been used the longest and in some of Adler's most important writings.

Striving for Success   Most holistically oriented psychologies recognize only one dynamic force as required for the conception of a unified self-consistent organism. Toward the end of his life, Adler (1937a) called this force the striving for a subjectively conceived goal of success. "This striving is anchored in the very structure of life." Many different terms preceded this last formulation: Wanting to be a man, the masculine protest, was the original formulation at the time of the secession from Freud. "Striving for power" was the unfortunate term which still clings to Adler's name, although he later explained that striving for power over others is the form of the general striving in the maladjusted. Later formulations were far better, striving from a felt minus to a felt plus situation, or striving for perfection or completion.

For many years this striving was anchored in inferiority feelings rather than "in the very structure of life," and seen as a compensatory effort for such feelings. This was deficiency motivation. But ultimately Adler rephrased this proposition, thereby doing justice to a concept of growth motivation (Maslow, 1962, pp. 19-41), by making the inferiority feelings secondary to the striving: "In comparison with unattainable ideal perfection, the individual is continually filled by an inferiority feeling and motivated by it. . . . Man is always in a state of psychical agitation and feels unsettled before the goal of perfection" (pp. 116-117).

Goal and Fictional Goal   The striving for success or perfection derives its direction from the goal of success which is influenced by all kinds of objective conditions but which is ultimately of the individual's own creation. The individual is generally only dimly aware of his goal or may never have conceptualized a goal so that he does not understand his own actions. In this case the goal, like the unconscious, is the psychologist's heuristic fiction. The function of the fictional goal is to provide the psychologist with a working hypothesis toward understanding a case. "Causes, powers, instincts, impulses, and the like cannot serve as explanatory principles. . . . Experiences, traumata, sexual development mechanisms cannot yield an explanation, but the perspective in which these are regarded, . . . which subordinates all life to the final goal, can do so" (p. 92). With regard to any kind of behavior in a person, the Adlerian will always ask himself not "How did he get that way?" but "What is he accomplishing or trying to accomplish by this?"

Masculine Protest   This term, coined by Adler, and later adopted by Freud with an important added implication, furnishes an excellent example of contrasting approaches. Both men had undoubtedly noted the frequent, often quite conscious or at least directly observable phenomenon, often confirmed since, that many women prefer to be men, while men would like to be "real men." This is what Adler called the masculine protest, "wanting to be a real man" (p. 108). Freud (1937), on the other hand, reaching for "depth," went on from here explaining the masculine protest as a function of the castration complex, which in the female takes the form of penis envy:

> We must not be misled by the term "masculine protest" into supposing that what the man repudiates is . . . the social aspect of femininity. . . . The "masculine protest" is in fact nothing other than fear of castration (p. 357n.).

Whereas Adler's logic remained operational, Freud's addition is, operationally seen, a mere redundancy because it has no other point of reference in the outside world beyond the one already contained in Adler's usage (Ansbacher, 1960).

Social Interest Every psychological theory must, in its model of man, account for the fact that man lives in society, and on what basis man responds to this. The various ways in which this accounting can be done, have been shown by Asch (1952, pp. 324-349). Adler chose in his mature theory the formulation that man has "an innate potentiality [for social living] which has to be consciously developed" (p. 134).

By this formulation Adler accomplished several points. (1) The assumption of an innate positive factor for social living is straightforward and logical, considering that after all language, culture, society have not been created otherwise than by individual men spontaneously interacting and co-operating with one another. (2) By conceiving of the social factor initially as a potentiality or aptitude, rather than a striving or a social motive, Adler took it out of the dynamic or conative realm and into the cognitive realm. This is required by an organismic, holistic theory which can recognize only one central dynamic force, certainly not conflict among opposing forces. (3) By saying the social disposition must be trained, Adler could account for the observation that under unfavorable conditions it is most often deficient, through having remained underdeveloped. (4) By saying that in mental disorders the social factor is only underdeveloped but still present as a potentiality, there is a starting point for the process of psychotherapy, which takes the form of belated education toward the kind of living in society, or with the community in mind, which is found in the mentally healthy.

Adler's formulation implies three developmental steps: (1) The social factor is initially a potentiality or aptitude. (2) When the potentiality has been developed through training, it becomes a proficiency or ability for

352 HEINZ L. ANSBACHER

social living. Behaviorally, this would be the skill of making contact with others and of cooperating with them. Intellectually, it would take the form of social understanding or discernment. (3) The developed social potentiality is likely to acquire secondary dynamic characteristics, as abilities generally may do (Allport, 1961, pp. 235-236; Woodworth, 1958, pp. 132-133), in the form of attitudes and interests. In this form it would influence the direction of the basic striving, by becoming part of the goal of success, but be no more in conflict with it than any other interest.

The social factor so conceived has been called by Adler *Gemeinschaftsgefühl*. This term has offered no mean difficulty to the translators, some Adlerians even having maintained it cannot be translated. But the difficulty is not so much with the translation as it is with the term itself, in either language. And here again, the first part, *Gemeinschaft,* for which community or society would do, is not really troublesome. It is the second part, feeling, that is difficult, because in either German or English it has both a cognitive meaning referring to insight, understanding, discernment; and a conative meaning referring to emotion in the sense of desire, craving, interest. The translation which Adler finally seems to have preferred is *social interest,* the term most appropiate to the third developmental step.

In Table 18-1, social interest has been analyzed according to its implied developmental sequence and corresponding attributes assigned to it by Adler. The table shows that this most distinguished term of individual psychology is heavily burdened. Yet structurally, its meaning complex does not differ from those which could be shown to exist around reading or skiing. Initially aptitudes, these may be developed into skills, and acquire secondary motivational attributes.

CLINICAL METHOD

The theory of individual psychology was constructed for understanding and treating the individual and is primarily idiographic; hence its name. It does, of course, include a considerable number of general, nomothetic principles. But these, says Adler, "should be regarded as nothing more than an aid to a preliminary illumination of the field of view in which the single individual can be found—or missed. Thus we assign only limited value to general rules, and instead lay strong emphasis on flexibility and on empathy into nuances" (pp. 194-195). In view of this emphasis, the nomothetic aspect was neglected by Adler and his followers, as far as methodology and research are concerned. Nevertheless many nomothetic research hypotheses can be derived from Adler's general observations as outlined by Rotter (1962). Many of Adler's general propositions have explicitly and more often implicitly been investigated by others, as shown in a review by Ansbacher (1947). Since this review, a considerable number of further such studies have been conducted.

TABLE 18-1. Analysis of "social interest" (*Gemeinschaftsgefühl*) according to implied developmental sequence and some corresponding attributes assigned to social interest by Adler

DEVELOPMENTAL SEQUENCE	CORRESPONDING ATTRIBUTES
Aptitude	Innate potentiality or substratum of social interest (p. 134)[a]; for cooperation (p. 135); for contact feeling (p. 295)
Ability Behaviorally	Ability to cooperate (p. 136); relating to others in a useful way (p. 139); contributing to common welfare (p. 155); behaving as part of mankind (p. 156); true compensation for all weaknesses (p. 154)
Intellectually	Understanding others (p. 137); empathy (p. 136); reason (p. 149); common sense (p. 149)
Secondary Dynamic Characteristics Attitudinally	Evaluative attitude toward life (p. 135); of harmony with the universe (p. 136); feeling at home on this earth (pp. 136 & 155); identification with others (p. 136); feeling of belongingness (p. 138)
Motivationally	Interest in others (p. 140); interest in community *sub specie aeternitatis* (p. 142); striving for an ideal community (p. 142); making spontaneous social effort (p. 134)[b]

[a] Page references are to Alder, 1956.
[b] These last attributes sharply distinguish social interest from social conformity. They allow for the striving for general betterment which implies changing existing norms rather than conforming to them. Mere conformity "would be nothing other than an exploitation of the accomplishments of the striving of others" (p. 107).

Adler's aim was to arrive "in an individualizing manner" at a self-consistent total portrait of a person (p. 10). "An individualizing examination became a main requirement" (p. 327). In the following we shall show what methods Adler and his followers used and developed for this purpose.

Phenomenology To understand an individual, it will be necessary to know his way of experiencing, his subjective world, his subjective "schema of apperception" (pp. 181-186). The chief method to accomplish this is, of course, the interview, which Adler conducted in a free and easy conversational manner as among equals. For Adler a prerequisite for a fruitful application of the phenomenological method was social feeling in the sense of empathy. "We must be able to see with his eyes and listen with his ears" (p. 340). Adler made two specific contributions for phenomenological investigation, his interpretations of dreams and of early recollections.

According to Adler (pp. 357-365) the dream metaphors are products of an individual's life style and, in turn, support this style. Dreams have a forward-looking, problem-solving function and thus must be interpreted in terms of the individual's orientation to his future. They are therefore well suited as an aid in diagnosing the life style. In recent years many others have accepted similar premises, and Ullman (1962) has shown that these are in essential agreement with our best present-day knowledge of the physiology of sleeping and dreaming.

To Adler (pp. 351-357) a person's earliest recollection represented a most conveniently available thumbnail sketch of his outlook on himself and life. Ruth Munroe (1955) considers Adler's routine request for a first memory "actually the first approach toward the projective-test methodology" (p. 428n.). The early recollection technique has been worked out and well described by Mosak (1958) and is finding increasingly wide application in research and diagnosis by workers of various theoretical orientations.

Natural History   The natural history or ecological approach refers to the study of the individual in his habitat, the situations to which he has been exposed, and how he responded to them. According to Dailey (1960) it makes observations in uncomplicated, natural ways and is interested in a science which can cope with everyday experience, as the phenomenological approach is. It reaches further than the latter in that it strives to make an objective representation of total situations. We would say that it is an individualized field-theoretical approach. "Natural history data tend to be concrete and specific. . . . They have the teeming richness of ordinary life" (p. 38). They differ from the conventional case history data in that they do not simplify according to an abstract conceptual scheme, are not mere rumination over one's past experiences, are not the result of laboratory testing and measurement.

Adler (1931) can be considered to have stood firmly on the ground of such an approach: "We are living on the crust of this poor planet, earth, and nowhere else, and must develop under the restrictions and with the possibilities which our place of habitation sets us" (p. 5). But man's natural habitat very much includes his social habitat. From this context, one can learn which factors have influenced him and how he responded to certain natural situations which have a control virtually built in because they are common in everybody's life. In this sense Adler speaks of the going-to-school "experiment" (p. 406) and other similar natural tests or experiments. Here, of course, nomothetic findings enter as points of reference.

Adler made two specific contributions to the natural history method, one biological, calling attention to an individual's organ inferiorities and his responses to them, and the other social, realizing the importance of a person's birth-order position and his reactions to it.

As is well known, Adler's first major contribution was his *Study of Organ Inferiority* (1907). Its lasting message is that the bodily hereditary or acquired characteristics and the individual's response to them must be taken fully into account for the understanding of the individual. Whereas our textbooks in general psychology have a section on the abstract mechanism of heredity which is hardly integrated with the rest of the subject matter, individual psychology is very definitely concerned with the concrete outcome of heredity with which the individual finds himself equipped for better or for worse. It calls attention to the reality of the soma, as Dreikurs (1948) and Neufeld (1953) have attempted to show, and how each individual deals in his own way with his somatic reality. This also includes illnesses. Yet Adler was far from overlooking the effect of the psyche on the soma, as stressed by prevailing psychosomatic medicine. He paid close attention to expressive movements, and when these took the autonomic pathway spoke of "organ dialect" (pp. 222-225).

The Adlerian approach to the reality of the individual's family constellation starts with his birth-order position and resulting interactions. As early recollections were the beginning of projective techniques, so early family interaction influenced by differential birth-order positions as a diagnostic method can be considered a prototype of the method of sociometry developed by Moreno. The family constellation in the Adlerian sense is "a sociogram of the group at home during the person's formative years" (Dreikurs, 1953, p. 109). How it may be used in personality diagnosis has been shown in great detail by Shulman (1962). It stands quite in contrast to the Freudian approach which reduces the full reality to the Oedipus situation and thereby regards every individual childhood situation as if it were that of an only child. While Adler's emphasis was, as always, individualizing, he started from nomothetic observations regarding birth-order position; research along such lines has recently been carried out and further promoted by Schachter (1959) and Toman (1959).

As an aid to the natural history method, Adler and associates devised an informal interview guide (pp. 404-409) which was reproduced in several of his books. Typical questions are: What was your situation when you first noticed your symptoms? What is your occupation? What illnesses did you have in childhood and how did you respond to these? What illnesses are there in your family background? Who was your father's or your mother's favorite? Parents of children were asked: Does he make friends easily? Does he like to be the leader? Who dominated the family? How is the supervision? There were, of course, also questions referring to birth-order, early recollections, dreams, and organ inferiorities.

Interpreting the Data As Dailey (1960) points out, both "phenomenology and natural history have a common philosophical ancestor in Dilthey" (p. 38), the originator of the term "understanding psychology."

But Adler (1920) finds that such psychologists fall short because "they always break off just when they should show us what exactly it is they have understood" (p. 6; translation modified according to the German original). He meant they fail to show what all the manifestations of the individual are aiming at and what his life plan is.

Adler requires that, as early as possible in the investigation, the clinician formulate a conception of the goal and life plan as an important aid for the proper interpretation of the clinical data. "If we know the goal of a person, we can undertake to explain and to understand what the psychological phenomena want to tell us, why they were created, what a person has made of his innate material" (p. 196). In other words Adler stipulates that the psychologist makes an individualized teleological interpretation, at the same time as he is trying to discover what the particular goal striving of the individual is.

This sounds like pulling yourself up by your own bootstraps. Adler believes this is possible by approaching the case with the general principles of individual psychology, yet remaining flexible enough to modify these principles as the case develops in its individuality. How can one do this and not be detrimentally biased by the general principles? There are several ways and conditions: (1) The psychologist must be aware of what he is doing and firmly try to counteract his theoretical bias. (2) Individual psychology being transactional rather than intrapersonal, its interpretations can always be validated by actual behavior. (3) Individual psychology being idiographic, prepares the psychologist for expecting the unexpected in a given case. (4) As a corollary of the preceding, the general principles of individual psychology are relatively few.

Guessing   The method of arriving early in the case study at a conceptualization of the individual's goal and life style based on initial information plus the psychologist's general experience and theory, and revising this conceptualization in the light of further data as these become available, was called "guessing" by Adler. "At first you have to guess at the [internal] cause. But then you have to prove it by other signs. If these do not agree, you must be severe enough with yourself to reject your first hypothesis and seek another explanation" (p. 327). "At the very first sentence of a history you have to think—you have to establish the whole situation in which the child can be seen" (Adler, 1941, p. 1). In other words, you must sharpen your observations by your guessing, and you must constantly check your guesses. Such guessing would, however, not be wild, but based on experience and theory, and could thus be learned.

Adler thought he was the first to have used guessing scientifically and to have adopted this method from the poets' intuition (p. 329). He did not know that it had already been given scientific standing under the name of stochastic method (Linus Pauling, 1962). Although mathematicians and statisticians have lately used the term stochastic in the sense of randomness, there was originally "not the slightest suggestion of the random. Instead, Aristotle, Plato, Galen, and other classical authors used it in the sense of endeavoring to arrive at a conclusion or a solution of a problem at hand by thoughts from within, by reflective thinking, making a good guess" (p. 46). Stochastic derives from a Greek word meaning apt to divine the truth by conjecture.

Pauling credits Alexander Smith with the term stochastic method and quotes from the latter's *Inorganic Chemistry,* 1909, p. 142: A stochastic hypothesis, the guess, "differs from the other kind in that it professes to be composed entirely of verifiable facts and is subjected to verification as quickly as possible" (1962, p. 46). E.g.,

> In the stochastic method of treating very complex crystals a plausible structure is guessed with the aid of hints . . . as well as knowledge of general principles . . . and the stochastic hypothesis that this is the actual structure of the crystal is thereupon either verified or disproved (1962, p. 46).

Adler's guessing or stochastic method of interpreting data is quite similar to the summary of clinical analysis presented by C. C. McArthur (1956). It is the development of special trial hypotheses about the person which are tested against further data, and to which the criterion of internal consistency is applied and re-applied. The aim is "to build from the data a clinical construct, . . . a 'special theory applicable to one person,' a model of that person . . . a formulation of the premises governing all of S's behavior . . . with which the person being studied had learned to face the world" (p. 101). This is almost a description of Adler's aim, the formulation of the individual's style of life. It is only not quite so teleologically conceived. But in any event the Adlerian would agree with McArthur that such personality diagnosis is a hypothetico-deductive process and as such "nothing but the application of the scientific method" (p. 101).

THERAPY

The concept of cure, the objective of psychotherapy, like all other concepts, was also defined by Adler operationally and socially: "As soon as the patient can connect himself with his fellow men on an equal and cooperative footing, he is cured" (p. 347).

The process by which the cure is brought about is a cognitive reorganization. "The cure or reorientation is brought about by a correction of the faulty picture of the world and the unequivocal acceptance of a mature picture of the world" (p. 333). On the basis of such a formulation of the process of the cure, Adler's individual psychology has correctly been identified by Sundberg and Tyler (1962, pp. 357-361) as probably the first among the cognitive change theories of psychotherapy. These authors mention as other therapy theories belonging in this group those of Albert Ellis (1962), Adolph Meyer (1958), F. C. Thorne (1950), G. A. Kelly (1955) especially, and E. L. Phillips (1956); also the existentialists like Rollo May (1958) and Viktor Frankl (1955); and O. H. Mowrer (1960).

Adlerian therapy consists in the art of imparting the understanding which the therapist has gained to the patient, the assumption being that the patient will then be able to correct his mistaken life style. At the same time, the therapist must strengthen the patient's social interest and thus enable him to gain the greater independence and courage necessary for the correction of his mistake (p. 119).

While thus in principle Adlerian therapy is not a very complicated process and relatively not very lengthy, still it is time consuming because the patient's schema of apperception is biased. It will be difficult for him to reorganize his perception of himself and the world and to modify his goal striving. Thus it becomes necessary to use the material from further interviews to interpret to the patient again and again how all his expressions fit his style of life. "The therapist must grasp the special structure and development of that individual life with such accuracy, and express it with such lucidity, that the patient knows he is plainly understood and recognizes his own mistake" (p. 335). Once this is accomplished, the patient will understand his specific incidents better than does the therapist (p. 336).

The first requirement is to provide the patient with a good human relationship, a situational requirement, to awaken his social interest. To provide him with insight into his mistaken style of life is only a second requirement. The contributive connection with and attitude toward one's fellow man is what counts, and the theory does not stipulate that this could come about only through insight. One's picture of the world and oneself could change without insight. If the individual could be "seduced" by certain situations toward a mistaken interpretation (pp. 138, 292), a different situation could seduce him toward a more adequate interpretation. This applies not only to social but also physiological factors. After all, individual psychology took its origin in the consideration of organ inferiorities and their possible psychological effects.

Special Techniques In view of such situational orientation, individual psychologists, beginning with Adler, were theoretically well prepared to accept any method which through manipulation of the patient's situation would bring him closer to the goal of connecting himself in a positive way with his fellow men. Examples of the various special techniques in which Adlerian psychotherapists have become interested or have pioneered are the following.

Drug therapy with psychotics, by interrupting unrealistic thinking, "may result in a more positive response to work, and an increased interest in human contact," according to Alexandra Adler (1957). A quite different and far less important kind of physical intervention, *plastic surgery,* is advocated by Adler (1936) because, "As we live in a group and are judged by the group, and as this group objects to any departure from normal appearance, it is clear that a facial deformity can have a very deleterious effect on behavior."

Milieu therapy with delinquents must provide a social environment which becomes conducive to better cooperation, not through permissiveness but by letting them experience the natural consequences of their behavior (E. Papanek, 1958). Likewise, the modern *mental hospital treatment* is consistently structured to facilitate more and better human connections for the patient (Brooks, Deane, & Ansbacher, 1960). In a similar vein, Bierer organized the first *therapeutic social clubs* (1949) and one of the first if not the very first *day hospital* (1951).

The manipulation of the *classroom* to ensure the better cooperation of problem children has been presented by Dreikurs (1957) and by Spiel (1962). *Art, play, and music therapy* are also the concern of Adlerians (Gondor, 1954; Dreikurs, 1960).

With its emphasis on the social factor in mental disorders, individual psychology has been quite naturally leading in *group psychotherapy* (Dreikurs, 1955, 1959), and the milieu aspect of group therapy has been pointed out by Helene Papanek (1961). Special forms of group therapy employed by Adlerians are *family counseling* (Dreikurs *et al.,* 1959; Deutsch, 1959), *multiple psychotherapy* (Dreikurs, 1950), and finally the application of Moreno's technique of *psychodrama* (Shoobs, 1956; Shulman, 1960).

SUMMARY

Individual psychology, an organismic psychology developed from the practice of psychotherapy, can be identified with the "open system" theories, particularly through its postulate of man's creative power. Through its emphasis on man's social embeddedness it is also a social science theory.

In methodology individual psychology is phenomenological and at the same time operational and pragmatic. Its key terms, including style of life, keep on a low level of abstraction. Social interest, the most distinguishing and difficult term, can be shown to refer to five different processes pertaining to man's relation to his fellow man.

The clinical data of individual psychology are concrete and specific and are obtained through the phenomenological and natural history approaches to which Adler made several distinctive contributions. The data are interpreted by formulating and testing stochastic hypotheses, a method also known as "guessing" and first recognized by this name in psychology by Adler.

Adler's theory of psychotherapy is essentially one of cognitive change. Through this, together with all the other aspects of the general theory, individual psychologists were well prepared to accept and to pioneer in any method of therapy which would bring the patient closer to a good relation to his fellow man, which is seen as the aim of therapy.

In conclusion we should like to point to what we consider the most characteristic feature of individual psychology. While it assigns central importance to man's self-transcending striving, it regards this striving as it actually or potentially feeds back positively into the general process of living.

REFERENCES

ADLER, A. *Study of organ inferiority and its psychical compensation: a contribution to clinical medicine.* 1907. New York: Mental Diseases Publishing Co., 1917.

ADLER, A. *The neurotic constitution.* 1912. New York: Dodd, Mead, 1926.

ADLER, A. *The practice and theory of individual psychology.* 1920. Paterson, N.J.: Littlefield, Adams, 1959.

ADLER, A. Vorrede. In *Studie über Minderwertigkeit von Organen.* (Reprint ed.) Munich: Bergmann, 1927.

ADLER, A. *Über den nervösen Charakter.* (4th ed.) Munich: Bergmann, 1928.

ADLER, A. *Praxis und Theorie der Individualpsychologie.* (4th ed.) Munich: Bergmann, 1930.

ADLER, A. *What life should mean to you.* 1931. New York: Capricorn Books, 1958.

ADLER, A. *Social interest: a challenge to mankind.* 1933. (a) London: Faber & Faber, 1938.

ADLER, A. Religion und Individualpsychologie. In E. Jahn and A. Adler, *Religion und Individualpsychologie.* Vienna: Passer, 1933. (b) Pp. 58-92.

ADLER, A. Die Formen der seelischen Aktivität: ein Beitrag zur individualpsychologischen Charakterkunde. *Int. Z. indiv. Psychol.,* 1934, **12,** 1-5.

ADLER, A. Introduction. In M. Maxwell, *New faces—new futures.* New York: R. R. Smith, 1936.

ADLER, A. The progress of mankind. 1937. (a) *J. indiv. Psychol.,* 1957, **13,** 9-13. Also in K. A. Adler and Danica Deutsch (Eds.), *Essays in individual psychology.* New York: Grove Press, 1959. Pp. 3-8.

ADLER, A. Psychiatric aspects regarding individual and social disorganization. *Amer. J. Sociol.,* 1937, **42,** 773-780. (b)

ADLER, A. Case interpretation. *Indiv. Psychol. Bull.,* 1941, **2,** 1-9.

ADLER, A. *The individual psychology of Alfred Adler.* New York: Basic Books, 1956.

ADLER, ALEXANDRA. Modern drug treatment and psychotherapy. *J. indiv. Psychol.,* 1957, **13,** 146-149.

ALLPORT, G. W. *Becoming.* New Haven: Yale Univ. Press, 1955.

ALLPORT, G. W. The open system in personality theory. *J. abnorm. soc. Psychol.,* 1960, **61,** 301-310.

ALLPORT, G. W. *Pattern and growth in personality.* New York: Holt, Rinehart & Winston, 1961.

ANDERSON, H. H. Personality growth: Conceptual considerations. In H. P. David and H. von Bracken (Eds.), *Perspectives in personality theory.* New York: Basic Books, 1957. Pp. 131-158.

ANSBACHER, H. L. Alfred Adler's place in psychology today. *Int. Z. indiv. Psychol.,* 1947, **16,** 97-111.

ANSBACHER, H. L. The "alienation syndrome" and Adler's concept of "distance." *J. consult. Psychol.,* 1956, **20,** 483-484.

ANSBACHER, H. L. Whose masculine protest? *Contemp. Psychol.,* 1960, **5,** 28-29.

ANSBACHER, H. L. On the origin of holism. *J. indiv. Psychol.,* 1961, **17,** 142-148.

ANSBACHER, H. L., & ANSBACHER, ROWENA R. Introduction: Individual psychology in its larger setting. In A. Adler, *The individual psychology of Alfred Adler.* New York: Basic Books, 1956. Pp. 1-18.

ASCH, S. *Social psychology.* New York: Prentice-Hall, 1952.

BIERER, J. (Ed.) *Therapeutic social clubs.* London: Lewis, 1949.

BIERER, J. *The day hospital: an experiment in social psychiatry and synthoanalytic psychotherapy.* London: Lewis, 1951.

BROOKS, G. W., DEANE, W. N., & ANSBACHER, H. L. Rehabilitation of chronic schizophrenic patients for social living. *J. indiv. Psychol.,* 1960, **16,** 189-196.

COLLIER, R. M. Independence: an overlooked implication of the open system concept. *J. Indiv. Psychol.,* 1962, **18,** 103-113.

DAILEY, C. A. Natural history and phenomenology. *J. indiv. Psychol.,* 1960, **16,** 36-44.

DEUTSCH, DANICA. Didactic group discussions with mothers in a child guidance setting. In K. A. Adler and Danica Deutsch (Eds.), *Essays in individual psychology.* New York: Grove Press, 1959. Pp. 247-255.

DEWEY, J. *Dictionary of education.* (R. B. Winn, Ed.) New York: Philosophical Library, 1959.

DREIKURS, R. The socio-psychological dynamics of physical disability: a review of the Adlerian concept. *J. soc. Issues,* 1948, **4** (4), 39-54.

DREIKURS, R. Techniques and dynamics of multiple psychotherapy. *Psychiat. Quart.,* 1950, **24,** 788-799.

DREIKURS, R. The psychological interview in medicine. *Amer. J. indiv. Psychol.,* 1953, **10,** 99-122.

DREIKURS, R. Group psychotherapy and the third revolution in psychiatry. *Int. J. soc. Psychiat.,* 1955, **1,** 23-32.

DREIKURS, R. *Psychology in the classroom: a manual for teachers.* New York: Harper, 1957.

DREIKURS, R. Early experiments with group psychotherapy: a historical review. *Amer. J. Psychother.,* 1959, **13,** 882-891.

DREIKURS, R. Music therapy with psychotic children. *Psychiat. Quart.,* 1960, **34,** 722-734.

DREIKURS, R., CORSINI, R., LOWE, R., & SONSTEGARD, M. (Eds.) *Adlerian fam-*

ily counseling: a manual for counseling centers. Eugene: Univ. Oregon Press, 1959.

ELLIS, A. Rational psychotherapy and individual psychology. *J. indiv. Psychol.,* 1957, **13,** 38-44.

ENGLISH, H. B., & ENGLISH, AVA C. *A comprehensive dictionary of psychological and psychoanalytic terms.* New York: Longmans, 1958.

FEIGL, H. Some major issues and developments in the philosophy of science of logical empiricism. In H. Feigl and M. Scriven (Eds.), *Minnesota studies in the philosophy of science.* Vol. 1. *The foundations of science and the concepts of psychology and psychoanalysis.* Minneapolis: Univ. Minnesota Press, 1956. Pp. 3-37.

FRANKEL, V. E. The doctor and the soul. New York: Knopf, 1955.

FREUD, S. Analysis terminable and interminable. 1937. In *Collected papers.* Vol. 5. London: Hogarth Press, 1950. Pp. 316-357.

FREUD, S. *The origins of psychoanalysis: Letters, drafts and notes to Wilhelm Fliess, 1887-1902.* Marie Bonaparte, Anna Freud, and E. Kris (Eds.). New York: Doubleday Anchor Books, 1957.

GONDOR, E. I. *Art and play therapy.* New York: Doubleday, 1954.

HALL, C. S., & LINDZEY, G. *Theories of personality.* New York: Wiley, 1957.

KELLY, G. A. *The psychology of personal constructs.* New York: Norton, 1955.

KLOPFER, B. Individualpsychologie, Wissenschaft und Weltanschauung. *Int. Z. Indiv. Psychol.,* 1925, **3,** 340. (Abstract.)

KOFFKA, K. *Principles of Gestalt psychology.* New York: Harcourt, Brace, 1935.

LANGMAN, L. Adlerian thought in Asch's social psychology. *J. indiv. Psychol.,* 1960, **16,** 137-145.

MCARTHUR, C. C. Clinical versus actuarial prediction. In R. F. Berdie (Chairman), *Proc. 1955 Invitational Conference on Testing Problems.* Princeton, N. J.: Educational Testing Service, 1956. Pp. 99-106.

MASLOW, A. H. *Motivation and personality.* New York: Harper, 1954.

MASLOW, A. H. *Toward a psychology of being.* New York: Van Nostrand, 1962.

MAY, R., ANGEL, E., & ELLENBERGER, H. F. (Eds.) *Existence.* New York: Basic Books, 1958.

MEYER, A. *Psychobiology: A science of man.* Springfield, Ill.: Thomas, 1958.

MILLER, G. A., GALANTER, E., & PRIBRAM, K. H. *Plans and the structure of behavior.* New York: Holt, 1960.

MOSAK, H. H. Early recollections as a projective technique. *J. proj. Tech.,* 1958, **22,** 302-311.

MOSAK, H. H. The getting type: A parsimonious social interpretation of the oral character. *J. indiv. Psychol.,* 1959, **15,** 193-198.

MOWRER, O. H. "Sin," the lesser of two evils. *Amer. Psychol.,* 1960, **15,** 301-304.

MUNROE, RUTH L. *Schools of psychoanalytic thought.* New York: Dryden Press, 1955.

MURPHY, G. *Historical introduction to modern psychology.* (Rev. ed.) New York: Harcourt, Brace, 1949.

MURPHY, G. *Human potentialities.* New York: Basic Books, 1958.

NAGEL, E. *The structure of science: problems in the logic of scientific explanation.* New York: Harcourt, Brace & World, 1961.

NEUFELD, I. Holistic medicine versus psychosomatic medicine. *Amer. J. indiv. Psychol.*, 1953, **10**, 140-168.

NUNBERG, H., & FEDERN, P. (Eds.) *Minutes of the Vienna Psychoanalytic Society.* Vol. 1. 1906-1908. New York: International Univ. Press, 1962.

PAULING, L. The genesis of ideas. In R. A. Cleghorn (Ed.), *Third World Congress of Psychiatry proceedings.* Toronto: Univ. Toronto Press, 1962. Pp. 44-47.

PAPANEK, E. Re-education and treatment of juvenile delinquents. *Amer. J. Psychother.*, 1958, **12**, 269-296.

PAPANEK, HELENE. Psychotherapy without insight: group therapy as milieu therapy. *J. indiv. Psychol.*, 1961, **17**, 184-192.

PHILLIPS, E. L. *Psychotherapy: a modern theory and practice.* Englewood Cliffs, N.J.: Prentice-Hall, 1956.

ROTTER, J. B. An analysis of Adlerian psychology from a research orientation. *J. indiv. Psychol.*, 1962, **18**, 3-11.

RUSSELL, E. S. *The interpretation of development and heredity.* New York: Oxford, 1930. As quoted by Nagel (1961, p. 433).

SCHACHTER, S. *The psychology of affiliation.* Stanford, Calif.: Stanford Univ. Press, 1959.

SHOOBS, N. E. Individual psychology and psychodrama. *Amer. J. indiv. Psychol.*, 1956, **12**, 46-52.

SHULMAN, B. H. A psychodramatically oriented action technique in group psychotherapy. *Group Psychother.*, 1960, **13**, 34-39.

SHULMAN, B. H. The family constellation in personality diagnosis. *J. indiv. Psychol.*, 1962, **18**, 35-47.

SIMPSON, G. G. *The meaning of evolution.* New York: Mentor Books, 1951.

SINNOTT, E. W. A biological basis for teleology. *J. indiv. Psychol.*, 1957, **13**, 14-23.

SKINNER, B. F. The operational analysis of psychological terms. In H. Feigl and May Brodbeck (Eds.), *Readings in the philosophy of science.* New York: Appleton-Century-Crofts, 1953. Pp. 585-595.

SKINNER, B. F. Critique of psychoanalytic concepts and theories. In H. Feigl and M. Scriven (Eds.), *Minnesota studies in the philosophy of science.* Vol. 1. *The foundations of science and the concepts of psychology and psychoanalysis.* Minneapolis: Univ. Minnesota Press, 1956. Pp. 77-87.

SMUTS, J. C. *Holism and evolution.* 1926. New York: Viking Press, 1961.

SPIEL, O. *Discipline without punishment: an account of a school in action.* L. Way (Ed.). London: Faber & Faber, 1962.

SUNDBERG, N. D., & TYLER, LEONA E. *Clinical psychology.* New York: Appleton-Century-Crofts, 1962.

THORNE, F. C. *Principles of personality counseling.* Brandon, Vt.: *J. clin. Psychol.*, 1950.

TOLMAN, E. C. *Purposive behavior in animals and men.* New York: Appleton-Century-Crofts, 1932.

TOMAN, W. Family constellation as a basic personality determinant. *J. indiv. Psychol.*, 1959, **15**, 199-211.

ULLMAN, M. Dreaming, life style, and physiology: a comment on Adler's view of the dream. *J. indiv. Psychol.*, 1962, **18**, 18-25.

VAIHINGER, H. *The philosophy of "as if"* (1911). London: Routledge & Kegan Paul, 1924.

VON BERTALANFFY, L. Theoretical models in biology and psychology. In D. Krech and G. S. Klein (Eds.), *Theoretical models and personality theory.* Durham, N.C.: Duke Univ. Press, 1952.

WOODWORTH, R. S. *Dynamics of behavior.* New York: Holt, 1958.

19 RICHARD S. PETERS

EMOTIONS, PASSIVITY,

AND THE PLACE OF

FREUD'S THEORY IN PSYCHOLOGY *

IN A PREVIOUS MONOGRAPH concerned with concepts and explanations in psychology (Peters, 1958), I argued that the basic concepts for the explanation of human actions must be related to what I called a purposive-rule-following model rather similar to the model of a rational man employed in classical economics. Though admitting the relevance of mechanical concepts for stating necessary conditions of actions, for postulating "mechanisms" by means of which purposes and the like are manifest in action, and for explaining certain kinds of breakdowns, I strenuously opposed psychological theories (for example, that of Hull). which claimed that the family of concepts connected with "action" could be translated into mechanical ones, or that actions could be sufficiently explained in mechanical terms. I still think that this basic thesis was correct, though it was open to misunderstanding on the issue of what is to be counted as a "sufficient explanation" (see Dodwell, 1960). Admittedly, not all my arguments for this thesis were good ones; but additional ones have since been produced by Melden in a later monograph in the same series (see Melden, 1961), which have strengthened my conviction about the truth of the basic thesis.

However, it is not my intention in this paper to refurbish a now familiar thesis. Rather, I want to elaborate and develop a point which I made at the end of the chapter on Freud's theory when I was considering the extent to which Freud employed a purposive-rule-following model or a mechanical one in his theory of the wish and the mechanisms of defense. I said:

---

* This chapter is based on a paper first read to the Boston Colloquium for the Philosophy of Science in 1961 and later published in the Proceedings of the Aristotelian Society, 1961-1962. Thanks are due to the Aristotelian Society for permitting me to reprint much of the material presented to them.

365

Freud spoke of mental processes, especially in his early work, in a language taken from the mechanical descriptions of physiology. But, when he developed his interest in ego psychology later on, he spoke increasingly in the 'as if' language based on a purposive rule-following model. . . . Perhaps Freud's lasting contribution to psychology lay not simply in the startling discoveries which he made, but also in showing, by implication, that neither the mechanical nor the rule-following purposive model of explanation are really adequate for conceptualizing his revolutionary insights (Peters, 1958, pp. 93-94).

I did not then appreciate the wider significance of this point for psychological theory. Subsequent work, however, on the concept and theories of "emotion" led me to see that this point could also be made about a much wider range of phenomena than those covered by Freud's original theory. A consideration of such phenomena and of the concepts necessary to explain them is not only interesting in itself; it also adds additional support to the main thesis of my original monograph that the phenomena of "behavior" are too disparate to be encompassed by any all-inclusive theory. What is needed are different types of theory to cover different ranges of phenomena. The phenomena with which I shall be particularly concerned in this paper are those in which the subject is "passive" but which are indisputably "mental" because they cannot be described without recourse to cognition or "awareness."

EMOTION AND COGNITION

The first point, then, that I must establish is that what we call "emotions" are not describable in mechanical terms because of the conceptual connection that exists between what we call "emotions" and cognition. When we speak of emotions those states of mind which we speak of in this way—such as fear, anger, jealousy, and so forth,—always imply some reference to an object. If we say that we are or feel afraid, angry, or jealous, it is always appropriate to ask "Of whom?" "Of what?" "With whom?" "With what?" This relationship is not a causal one of the type which has been canonized by mechanical theorists. It is not the product of external or internal conditions that as a matter of fact have been found to be connected with what is called the expression of emotion by relations of a purely spatiotemporal character. A man might always feel fear when the temperature sank below freezing point and angry when it rose above 100 degrees. But we would not then say that the man was afraid of cold or angry with heat. Such conditions might be necessary to having certain emotions, but would not be the object of emotions. For "being the object of" implies a cognitive relation. The conditions must be seen as or understood as being of a certain sort. We do, of course, use the word "cause" often enough in such cases as when we say things like "the sound of the safety catch being taken off was the cause of his fear." Indeed, Miss Anscombe has coined the term "mental cause" to cover this (and many other very *different* types of connection that we know "without observation"), which clearly do not fall into the category of mechanical causality (see Anscombe, 1957). But the term is used so widely that it only adds to the confusion about such matters.

The relationship between what a man sees a situation as and his fear, anger, and other such emotions is so close that it is plausible to suggest that the relationship is an internal one. It is difficult to state this point convincingly because our language for the different shades of emotions is too blunt. A man may "feel blue" on Monday morning; but we do not have a word for the shade of blue. "Fear," too, covers what a man might feel for a bull in one field, in the same field where there is an easy escape route inaccessible to the bull, and in a field where there is no escape route at all. The shades of emotion change with the perception of the differences in the situation; yet it is only possible to indicate the sort of fear with which a man is afflicted by drawing attention to relevant differences in the situation. This thesis is strengthened by the fact that certain descriptions of a situation rule out certain emotional reactions to it. As Mrs. Foot (1958-1959) has pointed out, a man cannot, without special explanation, feel pride for things like the sea which he has had no hand in bringing about. A man who does feel proud of the sea, we would say, must be the victim of delusions of grandeur—which is a special explanation of his plight. There is something peculiar about a woman who climbs up on a chest of drawers, trembling with fear, at the sight of a mouse. In such cases we begin to talk about the displacement of emotion; she can't be seeing a mouse as a mouse. And the notion of "displacement" only makes sense if we assume that the different emotions are intimately and properly connected with judgments about certain typical objects or situations.

But we can talk of "fear," "jealousy," and so on as motives as well as talking of them as emotions. The question is what is distinctive about talking of them as emotions. The standard uses of "emotion" and its derivatives might help us to see what is distinctive. And although, of course, the meaning of "emotion" is not to be equated with the standard uses of the term, nevertheless, such uses must surely provide important clues to the work done by the concept: the phrases in which the term "emotion" and its derivatives are not only natural but also almost indispensable are those used when we speak of judgments being disturbed, clouded, or warped by emotion, of people as being not properly in control of their emotions, being subject to gusts of emotion, being emotionally perturbed, upset, involved, excited, biased, and exhausted. In a similar vein, we speak of emotional outbursts, reactions, and upheavals. The suggestion in such cases is always that something comes over people when they consider a situation in a certain kind of light. Thus, though typical sorts of appraisals or "judgments" are involved in fear, anger, and love, "emotion" in the standard use of the term, rather than in that coined by philosophers and psychologists, is used to suggest mists on our mental windscreen rather than straightforward judgments. Emotions, like the weather, come over us and one of their main functions is to distort and cloud judgment. Indeed, if we say that a judgment is an expression of emotion, we are suggesting that it is a pretty sort of judgment.

EMOTIONS AND PASSIVITY

The tendency which I want to resist is to speak of "emotions" and "motives" as if they are classificatory terms for lumping together states of mind such as fear, anger, jealousy, and the like. Psychologists often set down what they consider man's instincts or basic drives to be. They then go on to catalogue his basic motives and emotions and are somewhat embarrassed to find that states of mind like fear and jealousy occur in both lists. So they try to make motives derivative from emotion, or emotion an aspect of, interference with, or facilitation of, motivated behavior. Alternatively, there is a tendency to do what Ryle does by putting "Emotion" as a chapter heading and classifying "feelings," "agitations," "moods," "motives," etc., as belonging to the general family of "emotion" (Ryle, 1949). All such treatments, in my view, misconceive both how the concepts of "emotion" and the concept of "motive" work. For these terms are not classificatory ones; they are rather terms which are used to relate states of mind such as fear, anger, and jealousy to distinctive frames of reference, those of activity and passivity.

There are what, for want of a better word, I will call "states of mind" like fear, anger, and jealousy, all of which imply reference to an object or situation and some kind of appraisal of it. When we are dealing with actions, we make reference to these states of mind either as reasons for action or, in special types of context which I have tried to make explicit (Peters, 1958, Ch. 2) as motives for acting. We act out of fear, jealousy, anger and the like. But we are sometimes overcome by fear, jealousy, anger, are disturbed by them, have our actions invigorated by them, have our judgments clouded, distorted, or heightened by them, and so on. When we relate fear and anger to this latter sort of framework, we are speaking of them as emotions. In such cases, the picking out of the characteristics in the implied appraisal is the reason for or cause of our being affected or acted on. We naturally use the term "emotion" and its derivatives to pick out our passivity.

The appraisal involved in using terms like "fear," "anger," and "jealously" is of objects or situations as being in various respects agreeable or disagreeable to us. (And they may *simply* be appraisals of a situation which issue in no actions and occasion no passive phenomena.) If we speak of them as "motives," these assessments are reasons for our actions; but when we speak of them as "emotions," there is no necessary connection with action. Indeed, typically these appraisals are connected with the functioning of our autonomic nervous systems, about which we usually speak in a metaphorical way, but in metaphors which are consonant with our passivity. We boil and fume with anger; we tremble and sweat with fear; we swell and glow with pride; we blush with shame and embarrassment; our eyes dilate with fear, sparkle with delight, and moisten with sorrow. Often, of course, the motor system is involved but, when it is, the manifestations typically take on an involuntary character. Our knees knock with fear, our teeth chatter with fright, and sometimes our limbs are paralyzed.

Fear, anger, etc., as emotions can be contingently rather than necessarily related to action in the sense that they can disrupt, heighten, and intensify motor performances. We can act in fear as well as out of fear. The preposition "in" draws attention to the manner of acting rather than to the reason or motive for acting. "He acted in anger" is different from "he was angry," which merely interprets the action as being of a certain sort, as well as from "he acted out of anger," which gives a reason or motive for acting beyond the initial characterization of the action as being of a certain sort. A man can act in anger who is also acting out of love. His manner of acting is affected by considering aspects of the situation, considerations which may distort or intensify his actions. And it is very nice when such gusts of emotions, as it were, speed us on our way rather than deflect us from our path. Thus there is no reason why "fear," or "anger," should not function both as motives and as emotions at the same time.

There are, too, the intermediary class of cases where people do not act altogether with reason, but where their reaction, which is typically of an uncoordinated protopathic type, springs from an intuitive type of appraisal of a situation. An example would be when a person lashes out in anger or starts with fear. These are not reactions to stimuli, like jumping when one receives an electric shock, because of their cognitive core. Neither are they actions in a full-blown sense; for there is no appraisal of means to an end, no careful consideration of the end to be achieved. They are what we call "emotional reactions." They are dissimilar, too, from acting on impulse; for we act on impulse when there is no such appraisal of a situation as is involved in emotional reactions. To say that a man acts on impulse is at least to deny that he acts deliberately. But it is not necessarily to class what goes on as being subsequent to the sort of appraisal which is involved in emotion. A hungry man might put his hand out and grab a banana in a store. This might be an action on impulse but it would be very strange to describe it as an emotional reaction.

In a similar way, there can be and often is a contingent relationship between perception, memory, and judgment on the one hand and emotion on the other. In such cases, the suggestion is that the appraisal which is necessarily connected with the emotion in question acts on the person so as to cloud or distort, or heighten or sharpen, the assessment which he is making. The appraisal of a situation as being in some way agreeable or disagreeable, which is involved in emotion, takes the attention away from or clouds over the relevant features of the situation, "relevance" being defined in terms of whatever criteria are involved in the type of judgment that is being made.

PSYCHOLOGICAL THEORIES OF EMOTION

My refusal to accept an internal connection between emotion and action flies in the face of almost every psychological theory. So it is at least incumbent on me to indicate the main features of such theories and to sketch my grounds either for rejecting them completely or for claiming that what is valuable in them can be accommodated within my theory. I find myself, for instance, very much in sympathy with Asch's (1959) view that "emotions express in the most striking manner the relation of conditions to us; they mark our awareness of what is happening to us." For he stresses the connection between emotion and passivity. Nevertheless, he seems to suggest more than a contingent connection between emotion and action when he says "Emotions are our ways of representing to ourselves the fate of our goals. They are a direct consequence of the understanding of our situation. One may say that emotions mirror the course of motivational events" (p. 112).

McDougall's theory, I suppose, is almost the classic case of a theory in which there is a necessary connection between emotion and some motivational concept; for he held that every instinct is felt as an emotion. Indeed, the specific emotional quale was, on his theory, the distinguishing mark of the different instincts. Instincts are aroused by cognition of an object that has significance for the animal because of its innate disposition, and the bodily changes which take place as the animal embarks on its characteristic responses are felt as emotion. Emotion is thus a commotion accompanying action which has a facilitating effect on it (McDougall, 1924). Why then, one might ask, are there not emotions accompanying hunger and thirst, which are the classic examples of such instinctive behavior—and the pillars of subsequent theories of motivation? And what about the disruptive effects of emotion? This latter type of objection was taken care of by more sophisticated theorists such as Leeper, who held that the function of emotion was to bring about the concentration of attention on an object, but that this might disorganize the action if it was too intense. Thus, normally emotions arouse, sustain, and direct activity; but they can disrupt activity if they are too intense (Leeper, 1955) Others stress the disruptive rather than the facilitating effect of emotion on behavior. On such a view, emotions may be looked on as what Ryle calls "agitations" occasioned by frustration in the pursuit of goals or by conflict between mutually incompatible tendencies. Paulhan (1930) held such a theory, and so did Dewey. P. T. Young included this stress on disruption in a much more sophisticated and subtle account which, apart from the necessary connection postulated with behavior, is largely acceptable (Young, 1956). On his view,

> An emotion is an acute effective disturbance within the individual as a whole, arising from psychological situations and manifest in conscious experience, behaviour, and especially through bodily changes which are regulated by the autonomic nervous system.

This is usually the result of a motivated action, for "In every emotional upset some motivating factor is thwarted, or satisfied, or excites the individual" (Young, 1943, p. 392). Here again is the suggestion, as in Asch's theory, that emotion occurs only in the context of action. Young held that such upsets occur when action is frustrated or when, in extremes of emotion, behavior becomes paralyzed or disrupted because intense sympathetic stimulation in the autonomic system interferes with muscular contractions. So emotion disorganizes behavior instead of having its usual function of arousing, organizing, or sustaining it.

The objection, surely, to all such theories is that emotion need not be occasioned by the frustration of behavior and it need not exhibit itself in the disruption or facilitation of behavior. It may simply affect a man's beliefs or judgment. Such theories write into the meaning of "emotion" a frequent occasion of its occurrence, which has the effect of blurring the distinction between talking of, say, fear as an emotion and as a motive. Or they point to a frequent effect of emotion—its interference with or facilitation of behavior. They show that anger, fear, jealousy, and so on can be viewed both as emotions and as motives. On such occasions action explained by references to, say, fear as a motive is facilitated or disrupted by fear functioning also as an emotion. But cognitive performances such as perceiving or remembering, which are not, strictly speaking, behavior, can also be enhanced, distorted, or disrupted by emotion. Such theories give no way of distinguishing what we mean when we talk of fear as an emotion rather than a motive. Neither do they establish that fear as an emotion must either be occasioned by a frustration of behavior or be exhibited in disrupted or facilitated behavior.

Behaviorists, understandably enough, have had little to say about emotion. For to be subject to emotion involves seeing or appraising a situation as being of a certain sort. And such appraisals, as well as the feelings which are often involved in experiencing fear as an emotion, for example, are excluded from any consistent behaviorist theory. Nevertheless behaviorists have, however consistently, given expression to views on the matter. Watson, for instance, regarded emotions as reactions to stimuli, such as loud noises, which involve changes in the visceral and glandular systems (Watson, 1924). Tolman, who conducted a protracted, if half-hearted love-affair with behaviorism, regarded emotion (1932) as the appearance in "conscious awareness" of organic and kinaesthetic sensations.

Such theories, which connect a watered-down notion of emotion with behavior, usually adopt some variant of a more promising type of theory which attempts to establish some kind of connection between emotion and the functioning of the autonomic system rather than with behavior in a proper sense. But the main theory in the field, that of James and Lange (1922), was vitiated by a bungling of the conceptual and empirical connections. Emotion on this theory, was regarded as felt visceral excitation (James) or felt vasomotor changes (Lange), involved in tendencies to approach and avoidance. These tendencies were regarded as reflexes built up into habits by association with previous perceptions of a situation in accordance with the traditional principles of association. Fear is thus the felt side of the tendency to run away in so far as the latter involves characteristic visceral changes. But the fact is that the physiological changes referred to usually come after the appraisal of a situation, and the appraisal of the situation is conceptually connected with whatever emotion is experienced, a connection which James regarded as empirical, to be explained in terms of his association theory. So both the empirical and the conceptual connections were bungled.

Perhaps the most comprehensive and careful theory of all is that of Magda Arnold, who regards emotions as the "felt tendency towards or away from an object" which is preceded by an appraisal of a situation as being of a certain sort that is harmful or beneficial to the agent. This attraction or aversion is accompanied by a pattern of physiological changes organized toward approach or withdrawal. This she calls an "excitation" theory; for although it stresses the connection between emotion and typical types of appraisal and the functioning of the autonomic system, it nevertheless makes an internal connection between emotion and a tendency to move toward or away from objects (Arnold, 1960). On her view it would be absurd, without special explanation, to say that a person is subject to, say, fear as an emotion without having any tendency to avoid the situation so appraised. And it certainly is more plausible to connect emotion with action in this way than in the ways previously suggested— that is as a facilitation or disruption of behavior. For there could well be an internal connection between the type of appraisal involved in emotion (as harmful, disagreeable, beneficial, agreeable or the like) and the tendency to approach or avoid. My own view is that the connection is not as strong as this. I hope, however, that by exhibiting what the connection is I shall be able not simply to develop a theory of my own but also to account for this persistent tendency to link emotion with action. But this must be tackled somewhat obliquely by means of a brief analysis of the distinction between "wishing" and "wanting" which, in my view, is the crux of the matter.

EMOTION AND THE DISTINCTION BETWEEN "WISHING" AND "WANTING"

It has been suggested that the type of appraisal that goes with emotion is of an object or situation as being in some way harmful, disagreeable, beneficial, agreeable. If "harmful" and "beneficial" are insisted on rather than "disagreeable" and "agreeable," it is very plausible to construe this appraisal as being necessarily connected with action via the concept of "want." For, it might be argued, to see something as beneficial is synonymous with seeing it as something that one might want, and to speak of "wanting" is to suggest that, in the absence of any special explanation, one will do something or take some conceivable steps to bring about or possess what is conceived of in this way. It is also to suggest that what is so picked out conforms to standards which make it an intelligible object for some action or performance. If a man says that he wants air, he suggests that there are steps which can be taken to get it and that, when he has got it, there is something, say breathing, that can be done with it. But with "wanting the moon," it is different. Children can reasonably be said to want the moon; for their understanding of distance and causal connections are limited and maybe they think they can bite a hunk out of it when they have it. But normally, talk of "wanting the moon" is a way of drawing attention to the extravagance, unreality, or unintelligibility of a person's wants. There are, however, no such strings attached to the concept of "wish." The optative mood "Would that X were the case," which is very closely connected with wishing, raises no questions of practicality or of possible operations that can be performed on or with what is wished for. Indeed, we usually say that we wish for things when we realize that they are impossible to have or when we rule out questions of practicality or possibility about them. We may say that we want a pet rhinoceros; but once we realize both the difficulties of getting one and the impracticality of having one as a pet we say, usually, that we wish for it, not that we still want it. For we can wish for things without any idea of how they can be got, which are in fact impossible to get, and which would embarrass us profoundly if we had them. Wishes may not only be bizarre but also riddled with logical contradictions. I have a highly respectable colleague, for instance, who wishes that he were monogamously married to eight women at once. This may be a strange wish, but it is not strange as a wish; for wishes can be like this, whereas wants, strictly speaking, cannot be.

To return, after this brief detour, to the concept of emotion: My suggestion is that the appraisal of a situation which goes with it is intimately connected with "wishing" rather than with "wanting," and that such situations are appraised as being in some way "agreeable" or "disagreeable" rather than "beneficial" or "harmful." When we speak of a person as being emotionally perturbed or overcome by fear, for example, his appraisal is certainly linked with a wish to be rid of the disturbing features of the situation. It is as if he exclaimed "Would that I were rid of this!" But there is no definite implication of any determinate steps that he envisages to put himself in such a position. To speak of fear as a motive, on the other hand, connects the appraisal with a course of action undertaken in the light of such an appraisal.

There is a further characteristic of such appraisals that links them more intimately with wishes than with wants, which is their tendency to be wild and un-realistic. Magda Arnold stresses what she calls the "intuitive" appraisal which characterizes emotion in which obvious distinctions are so often ignored. "Wishful thinking" is synonymous with thinking that proceeds according to principles of emotive congruence rather than those of logical or causal connection. Sartre (1948) regards emotion as "an abrupt drop into the magical" (p. 90). "Thus the origin of emotion is a spontaneous and lived degradation of consciousness in the face of the world" (p. 77). If, on the other hand, fear or anger are regarded as motives for action, there is the suggestion of a more discriminating appraisal; for the situation must be seen determinately enough for steps to be envisaged as leading up to or away from it.

What we call "emotional reactions" are typical manifestations of wishes. For when we start in fear or lash out in anger there is an appraisal of a situation, but it is of the blind, "intuitive," undiscriminating sort. And the movements involved in such reactions do not attain the level of coordination and grasp of means to ends necessary for them to qualify as actions; they are massive, protopathic and bordering on the involuntary. But, of course, wishes need not be displayed in anything resembling actions or in tendencies to action. They must, however, involve some kind of cognitive element, albeit of rather a wild sort. It is therefore very plausible to suggest a connection between "emotion" and "wishing," and, because there is such a close connection between "wishing" and "wanting" (which is in its turn necessarily connected with "action"), it is very easy to see how the connection between "emotion" and "action" has persisted in theories of emotions.

To summarize my thesis to date: (1) We may speak of, say, fear as an emotion, as a motive, or simply as an interpretation of a person's state of mind. (2) Reference to, say, fear or anger always implies an appraisal by the subject of a situation as affecting him in an agreeable or disagreeable way. (3) If we speak of fear, anger, or the like, as motives, we are linking a discriminating type of appraisal with an explanation of a man's action by assigning reasons to him of a certain sort (with the details of which we are not here concerned). (4) When we speak of fear as an emotion, we are linking a more intuitive type of appraisal with how it affects him, with his passivity. (5) There is no conceptual connection between being subject to an emotion and wanting to do whatever is appropriate, but there is such a connection between being subject to emotion and wishing for something of a more indeterminate sort. (6) A man who makes such an appraisal may be affected in a number of ways—bodily expressions of emotion, changes in the autonomic system, the disruption or facilitation of action, the disruption, facilitation, deflection, heightening, coloring, and distortion of cognitive performances such as thinking, perceiving, and remembering. He may also be subject to reactions such as starting, lashing out, and so on.

FREUD'S THEORY

The analysis of "emotion" that I am suggesting has many affinities with Freud's theory, insofar as it connects "emotion" with passivity and with wishes. It is difficult, however, to get to grips with his theory of emotion because it changed as Freud became more preoccupied with anxiety and because it was couched in the strange pseudophysiological language which marked Freud's early theorizing. Nevertheless, in spite of this gruesome terminology in which, for instance, wishes appear as currents in the mind, there is much of interest and value in his theory.

Freud conceived of emotions as expressions of discharge processes of psychic energy initiated by an incoming percept. ". . . Affects and emotions correspond with processes of discharge, the final expression of which is perceived as feeling" (see Rapaport, 1942, p. 29). He assumed that an unconscious process occurs between the perception of a situation and the physiological processes emphasized by the James-Lange theory. If no free pathway is open for the energy aroused by the incoming stimulus—as in cases where there is conflict of instinctual demands or where there is no suitable object for the aroused "drive"—discharge is found through channels other than those for voluntary motility. This provides what Rapaport calls the primary model of cognition and affect; drive at threshold intensity→absence of drive object→hallucinatory idea and/or affect discharge (Rapaport, 1959). This discharge of affect may take the form of emotional expression and its related physiological changes, the development of psychosomatic disturbances, disturbances of routine forms of behavior, characteristic organization of thought processes and memory in accordance with principles other than those of logical and causal relevance (Rapaport, 1942, pp. 37, 271).

The secondary model takes account of structural and adaptive features of the mind (necessary for what we call "action") which develop with the formation of the ego and the reality principle which characterizes this development. Rapaport characterizes this model as follows: "Drive at threshold intensity → structuralized delay → affect signals released by the ego from structurally segregated affect charges" (Rapaport, 1959, p. 76). Affect has now changed from a purely discharge phenomenon into a signal to help the ego deal with mounting drive tension. It may come to function as an autonomous motivating force in the way in which Leeper pictured emotion as intensifying goal-directed behavior.

All sorts of objections could be mounted against the manner in which this theory is expressed. Nevertheless, the notion of "discharge" places emotion squarely in the category of passivity. Emotion is also connected with the functioning of the autonomic nervous system and is regarded as disrupting, distorting, intensifying and "coloring" actions and performances, not as explaining them. There are also, in Freud's theory, all sorts of suggestions as to the types of laws which are relevant for the description of such passive phenomena.

THE LAWS OF EMOTION

Spinoza long ago made much of the distinction between activity and passivity, and he also claimed that emotions obey laws like lines, planes, and bodies. But he did not get very far with the task of working out what such laws would look like. Now Freud did make generalizations, albeit rather crude ones, about such phenomena. I want to get clearer about the conceptual character of such generalizations. My hope is that this might help to clarify a particular realm of psychological theorizing.

I have argued that there is a conceptual connection between wishes and being subject to emotion. And such a postulated link accounts very well for some of the characteristics of emotional appraisal on which Arnold (1960) and others have dwelt—what she calls "intuitive" appraisal in which obvious distinctions are so often ignored. Sartre (1948) regards emotion as a transformation of the world in which we live or try to live as magic, not by cause and effect. "We shall call emotion an abrupt drop into the magical" (p. 90). Indeed, he goes further; he thinks that fainting when a man is in a state of terror is a magical way of saving himself from the animal that is pursuing him and that flight is a fainting which is enacted (p. 63). Though this account of flight is rather fanciful, the linking of emotion with the magical view of the world is not. For it links it with the concept of wish, which is not subject to contradiction or to relations of cause and effect. And the more vivid the emotional experience, the more distorted is the view of the world along the dimension of wish-fulfillment. If such an experience is so intense as to be traumatic, it may be repressed beyond the recall of the sufferer. But it may trouble him in other ways. He may unaccountably veer away from situations or objects which are only remotely similar to the original traumatic one. His appraisal of situations is distorted in accordance with definite principles. He also may be deflected in some performance or make some strange slip. Or conversion hysteria may develop. Indeed, this sort of phenomenon was one of the crucial things in the development of Freud's theory; for he noticed that the paralysis of his patient's arm followed the line of her beliefs rather than a line predictable from a knowledge of anatomy and physiology. The sufferer too may project his fears or wishes on to the world or on to others; a reaction formation may develop against them. They may be sublimated, and so on.

Now these goings on—both wishes and the mechanisms developed to deal with them—have certain interesting characteristics in common. Firstly, they all involve cognitive appraisal of the "intuitive," often magical sort already mentioned. Whether one is speaking of a mental "mechanism" for dealing with a wish, or of the transformation of a wish as in its displacement to another object, or of its effect on bodily functioning as in conversion hysteria, what goes on cannot be described without mention of *some* cognitive appraisal on the part of the sufferer, however wild such appraisal may seem. This is what makes talk of mental *mechanisms* really quite inappropriate.

Secondly, these goings-on, though mental, do not fall within the category of action or performance. It does not make sense to say that they are efficiently or inefficiently, intelligently or stupidly, carefully or carelessly carried out. The subject has no grasp of means to an end. Thus, they are not techniques or stratagems any more than they are mechanisms. In repression, for instance, the traumatic experience just passes out of the sufferer's mind; he does not wittingly put it out of his mind, as a method of escaping from the horror of it. Similarly, a man who projects his fears on to something or someone else does not wittingly rig his environment. He just comes to see the world under an aspect such as that of threat. The phenomena, in other words, are indubitably mental because of their cognitive core; but they fall into the category of passivity.

I argued in my monograph (1958), adopting Ernest Jones' interpretation, that Freud's great discovery was not of the unconscious but of the fact that what he calls the "primary processes of thought," in terms of which the unconscious works, are of a quite different type from those of thinking proper. Indeed, as I think that Freud's greatest discovery was of the theoretical importance of the concept of "wish" and of some of the principles of its operation, I am not much concerned with the issue of whether or not we can recall such wishes, which is what he called the "criterion" of consciousness. What I am concerned with is what might be called the laws of passivity. To quote Ernest Jones:

Careful students of Freud have perceived that Freud's revolutionary contribution to psychology was not so much his demonstrating the existence of an unconscious, and perhaps not even his exploration of its content, as his proposition that there are two fundamentally different kinds of mental processes, which he termed primary and secondary respectively, together with the description of them. The laws applicable to the two groups are so widely different that any description of the earlier one must call up a picture of the more bizarre types of insanity. There reigns in it a quite uninhibited flow towards the imaginary fullfilment of the wish that stirs it—the only thing that can. It is unchecked by any logical contradiction, any causal associations; it has no sense of either time or of external reality. Its goal is either to discharge the excitation through any motor exit, or, if that fails, to establish a perceptual —if necessary, an hallucinatory—identity with the remembered perception of a previous satisfaction (Jones, 1954, p. 436).

The main principles in accordance with which the primary processes work is that of emotional equivalence based on the association of ideas, with a discharge of tension. These ideas can be displaced so that the object associated with the discharge of one type of instinctive excitation can serve as the object of another. Similarly, an object like a snake or spear can appear instead of its phallic prototype because of its emotional equivalence. The logical relation of "representing," which characterizes the symbols of conscious thought, is not employed in the same way. And, as Jones points out, logical, causal, spatial, and temporal categories do not characterize this sort of "thinking." These belong to conscious thought, to the development of the ego and the "reality principle" which is imposed on the "pure pleasure principle." This is connected with action and performance. As Freud put it, "The ego represents what we call reason and sanity, in contrast to the id which contains the passions" (Freud, 1927, p. 30).

I do not want to commit myself at all deeply to the details of Freud's theory. I think that, even if the eye is discreetly turned away from his physiologizing of mental concepts, many of his hypotheses are highly implausible. I cannot see, for instance, why aversion has to be regarded as presupposing some kind of a positive wish. Nevertheless, it might well be possible to restate the main features of his theory without committing oneself to some of its more objectionable details. And this would be done by making use of the two models which his theory suggests.

There would be, first of all, a rationality model roughly coincident with ego functions such as was used in classical economics. This would be required for explaining actions and performances. Assessment of situations in accordance with reality criteria (such as those involved in perceiving and remembering) would be presupposed together with the grasp of means and ends which conformed to standards of efficiency and social appropriateness. Explanations in terms of "motives" are a special class of explanations employing concepts taken from this model. There would be then the passivity model in which emotional appraisal and the goings-on subsequent to it (for instance, repression) would follow the laws of wishes. This passivity model would explain departures from actions and performances (such as characteristic errors and distortions of thought, perception, and memory, motor slips and breakdowns) and goings-on like dreaming and hysteria which do not rank as performances or actions at all. It would also explain the enhancement of such performances in various ways if they followed the lines of what was wished for. And, of course, it would also cover what might be called generally "emotional experience" and the processes both mental, bodily, or physiological, which are "caused" by them.

It might be said that, logically speaking, the passivity model is parasitic on the activity model in that we could not understand what a wish is unless we already had the concept of a reason, that we could not understand what principles of emotive congruence might be like unless we already understood what causal and logical connections were, that we could not understand what repression was unless we knew what it was to regulate impulses. This may well be true; for rendering anything intelligible presupposes relating it in some way to familiar concepts even if we then have to withdraw some of the cardinal features of what is familiar. This parasitic character of such explanations explains the tendency to talk of the unconscious in terms of "as if" or to say that it deals with the sort of thing for which one could have a reason (MacIntyre, 1958). All this may well be so. But I do want to assert that such an attempt to sketch a model of passivity is not just an exercise in conceptual clarification. The minds of children, for instance, may well work much more in accordance with this model than in accordance with the more familiar activity model. And adult minds often regress to this way of functioning; wishes and emotional appraisals disrupt and distort logical practical operations and have strange effects on the body. It is the task of empirical psychology to establish the laws of this form of "mental causality."

ACTIONS, PASSIVITY, AND THE ROLE OF EMPIRICAL GENERALIZATIONS

Indeed, it might be argued that this is peculiarly the task of empirical psychology in so far as it is concerned with what is specifically "mental." The ordinary man as well as the philosopher is rightly satirical when psychologists make attempts in technical jargon to explain the familiar phenomena of civilized life like crossing roads, making moves at chess, or looking for candy. For civilized life is constituted by a whole mass of rules and purposes and to have a mind means, to a large extent, to understand what these rules and purposes are, to have "internalized" many of them, to use a language into which all such knowledge is built in, and to be able to act in the light of such knowledge. There was at least this amount of truth in Hegel's doctrine of the "objective mind." Children are not born with minds; they have to develop them by being initiated into the language, rules, and purposes which constitute a civilized society. There may well be puzzlement, of course, about which particular purpose an individual has in mind or about what he sees as a means to achieving some particular purpose. But the general lines of such explanations introduce little that is novel, surprising, or a matter for careful empirical generalizations. There are two very good reasons why this must be so. Firstly we, as members of a society, have largely created for ourselves the content of purposes and rules, in terms of which actions are to be described and explained. Our lives are like a game of chess writ large. The explanation of a move must first of all be sought in the rules and purposes defining the game. Education consists largely in initiating people into the vast pattern of such rules and purposes which comprise a civilized life. By such a process of education we not only equip people to act in a civilized society; we also provide them with the wherewithal to understand the actions of others. Social anthropology is thus the basic "science" of human actions; for it is mainly concerned with filling in the content of the purposive-rule-following structure in societies different from our own, into which we have not been initiated in the usual ways.

Secondly, explanations of actions are *too good* to be formulated as empirical or "causal" generalizations. For to explain an action is to know what a man has in mind—what purpose he is trying to realize, what rule he is conforming to or acting on, what end he sees his action as a means to. Once we see that a man is doing X for the sake of Y, we explain his doing X, but our concept of his doing X has been transformed. It has now become part of his doing Y. If we explain a man's crossing of a road by saying that he is going to buy some tobacco, we can now describe him as "buying tobacco." His crossing of the road is part of a more general type of action. Actions have this open-ended character along many dimensions.

It might be replied that this is a characteristic of causal explanations of nature as well as of human actions. If the expansion of iron, it might be argued, is to be explained in terms of heat applied to it, we might then say, when the generalization "Iron expands when heated" is well established, that something could not be a piece of iron unless it expands when heated. The explanation alters our concept of "iron." This may be so. But the point about explanations of actions is that such an internal connection *must* be shown in order for it to be acceptable as an explanation. And accepting some particular purpose as a candidate for an explanation does not wait in the same way on the elaborate testing of the connection as an empirical law. Perhaps we would be reluctant to accept a particular purpose as an explanation if no one ever did such a thing for such a reason —say, if a man said that he was scratching his head in order to attract women. But our acceptance of it would not depend on establishing it as an empirical generalization of the form "Whenever men want to attract women they scratch their heads." Rather, it would depend on trying to establish some intelligible connection which the individual in question could see between the action and the desired result. It is quite different with causal generalizations about nature. For they do not *have to* exhibit an internal relation between cause and effect; such connections are simply *de facto* to start with; and if they are to be turned into internal connections, so that iron's tendency to expand when heated becomes one of its defining properties, the trick can only be done by empirical tests of the generalization.

To return, then, to the suggestion that passive phenomena are much more suitable candidates for fitting into empirical generalizations than actions, and hence preeminently the concern of psychologists. That a man's beliefs affect his actions is understandable enough; for the connection is internal, his "actions" being only describable in terms of what he believes, wants, hopes, fears, etc. But that a man's beliefs can issue in stomach ulcers, paralysis, facial tics, and the like, is not similarly understandable. The connections are empirical, not logical. For there is nothing about anxiety which makes its connection with ulcers, blood pressure, perhaps even with cancers, anything other than a brute *de facto* connection. Of course, if we knew enough about such connections, we might come to define some ulcers or cancers as psychosomatic. But the procedure here would be similar to that indicated above when an empirical connection passes over into a logical one. Indeed, the connection between the appraisal involved in fear and phenomena like shivering and rapid heartbeat is almost in this category. And if we speak of fear *as an emotion,* as I have argued, we postulate a connection between the appraisal of some situation as dangerous and some such passive phenomena under the control of the autonomic nervous system. But the details of all this are proper subjects for empirical investigation. That is why most work done by psychologists on "the emotions" is of a physiological type.

In a similar way, it was simply *discovered* by Freud that unacceptable wishes are repressed completely or pass beyond the reach of conscious recall, and that they lead to other passive phenomena such as slips of the tongue, lassitude, lapses of memory, phobias, distortions of perception, etc. Once the Freudian type of story is told, the connections, it is true, do begin to fit into bizarre pattern in which wild "intuitive" beliefs, like those of the small child or lunatic, have their place. But they are not connections which men have laboriously created like the rules of prudence, algebra, language, or the road, and into which children are initiated in the process of education. For, as I have argued, though to say that we wish for something is to withdraw considerations of means-ends practicability, possibility, temporal and spatial order, and even logical coherence, the positive workings of wishes have to be discovered. And that is where Freud's great importance lay—in his attempt to formulate positive laws of the operation of wishes and of "mechanisms" operating on them.

I am not claiming, of course, that such phenomena are the only ones fit for empirical investigation by psychologists in their search for "laws"! There are empirical generalizations to be made about how best actions and performances are learned, about techniques of training and about individual differences, about the underlying "mechanisms" in the body and brain, etc. There are also generalizations to be established about other passive phenomena—for example, pain, reflexes, reactions of a non-emotional sort—which cannot be explained in terms of Freud's minimal teleological concept of "the wish." Indeed, empirical psychology comprises an ill-assorted collection of inquiries into a number of extremely varied and disparate phenomena.

There was a time when it was fashionable to think that psychology could only progress if "behavior" was studied by "objective" methods and if "mentalistic" concepts were banished from explanation. This view derived from all sorts of misunderstandings about scientific method, but perhaps the basic objection to behaviorism is that behaviorists never properly faced the question of what constitutes "behavior." They concentrated on actions which they often confused with reactions to stimuli and failed to see that unless one knows what a person has "in mind," how he appraised a situation, what information about it he is employing, it is impossible to know what type of "behavior" is being studied. There is all the difference between one's arm being raised and raising one's arm. Also, "action" is an almost infinitely open-ended concept. One can raise one's arm to signal, to test the wind, to express amazement, and so on. "Behavior" also includes things like sweating and shivering, which could not, strictly speaking, even rank as actions. But there is a great difference between shivering because the temperature of the room is lowered and shivering because one hears a wolf howling. Similarly, there are important differences, as I have tried to show, between actions and emotional reactions. And emotional reactions must be distinguished from other sorts of reactions like withdrawing the hand from a red-hot poker. It is impossible to indicate the differences between all the phenomena to be explained unless one knows how the subject in question sees the situation. So "behaviorists" must employ "mentalistic" concepts in recognizing what is to be explained. They cannot merely luxuriate in them for the enjoyment of their nonlaboratory lives—as was often argued.

I have also suggested that, when explanations are given, "mentalistic" ones are not only appropriate in the sphere of action and performance. Another range of concepts associated with "the wish" is appropriate in the realm of some passive phenomena. And no doubt physiological and mechanical concepts are appropriate to explain other realms of phenomena. Psychology is surely more likely to progress, not by a Galilean "leap" or "breakthrough" in which one type of explanation is extended to cover all the varied and disparate phenomena of "behavior," but by looking carefully at the different categories of phenomena to be explained and by developing more limited theories, as did Freud, to explain classes of behavior that fall within the same category. This chapter has been an attempt to mark out one such category and to demonstrate Freud's importance as a theorist in elaborating explanation of phenomena within it that are neither of the purposive-rule-following nor of the mechanical type.

REFERENCES

ANSCOMBE, G. E. M. *Intention.* Oxford: Blackwell Scientific Publications, 1957.

ARNOLD, MAGDA. *Emotion and personality.* New York: Columbia Univ. Press, Vol. 1.

ASCH, S. *Social psychology.* Englewood Cliffs, N. J.: Prentice-Hall, 1959.

DEWEY, J. The theory of emotion, *Psychol. Rev. 1,* 553-569 and *2,* 13-22.

DODWELL, P. C. Causes of behaviour and explanation in psychology. *Mind,* January 1960.

FOOT, P. Moral beliefs. *Proc. Aristotelian Soc.,* 1958-1959.

FREUD, S. *The ego and the id.* London: Hogarth Press, 1927.

JAMES, W. & LANGE, G. C. *The Emotions,* Baltimore: Williams and Wilkins, 1922.

JONES, E. *Sigmund Freud, life and works,* Vol. 1. London: Hogarth Press, 1954.

LANGE, G. C. (See JAMES, W.)

LEEPER, R. W. A motivational theory of emotion to replace "emotions as disorganized response." *Psychol. Rev.* 1948, **55,** 5-21.

McDOUGALL, W. *Introduction to social psychology.* (19th ed.) London: Methuen, 1924.

MacINTYRE, A. *The unconscious.* London: Kegan Paul. 1958.

MELDEN, A. I. *Free action.* London: Kegan Paul, 1961.

PAULHAN, F. *The laws of feeling.* New York: Harcourt Brace, 1930.

PETERS, R. S. *The concept of motivation.* London: Kegan Paul, 1958.

RAPAPORT, D. *Emotions and memory.* Baltimore; Williams and Wilkins, 1942.

RAPAPORT, D. The structure of psycho-analytic theory: a systematizing attempt. In S. Koch (Ed.), *Psychology: a study of a science.* New York: McGraw-Hill, 1959. Vol. 3, pp. 55-183.

RYLE, G. *The concept of mind.* London: Hutchinson, 1949.

SARTRE, J.-P. *The emotions.* New York: Philosophical Library, 1948.

TOLMAN, E. C. *Purposive behaviour in animals and men.* New York: Appleton-Century-Crofts, 1932.

WATSON, J. B. *Behaviourism.* New York: People's Inst. Publishing Co., 1924.

YOUNG, P. T., Emotion as disorganized response—a reply to Prof. Leeper. *Psychol. Rev.,* 1949, **56,** 184-191.

YOUNG, P. T. *Emotion in man and animals.* New York: Wiley, 1943.

20 ROBERT D. CUMMING

THE EXISTENTIALIST PSYCHOLOGY
OF ACTION

ART AND THEORY

Philosophers, reading the title of this chapter, may be disconcerted by the tolerance of the editors and the brashness of this contributor. Presumably, this volume encourages philosophers to take stock, in the presence of scientific psychologists, of what is perhaps the most striking recent trend in Anglo-American philosophy—the virtual transformation of philosophy itself into philosophical psychology. This trend is striking because the progress of modern philosophy, beginning with Descartes and Locke, and continuing with Kant and Hegel and their successors, had been the development of philosophy of mind, which was (roughly speaking) what still seemed left to the philosopher as a subject matter when "natural philosophy" had become the science of physics. But this development had been halted by the beginning of the twentieth century; the collapse then of idealistic systems emancipated philosophy from "psychologism," and scientific psychology from philosophy. Anglo-American philosophers attempting nowadays to recapture a psychological subject matter should doubtless pause and consider what they are doing. And they might be expected to take into account the independent, but apparently parallel and equally paradoxical, transformation on the Continent of Husserl's antipsychologistic phenomenology into that psychological version of existentialism which is called "phenomenological existentialism." If, however, we consult the philosophical psychologists, we find the last book of Merleau-Ponty's—perhaps the tamest of the existentialists—reviewed in England as an "object-lesson in how not to do philosophy"; and we find A. D. MacIntyre (1962) concluding that there is something else which the existentialist Sartre can and should be doing:

> What makes Sartre's theoretical confusions more tolerable to him than they are to us is that he is really an artist and not a theorist. . . . The time has come for us to say to Sartre that what we need from him are fewer theories and more plays (p. 43).

384

Such unmitigated verdicts seem to leave no point of entry for existentialism in this volume. Anglo-American philosophers are concerned to exhibit their clarity, particularly when they are in the presence of scientists. They will not see much point in providing psychologists with theoretical confusions which are an object lesson in how not to do philosophy. Nevertheless, the presence of psychologists does raise an issue regarding the way in which MacIntyre dismisses Sartre. For MacIntyre (1958) also applies a distinction between art and theory to Freud. He can, in fact, cite Freud's own appraisal of his achievement:

> It still strikes me as strange that the case histories I write should read like short stories and that, as one might say, they lack the serious stamp of science. I must console myself with the reflection that the *nature of the subject* is evidentally responsible for this *rather than any preference of my own*. The fact is that local diagnosis and electrical reactions lead nowhere in the study of hysteria, whereas the detailed description of mental processes such as we are accustomed to find in the works of imaginative writers enables me, with the use of a few psychological formulas, to obtain at least some kind of insight into the course of the affection (p. 43).

Endorsing "this recognition by Freud of his place as being among the imaginative describers of human behavior," MacIntyre offers as one of his "main theses" that Freud is here giving "a correct account of his discoveries and of his method of achieving them," whereas he is giving an incorrect account when he appraises "his work 'as discovering the scientific method by which the unconscious can be studied.' " This scientific method MacIntyre does not rate a discovery; its adoption was not prompted by the nature of Freud's subject but by a "model" that was "drawn from physics," which as "the most advanced of the sciences, tends also to be taken as the type to which others should approximate."

Having applied to Freud a distinction between an imaginary description and a scientific explanation, why does MacIntyre not push the charge against Freud as far as he pushed the charge against Sartre, and perhaps conclude, for example, that since Freud is really an artist and not a theorist, Oedipus should have remained a character in a play, instead of having acquired a role in the construction of a theory? MacIntyre clearly feels that Freud is in some sense a theorist as well as an artist, because it is the nature of his subject which necessarily eludes scientific treatment and necessarily requires imaginative treatment, whereas when MacIntyre dismisses Sartre as really an artist and not a theorist, he is implying that the fact that Sartre is an artist is of no positive significance for his theories; it is an accident of his temperament and does not reflect any necessary requirements of a recognizable subject matter, but only helps to explain his readiness to tolerate theoretical confusions.

The issues which we face here seem to me to overlap those which are raised by the contemporary efforts of philosophers to recapture a psychological subject matter. I am not concerned with MacIntyre's particular version of the distinction between description and explanation; I am concerned with the fact that philosophical psychologists usually adopt some version of this distinction, not only when they reserve a place for Freud among the imaginative describers of human behavior, but also when they are presenting their own credentials as philosophical psychologists. Yet, although they sometimes characterize what they are doing as philosophers by some comparison with literary descriptions of human behavior, as well as with the descriptions implicit in the ordinary use of language, they rarely expend the care in arguing for the appropriateness to their subject of the literary model that they expend in arguing against the appropriateness of the causal model from physics. Indeed, the literary model sometimes seems to be adopted (for example, by John Wisdom) less as dictating any discernible procedure than as a way of securing our tolerance for quirks of temperament or personal preference.

The advantage of taking what Sartre is doing into account here is not just the obvious consideration that he, unlike Freud and philosophical psychologists, is a writer of imaginative literature in the quite ordinary sense. We shall see that his philosophy itself is a theory of human behavior as distinctively imaginative behavior; in fact he reaches the climax of this theory by raising the question, with regard to the imaginative writer, "Why does he write?" Thus, we need not linger with the "theoretical confusions" in Sartre's philosophy which MacIntyre exposes as "more tolerable to him than they are to us, because he is really an artist and not a theorist." We can worry instead over the theoretical status accorded by Sartre's philosophy to questions which we would be inclined to put to one side as a matter of an individual's temperament or preference—for example, the question of why Sartre writes plays.

THEORY AND ACTION

Concentrating mainly on Sartre might be supposed to have the advantage that his writings are more familiar to us than those of other phenomenological existentialists. But if we are to account for what he is doing by reference to the nature of his subject, the next difficulty we face is that the Sartre with whom we are familiar in this country is not the phenomenologist—the philosopher of mind—but simply the existentialist—the philosopher of action who accents freedom, commitment, and responsibility. One can hardly allude to this familiar Sartre, without having to deal with the familiar dismissal of his existentialism as an aftermath of the French experience in World War II. We have just escaped from the theoretical confusions which Sartre tolerates because he is really an artist, only to find him theoretically confused by German invaders. Eventually, I shall try to present the relation between art and action in Sartre's own terms. For the present, let me counter in passing with the fact that what has been imported of phenomenological existentialism into this country has been the existentialism. This fact could tempt the social historian. The vogue of existialism, as an accent on action, commitment, and responsibility, may be a reaction against our own moral apathy, for the one thing that American intellectuals are still not apathetic about is their apathy. Having lamented the end of ideology and the lack of commitment and responsibility in their American lives, they read an existentialist; unused moral muscles then flex, and they feel twinges of moral vigor. The moral truculence of existentialism administers momentary relief from their moral flabbiness.

In this volume, I trust, we are not to be tempted by such sociohistorical explanations, which can be extended to any trend in philosophy or psychology, but by the nature of our respective subject matters and the treatment they require. A more dignified explanation can accordingly perhaps be offered of the neglect by Anglo-American philosophers of the relation between the phenomenological and the existentialist components of phenomenological existentialism. The explanation may be the lack of relation between the two roughly corresponding subjects which are included within philosophical psychology: the philosophy of mind (in a restricted sense), which refurbishes such traditional epistemological problems as the nature of perception, and moral psychology, which refurbishes certain moral problems as to the nature of human action. Husserl's phenomenology had been primarily an analysis of perception; before World War II, Sartre was himself a phenomenologist who complained, in *L'Imagination* (1936b) and in *L'Imaginaire* (1940), that Husserl had failed to analyze the operations of the imagination, as distinguished from perception; it was only during World War II that Sartre became, in *L'Être et le méant* (1943), an existentialist preoccupied with the problem of action. But let me begin now with the more familiar—Sartre's existentialism—and then work back to its relation to Husserl's phenomenology, so that I shall finally be able to restore the relation between Sartre's own phenomenology of the imagination and his existentialism.

The mystique about action, the sense of exhilaration about commitment, which passes for existentialism in this country is an oversimplification. What is overlooked, for example, is Sartre's denunciation (1948) of the anti-Semite, as the man who wants to be, as the result of his actions, "a pitiless stone, a furious torrent, devastating lightening; in short, everything but a man." Other implications of this denunciation will have to wait and be disentangled later. Its larger implication is that one can significantly refer to what a man is. But what is a man in Sartre's existentialism, as opposed to the man of action who views his actions as making him all of one piece, transmuting him into a natural phenomenon? There is no answer to this question in Sartre which is obviously available, since he has never actually written *L'Homme*, which has long since been announced as the systematic presentation of his claim that *L'Existentialisme est un humanisme* (1946).

Furthermore, as soon as this question of man is raised, anthropologists, sociologists, as well as psychologists of various allegiances, protest that so sweeping a question blurs those specifications of subject matter which are indispensable to a scientific theory. And yet this does not seem to be the juncture at which moral psychologists can afford to lose patience with existentialism. Note the way they advance their claim that moral psychology is a subject which requires philosophical as distinguished from scientific treatment. Thus MacIntyre (1958) may concede, "To explain what human beings are and do in terms of a general theory is no doubt in some sense possible—the neurophysiologists will one day give us their full account." He adds, however, "Such an account . . . will state all the necessary conditions of human behavior, but it will mention nothing of the specifically human." If we go looking for the specifically human in the writings of moral psychologists, we find their immodesty disarming; the specifically human is what requires philosophical as distinguished from scientific treatment:

> The work of appraisal and argument that goes on in the mind affecting and altering all our conduct can never be adequately described in terms of stimulus and response, if only because—a Kantian insight—the validity of reasons as reasons cannot be dealt with in casual terms. . . . One may ask "Why?" and expect an answer in terms of reasons, intentions, purposes and the like; or one may ask "Why?" and expect an answer in terms of physiological or psychological determining antecedent conditions. This dichotomy remains untouched when the misleading character of other dichotomies such as that between the mental and the physical, or the inner and the outer aspects of human behavior, has been noted (p. 51).

In existentialism, too, the misleading character of these other dichotomies is usually noted, while intentional actions remain segregated to compose a distinctively philosophical subject matter. But, although this resemblance is sometimes asserted by bowdlerized translations of existentialism into the terminology of Anglo-Saxon moral psychology, what must not be overlooked is the fact that the term "intentional," which has become so definitive of the subject matter of action in moral psychology, does not enter existentialism from ordinary moral usage. It enters instead from Husserl's phenomenological analysis of perception, where it had acquired a range of technical implications, some of which are retained when it is applied by Sartre to human actions. Repugnant as some of these technicalities may be to Anglo-American taste, they cannot be shirked, for they will illustrate what is peculiar to phenomenological existentialism—the close relationship which holds between its phenomenological and its existential components, but which does not ordinarily hold, in Anglo-American philosophical psychology, between the treatment of the epistemological problems of perception and the moral problems of intentional action.

PERCEPTION AND INTENTION

The medieval Latin term *intentio* had been introduced into psychology by Brentano and then dropped, partly because he feared its acquiring misleading moral associations. The term was, nonetheless, retrieved by Husserl, who described the cognitive relationship between consciousness and its objects as an "intentional" relationship. The term here distinguishes "meaning-endowing" acts of consciousness as mental acts which refer intrinsically to their ideal "intentional objects," from actual mental occurrences which are responses to stimuli and so are subject to observation and causal correlation in the theories of scientific psychologists. Husserl segregates these intentional acts of consciousness, by noting that the object perceived is never completely given in any individual act of perception, or in any succession of acts of perception. The conclusion which he then reaches that perceptual experience (and hence scientific observation and scientific theories) is uncertain and indefinitely corrigible, has been traditional in epistemology. In Husserl, however, to become aware of the uncertainty and corrigibility of perceptual experience is not just to become aware of the limitations of scientific knowledge but is thereby also to transcend these limitations and enter on the experience of a transcendental realm of meanings or essences. The uncertainty and corrigibility of perception thus becomes one of the essential, and hence certain and incorrigible, characteristics of the act of perception itself, and justifies as distinctively philosophical the analysis of such characteristics. The most striking of these characteristics is the intentional relationship itself—the fact that in perception we are "conscious of something." The mental occurrences that can be discerned, in a causal explanation of the process of perception, are only its raw materials (such as sensory impressions), for they are only the successive subjective presentations of different "aspects" of what we are conscious of, and have to be organized and unified by the intentional acts, which supply the identifying reference to the object itself. In order to deal with its unity of meaning and objectivity for consciousness, the problem of the actual existence of anything corresponding to what we are conscious of (the problem as to whether or not, and by what causal sequence, perception provides us with knowledge of the external world) is bypassed or "bracketed," and we are provided instead with reflective knowledge of the essential structure of intentional acts of perception. Since these acts cannot be performed by a psychophysiological organism, whose responses belong to the scientific realm of causal explanation, the existing individual must also be bracketed, and Husserl accounts for the internal connectedness of experience as my experience by attributing these acts to the agency of a transcendental ego.

The merits of Husserl's procedure and attendant claims need not detain us, since they undergo considerable revision when his phenomenology becomes Sartre's phenomenological existentialism. All that survives from Husserl's analysis of "consciousness of something" is his analysis of the "of"—that is, the intentional relationship itself; or rather, Sartre draws within the scope of this relationship what for Husserl in different ways transcended it—both the existing thing and the ego.

On the one hand, Sartre draws within the intentional relationship the existing thing which Husserl had bracketed. Husserl's "consciousness of something" becomes consciousness of some thing; the raw materials for intentional acts of consciousness are no longer such subjective contents of consciousness as sensory impressions but actually existing things. Yet Husserl's distinction between meanings and existences survives in Sartre's verdict that "brute existences" are as such meaningless. Thus, the "meaninglessness of existence" which is native to existentialism is less what it is usually taken to be in this country—a moral reaction to the brutality of modern life, now that God is dead and the middle class is insecure—than it is the vulgarization (or naturalization, if you prefer) of Husserl's transcendental methodology into a psychological theory. For although Husserl's brackets are removed, the bracketing continues as the ordinary articulative and negating operations of intentional consciousness, which endows some thing with meaning by identifying it as this thing and *not* that thing. These operations Sartre describes as the emergence of a figure against a ground, for the removal of the brackets, which in Husserl protected the transcendental realm of meanings from "psychologism," enables Sartre to borrow from Gestalt psychology. (We shall later note similar borrowing from behaviorism, Freudian psychoanalysis, and role theory.) But the transcendental movement of consciousness survives this borrowing: Sartre repudiates Gestalt theory insofar as it is a causal explanation of the emergence of a figure against a ground; its emergence in Sartre is the spontaneous intentional movement of my consciousness of it, which transcends whatever is given as my response to a stimulus, by giving it meaning.

On the other hand, Sartre's removal of the brackets draws the existing individual within the intentional relationship. In Husserl the transcendental ego was located, so to speak, behind and above the existing individual's act of consciousness; its transcendental role was to unify, organize, and stablilize experience, making it mine and providing philosophy with an autonomous subject matter to reflect upon. No longer anchored to a transcendental ego, the transcendental structure of consciousness collapses in Sartre. The self is not something which exists, and it cannot be confronted by consciousness. It is given to consciousness as behind consciousness, but when I turn back toward it, I become conscious of it retrospectively only as having been implicit in my previous consciousness of something else.

The "I" is as "systematically elusive" in Sartre as it is in Ryle's behavioristic philosophical psychology. But in Sartre, the pursuit of this elusive self is also systematic. For self-consciousness in Sartre is still haunted by the privileged function which Husserl's transcendental ego performed in the systematic organization of experience, and is therefore conscious of its degraded status as necessarily contingent and relative to something which does exist. The meaning-endowing acts of consciousness which still articulate and organize our experience in Sartre are inherently the aspirations of the self to become a transcendental ego, although Sartre's removal of the brackets, which in Husserl segregated meanings from existence, permits Sartre to offer a vulgarized (or naturalized) version of this aspiration as the "desire to become God"—to confer necessary existence on my experience by becoming the creative source of all its meanings.

Yet Husserl's distinction between meanings and existence survives in Sartre's claim that existence is contingent and relative. The death of God in Sartre is not a transient historical episode—the weakening of contemporary man's faith—but is the necessary perennial frustration of the *mauvaise foi* which is implicit in faith in God. This "bad faith" is the refusal of consciousness to accept its contingency and relativity as consciousness of . . . In other words, this intentional movement, with which consciousness necessarily transcends itself, is disguised and disavowed when consciousness becomes faith in the prospect of arrival at something transcendent with which it can identify itself as the absolute source and final legitimation of its movement. Thus the intentional movement of consciousness becomes in Sartre a truncated dialectic: at once the recurrent transcendental aspiration of consciousness, as instanced by the transcendental structure that consciousness acquires in Husserl, and the recurrent collapsing of this structure, frustrating this aspiration.

REFLECTION AND ACTION

With this collapse, phenomenological problems can no longer be resolved by reflection and become existential problems of action. But this is precisely why we cannot disregard existentialism's inheritance from a phenomenological philosophy of mind, and regard it simply as a philosophy of action—some kind of unmotivated behest to commit oneself and take responsibility, whatever one's specific motives. The impetus to act, the urgency of action, and the fascination with acting are not practical, but methodological, in the sense that they derive from the inability of reflection by itself to structure and stabilize experience and satisfy the aspira-

tion of consciousness to become self-consciousness. The methodological impetus pulsates in the account Merleau-Ponty (1945) gives of the relation
between reflection and action:

> I can reflect and be assured of validly willing, loving, or believing, provided
> that I actually do will, love or believe. . . . If I do not, an irresistible doubt
> will spread over the world, and over my own reflections too. I should be end-
> lessly wondering whether my tastes, my volitions, desires, and undertakings,
> were really mine, for they would always appear fictitious, unreal, and frus-
> trated. Even this doubt would fall short of actual doubt, and I would not
> arrive at the certainty that I was in doubt (p. 162).

Merleau-Ponty cites the endless, indeterminate reflections of the heroine
of an existentialist novel:

> . . . But then, this also, this cynical distaste for her own role, was deliber-
> ately put on? and this contempt for that distaste which she was about to con-
> trive, was it not also play-acting? and this doubting of that contempt . . . ?
> (p. 162).

Her consciousness aspires, as it were, to come full circle reflectively, so
that she can become fully self-conscious, but her consciousness is continually frustrated by its rectilinear movement as intentional "conscious of
. . ." This transcending movement, continually recommencing, is the aspiration of her consciousness to perform the function of a transcendental
ego, which would provide what she is conscious of as herself with an
identity as stable and objective as that of something which exists and
which is identifiable, even though it is never completely given in any succession of acts of consciousness, but only its "aspects." The performance of
her self-consciousness, however, is no longer functional; there is no self to
support and interconnect the succession of her "aspects"; each successive
act of consciousness disconnects the previous act, and her self-consciousness becomes a succession of roles.

"The only way out," Merleau-Ponty concludes, is by "action" (le faire),
which he defines as "the violent transition from . . . what I am to what
I intend to be." With this transition, "intention" obtains its ordinary moral
reference to purposive action, but we will not appreciate the violence of
this transition, if we assume that "intention" is disowning its phenomenological inheritance. The mental acts which are features of the phenomenological philosophy of mind become moral actions in existentialism; more
accurately, intentional acts of consciousness become ingredients in overt
actions, but still retain phenomenological characteristics, which will explain why the resulting problems of action bear only a superficial resemblance to the problems of "intentional action" in Anglo-American moral
psychology.

The one common problem, as I have anticipated, is to demonstrate that problems of action are specifically human—that is, are of more than merely practical significance, because of their methodological peculiarity of requiring distinctively philosophical treatment. This common problem is perhaps most readily located in terms of one common but remote ancestor. We can follow out the reference to Kant with which Sartre makes his transition from phenomenology to existentialism, for we recall that the distinction with which MacIntyre rescued the problem of action from scientific psychology was the "Kantian insight" that "the validity of reasons as reasons cannot be dealt with in causal terms." Kant is in fact the last Continental philosopher who belongs to the Anglo-American tradition as well as to the Continental tradition, and his distinction between nature, as a subject matter that yields to scientific explanation, and the implications of human freedom, which compose a subject matter that transcends scientific explanation, has been a recurrent feature of both traditions.

In the Anglo-American tradition, the problem of freedom and of action has remained a Kantian problem in so far as it has remained a problem of the relation between scientific and practical reason, and is therefore to be treated as a problem of the kind of knowledge, the kind of rules, the kind of reasons which are practical as distinguished from scientific. The "reasons" in question are reasons for doing something, but they are still "reasons," and the primary issue to be settled is their "validity." An existentialism is, of course, honeycombed with abysses—with pockets of nothingness—and these abysses are variants of the Kantian gap between nature and freedom, although in Kant consciousness of one's freedom takes the quasicognitive form of respect (*Achtung*) for the moral law, whereas in existentialism consciousness of one's freedom is *Angest,* that is, consciousness of the gap itself, which has widened into an abyss that knowledge can no longer bridge, since there are no moral laws on the other side of the gap which are analogous to the laws of nature.

When intentional actions remain a problem of knowledge in Anglo-American moral psychology, they constitute a philosophical subject matter distinguishable from scientific psychology, inasmuch as intentions can be "known without observation." In existentialism, however, when the transcendental structure, which consciousness disclosed to reflection in Husserl, collapses, what had been a problem of reflective knowledge becomes a problem of action. My intentions, and the moral phenomenon accompanying them, are methodologically significant, not because they can be "known without observation," but because they cannot be known by reflection without the intervention of actions. As Merleau-Ponty (1945) puts it:

> My love, hatred, and will are not certain as mere reflections about loving, hating, and willing; on the contrary the whole certainty of these reflections is due to the acts of love, hatred, or will, of which I am quite sure because I

perform them (*je les fais*). Every inner perception is inadequate, because I am not an object which can be perceived, because I make (*fais*) my reality and rejoin myself only in action (p. 162).

PERCEPTION AND IMAGINATION

We have already found that for Sartre too "I am not an object which can be perceived." This is the conclusion that the anti-Semite was refusing to accept, when he tried to imagine himself, when he acted, "a pitiless stone, a furious torrent, devastating lightning—in short, everything but a man." The Kantian distinction between nature and freedom which is violated, when anthropomorphic traits are attributed to natural phenomena and naturalistic traits attributed to one's own character, is not the Anglo-American distinction between two kinds of knowledge, but a distinction between what can be perceived and a role which one can only imagine oneself playing. Here we might be reminded that the problem of the relation between nature and freedom was for Kant, not only the problem of knowledge that it has remained in the Anglo-American tradition, but also the problem of the imagination which it has remained in the Continental idealistic tradition. But we must recall Sartre's debt to Husserl's phenomenology and his criticism of Husserl for failing to distinguish the act of imagination from the act of perception.

The act of perception was, in Husserl, the specifically human and methodologically significant act of consciousness in that it served as a model for the analysis of all acts of human consciousness, including those higher-order acts of reflection embodied in this analysis itself, which he presented as a kind of transcendental analogue of acts of visual perception. Thus Husserl's repeated injunction, in guiding his reflections, was to "look at" and "see." When Sartre removes the brackets, which enabled Husserl's analysis to move up to this reflective transcendental level, Husserl's distinction between the actual existing thing perceived and the ideal intentional object survives in the vulgarized (or naturalized) form of a distinction between the act of perception, whereby we are conscious of something as already existing there, and the act of imagination, whereby we are conscious of something as not existing there. (For example, to *perceive* a portrait is to be conscious of a certain distribution of colors; to *imagine* the object portrayed, is to bracket and transcend the portrait as an actual existing thing, so that the distribution of colors becomes materials which are reidentified by consciousness as "aspects" of this object.)

In Sartre, the act of the imagination becomes the specifically human and the methodologically significant act of consciousness. Sartre loses methodological confidence in Husserl's visual metaphors, for the collapse of the transcendental structure of consciousness leaves Sartre with nothing there for reflection to "look at" and "see." But Sartre retains from phenomenology the imaginative procedure of "free variation"—the "free play of the imagination," on which Husserl had relied to eliminate the variable features of perceptual experience. In Sartre the method of "free variation" no longer terminates with arrival at the transcendental experience of a transcendental ego; the free play of the imagination continues unimpeded, and the method becomes vulgarized (or naturalized) as the stream of consciousness, whose flow is the perpetual, but unstable, imaginative restructuring of experience.

ART AND ACTION

The constructive activity of consciousness thus survives the collapse in Sartre of the transcendental structure of consciousness. The idiom of construction had been employed by Husserl in describing the way acts of intentional consciousness organize and objectify sensory materials. The idiom takes on additional scope and significance in Sartre's existentialism. Acts of intentional consciousness, having become constructive acts of imaginative consciousness, can be blended in as ingredients of overt intentional actions, because these themselves are constructive actions for Sartre. It is no accident that the example with which Sartre (1943) introduces his discussion of intentional actions is Constantine's construction of Constantinople, in order to provide the Roman Empire with a capital rivaling Rome. This overt construction includes as ingredients Constantine's intentional acts of consciousness, which structure the situation by reference to what he intends to do; and since what he intends to do is not yet actual, this structure is an imaginative reconstruction, which brackets, transcends, and thereby confers meaning on which is actually given. To be more specific, in the light of Constantine's intention of constructing Constantinople, Rome becomes a capital which is "not sufficiently secure from invasion," which is "too corrupt in its morals," and which is "still profoundly pagan."

A humbler example (Sartre, 1960) may perhaps clarify this incorporation, in intentional actions, of constructive acts of consciousness, and illustrate the place of the artifact constructed in Sartre's analysis of intentional actions. A friend who gets up and goes toward a window is performing an action which restructures our situation, endowing it with meaning —for instance, "the room is too warm." But an object in the room, if it has been made by man, has also been endowed with meaning in somewhat the same way that the intentional action of my friend has endowed the total situation with meaning: the window itself is the product of an intentional action; its structure indicates that it is intended to be pushed up or down or to be swung out, although my friend's action of opening the window is required to render explicit the intentions of the artisan which are crystallized in its structure, in somewhat the same way that reflection is required in Husserl's phenomenology to render explicit the intentional acts of consciousness which are implicit in routine perception. Thus intentional action, whether something is done or something is made, is a meaning-endowing gesture, which betrays its methodological inheritance. Intentional action has itself become phenomenological description.

We are finally able to follow out the implications of Sartre's sweeping references to man, which so disconcerted us originally. Although Sartre has never written the moral psychology which we would expect as a treatment of the problem of action, he has answered in another way the question as to the specifically human. The place *l'Homme* was to have had in Sartre's phenomenological existentialism has been taken by his existential psychoanalysis—in particular, of the playwright Jean Genet (Sartre, 1952). It is easy to confuse this work with the kind of psychoanalytic literary criticism which is prevalent today. But we can avoid this confusion, since we have determined the nature of the subject that Sartre inherits from the collapse of the transcendental structure of consciousness. This collapse has deprived knowledge of its primacy and brought forward the problem of action. If the reduction of theory to action were the only result of the collapse, Sartre's existentialism could pass as pragmatism. Sartre's sweeping references to man do sweep across the conventional distinction between theory and action, but the scope attained also involves the removal of the conventional distinction between art and action. Husserl's transcendental methodology has become a theory of consciousness that is, in effect, a theory of art, for it is a theory of the constructive activity of consciousness; and in this theory the distinction between man as an artist who makes something, and man as a moral agent who does something, is blurred by the French *faire*. (The deliberate blur can be noticed too in the last passage that I cited from Merleau-Ponty.)

We have to look back to Sartre's phenomenology for the only distinction with which we are left, between the aesthetic organization of experience and the moral organization of experience. It is the phenomenological distinction between intentional conscious of something and the self-consciousness that is implicit in intentional consciousness of something: the structure of the work of art is what the artist's consciousness articulates as his situation; but this structure is implicitly the artist's self-portrayal, his "choice of himself," since his consciousness is a succession of acts of consciousness of something, and as such intrinsically selective. The same distinction holds of an intentional action, in so far as it is assimilated to a work of art—that is, is also the product of the constructive activity of consciousness. If we return to the example of going to open the window, we find that the action not only defines the situation ("the room is too warm"), but at the same time also defines the agent. He has gotten up, say, before settling down to work, and his action is therefore a gesture which betrays, say, his intention of being methodical.

An intentional action is notoriously indeterminate; unlike a work of art, it cannot be hung for exhibition in a gallery. But the specific warrant for the privileged place of the artifact, and for the privileged role of the artist, in Sartre's analysis of intentional action, is that it is impossible in Sartre's analysis of consciousness as intentional to satisfy directly and explicitly the aspiration of consciousness to become self-consciousness—impossible to perceive and identify the agency of consciousness as itself something. The pursuit of a self therefore takes the form of self-expression; self-consciousness secures symbolic expression in my intentional consciousness of something else. It is at this juncture that Sartre borrows from psychoanalysis: reflective phenomenology's purely descriptive method has broken down, since the self is not something, and cannot be reflected upon and described. The self can only be symbolized. In other words, the individual's intentions have to be "deciphered," by interpreting what his actions indicate he is "conscious of . . . ," and they can only be readily and fully deciphered when these actions are the creation of a work of art in which his intentions are symbolically exhibited. Thus the meaning-endowing function of the transcendental ego has been inherited by the artist, whose constructive activity embodies the specifically human aspiration to organize and stabilize experience, making its structure his own.

THEORY AND ART

At last we recognize the trouble with MacIntyre's (1958) verdict, "What makes Sartre's theoretical confusions more tolerable to him than they are to us is that he is really an artist and not a theorist," and the trouble with MacIntyre's recommendation, "The time has come for us to say to Sartre that what we need from him are fewer theories and more plays." Without Sartre's theory of the way consciousness organizes experience, we could not appreciate the privileged role for Sartre of the artist, or even explain what Sartre is doing as an artist, when he writes plays rather than engaging in some other artistic activity. The transition which I have traced, from Sartre's phenomenological writings on the imagination to his later phenomenological existentialism, has been a transition in which Sartre has abandoned the novel in favor of writing plays. The change of genre has been a matter of finding a suitable vehicle, not just for his "real" temperament as an artist, but for his theory of consciousness. Like a phenomenological analysis, a novel is addressed to the reflective or imaginative consciousness of its reader; its "action" is merely imagined. But a play is acted. (I am neglecting other factors, which I have discussed elsewhere [Cumming, 1961], in the transition from reflection to action: the shift from visual to tactile imagery, and the fact too that seeing a play is a social situation, for I am not taking into account here the social dimension of Sartre's theory of consciousness.) The actor who brackets and transcends his

own experience, when he identifies himself by his actions with the character
he is playing, is exhibiting to the spectators interpreting his actions, not only
the fundamental distinction in Sartre's phenomenology between what is perceived (an actor acting) and what is imagined (the actions of the character
portrayed), but also the fundamental predicament of man in Sartre's existentialism: Man aspires to become a transcendental ego, but is in fact reduced to playing some particular role. (In one of Sartre's plays, *Kean*
[1954], the predicament itself is played up with an additional twist: the
hero is actually an actor but he aspires to become a man.)

Here again the transcendental character of this aspiration must not be
forgotten, even though it is so vulgarized (or naturalized) as to suggest
that Sartre is only borrowing from role theorists in his description, for example (1956), of the actions of a waiter:

> His movement is quick and forward, a little too precise, a little too rapid. He
> comes towards the patrons with a step a little too quick. He bends forward a
> little too eagerly; his voice, his eyes express an interest a little too solicitous
> for the request of his customer. Finally he returns, trying to imitate in his
> walk the inflexible stiffness of some kind of automaton, while carrying his
> tray with the recklessness of a tight rope walker by putting it in a perpetually
> unstable, perpetually broken equillibrium which he perpetually re-establishes
> by a light movement of the arm and hand. . . . He is playing at being a
> waiter (p. 59).

If the transcendental structure of consciousness in Husserl is forgotten,
we fail to recognize that the overt physical actions of the waiter are gestures
which embody and symbolize the transcending movement with which his
human consciousness perpetually re-establishes its perpetually unstable
and perpetually broken equilibrium.

The methodological significance which artistic experience acquires in
Sartre's analysis of the way consciousness organizes experience, is not an
idiosyncrasy of Sartre's. In his *Phenomenology of Perception,* Merleau-
Ponty (1945) analyzes the structure of perception with frequent reference
to the paintings of Cézanne. Even more startling is his analysis of the perceived structure of the human body, for he refuses to interpret what is perceived as merely a biological organism; he assimilates its structure instead
to that of a painting or a musical composition. Indeed just as Sartre's analysis of consciousness exploits, with a certain literalness, Husserl's idiom
of construction, so Merleau-Ponty exploits, with a certain literalness, Husserl's musical idioms (for instance, "thematic unity") to which Sartre is
philosophically deaf. If we had probed the issues over the structure of
consciousness, as they have developed within phenomenological existentialism, we should have found that they tie in with issues in the system of the
arts. Merleau-Ponty analyzes the techniques of specific arts in a different
way from Sartre, and the specific arts themselves are differently interre-

lated in his analysis; painting and music are philosophically privileged in the way that the literary arts (and I might add, sculpture) are by Sartre's analysis, so that the methodological issues separating Sartre and Merleau-Ponty seem comparable to some of the methodological issues over models, reductionism, and emergence, in the philosophy of science, when these are viewed as questions regarding the techniques, interrelations, and scope of specific sciences.

The implausibility of such a comparison at least points up the remoteness of phenomenological existentialism from Anglo-American philosophy. An empiricist like A. J. Ayer (1959) may view the phenomenological analysis of the organization of experience as embroidery on Gestalt psychology, and defend empiricism as if the phenomenological attack merely renewed the old charge that an associationist psychology pulverizes experience into atomistic sense impressions. In conducting this defense, Ayer argues that empiricism can allow patterns of experience to be perceived as units of meaning which are entering into further relationships. But phenomenological analysis does not remain at this rudimentary genetic level, and even experience at this level is tied in by the analysis with such patterns of organized experience as visual and literary works of art. There does not seem much hope of reducing the question of the juncture at which these "higher" forms of experience are to enter an analysis of the organization of experience to a question which genetic psychology can settle.

At any rate, we now see why it is difficult for Anglo-American philosophers to recognize what Sartre is doing as a philosopher as well as an artist. The organized forms of experience to which they accord general methodological significance are scientific theories. *What Is Science?* seems to them an admissible philosophical question, especially if its scope is restricted to the natural sciences. But they would be reluctant to accept as philosophical the question, *What Is Literature?*, which furnishes the title of one of Sartre's works (1949); and the question with which Sartre deals in this work—why certain novelists write the way they do and are justified in their techniques—would not seem to them comparable to the question, for example, of why scientists in a certain area, are justified in relying on mathematical equations. The scientist has a subject matter and his techniques are adapted to the nature of his subject. The artist has only a temperament, a cultural heritage, and a social setting, and when his techniques have been explained in these terms, nothing of general methodological significance emerges which is worth being philosophical about.

Resort to literary as well as to ordinary usage may enable the philosophical psychologist to protest that "a general theory . . . of human behavior" mentions "nothing of the specifically human." But the specifically human, when it is restricted to intentional action, does not itself become a subject matter for any general philosophical theory. Even the term "subject matter" proclaims too organized an undertaking, so the preferred emphasis of philosophical psychologists is on what a philosopher *does,* rather than on any general statement of his philosophical intentions. Philosophy is no more a methodologically significant form of organized experience than art is.

Philosophy takes the form instead of handling problems piecemeal, so that they become the debris left over from collapsed philosophical systems. Most Anglo-American philosophers do not credit any philosophy with even that kind of structural significance that the phenomenological organization of experience retains in Sartre, when its transcendental structure collapses, and yet its transcendental aspiration survives as a structural component of his existentialism. But I like to think that something besides my own temperament is at issue, when I prefer to interpret this collapse and surviving aspiration as a methodological restructuring of experience, in which a theory of consciousness becomes a theory of art—rather than as evidence that Sartre is tolerating theoretical confusions because he is not a theorist but really an artist.

REFERENCES

Ayer, A. J. Phenomenology and linguistic analysis. *Aristotelian Soc.* Supp. 1959, **33,** 114-116.

Cumming, R. D. The literature of extreme situations. In M. Philipson (Ed.), *Aesthetics today.* New York: Meridian Books, 1961.

MacIntyre, A. C. *The unconscious.* New York: Humanities Press, 1958.

MacIntyre, A. C. Review of the *critique de la raison dialectique. Listener,* March 22, 1962.

Merleau-Ponty, M. *Phénomenologie de la perception.* Paris: Gallimard, 1945. (Translation, *Phenomenology of perception.* New York: Humanities Press, 1962.)

Sartre, J. P. *La transcendance de l'égo. Recherches philosophiques* VI. 1936. (a) (Translation, *The transcendence of the ego.* New York: Noonday Press, 1957.)

Sartre, J. P. *L'Imagination.* Paris: Presses Univ. de France, 1936. (b) (Translation, *Imagination.* Ann Arbor: Univ. Michigan Press, 1962.)

Sartre, J. P. *L'Imaginaire.* Paris: Gallimard, 1940. (Translation, *The Psychology of Imagination.* New York: Philosophical Library, 1957.)

Sartre, J. P. *L'Etre et le néant.* Paris: Gallimard, 1943. (Translation, *Being and nothingness.* New York: Philosophical Library, 1956.)

Sartre, J. P. *L'Existentialisme est un humanisme.* Paris: Nagel, 1946. (Translation, *Existentialism.* New York: Philosophical Library, 1947.)

Sartre, J. P. *Réflexions sur la question juive.* Paris, 1946. (Translation, Anti-*Semite and Jew.* New York: Schocken Books, 1948.)

SARTRE, J. P. *Saint Genet Comédien et Martyr.* Paris: Gallimard, 1952.
SARTRE, J. P. *Kean.* Gallimard, 1954. (Translation, *Kean.* New York: Knopf, 1954.)
SARTRE, J. P. *Critique de la raison dialectique.* Paris: Gallimard, 1960.

21 CHARLES MORRIS

GEORGE H. MEAD: A PRAGMATIST'S PHILOSOPHY OF SCIENCE

THE PROBLEM OF THIS PAPER

The major pragmatists were eminent psychologists (James, Dewey, Mead) or at least much concerned with psychology (Peirce). As a group they were not so concerned to keep philosophy "pure" of psychology (Peirce is a partial exception to this) as much of contemporary analytic philosophy has been.

I have decided to stress the position of George H. Mead rather than to discuss the pragmatic movement as a whole in relation to science. Peirce's treatment of the sciences does not depend so much on his pragmatism, as does his pragmatism on his view of the meaning of scientific terms. James does not have much to say technically about science, though he is very careful not to oppose philosophical and scientific inquiry. Dewey was mainly concerned with scientific inquiry as seen within the context of a general theory of inquiry. These men, like Mead, looked at science as a cooperative social activity. They saw it as an advanced development of problem-solving inquiry—they are all "instrumentalists" in this sense. They are all "behaviorists" in a wide use of the term, though not denying all forms of self-observation. The movement was opposed from the beginning to a "dualism" of mind and body, and so to a psychology essentially based on introspection. I think it is fair to say that the pragmatist philosophers were a major force in preparing the climate of opinion characteristic of the present-day behavioral sciences. Nor do I know of anything done in the present-day behavioral sciences which requires a basic modification of the orientation of the major pragmatists.

Mead, however, seems to have a unique place with regard to this volume. In *The Philosophy of the Act,* Mead has presented a theory of human action (or behavior) more subtle and complex than any philosophical theory I know of. He has attempted to analyze such terms as "subjective," "private," "mental," "consciousness," "awareness," and "self" in behavioral terms. Our behavioral approach today becomes more sophisticated, and Mead has much to say that is relevant.

But more important for our present purpose is the fact that Mead, far more than other pragmatists, has tried in detail to show the place of science, its methods and concepts, within a general theory of human action. The analysis is difficult and in places hard to follow or to assess, but the general orientation is clear. And I hope what is said will lead some psychologists and philosophers of science to a consideration of Mead's *The Philosophy of the Act,* a book that has not received the attention it deserves.

MEAD'S CONCEPTION OF THE ACT

Mead's view is behavioral. It is not, however, "Watsonian," not written from the standpoint of keeping the human animal simply in front of one. It is in a certain sense "phenomenological," an account from the focus of the actor. The organism is always conceived as acting in "a world that is there." The act and the object to which it is directed are correlative. Mead distinguishes three stages of the act, and three correlative properties of objects.

What incites an act is often called an "impulse"; this is by Mead characterized as a disposition to act in a certain kind of way. Given such an impulse, the organism seeks objects which will satisfy the impulse, that is, permit the completion of the disposition to respond which it has. Hence the first stage of activity is *perceptual:* the organism scans the environment for clues as to objects relevant to the impulse. Then there follows a *manipulatory* phase of the act in which the actor acts on the object by ways which make it available for the satisfaction of its impulse. And finally, if all goes well, action reaches a *consummatory* stage in which the impulse is satisfied by an appropriate object, acted on in an appropriate way.

Corresponding to these three stages of the act are three properties of the object: the *distance* properties of the object, such as visual and auditory properties, which guide the perceptual phase of the act; the *contact* properties, which answer to manipulation; the *consummatory* properties by which the consummation of the act is completed. It is essential to Mead's position that these properties of the object are "real" relative to the stage of the act. Objects are "really" colored, "really" of certain sizes, "really" have certain values—relative to stages of the act. Hence Mead's position may be called an "objective relativism"; objects have different kinds of properties relative to the stages of action.

IMMEDIATE AND REFLECTIVE EXPERIENCE

The "world that is there," for humans, is a complex of immediate and reflective experience. Animals, perhaps almost wholly, and humans, at least occasionally, react to their world without symbols. Their experience is then said to be immediate. In this stage of experience there may be what Mead sometimes called "non-significant symbols." But the characteristic human symbol, which Mead called the "significant symbol," has the same signification to its producer as it has to the person to whom it is addressed. The growl of a dog may be significant to another dog who heard the growl but without having signification to the growler; the clenched fist held before an opponent has the same signification to both. It is, in Mead's terms, a "significant symbol."

Insofar as action is guided by significant symbols, it is reflective experience. Mead preferred to limit the term "mind" to behavior in which such significant symbols occurred. Mind is thus not something in the organism but a mode of behavior in which the organism's relation to the world that it is there is mediated by significant symbols.

This stress on "the world that is there" is fundamental to Mead's thought, including his conception of science. To use Peirce's terms, Mead's basic position is a form of "critical common-sensism." The world that is there is not merely immediate or unreflective experience: it varies with time and embodies the results of former reflection. Today we "see" the stars as large and far away, but only as a result of being participants in the tradition of Western astronomy. The world that is there is the unproblematic world, that which at any given stage of action is taken for granted. At our human level, the world that is there includes other persons with the same unproblematic status as oneself, physical objects with spatial and temporal characteristics, perceived qualities, and actual or potential consumations. Perceived qualities, physical objects, values are all part of the world that is there. It should be carefully noted that although this is a phenomenologically oriented behavioral position, it is not "psychologism" in any traditional sense. Mead's behaviorism never rejected self-observation. Indeed, Mead consistently regarded psychology as the concern for the experience of the individual as such. Even social psychology was concerned with such experience, but its study of changes in cults, vowel changes, and so on had to bring in the study of groups. So Mead's position is not in any narrow sense "psychological"; it is rather behavioral in the contemporary sense of the behavioral sciences. It is no more psychological than sociological. And even its behavioral orientation needs careful qualification. Action and object are correlative. Action occurs in the world that is there. The world that is there is for humans a common world, including other persons and physical objects. It is only within this common world that we can distinguish individual perspectives, and give meaning to such terms as "private" and "subjective."

SCIENCE AND THE WORLD THAT IS THERE

This conception of the world that is there, this version of critical common-sensism, gives the framework in which Mead must interpret science. Science for Mead, as for other pragmatists, is a social enterprise and obviously at the reflective level of experience. But what Mead especially emphasizes is that scientific thought always first occurs in the experience of some individual when expectations (and so his actions) are frustrated, that the concepts of science are to be explained in terms of aspects of actions, and that any hypothesis concerning the solution of the problem must be tested in the world that is there, such test involving the ongoing of the activity whose frustration was the occasion of the problem. Science, in other words, is to be interpreted in terms of the world that is there. Its results and methods cannot abrogate the reality of that world. Science is to be viewed as one form of action in the world that is there. Such is Mead's general orientation.

THE NEWTONIAN WORLD

As I write, my world that is there contains among other things trees visible outside the window, two dogs, furniture in the room, and me, my pen and pipe. These are all here simultaneously in some sense. But since my spatial-temporal relation to each object is in fact different, the sense of simultaneity becomes, on a behavioral orientation, a problem. Mead handles this problem as follows.

The distance qualities of objects (usually but not necessarily visual or auditory) which correspond to the perceptual stage of the act ordinarily in behavior function as "signs" of the manipulatory or contact properties of the distant objects, that is, set up in us the dispositions to actions that we would have in the actual presence of the objects in our manipulatory activities. Mead frequently writes of this as the "collapsing of the act." Since the temporal distances of the various objects are abstracted from, we obtain the Newtonian timeless space in which all objects can simultaneously exist. Correlative to this process we get the notion of a spaceless time which simply "flows." So on Mead's approach, the Newtonian distinction of absolute time and space is seen as a functional distinction explicable in behavioral terms. By the same token, the distinction need not be given another ("metaphysical") interpretation. The world that is there is spatial-temporal. It is only the "collapsing of the act" made possible by sign processes which behaviorally explains the bifurcation of space and time in Newtonian science.

This analysis also explains the historical bifurcation of primary and secondary qualities and the tendency of the Newtonians to perpetuate the mental-physical dualism. We tend to take the distance qualities of objects (such as those that are seen and heard) as signs of their contact or manipulatory qualities. These distance qualities vary with stages of the act and with various observers. The manipulatory properties on the other hand are less variable: there is general agreement on the weight and size of objects. Furthermore, whatever the purpose of the act, and however much these purposes differ among individuals, the consummation of the act must take account of the contact properties of the object. Hence the contact or manipulatory properties of objects assume a special importance. Such properties tend to be called "physical objects." The prevailing dualism of Western culture made it easy to then locate the distance and the consummatory properties of objects in the "mind." For Mead, this is again the conversion of a functional distinction relevant to phases of behavior into an unwarranted metaphysical dualism. For him distance, contact, and consummatory properties are all properties of objects relative to different phases of the act. All are "natural" and all are "real." Newtonian science pays special attention to the world of manipulation, and this is its legitimate task. But the confirmation of its theories is always within the world that is there, and this world is a world of experienced qualities and experienced consummations and frustrations.

THE WORLD OF RELATIVITY

Mead was greatly interested in the theory of relativity, especially as that theory was presented by Alfred North Whitehead. He liked Whitehead's stress on "perspectives," and their objectivity—a basic feature of objective relativism. Einstein seemed to Mead in contrast to be too "subjectivistically" inclined.

I vividly recall the astonishment of a group of social science students at the University of Chicago who attended Mead's course, "Social Psychology," during the first year that Mead was thinking about the relation of his views to the doctrine of physical relativity. The course in fact became a social psychology of relativity. The social science students did not expect this.

For Mead, the distinguishing characteristic of man lay in the behavior of the signicant symbol. In producing such symbols, man called out in himself the dispositions to response which such symbols called out in others. In this sense man could be said to "take the role" of the other. In telling a guest to "pull up a chair," one is inciting in oneself the dispositions one is inciting by the words in the guest, and may in fact find it difficult to restrain such dispositions if the guest delays in performing the action.

Reflection, for Mead, is essentially a role-taking process which involves, by symbols, the integration of perspectives. Thus in planning a shopping tour, one considers different courses of action with respect to the various objects or situations which one wishes to obtain, taking first one perspective and then others, until one finds a course of action (a sequence of actions) which will attain the complex of goals one wishes to accomplish. In this sense man, through symbols, "conditions" himself—he determines how he will respond to stimuli he will later encounter.

The same is true where action involves other persons. Here we need to know how things will appear in perspectives other than our own. In the Newtonian world we get a common world by collapsing the various acts to the stage of manipulation. We live in a timeless space in which objects exist simultaneously and which for all of us have the common properties they would reveal if we were in physical (that is, manipulatory) contact with them.

But when we consider the distance qualities of objects, the situation is different. We can throw up a ball in a moving train and watch its vertical fall; how will this fall be described by a person witnessing it outside of the train? Here we have the problem of translating between distance qualities of perspectives, and not the Newtonian problem of translation into a common manipulatory area. It was Mead's belief that the achievement of the theory of relativity was finding the translation formulas by which the distance qualities of one perspective could be predicted for another perspective. Thus relativity was brought within Mead's general theory of role-taking. The Newtonian world was an abstraction (by a collapse of the act) to the manipulatory realm: the world of relativity was essentially a transformation of the distance experiences between perspectives. The two doctrines are not expressions of metaphysical differences, but of functional differences within human action.

SCIENCE AND HUMAN ACTION

Mead was highly sympathetic to scientific inquiry. He regarded it as the most advanced form of inquiry, and he favored its extension into all moral and social problems. But there was no narrow "scientism" here. Just as in every scientific problem there are unproblematic beliefs taken for granted in the context of that problem, so in every value problem there are unproblematic values taken for granted in the context of that problem. Inquiry is always devoted to a specific problem in a specific context. Science as a phase of human action may minister to all other phases of human action, but it does not replace them. This point is exemplified in Mead's treatment of mechanism and teleology. Every action occurs under determinate conditions and it is the task of science to determine those conditions. Science is thus in principle deterministic. Action, however, is teleological, goal-oriented. And the discoveries, the knowledge, gained in scientific inquiry are but one more instrument used by man in seeking to choose and to fulfill his individual and social goals. The distinction between the mechanical and the teleological is thus, once again, a functional distinction within action, and not a metaphysical set of alternatives.

This persistent attempt of Mead to replace metaphysical dualisms by functional differentiations within phases of action is perhaps his most distinctive contribution to the philosophy of science.

INSTRUMENTALISM AND REALISM

Two distinctive features of Mead's philosophy of science are (1) his stress upon the appearance in some scientist's behavior of exceptions to what he had expected to experience (and hence the frustration of his behavior), and (2) the view that scientific behavior is essentially a process of discovery, an interpretation of such exceptions as will permit the frustrated behavior to continue.

The account is fundamentally behavioral. It is also fundamentally empirical, since the whole analysis is given in terms of problems appearing in a world that is there for someone or other. I shall not attempt to assess this analysis. I do not believe that any complete philosophy of science can deny or ignore the pragmatic aspect of scientific activity such as Mead has described it. But it is also clear that there are semantic and syntactic problems about the language of science which were not in the focus of Mead's attention. Perhaps they can be encompassed in his perspective, but perhaps not.

Ernest Nagel, in *The Structure of Science,* has discussed with acumen the instrumentalistic version realistic interpretation of scientific hypotheses and models. A statement of Mead's position on this problem would be very difficult. That the instrumentalist interpretation of scientific concepts, theories, and models is dominant in Mead's thought is evident. But it is also clear that Mead's cosmology, whatever his interpretation of science, is in a larger sense naturalistic and realistic. Life emerges out of prior processes, and mind emerges out of prior living processes. I think these views can be defended, but that is another problem. It is a problem of science, not of the philosophy of science.

PART III ISSUES

22 MICHAEL SCRIVEN

AN ESSENTIAL UNPREDICTABILITY
IN HUMAN BEHAVIOR *

IN THE HISTORY OF SCIENCE, there have been many memorable occasions when philosophers or scientists have laid it down that something cannot be done, or done in a certain way, for certain a priori reasons. We recall these cases chiefly for the dates when the claim was disproved.

But the practice is by no means as foolish as these failures are often thought to indicate. For the a priori is here no more than the level of fundamental theory, and to make predictions—including predictions about the impossibility of making predictions—is the proper task of fundamental theory. Indeed, the main problem with most fundamental theories, as Popper is prone to remark, is to squeeze any predictions out of them so that they *can*—in principle—be falsified. Furthermore, our memory is remarkably treacherous on this subject, since victories are sweeter than failures, and a careful survey of the history of science reveals a very different story. For example, as any new trend develops in a science, its prophets defend it by making pessimistic claims about the limited possibility of success with the older approach, and *these* impossibility claims have often proven well founded. A classic example is to be found in the history of psychology itself; with the advent of behaviorism and the experimental approach in general, the prediction was often made by the modernists that the old armchair introspectionist method would never get anywhere because it was incompatible with the quantitative objective tools of modern science. And so it came to pass, if we are to believe the current histories of psychology.

But even this coin has another side. For the actual success of the experimental method in psychology in producing an axiomatic theory has so far been very much less than its earlier proponents expected. It is perhaps

* Gratitude for stimulation or correction but no blame to the following, as well as those mentioned in the paper: Roger Buck, Dave Harrah, Frederic Mosteller (especially), Michael Polanyi, Meyer Shapiro, Lancelot Whyte, and the members of my X663 seminar at Indiana, especially John Cole, David Hull and Will Humphreys.

411

worth examining pessimistic prophecies about the prospects of the new Newtonian kind of psychology. Such prophecies are by no means new, and have attended the subject since birth, an event which—depending on one's point of view—occurred with Aristotle, Wundt, Pavlov, or Hull. Various reasons have been given for such pessimism. Human beings were alleged to transcend the kind of approach that was so successful with inanimate objects; they had souls, or free will, or required empathic understanding. We can safely say that these skeptical forecasts were *largely* based on beliefs which have not turned out to be well supported. But they are *partly* based on an instinctive appreciation of some sound points. In this chapter, I present a formal statement of one underlying truth that is closely related to these doctrines. To place it in context, I add that I think it is only one of several points that can be made in support of the view that the appropriate model for psychology is totally unlike Newtonian physics, that absurdly simple and atypical branch of science, and is much more like geology or geography with their limited developmental theories covering only the broad outlines of events and a mass of organized but non-lawlike information, much of it quite restricted in application.

DEVELOPMENT

The point I shall take up here arose from a study of the so-called self-defeating predictions (seldeps) of recent sociological theory (such as "Dewey will win": George Gallup) in the following very simple way. (Analogous remarks apply to self-fulfilling predictions (selfups) such as "There will be a depression": President Kennedy.)

The element in the seldeps that produces their falsification is not that they are predictions, nor is it their publication.[1] It is their comprehension and the assessment of their effect by listeners with a certain motivation and certain powers which brings about their defeat (perhaps unintentionally). Let us consider a family of examples related to the simple seldep. First example: instead of *telling* the subject exactly what I predict he will do, I so *act* as to make my predictive belief clear. To use individual cases for examples: as an insurance agent, I turn down, out of hand, the subject's application for automobile collision coverage after reviewing his extremely unsatisfactory record. The cognitive result is the same as if I announce my prediction; I believe, and he knows I believe, that he will probably have another serious accident. Thus my belief, a prediction, may lead

---

[1] Statements about the present can be affected in the same way; in obvious cases, because they take time to utter, for example, "Although there is a sign up there which says 'No Smoking,' several people here *are* smoking." There are other cases, however: "I know you can't bear to live without me." The sequel establishes the dispensability of publication.

him to take more care and so prove me and it wrong. This is in many ways the same process that the simple seldep instigates.

Second example: I act in a way that makes it clear that I have made *some* prediction, but not clear *what* prediction it is, for instance, I smirk and say knowingly, "I know what you are going to do about marrying that girl, even if *you* don't." The subject may ignore this and proceed as he would have done anyway. But it may be the case that the importance to him of showing me wrong is greater than any gains he can make by making his choice on the intrinsic merit of the alternatives (a common situation in cards, business, love, and war). I shall say that a subject whose utility-set is under this constraint is contrapredictive, or is contrapredictively motivated, or is a contrapredictive. (This is not at all the same as, though it overlaps with, being countersuggestible.)

Then a *good* strategy for him is to use a randomizer to determine his choice. If there are n alternatives open to him, this makes my chance of predictive success only $1/n$ which is presumably worse than it was. In principle, some randomizers are predictable (for instance, dice), but this is an uninteresting sense of "in principle" for the working scientist. Moreover, we can readily use a quantum randomizer, which is in principle unpredictable (on what I judge to be the best-supported current view of quantum theory). In the absence of access to such devices, it is comparatively easy to invent an *ad hoc* mental or physical randomizing procedure which will select a digit or letter in a way no more predictable than a roulette wheel.

So far we merely demonstrate that human choice behavior can be made at least as unpredictable as any physical system. In an important class of examples (which includes the last class), a stronger conclusion is demonstrable.

Third example: It may be that I do not indicate to the subject that I have made a prediction about his behavior, but that he suspects I *may* have done so—and is contrapredictively motivated at the time. His *best* strategy here (and in the preceding case) is to replicate my prediction, if he can. He may already know, or be able to infer, what I know about him; from this he draws any predictive conclusions that are possible. Then, of course, he acts so as to falsify my prediction. This strategy yields a gain in expected utility Δu (over the randomizing strategy) which is of course given by the formula $\Delta u = u/n$, where u is the utility of surprise, and is thus diminishingly important for choices between an increasing number of alternatives.[2]

---

[2] If the utility of surprise varies from alternative to alternative, being u_i for the ith alternative, $\Delta u = u_i/n$, and may therefore be larger for larger n.

SIGNIFICANCE

I shall try to give a precise statement of the conditions for this strategy in a moment. First we should examine the question whether such a case counts for anything against the predictability of human behavior as it is usually conceived. Psychologists have rarely been naïve enough to suppose that one can always announce one's predictions of behavior to the subject of the prediction without subsequent falsification: determinism does not mean this. And surely I am merely pointing out that the same conclusions apply when the subject can work out the prediction without being told it?

But the present case is more interesting. The idea that human behavior is "in principle" predictable is not seriously affected by the recognition that one may not be able to announce the predictions to the subjects with impunity (nor, more generally, can one allow them to be discovered). For one can make the predictions and keep them from the subjects. But in the present case, *one cannot make true predictions at all.* Secret predictions are still predictions; unmakable ones are not.

The behavior of an intelligent contrapredictive with adequate computer resources will never be *more* predictable than the best randomizer he can get hold of; but it is *absolutely* unpredictable, that is, the available data yields *no* predictive conclusion at all, unless certain very special conditions are met, namely, (i) the contrapredictive incorrectly believes he knows all the relevant data the predictor possesses about him; (ii) this presumed data implies a definite prediction (which *usually* means it does not include the fact of contrapredictive motivation); (iii) the data the predictor *actually* has enables him to predict the subject's behavior under conditions (i) and (ii).

For in any other case, the fact of contrapredictivity automatically nullifies any prediction the remaining data may imply, and also any implied by that fact *and* the other data.

PRECISE FORMULATION

Assume a rational intelligent predictor, P, whose task is to infer from information I_c the choice of an individual C, where:

(i) C is choosing rationally and intelligently (that is, so as to maximize expectations of utility) between alternatives $a_1, a_2, \cdots a_n, (n \geqslant 2)$ (that is, is physically capable of each [would do it if he decided to] and must do one).

(ii) C is a contrapredictive relative to P and a_i, that is, wishes to falsify any prediction made by P about his choice. Precisely, if $\bar{u}_i$ is the utility for C of a_i if a_i is predicted by P, and u is the utility for C of picking an unpredicted a, then "C is a contrapredictive" = "$u > [\max \bar{u}_i - \min \bar{u}_i]$." [3]

---

[3] The formula for the more general case, where u depends on the alternative chosen,

(iii) C knows that I_c is P's data and C has sufficient facilities to calculate any consequences of I_c with respect to C's forthcoming choice, prior to the time he must make the choice.

It immediately follows that I_c either implies an *incorrect* prediction as to which a_i will be chosen by C (that is, contains false information) or *none:* hence C's choice cannot be rationally predicted by P from I_c.

For assume the contrary: If $C(a_m)$ = C will choose a_m (definition) then the assumption gives us: (a) $I_c \to C(a_m)$ for some m; (b) $C(a_m)$ is true. Now C will know that P, since rational and accepting I_c, is making the prediction $C(a_m)$ (from (i) and (iii)). Hence C will in fact choose another alternative a_p, $p \neq m$. Hence $C(a_m)$ is false, contrary to the assumption. Hence either I_c does not imply $C(a_m)$ for any m or $C(a_m)$ is false.

QED

COMMENTS AND CLARIFICATIONS

A. "But much behavior is *already* known to be predictable, even when the prediction is known, for example, that of the compulsive, or the rational benevolent man, etc."

Granted: as long as condition (ii) does not apply, the theorem does not apply. (Other unpredictabilities: (i) K. R. Popper has suggested interesting similar results in other cases; (ii) quantum-uncertainty-dependent behavior.)

B. "Something *must* cause the eventual decision in the contrapredictive; and if we had enough knowledge, we would know what it is, and the effect it has."

Something does (in so far as determinism is true), but *what* it is, or rather what *effect* it has, we cannot know *in advance*. We could know it later, and this capacity for explanation is what I take determinism to mean: if it means "inferential predictability in principle," the theorem proves it false (see 4H and 5D below).

C. "But *we* can precisely predict C's behavior; C will always do the opposite of what P predicts."

1. The prediction task of the theorem is prediction of the precise alternative which C selects. Of course, for other prediction tasks, this result does not apply. For example, we can always predict that C will pick *some* a_i; this is guaranteed by (i). And we can predict with great confidence (for large n) that C will pick an a_i such that $1 \leq i \leq n - 1$; or that he will not pick a_n. As the information content goes down, the confidence level goes up, and vice versa. But the theorem tells us we can never achieve *high* confidence in a *highly specific* prediction, which is of course the kind we would

---

is min $(\bar{u}_i + u_i) > $ max $\bar{u}_i$. It is possible to regard this as the definition of strong contrapredictivity and discuss a weaker notion involving the probabilities P_i that P will predict a_i.

usually prefer to be able to make. If P predicts $C(a_m)$, we as third parties can still only predict "Not $C(a_m)$," which has vanishingly small information content for increasing n.

2. Moreover, P can't predict *anything* if he knows C is contrapredictive, unless he also knows C to be badly wrong as to what I_c is, so we never even get situation 1 in the important cases.

3. Even if P does predict something in the sense of selecting some a_m without proof, C can still actually do a_m since C knows P can't be rationally *sure* of $C(a_m)$.

D. "The proof assumes C's rationality, which is unrealistic."

1. The objection is irrelevant since the theorem can be taken as a *limit* theorem for rational methods; one does not raise a serious objection to the third law of thermodynamics (that absolute zero is unattainable) by saying "It practically never gets that cold."

2. If C is likely to be irrational, so is P; hence C is still likely to be unpredicted because P does not fully utilize his data.

3. There are in fact many practical occasions when the degree of rationality required is available and the theorem then represents a relevant practical consideration.

E. "Stochastic strategies are immune to publicity; hence the theorem only applies to exact prediction."

But C can falsify predictions about the statistical properties of his choice behavior just as easily as individual predictions: for example, if P concludes C will, *r% of the time,* choose an a_m where $1 \leqslant m \leqslant n/2$, then C can choose such an a_m just $(100 - r)\%$ of the time.

F. "One can't *prove* C is unpredictable; for P may just guess correctly or be a precognitive or prophet."

1. Guessing is not a procedure of predictive inference, since we cannot know when the guess is correct, that is, can have no confidence in predictions generated in this way. The theorem only refers to the impossibility of rational (correct) prediction, predictions in which we can have confidence.

2. If P finds his "guesses" are *significantly* more effective than they would be by chance alone, that is, that he can rationally have confidence in them, he has discovered a new fact about himself *and about C,* that P is a good instrument for predicting C's choices. This will—it could be argued—be part of I_c, hence C will know it. But this alone does not enable C to evade the prediction. Now we can plausibly take reliable intuition as a limit case of inference where the content of the intuition is itself part of the data, and this will then reduce to the case of announcing the prediction to C. Of course, a Helmholtzian would argue that P must be performing an *unconscious* inference. This is a misleading account in some ways, but it suggests an important distinction between supernatural precognition and supernormal prescience. The expert clinician's prognoses are not inferences,

nor are they normal perceptions—but nor are they supernatural. His brain is absorbing information and converting it into a prediction using a learned though not known transformation principle; if we cut him off from perceptual access to the patient or the patient's charts or his own past experience, he will fail. A prognostic computer operated by a medically naïve technician has the same dependency on stored information, so we may argue that the clinician and the technician are using this data in getting to their prediction, though not in a process of explicit inference which they themselves perform. I shall henceforth regard this as encompassed by the phraseology of the theorem preamble: "infer from information I_c" is to mean "explicitly deduce or infer from data I_c by means of laws, skills, or devices that incorporate transforming principles I_c ($I_c = I'_c + I''_c$)."

The crystal ball, however, operates in a different way. It does not require a data input, merely reflecting the shadows that coming events cast before them. And the same is true of the "true prophet," or the parapsychologist's precognitive. There is an *experimentum crucis* to distinguish the precognition from prescience; it is that used by the parapsychologists: can the agent predict events that are either fully random themselves, or determined by random events? If so, his powers are supernatural. The theorem, thus interpreted, applies to all prediction other than supernatural. As long as P's skill is inexplicable (but not supernatural), I_c will be unknown and hence the theorem cannot be applied since C cannot be in possession of I_c. Of course, he may still be able to duplicate P's prediction by finding a matching predictor P′; and he is highly secure in a random strategy. Thus, one consequence of replacing the idea of inferential prediction with that of using information to generate predictions is to put the P with a mysterious skill in the same category as the P with mysterious data; he can succeed only so long as the mystery is continued.

We conclude by stressing that making a rational prediction using a mysterious skill or instrument requires a testing period to establish the reliability of the "instrument," even if it is oneself. Supposing the instrument has a "pointer error," for example, indicates $C(a_j)$ whenever C actually chooses a_{j+1}. This emerges in such a trial period and is no handicap at all: and one might plausibly argue that, pointer error or none, the trial period establishes a correlational law from which together with subsequent pointer readings, the later predictions are *inferred*. If so, law and readings must be regarded as part of I_c and the earlier argument is unnecessary.

3. The above considerations have three interesting incidental consequences. (a) The term "data" should be distinguished from the term "information" since the latter is here used to include laws that are not inferrable from data in any systematic way. A computer may have the same data as another and not be able to generate the same predictions because it has not hit upon the same generalizations. In the theorem, I_c includes all information, including any well-confirmed generalizations, which is essentially

required for generating P's predictions. The fact remains that a brilliant computer or psychologist is the best weapon for getting one-up in the prediction war: a new insight is a new predicting algorithm, and like a new theorem, it tells us something we did not know and hence gives us new information, though it is not based on new data. (b) In the philosophical discussion of determinism, that doctrine has frequently been defined as predictability-in-principle. Now, a precognitive can by definition reliably predict anything, including the most random possible sequences, yet I think it unsatisfactory to suppose the existence of such a being would demonstrate determinism (an argument can be given, but it can be made very implausible by experimental ingenuity). I think determinism is much more nearly connected with predictions that use information. It is too narrow to require that the process be explicit: the existence of a prescient as defined above still shows determinism to be true. I give reasons below for thinking even nonsupernatural predictability-in-principle too strong a definition of determinism, but for forward-looking philosophers the present distinction is of some importance. (c) A mysterious predicting gadget may work perfectly during the trial period, but yet must fail thereafter, if I_c includes all the information from which P predicts. For during the trial, its readings are not an adequate basis for prediction and hence are not part of I_c: but thereafter, when they would yield good predictions in normal circumstances, they will not under the conditions of the theorem. The instrument, because it works, now must fail. This *ad hoc* way of falsifying predictions is reminiscent of the Maxwell demon's properties, and the peculiar defining characteristics of the Einstein-Podolski-Rosen *Gedankenexperiment*.

G. "A *third* person P' watching the P-C affair, can—in principle—predict everything that goes on, using the fact of contrapredictivity plus P's predictability."

Not if C is contrapredictive relative to P' and knows what P' knows about C, that is, not unless P' breaks condition (ii) or (iii). And objections from objection C above also apply. Of course, C will have to decide whether making P' wrong is more important than making P wrong, for $n = 2$; in general, C can only falsify one less predictors than he has alternatives.

H. "None of this really proves unpredictability, because that means the possibility of predictability by *someone*—if necessary, someone who *has* knowledge C doesn't know he has."

But Gödel's theorem is not a proof that a certain specific formula is not provable in any system; it is a proof that for certain common and important types of system, however they are strengthened, there is *at every given stage* an unprovable formula. The present proof is that under certain common and socially important conditions, as well as under certain ideal conditions (see 5D), however much is known about a subject's behavior, there are certain parts of it that will not be predictable. Increases in knowledge will make predictions possible; but with respect to each such increase in I_c, there will be new predictions which will be impossible. It seems not unreasonable to say this is an essential unpredictability in the same way that an essential unprovability is demonstrated by Gödel's proof.

I. "The proof begs the question; everything is packed into the 'free will' assumption that someone *can* do the opposite of whatever is covertly predicted of him by another. If we really knew *all* about a person, he would *have* to do what we predicted—or else we *wouldn't* know all about him."

I now undertake to prove the "free will assumption" for my own case. Notice first that it is here only necessary to demonstrate that, no matter what prediction is *announced,* I can do the opposite: for in the case where a prediction is made but not announced, I know what it is by replication (the possibility of which is guaranteed by the conditions) and hence am able to announce it myself, or have it announced to me, without change in the information parameters of the situation. Now we locate a predictor and we assign him the prediction task of saying whether I will turn my head left or right. He does not have very much information about me, but *even if he knew everything that can be known,* he would still have to predict either left or right. *By merely guessing, he has one chance in two of making the same prediction as if he were omniscient.* He makes his guess, and—to compensate for the fact that I would have been able to infer it—announces it. I then do the opposite. Now, if he had really had all the information, it might be that it would have led to the opposite prediction, which I would then have known to be his prediction. So the fact that I prove I can falsify his first prediction does not prove I could have falsified the correct prediction. But now there is only one chance in two of this. Let us continue the experiment, using the same prediction task. Many variables have changed significantly, but once again, there are only two possibilities. The predictor guesses again, or uses a randomizer to select one alternative. Once more I falsify his prediction. There is now only one chance in four he has not, on one of these occasions, made the same prediction as an omniscient psychologist. But I am not frozen by either prediction. We continue, and thus prove to any significance level that I have "free will" in this sense.

Of course, the point is obvious enough on other grounds since it is merely the claim that a man can be so sensitized as to respond with behavior B to the stimulus "You will do A" and conversely, which is a fairly trivial feat. But psychologists sometimes succumb to the "experimental demonstration" more readily.

It can here be noted that since full knowledge cannot lead to a correct prediction of a similarly informed contrapredictive, it cannot lead to any prediction at all (since false conclusions would imply false premises, that is, the "knowledge" would not be knowledge). Hence, the maximum possible knowledge the predictor can have of C cannot provide grounds for prediction. This is the limit version of the theorem.

J. "The result is easily circumvented since any psychologist knows that an observer can easily learn more about a subject than the subject knows about himself."

1. Knowing more may be easy, but knowing more in a direction that pays off in better predictions is more difficult and often impossible for the particular kind of choice we are trying to predict, for instance, whether to bluff at poker, what deployment of forces an unknown enemy strategist will select, and other nonneurotic cases.

2. What one observer can learn, another may; so the contrapredictive would obviously have to employ his own observers to study his own behavior, from whom he may be able to replicate the predictor's prediction, if any, and act so as to falsify it.

K. "To be realistic, C is quite likely to be wrong in his estimate of what P knows about him, and then the proof doesn't apply."

Such errors are likely to reveal themselves if P acts on his predictions of C, say, in a limited war situation. C then improves his replication or defensively moves to a random strategy. (A rider of this is that if P does acquire covert, predictively effective data about C, he should hold off using it until a very large gain is available by doing so, since he sacrifices later success when he does.) Whenever P has, for example, the results of standard tests done by C, plus public psychological theory about interpretation of these, the proof applies in full force, as to many cases of less data and of more. C can frequently but not always pursue optimum strategy by giving P the benefit of any doubts as to the content I_c and including the doubtful items.

L. "In view of the risk of underestimating the predictor's knowledge, the minimax strategy for C will usually be a wholly random choice between $a_1 \cdots a_n$."

1. It is not only underestimating but overestimating that is risky. A relatively ignorant P may have data which happens to imply that C will do what he actually does do, because C has assumed that P had more knowledge which would have indicated a different choice.

2. C's best strategy will indeed depend on (a) the likelihood of error in his estimate of P's data, and also on (b) the disparity between u and the set $u_1 \cdots u_n$, (c) the relative sizes of the u_i and (d) the size of n. He does take a risk by switching from a fully random strategy; but he generally has a chance of gain by doing so.

3. In general, where I_c includes the fact that C is contrapredictive, it cannot imply any specific prediction, hence errors in estimating I_c by C are unimportant since it has no consequences over this range. P will have to guess, and C knows this. It is no solution for P to weight his guesses with C's utility weights since C can ignore them.

4. This leads to some useful considerations for C. It is usually possible for C to structure a situation so as to increase the number of alternatives open to him. By thus increasing n, he increases his expectation of u, (the utility of surprise). This usually gives a net gain, even though the procedure for doing this also usually leads to some decrease in u or in the $\bar{u}_i$. For example, in a war Russia might see a choice of H-bombing New York City or Los Angeles. If all the antimissile missiles available are concentrated in one of these areas, they would have a good chance (75 per cent) of handling the attack—if divided, they almost certainly fail (95 per cent). The U.S. thus has a choice between two defense strategies, one of which offers a $50\% \times 75\% = 37\frac{1}{2}\%$ chance of success, the other a $50\% \times 5\% = 2\frac{1}{2}\%$ chance. Now, if the Soviet Union extends its range of choice to include three other major urban areas, the best strategy available to the United States gives only $20\% \times 75\% = 15\%$ chance of success. There is a possible loss to the Russians due to the diminished utility of killing a smaller city, but the gain to them considerably outweighs this if their utility is population-proportioned. The relevant strategic inequalities to decide whether Russia should (a) use a weighted stochastic strategy, (b) increase the number of alternatives further, are easily calculated. The crucial data in this large subfamily of cases is thus simply the set $a_i \cdots a_n$: C should (i) conceal it or misrepresent it, (ii) enlarge it, (iii) depending on u, u_i, etc., weight it, (iv) draw from it randomly, with or without weights.

5. Thus, in a large subclass of cases, but not all, the extent of the essential unpredictability is very close to being the same as that of the random unpredictability we first observed. But instead of being a way of avoiding prediction the strategy is adopted as a consequence of the impossibility of prediction.

6. One may ask: if prediction is impossible, why doesn't C simply pick the a_i which has maximum $\bar{u}_i$? I_c cannot contain the assertion that C, having seen P's impasse, will definitely select on this principle, because if it does, C's choice would be predictable by P, and this fact being known to C, he would do otherwise. Still, C *may* select on this basis; it has obvious merits. It cannot be definitely predicted that he will; but he may. Similarly for adjacent strategies. Similarly for any fixed ratio between them. Hence P can have no reliable grounds for supposing that C will deviate at all from a pure random choice between the a_i. This is not the same as saying that C will adopt this strategy. The situation is absolutely indeterminate. In practice, one might suppose that C should begin by using the high $\bar{u}_i$ strategies as much as he can until P bets on them and then changing: except that P can foresee this. The stable strategy for C will eventually be a mixture which is slightly biased toward the $\bar{u}_i$ weights by a factor which depends on what might be called P's sensitivity. This is a familiar proposition when applied to bluffing in poker.

7. The general conclusion here I take to be of considerable importance

in assessing models for psychological theories. I think we can establish on this and on other grounds that possibility-statements (here, the datum of the range of alternatives) are more important for psychology than universal statements (that is, exact laws). True and informative statements of the first kind are always more readily and sometimes solely available, and their availability more than compensates for their lack of intrinsic virtue.

M. "In the social sciences, we are rarely dealing with the behavior of a single person, and as soon as we switch to predictions of group behavior, H. A. Simon has shown that it is in principle possible to predict publicly not only the general behavior but the exact percentage of a group that will perform in a certain way, so the theorem has negligible impact."

1. In the social sciences, we are often dealing with the *effects* of the behavior of one or a few persons, the effects occurring to a large number of people.

2. What Simon's very interesting result shows is that *under some circumstances* precise selfups about group behavior are possible. This finding has been inaccurately summarized by himself and others (e.g., Simon, 1957, p. 86; Nagel, 1959, p. 142). There is a wide range of circumstances, including common electoral ones, where his results do not apply. A simple counterexample is this. Suppose that the underdog (or read "bandwagon") effect with respect to a particular candidate in a two-way fight operates in this way: the moment it appears from the announced prediction that he will win, a number of his supporters (or read "opponents") will decide to vote the other way. No predictions can be right in these circumstances unless the underdog or bandwagon motivated group is smaller than the uncontaminated majority would have been. (If both effects operate simultaneously, possibly for each candidate, the inequality must be generalized in an obvious way.) In Simon's terms, this corresponds to a discontinuity in the function giving the actual vote in terms of the predicted vote, at the point where the latter is 50 per cent; and it is highly plausible to suppose that just such a discontinuity exists at times since 50 per cent is the point at which the prediction's support switches from one candidate to the other. Other difficulties arise for Simon in the case of alliances, grapevine information and suspicion of manipulation.

3. Pure contrapredictive motivation is not usually involved in the bandwagon/underdog effects, only the reconsideration of one's own actions in the light of data about other people's actions, e.g., when wanting a candidate to know he has some support while not wanting him to get in, or preferring A to B and C, but being willing to vote for B against C if A has no chance at all, etc. The key to these effects lies in contrafactual belief, rather than contrapredictive motivation: the voters had voted as they did, because they did not think the facts about other people's votes (or the prediction) are as they subsequently turn out to be. It is also important that a vote can

serve more than one purpose: it can help to elect, or it can be used to show support when/because election is impossible.

4. The crucial reason for judging the Simon theorem irrelevant to the present theorem becomes clear when we realize that Simon's prediction succeeds *only* because he has two items of information about the electorate that they lack, namely, the uncontaminated vote and the functional relationship. The first datum is not hard to get, by replicating the poll if bribery fails; the second only a little harder. So a single (rich) contrapredictive in the group can foil the predictions.

5. A systematic study of published predictions referring to groups including some contrapredictives and/or some people with contrafactual beliefs reveals an extraordinary complexity. Some are susceptible to immediate disproof by a single individual's unaided act, others require collusion, others are highly vulnerable to random strategies, etc. No general conclusions emerge readily, but the mining rights look valuable.

6. Study of an apparently rather different kind of example is also illuminating and suggests conclusions about selfups. The family of paradoxical announcements—the paradox of the Class A blackout, the condemned prisoner, or the unpredictable examination (see, e.g., Martin Gardner, 1963) introduces an interesting consideration. If you tell someone you are going to give a party for him the following evening whose occurrence he will not be able to predict, he may conclude that the announcement is self-defeating. But is it? It looks as if he can predict the party from your announcement and hence it cannot be unpredictable. Since the only party your announcement guarantees is an *un*predictable one, it follows there can be no party at all. Having thus concluded that the party's non-occurrence is predictable, which entails that its occurrence is not predictable he is unfortunately vulnerable to the fact that if you give it, it will precisely fulfill your guarantee of an unpredictable party. One of the morals of this example is to stress the peculiar difficulty of inferences from what is announced by P to what is predicted by P: the main theorem of this paper does not involve any such inferences, whereas they are extremely important in this paradox and underdog effect. The secret of the success of Simonized predictions lies in almost the same peccadillo as the above paradox. The underdog voter may know the pollster's announcement is Simonized, but this cannot justify him in ignoring it since the likelihood of his ignoring it has also been taken into account. Of course, collusion can cause trouble in Simon's case and is irrelevant to the paradox.

SPECIAL APPLICATIONS

1. C = computer. The proof demonstrates that physical determinism is either false or does not imply predictability-in-principle of all systems

(contra Laplace). The motivational condition of contrapredictivity is a simple matter to program, and the parity of information easily arranged. K. R. Popper has given a most extensive—and a very interesting—treatment of limitations on determinism that arise from taking seriously the fact that the predicting computer is itself a physical system. His results are related to the present ones, but by no means the same; we develop these by taking seriously the fact that the predictee may be contrapredictively motivated.

In the early discussions of the contrapredictive effect, it was commonly thought to be unique to the social sciences. We have just observed its applicability to computers which might be thought to count against this; but I have argued elsewhere that the social sciences will ultimately include the study of molar computer behavior (Scriven, 1960). However, even *as it was originally defined,* the effect applies throughout science. The prediction that a comet will return on a certain date may provoke a successful effort to intercept and destroy it. What is unique to the social sciences is only that their predictions are often falsified by the action of those to whose behavior the prediction refers (directly, or indirectly as in bank and crop predictions). The contrapredictive effect, however, as I have tried to demonstrate, has some of its most interesting manifestations where no prediction is or can be generated at all; hence it is a more general concept than the self-defeating (published) prediction.

2. C = P. The problem whether one could ever know in advance how one was going to decide is a nice dilemma for determinists, and this aspect of the problem has been treated most illuminatingly by D. M. MacKay in many writings, with somewhat different conclusions from my own. His emphasis has been on the impossibility of the predictee's *believing* the predictions about his choices made by any observer including himself; I have discussed the impossibility of the observer even *inferring* a prediction under certain (narrower) conditions, a result which is stronger in one way, but more limited in its range (weaker) in another. The emphasis of the discussions by Popper, MacKay and myself is thus *primarily* on three kinds of ultimate limitations on predictions; computer limitations, belief limitations, and inference limitations. The existentialists have also sensed the logical indispensability of the act of genuine choice, despite determinism; and of course many others have felt this so acutely as to conclude that determinism must be false. But I do not think MacKay's denial that a single true account is possible, or the existentialist's nihilism, or the libertarian's antideterminism are required. The idea that determinism implies total predictability is, on this and other grounds indefensible and must be rejected. Taking it to mean only the universal rule of *some* kind of exact laws, it is falsified by quantum actions but not by the present argument (contrary to Paul Shiman's interesting suggestion which stimulated my thinking on this point). In particular, exact *explanation* of human and computer actions

is perfectly possible in principle although prediction is not, quantum effects apart. However, it is another question whether it is always worth searching for such explanations, or indeed practically possible to find them. I think the task of the social sciences is largely elsewhere, and (perforce) largely outside the prediction field. We could put the present point by saying that rational contrapredictive behavior is probably perpetually "emergent," that is, generates new "laws"; at any rate, new phenomena. At each stage we have to appeal to a higher element in the hierarchy of laws than any we have yet discovered; yet it can be an exact law, and it can be in turn explained. Atemporal laws are not necessary for explanation.

3. P = God. God can know what we will do only by preventing us from knowing what he knows, or depriving us of "free will" in the sense of the capacity for contrapredictive motivation. Thus his omniscience to some degree limits his exercise of omnipotence or benevolence. The theorem does show that monotheism is the only form of theism reconcilable with omniscience, under certain obvious conditions.

4. I_c = All possible information about C, that is, the ultimate goal of individual psychology. As for the mechanical and the supernatural predictors, so for the human ones. The present proof shows that psychology can never get to the point where its practitioners know enough to predict all the behavior of other psychologists, even if they could predict the behavior of all physical randomizers. Conversely, to insist that *predictive* determinism is true is to insist that it is impossible for some knowledge about C to be conveyed to him: which I take to be an empirical and false claim.

REFERENCES

GARDNER, M. Mathematical games. *Sci. Amer.*, 1963.
NAGEL, E. *The structure of science.* Glencoe, Ill.: Free Press, 1959.
SCRIVEN, M. The compleat robot, a prolegomena to androidology. In S. Hook (Ed.), *Dimensions of mind.* New York: New York Univ. Press, 1960.
SIMON, H. A. *Models of man.* New York: Wiley, 1957.

23 KARL H. PRIBRAM

PROPOSAL FOR A STRUCTURAL PRAGMATISM: SOME NEUROPSYCHOLOGICAL CONSIDERATIONS OF PROBLEMS IN PHILOSOPHY *

I HAD COMPLETED this chapter only to be plagued by a vague dissatisfaction. I had in hand four loosely connected sections, each in its own right the subject of an essay. Why this odd juxtaposition of memory, induction, mind-brain, and ethics—and why in this order? It finally occurred to me that my dissatisfaction stemmed not so much from the disconnectedness of the various sections, but from a feeling that a connection was there but that it remained unexpressed. Once this became evident, it was but a short distance to the identification of the connection.

I had been trying through these paragraphs and pages to discern my own posture toward certain problems in scientific philosophy. The consistencies and contrasts in this posture quickly crystallized—I was clearly a structural pragmatist.

How had this come about? To a physiologist, the choice is open as to whether he will gain understanding of the functions of the organ he is studying by (1) pursuing the reductive course to learn more and more about ever smaller units and processes, or (2) directing his efforts in a more holistic setting, to the examination of the relations between organ and organism. In choosing the holistic path, as a neurologist I was faced with

* If we are to take seriously the results of the Würzburg experiments, a *ms* such as this is as much due to those who pose the problems as to the author. I hope therefore that my uncle, Karl Pribram (*Conflicting Patterns of Thought,* Public Affairs Press 1949), Mrs. Elisabeth Wadleigh (with her perceptive editor's eye), George Miller (whose sharp distinction between normative and descriptive science "made" section III for me), Merton Gill (whose patient and continuing tutelage can be seen in section IV), and David Hamburg (who contributed in so many ways) will consent to share credit and responsibility for whatever has been accomplished.

the need for some sophistication in the experimental analysis of systematic variations made on behavior which it is the supposed office of the nervous system to control. As a neuro-behaviorist, I found much of use in the positivist, operationist approach. Pseudoproblems were uncovered (Pribram, 1954, 1958; Malis, Pribram, & Kruger, 1953; Pribram, Kruger, Robinson, & Berman, 1955-1956). Distinction between the levels of discourse that refer to the neural and the behavioral systems sharpened the way in which questions could be put in the laboratory and how the results of experiments could be communicated. I probably should have remained happy with some sort of neuro-behaviorism, were it not for a particular experience.

A patient had been given a bilateral removal of the anteromedial tip of the temporal lobe. In monkeys (and other mammals) such a surgical procedure is followed by a syndrome which includes excessive oral investigation of edible and nonedible objects and a marked increase in food intake (Pribram & Bagshaw, 1953). We had puzzled considerably and carried out many experiments to try to assess the factors responsible for the appearance of this disturbance. Had the operation impaired the sense of smell? The sense of taste? Had an increase in metabolism been effected? Or was it a decrease in the sensitivity of the satiety mechanism?

Here was an opportunity to go to the heart of the matter with a simple procedure. Ask the patient. She had been observed to put nonedible objects in her mouth and to eat excessively; she had gained over 100 pounds in weight. So, we inquired of her: are you excessively (or moderately) hungry (most of the time; right now; when shown food—candy, meat, etc.)? Always, the same answer: "Not especially; no more so than before surgery; not so I noticed it, Doctor."

Quite accidentally, an inquiry of this sort took place just before lunch one day. The door of the examining room opened onto the ward dining hall where other patients were already seated around a large table. Our woman took in this scene with a glance and made a beeline for the food-laden table, pushed others out of the way, and began to stuff herself, using both hands.

Immediately recalled to the examining room, her answers to our questions were as before. Further, when shown a piece of chocolate (which she was not allowed to grab), she gave no reaction such as "I'd love to have that," "I'm so hungry," or "That looks good." Rather, the piece was closely and intently scrutinized, described in detail and not mentioned again once put out of sight.

This patient was mentally ill, though communicative and cooperative. One would in any case be cautious in drawing conclusions from a single observation. But something stood out: there was more than an ordinary discrepancy of fact here. As a behaviorist, I should place my faith in the observed excessive eating behavior of my patient. I could actually weigh the results of her altered behavior. Verbal reports of introspections are notoriously untrustworthy—why should they be less so here? The evidence stood overwhelmingly in favor of the reliability and validity of the instrumental response—other patients had shown the same disturbances; so had two varieties of monkeys; we had produced a similar picture in dogs (Fuller, Rosvold, & Pribram, 1957); the literature showed the effect to be true of cats; and besides, this part of the forebrain is heavily connected with that region in the hypothalamus where injury classically leads to overeating. What, then, is the problem? Simply that I had believed the woman when she told me that she felt no hunger. Further, it makes a difference whether one ignores the verbal report or whether one comes to terms with it. And since it makes a difference, one cannot choose to ignore.

What is this difference? Primarily, the decision determines whether a body of evidence is shut out or admitted to inquiry. Such reports as those of Penfield (1958), where correlations are made between excitation of brain cortex and verbal reports of introspections, are inadmissible as evidence if the verbal report, with all its recognized limitations, is not good for *something*. On the other hand, if verbal report is indeed to be listened to, such nefarious borderline activities as medical psychoanalysis must, after all, fall within the province of the scientific study of behavior.

Since it did make a difference, I could no longer in good conscience ignore what patients told me—and the neuro-behaviorist was forced to become the neuropsychologist. Analysis of the woes and responsibility of neuropsychology—and its promise—are brought out elsewhere (Pribram, 1962a). And some of the consequences of this subjective-behavioristic approach to the problems of psychology have also been detailed, in collaboration with two equally troubled authors (Miller, Galanter, & Pribram, 1960). My stance as a systems neurophysiologist, neuropsychologist, and subjective behaviorist thus assured, I apparently had the temerity to accept the current assignment.

Why pragmatism? Pragmatism has, for many, come to mean, ". . . first, a method; and second, a genetic theory of what is meant by truth" (James, 1931, p. 65). Seen as a compromise between the tough-minded empiricist and the tender-minded rationalist, pragmatism has maintained the tough spirit in its methods and the tender heart in its aims.

The essence of the pragmatic method has been summarized by James:

> There can *be* no difference anywhere that doesn't *make* a difference elsewhere —no difference in abstract truth that doesn't express itself in a difference in concrete fact and in conduct consequent upon that fact, imposed on somebody, somehow, somewhere, somewhen (p. 50).

In method, then, pragmatism is a radical empiricism:

> Pragmatism represents a perfectly familiar attitude in philosophy, the empiricist attitude, but it represents it, as it seems to me, both in a more radical and in a less objectionable form than it has ever yet assumed. A pragmatist

turns his back resolutely and once for all upon a lot of inveterate habits dear to professional philosophers. He turns away from abstraction and insufficiency, from verbal solutions, from bad a priori reasons, from fixed principles, closed systems, and pretended absolutes and origins. He turns towards concreteness and adequacy, towards facts, towards action and towards power. That means the empiricist temper regnant and the rationalist temper sincerely given up. It means the open air and possibilities of nature, as against dogma, artificiality, and the pretense of finality in truth.

At the same time it does not stand for any special results. It is a method only. But the general triumph of that method would mean an enormous change in . . . the "temperament" of philosophy. Teachers of the ultra-rationalistic type would be frozen out, as the ultramontane type of priest is frozen out in protestant lands. Science and metaphysics would come much nearer together, would in fact work absolutely hand in hand (p. 51).

Why not pursue this line of reasoning, as has been done by others, to what would be its obvious conclusion: an operational logical positivism? The reason for hesitancy in adopting this course lies with the first and second sections of the body of this chapter. In a sense, these sections provide an ultraradical empiricism: data about the data forming process; facts about fact-making; the manner and form of the etchings on the *tabula rasa*. But a new quality is added: the empiricism takes on a nativistic flavor; hallowed distinctions give way to neurons. Both biology and philosophy gain. In a recent discussion of Milner and Olds' discovery that organisms will seek self-stimulation when electrodes are implanted in certain parts of the brain, I stated:

No longer can we say simply, "here is a pleasure center, here is a pain center in the brain," for stimulation of one and the same spot may produce behavior quite different depending upon the situation in which the organism finds itself. The arguments of the philosophers are taken out of the realm of the speculative and into the laboratory. The arguments remain the same, but now tissue is involved and the behavior of organisms studied. This new solidity has a two-fold effect. First, it shows that the arguments of the philosophers were not just "hot air," and secondly, it shows that the naïve materialism which has served the biologist so well thus far must be amplified, if not totally discarded, if his data are to make any sense to him or to anyone else (Pribram, 1959a, p. 5).

The step taken when brain tissue becomes involved in these issues has the feel about it that one has when going from a metalanguage to an object language. The techniques of logical analysis remain the same, but an additional dimension has been added. It is a matter of levels of discourse, of validity and of structure; and this is the substance of the third section.

In psychology, the operational approach has led to descriptive learning theory; to mathematical models of the psychological process; to postulates of variables and constructs that might intervene between observables to account for their lawful interrelation. But descriptive behavior theory has shown its weakness in definitions which are of necessity so narrowly circular that they lack meaning, that is, platforms for hypotheses or significant experiments; the mathematical modelers find themselves in the awkward opposite position that the very stimulus elements that compose their models defy even the loosest sort of definition; and intervening variable theorists admit their inadequacies when they grant that their variables really aspire to become constructs which in due time will become respectable, that is, physiological. This is not to say that these approaches have failed to contribute—it is only that they have stopped short. Many of their arguments ring hollow once it is recognized that the head is not.

Since there is this marked difference between the research on learning and memory generated by positivistic operationism and that generated by questions posed through a neuropsychological approach, the two cannot be identical. Both continue to be effectively pursued; what remains to be stated is the conviction that the pragmatic test, "Is there a difference that makes a difference," has proved a method more generally applicable than that which characterizes either biological science per se, or operationism per se.

But in spirit, pragmatism has never been merely a radical empiricism. The Jamesian pragmatist holds that knowledge is not just etched on a *tabula rasa*—knowledge is continuously *made* by a sentient being who acts on his universe. This genetic theory of what is meant by knowledge is the second characteristic of pragmatism:

> This new idea is then adopted as the true one. It preserves the older stock of truths with a minimum of modification, stretching them just enough to make them admit the novelty, but conceiving that in ways as familiar as the case leaves possible. An *outrée* explanation, violating all our preconceptions, would never pass for a true account of a novelty. We should scratch round industriously till we found something less eccentric. The most violent revolutions in an individual's beliefs leave most of his old order standing. Time and space, cause and effect, nature and history, and one's own biography remain untouched. *New truth is always a go-between, a smoother-over of transitions. It marries old opinion to new fact so as ever to show a minimum of jolt, a maximum of continuity.* We hold a theory true just in proportion to its success in solving this "problem of maxima and minima." But success in solving this problem is eminently a matter of approximation. We say this theory solves it on the whole more satisfactorily than that theory; but that means more satisfactorily to ourselves, and individuals will emphasize their points of satisfaction differently. To a certain degree, therefore, everything here is plastic (James, 1931, pp. 60-61) [italics mine].

Further, "theories thus become instruments, not answers to enigmas, in which we can rest. We don't lie back on them, we move forward, and on occasion make nature over again by their aid. Pragmatism unstiffens all our theories, limbers them up and sets each one at work" (James, 1931, p. 53).

How would the author of these remarks receive the results of the experiments on the orienting response, habituation and novelty? I am sure he would agree that at this juncture any differences between his statements and those made by neuropsychologists (and even some of those of Carnap on credence) would prove to be no differences at all. On this score, then, the label pragmatism is at least as good as any other; and the richness of the similarities between James' statement of the genetic theory of the meaning of truth and the evidence for the neurophysiological process now makes up for whatever lack of precision characterized the earlier formulation.

Moreover, the congruence of at least three different approaches—the introspective, the logical, and the neurological—must be attended. If it truly makes no difference whether the operations that define induction are made in the verbal, the mathematical, or the laboratory mode, how does this come about? What then is the essence of this congruence? The philosopher of science has met this circumstance before.

> It is sufficient to say that what physics ultimately finds in the atom, or indeed in any other entity studied by physical methods, is *the structure of a set of operations*. We can describe a structure without specifying the materials used; thus the operations that compose the structure can remain unknown. Individually each operation might be anything; it is the way they interlock that concerns us (Eddington, 1959, p. 262).

Inductive inference is, according to this analysis, a structure. And our pragmatism has taken a step.

That is why a *structural* pragmatism. The issue of structure is, of course, implicit in the examination of the mind-brain problem viewed as the relation between psychological and neurological science. This issue becomes explicit when the organization of behavior by the neural process is the subject of inquiry (Hebb, 1949), and comes to a focus in the problem of serially ordered behavior (Miller, Galanter, & Pribram, 1960). Whether or not the particular analysis presented in the third and fourth sections proves acceptable, the power of structure as a tool toward understanding is keenly felt. Pluralism is given form; monism loses its monolithic shapelessness; the reasons for a dual (mirror) appearance of the universe become evident. Infinite complexity can be approximated as a scientific idea; we are not stuck with just infinite chaos.

And this difference makes a difference. In the fourth section, the difference appears in the ethics of the classical *versus* that of the structural pragmatism. Classical pragmatism holds that:

> *"The true," to put it very briefly, is only the expedient in the way of our thinking, just as "the right" is only the expedient in the way of our behaving.*

Expedient in almost any fashion; and expedient in the long run and on the whole of course; for what meets expediently all the experience in sight won't necessarily meet all further experiences equally satisfactorily (James, 1931, p. 222).

Really, Prof. James, isn't this a hell of a fix for an ethics, and especially a pragmatic ethics which must draw its strength from its own impact, to get itself into? Small wonder American education and foreign policy, in their intuitive and often surprisingly effective pragmatism, have had so few explicit guideposts on which to base decision.

Structural pragmatism accepts the classical pragmatic method and the genetic view of the meaning of "truth" and "right." But in recognizing "structure," additional strength, that is, orderliness, is provided. Once structure is admitted, "truth" and "right," reliably established within the system in which they are formulated, become valid to the extent that they transcend that particular universe of discourse. In another connection, I used this example:

Recently there has been, in North America, a shift in popular connotation away from attitudinal determinants [of the meaning of words]: e.g. the term "honesty" no longer refers exclusively to "telling the truth," "respecting others' property" and such, but also to "behaving according to *how* one 'feels' and 'sees' the situation," even if this entails occasional lying or stealing (Riesman, Glazer, & Denny, 1950) (Pribram, 1959b, p. 284).

Each connotative meaning is true in its own right; each connotation right in its own truth. Confusion (and there is confusion; ask any perceptive and thoughtful teen-ager) results from (1) a failure to make explicit the distinction between the levels of discourse over which each meaning of truth and right holds; and (2) the assertion that one meaning, therefore one level of discourse, has a monopoly on the "really true and right." The structural pragmatist takes the difficult but eminently practical course that truth and right must be reliably and thoroughly established at each level separately and that only then, and in each instance that the issue is met, validity is attained through actions that mesh these levels.

For example, our courts have on occasion sanctioned a theft when this has occurred as an isolated act performed by a distraught parent who could find no other way to feed his children. Stealing has not become universally "good" as a result; nor has the more usual prohibition of robbery made it "right" to starve one's brood. The ordinary action that meshes these two levels of "goodness" and "rightness" is to work for pay which is spent for food. Through "work" and "money" a solid social structure is meshed. Both meanings of "good" and "right" have attained validity (have maintained their usefulness) through the operations "work" and "money." When these operations fail, others are invoked to maintain the mesh: the parent is declared to have been temporarily irresponsible for his actions due to duress. And we proceed to a more enduring engagement between the needs of the unemployed family and the society in which it functions: we act to remove the occasions for duress by appropriate social welfare legislation.

James is so close. The sentence following the passage quoted above reads: "Experience, as we know, has ways of *boiling over,* and making us correct our present formulas" (James, 1931, p. 222).

Neuropsychological researches and theories have recently provided several instances of such boiling over. As so often happens, the implications of this activity have gone unrecognized, since neurophysiologists and physiological psychologists work for the most part outside the main body of philosophic endeavor. Despite this, the neuropsychological effort has considerably aided in establishing man's altered view of his universe and even of himself as an ethical and moral entity. To make explicit the nature and extent of this effect is the job of philosophers. But an indication of the loci of "boil" and a preliminary analysis of their reach can be accomplished by the neuropsychologist.

ON THE NEUROBIOLOGY OF MEMORY STORAGE AND RETRIEVAL

Where or how does the brain store its memories? That is the great mystery. How can learning persist unreproduced, being affected by other learning while it waits? On the proper occasion what was learned reappears somewhat modified. Where was it in the meantime? The Gestalt psychologists speak of traces which may be altered before they are reproduced. The psychoanalysts speak of the unconscious or the foreconscious where the ideas await call in what Herbart described as a "state of tendency." *The physiology of memory has been so baffling a problem that most psychologists in facing it have gone positivistic, being content with hypothesized intervening variables or with empty correlations* (Boring, 1950, p. 670) [italics mine].

Of most immediate interest here are the rapid advances occurring in identification of a variety of material processes subsumed under the rubric "memory mechanisms." Techniques are now available to examine in detail the substrate that allows time binding, that is, an organism's capacity and infirmity to react to "experienced" events that cannot be identified in his momentary surround. As always when experimental techniques are brought to bear, there is a sharpening of the questions asked which in itself produces consequences in theory and practice.

First, an orientation. Evidence has accumulated during the past century and a half to support the proposition that the brain is the major organ controlling complex behavior and, in man, its immediate antecedents— thoughts and feelings. Much of this evidence has come from the clinic: injuries to brain substance are followed by behavior disturbances; electrical excitation of man's brain effects reports of alterations in introspections and of ongoing actions. In the laboratory, these techniques were refined to give further precision by extending the analysis of the brain's role in the organization of instrumental, nonverbal, complex behavior. But for the most part, the experimental laboratory was concerned with the electrical output of neural tissue. And the electrical events that could be studied were largely evanescent, transient phenomena. Examination of the more enduring structural changes assumed to underlie the memory mechanism could not be touched by these techniques. As a result of all this work, however, when neurochemical knowhow did offer an entrée into the problem, there was not much doubt as to where to focus attention: the brain (with its accessory organs) is the prime candidate for study.

Brain tissue can be divided into two types of components: neural and glial. Many nerves are characterized by the great physical length of their processes (in man, some are as long as three feet) and by the fact that electrical, chemical, and mechanical excitations are quickly propagated along this great length (in a matter of milliseconds). This striking characteristic preempted the attention of neurophysiologists for some time. Recently other more slowly changing attributes of neural tissue have been examined, and at the same time the affinities between neural and glial tissue have been explored. Changes having a time course of an hour or a week are now described, and even more permanent quantitative effects are selectively related to the conditions experienced by the organism:

I have elsewhere collated some of this recent work on the memory storage mechanism (Pribram, in press), and other views (Briggs & Kitto, 1962; Gaito, 1961) and reviews (Bach, 1962; Deutsch, 1962; Pribram, 1961) on the matter are available. Essentially, two major paths are presently discernible in this research.

(1) Most of the impetus for sustained interest has come from the experimental results that implicate ribonucleic acid (RNA) metabolism in neural-glial activity. Neurons have been shown to secrete RNA when active as a result of electrical excitation or physiological stimulation (Hydèn, 1961; Morrell, 1961). In fact, nerve cells have a vastly greater capacity to contain and to produce nucleic acids and proteins than do other cells in the body, so that this characteristic of nerve tissue is as conspicuous as is its ability to generate and transmit electrical potential changes (Hydèn, 1961). The well known role of the RNA molecule, together with its more stable sister substance, DNA, in the mechanisms of genetic "memory," stimulated the suggestion that RNA is somehow involved in the mechanisms of neural memory. Further, when the time course of minute chemical events is followed into the period after specific excitation has ceased, reciprocal changes in RNA concentration are observed to occur between neuron and enveloping glia (Hydèn, 1961).

Hydèn gently teases apart the neurons and the glia of the vestibular nucleus. He finds that the increased production of RNA in nerve cells concomitant with their excitation is coupled to a simultaneous decrease in RNA concentration in oligodendroglia. During this period of excitation, glia could provide the nerve cell with energy-rich compounds since the glia apparently resort, at least in part, to anaerobic metabolic routes such as glycolysis and lipid breakdown. In addition, however, Hydèn finds that after excitation ceases, the glia in turn increase their RNA production while that of the adjacent neurons diminishes. On the basis of other experiments, Hydèn suggests that the aerobic-anaerobic balance is maintained through competition for inorganic phosphates (the Pasteur effect), with the respiratory phase of the process dominant over the fermentative glucose degradation, and the phases in the neuron dominant over those in the glia. This phase lock-in mechanism is assumed to operate through pinocytosis. There is ample evidence of possible pinocytosis from high resolution analyses of the structural arrangements of the glial-neural border. In addition, pinocytosis has been observed in glia and nerve cell tissue cultures, where it can be induced by electrical stimulation.

Why this fuss about a glial-neural couplet? There are several reasons. For one, glial cells reproduce, while neurons do not. Should the memory storage mechanism turn out to be related to protein synthesis guided by RNA production, such stored protein could be replicated by glial cell division.

Second, nerve cells must remain constantly ready for new excitation. The time course of the effects of excitation is short, even when nerve nets rather than neurons per se are considered. In simulated nets, the difficulty has been to adjust the time an element "remembers" in such a fashion that "learning" can take place. Either the net remembers everything too much and so very quickly ceases to be sensitive to new inputs, or else, in the process of retaining sensitivity, so little is remembered that learning can hardly have been said to occur. This difficulty can be overcome in simulated "memistors" by adding a longer time-course storage device which sets a bias on the reception of new inputs and is in turn itself altered by those inputs (Widrow & Hoff, 1960). The glia could function in this fashion. Even their electrical responsivity is some thousandfold longer in duration than that recorded as impulsive activity from neurons. There is every reason to suppose that such graded electrical activity would influence the transmitted excitations of the adjacent neural net, which in turn, through the phase-lock-in biochemical mechanism, could alter the state of the glia.

Is there any evidence to support directly these notions? Most persuasive are the as-yet meager results of histological and histochemical analyses of neural tissue obtained from animals raised under conditions of sensory deprivation. Weiskrantz (1958) has shown that in the retinas of dark-reared kittens, Mueller fibers are scarce—and Mueller fibers are glia. Brattgård (1952), Liberman (1962), and Rasch, Swift, Riesen and Chow (1961) have all shown deficiencies in RNA production of the retinal ganglion cells in such dark-reared subjects.

Meanwhile, experiments by a group of "worm-runners" have added fuel to the RNA fire. Flat worms (planaria) were trained by McConnell, Jacobson and Kimble (1959) in a water filled trough illuminated from above. The animals were placed in the trough until they showed no reaction to the turning on and off of the light. Then each illumination of 3 seconds' duration was accompanied for the last second by an electric shock passed through the water. Initially the worms contracted and turned only when the shock was on; gradually, the frequency of such responses increased during the first 2 seconds, when only illumination was presented. Once a worm had reached criterion it was immediately cut in half transversely, the halves isolated and allowed to regenerate. About a month later, when regeneration was complete, all subjects were retained to the original criterion; whereas original training averaged 134 trials, subsequent to transverse sectioning the original head ends averaged 40 and the original tail ends, 43.2 trials. (A trained but uncut group showed about the same amount of savings; a group trained after the cut took more trials than did the original group's initial training, thus a sensitization effect was ruled out.)

On the basis of these and other similar results, McConnell and his collaborators suggest that whatever the physiological change responsible for this memory process, it must occur throughout the worm's body. Corning and John (1961) tested the hypothesis that RNA may somehow be involved in this mechanism. They immersed the halves of the trained worms in a weak solution of ribonuclease in order to destroy the RNA. The heads regenerated in ribonuclease showed savings as great as control heads; on the other hand, tails regenerated in ribonuclease showed no such savings. The brain-stored memory mechanism was apparently resistant to this exposure to ribonuclease, whereas the somatically mediated "worm memory" was destroyed.

So much for evidence that RNA is somehow involved in the memory storage mechanism. The suggestion is essentially that neural activity results in the rearrangement of the sequence of monomers on the nucleic acid molecule; or at least that a more or less permanent change takes place in the concentration of one or another of the specifically identifiable types of RNA. There is some reason to suspect that nucleic acids are insufficiently rich in alternatives and that their modification proceeds too slowly to handle all that is needed in the way of event storage—for example, to account for the results of experiments on the recall of tachistoscopically presented data. Yet it can be argued that the change in nucleic acids underlies the formation of polystable proteins, and that changes in these are then responsible for the changes in subsequent neuronal activity, and thus behavior.

(2) An independent, though also chemical, approach stems from the classical view of memory as the result of change in resistance to synaptic conduction. Here attention is focused on a neural transmitter substance, acetylcholine. Variations in concentration of acetylcholinesterase activity (presumably related to the amount of production of acetylcholine) are found related to learning by rats (Krech, Rosenzweig, & Bennett, 1956). Specifically, acetylcholinesterase activity has been found to correlate with genetic strain selected for "maze dull" and "maze bright" performance (Krech, Rosenzweig, & Bennett, 1959). Further, acetylcholinesterase activity is related to amount of varied experience available during early postnatal development. Finally, evidence has been presented that those parts of the brain known to serve a specific sensory mode through which experience is channeled, selectively show this increase in acetylcholinesterase activity.

Closely related to this series of studies are some recent results obtained in the neurohistological laboratory. Though the brain's nerve cells do not divide, they can grow new branches. This has been dramatically demonstrated (Rose, Malis, & Baker, 1961) in a study of the effects on brain of high energy radiations produced by a cyclotron. Minute, sharply demarcated laminar destructions (often limited to a single cell layer, and this not necessarily the most superficial one) were produced in rabbit cerebral cortex when high energy beams were stopped short by the soft tissue. The course of destruction and restitution was studied histologically. Intact nerve cells were seen to send branches into the injured area; these branches became progressively more organized until, from all that could be observed through a microscope or measured electrically, the tissue had been repaired.

The organization of the branches of nerve cells could well be guided by the glia that pervasively surround these branches. Such directive influences are known to be essential in the regeneration of peripheral nerves. Schwann cells, close relatives of glia, form a column into which the budding fibers must grow if they are not to get tangled in a matted mess of their own making.

The assumption could well be entertained that glial cell division is somehow spurred by those same activities recounted above as important to memory storage. The resulting pattern of the glial bed would form the matrix into which nerve cell fiber growth occurs. Thus guided, fiber growth is directed by its own excitation—the whole mechanism based, however, on the long-lasting intervention of glia. This dual mechanism for memory storage—RNA and synaptic facilitation—would account for the interfering effects obtained after the administration of electroconvulsive shock (Brady, 1951; Duncan, 1949; Madsen & McGaugh, 1961; Pearlman, Sharpless, & Jarvik, 1961; Poschel, 1957) and in the occurrence of spontaneous "restitution" as well: the growing nerve cell fiber is ameboid and can temporarily retract its tip, which is made up of a helical winding of small globular protein molecules. After the convulsive insult is over, first tentative, then more vigorous probings can again be resumed in some "random-walk" fashion by the nerve fiber tip, as has been suggested for normal growth by Von Foerster (1948). The glial substrate, assumed undamaged, will perform its guiding function to effect the apparent restitution.

These are but some of the data accumulating in neurobiological and neuropsychological laboratories. Work is proceeding on lasting changes produced on nerve membranes by activity (Robertson, 1961; Sjöstrand, 1960); on changes in relation between facilitation and inhibition as a result of continuous activity in small looped networks (Curtis & Eccles, 1960; Eccles, 1953; Landahl, McCulloch, & Pitts, 1943; MacKay & McCulloch, 1952; McCulloch, 1957; McCulloch & Pitts, 1943; Von Foerster, 1948; Wall, 1961); in the speeding of consolidation (Abt, Essman, & Jarvik, 1961; Breen & McGaugh, 1961; Madsen & McGaugh, 1961; McGaugh, 1961; McGaugh & Petrinovich, 1959; McGaugh & Thomson, 1962; McGaugh, Thomson, Westbrook, & Hudspeth, 1962; McGaugh, Westbrook, & Burt, 1961; McGaugh, Westbrook, & Thomson, 1962; Pearlman & Jarvik, 1961; Pearlman, Sharpless, & Jarvik, 1961); on delineating the differences between the neural mechanisms involved in learning from those involved in remembering (Kraft, Obrist, & Pribram, 1960; Stamm & Pribram, 1960, 1961; Stamm & Warren, 1961; Weiskrantz, in press).

There is little doubt that the questions asked have become specific: we are beginning to chart this area of ignorance with precision. No longer must we *assume* etchings on a *tabula rasa;* rather, we ask what the specific neurochemical and neurohistological processes involved are. No longer are we concerned whether the memory trace is indeed laid down in the brain; rather, we ask how many kinds of memory traces there are. No longer do we worry whether an act is rooted in an inherited biology or in an unobservable result of mental experience; the effects of experience are recorded in a biological process probably so akin to the instruments of inheritance that the geneticists are among the most actively interested in the memory mechanism.

We, neurological nativists by interest and empirical scientists by method, need no longer live as split personalities in our search for the laws that govern learning. The biological laboratory, having achieved the means for study of the modes through which experience is registered, asks immediately how experience registered might again be known, that is, appropriately retrieved. And, having posed this question, the need is to know more about other processes that determine knowledge.

ON THE NEUROLOGY OF KNOWLEDGE

I would propose that all forms of effective surprise grow out of combinatorial activity—a placing of things in new perspectives. But it is somehow not simply a taking of known elements and running them together by algorithm into a welter of permutations . . . (p. 20).

One final point about the combinatorial acts that produce effective surprise: they almost always succeed through the exercise of technique (Bruner, 1962, p. 22).

As already indicated, in his role of experimentalist the neuropsychologist at this stage of the development of his science works largely within an empiricistic frame. He makes much use of the inductive method to acquire knowledge, and is therefore apt to tackle the problem of knowledge by an interest in the process of inductive inference. In his own work, he asks simply phrased questions. These are often based on neuroanatomical considerations and/or introspections consensually validated. Greater precision is attained when the questions can be reformulated on the basis of manipulations of the variables that reliably alter some observable response of the neural tissue or of the behavior of the organism. He is wary of what he calls generalizations—and rarely resorts to deductions of any complexity. But the power of the inductive method is hardly questioned. Even though he recalls David Hume's injunctions, the experimentalist is somewhat surprised that the problem of inductive inference is still a thorny one for the philosopher. Further, when the experimentalist hears the philosopher of science solve the "causal" dilemma by invoking the notion of "subjective probability," his interest and concern are indeed piqued:

It seems to me that the view of almost all writers on induction in the past and including the great majority of contemporary writers, contains one basic mistake. They regard inductive reasoning as an *inference* leading from some known propositions, called the premises or evidence, to a new proposition, called the conclusion, usually a law or a singular prediction. From this point of view the result of any particular inductive reasoning is the *acceptance* of a new proposition (or its rejection, or its suspension until further evidence is found, as the case may be). This seems to me wrong. On the basis of this view it would be impossible to refute Hume's dictum that there are no rational reasons for induction. . . . I would think instead that inductive reasoning about a proposition should lead, not to acceptance or rejection, but to the assignment of a number to the proposition, viz., its [Credence] value. This difference may perhaps appear slight; in fact, however, it is essential (Carnap, 1962, pp. 316-317).

In this connection, Carnap defines "Credence" in terms of "the non-observable microstate of [a person's] central nervous system, not his consciousness, let alone his overt behavior" (p. 306). Already alerted, the neuropsychologist leaps at the words "non-observable microstate of the central nervous system." The philosopher has been forced by his logic to contend with the very thing the neuropsychologist is studying. The die is cast. As we will see, it is the neuropsychologist who must add credence to the philosopher's persuasive argument for credence.

Initially, the search for this nonobservable microstate must lead to the exposition of neural events coincident with phenomena heretofore treated as subjective (based on verbally reported introspections). The neuropsychologist, as well as the philosopher, has been faced with the problem that an individual's behavior is not easily described or predicted solely in terms of the probabilities of those occurrences in his environment which can be objectively analyzed. So often his behavior reaches concordance with such objective "reality" only by stages (Gibson & Gibson, 1955). This step by step procedure has been put to use by psychologists of the descriptive persuasion in the "shaping" of behavior (Ferster & Skinner, 1957).

The disparity between observed behavior and its more obvious determinants is most readily accounted for if one assumes the presence of a memory process that guides behavior, that memory process lawfully influenced by other ongoing processes in the organism and open to gradual, graded change by the objective events (Bruner, 1957; MacKay, 1956; Pribram, 1960b). But as long as such explanations rest on assumption, counter-arguments based on purely observable events, though less powerful explanatory tools, have the advantage of reliability. Once objective indices of "subjectivity" were available, this advantage would be lost. The neural sciences are now providing data to validate the presence of subjective states that intervene between experienced observables and observable actions determined by that experience.

First, the evidence that brain events take place concurrent with identifiable "states" in the absence of observable behavior. The most frequent and reliable data regard electrical records made from the precentral "motor" cortex of the brain. A change in electrical activity can be observed to accompany a subject's subsequently reported "thoughts" about preparing to move an extremity or a portion of it, even when the most careful observation (using electromyography) shows no muscular contractions to be taking place. The change in electrical activity is usually limited to the part of the brain cortex that controls the actions of the part "thought" about (Gurevich, 1961; Jasper & Penfield, 1949).

Such states can also be identified in animals (Adey, 1961). The subjects are cats. Fine wires are inserted into the depth of the brain and tied to the skull so that they can do no harm. The cats are placed facing a Y-shaped raised drawbridge. At the ends of the arms of the "Y" are two boxes about a yard apart, one of which contains food. As a flashing light is turned on above the box with the food, the drawbridge is lowered to form a path to each box.

During the first exposure to this situation, electrical recordings made from the brain of the cat disclose the characteristic pattern of alerting. With repeated exposure the recordings show increasing habituation. Since the cat begins to "expect" food when she reaches a box, the alerting pattern occurs only when she has chosen the empty box. The cat's performance can be judged as reliably from the recordings as from her observed behavior.

Occasionally, however, the electrical recording from the brain shows something is askew *before* the animal proceeds across the bridge. Whenever this record is observed, performance is again found to be at the chance level. In this instance, the brain record reflects uncertainty and *anticipates* the performance change: the "crucial microstate of the central nervous system" has been discerned.

But to go on with Carnap's logical analysis of credence. The quotation about the nonobservable microstate of the nervous system begun above continues:

> . . . Since his behavior is influenced by his state, *we can directly determine characteristics of his state from his behavior.* Thus experimental methods have been developed for the determination of some values and some general characteristics of the utility function and the credence function (subjective probability) of a person on the basis of his behavior with respect to bets and similar situations. Interesting investigations of this kind have been made by F. Mosteller, and P. Nogee and more recently by D. Davidson and P. Suppes and others (Carnap, 1962, p. 306) [italics mine].

If characteristics of the microstate can be obtained *directly* through operations on the behavior of the organism, what need is there for invoking the state at all—let behavior be a function of the operations imposed on the organism as the operationally inclined descriptive psychologists suggest. Gone is the very richness of the credence idea expressed in the sentence before: a microstate of the central nervous system, *"Not* his consciousness, *let alone* his overt behavior" [italics mine]. And lost are all of the fascinating determinants of microstate that are states in themselves, and not operations externally imposed on the behavior of the organism. Surely, Carnap does not want to lose as problems such possible determinants of betting as "level of activation" (Hebb, 1955; Lindsley, 1951; Magoun, 1958 and "tendency to explore" (q.v. below), both of which have ample neurological referents. And he need not. After all, it is this difficulty of what determines state which raised the issue of subjectivity in the first place—it is this issue which repeatedly drives psychologists into the neurological laboratory (for example, Neal Miller). And it is the work from the neurological laboratory that describes the formation and transformations of these important state variables.

Take, for instance, tendency to explore. Removal of a certain part of the brain cortex of monkeys has been shown to restrict their sampling of the environment (Pribram, 1959b). Normal subjects make choices out of a set of events that is, to a considerable extent, determined by their experience with that or a similar set. Damage to this particular part of the brain impairs the control which experienced events ordinarily exercise in delimiting such sets. The most extreme and therefore the clearest example of this process and its derangement comes from an analysis of the mechanisms that govern the appreciation of novelty.

An event is novel to an organism when it differs from prior events sufficiently to result in identifiable physiological and behavioral responses grouped together as the "orienting reaction." Repetition of the event leads to a gradual disappearance of the orienting reaction. The organism is said to habituate to the stimulus. However, habituation is not due to loss of reactivity: when, e.g., during repetition the intensity of a tone is suddenly diminished, the orienting responses reappear full blown. Also, when the duration of such a tone is suddenly shortened after habituation has occurred, an orienting reaction appears, but only after the tone has ceased, i.e., during the "silent period" which marks the difference between the length of this and the prior events (Sokolov, 1960).

These experiments and others leave beyond doubt that habituation of the orienting reaction reflects an active process guided by neural events that are now under study. This active process involves a continuous matching of the current sensory (sense organ) input to some state that is the result of prior inputs. This state has sufficient precision of detail encoded from these prior inputs to warrant the label "model" or "representation." It thus serves as the ground against which events attain sign(al)ificance—the set from which the environment can be sampled.

But there is more. This state, the psychologist's "set," which can be modified both by other organismic states and by the current input, has identifiable neurological determinants. Two basic mechanisms interact at the several levels of the nervous system. The first leads to progressive differentiation by the convergence of signals from disparate sources onto a common neuronal pool. The action of these pools is to admit and relay "this input or that," canceling out the other. The laws which govern such switching mechanisms are for the most part still to be formulated. The result of their action is better known: behavior comes for a period under the control of one or another set of input variables.

The second mechanism is possibly the more primitive. Even at the receptor, contrast is enhanced by inhibitory interaction extending laterally among neuron sheets. When the energy form, to which the receptor is sensitive, is distributed along a gradient, such lateral inhibition markedly steepens the gradient by effecting a diminution of the normal, spontaneous excitation of all elements except those most centrally located in the field (Hartline, Wagner, & Ratliff, 1956).

Some of the richness gained by the operation of these mechanisms even at the brain stem level of the nervous system (of relatively uncomplicated frogs) can be appreciated from the following experiments:

"Newness" neurons: These cells have receptive fields about 30 degrees in diameter. . . . They are distributed so as to map continuously the visual field with much overlap. Such a neuron responds a little to sharp changes in illumination. If an object moves across the receptive field, there is a response whose frequency depends on the jerkiness, velocity, and direction of the movement, as well as on the size of the object. There is never an enduring response (p. 773).

"Sameness" neurons: Let us begin with an empty gray hemisphere for the visual field. There is usually no response of the cell to turning on and off the illumination. It is silent. We bring in a small dark object, say 1 to 2 degrees in diameter, and at a certain point in its travel, almost anywhere in the field, the cell suddenly "notices" it. Thereafter, wherever that object is moved it is tracked by the cell. Every time it moves, with even the faintest jerk, there is a burst of impulses that dies down to a mutter that continues as long as the object is visible. If the object is kept moving, the bursts signal discontinuities in the movement, such as the turning of corners, reversals, and so forth, and these bursts occur against a continuous background mutter that tells us the object is visible to the cell.

When the target is removed, the discharge dies down. If the target is kept absolutely stationary for about two minutes, the mutter also disappears. Then one can sneak the target around a bit, slowly, and produce no response, until the cell "notices" it again and locks on (Lettvin, Maturana, Pitts, & McCulloch, 1961, p. 774).

The ubiquity of the mechanisms is attested by the following quotations:

The organization of visual neurons in the cortex may be explained by two principles of inhibition, which were first described in the retina: (a) reciprocal inhibition of antagonistic neurons in the same region; and (b) lateral inhibition of synergistic neurons in neighboring regions (Jung, 1961, p. 668).

Evidence has been presented to support the conception that the posterior and the frontal intrinsic systems serve different aspects of the problem-solving process. The argument has been forwarded that two major classes of behavior can be distinguished, differential and intentional. . . . The distinction between neural mechanisms that serve differentiation and those that subserve intention is not a new one. Sherrington makes this distinction in his description of the coordination of reflexes (1947): The "singleness of action from moment to moment is the keystone in the construction of the individual." This singleness of action comes about in two ways—"interference" between and "allied combinations" of reflexes. In his analysis of "interference" (or antagonism) between reflexes, Sherrington forwards concepts such as inhibition, induction and spinal contrast—concepts which have relevance to discriminative behavior (for example . . . the use of the concept "induction" by Skinner [1938] for the occurrence of the "hump" in the graphical representation of complex discrimination learning). Sherrington uses these concepts to provide an understanding of the differences between reflex behaviors to different inputs. On the other hand, Sherrington's discussions of "allied combinations" of reflexes are an attempt to understand behavior regulated by outcomes: "the new reflex breaks in upon a condition of equilibrium, which latter is itself a reflex," a notion which has been enlarged upon by Cannon (1941) and more recently by Wiener (1949). In discussing allied combinations of reflexes, concepts such as reinforcement, convergence, summation and facilitation are used by Sherrington—concepts which have relevance to intentional behavior (Pribram, 1960a, p. 1340).

One thing stands out: a most important effect of these interacting mechanisms is continuous redundancy reduction (Barlow, 1961). The nervous system seems to ask, at every level, "Is this news?" As a whole, its activity has been compared to that of an editor whose function it is to communicate only that which is newsworthy. But news must be "fit" to communicate, that is, it must fit within the context of the encoded residuals of prior inputs, yet be insufficiently "same" to result in a signal of "mismatch." The accepted must not be too far beyond the expected.

These data have a fundamental bearing on the choice of theory used to subsume the data that have been accumulated by experimenting empiricists dealing with the problems of knowledge: with perception, learning, and decision. Again and again such theorists have found it necessary to postulate some mediating states, events intermediating between those to be perceived or learned and the responses made by the organism to these events. But always this need has come up against the operationist's unease with nonobservables. Only theorists of the "cognitive" persuasion have steadfastly and clearly maintained that there is no other way out of the dilemmas posed by the richness and orderliness of individuals' variability in reactions to apparently identical situations. And now, the new neurology suddenly places these cognitivists with their sets, expectancies, plans, and credences, on solid operational ground. Meanwhile, descriptive behavior theorists and professed nontheorists have reached the awkward position of inability even to properly define "stimulus events," much less their state variables and, most importantly, the reinforcers without which they cannot work. Neuropsychology here has the role not so much of theory-building, as of selection among otherwise equally persuasive (and each in its own way defective) approaches to the same body of knowledge. Without question the decision, for this season at least, goes to the cognitive theorists—provided they adhere to the golden operational rules of the behaviorist. This is after all what a neuropsychologically based, empiricistic, subjective behaviorism is about (Miller, Galanter, & Pribram, 1960).

The old puzzle of induction consists in the following dilemma. On the one hand we see that inductive reasoning is used by the scientist and the man in the street every day without apparent scruples; and we have the feeling that it is valid and indispensable. On the other hand, once Hume awakens our intellectual conscience, we find no answer to his objection. Who is right, the man of common sense or the critical philosopher? We see that, as so often, both are partially right. Hume's criticism of the customary forms of induction was correct. But still the basic idea of common sense thinking is vindicated: induction, if properly reformulated, can be shown to be valid by rational criteria (Carnap, 1961, p. 318).

ON BRAIN AND THE STRUCTURE OF MIND

There has been a great deal of speculation in traditional philosophy which might have been avoided if the importance of structure, and the difficulty of getting behind it, had been realized (Russell, 1956, p. 61).

These considerations of neuropsychologically based subjective behaviorism lead directly into a discussion of the ever vexing dichotomous formulation of mind versus brain. I have dealt with this subject extensively elsewhere (Pribram, 1962a). Some additional comments can now be made, however. The argument was forwarded that the mind-brain gap would be closed by experimental results obtained when variables in two adjacent universes of discourse (for instance, the neural and the behavioral) are simultaneously manipulated. Reference terms between these universes result. The caution was voiced that communication would never amount to complete transliteration. The limitations encountered in any communication (even within the same universe of discourse) have been ably discussed by Quine (1960). These limitations apply to an even greater extent when the levels at which the discourse is directed are disparate. But it is in the very recognition of these limitations that the problem becomes resolved: pseudo-monistic identity of the material with the mental process (or the converse) and dualistic parallelism are no longer possible solutions. Once levels of discourse are recognized as such, and the potentialities and limitations of communication between them are accepted, the only recourse is to a truly monistic, seemingly pluralistic, multilevel *structural* mindbrain. As one scientist-philosopher (Rioch, personal communication) aptly put it, to have mind there must be at least two brains.

Mental terms are primarily derived from propositional verbal reports of introspection; these verbal reports must be analyzed in the linguistic social context within which the speaker and listener communicate, and interpreted in conjunction with nonpropositional aspects such as the kinesics of the verbal report and other instrumental behaviors supplied by the reporter. But validity is a level loving thing; when levels can become meshed

we are apt to consider a report valid. So, to the extent that neural (or
other organ system) data extend validity into the biological realm of discourse, mental terms become respectable even to the tough minded physicalist. Ask any physical or biological scientist to discuss vision and he won't
bat an eyelid, though this term is no less mental than is its generic concept, perception; and if we recognize perception, what about emotion,
cognition, or volition? The difference is, of course, the degree to which
meshing of levels of discourse has taken place. In the case of vision, the
physical descriptions of the energies that activate the eye, the minute
structure of the eye, the afferent paths into and through the central nervous
system, and the central control over the optic mechanism are all thoroughly in hand, as are some of the relations between these structures. Furthermore, these descriptions go into the structure of the perceptual events
in detail; knowledge at different levels is available about color, pattern,
brightness, and visual field. Finally, level by level reference terms are
daily encountered, not only in the ophthalmological and neurological clinics,
but as well in the daily experience of everyone who does bat his eyelids to
demonstrate the relation between "I see" and "eye."

Structure, hierarchically arranged by reference terms among levels:
this is what the biologist usually refers to as process or mechanism. When
mechanism is so conceived, it does not violate logic and experience as
does the usual extreme mechanistic, reductionist position. The Beethoven
symphony to which I am at the moment listening is not in one sense reducible to the mechanics of the score, nor of the recording, receiver, ampli-
fier, and speaker system which is emitting it; nor is it completely described
by the contortions set up in my auditory apparatus by the describable
wave patterns impinging on my ears. All these and more are components—
but something more than this constitutes the symphony. This something
more is not mystical. Musicians call it structure.

I do not consider the mystery of the symphony the more (nor the less)
mysterious for the fact that one very crucial element in the structure of its
reproduction is a piece of light cardboard shaped in a cone, whose crucial
characteristics are difficult to pin down. I do not invoke the epithet "men-
talist" at the British Industries Corporation, nor call them less competent
engineers because they say:

> Your own ear is the best judge of the ability of a speaker system to recreate
> the emotional impact of the original musical performance. Technical details
> can not be expected to answer the question "Does it sound natural?" Each
> person must listen and judge for himself (British Industries Corporation,
> 1962, p. 77).

I merely validate their experience with my own—which if possible includes running pure tones, harmonics, and complex sounds through portions of the equipment, to satisfy my desire for minimal distortion. But

I also listen to the symphony. And, in the same way, I also unashamedly listen to my own introspections and to verbal reports of others, as well as to the records of instrumental behavior and to the responses of neurons, to build my multilevel monistic structure of the neuropsychological apparatus.

And your reply, rightly, may well be, "Bully for you, but why should I accept your view of the universe and the way it ought to be constructed?" Or, to put it another way, can the search for constants or invariants in the exact natural sciences be properly extended to include the problems faced by the social disciplines? As a *neuro*psychologist my answer is a resounding yes. I would not deny Eve her root biological entity, her identity and unity. Yet the many faces shown by the social Eve are nonetheless real for their evanescence. Physics has gracefully accepted the principles of complementarity and of indeterminacy: one way of looking at the natural world complements, not necessarily supplements, another; what at one level of analysis appears structurally stable and ordered may, at another level, reveal a goodly amount of chaos—and structure is often shown to emerge from the very probabilities that describe the amount of this chaos.

Are matters so utterly different in the biological-social science enterprise which comes to a focus in neuropsychology? If the answer were a simple "no" it should have been given easily by now. Wherein lies the difficulty? I believe that the complication lies in the fact that the behavioral, biological-social scientist interested in the mind–body problem finds his universe to be a mirror image of the universe constructed by the physical scientist who deals with the same problem. And it should not come as a surprise when each of these isomers, the one produced by the physicist and the one produced by the behavioral scientist, on occasion displays properties that differ considerably from one another, much as do optical isomers in organic chemistry.

I believe these images are mirrors because of differences in the direction generally pursued from each investigator's effective starting point, his own observation. The physical scientist, for the most part, constructs his universe by ever more refined analysis of systems of input variables, that is, sensory stimuli to which he reacts. The form of the reaction (cathode-ray tube, solid-state device, chromatography, or galvanometer) is unimportant, except that it provides a sufficiently broad communicative base. Constancies are gradually retrieved from manipulations and observations of these input variables under a variety of conditions. As these constants achieve stability, the "correctness" of the views that produced them is asserted: the physical universe is properly described.

In the social disciplines the direction pursued is often just the reverse. Analysis is made of *action* systems (cf. Parsons & Bales, 1953). The exact nature of the input to the actor (including the observing scientist) is of little consequence, provided it has sufficient communicative base; the effect of action on the system is the subject of analysis. It matters little (perhaps because the cause is usually multiple and/or indeterminable) if a currency is deflated because of fear of inflation, depression, personal whim, or misguided economic theory. The effects of deflation can be studied, are knowable. And once known, the action *becomes* corrective; the resulting stabilization, constancy, is interpreted as evidence for the "correctness" of the action that produced the correction. Appropriate norms for the social universe become established.

One striking difference between the two images thus formed is immediately apparent. The physicist's macroscopic universe is the more stable, predictable one: "It does not hurt the moon to look at it" (Eddington, 1958, p. 227). For the most part, it is as he moves to ever more microscopic worlds that uncertainties are asserted. The scientist concerned with social matters finds it just the other way round: it seemingly does little harm to the man to look at him; but seriously look at his family, his friendships, or his political-economic systems and what you had started out to look at changes with the looking. Here indeterminacy comes to plague the macrostructure; it is in the stabilities of microanalysis that the mirage of safety appears.

The philosopher of science and the neuropsychologist, interested as they must be in the mind-brain problem, stand by necessity squarely between these two mirror images. If they deny the evidence that there are two images by showing interest in only one, or by denying the "reality" of the other, they are in dangerous waters and liable to shipwreck in the strong currents of mentalism, physicalism, and dualism. Their searches for the one "real" world and its mirror image may well be interminable, since an alternative possibility is equally likely to be a correct one.

The problem can be grasped, however, if it is dealt with in terms of isomeric forms of the same event universe—isomers differing in that their *structures* mirror each other. Put another way, the problem resolves itself into a meshing of the descriptive and the normative sciences. The suggestion is that structure in descriptive science ordinarily emerges from the analysis of the relations between systems and their subsystems; that in the normative sciences, it is largely the other way round: structure emerges when the relation between a system and its "supersystem" is studied.

If this view is correct, we should find normative statements about the nature of the physical world when these are constructed from the examination of relations between a set of systems and a higher order system. Is not relativity just this sort of statement? This is not a social scientist speaking about the "criterion problem":

The modest observer . . . [is] faced with the task of choosing between a number of frames of space with nothing to guide his choice. They are different in the sense that they frame the material objects of the world, including the observer himself, differently; but they are indistinguishable in the sense that the world as framed in one space conducts itself according to precisely the same laws as the world framed in another space. Owing to the accident of having been born on a particular planet our observer has hitherto unthinkingly adopted one of the frames; but he realises that this is no ground for obstinately asserting that it must be the right frame. Which is the right frame?

At this juncture Einstein comes forward with a suggestion—

"You are seeking a frame of space which you call the *right* frame. In what does its *rightness* consist?"

You are standing with a label in your hand before a row of packages all precisely similar. You are worried because there is nothing to help you to decide which of the packages it should be attached to. Look at the label and see what is written on it. Nothing.

"Right" as applied to frames of space is a blank label. It implies that there is something distinguishing a right frame from a wrong frame; but when we ask what is this distinguishing property, the only answer we receive is "Rightness," which does not make the meaning clearer or convince us that there is a meaning (Eddington, 1958, p. 20).

Obversely, we should find descriptive statements about the nature of the social world when these derive from a study of the relations between a system and its subsystems. Doesn't the following passage fit this requirement?

Role behavior depends first of all on the role positions that society establishes; that is certain ways of behaving toward others are defined by different positions (Hilgard, 1962, p. 482).

Aren't statements about roles unambiguously descriptive?

Attention to structure has left the neuropsychologist, perhaps a bit dizzily, contemplating two mirror images of a universe. By looking to the right, he has profited greatly from the researches of his neurobiological colleagues in matters concerning memory mechanisms. Is there any substantial insight to be reaped from a look to the left?

ON AN EFFECTIVE ETHIC
—A NEUROPSYCHOLOGICAL DIVIDEND

Considered in the main, the best communities are those which have the best men for their members, and the best men are the members of the best communities. Circle as this is, it is not a vicious circle. The two problems of the best man and best state are two sides, two distinguishable aspects of the one problem, how to realize in human nature the perfect unity of homogeneity and specification; and when we see that each of these without the other is unreal, then we see that (speaking in general) the welfare of the state and the welfare of its individuals are questions which it is mistaken and ruinous to separate. Personal morality and political and social institutions cannot exist apart, and (in general) the better the one the better the other. The community is moral because it realizes personal morality; personal morality is moral because and in so far as it realizes the moral whole (Bradley, 1951, p. 123 [1876]).

The argument presented, if it has merit, should prove supportable by evidence. The nature of this evidence ought to demonstrate an effective influence felt in the social disciplines as a result of knowledge held on the neuropsychological level. Is there any such evidence?

There is, and it comes from an unexpected and controversial quarter. The fact of controversy in itself attests to effective influence; the unexpectedness demonstrates the little recognized importance of the neuropsychological aspects of the contribution.

I am of course speaking of Sigmund Freud and of psychoanalysis. I have elsewhere (Pribram, 1962b) reviewed the *Zeitgeist* in Vienna, the setting in which Freud made his contributions. This setting included the activities of the Viennese functionalists, especially in the person of Brentano, heirs to the issue of the elusive activity of thinking versus the determinable content of the thought process, which had been raised by the Würzburg school.

In one sense, psychoanalysis is a *technique* whereby the activity of thinking can be explored: whereas the Würzburgers provided a set, in the form of a problem to be explored by the thinker, the psychoanalytic method allows exploration among many possible sets. The Würzburgers thus arrived at lawful descriptions of content within the sets they had presented; the psychoanalysts, by contrast, have attempted to describe a lawful, developmental process of formation of sets (and subsets) by eliciting a variety of partitions, graded according to accessibility, to which content can be subject. Basic to the success of the psychoanalytical approach was an uncompromising faith in the lawfulness of the relation between accessibility (availability to conscious introspection and thus to verbal report) and the structure of psychological processes. This faith presupposed a thorough acquaintance both with the mechanisms by which experience leaves its mark and by which it is utilized: in other words, with the mechanisms that determine memory storage and retrieval.

Only within the past decade has it become generally known that Freud indeed relied heavily on a model of the way in which experience leaves its mark on the nervous system. As a rule, Freud's contributions to basic neurology have been ignored except to point out that he left them behind to go on to endeavors felt to be really "important" or "misguided" according to whether the viewer came from a soft or a hard science background. Careful examination of Freud's *Project for a Scientific Psychology* (1954) and perusal of later works (in collaboration with Dr. Merton Gill) shows that despite protestations to the contrary, Freud repeatedly turned to neurology for his model—that indeed his model, though altered in detail and emphasis, remained in most essentials the model first conceived as "The Project." (As Gill has pointed out, the difference between the structural and topographic models is one of emphasis: during the structural phase Freud deals primarily with the relative accessibility to consciousness of experienced events; during the topographic phase he deals primarily with the relation between drive and satisfaction, irrespective of accessibility. The model changes little. It is viewed from different vantages. And it continues to be neurological.)

The question remains to be answered as to whether this model performed some service other than to sustain Freud's morale (in the paradoxical sense that he could blame many of his creative woes on its inadequacy). Another way to put this question is to ask whether the neurological model is essentially, crucially, though in unrecognized form, involved in psychoanalytic dogma.

Neurology has little to contribute to the study of consciousness even today. Whatever neurologizing is done depends on a very few facts: the *déjà vu* phenomenon when epilepsy stems from an anterior temporal lobe focus; loss of awareness when the structures around the midline cerebral ventricles are manipulated; interruption of ongoing actions (including verbal) by excitations of certain locations on the brain cortex. These are not the threads from which any richly woven theory of consciousness, psychoanalytic or other, can be derived. Freud had to base his ideas in this area on the behavioral reports obtained from his patients, his knowledge of hysterical phenomena, and on his introspections.

Drive is certainly biologically conceived, and most psychologists, whether of analytical persuasion or not, feel that Freud's neurological background led to his emphasis on *Triebe* factors in the development and determination of behavior. Close reading of the Project shows this to be a half-truth. Drive is mentioned only once as such. Freud did speculate on the mechanism of *Unlust,* but to do this, he had to postulate a neurology of internal receptors and key (secretory) neurons only sparsely supported by the facts of his or our day. The neurological model is consonant with a mechanism of drive—but "drive" cannot be constructed from the neurological facts. Behavioral observation, especially of the infant, had a great deal to do with the construction of this part of the model in the Project.

Not the "unconscious"; not "instinct or drive"; what then is peculiarly neurological about psychoanalytic theory? Surprisingly, it is the mechanisms of defense. Composed as they are of the processes that determine memory and motive, which in turn were derived by Freud from the neural properties of resistance (to neural impulse conduction at the synapse) and cathexes (the graded potential changes to which neural tissue is subject), defenses are structures which would not have been conceived as such except by someone deeply concerned and conversant with the neural regulation of behavior.

The neurological nature of the conception "defense" can be recapitulated as follows: *At the tissue level*, Freud accepts the neuron doctrine—nervous tissue is made up of cells separated from one another by contact barriers (these were later called synapses by Sherrington). Contact barriers have the property, resistance. Resistance hinders the transmission of propagated, impulsive neural excitation—the nerve impulse—across the synapse. Neurons have two properties: (1) they transmit impulses along their extent and (2) they change their excitatory state in another, local, nontransmitted fashion. This second property, cathexis, plays a major role in all of Freud's thinking and, as I have indicated elsewhere, is a scientifically well-established, though until recently neglected, aspect of nervous tissue function.

At this level, Freud considers the memory trace as formed by selective lowering of synaptic resistances at locations subject to large and/or repeated excitations of the impulse type.

This has consequences at the brain system level. Within the core of the brain there are diffusely organized systems, within which neurons branch profusely and make contact more or less randomly with many other neurons (Freud provides a drawing). These he labels ψ or "nuclear." From the fact that behavior is selective, Freud reasons that the lowering of resistance must occur selectively among these contacts. Preferred paths develop along which excitation is propagated: the structure of the sum-total of these paths provides the retentive and selective control exercised over behavior by the nervous system, that is, this structure is the mechanism for memory and motive.

Two groups of factors determine the form of the memory-motive structure. Its location at the core of the brain makes it especially receptive to stimuli concerned in the regulation of the body's internal milieu (the work begun by Claude Bernard which led later to the enunciation by Cannon of the notion of homeostasis). These are Freud's drive factors and he spells out their presumed operation in detail. The second group of factors influences the ψ nuclear systems through another set, the projection systems, concerned more directly with sensory-motor relations between the organism and its external environment.

The reasoning then proceeds: since little can be done to alter the internal environment when this becomes necessary (for example, when the organism is hungry) except through changes made in the external, the two sets of factors come to converge (by simultaneity) in their effect on the ψ nuclear systems. This is especially the case in the human infant, dependent as he is on a caretaking person to effect those changes in his external environment necessary to his internal stability (or well being). Man's memory-motive structure, therefore, is laden with these doubly-determined pathways which "defend" his well being, that is, allow him to make adjustments in his external environment such that his milieu interieur does not suffer radical disequilibration. This part of the memory-motive structure is referred to by Freud as the defense mechanism—neural configurations based on experience that give selective direction to behavior.

At least three levels of defense are recognized. (1) Reflex defense, which is really no defense at all: this consists of an infant's built-in mechanism that distributes excitation generally throughout the nervous system, and so to effectors whose activity calls the attention of the caretaking person to the infant's distress. (2) Primary defense, which is a partial defense: this mechanism is operative when a memory trace has become established consequent to the experience of pain or "unlust." During primary defense, these memory traces are rapidly decathected, that is, they lose their excitatory potential. This is due to a precipitous discharge (much as that of a condensor) when the excitation in passage becomes overly great. The memory trace thus becomes temporarily inoperative (for example, it cannot affect awareness, thus memory; guide action, and so on). Nor is distress (pain, *Unlust*) prevented—but, since excitation shunts past the memory mechanism, this at least does not add to the generation and maintenance of the disequilibratory process. (3) The third, ordinarily operative, adult defense: here the network of memory traces consequent on the distressful experience has grown to sufficient proportions that excitation is "bound" within the network. Precipitous discharge does not occur and the cathected memory-trace network can exert a delaying and selective influence on more localized and patterned neural discharges (nerve impulses), and so control behavior.

This, then, is the structural nature of defenses. To complete the argument, the question must be posed as to whether this particular facet of psychoanalytic theory has had social impact. Much has been made recently of the replacement or dilution of the Protestant ethic by what is called the Freudian (Rieff, 1959). A case can be made for the proposition that the two ethics differ essentially in the way they conceive the interaction of the two types of determinants that compose the structure of human motive. Paradoxically, the Protestant ethic considers that (internal) drive factors need be defended *against* by socially (externally) imparted directives; the Freudian, because he believes that drive and social directive are symbiotic in establishing motive structure in the nervous system, comes to a less defensive view of defenses. In the Protestant ethic, control of behavior is based largely on the role of social determinants; control of behavior for the Freudian is exercised by a memory-motive structure which results from inexorable intermeshing of drive and social determinants. This structure is defensive only in that it defends against breakdown of the organism's homeostasis, with a consequent threat to the social fabric.

In the extreme sense, this structure neither defends society against man's drives (his "baser" nature) nor man against his society—though both claims have been made for it. Yet, in a special sense, the Freudian conception of defense does both, by the strength of recognition of each and of the mesh between the two. This is the strength that has had the power to make itself felt as an ethic; this is the strength that has led to effective impact. And this strength results to a remarkable extent from the highly detailed and accurate neurological origins of the conception.

"Considered in the main, the best communities are those which have the best men for their members, and the best men are the members of the best communities." And these best men possess the best defenses—best in that they mesh, through the neurological process, their biological and social systems. In the same sense, the best communities are also those which possess the best defenses—best in that they mesh, through accurate awareness of the structure of the political-economic process, their internal and international systems. Neuropsychology provides this model for an effective ethic.

In the preface to that admirable collection of essays of his called "Heretics," Mr. Chesterton writes these words: "There are some people—and I am one of them—who think that the most practical and important thing about a man is still his view of the universe. We think that for a landlady considering a lodger it is important to know his income, but still more important to know his philosophy. We think that for a general about to fight an enemy it is important to know the enemy's numbers, but still more important to know the enemy's philosophy. We think the question is not whether the theory of the cosmos affects matters, but whether in the long run anything else affects them." I think with Mr. Chesterton in this matter (James, 1931, p. 3).

REFERENCES

ABT, J. P., ESSMAN, W. B., & JARVIK, M. E. Ether induced retrograde amnesia for one-trial conditioning in mice. *Science,* 1961, **133,** 1477-1478.

ADEY, W. R. Studies of hippocampal mechanisms in learning. In *Brain mechanisms and learning.* Oxford: Blackwell Scientific Publications, 1961.

BACH, L. M. N. Regional physiology of the central nervous system. In E. A. Spiegel (Ed.), *Progress in neurology and psychiatry.* Vol. 17. New York: Grune & Stratton, 1962. Pp. 43-71.

BARLOW, H. B. Possible principles underlying the transformations of sensory messages. In W. A. Rosenblith (Ed.), *Sensory communication.* New York: M.I.T. Press and Wiley, 1961. Pp. 217-234.

BORING, E. G. *A history of experimental psychology.* (2nd ed.) New York: Appleton-Century-Crofts, 1950.

BRADLEY, F. H. My station and its duties (1876). In F. H. Bradley, *Ethical studies.* New York: Liberal Arts Press, 1951.

BRADY, J. V. The effect of electroconvulsive shock on a conditioned emotional response: the permanence of the effect. *J. comp. physiol. Psychol.*, 1951, **41**, 507-511.

BRATTGÅRD, S. The importance of adequate stimulation for the chemical composition of retinal ganglion cells during early post-natal development. *Acta Radiol.* Suppl. 96, 1952.

BREEN, R. A., & McGAUGH, J. Facilitation of maze learning with posttrial injections of picrotoxin. *J. comp. physiol. Psychol.*, 1961, **54**, 498-501.

BRIGGS, M. H., & KITTO, G. B. The molecular basis of memory and learning. *Psychol. Rev.*, 1962, **69**, 537-541.

BRITISH INDUSTRIES CORPORATION. Advertisement for the Wharfedale W60 achromatic speaker system. *High fidelity*, 1962, **77**, 77.

BRUNER, J. S. On perceptual readiness. *Psychol. Rev.*, 1957, **64**, 123-152.

BRUNER, J. S. *On knowing.* Cambridge: Harvard Univ. Press, 1962.

CANNON, W. B. The body physiologic and the body politic. *Science*, 1941, **93**, 1-10.

CARNAP, R. The aim of inductive logic. In E. Nagel, P. Suppes, and A. Tarski (Eds.), *Logic, methodology, and philosophy of science.* Stanford, Calif.: Stanford Univ. Press, 1962.

CORNING, W. C., & JOHN, E. R. The effects of ribonuclease on retention of conditioned response in regenerated planarian. *Science*, 1961, **134**, 1363-1365.

CURTIS, D. R., & ECCLES, J. C. Synaptic action during and after repetitive stimulation. *J. Physiol.*, 1960, **150**, 374-398.

DEUTSCH, J. A. Higher nervous function: the physiological bases of memory. *Annual Rev. Physiol.*, 1962, **24**, 259-286.

DUNCAN, C. P. The retroactive effect of electro-shock on learning. *J. comp. physiol. Psychol.*, 1949, **42**, 32-44.

ECCLES, J. C. Prolonged functional changes (plasticity) in the nervous system. In J. C. Eccles, *The neurophysiological basis of mind.* Oxford: Clarendon Press, 1953. Pp. 193-227.

EDDINGTON, A. *The nature of the physical world* (1927). Ann Arbor: Univ. Michigan Press, 1958.

EDDINGTON, A. *New pathways in science* (1934). Ann Arbor: Univ. Michigan Press, 1959.

FERSTER, C. B., & SKINNER, B. F. *Schedules of reinforcement.* New York: Appleton-Century-Crofts, 1957.

FREUD, S. Project for a scientific psychology. Appendix in *The origins of psychoanalysis: letters to Wilhelm Fliess, drafts and notes, 1887-1902.* New York: Basic Books, 1954.

FULLER, J. L., ROSVOLD, H. E., & PRIBRAM, K. H. The effect on affective and cognitive behavior in the dog of lesions of the pyriform-amygdala-hippocampal complex. *J. comp. physiol. Psychol.*, 1957, **50**, 89-96.

GAITO, J. A biochemical approach to learning and memory. *Psychol. Rev.*, 1961, **68**, 288-292.

GIBSON, J. J., & GIBSON, E. J. Perceptual learning: differentiation or enrichment. *Psychol. Rev.*, 1955, **62**, 32-41.

GUREVICH, B. KH. Electrical indicators of the "tuning-regulatory" activity of the parietal association areas. *Doklady Akademii Nauk USSR*, 1961, **141,** 505-508.

HARTLINE, H. K., WAGNER, H. G., & RATLIFF, F. Inhibition in the eye of limulus. *J. gen. Physiol.*, 1956, **39,** 651-673.

HEBB, D. O. *The organization of behavior.* New York: Wiley, 1949.

HEBB, D. O. Drives and the CNS (conceptual nervous system). *Psychol. Rev.*, 1955, **62,** 243-254.

HILGARD, E. *Introduction to psychology.* (3rd ed.) New York: Harcourt, Brace & World, 1962.

HYDÈN, H. Biochemical aspects of brain activity. In S. M. Farber and R. H. L. Wilson (Eds.), *Man and civilization, control of the mind.* New York: McGraw-Hill, 1961.

JAMES, W. *Pragmatism—a new name for some old ways of thinking.* (1907). New York: Longmans, 1931.

JASPER, H., & PENFIELD, W. Electrocorticograms in man: effect of voluntary movement upon the electrical activity of the precentral gyrus. *Arch. Psychiat. Z. Neurol.*, 1949, **183,** 163-174.

JUNG, R. Neuronal integration in the visual cortex and its significance for visual information. In W. Rosenblith (Ed.), *Sensory communication.* New York: M.I.T. Press and Wiley, 1961. Pp. 627-674.

KRAFT, MARCIA S., OBRIST, W. D., & PRIBRAM, K. H. The effect of irritative lesions of the striate cortex on learning of visual discriminations in monkeys. *J. comp. physiol. Psychol.*, 1960, **53,** 17-22.

KRECH, D., ROSENZWEIG, M. R., & BENNETT, E. L. Dimensions of discrimination and the level of cholinesterase activity in the cerebral cortex of the rat. *J. comp. physiol. Psychol.*, 1956, **49,** 261-268.

KRECH, D., ROSENZWEIG, M. R., & BENNETT, E. L. Correlation between brain cholinesterase and brain weight within two strains of rats. *Amer. J. Physiol.*, 1959, **196,** 31-32.

LANDAHL, H. D., McCULLOCH, W. S., & PITTS, W. A. statistical consequence of the logical calculus of nervous nets. *Bull. Mathematical Biophysics*, 1943, **5,** 135-137.

LETTVIN, J. Y., MATURANA, H. R., PITTS, W. H., & McCULLOCH, W. S. Two remarks on the visual system of the frog. In W. Rosenblith (Ed.), *Sensory communication.* New York: M.I.T. Press and Wiley, 1961. Pp. 757-776.

LIBERMAN, R. Retinal cholinesterase and glycolysis in rats raised in darkness. *Science,* 1962, **135,** 372-373.

LINDSLEY, D. B. Emotion. In S. S. Stevens (Ed.), *Handbook of experimental psychology.* New York: Wiley, 1951. Pp. 473-516.

MacKAY, D. M. The epistemological problem for automata. *Automata studies.* Princeton Univ. Press, 1956. Pp. 235-252.

MacKAY, D. M., & McCULLOCH, W. S. The limiting information capacity of a neuronal link. *Bull. math. Biophysics,* 1952, **14,** 127-135.

MADSEN, M. C., & McGAUGH, J. L. The effect of ECS on one-trial avoidance learning. *J. comp. physiol. Psychol.*, 1961, **54,** 522-523.

MAGOUN, H. W. *The waking brain.* Springfield, Ill.: Charles C. Thomas, 1958.

MALIS, L. I., PRIBRAM, K. H., & KRUGER, L. Action potentials in "motor" cortex evoked by peripheral nerve stimulation. *J. Neurophysiol.,* 1953, **16,** 161-167.

McCONNELL, J. O., JACOBSON, A. L., & KIMBLE, D. P. The effects of regeneration upon retention of a conditioned response in the planarian. *J. comp. physiol. Psychol.,* 1959, **52,** 1-5.

McCULLOCH, W. S. The stability of biological systems. In *Homeostatic mechanisms* (Vol. 10, *Brookhaven Symposia in Biology*). Upton, N.Y.: 1957. Pp. 207-214.

McCULLOCH, W. S., & PITTS, W. Logical calculus of the ideas immanent in nervous activity. *Bull. math. Biophysics,* 1943, **5,** 115-133.

McGAUGH, J. L. Facilitative and disruptive effects of strychnine sulphate on maze learning. *Psychol. Rep.,* 1961, **8,** 99-104.

McGAUGH, J. L., & PETRINOVICH, L. The effect of strychnine sulphate on maze-learning. *Amer. J. Psychol.,* 1959, **72,** 99-102.

McGAUGH, J. L., & THOMSON, C. W. Facilitation of simultaneous discrimination learning with strychnine sulphate. *Psychopharmacologia,* 1962, **3,** 166-172.

McGAUGH, J. L., THOMSON, C. W., WESTBROOK, W., & HUDSPETH, W. A further study of learning facilitation with strychnine sulphate. *Psychopharmacologia,* 1962, **3,** 352-360.

McGAUGH, J. L., WESTBROOK, W., & BURT, G. Strain differences in the facilitative effects of 5-7-diphenyl-1-3-diazadamantan-6-ol (1757 I.S.) on maze learning. *J. comp. physiol. Psychol.,* 1961, **54,** 502-505.

McGAUGH, J. L., WESTBROOK, W., & THOMSON, C. W. Facilitation of maze learning with posttrial injections of 5-7-diphenyl-1-3-diazadamantan-6-ol (1757 I.S.). *J. comp. physiol. Psychol.,* 1962, **55,** 710-713.

MILLER, G. A., GALANTER, E., & PRIBRAM, K. H. *Plans and the structure of behavior.* New York: Henry Holt, 1960.

MORRELL, F. Lasting changes in synaptic organization produced by continuous neural bombardment. In UNESCO Symposium (1959), *Brain mechanisms and learning.* Oxford: Blackwell Scientific Publications, 1961. Pp. 375-392.

PARSONS, T., & BALES, R. F. The dimensions of action-space. In T. Parsons, R. Bales, & E. Shils (Eds.), *Working papers in the theory of action.* New York: Free Press, 1953. Pp. 63-110.

PEARLMAN, C. A., & JARVIK, M. E. Retrograde amnesia produced by spreading cortical depression. *Federal Proc.,* 1961, **20,** 340. (Abstract)

PEARLMAN, C. A., SHARPLESS, S. K., & JARVIK, M. E. Retrograde amnesia produced by anesthetic and convulsant agents. *J. comp. physiol. Psychol.,* 1961, **54,** 109-112.

PENFIELD, W. Functional localization in temporal and deep sylvian areas. In H. Solomon, S. Cobb, & W. Penfield (Eds.), *The brain and human behavior* (Assn. Nerv. Ment. Dis., Vol. 36). Baltimore: Williams & Wilkins, 1958. Pp. 210-226.

POSCHEL, B. P. H. Proactive and retroactive effects of electroconvulsive shock on approach–avoidance conflict. *J. comp. physiol. Psychol.,* 1957, **50,** 392-396.

PRIBRAM, K. H. Toward a science of neuropsychology: method and data. In *Current trends in psychology and the behavioral sciences.* Univ. Pittsburgh Press, 1954. Pp. 115-142.

PRIBRAM, K. H. Neocortical function in behavior. In *Biological and biochemical bases of behavior*. Madison: Univ. Wisconsin Press, 1958. Pp. 151-172.

PRIBRAM, K. H. Neuropsychology in America. In *The Voice of America forum lectures* (Behavioral Science Series 9). Washington, D.C.: U. S. Information Agency, 1959. (a)

PRIBRAM, K. H. On the neurology of thinking. *Behav. Sci.*, 1959, **4**, 265-287. (b)

PRIBRAM, K. H. The intrinsic systems of the forebrain: an alternative to the concept of cortical association areas. In *Handbook of physiology, neuropsychology, II*. American Physiological Society, 1960. Pp. 1323-1344. (a)

PRIBRAM, K. H. A review of theory in physiological psychology. In *Annual review of psychology*. Palo Alto, Calif.: Annual Reviews, Inc., 1960. Pp. 1-40. (b)

PRIBRAM, K. H. Regional physiology of the central nervous system (the search for the engram—decade of decision). In E. A. Spiegel (Ed.), *Progress in neurology and psychiatry*. Vol. XVII. New York: Grune & Stratton, 1961. Pp. 45-57.

PRIBRAM, K. H. Interrelations of psychology and the neurological disciplines. In S. Koch (Ed.), *Psychology: a study of science*. Vol. 4. *Biologically oriented fields: their place in psychology and in biological sciences*. New York: McGraw-Hill, 1962. Pp. 119-157. (a)

PRIBRAM, K. H. The neuropsychology of Sigmund Freud. In A. J. Bachrach (Ed.), *Experimental foundations of clinical psychology*. New York: Basic Books, 1962. (b)

PRIBRAM, K. H. Neural mechanisms in memory and thought. In G. H. Glaser (Ed.), *EEG and behavior*. New York: Basic Books, 1963. Pp. 149-173.

PRIBRAM, K. H., & BAGSHAW, MURIEL. Further analysis of the temporal lobe syndrome utilizing fronto-temporal ablations. *J. comp. Neurol.*, 1953, **99**, 347-375.

PRIBRAM, K. H., KRUGER, L., ROBINSON, F., & BERMAN, A. J. The effects of precentral lesions on the behavior of monkeys. *Yale J. Biol. Med.*, 1955-1956, **28**, 428-443.

QUINE, W. O. *Word and object*. New York: Wiley, 1960.

RASCH, E., SWIFT, H., RIESEN, A. H., & CHOW, K. L. Altered structure and composition of retinal cells in dark-reared mammals. *Exp. Cell Res.*, 1961, **25**, 348-363.

RIEFF, P. *Freud; the mind of the moralist*. New York: Viking Press, 1959.

RIESMAN, D., GLAZER, N., & DENNY, R. *The lonely crowd: a study of the changing American character*. New Haven: Yale Univ. Press, 1950.

ROBERTSON, J. D. Cell membranes and the origin of mitochondria. In S. Kety & J. Elkes (Eds.), *Regional neurochemistry*. New York: Pergamon Press, 1961. Pp. 497-534.

ROSE, J. E., MALIS, L. I., & BAKER, C. P. Neural growth in the cerebral cortex after lesions produced by monoenergetic denterons. In W. Rosenblith (Ed.), *Sensory communication*. New York: M.I.T. Press and Wiley, 1961. Pp. 279-301.

RUSSELL, B. *Introduction to mathematical philosophy*. 1919. London: Allen & Unwin, 1956.

SHERRINGTON, C. *The integrative action of the nervous system.* 1906. New Haven: Yale Univ. Press, 1947.

SJÖSTRAND, F. S. Electron microscopy of myelin and of nerve cells and tissue. In J. N. Cumings (Ed.), *Modern scientific aspects of neurology.* London: Edward Arnold, 1960. Pp. 188-231.

SKINNER, B. F. *The behavior of organisms: an experimental analysis.* New York: Appleton-Century-Crofts, 1938.

SOKOLOV, E. N. In M. A. B. Brazier (Ed.), *The central nervous system and behavior: transactions of the third conference.* New York: Josiah Macy, Jr., Foundation, 1960.

STAMM, J. S., & PRIBRAM, K. H. Effects of epileptogenic lesions in frontal cortex on learning and retention in monkeys. *J. Neurophysiol.,* 1960, **23,** 552-563.

STAMM, J. S., & PRIBAM, K. H. Effects of epileptogenic lesions in inferotemporal cortex on learning and retention in monkeys. *J. comp. physiol. Psychol.,* 1961, **54,** 614-618.

STAMM, J. S., & WARREN, ANN. Learning and retention by monkeys with epileptogenic implants in posterior parietal cortex. *Epilepsia,* 1961, **2,** 229-242.

VON FOERSTER, H. *Das Gedächtnis.* Vienna: Franz Deuticke, 1948.

WALL, P. D. Two transmission systems for skin sensations. In W. Rosenblith (Ed.), *Sensory communication.* New York: M.I.T. Press and Wiley, 1961. Pp. 475-496.

WEISKRANTZ, L. Sensory deprivation and the cat's optic nervous system. *Nature,* 1958, **181,** 1047-1050.

WEISKRANTZ, L. Presentation at Conference on RNA and Brain Function, Los Angeles, November 1962, in press.

WIDROW, B., & HOFF, M. E. *Adaptive switching circuits.* Stanford, Calif.: Stanford Electronics Laboratories, 1960.

WIENER, N. *Cybernetics.* New York: Wiley, 1949.

24 JEAN-BLAISE GRIZE

GENETIC EPISTEMOLOGY
AND PSYCHOLOGY

IT IS A CURRENT PRACTICE to divide speculative philosophy into two branches: metaphysics which, according to Aristotle's definition, "studies Being as being" (*Metaphys.*, Γ, 1, 1003a21), and epistemology "which investigates the origin, structure, methods, and validity of knowledge" (Runes, 1942, article on *Epistemology*). More particularly, *genetic epistemology,* in Piaget's sense of the term (Piaget, 1950, 1957), proposes to give answers to the fundamental problems of the theory of knowledge while wishing to be, at the same time, a "positive science." The intention of treating questions of a clearly philosophical nature in a rigorously scientific manner raises a preliminary question: does there exist a method which satisfies all the requirements of being a true science but whose doctrines are capable of furnishing answers to problems which seem, at the very least, to escape every attempt at experimental control? Piaget's answer to this question is in the affirmative, and he feels that he has found such a method in the genetic psychology of intelligence.

That genetic psychology is a scientific discipline is beyond doubt. On the other hand, it is a more delicate matter to establish the way in which its doctrines can lead to answers of a philosophic import. Indeed, one can question the legitimacy of wishing to use facts, which are fundamentally contingent in nature, as a basis for drawing necessary relationships.

Thus, we will proceed by first examining the sense in which genetic epistemology has recourse to psychology. Then we will illustrate the method by the example of the natural numbers. Finally, we will return to consider the nature of genetic epistemology itself.

THE RECOURSE TO PSYCHOLOGY

Consider the problem of the foundations, for example, of a branch of mathematics such as arithmetic, the geometry of Euclid, or the calculus of

460

probabilities. In the scientific world of today, there is universal agreement
that such a discipline is not technically founded until it has been axioma-
tized and even formalized. But if such a condition is generally admitted to
be necessary, it is easy to see that it would not be sufficient. There are
two simple and immediate reasons why this is so.

The first of these reasons is contained in the plurality of possible formalizations of a single theory. Indeed, that one can be led, on the basis
of principles which are often extremely different, to equivalent formal
systems (equivalent in the sense that they contain the same set of
theorems) clearly shows that no one system is forced upon us and that
the choice of the elements of the construction depend on the point of
view adopted. Thus, to take geometry as an example, Hilbert (1930) begins with three primitive notions and five groups of independent axioms,
while Beth and Tarski (1956) realize their construction on the basis of a
single primitive notion. The former system is more concerned with respecting the "natural" procedures of geometrization, while the latter is more
given to simplicity and logical elegance. But, needless to say, neither of
these systems can claim—and they are careful not to do so—to encompass
all the effective processes put into play by human intelligence.

The second reason has appeared more recently, but is even more significant. It rests in the fact that the techniques of formalization are incapable
of being entirely formalized themselves. Thus, for example, no formal
system which is conceivable at this time can be constructed such that the
theory of the predicate "true" is formalizable in that theory (Tarski, 1939).

From these remarks, it follows that there is always a moment when the
very processes which tend to assure the foundations of a body of knowledge
are themselves questioned and thus considerations of a metatheoretical
nature make their appearance. Can we say that these considerations themselves constitute philosophical questions? Obviously, the answer depends
on the sense which we give to the word "philosophy." But in the measure
that we define philosophy as that sort of knowledge which makes no appeal
to anything but itself for its justification, knowledge which is intelligible
in itself, the answer is in the affirmative.

But this necessary appeal to philosophy immediately encounters two
kinds of difficulties. The first can be expressed in sum by the remark that
the philosopher never furnishes the scientist with the kind of answer of
which the latter has need. By virtue of his own particular arguments, the
philosopher may well be able to show, for example, the logician that,
when he poses the problem of truth, he has necessarily presupposed this
problem already, but this will not give the logician any way of going beyond the theorem of Tarski. The philosopher ascertains, in his way, the
difficulty, but he does not explain it. He furnishes a reason to bow before
a necessity more than he clarifies it.

All of this leads to the second difficulty, which rests in the lack of agreement of philosophers among themselves. It is extremely rare, in history, to find a philosophy which is a true extension of another. More often, each philosophy opposes the ones which have preceded it, rejecting certain principles in order to substitute others, only to meet later on with the same fate itself.

Without doubt, the nature of philosophy is not to furnish results. "To philosophize means: to be *en route*" (Jaspers, 1950, p. 14). But even so, philosophic epistemology poses questions of a generality which is too great for the scientist to find in it adequate answers to his problems. It insists on attempting to solve a priori the completely general form of the problem of knowledge instead of posing, in a clearly limited framework, some more particular epistemological problem.

From the above, it follows that the solution to problems of an extremely precise nature, issuing from the preoccupations of scientists, must be looked for in a completely different direction and must make use of methods which are very different from those of traditional philosophy.

The only method which today seems capable of giving satisfaction, in the double sense of giving precise answers and at the same time permitting a certain agreement between different minds, is the experimental method. It is to facts that one must go to assure epistemological foundations; temporary foundations perhaps, since they are always partial, but foundations which are sufficient under the double condition (1) that such facts do exist, and (2) that they can be understood by methods which are rigorous.

One must first carefully distinguish between two types of problems. The first are of a purely technical nature and require only the competence of the scholars of the science under consideration. Thus, for example, it is for the mathematician to decide whether he wishes to place the commutative law of arithmetic addition among the axioms or if he wishes to deduce it from another property. But the second type of question is of a clearly epistemological character. Is or is not the commutative law of addition intellectually primitive? If not, does it follow from the law of the union of classes, from the principle of complete induction, or from yet another principle?

Relative to this second kind of questions, one remark immediately commands attention. It is that, at the level of spontaneous thought, the problem is resolved. Neither humanity in its history nor the child in his development have waited for the pronouncement of epistemology in order to establish, by certain methods, that $a + b = b + a$. This fundamental property is so firmly established that one who has not reflected at length on the question might very well believe it is a law written somewhere in the heaven of Ideas.

But it is clear that the appeal to the spontaneous solution of questions of this kind requires that one dispose of an appropriate technique of analysis, a technique capable of revealing the solution without deforming it, of disengaging its structure, and above all of discovering its genesis. It is this genesis alone which will permit us to distinguish between what may be innate and what is acquired. Two methods seem to satisfy these requirements: historico-critical analysis and psychological analysis.

This is not the place to compare the merits of each method. Let us note only that, whatever may be the services rendered by the first, it will only be able to bring very little information on the early beginnings of knowledge, and this because of a lack of documentation. Let us notice also that, in a certain sense, it appeals ultimately to the second. Indeed, the texts which we possess are the expression of what one may call a social subject, that is, a subject who is a function of the *milieu* and the *époque* in which he wrote, but also a function of the individual himself, for authors of scientific works do not constitute a representative sample of a population. Finally, it is easy to see how much certain authors have a tendency to underestimate the difficulties that they have encountered, how many others are discreet concerning their methods of discovery and finally, how many, the most desirous of sincere introspection, have difficulty in practicing it. From all this it follows that the fundamental instrument which will permit an objective clarification of central epistemological problems, which if it does not bring solutions, will at least, as Piaget (1960) prudently states "lead to instructive results" (p.1), can only be psychology itself.

There remains, however, a fundamental difficulty. It is situated in the absolute obligation to avoid every form of psychologism, i.e., every attempt "to resolve a mathematical or logical problem by using results borrowed from psychology" (Beth & Piaget, 1961, p. 143). Indeed, there can be no question of dictating to the logician or the mathematician—nor to any other scientist for that matter—what, in the name of psychology, he must do. Psychology arrives only at facts, and it cannot transform them into norms by some magic operation. It is useless to take up again the always valid criticisms that Husserl (1900) addressed to the well-known attempts of J. S. Mill, Sigwart, Wundt, and others. The role of psychology is not to decide for the scientist on the terrain where he is the absolute master, it is to suggest to him that he look for certain solutions by furnishing him the real genesis of basic notions, by presenting to him the lived relations between the subject of knowledge and its object.

All of this leads to the usage of a particular psychology which one can describe by three principal aspects.

The child, in the course of his development, encounters certain difficulties which can be of fairly different natures. The content of these difficulties is not, however, the most important thing here. It is even possible that the obstacle be exterior to the problem studied. This has little importance in the measure that psychology can establish the types of conduct which, by progressive structuring, permit the subject to surmount the obstacle. Thus, one has often drawn attention to the fact that, in problems of conservation, for example, the questions posed to the child present a certain ambiguity. Piaget and Szeminska (1941) or Gréco (1962a), after having placed two series of objects A and B in visual one-one correspondence, bunch up the elements of one of the series and ask the child whether it is "still the same thing with A and with B." One can well understand that the child responds by the negative. Something has changed, not of course, the quality of number on which the experimenter centered his attention, but the configuration of the objects. One can certainly affirm that the child has simply not understood the question that one thought to ask him. However, and this is the essence of the method, the same question posed to subjects a few years older is not only immediately understood in the right way, but it is just as quickly solved correctly. This, of course, is only an example. But it does permit us to understand why the psychology required must necessarily be, from the beginning, *genetic*.

Every genesis will not be, however, equally interesting to study and the kind of problems with which this psychology will concern itself is characteristic. They are not chosen in terms of the interests of the subject who is questioned, but as a function of the interests of the epistemologue. In particular, it is the study of the development of a certain number of *notions* which first appears fundamental. What is important for the theory of knowledge is not to know in what measure the child experiences difficulties in adapting himself, for example, to a school society which is new to him, nor how emotional problems which he must solve are going to more or less hamper his learning of arithmetical operations. What is revealing is the way in which he proceeds, an abstraction made precisely from a whole set of factors, factors which are justly considered, the greater part of the time, as properly "psychological." In this sense, one can say that it is a question of a *pure* psychology, as one speaks of pure mathematics as opposed to applied mathematics.

Finally—and it is here that the danger of psychologism is definitely avoided—the subject of the psychology necessary to epistemology is of a very particular nature. In the first place, it is not a question of the individual subject. The behavior of some particular child, with his own set of characteristics, with his personal history, with the portion of information that his family and his school have brought him, cannot in any way enlighten the epistemologist, any more than the average subject could. Neither the average inhabitant of Geneva nor even the average American possess the truth concerning the nature of number. It would be infinitely more useful to interview one man such as Prof. Quine than ten thousand readers of *Life* magazine! The subject with which we are concerned here is the one Piaget calls the *epistemic subject,* a subject which reflects "what there is in common with all subjects" (Beth & Piaget, 1961, p. 254). It is fundamentally the transcendental subject. In this latter sense, the psychology in question is *general*.

Genetic psychology, pure and general, such is the instrument which will thus permit us to suggest objective answers to problems which are posed by the establishment of the foundations of knowledge.

THE EXAMPLE OF THE NATURAL NUMBERS

The problem of the nature of the natural numbers will permit us to illustrate concretely the general considerations above. We choose this example for several reasons. On the one hand, it is a problem of considerable importance because the mathematicians know how to construct all numbers on the basis of the natural numbers. On the other hand, Piaget and his collaborators have consecrated much work to the natural numbers, experimental as well as theoretical. Moreover, the nature of the natural numbers has excited the imagination of many of the most famous philosophers from Aristotle to Kant, not to mention the mathematician-philosophers such as Helmholtz, Poincaré, and Russell. Finally, agreement is far from established today on the foundations of arithmetic and, more generally, on the foundations of mathematics. It is thus particularly instructive to examine how genetic epistemology can, by the intermediary of psychology in the above sense, realize its contribution to the problem.

But, since genetic epistemology never begins with a priori questions, it is convenient to recall here at first, in summary fashion, the principles of the three leading schools which still divide the allegiance of mathematicians.

The logistic school, with Russell and more recently Quine, proceeds by a reduction of mathematics to logic. This means, in particular, that the notion of number and the principle of complete induction are defined in purely logical terms. Mathematics appears thus as a branch of logic.

For the intuitionist school of Brouwer, on the other hand, logic appears rather as a part of mathematics. The former is, indeed, considered as the set of general rules which permit the engendering of mathematical theorems, and these rules have no sense even outside of mathematics. Number, or more particularly the sequence of natural numbers, is the object of a direct and specific apprehending of the mind.

Finally, for the formalist school of Hilbert, logic and mathematics are placed on the same footing, in the sense that they are formalizable together. It should be mentioned that, in the opinion of Hilbert himself (Hilbert, 1926), not all formal judgments are "real" in the sense that they do not all have intuitive meaning.

Each of these three positions has its own value; it clarifies a certain aspect of mathematical reality. Taken from a general point of view, however, they are incompatible with each other and, in the measure that they make appeal to other principles besides purely logical and mathematical ones, thus in the measure that they represent judgments of an epistemological nature, it is legitimate to submit them to experimental test. True, one could object that psychological experiments, even in the sense that we have made precise, is not the kind which is needed. This argument has little force, however, in view of the fact that the representatives of each of the three schools themselves support their arguments by a whole set of affirmations of a clearly psychological character.

Thus, for example, Whitehead and Russell (1910) feel that the notions and primitive propositions of the *Principia Mathematica,* although formal, have also a certain character of obviousness and, speaking of the theory of types, they write: "It has also a certain consonance with common sense which makes it inherently credible" (Vol. I, p. 39). Similarly, Heyting (1956), in explaining the position of Brouwer with respect to the numbers, writes: "We . . . state the fact that the concepts of an abstract entity and of a sequence of such entities are clear to every normal human being, even to young children" (p. 13). Finally, Kleene (1952), taking up in turn the project of formalizing mathematics, notes that "we cannot hope to study in exact terms what is in the mathematician's mind" (p. 59).

It is clear that "common sense," the "normal human being" and the "mathematician's mind" appeal to psychology. And it is even more important to emphasize that the judgments cited here—among many others— do not have an accidental character but express adequately the totality of the postitions there defended.

Now that we have thus assured ourselves of the legitimacy of psychological experimentation, let us examine its significance by taking what is probably the most famous example, that of the construction of the numbers by Russell. We will retain five principal aspects of this construction:

(1) Cardinal numbers are classes of classes.

(2) Ordinal numbers are classes of serial relations.

(3) "The logical definition of the cardinals is wholly independent of the ordinals" (Russell, 1956, p. 241) and, conversely, the ordinals "can be defined without any appeal to the cardinals" (p. 242).

(4) Mathematical induction is reducible to the logical notion of the ancestral relation.

(5) This relation is also the principle "upon which depend, so far as ordinals are concerned, the commutative law and one form of the distributive law" (p. 240).

It is impossible, in the space of this brief study, to give an account of the experimental techniques by which Piaget and his collaborators have undertaken the systemic study of the genesis of the nature of number. We will content ourselves with an indication of the epistemological conclusions which they have drawn from them while providing the reader with the sources where he will be able to find any complementary information.

To begin with, genetic psychology shows (Piaget & Szeminska, 1941) that the only materials of which the child makes use in order to elaborate the notion of number are, indeed as the logicians affirm, of purely logical nature: it is a question of classes and asymmetrical relations. However this means neither that the numbers are logically reducible to classes and relations nor that the cardinals may be constructed independently of the ordinals. Much to the contrary, the detailed examination of the preoperational arithmetic of the child, that is to say the numerical behavior before seven years, as well as experimentation on the very beginnings of operational arithmetic (Gréco, 1960, 1962a) speak in favor of a certain specificity of number.

In order to understand how these two conclusions can be reconciled, we must insist with Piaget (1960) that "the fundamental psychological reality . . . is the system and not the atom" (p. 11). This signifies that neither classes nor relations have a psychological existence outside of a system of operations. More precisely, this means that the child never deals with objects, whether classes or numbers, which he adds or substracts, but that operations and the objects which are operated on are completely interrelated from the beginning.

On the other hand, the logical structures of the systems thus constituted continue to enrich themselves progressively, though they pass through certain stages, or plateaus of equilibrium, which are characteristic. Thus, for example, toward seven–eight years, on the level of concrete operations, classes and relations form a particular type of structure which Piaget calls "groupings."

These groupings exhibit three fundamental aspects. (1) The operations are not everywhere defined, in the sense that only those elements can be composed which are linked by a certain relation of partial order. And even then the composititions are carried out in an iterative manner, that is if $a \subset b \subset c$, then the composition of a with c passes by b. (2) They exhibit certain properties of mathematical groups: identity element, inverse elements. (3) They contain a semi-lattice (Piaget, 1942, 1949; Grize, 1960).

Since the natural numbers that the child begins to construct at this age form a semigroup with respect to addition, it is easily understood that it is in the passage from groupings of classes and relations to the semigroup of numbers that arithmetical specificity will appear and it is on this passage that recent experimentation has been concentrated (Piaget, 1960).

To begin with, groupings of classes and groupings of relations are incompatible in the sense that one can neither reduce one to the other nor incorporate the two in a third. In another way, the semigroup of numbers is itself also incompatible with the groupings. It follows from this that the child must, in order to pass from classes and relations to numbers, bring about a real synthesis, real since it consists in going beyond a whole set of incompatibilities and even contradictions.

Let us consider only a single point, the passage from the union of classes to the addition of numbers. If, beginning with qualitatively distinct classes $a, b, c, \ldots$, the child constructs a single class by neglecting the qualities which permitted him up to then to distinguish the classes, he will be led to the law of tautology: $a \cup a = a$. But what is specifically numerical is that, if n is a number, one will have: $n + n = 2n$. Thus, the child must find a way of enumerating the objects by making abstractions from their particular qualities in order to treat them as equivalent units and, at the same time, to consider them as distinct. Now the only way psychologically possible to maintain a distinction under these conditions is to make appeal to the order of the elements: *one* first object, with *one* which follows, makes two *ones*. The child is thus necessarily led, in spite of the incompatibilities which we have pointed out, to make use, not only of the grouping of classes, but also of the grouping of relations.

Thus, the specificity of number explains itself by an original synthesis of classes and relations at the same time that the impossibility of reducing the cardinals to classes alone (first aspect) and the ordinals to relations (second aspect) makes its appearance. Similarly, it is impossible to defend the independence of the two constructions (third aspect), constructions which reveal themselves, to the contrary, as being always fundamentally complementary to each other.

If this really is the case, one should find also a specificity of arithmetical induction with respect to purely logical induction. This is exactly what a group of recent studies has shown (Gréco, 1960, 1962b; Morf, 1962). These studies indicate recursive reasoning on the numbers as early as between seven and nine years according to the material used, but in any case before the subjects are capable of complete hypothetico-deductive reasoning. The most plausible explanation of this precocity is to admit that the child bases his reasoning on that which constitutes the particular character of the numbers, that is, on the law of iteration which constitutes the sequence 1, 2, 3, . . . , and thus to reinforce the idea of a properly numerical specificity. In the nature of a control, let us mention that Matalon has studied, in some research which is to appear, inferences of the type "Atrides" (if the son of Atreus is an Atrides, the son of the son of Atreus is an Atrides, and so forth). He arrives at the conclusion that such a problem is only resolved towards eleven–twelve years and that, consequentially, the mechanics here in play have absolutely nothing of a primitive quality. It thus follows that the fourth aspect that we have retained of the Russellian construction is hardly admissible in the presence of the doctrines of psychology.

One must not conclude, however, from these examples that genetic epistemology is systematically led to reject the conclusions of logical analysis. It does lead, without doubt, to a rejection of certain a priori hypotheses or to a refusal to the logician of the right to see in certain of his formulas anything other than formal procedure. But it also gives a concrete and real content to numerous analytic results. Thus, it confirms, as we have seen, the close link that logicism has tried to see between mathematics and logic. It also gives real meaning to the intuitions of Brouwer, not being content to call intuition "the faculty of considering separately certain concepts and conclusions which intervene normally in our habitual thinking" (Heyting, 1934, p. 12), but by giving foundations to this "normally" and by explaining the genesis of these intuitions. Finally, it is very much, in its way, what Hilbert wanted the metascience to be: a systematic method for studying knowledge as an object, a method which operates simultaneously on the logical plane and on a plane which, if it is not generally mathematical, is at least arithmetical.

This last remark will now permit us to make more precise the nature of genetic epistemology.

THE NATURE OF GENETIC EPISTEMOLOGY

Genetic epistemology is thus seen in a double aspect. It is scientific by its usage of psychology, but it is philosophic by the questions that it poses and by the kind of responses that it gives to these questions. It thus offers certain incontestable analogies with the current of logical empiricism with respect to which it will be useful to situate the position of genetic epistemology.

To begin with, the fact that the problems which are submitted to experimentation have their origin in the heart of scientific technique and are never issued from a priori speculation, assures genetic epistemology that it will not encounter pseudoproblems, questions void of real meaning because they result simply from an imprecise or maladroit use of language. The problem which genetic epistemology treats are authentic in Ayer's sense of the term (Ayer, 1936), in that they are not only theoretically susceptible to receiving a solution, but that they have already received that solution, as we have seen, on the level of spontaneous thought.

And again, still in resemblance to logical empiricism, genetic epistemology submits itself entirely to the jurisdiction of facts, in the framework of a precise and rigorous experimental technique, and thus gives a large place to methods of statistical and even logical analysis. But it is also true that these methods are not sufficient for genetic epistemology, and it does not claim to confine itself only to those statements which are translatable into a given logico-mathematical language. Thus, if on the one hand it subscribes to some of the fundamental requirements of neopositivism, it strictly avoids, on the other hand, their consequences.

The difference is found in the way of envisaging the idea even of fact. Indeed the experience to which genetic epistemology submits itself in principle shows without any possible doubt that there exists nowhere a phenomenon which could be considered as a fact free from all theory, isolated from every other fact. Consequently, it is impossible for it to distinguish—except at the end of particular analysis—between a formal, linguistic background and facts which are known by another means and which come, as from the outside, to "fill up" the background. Much to the contrary, to the degree that its investigations are refined, genetic epistemology exhibits more and more clearly the link which exists, at every level of development, between what one can call a naïve component and a formal component of knowledge.

It follows from this that the purely formal component is not greater than the brutally factual component and that one encounters only a series of successive formalizations without the possibility of discerning a primitive state or a final one. The most elementary perception in appearance already presupposes a portion of intelligent activity on the part of the subject, and the most abstract conduct imaginable is still the result of the abstraction *from something* (Piaget, 1961).

In another regard logical empiricism, or in any case some of its most eminent representatives, profess to refuse on principle to examine any metaphysical question. In reality, things are not so simple. The taking of such a position, prior to all systematic investigation, can result only from a judgment which is itself metaphysical. Even the name of empiricism shows that those who belong to the movement have, for their part, resolved at least the problem of the origin of our knowledge. On the other hand, genetic epistemology does not presuppose any philosophical position at the beginning, and when agreement occurs among the researchers, it has not come from the prior acceptance of a few principles, but it has come only as the result of objective research.

Insofar as accord is realized on the basis on the immediate results of experimentation, there is no difference between genetic epistemology and other science. It suffices that everyone assure himself that the experiment was conducted according to commonly accepted standards. But when it is a question of agreement on questions of a clearly philosophical nature, such as on the relationship between the subject and the object, for example, one finds oneself before a rather serious problem. Indeed, it is difficult to see immediately how science and philosophy can be reconciled. For a scientific discipline is never self-sufficient in the sense that it always needs a corresponding metadiscipline in order to establish itself. However, in compensation for this lack of self-sufficiency, it gains the right, or in any case the fact, of being hypothetico-deductive. On the other hand, philosophy could never relegate, without being absurd, the solution of its problems to a metaphilosophy. But genetic epistemology effectuates the union of these two types of thinking and it is probably in this that it is the most fruitful.

The key idea which permits genetic epistemology to avoid the obvious contradictions which would result from a simple juxtaposition of the analytic procedures of science and the discursive procedures of philosophy is found to be the epistemic subject. It is because, as a subject, he is essentially active that he affords the researchers the possibility of playing two games, so to speak. In other words, it is because the epistemology of Piaget is genetic that it can be science and philosophy at the same time. It can thus benefit from the rigor of science on the one hand, taking account of its analytic processes, and it can conserve on the other hand the advantages of a structural and synthetic viewpoint, a viewpoint which is the source of the intelligibility of the notions studied.

Indeed, in opposition to an epistemology which would analyze static states, genetic epistemology centers its attention on the passage from one state to the next. The description of each state—sensory-motor, concrete-operational, hypothetico-deductive—can and even must give way to a logical analysis. But the filiation between these states appeals to another kind of thought, a thought properly dialectic. It thus follows that genetic epistemology never encounters real contradictions, situations where everything is suddenly found to be emptied of all content. In fact, two propositions can be contradictory in this paralyzing sense only in the context of a system which is clearly marked out and closed on itself. But in a context where the subject of knowledge itself figures explicitly and fundamentally, contradictions, far from having this sterilizing effect, are, on the contrary, the evolutionary force. The subject overcomes every contradiction by his *praxis* and it is finally, in the study itself of these acts of overcoming, that genetic epistemology finds answers to the problems that it poses. The passage from classes and relations to the numbers gave us a characteristic example of this.

It thus follows, to take up the distinction which is classical since Morris (1955) between syntactics, semantics, and pragmatics, that genetic epistemology presents itself as a complete system of pragmatics. It is exactly what Morris meant by this term: a "science of the relation of signs to their interpreters" (p. 108). It finds its problems in that which "while not strictly semiotical, cannot be defined in syntactics or semantics; in the clarification of the pragmatical aspect of various semiotical terms; and in the statement of what psychologically, biologically, and sociologically is involved in the occurrence of signs" (p. 112).

Genetic epistemology is thus the metascience of the whole of scientific knowledge. What metalogic is for logic and metamathematics is for mathematics, genetic epistemology wishes to be for each one of the sciences. And so it can be, without for that reason incurring the dangers of a purely philosophical epistemology, in the measure that, beyond its diversity, all scientific knowledge has common characteristics. These characteristics are primarily concentrated in logic and mathematics, not that these disciplines are only empty languages, but because they express the most general coordinations of the actions of the subject (Beth & Piaget,

1961). This is why the work of Piaget accords a predominant importance to these two sciences. But if we examine the *Introduction à l'épistémologie génétique* (Piaget, 1950), we see immediately that this is only a point of departure, the intention being to do for each science what has already been done for logic and mathematics.

Needless to say, the project of a general metascience outstrips the knowledge of any one man. The necessity for epistemology to begin always, as we have shown, from problems whose origins are internal to each particular science requires the possession of information that a single man —even a philosopher!—could never have. Even more, only the specialists can, not only determine the exact nature of the difficulties encountered, but appreciate the results of the experiments that psychology has done. It thus follows that genetic epistemology can only be the work of a group of researchers, some of which perfectly dominate psychological techniques while others belong to each particular science.

Thus, as a theory of knowledge, genetic epistemology always directs its experimentation and its reflection, not only on precise points, but in the same way on problems which continually renew themselves. The sciences themselves from which it always begins, evolve incessantly, and genetic epistemology is also in continual development. Needless to say, this does not mean at all that it cannot consider certain very general results as acquired. To the degree that human intelligence guards a certain self-similarity in its diverse expressions, it is always subject to the same laws. On the other hand, as soon as that same intelligence creates a new instrument, from the moment that a new relationship between the subject of knowledge and its object is manifest, genetic epistemology must face up to new problems, but always by using that method "which does not seek to escape from such a circle by the hope of a direct leap into absolute knowledge, but which charges itself with the task of following step by step, under all their observable forms, the development of that continuous interaction between the subject and the object" (Piaget, 1957, p. 84).

REFERENCES

AYER, A. J. *Language, truth and logic.* London: Gollancz, 1936.
BETH, E. W., & PIAGET, J. *Epistémologie mathématique et psychologie.* Paris: Presses Univ. de France, 1961.
BETH, E. W., & TARSKI, A. Equilaterality as the only primitive notion of Euclidean geometry. *Indagationes Mathematicae,* 1956, **18,** 462-467.
GRÉCO, P. Recherches sur quelques formes d'inférences arithmétiques et sur la compréhension de l'itération numérique chez l'enfant. *Études d'Épistémologie gén.,* 1960, **11,** 149-213.

GRÉCO, P. Quantité et quotité. *Études d'Épistémologie gén.*, 1962, **13,** 1-70.

GRÉCO, P. Une recherche sur la commutativité de l'addition. *Études d'Épistémologie gén.*, 1962, **13,** 151-227.

GRIZE, J. B. Du groupement au nombre: essai de formalisation. *Études d'Épistémologie gén.*, 1960, **11,** 69-96.

HEYTING, A. *Mathematische Grundlagenforschung, Intuitionismus, Beweistheorie.* Berlin: Springer, 1934.

HEYTING, A. *Intuitionism, an introduction.* Amsterdam: North-Holland Publishing Co., 1956.

HILBERT, D. Über das Unendliche. *Mathematische Annalen,* 1926, **95,** 161-190.

HILBERT, D. *Grundlagen der Geometrie.* (7th ed.) Leipzig and Berlin: Teubner, 1930.

HUSSERL, E. *Logische Untersuchungen.* Vol. 2. Halle, 1900-1901.

JASPERS, K. *Einführung in die Philosophie.* Zurich: Artemis-Verlag, 1950.

KLEENE, S. C. *Introduction to metamathematics.* Amsterdam: North-Holland Publishing Co., 1952.

MATALON, B. Étude du raisonnement par récurrence sur un modèle physique. *Études d'Éspistémologie gén.,* **17,** 283-316.

MORF, A. La découverte d'une loi numérique simple dans une situation de partition spatiale. *Études d'Épistémologie gén.,* 1962, **13,** 105-150.

MORRIS, C. W. Foundations of the theory of signs. In *International Encyclopedia of Unified Science.* (Combined ed.) Vol. 1. Chicago Univ. Press, 1955. Pp. 77-137.

PIAGET, J. *Classes, relations, et nombres.* Paris: Vrin, 1942.

PIAGET, J. *Traité de logique.* Paris: A. Colin, 1949.

PIAGET, J. *Introduction à l'épistémologie génétique.* Paris: Presses Univ. de France, 1950. 3 vols.

PIAGET, J. Programme et méthodes de l'épistémologie génétique. *Études d'Épistémologie gén.,* 1957, **1,** 13-84.

PIAGET, J. Problèmes de la construction du nombre. *Études d'Épistémologie gén.,* 1960, **11,** 1-68.

PIAGET, J. *Les mécanismes perceptifs.* Paris: Presses Univ. de France, 1961.

PIAGET, J., & SZEMINSKA, A. *La genèse du nombre chez l'enfant.* Neuchâtel: Delachaux & Niestlé, 1941.

RUNES, D. D. *The dictionary of philosophy.* New York: Philosophical Library, 1942.

RUSSELL, B. *The principles of mathematics.* (7th impression) London: Allen & Unwin, 1956.

TARSKI, A. On undecidable statements in enlarged systems of logic and the concept of truth. *J. sym. Logic,* 1939, **4,** 105-112.

WHITEHEAD, A. N., & RUSSELL, B. *Principia Mathematica.* London: Cambridge Univ. Press, 1910-1913. 3 vols.

25 G. J. WARNOCK

LOGICAL ANALYSIS AND THE
NATURE OF THOUGHT

IT APPEARS THAT, when in recent years philosophers have addressed themselves to the topic of thinking, three questions in particular have engaged their concern. These are:

What is it to think *about* something? Or, how is it possible for our thinking to be *about* what we would customarily take it to be about?

What is the nature of those particular episodes in which (presumably) thinking, or the process of thought, consists?

When, for instance, a man speaks or acts and, as we say, thinks what he is saying or doing, what, if anything, must then be supposed to be occurring besides, or in addition to, or in conjunction with his *just* speaking or acting?

Philosophers who have handled these questions have no doubt been correct in their supposition that they are not wholly independent of one another; it is difficult, however, to resist the suspicion that they have not always been clearly perceived to be different. In particular, some discussions of the first and last questions have appeared to incorporate an unrecognized, perhaps inadvertent, and certainly false assumption concerning the answer to the middle question. The second has, in fact, been accorded comparatively little explicit discussion. This may be thought natural, and indeed quite proper, for the reason that the question appears to ask for quite straightforward (though doubtless somewhat elusive) empirical information of a kind which the armchair cogitations of philosophers are not well suited to supply: however, as will appear, the question has certain peculiarities which may qualify philosophers, not indeed to answer it, but to issue with reference to it some highly pertinent warnings.

We may begin our survey with a brief word or two about H. H. Price's *Thinking and Representation* (1946)—brief, since this lecture deals somewhat unsatisfactorily with problems much more adequately discussed in the same author's book *Thinking and Experience*. The question to which Price appears to be addressing himself here is the first question above. Thinking, he says without argument, is to be contrasted with observation as

474

"cognition by means of symbols"; it is "cognition in absence," in which "the only entities directly present to our minds are the symbols themselves." The question then is: "How is such purely symbolic awareness possible at all? How is it that by merely operating with symbols we become aware of what is absent, and are brought into touch with objects which we do not see or feel?" "It makes no difference," Price adds, "whether the symbolic operations are public, as when you speak aloud or write, or whether they are conducted in the privacy of your own mind by means of verbal or other imagery"; in either case, exactly the same question arises.

It will be observed that some very strange assumptions are made here. First, thinking is taken to be some kind of *cognition*—which, if the obscure term "cognition" is intended to bear its etymologically appropriate sense of "knowing," it is plain that not all thinking is. Second, stress is evidently laid on the phrase "in absence"—yet, to the question what, say, thinking about my cat consists in, it is hard to see that it makes the faintest difference whether my cat is on the mat before me, or out prowling the neighborhood. Thinking, as Price begins by saying, is no doubt to be distinguished from, and may even be contrasted with, observation: but it does not follow that my observation of X *excludes* my thinking about X, or vice versa.

It is, however, a more important and more pertinent comment that Price's question, contrary to his evident assumption, appears not to be particularly concerned with the nature of thinking at all. For the question Price initially asks, and throughout attempts to answer, is really this: What is it for "a symbol" to have, and to be used and understood as having, a meaning? The "symbols" to which most of his discussion is actually directed are, it seems, words—these being, as he says, "incomparably the most important sort" of symbols. And thus, as indeed Price says himself in effect, his question might have been posed just as well by asking how it is possible to *speak or write* about an "absent" object. He is actually investigating, that is to say, the theory of meaning; and the procedures of talking or writing raise problems about meaning just as well as, and probably more perspicuously than, that of thinking does.

To this, on the evidence of his text, Price would presumably reply that we are making a distinction without a significant difference; for in talking or writing, usually at least, we *are* thinking—aloud or actively; and whether we do so aloud or actively, or merely "in the privacy of our own minds," makes no relevant difference. This, however, is not so. For, first, it would be highly imprudent, not to say grossly mistaken, to assume (as perhaps Plato did, though Price certainly does not) that all thinking is merely inward, unvocalized talking and therefore, if talking is discussed, needs no separate discussion; and second, if the suggestion is, not that whenever we think about anything we (inwardly) talk, but merely that whenever we talk about anything we think, it must be pointed out that this suggestion implies concentration upon *formulated,* expressed or ready-to-be-expressed, thoughts or processes of thought, to the evident neglect of (among other things) those as it were exploratory, questing, or tentative thinkings in the course of which we do not talk, since we have not—yet—anything to say. Thus it seems clear that, if we produce an answer to the question what it is for "a symbol" to have a meaning, we certainly have not exhausted, and may even have said little of particular relevance to, the problem of thinking: what Price in his lecture speaks of as "theories of thinking"—nominalism, conceptualism, and imagism—are in fact not theories of thinking, but theories of meaning; and though, as stated by Price, these theories of meaning do incorporate (and perhaps have historically incorporated) doctrines as to the nature of thinking, it may well be thought that they are neither the better nor the worse for that—not better, since the doctrines for the most part are evidently inadequate; and not worse, since they are, in theories of meaning, entirely unnecessary.

That theories of meaning are to be distinguished from theories of thinking is recognized by Price, though perhaps somewhat insecurely, in *Thinking and Experience* (1953). Most of that book, like most of his earlier lecture, is actually concerned with theories of meaning. The question chiefly canvassed is the question what it is for something to be, and to be employed and construed as, a symbol; symbols are carefully compared with, and distinguished from, signs; the role of images as symbols and in symbol-using is examined, and so on. Now, in most of this discussion Price appears to assume—as the titles both of his book and of its chapters suggest in themselves—that he has been considering the nature of *thinking;* he appears to have been making, as he had earlier made, the bold assumption that thinking just *is* the occurrence of symbols, so that any theory about symbols is *ipso facto* a theory about thinking. Now, however, he points out convincingly not only that this is an assumption, but that it is probably a false one. According to what Price calls the "classical theory" of thinking, the use or occurrence of symbols can never be *identified* with any process of thinking; symbols, when they occur, are merely the vehicles, and sometimes the medium of communication, of thinking, which in principle can and sometimes does occur entirely without them. Price does not indeed accept the full-blown doctrine "classically" erected on this basis—that thinking really consists in the intellectual inspection of a distinctive species of "objects of thought"—but he does accept a good deal of the basis itself. In particular it is, as he concedes, simply not the case that, whenever we think about topic A, there actually occurs, in our minds or anywhere else, a complete, as it were fully-dressed set of symbols *meaning* topic A, or what we think about that topic. We do not usually, for instance, in thinking *out* an argument, produce straight off, or even step by step, a full-dress formulation *of* the argument; nor do we do so when, as it were in a flash, we think *of* a perhaps elaborate argument with which we are familiar and which, if need be, we could fully formulate.

It is only rehearsed thinking which ever has a full dress and fully formulated character. But it is unrehearsed thinking which is important. . . . And in unrehearsed thinking our symbols are particularly scrappy and sketchy. Some symbols, no doubt, are present even then. But could it not be said that when we think most, we symbolize least?

Price makes these observations as tending to show that "the classical theory of thinking" cannot at any rate be dismissed out of hand: and perhaps they do show this: but they also show that such theories of meaning— theories about the meaningfulness or significance of "symbols"—as nominalism, conceptualism, and so on should not have been regarded as theories of *thinking* at all. No doubt there is some sense in which it would be true to say that the employment of, or at least the capacity to employ, "symbols" is essential to all thinking: but exactly *how* "symbols" enter into thinking of this or that kind appears to be a centrally relevant question, toward answering which it is plain that nothing is done by the production of a general "theory of symbolization."

It may be said, on similar grounds, of A. J. Ayer's *Thinking and Meaning* (1947) that it has a good deal more to do with meaning than with thinking. This lecture is an avowed exercise in philosophical Occamism, of a type perhaps more common before World War II than after it. What, Ayer asks, is really involved in the occurrence of thinking? There is involved, we may concede, a person, the person who thinks. But we need not add, as a separate item, this person's mind, for the mind is not to be thought of as an instrument with which we think, still less as an entity which does our thinking for us: indeed, to say that we have minds at all is only to say (among other things) that we think. Further, Ayer is inclined to hold that we should not distinguish, as two items, the process of thought and the expression of it; for, he suggests, at least in the case in which a thought is given expression—whether privately or overtly—"the expressing and the thinking merge into a single process . . . The thinking is not a reduplication of the talking." What is it, then, for a thought to be *about* something? "In every case," Ayer answers, "it will be found that the questions whether the thought has an object, and what object it has, are questions about the use of certain symbols, and fundamentally about nothing else at all." And so we are back again with the theory of meaning: thinking has been (with certain reservations) equated with symbol-using; and "the question which then arises is what is meant by saying that something is designated by a symbol."

There is a further question, however, on which Ayer in his lecture has something to say. Suppose that we have produced an account of meaning in terms of which we are in a position to explain how the words, say, "There is a tiger in that cage" have the meaning that they do have: there are surely further questions that arise concerning trains or processes of thought in which those words may be supposed to occur. One may, for instance, suspect, or doubt, or believe, or know, or merely entertain the idea, that there is a tiger in the cage; and how do these cases differ from one another? Must it not be supposed, if these cases are to be differentiated, that there occur from time to time mental *acts* of suspecting, doubting, believing, knowing, entertaining? Ayer's own views on this question are not entirely clear, no doubt because they are sketched only very briefly indeed; it is plain, however, that he wholly rejects the conception of "mental acts." Knowing, believing, doubting, and so on are, he insists, not different *acts*, but different *dispositions*—"to say of someone that he knows, or believes, or doubts something is not to say that he is *doing* anything at all"; but further, even when we do actually "have in mind" what it is that we are said to know, or believe, or doubt, there may be no distinctive act, or state, of mind—"I think that what are taken in this context to be different states of mind may be nothing more than different sets of dispositions. If there is a further difference, then I suppose that it consists in the presence or absence of certain feelings." Nor, Ayer adds, does *understanding* the symbols we use "consist in the presence or absence of anything that could be reasonably described as a cognitive act": understanding also is "purely dispositional." It seems, then, to be implicit in all this that what, in Ayer's view, thinking consists of—what actually constitutes processes of thought—is *just* the occurrence, whether private or public, of certain "symbols": what gives to thought a reference, or an object, is merely the fact that symbols have meanings; and the basis for distinguishing one variety of thought from another lies, not in episodes internal to the thinking, but in dispositions which the thinker may manifest from time to time, elsewhen and elsewhere.

So far, then, we have found, in Price and Ayer, certain somewhat inexplicit views on the nature of thinking, their interest in this matter being in each case subordinate to a primary interest in the problem of meaning. We may mention next a very valuable discussion (Murdoch Lloyd, & Ryle, 1951) in which the nature of thinking is explicitly canvassed.

The problem is posed by Iris Murdoch. Thinking, she assumes, is surely "a private activity which goes on in our heads"; but what *is* this activity, how is it to be described? "We might at first be tempted to say that thought is the uttering of mental words. We could then divide the mental region between obscure drifting images and clear verbal thought whose meaning is determined in accordance with simple overt criteria." But this course (which from time to time tempts both Ayer and Price) would, she thinks, be mistaken: "vague floating images" and "fully verbalized thought" are more like two extremes, between which falls a wide variety of diversely intermediate cases; and surely there are also cases in which we have a "fully verbalized" thought in mind, and are yet conscious of its *inade-quacy* to express or encompass what, in some sense, we "really" think. But there is, she holds, one valuable general point to be made; when we do attempt to describe the actual course of our thoughts, though we may well not offer just the same descriptions, "we naturally use a metaphorical mode of speech." And it is important that in these terms we do understand each other: the inner course of our thoughts does not consist merely of "obscure private communings about which nothing can be said." It is, at any rate, *"as if* our thoughts were inner events, and it is *as if* these events were describable either as verbal units or in metaphorical, analogical terms. We constantly recover and fix our mental past by means of a descriptive technique, whose justification is its success." Moreover, "in such a context metaphor is not an inexact *faute de mieux* mode of expression, it is the best possible . . . the language which does the 'fixing' is already soaked in the sensible, from its occurrence in the strugglings of private thought"—so that it would be, she appears to conclude, a mistake dogmatically to insist that there must be some quite *literal* description of thoughts, quite free from the colorful, pictorial, metaphorical style of the descriptive idioms that we naturally employ.

Gilbert Ryle, in an excellent paper commenting on Miss Murdoch's, begins by accepting her formulation of the problem: there is indeed "usually an ostentatious picturesqueness" in the idioms in which we describe "stretches of our ponderings and musings, and it is puzzling that we seem unable to find unpicturesque paraphrases for them . . . We cleave instead to such expressions as 'bogged down,' 'losing the thread,' 'casting around,' 'seeing daylight,' 'germinating,' 'dawning,' 'floundering,' 'consolidating,' and a thousand others. So what stops us describing what has been going on in nongraphic terms? If the concrete incidents of fruit-picking and fishing can be unpicturesquely reported, why do the concrete incidents of a stretch of thinking appear to be so shy?" Miss Murdoch, so far as she offered an answer to this question, appeared to suggest that the "concrete incidents" of thinking resisted unpicturesque description for the reason that they (very often) were themselves irreducibly picturesque in character—"soaked in the sensible"; Ryle believes that something more can be said than this.

First, he stresses that "the concept of *thinking* is polymorphous." If we are asked in what, say, apple-picking consists, we are in a position to say, no doubt somewhat roughly, what sorts of particular episodes must successively occur in any process of picking apples: by contrast, the question "What does working consist of?" quite plainly does not admit of any general answer, for there is practically no limit to the number and diversity of activities (or even inactivities) which at one time or another, for this person or that, might constitute working: in this sense, *working* is a highly "polymorphous" concept. Similarly, though perhaps not quite to the same degree, with thinking—"there are hosts of widely different sorts of toilings and idlings, engaging in any one of which is thinking. . . . Just as there are hundreds of widely differing operations, including apple-picking, to be occupied in any one of which is to be doing farm-work: so there are lots of widely differing operations, including multiplying, all of which are proper specimens of thinking." Thus we cannot say simply, for instance, that "in thinking the soul is talking to itself." Words may, as we say, run through my head—dialogue, perhaps, that I have learned by heart as an actor—without its being true on that account to say that I am thinking: or again, I may be engaged in thinking out *what* to say, while not *yet* being in a position to say anything, even to myself: and further, not all thinking essentially involves talking at any stage—for instance, an architect, or sculptor, or musician may well think out solutions to their problems without either saying anything in the course of doing so or subsequently being able to say how their deliberations went. It may be true that thinking *about philosophy* both largely consists in, and is often intended to culminate in, talking; but philosophers are in error if they assume that *all* thinking *must* have the same highly verbalized character. In some thinkings the soul is "only stammering to itself," and in yet others it may be, though busily occupied, silent.

But, Ryle next suggests, in the extreme polymorphousness of thinking we have a large part of the explanation of the peculiarly and persistently graphic character of the idioms in which our "ponderings and musings" are apt to be reported. There is a sense in which it is surely true to say that the aims, or goals, or points of thinking are enormously less diverse than are the actual episodes of which this or that tract of someone's thinking may consist: and moreover, since those actual episodes are usually neither necessarily involved in nor proprietary to this or that particular bit of thinking, it would seldom be particularly relevant or informative to produce, or try to produce, an exhaustive chronicle of them.

> If we ask a soldier to tell us about a battle, we do not expect to be told all or many of the myriad details of which the battle and the battle-field happened to consist. We do not care which of his boots he wore, when he had a cigarette, over what tussocks of grass he walked or what he said to the sergeant during a lull in the fighting. We want to know how the battle went, and why it went that way. We want the tactical and strategic plot of the story of the battle, and the telling of this requires careful neglect of its negligible detail.

Very similarly, what we require in reports of people's thinking are "histories," not "chronicles"; we want to know, for instance, their goal and the strategy of its pursuit, not the inessential and unilluminating details of all the particular happenings en route. But, the suggestion is, if this is the nature of our usual interests, then the use of metaphor in our reports is entirely natural—"to tell the plot without the detailed incidents requires the employment either of idioms so general as to be lifeless or of graphic idioms which show the point by illustrating it." At least one good way of conveying what we usually wish to convey about our thinking is "to borrow some of the non-polymorphous expressions for specific proceedings"—for example, "wander," "grope," "grasp," "pursue"—"the concrete detail of which is meant to be discounted." Thus, Ryle suggests, it is not that the episodes which constitute our thinkings are in some peculiar way "ineffable, private, or gossamery," still less that they possess "the odd property of baffling literal description"; it is true that we do not often give such a description, but this is mostly because we scarcely ever have any interest in doing so; furthermore, if we find it a very difficult thing to do, this may be because to do it requires that we should attend to detailed happenings which, for quite understandable reasons, we are quite unaccustomed to according any careful scrutiny.

This, then, is how, in Ryle's view, we may be led erroneously to suppose that there is something mysteriously *indescribable* about what goes on when people think. Earlier, in his justly famous book *The Concept of Mind* (1949), he had argued against the contrary tendency, namely that of foisting upon thinking a definite but more or less inappropriate form of description. There is, Ryle argues in a valuable section of that book, a large number of idioms in which we may describe, criticize, anatomize, and logically chart what may be called the finished products of thinking—for example, a lecture publicly delivered, a theory stated, or perhaps merely an opinion expressed; and in doing so we are (in one sense) describing what some person thinks. But it is, Ryle suggests, a tempting and prevalent philosophical error to construe such talk as if it related, not to the finished products of thinking, but to the processes of constructing or arriving at those finished products—as if it related, not to what some person thinks, but to what (in another sense) he *was thinking* over some particular stretch of time. From the fact that, in an expounded argument, a speaker may be said to deduce from certain premises that so-and-so, and after various intermediate steps to conclude that such-and-such, we jump misguidedly to the conclusion that, in the course of his own pondering, he must have performed certain "mental acts" of which, for instance, "deducing" and "concluding" would be the names. But these, as Ryle puts it, "are 'referees' nouns, not 'biographers' nouns"; their application is to the argument as the speaker ultimately expounds it, not to the antecedent ponderings which, in all probability, he neither narrates nor himself recalls. The formidable battery of alleged "mental acts" supposed to have been discovered by "the inferences and divinations of expert epistemologists" is really, in Ryle's view, a pure invention, attributable to a very natural desire to find nominees for a set of familiar but misconstrued expressions: and the picture of thinking which results is a theorists' myth.

Ryle returns to this subject in his lecture *A Puzzling Element in the No-tion of Thinking* (1958). The puzzling element with which he is here con-cerned is that, whereas we usually have no difficulty in identifying, and if necessary in reporting, the particular items or episodes of which our ac-tivities consist, we do encounter difficulty in the particular case of thinking. If, for instance, I have been engaged in singing a song, I have no difficulty in specifying, if necessary, that this activity actually consisted in the vocal production of an ordered sequence of noises: but if I have been thinking, in what exactly did *that* consist? It is not that I would usually have much difficulty in reporting what I was thinking: I may do this quite easily in, for instance, a couple of hundred words of English prose. But it is exceedingly unlikely that my thinking actually consisted in my inwardly saying to myself those words: but if not, in what *did* it consist? What, in general, are the items, incidents, or episodes which constitute thinking?

Now an answer to this question which we have seen to be popular with philosophers is that we think "in symbols"—not necessarily in words, or not at least in consecutive and grammatical words, nor yet in images, or not at least in detailed and well-defined images, but nevertheless in symbols of some kind. But this notion, Ryle suggests, vague and noncommittal though it is, can yet be seen to rest on a presupposition that he finds ob-jectionable—the presupposition, namely, that thinking must be carried on "in" mental vehicles of some sort or other. "I want to deny," Ryle now says, "that it even makes sense to ask, in the general case, what special sort or sorts of things we think *in*." A large part of the ground for this denial is, in Ryle's argument, that thinking is not a "special or proprietary ac-tivity" in the way that, say, singing is. Singing, that is, is a quite specific activity in which we may or may not engage from time to time, and such that, if we do engage in it, certain specific episodes—namely the production of sounds—must occur in the course of our so doing: but "thinking is not a rival occupation to these special occupations. . . . Its proper place is in all the departments—that is, there is no particular place which is its proper place, and there are no particular places which are not its proper place." Ryle argues that "adverting to anything whatsoever can be what puts a person, at a particular moment, in mind of something or other"; and he proposes the slogan "No thinking without adverting to something or other, no matter what"—it is true that this slogan does not really answer the question in what thinking consists, just as "Food" does not really an-swer the question what people eat. But then the question in what thinking consists does not really, any more than the question what people eat, admit of any worthwhile, quite general answer.

Allusions to philosophical problems about thinking are numerous in the writings of Wittgenstein, but, in his characteristic manner, they are scattered and discontinuous: they occur from time to time in his *Philosophical In-vestigations* (1953) and also in *The Blue and Brown Books* (1958).

There is a sense in which it might be said that his concern with these problems is mainly negative: that is, his purpose in those passages in which they crop up is, usually, not that of directly analyzing and elucidating the concept of thinking, but rather that of issuing warnings or protests against what he takes to be prevalent and tempting misunderstandings. These misunderstandings, further, are sometimes misunderstandings of the concept of thinking itself, but also, and perhaps more frequently in his references to the subject, misunderstandings of other topics brought about by, or partly consisting in, tacit misconstructions of the concept of thinking.

First, it is not his concern, Wittgenstein insists, to *describe* processes of thought: "We are not analysing a phenomenon (e.g., thought) but a concept (e.g., that of thinking), and therefore the use of a word." The attempt to describe the actual process of thinking he evidently regards as quite unfruitful: he speaks, for instance, of "that dead-end in philosophy, where one believes that the difficulty of the task consists in this: our having to describe phenomena that are hard to get hold of, the present experience that slips quickly by, or something of the kind." Presumably, Wittgenstein did not mean by this that actual processes of thinking are somehow not describable: nor, perhaps, would he have regarded as totally uninteresting those questions concerning the description of thought processes to which, for example, Miss Murdoch addressed herself. His point is rather that our philosophical difficulties typically arise, not because we are too clumsy to grasp the fragile and evanescent constitutents of our thinking as they flash by, but because we are confused or unclear about the *concept* of thinking. We need, not more dexterity in the pursuit of the fleeting, but more clarity in our understanding of the very familiar.

Unclarity, Wittgenstein suggests, is liable to assail us at the very outset of any reflection on the notion of thinking. We may begin, for instance, with what we may take to be the incontestable, though indeed somewhat vague and even platitudinous, idea that thinking is at any rate a "mental process"; but this is already, he suggests, dangerous in two ways.

> We talk of processes and states and leave their nature undecided. Sometime perhaps we shall know more about them—we think. But that is just what commits us to a particular way of looking at the matter. For we have a definite concept of what it means to learn to know a process better. . . .

Should we not, for instance, expect to get to know more about a process by observing it very carefully while it takes place? So "we watch ourselves while we think; what we observe will be what the word means!" But of course it will not be: it will be only a (probably) odd and untypical instance of one kind of case in which the word might be employed. Again, the word "mental" is liable to be somewhat misleading: it may suggest that thinking is something that we do *with* our minds, or that takes place *in* our minds; and these forms of expression may suggest a host of bad analogies with, for instance, things that we do with our hands, or with processes that take place in our brains. "One might say 'Thinking is an incorporeal process' . . . if one were using this to distinguish the grammar of the word 'think' from that of, say, the word 'eat.' Only that makes the difference between the meanings look *too slight*"—it tends to saddle us with the misleading idea that thinking is a quite specific process or activity of *some* kind, merely differing in certain particular respects from, say, eating: "an unsuitable type of expression is a sure means of remaining in a state of confusion," and even the harmless-looking "mental process" *may* be—not of course in all contexts or for every purpose—an expression of just such an unsuitable type.

There are, however, two other themes to which Wittgenstein constantly returns, and which are indeed centrally characteristic of his philosophical views. The first is this. When we talk about meaning, about language and the understanding of language, or indeed when we talk about any form of intelligent behavior, there inevitably arises the question, how *merely* saying or hearing certain words, or *merely* carrying out certain bodily movements, is to be distinguished from doing these things intelligently, with understanding—thinking, as we sometimes say, what we are doing. We say that people speak without thinking, or hear without understanding: what account, then, are we to give of speaking *and* thinking, hearing *with* understanding? And here Wittgenstein discerns a standing temptation to misrepresent the state of the case. We may be struck by the grammatical analogy between the expressions "say something," "hear something," "mean something," "understand something," and so be led to the idea that meaning something is a process that runs *parallel* with that of saying something; or that, when I hear and understand, two *concurrent* processes occur in me, (1) hearing, and (2) understanding. But this idea can be attacked on at least two grounds, and probably more. First, it is entirely unclear *how* a process or performance, say, hearing or saying, could be rendered "intelligent" merely by the occurrence simultaneously with it of some *other* process or performance: indeed, if we say that a concurrent thinking-process is what renders a saying-process "intelligent," does not the question immediately arise what makes the thinking *itself* intelligent? Must we suppose yet another sense-conferring process to run parallel with the thinking? But here we are evidently well launched on an infinite regress. Wittgenstein suggests that philosophers shy away from such questions because they take the word "mental" (in such phrases as "Understanding is a *mental* process") as "indicating that we mustn't expect to understand how these things work": but why not? May it not be a mere confusion, rather than an actual mystery, that puzzles us?

But, further, though certainly Wittgenstein does not deny that there may *be* processes, feelings, mental states which accompany (sometimes) saying or hearing, it is evident, he repeatedly insists, that it is not *these* which distinguish understanding from not understanding, thinking from not thinking, meaning something from meaning something else, or from mere senseless babbling. For such accompaniments are neither necessary nor sufficient for the purpose. Suppose that, on some occasion when I speak the word "Oxford," there occurs in me concurrently some kind of sensation, which I may be inclined to call a feeling "of familiarity": does this, or does any such, accompanying occurrence constitute my then *meaning,* in saying "Oxford," the city with which I am, in fact, familiar? Plainly not: for, firstly, there is no doubt that I often use the name "Oxford," meaning that city, without any such feeling of familiarity occurring, and second, I might well, perhaps owing to some sort of association of ideas, have just that feeling of familiarity in saying "Oxford" when I actually mean the, to me, wholly strange town of Oxford, Mississippi. What we need to ask here is: what *does* in fact settle what I meant when I said "Oxford"? What *does* settle whether or not someone has understood me, or that I myself knew, or was thinking, what I was saying? We then see that it is not a question at all of what occurred, if anything did, concurrently with the speaking or hearing. "If we scrutinize the usages which we make of such words as 'thinking,' 'meaning,' 'wishing,' etc., going through this process rids us of the temptation to look for a peculiar act of thinking, independent of the act of expressing our thoughts, and stowed away in some peculiar medium. We are no longer prevented by the established forms of expression [that is, by certain misleading grammatical analogies] from recognizing that the experience of thinking *may* be just the experience of saying. . . ." We shall no longer feel constrained to conjure into existence, in each such case, a "mental" act or process "which seems to perform in a miraculous way what could not be performed by any act of manipulating symbols."

This is closely related to a more general contention on which Wittgenstein also lays great emphasis. Suppose, for example, I say "I have been expecting him to arrive for the last hour": that is, to put it more tendentiously, it has been true of me, at all times during the last hour, that I was expecting him to arrive. Now we may be tempted to assume in such a case, Wittgenstein suggests, that, since I have been expecting him all that time, any cross section of my thoughts, or of my "state of mind," taken within that period of time must somehow contain, or exhibit, just that expectation: there must be, we think, something "in my mind" which *makes* it true that I was expecting him, as distinguished from, say, merely wondering whether he would arrive, or again from expecting somebody else. But of course this is not so. "An expectation is imbedded in a situation": what I say to myself, what I feel, what I do from time to time during the hour would not, if considered so to speak in isolation or out of context, be *recognizable* as "expecting him to arrive." It is not exactly that what is

happening in me at any particular moment does not matter, or has no significance—"what is happening now has significance—in these surroundings. The surroundings give it its importance." Rather similarly, "what I
meant" by a certain expression is not made clear by an account, if any
could be given, of what was going on in me *when* I used that expression:
what I meant is made clear by the setting in which I spoke, by the whole
tenor of my talkings and doings at that and other times. "What I was thinking" has in common with a vast number of related expressions—"what I
meant," "what I wished," "what I expected," "what I intended"—that its
reference, its use, cannot be made clear in terms of any momentary, isola-
ble "mental acts," "mental processes," or "states of mind." "When I think
in language, there aren't 'meanings' going through my mind in addition to
the verbal expressions: the language is itself the vehicle of thought":
and if the objection is made that the words which occur in my thinking
might well be meant, or understood, in more than one way, the answer is
that although this is undeniably the case, how they *are* meant is not to be
discovered by searching for "meanings" in the thinker's mind concurrent
with his words, but by investigating the whole setting in which his words are
imbedded. If his words were accompanied by, say, mental images, this
would solve no problems; for images too can be interpreted, or made use
of, in various ways; they do not contain their own sense.

This survey, already of course sketchy, may perhaps be usefully summarized by reference back to the three questions which were distinguished
at the outset.

What is it to think *about* something? This question has been debated at
length by philosophers, particularly, among those mentioned here, by Price
and Ayer. I have suggested, however, that this question inevitably turns into
the question what it is for something—a "symbol"—to have a reference
or a meaning, and that this question, though certainly difficult enough and
central to many philosophical problems, has no *particular* connection with
problems about thinking. Failure to see this may well, indeed, obfuscate
such problems, by encouraging an undue assimilation of thinking to
talking.

What is the nature of those particular episodes in which thinking consists?
On this question there is, I think, more general agreement than might appear at first sight. Many philosophers seem to hold, with varying degrees of
explicitness, that thinking consists in operations with "symbols"; and,
though Ryle has objected to that word as inappropriate and potentially misleading, its use seems quite compatible with the view, which he accepts,
that *almost anything* may, in the course of some piece of thinking, actually
occur: for practically no restriction can be placed, in this connection, on
the kinds of items which may occur as "symbols." We find, however, that
while some writers (for example, Miss Murdoch and Ryle) have interested
themselves in the actual nature of thought-processes and our descrip-

tions of them, others (particularly Wittgenstein) have tended to dismiss this question as philosophically unrewarding. In Wittgenstein's view—with which, indeed, Ryle largely concurs—it does not vitally matter what is actually going on *when* a person thinks, for the reason that even a detailed answer to that question, even if we could give one, would not by itself put us in a position to say *what* he was thinking. The constituent episodes have the "significance" they have only in the wider setting in which they take place: and in a sense that setting has much the *more* significance, since the plot, or tenor, or purport of a piece of thinking is central to its being a piece of thinking of that kind, in a way in which its particular constitutents, whatever they may be, are not.

When, for instance, a man speaks or acts, and "thinks" what he is saying or doing, what, if anything, must be supposed to be occurring besides, or in addition to, or in conjunction with, his *just* speaking or acting? On this question also, which is perhaps the predominant concern in this field of both Wittgenstein and Ryle, there appears to be a large measure of agreement. It appears to be widely agreed that, as both those philosophers have powerfully argued, it is a mistake to succumb to the temptation to assume that *anything at all* must be going on. To put it very briefly indeed—to talk significantly, to act intelligently, is not to talk *and* think, to act *and* think: there is not, nor need there be, any "mental" shadow-process running concurrently with, and in some mysterious way conferring intelligence on, the processes of speaking or doing. It may be said, as Ayer has said, that the difference between one who speaks with, and one who speaks without, understanding really resides, not in the concurrent "mental states," but in the "dispositions," of the two speakers: and this, though of course it is nothing more than a highly unspecific blueprint for a possible philosophical view, would as such, I believe, be accepted without demur by most philosophers in the contemporary tradition with which we have here been concerned.

REFERENCES

AYER, A. J. *Thinking and meaning.* London: H. K. Lewis, 1947.
MURDOCH, I., LLOYD, A. C., & RYLE, G. *Thinking and language.* Proc. Aristotelian Soc., Supplementary Volume XXV, 1951, pp. 25-82.
PRICE, H. H. *Thinking and representation.* London: Oxford, 1946. (Reprinted from *Proc. Brit. Acad.,* Vol. XXXII.)
PRICE, H. H. *Thinking and experience.* London: Hutchinson, 1953.
RYLE, G., *The concept of mind.* London: Hutchinson, 1949.
RYLE, G., *A puzzling element in the notion of thinking.* London: Oxford, 1958. (Reprinted from *Proc. Brit. Acad.* Vol. 44.)

WITTGENSTEIN, L. *Philosophical investigations*. Oxford: Blackwell Scientific Publications, 1953.

WITTGENSTEIN, L. *The blue and brown books*. Oxford: Blackwell Scientific Publications, 1958.

26 DAVID M. ARMSTRONG

A THEORY OF PERCEPTION

1. *Perception is the acquiring of knowledge of our environment.* If we want to know what sense perception *is,* it may be helpful to ask what the senses *do* for us. The answer to this second question is obvious: the senses give us information about our environment, including our own body. This suggests the possibility of saying that sense perception is simply *a flow of knowledge or information about our environment;* or, in the case of sensory illusion, *a flow of false beliefs or misinformation.*

I shall first try to work out this conception more fully, then I shall consider some obvious objections. I hope to show that all these objections can be met, provided that the original conception is complicated and modified a little.

2. *The knowledge acquired is subverbal:* it is clear that the knowledge acquired in perception need not be put into words. I can see that there is a horse before me without saying anything, and without any words passing through my mind. Vision, in particular, yields such a continuous flood of information that it would be impossible to put it all into words. Again, animals can perceive, sometimes better than we can, yet they entirely lack words. So, if we conceive of perception as the acquiring of knowledge, we must say that it is *subverbal* knowledge.

3. *But perception involves concepts.* If perception is the acquiring of knowledge or information about the environment, then it must involve an awareness of resemblances and differences among the objects perceived. This in turn means that it must involve some *sorting* and *classifying* of objects, even although the sorting and classifying is not a matter of applying *words* to things. And this justifies us, I think, in saying that perception must involve *concepts,* although they may be only subverbal concepts. (Here, perhaps, I am doing no more than *recommending* that we speak of perceptual awareness of resemblances and differences as "involving concepts." But it seems a natural way of speaking.)

4. *Perceiving is always perceiving that something is the case.* Verbs of perception take two different sorts of accusative. We say we see *a horse,* and we also say we see *that there is a horse before us.* In the first case, the

489

accusative of the verb "to see" is a *thing*. It could also be an *event*. ("I see the horse overtaking another horse.") But in the second case the accusative of the verb is a fact about the world.

Some philosophical accounts of perception seek guidance from the first idiom, others from the second. Those accounts which are influenced by talk of perceiving *things* or *events* take the essential feature of perception to be a direct confrontation of some object: either sense impression or physical thing. Russell's "knowledge by acquaintance" is an example of such a theory. "Perceiving that" is then taken to be a matter of forming judgments which are *based upon* this simpler mode of cognition. By contrast, theories influenced by the second idiom take perception, even in its simplest form, to be essentially judgmental.

If perception is said to be a flow of knowledge or information, then it is clear that we must be guided by the second idiom. We must say that all perceiving entails perceiving that something is the case. To smell a smell is to smell *that* there is a smell in our vicinity now. To hear a noise is to hear *that* there is a noise within earshot. And so for all cases where we are said to perceive things or events.

Our theory must explain why there are, nevertheless, the two distinct modes of speech. One obvious reason for speaking of perceiving *things* is brevity. It is quicker to say "I smell cooking" rather than "I can smell that there is cooking going on." But there is also a rather more interesting reason why we do not always speak of *"perceiving that. . . ."* We speak of perceiving things or events, not simply for brevity, but also because this idiom is a *noncommittal* one. If I say I perceived a horse, this does not commit me to saying just what information it was that I acquired. It does not even commit me to saying that I acquired the information that there was a horse before me. For it is possible to say "I saw a horse, but failed to realize that it was a horse." (If I say "I saw that there was a horse before me" I cannot add "but I failed to realize that it was a horse.") Now in view of the overwhelming flood of information that we are constantly gaining by means of the senses—information that differs from person to person even when their senses are trained on exactly the same object or event—it is very important to have a noncommittal way of speaking. Without such a way of speaking, communication about perceptions would become intolerably complicated.

5. *Perception can be indeterminate.* The philosophically notorious case of the speckled hen shows that perception can be indeterminate. I can see the speckles, but I cannot see just how many speckles there are. This is a serious difficulty for the view that perception is a nonjudgmental confrontation of an object. Such theories seem forced to postulate an *indeterminate* object of perception to account for the case of the speckled hen.

But such cases can be easily explained if we take the view that perception is the acquiring of knowledge. For there is not the slightest objection to knowledge being more or less determinate. When I turn my eyes toward the hen, I acquire the knowledge that it has *a considerable number of speckles,* without acquiring the knowledge that it has ninety-three speckles.

6. *Knowledge is dispositional, but the acquiring of knowledge is an event.* Modern philosophy (and, in particular, the work of Wittgenstein) has made us realize *clearly* that to say a man knows that something is the case does not entail that something is currently going on in his mind, or that he is currently engaging in any relevant behavior. We can say of a sleeping man that he knows when Columbus discovered America. To say that A knows *p* is to attribute only a *dispositional* property to A. This may seem to be a difficulty for our theory of perception, because it seems obvious that if A perceives an object or event then something actually happens in his mind. But in fact our theory does not prevent us from treating perception as a mental *event.* For perception is not knowledge, but is the *acquiring* of knowledge, and the acquiring of a disposition is an event. If, for instance, a glass becomes brittle at times T_1, that is an event, even although brittleness is a mere disposition of the glass.

Now the word "event" is sometimes used to apply to something that covers a stretch of time. But the word is also used to refer to the instant of transition from one state of affairs to another. To win a race is an event in this second sense. Up to a certain instant, the winner has not yet won the race, although he may be winning. After that instant, he has won the race. "The winning of a race" is thus an event, but not an event that takes time. Perception is also an event of this sort. Up to a certain moment I have not yet perceived a certain state of affairs, from that moment on I *have* perceived it. And, of course, this fits our theory of perception very well. Up to a certain moment I have not yet acquired a certain piece of knowledge about my environment, from that moment on I have acquired it.

We owe the recognition that perception is an event, in the sense in which winning a race is an event, to Gilbert Ryle. He put the point by saying that verbs of perception are "achievement words." His contention is sometimes attacked by pointing out that we can perceive an unchanging scene for a period of time. To espy a robin may be an achievement, but where, it is asked, is the achievement involved in staring at a brick wall? However, if we think of perception as the acquiring of knowledge, and if we remember that we cannot stare at a wall *without time passing,* this objection is easily met. At T_1 we acquire the information that there is a wall before us at T_1. At T_2 we acquire the information that the wall is still before us at T_2. This is new, even if not unexpected and somewhat monotonous, information. And so for every distinguishable instant that we are gazing at the wall.

Ryle's insight here is sometimes confused with a much more familiar point which he also makes. We often use the word "perceive," and its determinates "see," "hear," and so on to imply that the perception reported is *veridical*. If I perceive something, that thing has physical existence. Now when Ryle compares verbs of perceiving to words like "winning" this may mislead us into thinking that he is simply calling attention to the "success-grammar" of such words. But this is a mistake. For the word "know" has the same "success-grammar" as "see" and "hear." What I know must be true, and if something I claim to know turns out not to be true after all I must withdraw the word "know." But, as we have already mentioned, to know that something is the case is *not* an event. The important point about perception is that it is a *getting* to know, it is an *arrival* at success. This becomes clear if we remember that misperception, if it is conceived of as the acquiring of false beliefs, is *also* an arrival, an arrival at failure. But an arrival at the wrong terminal is still an arrival, and losing a race is as much an event as winning one.

7. *The knowledge acquired in perception is manifested in behavior.* The brittleness of glass is manifested, when it is manifested, by the breaking of the glass under the stress of comparatively small impacts. Now, if perception is the acquiring of knowledge, and if knowledge is a dispositional property of persons, in what way is this knowledge manifested, when it is manifested?

In human beings the knowledge acquired may be manifested in words, and in thoughts that are naturally expressed in words. But there can be no such manifestation in animals, and even in the case of human beings much that they perceive eludes verbalization. I believe that the primary manifestation of the knowledge acquired in perception is certain sorts of nonverbal *behavior*.

Suppose that a human being or animal is presented with otherwise similar objects that have different colors. If, by the use of its eyes, it is able to behave in a systematically different way to objects with a different color, for instance, by putting all objects of the same color together, then we say that it can *see the difference* between the different colors. Now it may be said that such behavior is a mere *inductive sign* that the person or animal can see colors. But I am suggesting that the relation between the behavior and perception is more intimate than that. In default of some very unusual circumstances being described, the occurrence of such behavior *entails* that the organism has perceived the differences of color. In just the same way, if a glass breaks when it is given a very light tap, then, in default of some very unusual circumstances being described, this *entails* that the glass has become brittle. The *tests* by which we determine whether human beings and animals can or cannot make certain discriminations by means of their senses, have a *logical* relevance to the question what knowledge they have acquired by their senses.

So, when we perceive, we acquire the capacity to manifest certain discriminating behavior toward the things in our environment. When this discriminating behavior corresponds to actual resemblances and differences among objects in our environment, it is veridical perception. Where it fails so to correspond, it is misperception.

This account of perception as the mere acquiring of capacities to manifest discriminating behavior is exposed to very obvious objections, which can only be met by in some degree modifying the theory. But, before considering these objections, I shall develop the theory still further.

8. *The role of the sense organs is causal only*. We speak of seeing *with* our eyes, or hearing *with* our ears. According to the theory I am developing, this simply means that stimulation of the sense organs *causes* us to acquire knowledge about our environment. As a causal result of my having eyes, and their being open and otherwise in a normal state, I acquire the knowledge that there is a horse before me. We learn to manipulate our eyes and other sense organs in certain ways, because we discover by experience that this is an effective way of gaining knowledge of certain things that go on in our environment.

To this it may be objected that there is more than a contingent connection between seeing and having eyes, smelling and having a nose, tasting and having a tongue, hearing and having ears. To say I see with my ears sounds not merely false, but nonsense. It seems to break a rule of language. But I think that this linguistic rule is based solely on our extreme familiarity with the causal connection between the possessing of certain organs, on the one hand, and the acquiring of certain sorts of knowledge about the environment, on the other.

It is worth noticing, in any case, that there is one species of perception with which no sense organ is naturally associated. This is bodily perception. We can perceive that our body temperature is up, or that our legs are crossed, or our stomach distended, without being able to say what we perceive these things *with*. This reinforces the view that the role of the sense organs in perception is purely causal.

9. *Immediate and mediate perception:* I must now draw the very important distinction between what is *immediately* and what is *mediately* perceived. It is natural to say, when we start to think about perception, that the only things that can be perceived by sight (to take one sense as an example) are the colors, shapes, and spatial relations of things. And so for every other sense: it is natural to say that each is restricted to what Aristotle called the "proper sensibles." Yet, at the same time, reflection on the way we actually use words like "see" makes this claim appear absurd. I do not say I see things having a certain color and shape, but instead that I see a horse or a house, which are far more than things of a certain color and shape.

We may try to reach a fair compromise by distinguishing between *immediate* and *mediate* perception. We may say, as a first attempt, that what happens in visual perception is that we immediately percieve a thing of a certain shape and color, and that we then go on to *infer* that this thing is a horse, which we say is mediately perceived. Put in terms of our own analysis of perception, this would come down to saying that we first acquire the information that there is a thing of a certain shape and color before us, and then go on to infer that this thing is a horse.

But to talk of "inference" brings to mind a process that is self-conscious and that takes time. Following Berkeley, we might consider the word "suggestion." I acquire the information that there is a thing of a certain shape and color before me, and this *suggests* to me that this thing is a horse. But even this word has misleading overtones. The "transition" from immediate to mediate perception is normally perfectly automatic and perfectly instantaneous.

The mention of Berkeley must not mislead. Berkeley took the immediate objects of perception to be *mental* objects: "ideas" or sensations. My distinction between the objects of immediate and mediate perception is a distinction between different *objective states of affairs*. By using my eyes, I acquire the knowledge that there is a physical existent of a certain color and shape before me, and I automatically and instantaneously pass from this knowledge to the further knowledge that it is a horse.

We can draw a parallel distinction in the case of misperception. Having an hallucination as of a cat before us, for example, can be analyzed in the following way. Due to aberrations in my central nervous system, I acquire the false belief that there is a thing of a certain shape and color before me, and I pass automatically and instantaneously to the further false belief that this thing is a cat. (It is also possible to have cases where immediate veridical perception leads to illusory mediate perception, and even cases where illusory immediate perception leads to veridical mediate perception.)

(There is one phenomenon, that we might be tempted to call mediate perception, which is not an acquiring of knowledge. If I immediately perceive certain markings on a surface, I may *see* them as forming a picture of something. This might be called mediate perception, but it is scarcely an acquiring of knowledge. What happens here, I think, is that, instead of automatically and instantaneously *acquiring further knowledge* of the objects perceived, I am automatically and instantaneously *reminded of* or *put in mind of* further objects by the objects immediately perceived. This point requires to be worked out much more fully, but I lack space. Wittgenstein's remarks on "seeing as" would be very important here.)

If our previous contention, that the knowledge acquired in perception is primarily manifested in behavior, is accepted then both immediate and mediate perception will be acquirings of knowledge manifested in certain sorts of discriminatory behavior. Suppose an animal can discriminate between doors painted green, beyond which lies food, and doors painted red, beyond which no food lies. Its behavior tells us it has an immediate perception of green and of red, and that it has a mediate perception that there is food behind the green object.

10. *Perception can be unconscious.* The difficulty that many people feel about this distinction between immediate and mediate perception is that immediate perception, as we have described it, bulks so little in our consciousness. Consider the following case. I pass quickly through a room, and while doing so my eyes rest briefly on a chair. Afterward I can say that there was a chair there, but am quite unable to say anything about its shape and color. Did I really have an immediate perception of its shape and color? [1]

But, it is interesting to notice, in such a case we are not inclined to say simply that we did not perceive the shape and color. Rather, what we are inclined to say is that, although we have no memory of it, we *must* have seen the shape and color of the chair. Why do we say this? I think we do so because we are very unwilling to give up the contention that all visual perception starts from a perception of the visual "proper sensibles": color, shape, etc. It is an elementary piece of *psychological theory* which has proved its worth in so many other ways that we are reluctant to give it up here.

I think we are quite right not to give the theory up. And we shall find it much easier to stick to the theory once we accept the notion that perception need not be *conscious.* Consider another case, also suggested to me by Noel Fleming. I am walking along deep in conversation, and, while doing so, step over a log that lies in my path, with every appearance of care and concentration. Yet I remain completely unaware that I have done so. A remark about the log made the next moment by my companion draws the response "What log?" I think we must say here that I saw the log, although I was completely unconscious of doing so. In this case, not only was I unconscious of acquiring the knowledge that there was a log before me, but I was also unaware of the behavior in which my knowledge was manifested (carefully stepping over the log). There could also be cases where my unconsciousness was less complete. Suppose I pass a hoarding on the street, but am not aware of seeing what was written on it. But, when I am asked what was written on it, I find to my surprise that I can answer readily. Here the acquiring of knowledge was unconscious, but the manifestation of the knowledge is not. Similarly, there could be cases where the acquiring of the knowledge was conscious, and the knowledge was manifested, but we were unconscious of the manifestation.

Now "seeing a log" or "seeing what was written on a hoarding" are cases of *mediate* perception. But the cases were introduced simply to show that there is nothing objectionable in the notion of *unconscious* perception. Hav-

---

[1] This case was put to me by Noel Fleming. The first draft of this paper was written at Yale University, and I benefited greatly from conversations with Noel Fleming and Wilfrid Sellars. They may think that I could have benefited further.

ing shown this, we can turn round and suggest that the peculiar "transparency" of our immediate perceptions reflects the fact that they are normally perceptions of which we are hardly conscious, or even, sometimes, totally unconscious. It is in the case of *sight* particularly that our immediate perceptions are little regarded. Sight presents us with a flood of information about the visual qualities of things; but it is information in which we are little interested for its own sake, our concern being with the objects that these visual qualities are qualities of. So the knowledge acquired in immediate visual perception fades very fast, and, on many occasions, we are even unconscious of acquiring it.

11. *The role of causality in perception.* It is part of our concept of veridical perception that what is perceived is causally responsible for the perception of it. Suppose that I have visual experiences as of an orange before me, and suppose that there really is an orange before me that corresponds to my visual experiences. Does this entail that I am perceiving the orange? I do not think it does, because it is at least conceivable that evidence might be produced to show that I would have had that "perception" even if there had been no orange before me. (My brain was being probed in just the right way.) In order to eliminate this possibility, it must be added that it is the orange before me that actually *brings it about* that I have the visual experience as of an orange before me. In veridical perception, the objects perceived are the causes of the perception.

If we ask just what it is in the objects we perceive that is responsible for our perceptions of them, we are led back once more to the special role of the objects of *immediate* perception. It is clear that the whole orange was not *necessary* for the bringing about of our perception. What was essential was the portion of the orange that was actually in the visual field: a part of its surface. It was light waves from this surface that actually acted on our eyes, and so on our mind. But equally it was this surface that was the immediate object of sight. So we can say that, in veridical perception, the objects immediately perceived act on our sense organs to produce the perception.

12. *Objection: perception is a mental experience.* But now let us begin to develop objections to the theory sketched so far. It may be objected that the theory is a purely behavioristic theory of perception. For perception is defined in terms of the acquiring of knowledge, knowledge is said to be a mere disposition or capacity, and this disposition or capacity is manifested in terms of behavior. And surely this leaves out of account the *mental experience* of perceiving? Acquiring a certain disposition or capacity may be an event, in the sense in which winning or losing a race is an event, but surely perception is, or involves, a *private mental event* of which only the perceiver is directly aware? It is true that we have argued that perception can, on occasion, occur without our being aware of it, but to say this is to

imply that sometimes we *are* aware of perceiving. And how can that be reconciled with our theory?

Now I do not want to put forward a purely behavioristic account of perception. I agree that, on many occasions, when we perceive we are introspectively aware of an inner mental event, and that that event is a perception (or a misperception, as the case may be).

But now the question arises "How are the inner mental events given to introspection to be *characterized?*" According to some philosophers, a perception of something blue can itself be characterized as being *blue,* or a perception of something round can be characterized as being *round.* I think this is a complete mistake. When I perceive a blue wall I have a perception *of* something blue, but not a blue perception. So how can we describe a perception? What is it, as it is given to us in introspection?

I do not believe that we can say anything of the nature of the perception of something blue, as it is given to introspection, except that it is the *experience* of acquiring the information or misinformation that there is a blue thing before me now. And if we are asked to describe the experience further, then I think all we can say is that it is "that which manifests itself, if it does manifest itself, in certain sorts of behavior—in particular, in blue-discriminating behavior."

An imaginary example may help to make what I am saying a little clearer. Suppose there are glasses which, at a certain point in their history, become brittle. (This will be due to a change in the molecular structure of the glass.) It is imaginable that I should have the ability to say, and say truly, on the basis of no evidence whatsoever, when this change for the worse takes place. I should be directly aware of the occurrence of an event within the glass. But, it might be, I could characterize the event *only* by saying that it is the acquiring of brittleness, and could characterize brittleness only as that which is manifested, if it is manifested at all, by the breaking of the glass under the impact of comparatively small forces. Now, I am claiming, introspective awareness of perception is simply a direct awareness of an event within us which can be characterized only as a disposition or capacity manifested, if it is manifested at all, in certain sorts of behavior.

We can perhaps put the matter this way. What we acquire in perception may be said to be a *map* of our physical environment, including our own body. Where the map acquired is accurate, this is veridical perception, where inaccurate, it is misperception. But when we are aware of our own perceptions, the *intrinsic* nature of this map is not given to us. We are simply aware that there is something within us which maps the world, whether well or ill, and so allows us to treat different parts of the environment differently.

What in fact is this inner happening which is apt for certain discriminatory activities toward our environment? I cannot possibly develop and defend my answer here, but I should be prepared to argue that it is, as a matter of empirical fact, a *structure in the brain.* I should further maintain that introspective awareness of this structure is itself a further process in the brain. It is possible, however, to maintain that the inner happening, and our introspective awareness of the happening, are nonmaterial or spiritual processes. I do not think that *unaided* introspection can do anything to settle the point.

13. *The nature of sense impressions.* It is tempting to say that what I was doing in the previous section was putting forward a theory of what it is to be aware of having *sense impressions.* But while this would be on the right track, I do not think it is absolutely accurate. I was trying to give an account of what it is to be aware of our *perceptions,* and we cannot identify sense-impressions with perceptions *simpliciter.*

We can find cases when we might be prepared to grant that two people have more or less qualitatively identical sense impressions, yet have quite different perceptions. Consider the case where two people look at a printed page, and one knows what the words mean, but the other cannot read. It is clear that they have different *perceptions.* The one sees meaningful words, the other nothing but black marks on white paper. But is it not possible (whether or not it is true) that they are having the same visual sense impressions?

Once again, the matter can be cleared up by appealing to the distinction between immediate perception or misperception, on the one hand, and mediate perception or misperception, on the other. When we speak of sense impressions, I suggest, we are speaking of our perceptions, but we are confining ourselves to our *immediate* perceptions, the information or misinformation which is *immediately* acquired, and which is restricted to the "proper sensibles." They are the immediate *impressions* that the environment, acting like a seal on a block of wax, makes on the mind. But these impressions can be characterized only by saying that they map a part of our physical environment, more or less accurately, and so enable us to treat different features of that environment in systematically different ways.

Notice that our sense impressions are not to be conceived of as the *evidence* for our immediate beliefs about the environment. For, it is noted that these sense impressions are themselves the acquirings of these immediate beliefs.

There are certain cases where perception occurs, but there is no acquiring of true or false beliefs.

In the first place, it is often pointed out that it is possible to have perceptions that do not correspond to reality, yet quite fail to be *deceived* by them, that is, quite fail to acquire false beliefs. In the case of visual perception, this is a familiar experience. When we look into a mirror, the visual appearance that we are presented with is that of a mirror-*Doppelgänger* behind the glass. Yet, whatever may be the case for anyone unfamiliar with mirrors, mirror images do not normally deceive us.

The same thing can happen, although it is rarer, in the case of veridical perception. If I am told that the conditions for viewing a certain pond are such that, although it is round, it looks elliptical, then I may *believe* that it is round, although it looks elliptical to me. It may nevertheless be the case that viewing conditions are perfectly normal, and the pond really *is* elliptical. Here we have veridical perception, but no acquiring of knowledge.

In the second place, there are cases where we cannot speak of *acquiring* knowledge or false belief, because we *already have* that knowledge or false belief. Here the normal cases are the ones involving veridical perception. Thus, if I am looking at a red book, I may know with perfect certainty that it will continue to be red during the next instant. So, when my eyes are still resting on the book during that instant, I cannot be said to *acquire* the knowledge that it is now red, because I already knew that it would be red during that instant.

It is possible, although less common, to have the same sort of thing occur in the case of *misperception*. If a pond looks to me to be elliptical, and I believe it to be elliptical, although in fact it is not, I may be perfectly certain that it will be elliptical the next instant. And if I look at the pond at that instant, I cannot be said to *acquire* a false belief, because I already believed that it would be elliptical during that instant.

But I think we can give an account of these cases without having to make major modifications in my theory. In all these cases, it must be admitted, there is *perceptual experience* without the acquiring of knowledge or false belief. But how is this perceptual experience to be characterized? According to our argument in the preceding section, it can only be characterized as the experience of acquiring knowledge or false beliefs. And according to that argument, this knowledge or false belief is a disposition or capacity primarily manifested, if it is manifested, in certain discriminatory behavior. So what we have to say is that, in the cases we are now considering, we have experiences which can only be characterized as being of the *belief-acquiring sort* (beliefs manifested, when they are manifested, in behavior), but without the actual acquiring of the belief.

There are some considerations which may make this solution of the problem more plausible than it seems when it is stated in a bare way.

In all these cases of "perception without the acquiring of belief," be it noticed, it is only because we already have certain other beliefs, independently acquired, that there is no acquiring of belief. We do not believe that our mirror-double stands before us, because we have a great deal of other knowledge about the world which contradicts the belief that there is any-thing like the object we seem to see behind the surface of the glass. These other beliefs, we may say, suppress the false belief that the object we seem to see behind the surface of the mirror is really there. But they do not suppress it entirely, because we are still left with an experience which can be characterized only as a certain sort of belief-acquiring experience, even although it is not accompanied in fact by any belief. In earlier writings on perception, I have spoken of these belief-experiences without belief as "inclinations to believe." This may fit some cases, but in the case of the mirror-image, for example, it is, to say the least, misleading to speak of an inclination to believe that our mirror-double is behind the surface of the glass. It is better to describe it as the *experience* of acquiring a belief with-out any actual acquiring of belief.

A parallel to this logically rather peculiar situation may be found in other fields of our mental life. For example, it is possible to know that one has turned off the gas, yet still be unable to shake off the feeling that one has not done so. This feeling may become so strong as to induce one to take what one *knows* to be the totally irrational action of going back to see if the gas really was turned off. How is this feeling to be characterized? *Only,* I think, as "the feeling that one has not turned off the gas." Yet this feel-ing can co-exist with the *full* knowledge that the gas *has* been turned off. I suggest that this is a model for cases where we have perceptual experiences without the acquiring of beliefs.

The cases where we cannot be said to acquire a belief because we have it already, can be described as the *experience* of acquiring beliefs without any actual acquiring. In the case of our *immediate* perceptions, that is our sense impressions, where the image of the environment acting on our mind like a seal on wax is appropriate, we can think of the seal acting upon the wax a second time, but this time producing no change in the wax, be-cause it simply fits into the imprint it has already made.

14. *"Small perceptions."* Even a reader who is sympathetic to the general line of my argument may still be troubled by a doubt. The doubt may be put this way: talk about acquiring knowledge or false beliefs is too high-flown a way of characterizing much of our perception. In the case of objects that are the center of our attention and interest, speaking of "acquir-ing of knowledge" may seem quite appropriate. But many, perhaps the vast mass, of our perceptions are "small perceptions" that hardly deserve such an honorific description. Consider, in particular, the great flood of de-tail that is involved in our immediate visual perception. Can we say that it is all an acquiring of knowledge or false belief?

The words "small perceptions" recall Leibniz' phrase *"petites percep-tions."* But I have deliberately not used his French words, because I am not referring to the same range of phenomena. "Small perceptions" are "small" not because we are unconscious, or only marginally aware, of them. (In the case of the log that was carefully stepped over, the perception was unconscious, but I do not want to call it a "small perception." For in this case, it is natural to say that *knowledge* was acquired, even though unconsciously.) But, by contrast, even when I recall myself from practical concerns and force myself to become *fully conscious* of the profusion of detail offered by immediate visual perception, I may still want to describe most of these perceptions as something less than the acquiring of knowledge or false belief.

It does seem that it is only the *central* cases of perception that can quite naturally be described as the acquiring of nonverbal knowledge or false belief. But now the problem arises: how are the cases that are not central to be described? It seems to me that they can be characterized only by their resemblance to the central cases. We can say of them only that they resemble the acquiring of knowledge or false belief without fully being such cases. The rapid succession of a huge number of perceptual experiences that I can make myself aware of as my eyes move over the objects in front of me, can only be characterized as events approximating to the acquirings of knowledge or false belief. But they are of too slight and evanescent a nature to deserve fully such description. The environment makes an impression on my mind, but although it is of the same sort as that made in the acquiring of immediate knowledge by the senses, the impression made is less deep and lasting.

15. *Systematic change in the quality of our perceptions.* It appears to be logically possible that the qualities of the objects that we perceive should seem to us to change *in a systematic way.* By this I mean that it seems logically possible that the qualities should seem to change, but that all *relations* that hold between the objects, and their qualities, should seem to remain exactly as before. If this is admitted, then an old problem reappears. Is it not possible that what looks red to you looks green to me, and vice versa, but that the completely systematic difference between our perceptions makes the difference impossible to detect? Yet to allow this possibility seems to falsify my theory of perception. For, in such cases, yours and my *perceptual experience* would differ when we looked at the same surface, but there would be no relevant difference in our behavior toward the object. For instance, we would both apply the word "red" to the top traffic light, and would stop our cars when it shone. But, according to my theory, perceptual experience can only be characterized as the acquiring of certain sorts of knowledge or false beliefs, knowledge and false beliefs *which are manifested in behavior.* But if our actual or potential behavior toward the top traffic light exhibits no relevant difference, it follows that our perceptual experience is qualitatively *the same,* which is contrary to hypothesis.

In fact, however, I believe that the difficulty is not very serious. For I think the case presented is simply a case where the particular sort of inner process that is apt for green-selection behavior, is, in the case of a person with reversed color-experiences, apt for red-selection behavior. Contrariwise, the inner experience that in normal persons gives them a capacity for red-selection behavior, gives him a capacity for green-selection behavior. As we may say, for the person who has reversed color experiences, the wires are crossed. The same behavior, or capacity for behavior, in him and us, springs from different causes in him and us. Once we give up the lurking notion that to have a perceptual experience as of something green is actually to have *something green within us,* this is what difference of perceptual experience must come to.

We can even make sense of the idea that you may perceive a set of qualities, completely different from, but systematically correlated with, the ones that ordinary persons perceive; although this difference is undetectable in speech and behavior. This comes down to the possibility that the inner experiences which give us the capacity to discriminate between a range of objects (for instance, the objects which we all *say* "have different colors") are systematically different processes in you from what they are in normal persons.

What is the ground of the knowledge acquired in veridical perception? I consider a final objection to the theory of perception put forward here. Such a theory, it may be said, can account for our acquiring true and false *beliefs* by means of the senses, but it cannot account for the fact that, by means of the senses, we gain empirical *knowledge.* For, on my view, our immediate perceptions are mere acquirings of belief *that are not based on any evidence.* But if they are not based on any evidence, then they cannot be said to be *knowledge.* We must therefore admit the existence of perceptual experiences which are not mere acquirings of beliefs about the environment, but which form the *evidence* or *ground* on which these beliefs are based.

The first answer to this objection is that, if we accept the existence of such perceptual experiences, we are saddled with the insuperable problems either of the representative theory of perception, or of phenomenalism. For if *experiences of ours* are the ultimate evidence on which all knowledge gained in perception is based, then we have only two alternatives. In the first place, we can make physical objects something distinct from our experiences. But this raises the puzzle how we *infer* from the experiences the physical events which cause them, and so brings up the skeptical problems of a representative theory of perception. Alternatively, we can solve the skeptical problem by identifying physical reality with our experiences "of" that reality. This involves embracing the still greater implausibilities of phenomenalism.

But, in any case, the demand that knowledge, to be knowledge, be always backed up by further good reasons reflects a false view of the nature of knowledge. It is often argued that if A is to know that p is true the following conditions must be satisfied:

1. A believes p.
2. p is true.
3. A has good reasons for p.

But it should be at once evident that this account cannot fit *all* cases of knowledge. The trouble lies with the third condition. To have evidence or good reasons for a proposition p implies that we *know* a proposition q, which is a good reason for p. If this new knowledge is to be analyzed according to the same formula, then, in order to know anything, it will be necessary to know an infinite number of things.

The vicious regress could be brought to an end, and the problem solved, if we could reach ultimate evidence which was absolutely self-evident, that is, logically indubitable. Such evidence would not need to be backed up by further evidence. And it is often argued that our perceptual experiences *do* yield us logically indubitable knowledge which is the ultimate basis for all empirical knowledge. However, although I lack space to argue the point here, I hold that the notion of logically indubitable knowledge is an incoherent one. Records of current sense experience are no more logically free of error than any other form of knowledge.

It seems, then, that if we want to avoid an infinite regress of good reasons, some of the things we know must be known without evidence, yet not be logically indubitable. Our problem then becomes: in the case of such "knowledge without good reasons," what distinguishes it from *mere true belief?*

I believe that the answer must be sought along the following lines. (I lack space to be anything but dogmatic.) If a true belief for which we have no reasons is to count as knowledge, there must exist a *reliable correlation* between holding a belief of that sort and beliefs of that sort being true. The true belief cannot simply be true *by accident*. It must be possible to repeat the belief-performance. Put into the same sort of situation again, I must be capable once again of coming to the same sort of true belief. But I need not *know* that my true belief has this sort of reliability, so there is no regress of reasons.

So we can say that A knows p, yet has no good reasons for p, provided that:

1. A believes p.
2. p is true.
3. A's belief is *reliably correlated* with the truth of p.

Now to apply this to the case of immediate veridical perception. Here, as we have already seen, we not only acquire a true belief about the environment, but, furthermore, that feature of the environment about which we acquire the true belief *causes* us to acquire that belief. The object makes us perceive it. But since like objects, acting on like objects, produce like effects, this means that, in normal circumstances, there is a reliable correlation between our acquiring true beliefs about the objects before us, and the existence before us of the objects. So immediate veridical perception is capable of being an acquring of *knowledge* without good reasons.

It is true that there can be exceptions. Consider the case, suggested to me by Max Deutscher, of an unsophisticated person watching a conjuror. He may have *veridical* immediate perceptions which a more worldly spectator would be properly inclined to discount because of familiarity with the many tricks of conjurors. I think we would say that the unsophisticated spectator's perception was an acquiring of true belief, but not an acquiring of knowledge. Here we have a case of *mere* true belief where, nevertheless, the object of the true belief *causes* the belief. (Incidentally, this is an—unimportant—exception to an account of veridical perception as the acquiring of *knowledge*.) But this case proves only that the causal action upon us of the object perceived does not *invariably* produce that reliable true belief which constitutes knowledge. There remains a very close connection between the fact that, in veridical perception, the object is the cause of the perception, and the fact that veridical perception is normally an acquiring of *knowledge*.

The *skeptic* may still ask how in fact we can be sure that we have *got* knowledge in any particular case of immediate perception. If he is sufficiently pertinacious, he will question any *reason* we advance, asking how we know it to be a good reason. Our answer to him, in the end, can only be that there are certain things we *do* know. If he torments us on the question of perception, we shall, with equal justification, torment him about his knowledge of the existence of a past. If he assaults perception, we shall assault memory, including memory of past perceptual experiences. In the end, we will reduce him to the literally inexpressible doctrine of solipsism of the present instant.

16. *Further problems.* A complete philosophy of perception demands a complete unfolding of a philosophy of mind. I have been able to do no more than indicate the line along which I believe a full account of perception could be developed. And there are certain further problems that naturally arise when we are considering perception, which any complete theory of perception may reasonably be expected to answer. These are the problems of the nature of *bodily sensations, dreams,* and *mental images.*

Of bodily sensations I will say only that I take them to be a species of sense impression. They are sense impressions of *bodily sense,* accompanied, in certain cases, by the taking up of certain attitudes to the having of the impression. I have developed this view in detail in "Bodily Sensations" (1962). If this is correct, they can be brought under my general theory of perception.

Dreams, in so far as they are *sensory* phenomena at all, I take to be hallucinations occurring during sleep, and so also to fall under the general theory. This view of dreaming would need to be defended against the un-true-story-told-on-waking account recently advanced by Norman Malcolm, and what might be called the "idiosyncratic view" at least suggested by the late John Austin (1962, p. 27): ". . . dreams are *dreams*. . . ."

There remains, finally, the interesting question of what account we should give of the *mental images* that are often involved in memory, thinking, and reverie. At present I do not know what to say about the having of these experiences, at once so like, and yet rather different from, the having of sense impressions. But a complete philosophy of perception must include a theory of mental images.

REFERENCES

ARMSTRONG, D. M. *Bodily sensations*. London: Routledge and Kegan Paul, 1962.
AUSTIN, J. *Sense and sensibilia*. Ohio: Ohio Univ. Press, 1962.
MALCOLM, N. *Dreaming*. London: Routledge and Kegan Paul, 1962.

27 MORTON DEUTSCH

SOME PSYCHOLOGICAL ASPECTS
OF SOCIAL INTERACTION

THIS PAPER IS DIVIDED into three sections. The first section outlines some theoretical notions concerning social interaction, the second discusses some critical problems in the initiation of cooperation, and the third summarizes the theoretical notions presented in this paper and comments on the role of "loose theory" in a developing science.

SOCIAL INTERACTION

I start off with the intuitive notion that a key determinant of the nature of social interactions is the way that people perceive their goals to be interrelated. I distinguish two basic ways in which the goals of people may be perceived as being linked. They may be perceived as being linked so that a gain (loss) in the amount or probability of goal attainment for one person implies a gain (loss) for the other person; the term "promotively interdependent linkage" ("co-link") is used to refer to this type of linkage. Or they may be perceived as being linked so that a gain (loss) in the amount or probability of goal attainment for one implies a loss (gain) for the other; the term "contriently interdependent linkage" (abbreviated as "contra-link") is used to refer to this type. A perceived lack of linkage is "no-link." The linkages between two people, "A" and "B," may be symmetrical or not, they may be perceived concordantly or not by the people involved, and they may be perceived veridically or not.

The degree of perceived linkage of A with B is indicated by the magnitude of the perceived correlation between the changes which occur in the amount or probability of A's goal attainment when changes occur in the amount or probability of B's goal attainment. A co-link can vary in degree from 0 to $+1$; a contra-link can vary in degree from 0 to -1. The strength of a linkage for an individual is the product of the degree of perceived linkage and the importance of the individual's goal which is involved in the linkage. (Importance is conceived to be a function of the

506

subjective utility of the goal and of the perceived difficulty of finding a satisfactory substitute for it.) When an individual is linked to another by more than one goal, the resultant linkage is determined by the sum of the strengths of the various goal linkages: the sign of the resultant indicates the type of the over-all linkage, its magnitude indicates its intensity. The ambivalence of a resultant linkage is equal to the strength of the weaker linkage type multiplied by the ratio of the strengths of the weaker to the stronger linkage type.

Although in the preceding paragraphs I have indicated that linkages of either type are not necessarily all-or-none and that the relationship may be asymmetrical and may be perceived discordantly, I shall limit myself in this paper to the consideration of the pure cases of complete promotive and contrient interdependence which are symmetrical and which are perceived consonantly. I employ the term "cooperative situation" to refer to situations in which individuals mutually and concordantly perceive their symmetrical co-linkages; the term "competitive situation" is analogously applied to situations involving contra-linkages. Figure 27-1 illustrates a case

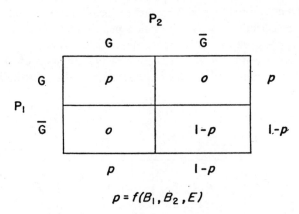

$$p = f(B_1, B_2, E)$$

Figure 27-1. Pure promotive interdependence.

of complete symmetrical co-linkage; concordant perception implies that the relationship is perceived by both persons (P_1 and P_2) to be promotively interdependent. Figure 27-2 illustrates the case of complete, symmetrical contra-linkage. Figure 27-3 illustrates the case of noninterdependence or no-link between the goals of P_1 and P_2.

It may be noted that few real life situations correspond to our definitions of a complete or pure cooperative or competitive situation. Most situations of everyday life involve a complex set of goals and subgoals. Consequently, it is possible for individuals to be promotively interdependent with respect to one goal and contriently interdependent with respect to another. Members of a basketball team may be cooperatively interrelated with respect to win-

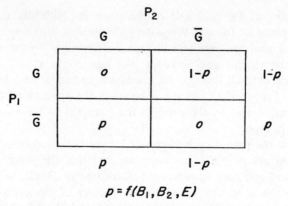

$$p = f(B_1, B_2, E)$$

Figure 27-2. Pure contrient interdependence.

ning the game but competitive with respect to being the "star" of the team. Also, people may be co-linked with respect to subgoals and contra-linked with respect to goals, or vice versa. For instance, firms manufacturing the same product may be cooperative with regard to expanding the total market but competitive with regard to the share each obtains. Moreover, there are certain situations in which people may compete about the terms of their cooperation, as in bargaining. Except for this latter type of situation, which is critical to the discussion of the initiation of cooperation, situations which contain mixtures of cooperation and competition will not be considered.

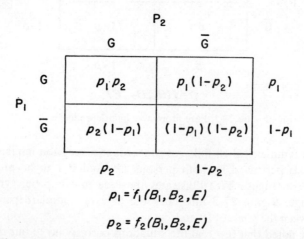

$$p_1 = f_1(B_1, B_2, E)$$

$$p_2 = f_2(B_1, B_2, E)$$

Figure 27-3. Noninterdependence. Each matrix depicts the relationship between the probabilities of goal attainment of two people, P_1 and P_2. Ge $\pm$ goal attainment; Ga = lack of goal attainment. p, p_1, p_2 refer to probabilities and are conceived to be some function of B_1, the behavior of P_1; B_2, the behavior of P_2; and E, events outside the control of P_1 and P_2.

For the purpose of stating hypotheses about the direction and strength of behavior tendencies which result from the two basic types of goal linkages, it is necessary to make some assumptions. First of all, to simplify matters, I shall assume that we are dealing with self-contained systems in which the perceptions of individuals involved in the situation are largely veridical to the situation and to the events which occur in it. Thus, my discussion is of idealized situations which do not have the perturbations and complexities of cooperative and competitive situations found in everyday life. Secondly, I shall assume that the probability and intensity of promotive or contrient behavior upon the part of "A" in relation to "B" is, at any given time, a positive function of: (1) the strength of A's linkage to B; (2) the increase in the likelihood of attaining his goal that A believes would result from engaging in such behavior; (3) his perceived likelihood of goal attainment if he engages in such behavior; (4) the perceived intrinsic attractiveness and lack of cost of the behavior; and (5) the perceived immediacy of goal attainment if he engages in such behavior.

From the assumptions in the preceding paragraph, it is apparent that such factors as goal importance, perceived power to affect one's chances of goal attainment and the like, will be important determinants of behavior in the cooperative and competitive situations. Moreover, differences in goal importance, in perceived power, etc., among the individuals in a given situation will have important consequences. However, let us assume initially that the participants in the situation have approximately equal power and equally important goals involved and let us consider the effects of the two different types of goal interdependence.

Effects of Cooperation and Competition among Equals   From the definition of mutually perceived promotive interdependence, it follows that when any individual behaves in such a way as to increase his chances of goal attainment, he increases the chances that the others (with whom he is co-linked) will also attain their goals. In the case of complete co-linkage between the goals of P_1 and P_2, the co-linked goals may be thought of as the *common goal* of both since the attainment of both goals is a necessary condition for the attainment of either of the individual goals. Several psychological consequences may be expected to follow from the perception of this state of affairs, (see Deutsch, 1949a, for an elaboration of the rationale underlying these expectations):

Substitutability.   If P_1 has moved toward his goal as a consequence of P_2's actions, there is no longer any necessity for P_1 to perform any action which is functionally identical to P_2's: P_2's actions are substitutable for similarly intended actions by P_1 and repetition would be perceived as superfluous. Here, of course, I assume that P_1 has no intrinsic desire to perform the superfluous action and that performing it would involve some cost or delay other actions which would expedite his goal attainment.

Positive Cathexis. If P_1 has moved toward his goal as a consequence of P_2's actions, it seems likely that P_1 will cathect positively P_2's actions and may generalize the cathexis to P_2. Here, I assume that people tend to like events and the perceived causes of events which contribute to their goal attainment.

Inducibility. If P_2's actions move P_1 toward his goals, it may be expected that P_1 will facilitate P_2's actions and will be receptive to P_2's attempts to induce him to engage in behavior which will facilitate P_2's actions. In other words, P_1 will be willing to contribute to the attainment of the common goal.

One may expect just the opposite of substitutability, positive cathexis, and positive inducibility if P_1 perceives that P_2's actions are *decreasing* rather than increasing his chances of goal attainment. He will hinder rather than facilitate, be negatively rather than positively influenced, dislike rather than like, correct rather than be satisfied with P_2's actions. In other words, one may expect radically different forms of behavior in the cooperative situation depending upon whether the actions are seen as increasing or decreasing the chances of goal attainment.

In some respects, the situation of mutually perceived competition resembles the situation of unsuccessful action in the cooperative situation, except that here P_1 will have his chances lessened by P_2's *successful* actions. P_2's successful actions will not be substitutable for similarly intended actions of P_1. P_1 will not cathect such actions positively, nor is he likely to be induced to facilitate such actions. On the other hand, if P_2's actions are bumbling and unsuccessful, one could expect that P_1 would have no need to duplicate them, would be pleased by such actions, and could be induced to facilitate P_2's bumblings or obstruct P_2's successful actions. It should be noted that in these characterizations, we are assuming "pure" situations of promotive or contrient interdependence. Real life situations mostly contain mixtures of both types. Thus, a bumbling competitor may lessen the joy of a sporting contest in which the participants are contriently interdependent with respect to victory, but promotively interdependent with regard to having a challenging contest.

I shall now turn to a consideration of some of the valuable and dysfunctional consequences of "substitutability," "positive cathexis," and "inducibility" for social life and organized collective effort.

Substitutability permits the division of labor and the development of role specialization which seem necessary to the origin and survival of social groups. Role specialization may develop from initial differences in abilities, skills, knowledge, and preferences among individuals in a cooperative situation. With experience of these differences, they may arrive at a crude matching of individual characteristics and task requirements. A poor matching presumably would be corrected because the actions of someone who was inadequate in his specialized role would not be seen as substitutable for similarly intended actions by others and, hence, there would be a tendency to redo the actions necessary to goal attainment. In effect, some-one else would be performing the activities that were initially done inade-quately. Role specialization could, of course, develop accidentally or by arbitrary assignment and training; but, once it had occurred, it would be likely to generate further differences in knowledge, skills, and preferences among individuals performing different functions.

Earlier, I assumed that if an individual's actions increase the chances that others will attain their goals, his actions will be cathected positively. If we make the further assumption that an individual desires to be the object of positive cathexis, we may expect that once an individual has experienced success in a given social role, he will tend to value it and seek out occasions which will permit him to perform it. The result of this process, repeated over time, is that individuals develop predispositions to perform certain roles and they come to value the opportunities and conditions which permit them to perform their roles. Thus, the process of cooperative interaction is, in its idealized form, one in which cooperating individuals perform specialized but complementing activities which are motivated in part by values and expectations deriving from prior experiences in coop-erative situations.

The molding of personality predispositions and personal goals so that they support the behavior in a given social role is, of course, a great asset in developing a stable system of cooperative interactions. However, it may also have an important dysfunctional consequence. To the extent that an individual comes to value a given role per se rather than for its contribution to the attainment of goals around which the cooperative sys-tem is based, a potentially disruptive motivational element has been intro-duced into the system. The development of vested interests in roles may make it difficult to restructure the activities comprising a role or to reallo-cate roles in the light of changing experience. This may lead to the devel-opment of contrient interdependence *vis-à-vis* the allocation of internal resources to the different roles. I term this type of dysfunction: the pa-thology of vested interest.

A cooperative system may survive the potentially disruptive influences of individual commitment to specific social roles if it exists in a relatively stable, unchanging environment. In the absence of such a benign environ-ment, it must develop a unifying influence sufficiently strong to counteract divisive individual interests. One such unifying influence inheres in the development of a commitment to and positive valuation of the cooperative system per se. Depending upon the kind of system involved, this type of commitment is referred to as "we-feeling," "team spirit," "group identifi-cation," "company loyalty," "patriotism," and so forth.

Although the perception of cooperative interdependence may be neces-sary to the development of "group identification," it may not be sufficient by itself. I would suggest that, in addition, there must be the perception of an entity which is valued in common by different individuals for its diffuse instrumentality in relation to varying goals and which can, as a consequence, induce common goals relating to the maintenance and survival of the collective entity. The perception of a cooperative system as an entity and its positive evaluation are fostered by many factors. These are probably analogous to the factors which give rise to the sense of the self as an entity in the course of individual development; for instance, the reactions of people outside the cooperative system to the system as an entity, the cognition of other cooperative systems as entities, and the like.

One might speculate that the primary social functions of leadership are concerned with creating and maintaining a sense of unity despite the existence of divisive individual interests. Presumably, then, the emergence of leadership as a function which creates and maintains an over-all sense of organized purpose and coordinated effort is made more likely by the development of specialized roles and the division of labor. As history has amply demonstrated, the thesis that individuals tend to develop vested interests in their social roles is also applicable to the roles connected with leadership functions. This, in turn, creates the potential dysfunctional consequence of a divergence between the goals of the leaders and the goals underlying the cooperative system: the pathology of self-perpetuating leadership.

Positive cathexis contributes to the development and maintenance of organized collective effort by creating new motives for participation in the system of cooperation. To the extent that individuals repeatedly experience an association between their own gratifications and the gratifications of others, they are likely to come to value one another's gratifications and, hence, a new basis for cooperation emerges. That is, when there is development of mutual positive interest in one another's welfare, each person receives vicarious pleasure from the other person's pleasure or satisfaction. Under such conditions, even if the original individual goals around which cooperation developed are attained or changed, a continuing basis for cooperative relations is created. In other words, the development of an interest in the welfare of the other provides a source of motivational stability to a cooperative system which buttresses it against the otherwise debilitating effects of changing individual goals. Thus, it may be said that, though a mutual interest in the other's welfare is not initially a condition of cooperative relations, such mutual interest may arise as a consequence of cooperation and may, then, provide a basis for continuing cooperation.

The developments of personal relations among cooperators also may have dysfunctional consequences—the pathology of favoritism. This pathology is particularly likely to have harmful consequences in situations characterized by rapid change, high mobility, or considerable complexity. In such situations, personal ties may be an impediment to change, a source of internal conflict when mobility is required, and a basis for the erosion of universalistic rules by the obligations of the particularistic ties of a personal relationship. Thus, there is some evidence that one of the personality requirements of upward social mobility is the ability to join and to leave social groups easily—the ability to avoid or resolve a strong emotional attachment to the social groups one has to leave in order to move upward.

Inducibility provides the basis for normative control of individual behavior in the cooperative situation. An individual will be receptive to the influence attempts of others to the extent that he perceives attainment of his goals as promotively linked to theirs and/or dependent on the existence of the cooperative system per se. Normative control functions to elicit cooperative behavior aimed at facilitating the promotive behavior of others or at obstructing the actions of others that are contrient with respect both to goal attainment and to the continued existence of the system. Similarly, the individual should expect that others will be receptive to his attempts to influence them. Thus, mutual inducibility provides the psychological basis for channeling individual effort into a coordinated system of action, moving the group toward goal attainment while maintaining the viability of the cooperative system itself.

Although inducibility is necessary to effective coordinated action, it may give rise to important dysfunctional consequences. This possibility has been dramatically illustrated in the Asch-type experiments where an individual may be induced to make an incorrect judgment in order to conform with the opinion of a majority. We have elsewhere (Deutsch & Gerard, 1955) made the point that most Asch-type experiments involve little in the way of cooperation or "group" influence. However, our results indicate that when promotively interdependent goals are introduced into the Asch situation, conformity tendencies are markedly increased. In effect, inducibility may come to be valued for its own sake or as a sign of one's general cooperative orientation toward others. Under such conditions, an individual may facilitate the actions of others even when it would be more useful to obstruct them, he may agree even when it would be more appropriate to disagree. Groups which arrive at consensus and concerted action based on values which make it difficult for a minority to influence the majority are deprived of the insights which reside in individual judgment.

Effects of Cooperation and Competition on Group Process   Elsewhere (Deutsch, 1949a), I have drawn out the implications of my discussion of substitutability, cathexis, and inducibility to characterize in further detail the effects of cooperation and competition on group process. Results of experimental work (Deutsch, 1949b) have provided substantial support for this characterization. These results indicated that groups of individuals who were promotively oriented to one another, as compared with groups of individuals who were contriently oriented to one another, showed: (1) more coordination of efforts; (2) more diversity in amount of contributions per member; (3) more subdivision of activity; (4) more achievement pressure; (5) more communication to one another; (6) more attentiveness to fellow members; (7) more mutual comprehension of communication; (8) more common appraisals of communication; (9) greater orientation and orderliness; (10) greater productivity per unit time; (11) better quality of product and discussions; (12) more friendliness during discussions; (13) more favorable evaluation of the group and its products; (14) more behavior directed toward helping the group improve its functioning; (15) greater feeling of being liked by fellow members; and (16) greater feeling of obligation and desire to win the respect of others. Other studies have replicated many of these findings (e.g., Back, 1951; Berkowitz, 1957; Gerard, 1953; Gottheil, 1955; Grossack, 1954; Levy, 1953; Mizuhara, 1952; Mizuhara and Tamai, 1952; Schachter, 1951).

In the discussion so far, I have assumed that all participants were equally motivated to attain their goals and were equally capable. These assumptions are, at best, only roughly met in real life situations. Let us now turn our attention to some of the potential effects upon the cooperative process of differences in motivation and capability.

Effects of Differences in Motivation and Capability on the Cooperative Process Let us consider the case where the behavior of P_1 largely determines the probabilities of goal attainment and P_2's behavior is largely irrelevant (or vice versa). An example of this is where a husband and wife both want to live in a given community and the chances of doing so are determined by the husband's efforts to get a job there. Here, the wife's fate is dependent upon the husband's behavior, but the husband alone can produce the outcome. Under these conditions, assuming that both are equally motivated to move to the new community, it may be expected that the power of the husband to *induce* behavior in the wife will be greater than his wife's power over him. This discrepancy in power will present no problem to the wife, since the husband is strongly motivated to relocate. In general, unequal power among cooperators presents no problem when those who have the most power to determine the outcome have equal or stronger motivation for goal attainment than those with lesser power (Rosenberg, 1960). However, consider a situation where the husband has the power to determine the outcome but not sufficient motivation to use his power, while the wife has little power but strong motivation. Here, one may expect the wife either to attempt to increase her husband's motivation, to increase her own power to achieve her goal, or to reduce the strength of her own motivation; one may expect the husband to attempt to reduce his power and/or decrease his wife's perception of his power. I shall not consider the strategy and tactics of influence attempts (see Thibaut and Kelley, 1959, Ch. 7, for a discussion of these matters).

The general principle that I wish to assert is that a stable cooperative relationship exists when there is a strong positive relationship between the amount of power an individual has to determine a group's outcome and the strength of his motivation to achieve that outcome. Thus, if P_1's power is greater than P_2's power and his motivation is weaker, an unsettled situation exists. To bring it into balance, P_2 will attempt to augment his own power, or to augment P_1's motivation, or to reduce his own motivation; and/or P_1 will attempt to reduce his own power, or reduce P_2's motivation, or augment P_2's power, or augment his own motivation. If the attempts to establish a more stable relationship between power and motivation do not succeed, one would expect to find symptoms of dissatisfaction and further attempts to change.

The thesis which I have advanced in the preceding paragraphs is not unfamiliar. It has often been stated that those who control power also control the benefits to be derived from its exercise (Laski, 1935) and, of course, there is considerable statistical evidence to support the view that power and such benefits as income, prestige, educational opportunity, and the like do vary together. However, the point that I am making is somewhat more general; namely, that there is a stabilizing process in cooperative systems which functions to keep motivation and power in balance. When motivation is low and power is high in a given member, other members may attempt, for example, to increase his motivation, whereas he may attempt to decrease his power; when motivation is high and power is low, a member may attempt to increase his power, whereas the others may attempt to decrease his motivation.

Noninterdependence of Goals, Dependence with Regard to Means Figure 27-3 depicts a situation in which the probabilities of goal attainment for P_1 and P_2 are independent. In such a situation it is, nevertheless, possible for a number of different types of relationships to exist between P_1 and P_2. For example, P_1's behavior toward P_2 may determine P_2's chances of attaining his goal and not have any effect on his own chances, E controlling P_1's chances. This would be a case of unilateral dependence. An illustration of this might be an assembly line in which each worker may affect the worker behind him but be affected by the one preceding him. A case of mutual dependence would be illustrated by a situation in which P_1's work determined how much P_2 was paid but did not affect his own pay and, similarly, P_2's work determined P_1's pay but not his own.

The situation in which P_2 is unilaterally dependent upon P_1 may be thought of as an extreme case of "cooperation under conditions of differences in motivation and capability." P_2's power is zero, P_1's power is critical; P_2's motivation is high, P_1's motivation to produce the behavior desired by P_2 may be negligible. One would expect that if P_1 does produce the desired behavior, it would create in P_2 substitutability, inducibility, and positive cathexis. However, one could also expect that the perceived imbalance between power and motivation would result in stabilizing attempts on P_2's part to increase P_1's motivation to produce the desired behavior and/or to increase his own power.

It is apparent that the situation of perceived mutual dependence with regard to means is quite similar in many respects to the situation of perceived promotive goal interdependence; these similarities require no elaboration and have been demonstrated by Thomas (1957). Moreover, it is evident that, over a period of time, the situation of successful mutual dependence will turn into one of promotive interdependence, as each person comes to acquire vicarious satisfaction in the other person's goal attainment. However, there are important differences between the two types of situations. Consider the case in which P_1 is very capable and P_2 is incompetent. If they are promotively interdependent, P_2's incompetence may spur P_1 on to exert additional effort in the attempt to compensate for P_2's inadequacies; in the mutually dependent case, P_2's incompetence would be likely to dampen the effort P_1 would make. Also in the situation of mutual dependence, if P_3, a third person, contributes to P_1's goal attainment, it does not necessarily help P_2; in the situation of promotive interdependence, it does.

CRITICAL PROBLEMS IN THE INITIATION OF COOPERATION

Tinbergen, in his book, *Social Behaviour in Animals* (1953), in answer to the question of how does cooperation originate, asserts (p. 105): "Cooperation is ensured by a system of innate activities in the actor, and of (usually innate) responsiveness to the actor's behaviour in the reactor." The situation for man is, of course, radically different: complementing innate mechanisms do not "coerce" coordination and social cooperation. The paramount fact about human cooperation is, as Asch (1952, p. 162) has pointed out, that it is based on the human "capacity to perceive a situation that includes others and ourselves and to perceive others as referring themselves to the same situation." In contrast to bio-social forms of interaction, which are dependent on innate signal and releasing tendencies, human interaction is founded on the fact that the happenings in a social encounter can be psychologically represented in each of the participants, on the enlarged capacity of humans to take into account the joint situation of oneself and the other.

The human choice to cooperate or not, thus, frequently has as its context an awareness that cooperation with another cannot be consummated unless the other's choice is consonant and coordinated with one's own.

The problems involved in achieving mutuality of choice do not, of course, arise in choosing an inanimate object. For example, if one chooses to eat a strawberry pie, one does not have to be chosen by it in order to eat it. Since cooperation depends on mutual and consonant choices, when an individual makes his choice to cooperate or not he is faced with three critical problems—the problem of trust, the bargaining problem, and the problem of coordination. Each are discussed below in terms of the question which it poses for the potential cooperators:

1. Can he and the others trust one another sufficiently to take the risks involved in initiating cooperation? Cooperation will not develop unless at least one person initiates it through actions which are clearly recognizable as contributing to the attainment of the mutually interdependent goals. Taking the initiative, however, may involve a cost which the individual would not be willing to bear unless he felt that the others were sufficiently trustworthy to reciprocate with further cooperative actions. Figure 27-4 illustrates the problem of trust. P_1 has to choose between rows A and B and has to announce his choice before P_2 chooses. Clearly, unless he can trust that P_2 will choose column X in response to his choice of row A, he is likely to choose row B.

Figure 27-4. The trust problem. This and the following matrixes should be read as follows: P_1 chooses between rows A and B, P_2, between columns X and Y. P_1's payoffs are the first numbers in the cell; P_2's, the second.

Using the experimental game illustrated in Figure 27-4, my colleagues and I (Deutsch, 1957, 1958, 1960a, 1960b; Loomis, 1959; Solomon, 1960) have conducted a series of theoretical and experimental investigations bearing on the determinants of trusting behavior. The essential psychological feature of the game is that there is no possibility for "rational" individual behavior in it unless the conditions for mutual trust exist. If each player chooses to obtain either maximum gain or minimum loss for himself, each will lose. But it makes no sense to choose the other alternative, which could result in maximum loss, unless one can trust the other player. If one cannot trust it is, of course, safer to choose so as to suffer minimum rather than maximum loss, but it is even better not to play the game. If one cannot avoid playing the game and if one cannot trust, there may be no reasonable alternative except to choose "the lesser of two evils" and/or attempt to develop the conditions that will permit mutual trust.

There are many social situations similar to the game, in the sense that they do not permit rational individual behavior unless the conditions for mutual trust exist. Any social situation in which an individual may enhance his own satisfactions to the disadvantage of another by not adhering to the normative expectations or "social rules" governing the situation is of this sort—e.g., buyer–seller transactions, husband–wife relationships, pedestrian–driver interactions, a crowd in a theater when there is a fire, disarmament negotiations. In everyday situations, mutual trust is predicated on the existence of socialized motives (for instance, an interest in the welfare of others, a desire for social approval, a conscience), external authority, or other arrangements that will provide the participants with an incentive for adhering to the rules. Generally, if people who are willing to adhere to the rules cannot trust other participants in the situation to do so, there is little possibility for rational behavior except to attempt to develop the conditions under which mutual adherence to the rules will occur.

In such a situation, what are the conditions which lead to mutually trusting behavior? From our experimental and theoretical studies of trust I would draw the following over-all generalizations: (1) Mutual trust is most likely to occur when people are positively oriented to each other's welfare. (2) Mutual trust can occur even under circumstances where the people involved are indifferent to each other's welfare (i.e., neither cooperatively or competitively oriented to one another), provided that one or more of the following conditions exist: (a) There is opportunity for each person to know what the other person will do before he commits himself irreversibly to a trusting choice. (b) There is opportunity and ability to communicate fully a system for cooperation which defines mutual responsibilities and also specifies a procedure for handling violations and returning to a state of equilibrium with minimum disadvantage if a violation occurs. (c) Each person has power to influence the other person's outcome and hence to reduce any incentive he may have to engage in untrustworthy behavior. (d) There is a third person whose relationship to the two players is such that each perceives that a loss to the other player is detrimental to his own interests *vis-à-vis* the third person.

2. Can he and the others resolve differences in preferences or conflicts of interests over the various cooperative agreements that might be made? This is the bargaining problem, which is illustrated in Figure 27-5. P_1 would obviously prefer an agreement in which he chose row B and P_2

chose column X; P_2 would obviously prefer an agreement which involved the choices of row A and column Y; both players are clearly better off if they reach agreement than if they do not.

P_2

		X	Y
	A	0,0	+2,+4
P_1	B	+4,+2	0,0

Figure 27-5. The bargaining problem.

The outcome of a bargaining process—whether or not agreement is reached and if so on what terms—depends, I believe, on two broad sets of factors: (1) the factors determining the relative strengths of the bargainers' respective cooperative and competitive interests and (2) the abilities, resources, and freedom the bargainers have available for the invention and communication of potential bargaining agreements which might affect the strengths of their cooperative and competitive interests.

We have recently initiated a program of research on some of the factors affecting the outcome of a bargaining process (Deutsch & Krauss, 1960; Deutsch, 1961; Deutsch & Krauss, 1962). This research has, so far, been concerned with study of some of the factors that influence the strength of the cooperative and competitive interests of the bargainers. We have employed an experimental bargaining game in which a pair of subjects are presented with a bargaining problem which requires the development of a cooperative agreement in order to maximize the amount of (imaginary) money won. Subjects undergo twenty repetitions of the same bargaining problem.

In the first of several experiments, we examined the effect of the availability of threat on our subjects' behavior. Three conditions of threat were employed: no threat (neither player could threaten the other); unilateral threat (only one player had a means of threat available); and bilateral threat (both players had a means of threat).

The results of Experiment I indicated that the difficulty in reaching an agreement, as well as the amount of money lost individually and collectively, was greatest in the bilateral threat condition and next greatest in the unilateral threat condition. Only in the no threat condition did the players make an over-all profit. In the unilateral threat condition, the player with the threat capability did better than the player without the threat capability. However, comparing the bilateral and unilateral threat conditions, the results also indicate that when facing a player who had a threat capability one was better off *not* having than having the capacity to retaliate in kind.

In a second experiment, we investigated the effect of communication upon the subjects' ability to reach agreements. The same task was employed as in the previous experiment, except for the fact that subjects were permitted to talk over an intercom system. The results indicated that the communication variable had no effect on the difficulty of reaching agreements in our bargaining game, although the results of Experiment I with respect to the effects of threat were replicated. Players only infrequently availed themselves of the opportunity to communicate; on the average, players communicated on fewer than one-quarter of the trials. Communication was most frequent in the no threat condition and about equally frequent in the bilateral and unilateral threat conditions, although these differences were not statistically significant.

Because subjects in Experiment II communicated so infrequently, any conclusions based upon these results would relate to the opportunity to communicate per se. In a third experiment, we attempted to overcome this difficulty by running a treatment condition in which subjects were compelled to communicate on every trial. We call this treatment "compulsory communication" and the treatment employed in Experiment II "permissive communication." All other aspects of the experiment remained the same.

The results of Experiment III indicated that compulsory communication significantly improved performance in the unilateral threat condition, as compared to the unilateral threat condition under both permissive communication and no communication.

Our interpretation of these experimental results places emphasis on the assumption that the use of threat strengthens the competitive interests of the bargainers by introducing or enhancing the competitive struggle for self-esteem. This assumption is based upon the view that to allow oneself to be intimidated, particularly by someone who does not have the right to expect deferential behavior, is (when resistance is not seen to be suicidal or useless) to suffer a loss of social face and, hence, of self-esteem; and that the culturally defined way of maintaining self-esteem in the face of attempted intimidation is to engage in a contest for supremacy *vis-à-vis* the power to intimidate or, minimally, to resist intimidation.

3. Can he and the others coordinate their actions in such a way that they will mutually benefit? This is the problem of coordination. Figure 27-6 illustrates the coordination problem. P_1 has to choose among rows A, B, C, and D; P_2 has to choose among columns W, X, Y, and Z. If their choices are coordinated appropriately, each will profit; lack of coordination may produce mutual loss or no gain. In such a situation, P_1's best course of

action depends on the action he expects P_2 to take, which depends in turn on P_2's expectation of P_1's action. Each must try to guess what the other guesses he will guess the other to guess, and so on. What permits the convergence of expectations, rather than the endless spiral of "second-guessing" the other, to occur?

P_2

	W	X	Y	Z
A	+4,+4	0,0	0,0	−4,−4
B	0,0	+4,+4	−4,−4	0,0
C	0,0	−4,−4	+4,+4	0,0
D	−4,−4	0,0	0,0	+4,+4

P_1

Figure 27-6. The coordination problem.

Communication is an obvious way of solving the coordination problem —for example, P_1 says to P_2: "You choose column W and I'll choose row A." However, there are many situations in which communication is impossible or too costly and coordination has to be accomplished tacitly rather than explicitly. Moreover, even when communication is feasible, there is often some necessity for selecting what one communicates from that limited range of possibilities which are likely to be mutually acceptable. Thus, Schelling (1960, p. 70) has pointed out:

> Most bargaining situations ultimately involve some range of possible outcomes within which each party would rather make a concession than fail to reach agreement at all. . . . The final outcome must be a point from which neither expects the other to retreat; yet the main ingredient of this expectation is what one thinks the other expects the first to expect, and so on. . . . These infinitely reflexive expectations must somehow converge on a single point, at which each expects the other not to expect to be expected to retreat.

Schelling (1960, Ch. 3), in a very interesting series of pilot experiments, has demonstrated that it is possible for people to converge their expectations and coordinate their actions even though they have no opportunity to communicate. This was true in situations where the interests of the subjects were purely cooperative (as, "Name 'heads' or 'tails.' If you and your partner name the same, you both win a prize.") and also true in situations which involve tacit bargaining (as, "You and your partner are to be given $100 if you can agree on how to divide it without communicating. Each of you is to write the amount of his claim on a sheet of paper, and if the two claims add up to no more than $100, each gets exactly what he claimed. If the two claims exceed $100, neither of you gets anything. How much do you claim?").

Schelling (1960, p. 70) advances the proposition that certain alternatives serve as focal points around which expectations converge because they enjoy "prominence, uniqueness, simplicity, precedent, or some rationale that makes them qualitatively differentiable from the continuum of possible alternatives." The existence of qualitatively distinct focal points permits tacit coordination in the situation of pure coordination and gives certain outcomes a greater intrinsic magnetism in bargaining situations. Unfortunately, there has been little adequate theorizing or research on the determinants of the convergence of expectations or in the perception of focal points. I suspect that the research by Gestalt psychologists on the determinants of figure-ground relations in perception and by social psychologists on acculturation processes may provide the best leads for understanding the processes leading to the convergence of expectations in situations of tacit coordination.

SUMMARY AND COMMENT

In the first two sections of this paper, I have attempted to develop the notion that an important determinant of social behavior is the way in which the goals of interacting individuals are related. Three fundamental properties of social interaction have been focused upon: substitutability (i.e., the readiness to accept another person's actions as substitutes for one's own); cathexis (i.e., the tendency to develop positive or negative sentiments toward another); inducibility (i.e., the tendency to accept or reject the other's influence attempts). The extent to which one individual's behavior improves or worsens another's chances of goal attainment will determine the direction of the effect of these three mediating variables. The likelihood that A's behavior will improve B's chances is, I have pointed out, determined by the type of linkage between B's goal and A's goal (cooperative or competitive) and by its effects upon A's chances or degree of goal attainment. The magnitude of the effect of A's behavior on B will be determined by the degree of improvement (or worsening) in B's chances or degree of goal attainment which results from A's behavior and the importance of B's goal to B. I have further indicated that the extent to which A's behavior will affect B's chances is determined by the degree of linkage between B's goal and A's goal and by the expected utility of A's behavior in relation to his goal and by A's power or capability to act in relation to his goal.

In the first section, I took as a premise that the people were objectively linked in a given type of interdependence and that they mutually and veridically perceived the nature of this interdependence. In the second section, I considered some of the problems—the problem of trust, the bargaining problem, and the coordinative problem—which may arise in the process of attempting to establish mutual cooperation. Our experimental results suggest that these problems are much easier to resolve if the potential cooperators each have a stake in the other's welfare. The development of mutual interest in one another's welfare is, in turn, fostered by the experience of successful cooperation.

An examination of the ideas presented in this paper would suggest that I have presented what might be termed a "loose theory." The ideas presented form a theory to the extent that they contain a number of concepts which are interrelated so as to lead to a variety of predictable consequences if empirical coordinations are made with the concepts. The theory is a loose one because neither the concepts, nor their interrelations, nor their empirical coordinations are precisely or unambiguously defined. In terms of the criteria for a theory often specified in books on the philosophy of science, it is admittedly a woefully deficient theory. Yet "loose theories" of this kind are rather prevalent in the social sciences. I suggest that their prevalence does not merely indicate the intellectual deficiencies of the theorists but expresses a genuine need of relatively immature sciences.

The very "looseness" of such theories has, of course, an important function. It enables the scientist to keep in contact with phenomena which common sense, experience, and personal intuition suggest are central to his discipline, but which cannot as yet be apprehended in a form sufficiently rigorous for "tight" formalization. An alternative to this, of course, is for the scientist to consciously delimit himself to those aspects of his discipline which can be rigorously apprehended. Such an approach is not without its own pitfalls. The attempt to construct a formalized theory before an appropriate logico-mathematical apparatus has been developed or before there is a rich intuitive grasp of the phenomena being investigated may distract attention from the problems indigenous to one's subject matter. It also may lead to a focus on problems which are "scientifically" tractable in the sense that they enable the investigator to be adequate to an image of science which is modeled after the relatively mature portions of physics. The functions of "theory" in "loose theory" are similar to those of any plausible system of explanation; namely, to provide a communicable framework for integrating experience and empirical research, for stimulating and guiding new research, and for generating novel insights which are not immediately apparent from or necessarily consistent with common sense or personal intuition.

A loose theory to be useful has to be fertile and communicable. But how can a theory which is ambiguous and imprecise achieve these objectives? It would be valuable indeed if students of science turned their attention to this question because there is little doubt that various "loose" theories (such as psychoanalytic theory, G. H. Mead's symbolic interactionism theory, Durkheim's theory of anomie) have been both fertile and communicable.

REFERENCES

ASCH, S. *Social psychology.* New York: Prentice-Hall, 1952.

BACK, K. Influence through social communication. *J. abnorm. soc. Psychol.,* 1951, **46,** 9-23.

BERKOWITZ, L. Effects of perceived dependency relationships upon conformity to group expectations. *J. abnorm. soc. Psychol.,* 1957, **55,** 350-354.

DEUTSCH, M. A theory of cooperation and competition. *Human Relat.,* 1949, **2,** 129-151. (a)

DEUTSCH, M. An experimental study of the effects of cooperation and competition upon group process. *Human Relat.,* 1949, **2,** 199-231. (b)

DEUTSCH, M. *Conditions affecting cooperation.* Final Technical Report for the Office of Naval Research, Contract NONR-285[10], February 1957.

DEUTSCH, M. Trust and suspicion. *Conflict Resolution,* 1958, **2,** 265-279.

DEUTSCH, M. The effect of motivational orientation upon trust and suspicion. *Human Relat.,* 1960, **13,** 122-139. (a)

DEUTSCH, M. Trust, trustworthiness, and the F scale. *J. abnorm. soc. Psychol.,* 1960, **61,** 138-140. (b)

DEUTSCH, M. The face of bargaining. *Operations Research,* 1961, **9,** 886-897.

DEUTSCH, M., & GERARD, H. B. A study of normative and informational social influences upon individual judgment. *J. abnorm. soc. Psychol.,* 1955, **59,** 629-636.

DEUTSCH, M., & KRAUSS, R. M. The effect of threat upon interpersonal bargaining. *J. abnorm. soc. Psychol.,* 1960, **61,** 181-189.

DEUTSCH, M., & KRAUSS, R. M. Studies of interpersonal bargaining. *Conflict Resolution,* 1962, **6,** 52-76.

GERARD, H. B. The effect of different dimensions of disagreement on the communication process in small groups. *Human Relat.,* 1953, **6,** 249-271.

GOTTHEIL, E. Changes in social perception contingent upon competing or cooperating. *Sociometry,* 1955, **18,** 132-137.

GROSSACK, M. Some effects of cooperation and competition on small group behavior. *J. abnorm. soc. Psychol.,* 1954, **49,** 341-348.

LASKI, H. *State in theory and practice.* New York: Viking Press, 1935.

LEVY, S. Experimental study of group norms: the effects of group cohesiveness upon social conformity. Unpublished doctoral dissertation, New York Univ., 1953.

LOOMIS, J. L. Communication, the development of trust, and cooperative behavior. *Human Relat.*, 1959, **12**, 305-316.

MIZUHARA, T. Experimental studies of cooperation and competition. II. *Jap. J. Psychol.*, 1952, **23**, 170-172.

MIZUHARA, T., & TAMAI, S. Experimental studies of cooperation and competition. *Jap. J. Psychol.*, 1952, **22**, 124-127.

ROSENBERG, S. Cooperative behavior in dyads as a function of reinforcement parameters. *J. abnorm. soc. Psychol.*, 1960, **60**, 316-333.

SCHACHTER, S. Deviation, rejection, and communication. *J. abnorm. soc. Psychol.*, 1951, **46**, 190-207.

SCHELLING, T. C. *The strategy of conflict.* Cambridge: Harvard Univ. Press, 1960.

SOLOMON, L. The infleunce of some types of power relationships and game strategies on the development of interpersonal trust. *J. abnorm. soc. Psychol.*, 1960, **61**, 223-230.

THIBAUT, J. W., & KELLEY, H. H. *The social psychology of groups.* New York: Wiley, 1959.

THOMAS, E. J. Effects of facilitative role interdependence on group functioning. *Human Relat.*, 1957, **10**, 347-366.

TINBERGEN, N. *Social behaviour in animals.* New York: Wiley, 1953.

28 FREDERICK B. DAVIS

INTERPRETATION IN MEASUREMENT

PSYCHOLOGICAL MEASUREMENT has attracted the attention and efforts of so many gifted and ingenious workers during the past quarter of a century that the array of techniques and instruments now available in the field is almost bewildering. In fact, this situation has created what may be regarded as a major problem for students, test users, and research workers—that of matching specialized techniques with occasions that particularly call for their use. For test users, the problem is especially troublesome; students ordinarily can turn to their instructors for guidance, and research workers can usually find models to follow. Therefore, techniques for interpreting individual scores and the logical and statistical bases of these techniques will be considered in this chapter.

Almost all interpretations of test scores involve the estimation and evaluation of differences. For example, an individual's score may be compared with those of other individuals to determine whether his performance is better than theirs. His score may be compared with the average of a defined group or with some percentile in that group. If more than one test is administered to the individual, comparable scores may be compared to determine on which test or tests his performance was better than on others. Appropriate comparisons of this kind lead to inferences about possible overachievement or underachievement. When a period of learning takes place between administration of equivalent tests, the difference may be used to estimate the individual's progress. In short, the interpretation of test scores rests very largely on the estimation and evaluation of differences among scores.

It is a truism in educational and psychological measurement that difference scores are apt to be misleading and unreliable; and so they are. This fact plus the inescapable need for using them in the process of test interpretation explains why this chapter is devoted to the estimation of true differences of several types that are commonly used for interpreting individual test scores and to the determination of their statistical significance.

526

BASIC DATA

Three fundamental types of data that must be used if the statistical significance of differences between individual scores, individual scores and group means, and between group means are to be determined are:

1. The standard deviation of the differences between the average score of an individual and each of his obtained scores on an indefinitely large number of equivalent forms of a test administered while no change takes place in the individual's status in the functions measured. This statistic is commonly termed the standard error of measurement.

2. The standard deviation of the differences between the true mean of a sample and the obtained means in the same sample on an indefinitely large number of equivalent forms of a test. This statistic may best be termed the standard error of measurement of the mean.

3. The standard deviation of the differences between the mean score of a test in a population and the means on an indefinitely large number of forms of the same test in samples drawn at random from the population. This statistic is commonly termed the standard error of the mean.

Introduction: The Standard Error of Measurement. Because decisions regarding the significance of any difference involving a test score of an individual are affected by the numerical value of the standard error of measurement of the score and because this value is affected by the method used to estimate it, a thorough understanding of the fundamental nature of this statistic and of methods that may be used to estimate it is essential for anyone who expects to interpret test scores in more than a superficial way. For this reason, the concept of the standard error of measurement and some methods that may be used to estimate it will be presented in a way that, it is hoped, will show the assumptions underlying these methods.

Theoretical basis. Let J_o represent the obtained score of one examinee, and J_t represent his true score on Test J. By definition, an individual's true score is the mean of his scores on an indefinitely large number of equivalent tests, provided that his ability in the function measured does not change throughout the testing. For purposes of this discussion, equivalent tests are defined as those yielding distributions of scores that measure the same functions and that have identical means, variances, and shapes when they are administered to the same sample of examinees. Given J_o and J_t for one examinee, we may write

$$J_o = J_t + J_e \tag{1}$$

where J_e is an error of measurement on Test J. Then, rearranging Equation 1, we may write

$$J_e = J_o - J_t \tag{2}$$

Suppose that an indefinitely large number, *n,* of tests equivalent to Test J
were administered to this examinee. If we assume that the true ability of
the one examinee tested with *n* equivalent forms of Test J remains the same
with respect to the functions measured by Test J throughout the *n* testings,
the variance of errors of measurement in obtained scores on Test J is

$$\sigma^2_{Je} = \sigma^2_{(Jo-Jt)} = \sigma^2_{Jo} + \sigma^2_{Jt} - 2\sigma_{Jo}\sigma_{Jt}\rho_{(Jo)(Jt)} \tag{3}$$

where σ^2 represents a population variance and ρ represents a product-
moment coefficient of correlation in the population. Since the examinee's
true scores are identical, their variance, σ^2_{Jt}, is equal to zero. Hence,

$$\sigma^2_{Je} = \sigma^2_{Jo} \tag{4}$$

and

$$\sigma_{Je} = \sigma_{Jo} = \sigma_{\text{meas } J} \tag{5}$$

where $\sigma_{\text{meas } J}$ is the population standard error of measurement.

If the examinee mentioned was only one of a large sample of examinees
representative of a defined age or grade group, a value for σ^2_{Je} would be
obtained for each examinee. The average of these values would constitute
an over-all variance error of measurement for Test J.

In practice, it is obviously impossible to administer an indefinitely large
number of equivalent tests to any one examinee, much less to a large representative sample of examinees. As a matter of fact, it is impossible to administer even a few equivalent tests of most kinds to any examinee without affecting his true ability or altering his attitude and motivation in such
a way as to change his performance from test to test. Consequently, a different procedure for estimating the standard error of measurement must be
employed.

Practical procedures for speeded or unspeeded tests. Instead of administering to one examinee an indefinitely large number, *n,* of equivalent
tests, we may adopt the procedure of administering in separate time limits
to an indefinitely large number, *N,* of examinees two tests that can plausibly be regarded as yielding distributions of scores like those of equivalent
tests, as defined previously. To make the two tests as nearly equivalent as
possible, each should be composed of the same number of items; these
should be drawn from a common pool in such a way that pairs of items covering each point in the test outline are obtained. Both items in each pair
should be of approximately the same level of difficulty and should have
approximately the same correlation with the total scores on the tryout
test in which they were given to examinees like those for which the final
tests are intended. It should be noted that items for the two tests intended
to be equivalent should *not* be drawn at random from the pool of available
items. Instead, their selection should rest partly on objective item-analy-

sis data, partly on subjective judgment exercised by the test constructor regarding the content measured, and partly on random assignment to one of the tests.

Let the two tests intended to be equivalent be designated J and K. The difference between obtained scores for any examinee may be expressed as:

$$J_o - K_o = (J_t + J_e) - (K_t + K_e) \tag{6}$$

The variance of the N differences will be

$$\sigma^2_{(Jo-Ko)} \equiv \sigma^2_{(Jt+Je-Kt-Ke)} = \tag{7}$$

$$\sigma^2_{Jt} + \sigma^2_{Je} + \sigma^2_{Kt} + \sigma^2_{Ke}$$

$$- 2\sigma_{Jt}\sigma_{Kt}\rho_{(Jt)(Kt)} + 2\sigma_{Jt}\sigma_{Je}\rho_{(Jt)(Je)}$$

$$- 2\sigma_{Jt}\sigma_{Ke}\rho_{(Jt)(Ke)} - 2\sigma_{Kt}\sigma_{Je}\rho_{(Kt)(Je)}$$

$$+ 2\sigma_{Kt}\sigma_{Ke}\rho_{(Kt)(Ke)} - 2\sigma_{Je}\sigma_{Ke}\rho_{(Je)(Ke)}$$

This equation can be greatly simplified if we are willing to make four assumptions pertaining to scores on tests J and K. First, we make the plausible assumption that the ratio of error variance to obtained variance is the same in the equivalent tests; that is,

$$\frac{\sigma^2_{Je}}{\sigma^2_{Jo}} = \frac{\sigma^2_{Ke}}{\sigma^2_{Ko}} \tag{8}$$

Whether σ^2_{Jo} and σ^2_{Ko} could be identical may be inferred by testing the significance of the difference between their sample estimates, as follows:

$$t_{(M-2)} = \frac{\left(\hat{s}^2_{Jo} - \hat{s}^2_{Ko}\right)\sqrt{M-2}}{\sqrt{4\hat{s}^2_{Jo}\hat{s}^2_{Ko}\left(1 - r^2_{(Jo)(Ko)}\right)}} \tag{9}$$

where M is the number of cases in the finite sample.

If $\hat{s}^2_{Jo}$ and $\hat{s}^2_{Ko}$ are found to be insignificantly different at a designated level of probability, it is not unreasonable to infer that σ^2_{Jo} is equal to σ^2_{Ko}. If $r_{(Jo)(Je)} = r_{(Ko)(Ke)} = 0$, it can be shown that

$$\sigma^2_{Jt} = \sigma^2_{Jo}\left(1 + \frac{\sigma^2_{Je}}{\sigma^2_{Jo}}\right) \tag{10}$$

and

$$\sigma^2_{Kt} = \sigma^2_{Ko}\left(1 + \frac{\sigma^2_{Ke}}{\sigma^2_{Ko}}\right) \tag{11}$$

Under the circumstances, σ^2_{Jt} and σ^2_{Kt} in equation 7 may be equal. If conscientious efforts have been made to match the content of tests J and K, it is reasonable to assume that their true scores measure identical functions and have a product-moment correlation that equals unity.

It is also plausible to assume that true scores on Test J have identical correlations with errors of measurement in tests J and K and that true scores on Test K have identical correlations with errors of measurement in tests J and K. Note that these identical correlations need not be zero and need not be the same for true scores on tests J and K.

We may now simplify equation 7, since the first and third terms on the right-hand side will cancel the fifth; the sixth term will cancel the seventh; and the eighth term will cancel the ninth. Equation 7 becomes

$$\sigma^2_{(Jo-Ko)} = \sigma^2_{Je} + \sigma^2_{Ke} - 2\sigma_{Je}\sigma_{Ke}\rho_{(Je)(Ke)} \tag{12}$$

which may also be written as

$$\sigma^2_{(Jo-Ko)} = \left[\sigma^2_{Je} - \sigma_{Je}\sigma_{Ke}\rho_{(Je)(Ke)}\right] + \left[\sigma^2_{Ke} - \sigma_{Je}\sigma_{Ke}\rho_{(Je)(Ke)}\right] \tag{13}$$

In equation 13, the first term on the right-hand side represents the error variance of scores derived from Test J and the second term represents the error variance of scores derived from Test K.

To simplify equation 13, we may consider the probable value of $\rho_{(Je)(Ke)}$. If the errors of measurement in tests J and K, of which the standard deviations are σ_{Je} and σ_{Ke}, result only from chance, their correlation will be zero. Such "chance errors of measurement" come from sources like sampling variations in the items drawn from the common pool or from pure guessing on the part of examinees. Unfortunately, however, systematic errors of measurement may contribute to the variance of J_e and of K_e. Suppose, for example, that an examinee has a severe headache while he is taking both tests J and K. His performance on both tests may be adversely affected, so that the error of measurement (e.g., $J_o - J_t$) in each of his obtained scores is negative. Any systematic influence, except true ability, in the function measured by tests J and K (or some variable that correlates perfectly with it) that increases any examinee's obtained scores on both tests or that decreases his obtained scores on both tests by amounts that vary to some degree from examinee to examinee will cause $\rho_{(Je)(Ke)}$ to take a positive value. It may be noted in passing that, if the obtained scores of all examinees are influenced to the same extent on either Test J or Test K (or both of them) by some systematic error, the value of $\rho_{(Je)(Ke)}$ will not be affected thereby.

If $\rho_{(Je)(Ke)}$ takes a positive value, the error variance of the difference between scores on tests J and K decreases as the value of the correlation coefficient increases. Error variance in scores from each test can be masked, thus making the obtained scores seem more reliable than they actually are. Consequently, every effort must be exercised to reduce the value of

$\rho_{(Je)(Ke)}$ to zero or as close to zero as possible. To do so, the examinees must be cooperative and well motivated and the administration of the tests must be properly conducted with careful adherence to time limits. The time interval between administrations of the two equivalent tests should be long enough so that transitory influences, such as headaches or moods, will not affect performance on both tests, but short enough so that the true abilities of the examinees will not change appreciably. It would not matter if the true scores of all the examinees increased by the same amount, but examinees of high aptitude tend to increase their true scores with practice more rapidly than examinees of low ability. Consequently, the assumption that $\sigma^2_{Jt} = \sigma^2_{Kt}$ is likely to be violated if the examinees are learning the tasks measured by the tests during the interval between administrations.

Determination of the length of the interval poses something of a dilemma since the major requirements are often incompatible. If the function measured is one that is not subject to rapid learning, such as word knowledge or comprehension in reading, an interval of perhaps a week may be suitable. Cureton (1958), among others, has suggested separating the two administrations by at least a week and giving one test in the morning and the other in the afternoon, thus taking into account both day-to-day and morning-to-afternoon variations in performance. If the function measured is one in which considerable learning can take place with short but concentrated practice periods, such as accuracy and rapidity of arithmetic calculation, the two equivalent tests may be administered on two successive days or in the morning and afternoon of the same day. For some psychomotor functions, the testing periods may serve as practice periods. For tests of this type, any estimate of reliability may be unsatisfactory because one or more of the basic assumptions has been violated. Ordinarily, enough practice is provided before the testing is begun so that the examinees will have reached a level of performance close to the maximum possible for them. This procedure is probably optimal since the interval between testings can be long enough to take day-to-day variations in performance into account.

If proper precautions have been taken to reduce $\rho_{(Je)(Ke)}$ to zero, or essentially zero, equation 13 becomes

$$\sigma^2_{(Jo-Ko)} = \sigma^2_{Je} + \sigma^2_{Ke} \qquad (14)$$

We may now consider whether σ^2_{Je} equals σ^2_{Ke}. If the assumption expressed in equation 8 is accepted and σ^2_{Jo} and σ^2_{Ko} are found to be insignificantly different at a specified level of probability, σ^2_{Je} and σ^2_{Ke} must also be insignificantly different at the same level of probability. Under these circumstances, equation 14 may be rearranged to read:

$$\frac{\sigma^2_{(Jo-Ko)}}{2} = \sigma^2_{Je} = \sigma^2_{Ke} \qquad (15)$$

The best estimate of σ_{Je}^2 is

$$\hat{s}_{Je}^2 = \frac{Ns_{(Jo-Ko)}^2}{2(N-1)} \tag{16}$$

The square root of equation 16 constitutes the standard error of measurement of either Test J or K, namely:

$$\hat{s}_{\text{meas } J} \equiv \hat{s}_{\text{meas } K} = s_{(Jo-Ko)} \sqrt{\frac{N}{2(N-1)}} \tag{17}$$

For practical purposes, with samples of 200 or more, $N/(N-1)$ is so nearly unity that equation 17 is closely approximated by

$$s_{\text{meas } J} \equiv s_{\text{meas } K} = \frac{s_{(Jo-Ko)}}{\sqrt{2}} \tag{18}$$

Equation 18 defines the standard error of measurement of obtained scores from tests J and K, provided that the conditions described are met. These included four assumptions and two conditions. The assumptions were that: (1) true scores on tests J and K measure the same functions; (2) the ratio of error variance to obtained variance is the same for both tests J and K; (3) true scores on Test J have identical correlations with errors of measurement in tests J and K; true scores on Test K have identical correlations with errors of measurement on tests J and K; (4) the correlation of errors of measurement in scores from tests J and K is zero with each other and with the obtained scores. The two empirically determinable conditions were: (1) evidence that the obtained-score variances of scores from tests J and K are insignificantly different at a specified level of probability; (2) use of a large number of cases.

Unfortunately, there is no entirely satisfactory way of estimating the standard error of measurement when the obtained-score variances of two equivalent tests are significantly different in the same sample of examinees. An approach to the problem that has been suggested (Angoff, 1953) may often be useful. Beginning with the correlation of Test J and the sum of n parallel tests of the same effective length as Test J (any one of which may be represented by T), he notes that

$$r_{J(A+B+\cdots+N)} = \frac{n(\overline{s_J s_T r_{JT}})}{s_J s_{(A+B+\cdots+N)}} \tag{19}$$

He assumes that the variance of any one of the n tests is equal to their average variance, that the covariance of any pair is equal to the average covariance of all pairs, and that the average covariances of parallel tests of the same effective length are equal.

He has shown that

$$n = \frac{s_J(s_J + r_{JK}s_K)}{s_K(s_K + r_{JK}s_J)} \tag{20}$$

and that the reliability coefficients of tests J and K may be expressed as

$$r_{JJ'} = \frac{(s_J + r_{JK}s_K)r_{JK}}{s_K + r_{JK}s_J} \tag{21}$$

and

$$r_{KK'} = \frac{(s_K + r_{JK}s_J)r_{JK}}{s_J + r_{JK}s_K} \tag{22}$$

A conventional procedure for estimating the standard error of measurement may then be employed to obtain values for $s_{\text{meas } J}$ and $s_{\text{meas } K}$, as follows:

$$s_{\text{meas } J} = s_J \sqrt{1 - r_{JJ'}} \tag{23}$$

$$s_{\text{meas } K} = s_K \sqrt{1 - r_{KK'}} \tag{24}$$

Practical procedures for unspeeded tests. The standard error of measurement of an unspeeded test may be estimated from data gathered in one administration by any of several procedures. One of these consists of creating two matched halves in a single test. Pairs of items should be matched as closely as possible for content, correlation with total score, and difficulty. The two scores derived from these matched halves are then used to estimate the standard error of measurement. The line of reasoning is similar to that which led to equation 13. If we let A_o and B_o represent obtained scores on the two matched halves of Test J, and A_e and B_e represent errors of measurement in halves A and B, respectively, the analogue of equation 13 reads:

$$\sigma^2_{(Ao-Bo)} = \left[\sigma^2_{Ae} - \sigma_{Ae}\sigma_{Be}\rho_{(Ae)(Be)}\right] + \left[\sigma^2_{Be} - \sigma_{Ae}\sigma_{Be}\rho_{(Ae)(Be)}\right] \tag{25}$$

The first term on the right-hand side of equation 25 represents the contribution of half A to the variance error of measurement and the second term on the right-hand side represents the contribution of half B. Hence, we may write

$$\sigma^2_{\text{meas } J} = \sigma^2_{(Ao-Bo)} \tag{26}$$

The best estimate of the standard error of measurement of Test J is, therefore,

$$s_{\text{meas } J} = s_{(Ao-Bo)} \sqrt{\frac{N}{N-1}} \tag{27}$$

Again, if a large number of cases is used in computing $s_{(Ao-Bo)}$, the radical term will approach unity so closely that it may be dropped, leaving as a practical computing formula:

$$s_{\text{meas } J} = s_{(Ao-Bo)} \tag{28}$$

It should be recalled that influences tending to create positive or negative errors of measurement in obtained scores from both halves A and B will cause $\rho_{(Ae)(Be)}$ in equation 25 to take a value other than zero. These influences are likely to operate because responses to the items in halves A and B are made during the same testing period. Consequently, equations 27 and 28 are likely to yield standard errors of measurement smaller than equations 17 and 18 for the same tests in the same samples. Since it is usually desirable to have the standard error of measurement reflect all sources of error in measurement (including day-to-day variation) which may cause an individual's obtained score to deviate from his true score, the techniques leading to employment of equations 27 and 28 should ordinarily be used only when it is impracticable to administer equivalent tests on two different days or when learning of the function measured is occurring at a rapid rate among the examinees.

Another procedure for estimating the standard error of measurement of unspeeded tests in which all of the items are scored 1 point for a correct response and 0 points for an incorrect response on the basis of only one test administration has been widely used (Lord, 1955). This has been extended to cover unspeeded tests in which the items are scored 1 point for a correct response and $(-a)$ points for an incorrect response, where a ordinarily (but not necessarily) represents $1/(k-1)$ with k equal to the number of choices in each item (Medley, 1962). The negative score for an incorrect response, consisting of $-1/(k-1)$ points, is the conventional correction for chance success on one item. It has been shown that, if the examinees respond solely on the basis of either knowledge or chance and if these responses distribute themselves binomially, the conventional correction for chance provides a maximum-likelihood estimate of the examinee's true score (Lyerly, 1951). It has been pointed out (Davis, 1951) that when the first assumption is not satisfied because the examinees use partial information or misinformation, these two influences tend to cancel each other.

Medley's equation for the over-all standard error of measurement of an obtained score derived from, say, Test J is as follows:

$$\hat{s}_{\text{meas } J} = \sqrt{\frac{\overline{J_o}(n - \overline{J_o}) + n\overline{W}a(a + 1) - \hat{s}_{Jo}^2}{n - 1}} \tag{29}$$

where: $J_o = R - aW$, and represents an individual obtained score corrected for chance success; R represents the number of items marked correctly in Test J by one examinee; W represents the number of items marked incorrectly in Test J by one examinee; a represents a multiplier, usually $1/(k-1)$ with k equal to the number of choices per item; n represents the number of items in Test J; $\bar{J}_o$ represents the mean score on Test J in the sample; $\overline{W}$ represents the mean number of items marked incorrectly on Test J in the sample; $s^2_{J_o}$ represents an estimate of the population variance of scores on Test J. It may be noted that, if the scoring procedure assigns a zero to each incorrect response, a becomes zero and equation 29 simplifies to:

$$\hat{s}_{\text{meas } J} = \sqrt{\frac{\bar{J}_o(n - \bar{J}_o) - \hat{s}^2_{J_o}}{n-1}} \tag{30}$$

Equation 30 is an appropriate estimator for the standard error of measurement only if the scores are obtained from an unspeeded test comprising multiple-choice items scored with 1 point for a correct response and 0 points for an incorrect response. Like the standard error of measurement estimated by means of equation 28, those estimated by means of equations 29 and 30 do not include as error variance any variation from day to day or from one testing session to another. This tends to make them smaller than estimates obtained by means of equations 17 and 18. However, the estimation of standard errors of measurement by equations 29 and 30 implicitly involves only the average covariance of all possible pairs of items in Test J, whereas this estimation by equations 17 and 18 implicitly includes the average covariance of pairs of matched items, one of each pair in Test J and one in Test K. To the extent that the average covariance of the pairs of matched items exceeds that of pairs chosen at random from Test J, a standard error of measurement yielded by equation 29 or 30 tends to be larger than one yielded by equation 17 or 18. In general, one would expect the average covariance of pairs of matched items to be larger than that of pairs chosen at random, but the homogeneity of items in most well-constructed tests and the low reliability coefficients of single items tend to keep the averages more nearly the same than might, at first thought, be expected. A few tests, such as those intended to sample an examinee's knowledge of diverse sports and hobbies, include items that have intercorrelations lower than usual and difficulty levels more disparate than usual; consequently, estimates of their standard errors of measurement are likely to differ more than those of most tests if the estimates obtained by equations 29 and 30 are compared with those obtained by equations 17 and 18.

The effects of eliminating *or* including day-to-day (or session-to-session) variance and of involving the average covariance of pairs of items drawn at random *or* of pairs of matched items, tend to counterbalance one another, but their relative influences vary from test to test and from one type of examinee to another. Experimental data support the generalization that standard errors of measurement estimated by equations 29 and 30 tend to be larger than those estimated by equations 17 and 18.

Variation of Standard Error of Measurement with Score Level. Throughout the preceding discussion, the standard error of measurement of obtained scores on a given test has been regarded as applicable to scores of all possible values. The computational procedures described do, in fact, yield over-all standard errors of measurement. One of these constitutes the best estimate for use with any obtained score drawn at random from a distribution, yet the standard errors of measurement properly applicable to specific obtained scores may, and in practice ordinarily do, vary with the values of different obtained scores. It may be noted in passing that, because errors of measurement in individual obtained scores take both positive and negative values, the existence of a relationship (such as might be indicated by a correlation ratio significantly different from zero) between absolute size of standard error of measurement and obtained-score value does *not* necessarily establish the existence of a product-moment correlation between errors of measurement and obtained scores in the sample tested.

If a sample were large enough, it would be practicable to estimate a standard error of measurement by equation 17, 18, 27, or 28 applicable to any obtained score at each different score value over a wide range. For practical purposes, it would be necessary only to enter equation 17 or 18 with data based on examinees whose obtained scores on one of the two equivalent tests were the same. Equation 27 or 28 would be entered with data based on the scores of examinees whose half-scores summed to the value for which the standard error was desired. Inasmuch as the number of examinees at each score level would vary, the accuracy with which the standard errors of measurement were estimated would vary accordingly. In fact, the number of cases at some score levels might be too small to warrant their computation. This is apt to be the case for scores near the ends of the possible range where, in any event, the restrictions imposed on score variation impair the meaningfulness of standard errors of measurement. Given the sample sizes that are commonly practical, obtained scores within a range of 5 to 10 points centered at, say, three different points in the distribution are suggested as a basis for entering equations 17, 18, 27, and 28. The three ranges are often centered around the mean of the distribution and around obtained scores corresponding to points one and one-half standard deviations above and below the mean.

Standard errors of measurement applicable to any possible obtained score that are analogous to the over-all standard errors of measurement yielded by equations 29 and 30 may easily be estimated by an equation (Medley, 1962), which is as follows for Test J:

$$\hat{s}_{\text{meas } Jo(p)} = \sqrt{\frac{J_o}{n-1}(n - J_o) + \frac{nWa(a+1)}{n-1}} \qquad (31)$$

where the notation is the same as in equation 29, except that $J_{o(p)}$ represents a particular value of J_o.

If the scoring procedure assigns a zero to each incorrect response, the second term under the radical drops out and equation 31 simplifies to

$$\hat{s}_{\text{meas } Jo(p)} = \sqrt{\frac{J_o}{n-1}(n-J_o)} \qquad (32)$$

It will be noted that equation 32 can be used to estimate the standard error of measurement for any particular obtained score even before the test has been administered.

Equations 31 and 32 yield standard errors of measurement for raw scores on most tests that are larger for scores at the middle of the possible range than toward the ends of that range. This result is in agreement with theoretical formulations (Lawley, 1942–1943; Mollenkopf, 1949) and with empirical findings. However, if raw test scores are transformed into derived scores that more nearly approximate interval scales with respect to the functions measured (such as Cooperative Scaled Scores, Gardner's K Scores, or some normalized standard scores), the standard errors of measurement for scores toward the ends of the range of possible scores will usually tend to be larger in terms of the derived-score units than for scores near the middle of the range. This is because raw-score units near the middle of the range of scores on most tests cover a narrower band of ability with respect to the functions measured than do units near the ends of the range. A glance at the fan keys formerly supplied with various forms of the *Cooperative Reading Comprehension Test* will illustrate how this phenomenon displays itself (Davis *et al.*, 1940). Test interpreters should recognize that most tests measure more accurately near the middle of their ranges of scores than toward the ends of their ranges, despite the misleading impression to the contrary that may follow an inspection of standard errors of measurement at various raw-score levels.

The Standard Error of Measurement of the Mean and the Standard Error of the Mean The standard error of the mean is well known and widely used, but the standard error of measurement of the mean has rarely been used in the interpretation of test scores even though it is needed for making meaningful comparisons of the mean performances of particular groups or of the performance of an individual with that of a particular group. Its derivation has been provided (Huffnaker & Douglass, 1928). Hence, a brief sketch will suffice to show its relationship to the standard error of the mean.

Let J_o represent an obtained score of one examinee on Test J. As indicated by equation 1, we may substitute for J_o the expression $(J_t + J_e)$. Suppose that Test J were administered to an indefinitely large number, n, of samples of N examinees, each sample being drawn at random from a population. The n sample means would be distributed normally around the mean of their means, which would approach the population mean as a limit. The variance of this distribution of means may be written as

$$\sigma_{\bar{J}_o}^2 = \left[\frac{\overset{n}{\Sigma}[\bar{J}_o - \bar{\bar{J}}_o]^2}{n}\right] = \left[\frac{\overset{n}{\Sigma}[\bar{J}_t + \bar{J}_e - \bar{\bar{J}}_t - \bar{\bar{J}}_e]^2}{n}\right] \tag{33}$$

where $\bar{\bar{J}}_o$, $\bar{\bar{J}}_t$, and $\bar{\bar{J}}_e$ represent mean scores in the population. For each of the n samples,

$$\bar{J}_o = \frac{\overset{N}{\Sigma}(J_t + J_e)}{N} = \left[\frac{J_{tA}}{N} + \frac{J_{tB}}{N} + \cdots + \frac{J_{tN}}{N}\right] + \left[\frac{J_{eA}}{N} + \frac{J_{eB}}{N}\right.$$
$$\left. + \cdots + \frac{J_{eN}}{N}\right]$$

If the mean true score of the population divided by N is subtracted from the true score of each individual and the mean error score of the population divided by N (a quotient which will by definition equal zero) is subtracted from the error of measurement in each individual's obtained score, equation 33 becomes:

$$\sigma_{\bar{J}}^2 = \frac{\overset{n}{\Sigma}\left[\frac{\overset{N}{\Sigma}j_t}{N} + \frac{\overset{N}{\Sigma}j_e}{N}\right]^2}{n} \tag{34}$$

where j_t and j_e represent deviations from the mean true score and the mean error score in the population.

When the numerator of equation 34 is expanded, all cross-product terms vanish for two reasons. First, there is zero correlation between a set of scores obtained by one sample of N examinees drawn at random from the population and a set of scores obtained by another sample of N examinees drawn at random from the same population. Second, we assume, as is customary, that there is zero product-moment correlation between true scores and errors of measurement in a set of obtained scores from an indefinitely large population. Therefore, equation 34 reduces to

$$\sigma_{\bar{J}}^2 = \frac{\overset{N}{\Sigma}\sigma_{Jt}^2}{N^2} + \frac{\overset{N}{\Sigma}\sigma_{Je}^2}{N^2} \tag{35}$$

Since the n examinees whose scores determine each of the variances in equation 35 constitute a random sample of the population, all true-score variances and all error variances will be equal. Then each of the summation signs in equation 35 may be replaced with N, and the equation becomes:

$$\sigma^2_{\bar{J}} = \frac{\sigma^2_{Jt}}{N} + \frac{\sigma^2_{Je}}{N} \tag{36}$$

The first term on the right-hand side of equation 35 represents variance attributable to differences in the true means of the n samples drawn from the population while the second term represents variance attributable to differences in the mean errors of measurement of the n samples. The latter variance may be defined as the population variance error of measurement of the mean. It may be estimated in the usual manner as follows:

$$\hat{s}^2_{\text{meas } \bar{J}} = \frac{s^2_{\text{meas } J}}{N - 1} \tag{37}$$

Its square root constitutes the standard error of measurement of the mean, as follows:

$$\hat{s}_{\text{meas } \bar{J}} = \frac{s_{\text{meas } J}}{\sqrt{N - 1}} \tag{38}$$

Since errors of measurement and true scores in an indefinitely large number of obtained scores have been assumed to be uncorrelated, $\sigma^2_{Jt} + \sigma^2_{Je} = \sigma^2_{Jo}$. Therefore, equation 36 may be written as

$$\sigma^2_{\bar{J}} = \frac{\sigma^2_{Jo}}{N} \tag{39}$$

for which the best estimate is

$$\hat{s}^2_{\bar{J}} = \frac{s^2_{Jo}}{N - 1} \tag{40}$$

The square root of equation 40 is the familiar standard error of the mean:

$$\hat{s}_{\bar{J}} = \frac{s_{Jo}}{\sqrt{N - 1}} \tag{41}$$

If inferences about the mean of a population are to be made on the basis of data from a sample drawn from it at random, the standard error of the mean should be used for the purpose. However, if inferences about the true mean of a sample are to be made on the basis of data from the sample itself, the standard error of measurement of the mean should be used for that purpose. The former purpose is characteristic of research workers making experimental studies. The latter is often the chief concern of test interpreters interested in comparing the mean performances of intact groups, such as school classes or grades or in comparing the performance of a single examinee with that of one or more groups.

INTERPRETATION OF INDIVIDUAL TEST SCORES

Two Approaches As stated at the beginning of this chapter, virtually any meaningful interpretation of test scores, whether they are those of individuals or groups, requires the comparison of two or more scores. The comparison usually takes the form of a difference, so the interpretation of differences is the key to test interpretation. There are two main approaches to the interpretation of differences, which are not irreconcilable.

The first approach is to obtain the best possible estimate of the true scores of individuals or groups and, in effect, to interpret these as though they were true scores. Differences among true scores are true differences, so even the smallest of them carries meaning. The phrase "in effect" was used advisedly in the sentence above because sophisticated test interpreters who take this approach recognize that, since obtained test scores are not infallible, inferences drawn from them and from differences among them are subject to error. Nonetheless, as these interpreters point out, the best estimates of true scores that can be obtained cannot be improved on. Therefore, those who advocate this approach make inferences from them as though they were true scores. It is argued that inferences to the effect that certain differences are real when they are, in fact, merely the result of chance ordinarily result in no less desirable practical consequences than inferences that certain differences are merely the result of chance when they are, in fact, real (that is, attributable to something other than chance).

The second approach is to obtain the best possible estimate of the true scores of individuals or groups, select a level of probability for tests of significance, and determine how large a difference of the type being considered must be before it can be considered significant. Only differences that meet (or exceed) this level are taken as evidence that one pupil is superior to another, that one group is superior to another, or that a pupil is above or not above the average of a group. In practice, the sophisticated interpreter gives greater credence to differences as they become larger than the minimum required by his preselected level of probability. He also makes a mental note of those differences that come close to the preselected level because he knows that his chances of making incorrect inferences from the data are greatest for differences at this level. The procedures for determining these chances at any given level have been presented and discussed (Cronbach & Gleser, 1959). It should be noted that nothing has been said as yet about the level of probability to be employed. It may be varied in the light of the effect of the decisions to be made, the weight given to these inferences in making decisions, and the temperament of the interpreter. At one extreme, the probability of making errors in inferring that a random selection of differences are real when, in fact, they are merely chance deviations from zero may be reduced almost to zero—say, to one in a hundred. At the other extreme, the probability of making such errors may be allowed to rise to the point where it approaches unity.

The interpretation of differences is complicated, however, by the fact that the interpreter can not only make an error of the type described (inference that a difference is real when in fact it is merely a chance deviation from a true difference of zero) but also can make a second type of error, namely, that a difference is merely a chance deviation from zero when, in fact, it is evidence of the existence of a true difference other than zero. Other things being equal, as the chances of making the first type of error are *decreased* by using a larger difference as the minimum for inferring the existence of a true difference other than zero, the chances of making the second type of error are *increased*. Thus, choice of a level of probability involves weighing the penalties for making the first kind of error against those for making the second kind of error.

The Differences between Scores Obtained by One Examinee   It has been shown that the difference between two obtained scores of one individual is often misleading evidence regarding the difference between his true scores (Lord, 1956). For this reason, it is desirable to estimate a true difference whenever the data permit this. The best estimate, in a least-squares sense, of a true difference for any individual in a sample can be obtained by means of a multiple-regression equation, using the individual's obtained scores as predictors. The standard deviations, reliability coefficients, and intercorrelations of the predictor scores and the true differences in the sample are also used. The rectilinearity of the regression lines of the intercorrelated variables is assumed. Lord's procedure forms the basis for the estimation technique presented here, but the two are not identical. The symbols to be used are interpreted as follows: J_o and K_o represent obtained scores on tests J and K, which are administered in that order; J_t and K_t represent true scores on tests J and K; T represents the difference between J_t and K_t, namely $K_t - J_t$; D represents an estimate of T. Each of these scores expressed in terms of standard measures is represented by a lower-case letter.

As is customary, β and b are used to denote multiple-regression coefficients in standard-score and obtained-score form, respectively. Also: $\bar{J}_o$ and $\bar{K}_o$ represent the mean obtained scores on tests J and K, respectively, in the sample; s_J and s_K represent the standard deviations of obtained scores on tests J and K, respectively, in the sample; s_T represents the standard deviation of true differences, $K_t - J_t$; s_D represents the standard deviation of estimates of these true differences; $r_{JJ'}$ and $r_{KK'}$ represent the reliability coefficients of obtained scores in the sample; $r_{DD'}$ represents the reliability coefficient of the estimates of true differences in the sample; r_{JK} represents the product-moment correlation of obtained scores on tests J and K.

The multiple-regression equation for estimating T for each examinee may be written as

$$D = b_{TK \cdot J}K_o + b_{TJ \cdot K}J_o + (\bar{K}_o - \bar{J}_o - b_{TK \cdot J}\bar{K}_o - b_{TJ \cdot K}\bar{J}_o) \quad (42)$$

or in standard-score form as:

$$d = \beta_{tk \cdot j}k_o + \beta_{tj \cdot k}J_o \quad (43)$$

It is well known that:

$$\beta_{tj \cdot k} = \frac{r_{JT} - r_{KT}r_{JK}}{1 - r_{JK}^2} \quad (44)$$

$$\beta_{tk \cdot j} = \frac{r_{KT} - r_{JT}r_{JK}}{1 - r_{JK}^2} \quad (45)$$

$$b_{TJ \cdot K} = \beta_{tj \cdot k}\frac{s_T}{s_{Jo}} \quad (46)$$

and

$$b_{TK \cdot J} = \beta_{tk \cdot j}\frac{s_T}{s_{Ko}} \quad (47)$$

It can easily be shown that

$$s_T = \sqrt{s_J^2 r_{JJ\prime} + s_K^2 r_{KK\prime} - 2s_J s_K r_{JK}} \quad (48)$$

$$r_{JT} = \frac{s_K r_{JK} - s_J r_{JJ\prime}}{s_T} \quad (49)$$

and

$$r_{KT} = \frac{s_K r_{KK\prime} - s_J r_{JK}}{s_T} \quad (50)$$

If the expressions on the right-hand sides of equations 44, 45, 48, 49, and 50 are substituted appropriately in equations 46 and 47, these may be written as

$$b_{TJ \cdot K} = \frac{s_K r_{JK}(1 - r_{KK\prime}) - s_J(r_{JJ\prime} - r_{JK}^2)}{s_J(1 - r_{JK}^2)} \quad (51)$$

and

$$b_{TK \cdot J} = \frac{s_K(r_{KK\prime} - r_{JK}^2) - s_J r_{JK}(1 - r_{JJ\prime})}{s_K(1 - r_{JK}^2)} \quad (52)$$

Equations 51 and 52 make possible the computation of an estimate of a true difference, D, by equation 42. It should be noted that the latter is far less troublesome to use than a first glance might suggest. First, the terms in the parentheses form a constant for the estimation of all the differences in a sample (or, indeed, in similar samples). In the same way, regression coefficients $b_{TK \cdot J}$ and $b_{TJ \cdot K}$ are constants. Second, the estimation of a true difference is identical for all examinees whose obtained scores are identical. Some remarks concerning the applications of equation 42 follow.

Case 1. A difference between scores on two equivalent forms of the same test administered to one individual. This sort of difference ordinarily occurs when equivalent forms of a test are administered before and after a learning period to assess the change that has taken place in the learner. The technique recommended does not assume that the standard deviations or the reliability coefficients of the two sets of scores will be the same.

Case 2. A difference between scores obtained by one individual on two different tests that yield comparable scores. Comparison of an individual's standing in two different subject-matter fields or in two different kinds of mental skills involves this type of difference. For example, an estimate of the true difference between an individual's verbal and nonverbal IQs derived from the same test may be obtained. An estimate of the true difference between scores on an achievement test and a mental-ability test constitutes one kind of measurement of overachievement or underachievement, provided that the tests yield comparable scores and that the mental-ability test is appropriate for the purpose. In equation 42, the mental-ability test would ordinarily be represented by Test J.

The standard error of measurement of an estimate of a true difference, $s_{\text{meas } D}$, yielded by equation 42 may be obtained from the following equation:

$$s_{\text{meas } D} = \sqrt{b^2_{TJ \cdot K} s^2_{\text{meas } J} + b^2_{TK \cdot J} s^2_{\text{meas } K}} \tag{53}$$

It may be noted that

$$s_D = \sqrt{s^2_{Jo} b^2_{TJ \cdot K} + s^2_{Ko} b^2_{TK \cdot J} + 2 b_{TJ \cdot K} b_{TK \cdot J} s_{Jo} s_{Ko} r_{(Jo)(Ko)}} \tag{54}$$

and

$$r_{DD\prime} = \frac{s^2_{Jo} b^2_{TJ \cdot K} r_{JJ\prime} + s^2_{Ko} b^2_{TK \cdot J} r_{KK\prime} + 2 b_{TJ \cdot K} b_{TK \cdot J} s_{Jo} s_{Ko} r_{(Jo)(Ko)}}{s^2_D} \tag{55}$$

As an illustration, equations 42 and 53 will be used for evaluating a difference between verbal and performance IQs obtained on the Wechsler Adult Intelligence Scale by Roger, an eighteen-year-old student. His verbal IQ was 104 and his performance IQ was 94. The means and standard deviations of both IQ scores in the sample of which Roger was a member were 100 and 15, respectively. The correlation of the verbal and performance IQs in the sample was .77; the reliability coefficients were .96 for the verbal IQs and .93 for the performance IQs. For the difference between Roger's IQs, Equation 42 yields a value of 7.58 if his verbal IQ is represented by K_o and his performance IQ by J_o. Thus, his obtained IQ difference of 10 points leads to the estimation of a true difference of 7.58.

If we adopt the first approach to test interpretation mentioned earlier in this chapter, we simply note that, with the data available, this is the best estimate of Roger's true difference that we can obtain and conclude that his verbal ability is superior to his performance ability. If we adopt the second approach to test interpretation, we also obtain the standard error of measurement of the difference between his two scores. Equation 53 yields a value of 3.77. Now we must consider whether it is more undesirable to accept the conclusion that his verbal and performance abilities are different when they really are the same, or whether it is more undesirable to accept the conclusion that they are the same when they really are different. The personal and social consequences of diagnostic decisions or administrative actions, for example, must be weighed. In general, it seems inefficient and unwise to make diagnostic decisions or to take action with respect to a client or pupil that follow from the presence of an obtained difference in measured abilities, skills, or achievements when the difference can readily be ascribed merely to chance. On the other hand, it is unfortunate to deny to clients or pupils the benefits (if any) of the consequences of these decisions or actions if there is even a reasonable possibility that they are justified. This is particularly true if no special harm is done by the decisions or actions in those cases where there is no true difference.

In the interpretation of test scores, the penalties of making errors of the first and second types are usually more nearly balanced than in experimental research. Nonetheless, the principle of explaining phenomena in the simplest possible terms favors an emphasis on reducing errors of the first type, as does reluctance to take practical action on the basis of an observed difference that could easily have arisen by chance from a true difference of zero, or indeed from a true difference in the opposite direction. These considerations suggest the choice of a level of probability for rejecting the null hypothesis that is more lenient than levels commonly used in experimental studies and yet more stringent than the level that is implicit in the interpretation of small estimates of true differences (crude or refined) as true differences. The exact level should be adjusted to suit the nature of the tests being interpreted and the purposes for which they are being used.

The 15 per cent level of significance is a moderately lenient value that has demonstrated practical utility in many problems in test interpretation. If this level is used with the data pertaining to Roger's IQ scores, we find that differences of 5.43 points, or larger, are significant. We conclude, therefore, that the difference between Roger's verbal and performance

IQs is not attributable to chance and use this conclusion with other data in making a diagnosis of his mental abilities. We also note that the difference is far greater than the minimum included by the critical region and attach added confidence to it.

Differences between Scores Obtained by Two Examinees Estimation of a true difference between scores obtained by two different examinees differs from the estimation of a true difference between two scores obtained by the same examinee for the obvious reason that we cannot predict one examinee's score on a test from knowledge of another's score. Therefore, r_{JK} in equations 51 and 52 becomes zero. Equation 42 can then be simplified for two cases that may commonly arise.

Case 3. A difference between scores on one test obtained by two different examinees drawn from the same population. This kind of difference is one of those most used in interpreting test scores; it is involved in a comparison of the levels of performance of two individuals drawn from the same age or grade group who were tested at the same time. Under these circumstances, equation 42 becomes

$$D_3 = r_{JJ'}(J_{o(1)} - J_{o(2)}) \qquad (56)$$

where $J_{o(1)}$ and $J_{o(2)}$ are the obtained scores of examinees 1 and 2 on Test J.

It can easily be shown that, in this special case, the standard error of measurement of D_3 becomes:

$$s_{\text{meas } D3} = \sqrt{2r_{JJ'}^2 s_{\text{meas } J}^2} \qquad (57)$$

It is interesting to note that the computation of estimates of true differences by means of equations 56 and 57 can be accomplished with the expenditure of scarcely any more labor than that of obtained-score differences. However, since the rank orders of the two kinds of differences are the same, the use of estimates of true differences in case 3 is not so important as it is in cases 1 and 2.

Case 4. A Difference between Scores on One Test Obtained by Two Different Examinees Drawn from Different Populations. If the two examinees are drawn from different populations, the reliability coefficients and the means on the test need not be the same in the samples drawn from the different populations. Accordingly, equation 42 becomes

$$D_4 = r_{J(2)J(2)'}J_{o(2)} - r_{J(1)J(1)'}J_{o(1)} + (\bar{J}_{o(2)} - \bar{J}_{o(1)} - r_{J(2)J(2)'}\bar{J}_{o(2)} +$$
$$r_{J(1)J(1)'}\bar{J}_{o(1)}) \qquad (58)$$

where $r_{J(2)J(2)'}$ and $r_{J(1)J(1)'}$ are the reliability coefficients and $\bar{J}_{o(2)}$ and $\bar{J}_{o(1)}$ the means in the samples of which examinees 2 and 1 are members, respectively.

The standard error of measurement of D_4 is given by:

$$s_{\text{meas } D4} = \sqrt{r^2_{J(1)J(1)} s^2_{\text{meas } Jo(1)} + r^2_{J(2)J(2)} s^2_{\text{meas } Jo(2)}} \tag{59}$$

Equation 58 should be used to estimate a true difference between scores on the same test for two individuals in different age or grade groups or even for two individuals in the same age or grade group if they have markedly different social or economic backgrounds.

Differences between Individual and Mean Scores The interpretation of individual scores ordinarily requires that some standard of comparison or norm be set up. The difference between this norm and each individual's score can then be interpreted. The norm can be one of several statistics. If it is the mean, it may be the mean of the sample made up of the individuals whose scores are to be interpreted or it may be the mean of a sample of different individuals. In the latter case, the interpreter may be interested in comparing an individual's score with the mean performance of the particular group of examinees constituting the sample or he may be interested in using the mean of the sample only to represent the mean of the population from which the sample was drawn at random. Each of these three objectives of the interpreter requires a different standard error term for determining the statistical significance of a difference.

Case 5. A difference between the mean score of a group and the score of one individual in the group. Let $J_{o(1)}$, $J_{o(2)}$, $\cdots J_{o(N)}$ represent obtained scores of N examinees on Test J and let $\bar{J}_o$ represent the mean of these scores. Assume that an indefinitely large number (n) of equivalent tests are administered to the N examinees and that their true scores remain the same throughout the testing. For any one examinee drawn at random, an essentially normal distribution of differences will be generated between the mean of the n test means and the examinee's scores on the n tests. The mean of this distribution of differences will approach $\bar{J}_t - J_t$, where $\bar{J}_t$ is the true mean of the N examinees and J_t is the true score of any one examinee. The variance of the distribution around this mean difference is the variance error of measurement for the obtained difference of any one examinee:

$$\sigma^2_{(\bar{J}o - Jo)} = \sigma^2_{\bar{J}e} + \sigma^2_{Je} - 2\sigma_{\bar{J}e}\, \sigma_{Je}\, \rho_{(\bar{J}e)(Je)} \tag{60}$$

where $\sigma^2_{\bar{J}e}$ is the population variance error of measurement of the mean, σ^2_{Je}/N, as defined by the second term on the right-hand side of equation 36. It is easy to demonstrate that $\rho_{(\bar{J}e)(Je)} = 1/\sqrt{N}$. Substituting these values in equation 60, we obtain

$$\sigma^2_{(\bar{J} - Jo)} = \left(\frac{N-1}{N}\right)\sigma^2_{Je} \tag{61}$$

This may be estimated in the customary way as

$$\hat{s}^2_{(\bar{J}-Jo)} = \frac{(N-1)(N_p)}{(N)(N_p-1)} s^2_{Je} \qquad (62)$$

where N represents the number of examinees whose scores were averaged and N_p represents the number used for the computation of s^2_{Je}. In practice, if s^2_{Je} has been computed on a large number of cases (as it should be), $N_p/(N_p-1)$ approaches unity. Then, the square root of equation 62 may be used as a serviceable estimate of the standard error of measurement of the difference between the mean of the sample and the obtained score of any examinee in the sample. It may be written:

$$s_{\text{meas}(Jo-Jo)} = s_{\text{meas} Jo} \sqrt{\frac{N-1}{N}} \qquad (63)$$

Whether the score of any examinee in the sample is significantly different from the mean may be ascertained for any level chosen by the interpreter as appropriate for his purposes.

Case 6. A difference between the mean score of a group and the score of one individual not included in the group. If the individual whose score is to be compared with the mean of a group is not a member of the group, the covariance term in equation 60 will be zero. The standard error of measurement of the difference between any such individual's score and the mean may be estimated, when $s_{\text{meas}Jo}$ was computed in a large sample, by

$$s_{\text{meas}(Jo-Jo)} = s_{\text{meas} Jo} \sqrt{\frac{N+1}{N}} \qquad (64)$$

This statistic may be used in conventional ways to infer whether an examinee's score is above or below the mean of a particular sample of which he is not a member. It should not be used to infer whether his score is above or below the mean of the population from which the particular sample was drawn at random.

Case 7. A difference between an estimate of the mean score of a population and the score of an examinee not included in the sample used for estimating. Most comparisons of the test scores of individuals with norms fall in this category. Consequently, it is important to have the proper standard error of measurement for this sort of difference. The analogue of equation 60 follows:

$$\sigma^2_{(\bar{Jo}-Jo)} = \sigma^2_{\bar{Jo}} + \sigma^2_{Je} - 2\sigma_{\bar{Jo}} \sigma_{Je} \rho_{(\bar{Jo}-Je)} \qquad (65)$$

where $\sigma^2_{\bar{Jo}}$ is the variance error of the mean, shown in equation 39 as equal to σ^2_{Jo}/N. Making this substitution in equation 65, recognizing that the covariance term equals zero, and making unbiased estimates of the population values, we obtain:

$$\hat{s}^2_{(\bar{J}o - Jo)} = \frac{s^2_{Jo}}{N-1} + \frac{N_p}{N_p - 1} s^2_{Je} \tag{66}$$

where, as previously, N represents the number of examinees whose scores were averaged and N_p represents the number used for the computation of s^2_{Je}. If N_p is large, $N_p/N_p - 1$ approaches unity, and the square root of equation 66 is closely approximated by

$$s_{\text{meas}(\bar{J}o - Jo)} = \sqrt{\frac{s^2_{Jo}}{N-1} + s^2_{\text{meas } J}} \tag{67}$$

By means of equation 67, it is possible to determine, at any desired level of probability, the likelihood that one individual's obtained score differs from the norm.

SUMMARY

The development of statistical techniques essential for the interpretation of pychological test scores has far outrun their application by clinicians and other test users. This lag constitutes one of the most serious problems in measurement at present. The first step in solving the problem is to recognize that almost all interpretations of an individual's scores that are not trivial involve comparisons of these with mean scores (or percentiles) or with the scores of other individuals. The comparisons consist of differences between individual scores or between individual scores and mean scores (or percentiles).

It is well known that differences between scores are often unreliable. Less well known is the fact that point estimates of true differences are often misleading when they consist (as they usually do) of simple algebraic differences between obtained scores. To aid test users, this chapter has presented sophisticated point estimates of four kinds of differences between individual scores (cases 1, 2, 3, and 4) and their standard errors of measurement. In addition, three kinds of differences between individual scores and means that are commonly needed in test interpretation have been delineated (cases 5, 6, and 7), and their standard errors of measurement have been presented.

Three parameters basic to an understanding of the standard errors of measurement of differences and the standard errors of differences have been considered in detail, and methods for estimating them have been outlined. These are the standard error of measurement of an individual obtained score, the standard error of measurement of a mean, and the standard error of a mean.

The logical problems underlying the choice of a level of probability for accepting an estimated true difference as evidence of the existence of a true difference other than zero have been explored. No one level can be specified as optimal or even as reasonably suitable for all kinds of situations. The most important consideration is that a clinician or test interpreter realize the effect of the level that he adopts on the incidence of the kinds of errors he will make in his interpretations and, therefore, on the social consequences of the decisions these interpretations lead him to make.

REFERENCES

ANGOFF, W. H. Test reliability and effective test length. *Psychometrika*, 1953, **18**, 1-14.

CRONBACH, L. J., & GLESER, G. C. Interpretation of reliability and validity coefficients: Remarks on a paper by Lord. *J. educ. Psychol.*, 1959, **50**, 230-237.

CURETON, E. E. The definition and estimation of test reliability. *Educ. psychol. Measmt*, 1958, **18**, 715-738.

DAVIS, F. B., et al. *Cooperative Reading Comprehension Test*, Form Q, Lower and Higher Levels. New York: Cooperative Test Service, 1940.

DAVIS, F. B. Techniques of item selection. In E. F. Lindquist (Ed.), *Educational measurement*. Washington: American Council on Education, 1951. Pp. 266-328.

HUFFNAKER, C. L., & DOUGLASS, H. R. On the standard errors of the mean due to sampling and to measurement. *J. educ. Psychol.*, 1928, **19**, 643-649.

LAWLEY, D. N. On problems connected with item selection and test construction. *Proc. roy. Soc. Edin.*, 1942-1943, **61**, (Section A, Part III), 273-287.

LORD, F. M. Estimating test reliability. *Educ. psychol. Measmt*, 1955, **15**, 325-336.

LORD, F. M. Measurement of growth. *Educ. psychol. Measmt*, 1956, **16**, 421-437.

LYERLY, S. B. A note on correcting for chance success in objective tests. *Psychometrika*, 1951, **16**, 21-30.

McNEMAR, Q. On growth measurement. *Educ. psychol. Measmt*, 1958, **18**, 47-55.

MEDLEY, D. M. The effects of item heterogeneity and guessing on the accuracy of a test score. *Amer. Psychologist*, 1962, **17**, 368.

MOLLENKOPF, W. G. Variation in the standard error of measurement. *Psychometrika*, 1950, **15**, 291-315.

29 BENOIT MANDELBROT

INFORMATION THEORY
AND PSYCHOLINGUISTICS

THIS CHAPTER WILL TELL the story of the brief encounter between two important streams of thought. All the elements of a long and successful association seemed to be present, and the encounter was indeed most exciting. But it was not durable, and the two protagonists have gone their own separate ways, leaving a few fruits that may enjoy some permanency. This chapter will describe a theory of word frequencies thus born out of contact between information theory and psycholinguistics.

The stage having been set, let us introduce the actors.

The great distinction of information theory, born fully armed in 1948 from two celebrated papers by Claude Shannon, was the novel manner in which it recombined two of the oldest and most fundamental ideas of formalized science: the concept of algorithm and the concept of chance. These two ideas have of course never been far from each other, starting with games of pure chance in the seventeenth and eighteenth centuries and continuing through statistical mechanics and quantum theory, around 1900 and 1925, respectively. Therefore, Shannon's theory was in no way the beginning of something entirely new, and now—as time goes by—it begins to fit very well within probability theory as another interesting chapter. However, before 1948, there were only a few scattered attempts to formalize the fact that human discourse is both something highly structured and something highly unpredictable. Shannon's work stressed the possibility of describing its structure by the algorithms of coding and of describing its unpredictability by a systematic exploitation of Markov's pure-chance model of Pushkin's novel *Eugene Onegin;* By reinterpreting the physical concept of entropy as a measure of "quantity of information," Shannon also showed a way of describing the degree of structure of a system by its degree of disorder, itself measured by a function of the probabilities of various events. Of course, it was never claimed that "quantity of information" exhausted the loose verbal idea of "information"; many experts soon found that the best way of presenting Shannon's theory was to follow

550

that author in *not* giving top billing to "quantity of information." It is true, also, that "information theory" was meant to be applicable not only to human discourse, but to every type of message; but the actual techniques of the theory have turned out to be most inconvenient, except for messages similar to discourse.

The importance of Shannon's contribution has always been obvious. But, fifteen years later, it is difficult and somewhat puzzling to think of one's reactions and of those of one's peers, when the original papers appeared, a part of the backlog of novelties accumulated during the war and readied for publication during the three years from 1945 to 1948. The supply and the demand for new things being then at their highest, the ink was not yet dry when enthusiasts started going around promising prompt rewards from the application of information theory to any problem one could think of. Conservatives balked, some saying that it would be too easy to be true, and others adding that one should really not expect that much from a mathematical panacea of which professional mathematicians were taking such an indifferent view. These quarrels have now died, since —as is often the case—most predictions were rather poor. Indeed, application of information theory turned out not to be easy, and it did not solve everything; but the honest toil which it generated has—in our opinion— served as a most effective wedge through which mathematics was helped to conquer ever new fields of application. As to professional mathematicians, they sought to compensate, by great activity, their lateness in getting involved in these problems. To sum up, information theory has indeed become quite well established as a chapter of the calculus of probability. In the meantime, the limitations of its practical usefulness in its field of origin have also become fairly clear.

Let us now turn to the second actor of our story. The term "psycholinguistics" fits him well. But we are not so sure about "linguistics" taken alone, since our story belongs to that margin of problems which were of no concern to the linguists of yesteryear, and of which nobody could know today whether those who will study them tomorrow will choose to be called linguists. What, indeed, is the definition of linguistics? The answer to this question has lately lost the clarity which it seemed once to enjoy. The poet, the philologist, the philosopher, and their traditional associates have ceased to be the only ones concerned with the structure of human discourse. Increasing numbers of mathematicians and of engineers have joined them, attracted by technological problems, formerly ignored or considered trivial, suddenly become so important that they elude traditional barriers between fields, even those which merely contained intellectual curiosity. All this, however, is not enough to make linguistics into what has been called an "interdisciplinary field." In a healthy relation between sciences and technologies, the latter must not determine the limits between the former. Techniques such as applied mathematics may well remain forever at a crossroads between sciences, but the definitions of sciences must be more intrinsic. But, whenever any field enters a period of rapid flux, its definition necessarily becomes vague. Hence, we can neither tell what "linguistics" is really about today nor predict what science or what sciences will be born of the gestations which we are now witnessing. Therefore, we should not venture to prescribe what the word "linguistics" should really mean.

In particular, no one can predict the most important meeting ground between information theory and psycholinguistics, namely, an astonishing statistical law, the discovery of which is associated with the names of Jean-Baptiste Estoup and of George Kingsley Zipf.

Let us again begin with a bit of history. Among the technological problems concerning natural discourse, the most ancient are without question those of cryptography and of stenography or telegraphy. All these problems have now become parts of information theory, but one may question whether they are parts of linguistics. We wish to show that they ought indeed to be considered as such. For that, let us recall the purposes which the cryptographer and the stenographer set for their special transformations of the usual phonic and graphic signs—which are of course quite "arbitrary" in de Saussure's sense. The cryptographer wishes to achieve a code as devoid as possible of any kind of structure that may be used by his adversary to break the secrecy of his message. As to the stenographer and telegrapher, their common aim is to achieve a code in which encoding is as rapid as possible. We must investigate these two kinds of code somewhat more closely.

First of all, we shall neglect the technological constraints which are obviously present in both cases. To that end, let us grant for the moment that the encoding and decoding machines may be as complicated as the designer may wish, and that the memory of the human links—using the common sense of the word "memory"—is unbounded. Under those ideal circumstances, it is obvious that any improvement of our understanding of the structure of language and of discourse will bring a possibility of improvement of the performance of the cryptographer or stenographer. For example, a knowledge of the rules of grammar will show that a given phrase will never be encountered in grammatically correct discourse; thus, if his employer were to speak only grammatical English, a stenographer would not need any special set of signs to designate the incorrect sentences. Similarly, a knowledge of the statistics of discourse will suggest that the "clichés" be represented by special short signs; in this way, the stenogram will be shortened and—since deciphering is very much helped by clichés—the code will be strengthened. That is, the ideal cryptographer and stenographer should make the utmost use of any available linguistic information. Conversely, the empirical findings of language engineers should widen our knowledge of language and of discourse. (Moreover, this interplay between theory and practice should be widened to include the role of another group of language engineers: those concerned with helping translation from one language to another with the help of automatic dictionary look-up. However, the scope of the present work excludes this question and any other topic of the field of "mechanical translation.")

Let us indulge at this stage in a brief epistemological aside, pointing out that one could hardly have expected the empirical facts most important to language engineers to be those that most interest traditional linguists. As a matter of fact, the following is likely to happen and has indeed been observed: using the margin of error allowed by empirical observation, gramarians and language engineers may very well envision their common object of study in such divergent ways that their final theories are, strictly speaking, logically incompatible. The discovery of such occurrences has had a rather traumatic effect on some linguists, whose previous experience did not include logical deductions sufficiently long to ever lead to logical contradiction. Practitioners of supposedly "hard" fields, such as physics, are on the contrary very familiar with the fact that a total description of a given reality may require the use of several logically incompatible theories. There is also good reason for the psychologist to envy the physicist's luck, in his attempts to explain complicated facts on the basis of very simple assumptions: after all, practitioners of the "hard science" of physics have succeeded—for centuries—in being excused for using arguments about the imaginary realm of atoms; no one could check the properties assumed for these entities, so that the philosophers' strictures against such "non-operational" procedures were paid little heed to.[1]

Feeling sure that nobody will take quite seriously this aside, let us resume our examination of the cryptographer and the stenographer. It is clear that they work under such obvious practical constraints that they could seldom take advantage of the possibilities of making use of liguistics, which we have described. Conversely, the professional literature of those fields is hardly known to outsiders, so that their discoveries are, hardly well known. There are a few exceptions; from the viewpoint of information theory, the most important are the frequency properties based either on "average samples of discourse" from mixtures of various sources, or on samples from well-determined authors. The striking fact here is the difference in simplicity between the two most commonly studied "articulations," namely, that of the letter or phoneme, and that of the word.

The frequencies of single letters, and of "*n*-grams" made up of *n* suc-

---

[1] This is a good example of what the physicist Eugene P. Wigner refers to as "the unreasonable effectiveness of mathematics in the natural sciences." How embarrassing, by contrast, is the situation encountered in the social sciences: any set of asssumptions —however fruitful, reasonable, and useful it may be—is suspectible of some kind of experimental verification, which—however rough it may be—is very likely to show the inapplicability of these assumptions.

cessive letters, have been taken into account by cryptographers and teleg-raphists since earliest times. Decades before the justification provided by information theory, Samuel Morse knew that he should use the shortest combinations of dots and dashes to designate the most frequent letters; cryptographers dealt with letter frequencies centuries before information theory. Moreover, recurrent attempts have been made to relate the fre-quency of a phoneme to some measure of its articulatory "difficulty." But all this has not taken us very far. Indeed it seems that, from the viewpoint of statistical model-making, isolated letters are too small to be intrinsic units: little is implied about longer bits of discourse by knowing the fre-quencies of its contributing letters. As to n-grams, they are more useful, but linguistically very artificial.

Words are better bets for the theoretician: although their exact linguistic standing is not without problems, there is no question that perception of discourse is based on units of the approximate length of a word, and there is good practical reason for beginning the study of those units by examin-ing the words defined as the sequences of letters between two successive space-symbols.

Such a study was performed quite early; according to our sources, the first worker in this area was a stenographer of the French Parliament, Jean-Baptiste Estoup. His work seems to have been motivated by a politico-technical dispute concerning the respective advantages of several systems of French stenography and—very commendably—he sought scientific fact to support the design which he favored. Similar investigations were re-peated, this time for the sake of healthy intellectual curiosity, by many other investigators. But theirs were isolated and brief efforts in compari-son with the lifetime of toil devoted to the question of word frequencies by George Kingsley Zipf, the author of several books that combine fact and folly in an unusually intimate fashion. To describe the findings of these various authors, take a long sample of discourse from a given individual, and rank all the words that occur in this sample in the order of decreasing frequency. The word given rank 1 is the most frequently observed sequence of letters contained between two successive space-signs; in English, it is usually "the," but for some subjects it is "I." The word given rank 2 is that which becomes the most frequent when the word of rank 1 has been put aside. The word of rank 3 is the most frequent when one excepts those of ranks 1 and 2, and so on. Let us designate by the symbol W (r) the word that occupies the rank number r in this special ordering. We should note that, when one gets down to rare words, one finds many that occur only once or twice in the given sample. The order of rare words is indeter-minate but also indifferent; that is, these words can be ranked arbitrarily. Using the definitions given above, the empirical findings can be expressed as follows:

In the first approximation, the ratio $i(r,k)/k$, which is the relative number of repetitions of the word $W(r)$ in the sample of length k, is inversely proportional to 10 times r:

$$i(r,k)/k = 1/(10r)$$

This is supposed to hold for every writer regardless of the language that he uses. The usual way of checking relationships of this form is to use logarithmic paper, in which the abscissa is the logarithm of r and the ordinate is the logarithm of $i(r,k)$. The first-approximation law of word frequencies is expressed by stating that the graph of $\log [i(r,k)]$ as a function of $\log r$ is a straight line of slope -1, that is, parallel to the second bisectrix of the coordinate axes, as shown by the solid line of Figure 29-1.

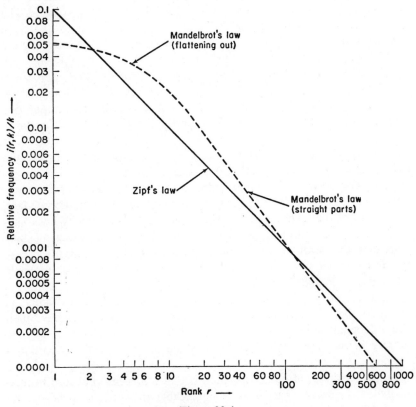

Figure 29-1.

In the second approximation, one finds that most empirical graphs differ markedly from a straight line of slope -1. *First of all,* the first few words seem not to follow the law at all. As a matter of fact, in languages such as French, the definition of "word" is unclear in the case of abbreviated forms such as *l'*, which are among the most frequent, so that "the" distribution of the most frequent words is ill determined. One finds, moreover, that the bulk of the graphs of log $[i(r,k)]$ are not parallel to the second bisectrix, and that their slope depends upon what is loosely referred to as the "wealth of vocabulary" of the subject. Such a dependence is hardly unexpected. To sum up, data can be analytically represented by the following formula (the reader may prefer to skip this formula; we hope that he will be able to follow the sequel anyway):

$$i(r,k) = Pk(r + V)^{-B}$$

The rank, r, has been defined. As to P, V, and B, they are "parameters": that is, they are fixed for a given subject, but are different for different subjects; they do not characterize a language, although it may well be that different languages favor different ranges of values for the parameters. The easiest to measure is parameter B, which is the absolute value of the slope of the logarithmic graph of log $[i(r,k)]$ as a function of log r (excluding the most frequent words). In the first approximation, $B = 1$ and $V = 0$.

Social science statistics being what it is, the foregoing second approximation is among the best-established results of that field. One still finds some authors, however, who say that it is either false, absurd, or self-evident; one author even says that it is partly false, partly absurd, and partly self-evident.

But actually there is nothing obvious in the law of word frequencies: Of course, by their very definition, the quantities r and $i(r,k)$ vary in inverse *directions,* but this is not the same as to say that they vary in inverse *proportion,* as suggested by the first approximation. As a matter of fact, distributions of the form above are closely related to probability laws having an infinite first moment; without needing to know the exact meaning of this technical term, the reader may be assured that the occurrence of such laws was felt until very recently to be practically never observed in practice, rather than to be obvious.

Note also that the double logarithmic graphs have been so misleading, at times, that they have come to be distrusted at all times; actually, their validity depends entirely upon the value of the coefficient B, and they are very safe in the range of values of B which are observed for word frequencies.

The final criticism of our distribution is that it is a priori absurd to imagine that any general law could be applicable to word frequencies. But there is actually no such conflict between the facts and most people's "intuition" of the properties of discourse. Let us discuss this in detail.

To fix our ideas, consider the word "coffee." It is usually observed when the subject wishes to express some idea, without reference to any desire to attribute a given frequency to the sequence of letters "c-o-f-f-e-e." But, first of all, the probabilistic conception of the structure of discourse determines the relative frequency of a word only on the average. To say that "coffee" occurs exactly once every 1,770 words implies belief in a nonstochastic structure. This is very similar to well-known facts concerning the tossing of coins or of dice: if the ace appears exactly once for each play in a long succession of plays (each made up of 6 tosses), one may be sure that the game is unfair. In the ideal model of random tosses, the observed frequencies of the ace must vary (or fluctuate) around the ideal value (1/6). Similarly, the observed frequencies of words should be expected to fluctuate. Naturally, as seen by the emitter, the fluctuations of word frequencies are not generated by "pure chance" but rather are associated with what he "has to say"; but, as seen by the receiver, the occurrences of the words are (hopefully) at least partly unpredictable, and "pure chance" is nothing but a model of unpredictability. One may very well find that this model is inadequate for certain refined purposes, but one can certainly not say that it is a priori absurdly in conflict with any kind of intuition.

Let us proceed. The law $i(r,k) = Pk(r + V)^{-B}$ does not limit itself to saying that every word has a well-defined frequency; it also proposes a

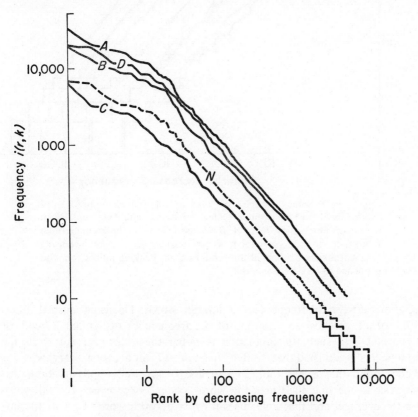

See page 558 for explanation of this part of the figure.

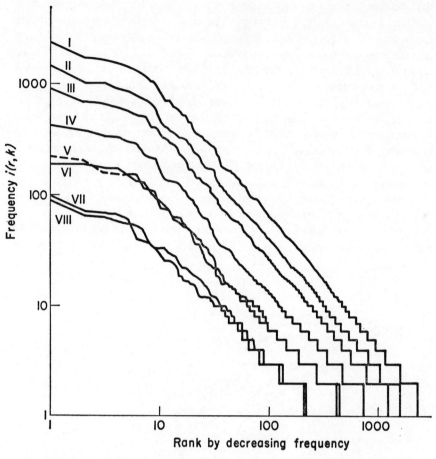

Figure 29-2. Some examples of plots of the frequency of a word (vertically in the logarithmic scale) versus its rank (horizontally in the logarithmic scale). *First: A, B, C,* and *D* are samples from German writers, N, from a Norwegian writer; *second:* samples of increasing length from the writings of the same English-speaking individual, who happened to be a schizophrenic.

relation between the frequencies of different words. This is not absurd either. First of all, the law says nothing of the frequencies of "coffee," "tea," or "chocolate" as such. Its prediction is rather the following: Paul tells me that he has established that "coffee" has rank 177 in his vocabulary; whereas Peter found that it has rank 315 in his. In the first approximation, this suggests to me that Paul uses the word "coffee" once every 1,770th word on the average, and that Peter uses it every 3,150th word. That is, the law of word frequencies relates to the entire system of Peter's or Paul's words, taken as one whole. Moreover, "system of words" is in no way synonymous with "system of ideas." The correspondence between the two is sufficiently "arbitrary" to allow one system of words to represent many systems of ideas, and conversely.

Having hopefully convinced the milder skeptics of the reasonableness of the existence of a law of word frequencies, it remains to "explain" why this law takes the form which we have described above. It happens that this expression is, formally, one of the simplest encountered by statisticians; but most professionals neglected it until recently, so that almost all the explanations (beginning with Zipf's "least effort" arguments) used very primitive tools, or handled the mathematics incorrectly. Hence—so far as we know—the only acceptable models are the numerous variants of an idea which I suggested in 1951 and which was developed in various directions by several writers. These variants are fully equivalent mathematically, but they appeal to such different intuitions that the strongest critics of one may be the strongest partisans of another; certain variants were in fact rediscovered by constructive critics! (I have long since given up trying to determine which is best.) It is useful to note here that a problem of prediction is called "well posed" in physics if slight changes in initial conditions do not change the result more than slightly. Similarly, our "explanatory" setup may be called well posed, since changes in assumptions do not lead to disproportionate changes in the results. (This outlook is not as obvious as it may seem: one incorrect model of the law of word frequencies considers as an asset the fact that, by changing its assumptions slightly, one could also obtain any one of several other laws which share none of the deeper properties of the distribution actually observed.) Let us now examine a few of the variants of our model.[2]

Two of the variants are readily interpreted in terms of the problems of cryptography and telegraphy mentioned earlier. We can prove this: suppose that the cryptographer or the telegraphist are forced to use a given coding alphabet and that they must encode word by word, the code of each word being followed by a special symbol that plays the same role as the "space" of ordinary spelling. Then, it is shown by information theory that the same rule of coding is best for both secrecy and economy (because any symbols that could be spared for purposes of economy might also provide the clue for deciphering). Let us now examine the constraint imposed by the use of word-by-word coding. This requirement may be expected to yield decreased economy and decreased strength, as compared to coding procedures that cut across words and use longer units. However, in the case of actually observed word statistics, and in this case alone, no loss whatsoever is entailed by the need to use word delimitations and to follow

---

[2] For the details of the various derivations, the reader is referred to Mandelbrot, 1961. Less complete account but probably better-written is the account given in Miller and Chomsky, 1963. For further developments addressed to the philosopher of science, see Mandelbrot, 1957.

the words by "space" symbols. That is, we may say that, insofar as the use of a space is intrinsic to the concept of a word, the only case where the word is a natural segment of discourse is when its statistics follow the law which they happen precisely to follow.

The form of these criteria is very familiar in physics, which is quite inclined to characterize the observed facts with the help of such statements as "the principle of least action," "the principle of largest entropy," "the principle of smallest entropy production," and the like. Of course, the initial idea of those principles was borrowed from introspective criteria of optimal human behavior, and, after a long detour through physics, they returned to social science under the guise of such things as Zipf's "principle of least effort." As a matter of fact, I acknowledge that it is the title of Zipf's book that triggered my first derivation of the law of word frequencies, a model in which "telegraphic optimality" was characterized by maximizing Shannon's "quantity of information" under certain constraints. Unfortunately, it seems that many readers were greatly confused by the inevitable association of such a model with Zipf's peculiar idea of a perfect world and by the inevitable association of Shannon's "quantity of information" with the many aspects of the word "information" (which Shannon never remotely claimed to cover). It turned out, therefore, to be more politic to stress the optimality of observed word statistics with respect to cryptography, an activity less readily associated with the idea that the works of man are perfect.

A third variant of our basic model also deserves brief mention. It is clear indeed that, as time goes by, the structure of the system of word frequencies slowly changes, both for individuals and for the averages relative to groups. Concerning the nature of this change, I made certain hypotheses that are simple and would have seemed reasonable in the framework of the "unreasonable effectiveness of mathematics in natural science" to which we have referred. Since, as mentioned, the model thus obtained is only a reinterpretation of the two criteria of "optimality," it leads again to the empirically observed law. Again, there is little chance of a universe generated by haphazard diachronic chance being considered "perfect" in any real way.

As we near the end of our tale, we realize that we have not done justice to psychology as such. Let us therefore end by commenting on a curious and controversial aspect of some of our models. Independently of the specific variant that one may prefer, our models ultimately rest upon the decomposition of words into more elementary units. For example, in the last analysis, the cryptographic or telegraphic optimality implies the representation of words with the help of such special signs as Morse dots and dashes. As a matter of fact, this decomposition into parts is the key to the success of our models since, using appropriate new forms of (roughly) the "law of large numbers," we could show that the same law of word frequencies should correspond to a wide range of microscopic structures; this is an application to linguistics of a method of "macro-model" making in the absence of "micro-data," which is one of the most powerful tools of the physicist (a different tool bearing the same name is greatly used in economics). This being granted, and even though word frequencies are surely independent of the technical details of Samuel Morse's contraption, one could have expected them to be linked to phoneme frequencies and—in the first approximation—to letter frequencies. For example, most of our variants require a concept of "the cost" of a word, and it would be tempting indeed to identify the cost of a word with the number of letters which it contains. Unfortunately, this is impossible, and the best that one can do is to look for the cost within the recoding of discourse by the higher nervous system of the receiver of the message and perhaps even of its emitter.

Even though hardly anything is known about those stages, it is likely that this recoding uses certain "units" shorter than the phrase or the "idea" and longer than the phoneme or the letter. It is natural to try to determine whether these units are the words; if so, our models would refer to the mutual "adaptation" between the codes of those words and their frequencies. Unfortunately, the only simple tests of this hypothesis are the tachistoscopic measurements of the time required in order to identify words. These tests are favorable to our hypothesis, but the recourse to higher brain functions may still seem to be a dodge. Let us hope, however, that the situation is no worse than that of statistical physics in the heyday of the energetists: those who dared oppose the philosophers of science spoke freely of the effects of the shape of the unobservable atoms; the more cautious scholars preferred to work with the so-called "phenomenological" method, for which theories that predict well the results of possible experiments need not be "explained" any further. As it happens, I personally am rather in favor of phenomenology, these days, so that we shall not continue our tale any further.

REFERENCES

ESTOUP, JEAN-BAPTISTE. *Les gammes sténographiques.* Paris: privately printed for the Institut Sténographique, 1916.
MANDELBROT, BENOIT. Adaptation d'un message à la ligne de transmission. *Comptes Rendus des Séances Hebdomadaires de l'Académie des Sciences de Paris,* 1951, **232,** 1638-1640.
MANDELBROT, BENOIT. Linguistique statistique macroscopique. In L. Apostel, B. Mandelbrot, and A. Morf, *Logique, langage et théorie de l'information.* Paris: Presses Univ. de France, 1957, Pp. 1-80.
MANDELBROT, BENOIT. On the theory of word frequencies and on related Marko-

vian models of discourse. In Roman Jakobson (Ed.), *Structure of language and its mathematical aspects, proceedings of symposia on applied mathematics*. Vol. 1. Providence, R. I.: American Mathematical Society, 1961.

MILLER, GEORGE A., & CHOMSKY, A. NOAM. Finitary models of language users. In R. R. Bush, E. Galanter and R. D. Luce (Eds.), *Handbook of mathematical psychology*. Vol. 2. New York: Wiley, 1963.

SHANNON, CLAUDE. A mathematical theory of communication, *Bell System Technical J.*, 1948, **28**, 379-423, 623-656.

ZIPF, GEORGE KINGSLEY. *Human behavior and the principle of least effort.* Reading, Mass.: Addison-Wesley, 1949.

30 BENJAMIN B. WOLMAN

PRINCIPLES OF MONISTIC TRANSITIONISM

THE TERM "REDUCTIONISM" can be applied either to research methods or to a theory. This chapter is an examination of the problems of reductionism in psychological theory. As its name suggests, reductionism is a belief that (1) the subject matter of psychology can presently be presented in terms of the subject matter of another science, for example, neurophysiology, (2) future research may discover that such a reduction is feasible, or (3) the scientific propositions and theories derived from empirical studies in psychology could and should be presented as logical consequences of scientific propositions of other sciences. The radical reductionist may be said to believe that *"Der Mensch ist was er isst"* (Man is what he eats). Thus the subject matter of psychology—human personality—is reduced to biochemical processes related to nutrition.

Not all psychologists share the belief that such a reduction is possible at the present time, and oppose *radical reductionism* on methodological grounds. They feel that radical reductionism is presently an untenable hypothesis, yet they share the belief that such a reduction may become possible in the future. This belief, which we shall call *hoped-for reductionism,* is widely accepted in psychology.

A third alternative is to deal with the problem on a formal basis. *Logical reductionism* tries to reduce the formal logical propositions derived from empirical studies and conceptualization of psychological theory to scientific propositions of other sciences.

A fourth point of view, *monistic transitionism,* is introduced in this discussion.

Radical reductionism insists that events described by the "science to-be-reduced" are mere appearances or illusions. Actually, these events are better and more truthfully explained in terms of the other, "reducing" science. The facts as described by the "science-to-be-reduced" are believed to be unreal and have to be replaced by scientific data described by the "reducing" science. The reducing science, so to speak, has to take over and dispossess the science to be reduced.

The history of philosophy and science offers many examples of such developments. The pre-Socratic philosophers introduced the concept of four elements in an effort to reduce the universe of the sensorily perceived variety of phenomena to the four elements which constituted the "true" world. In Plato's philosophy, the material world was believed to be a mere reflection of the world of ideas. So it was in Hegel's philosophical system. Galileo's theory of falling bodies has been "reduced" or taken over by Newton's theory of gravitation and mechanics. In our times, metabolic processes are being reduced to chemistry.

The radical reductionist assumes an identity in the subject matters described in both sciences. He may express the belief that chemical processes are really physical quanta processes and that ultimately chemistry will be abolished and its empirical data supplanted by data derived from physics.

Although the efforts to solve the psyche-soma dichotomy can develop in either direction, reducing body to mind or mind to body, the latter has been more common in modern times. Consider La Mettrie's *L'Homme Machine* and Karl Vogt's *Vorlesungen über den Menschen* (1863). In this volume, Vogt defended the idea that consciousness should be regarded as one of the many brain functions. Earlier, Vogt had blatantly asserted that human thought is related to the brain as gall is to the liver. Similar ideas were expressed by J. Moleschott: "No thought without phosphorous." Moleschott, in his *Kreislauf des Lebens* (1852), made an effort to re-establish the unity of the universe instead of the "hopeless" division of the world into material and spiritual which, he believed, was a division between the real and the imaginary. Herbart also advocated radical reductionism (Wolman, 1942).

This radical point of view has considerably influenced contemporary psychological theory. Radical reductionism in psychology assumes that so-called mental phenomena should be reduced to phenomena known from other, more basic sciences. The difference between psychology and physiology, as Watson saw it (1919, p. 20), was that physiology dealt with separate physiological functions whereas psychology dealt with the functions of the organism as a whole. "The findings of psychology become the functional correlates of structure and lend themselves to explanation in physico-chemical terms" (Watson, 1913). Bekhterev (1913, pp. 45ff.) believed that consciousness *is* a state of physical energy related to central inhibition and resistance in cortical processes. Hebb (1949) wrote about "the kind of activity *throughout the cerebrum* which we call consciousness" (p. 219). He also believed that "interest or motivation" can be "provisionally translated into the stability and persistence of the phase sequence" in nerve cells (p. 223). Pratt (1948) expressed the belief that psychology will become a truly scientific system when it will "resolve" itself into a basic science such as physiology.

The opposition to radical reductionism has come from diverse sources and for a variety of reasons. Skinner (1950) stated that in modern science "the picture which emerges is almost always dualistic. . . ." Yet the study of human behavior need not be described in physiological terms, related to "events taking place somewhere else, at some other level of observation, described in different terms, and measured, if at all, in different dimensions."

Freud (1949) felt that such a reductionism was of no help toward understanding of mental phenomena. Psychology must therefore develop its own "fresh hypotheses" and "fresh concepts" (p. 36).

Pavlov believed that his research dealt with the physiology of the central nervous system, that is, with objective facts—facts existing in time and space. Physiological concepts are "necessarily spatial," whereas the psychological are "subjective states." Thus the position of psychology was "absolutely hopeless" (1928, p. 219).

Yet it is evident that why John married Elisabeth instead of Mary, or why George decided to study law and not accounting, are not the practical concern of neurology. Neither neurology nor biochemistry can report what Tom thinks about Kant's philosophy or why he voted for President Kennedy. One may conclude the discussion of the radical reductionism with the remark of Charles Sherrington, who doubted whether the gap between brain and mind could ever be closed. Because, wrote Sherrington (1941), "the two for all I can do remain refractorily apart" (p. 312.)

THE HOPED-FOR REDUCTIONISM

Some research workers, although renouncing "here-and-now" radical reductionism, have not abandoned the idea that ultimately psychological propositions can and will be presented in terms of the physicochemical sciences. In fact, such a hoped-for reductionism is very much in vogue today and is stated, explicitly or implicitly, by a majority of psychologists whether they are learning theorists, psychoanalysts, or of any other persuasion.

Freud hoped for an ultimate victory of reductionism. His hoped-for reductionism was clearly stated in his last work where he wrote that "the future may teach us how to exercise a direct influence, by means of particular chemical substances, upon the amount of energy and their distribution in the apparatus of mind" (1949, p. 79).

It is worthwhile mentioning that ethologists also have not, as a rule, joined the ranks of the immediate, radical reductionists. For the ethologist, as Hinde (1959) summarized the situation, "analysis down to a physiological level is a desirable, but not at present usually attainable aim" (p. 565).

Pavlov expressed a similar hope. Pavlov dealt with behavior from a neurological point of view and his data were derived from observation and experimentation with the nervous system; Pavlov's theory operated with neurological terms. If it was speculative (cf. Wolman, 1960, pp. 62ff.), it was a speculation regarding the functioning of the nervous system. Yet Pavlov expressed the hope that some day psychology would be built as a "superstructure" on physiological foundations.

Hull's theory likewise belongs to the category of hoped-for reductionist systems. Hull believed that at the present time psychology must be a molar theory, dealing with behavior as a whole. "Students of the social sciences are presented with a dilemma of waiting until the physico-chemical problems of neurophysiology have been adequately solved before beginning the elaboration of behavior theory" (1943). Hull did not wait, and developed a theory independent of neurophysiology with the hope that some day the reduction would take place.

The efforts to reduce psychology to other sciences are in full swing. At the present, neurophysiological propositions are largely interpreted in terms of physics and chemistry. Should psychology be reduced to neurophysiology, it could *eo ipso* join the physicochemical kingdom of pure science. The methodological advantages of such a reduction cannot be overestimated.

Scores of workers are driving toward this goal, and serious efforts are being made in the direction of reducing psychology to neurophysiology and behavior to brain. Pribram (1954), for example, has tried to resolve this problem by experimental work that manipulated both the central nervous system and the environmental conditions in their interaction with behavior of the organism in the hope that such a procedure would eventually lead to a science of neuropsychology.

Several research workers, concerned with psychosomatic disorders, have attacked the problem of reductionism. Yet, despite the most thorough research work, reported by F. Alexander (1950), F. Deutsch (1953), Grinker and Robins (1954), and many others, we are not one whit closer to "reduction" of mental processes. We know more precisely that worries and anxieties *can* produce physical symptoms. Yet all this prolific and productive research did not bring us any closer to reductionism.

The moderate, hoped-for reductionism assumes that some day the psychological proposition "John understands Proust's novel" will be translated into "Such or such processes take place in John's cells and tissues." But there is, as of today, not much hope that the understanding of Proust's ideas can ever be translated into metabolic or biochemical terms, or that the most thorough blood, urine, or gall examination can ever be translated into political, religious, or aesthetic convictions. It seems that, today as yesterday, the two empirically distinct phenomena, expressed as "John's metabolic rate or blood chemistry is so and so" and "John prefers Beethoven to Bach," for example, are mutually untranslatable and irreducible, and the hope for a future solution is just about a hope and nothing else.

The gravity of the issue is underscored by the fact that reductionism in psychology represents the monistic conception of the world whereas a nonreductionistic psychology inevitably leads to dualism. The mind–body dualism is certainly not what psychological science is likely to thrive on. Such a dualism presents a knot of problems that have perplexed philosophers and psychologists since Descartes and Geulincx. Philosophy, since its early pre-Socratic days, has always tried (with a few exceptions) to find unity in the universe, despite the empirical diversity. Although a monistic theory of universe cannot easily be proven, a dualistic or pluralistic theory can be neither proven nor proposed without finding the means of "communication" between the two separate worlds. It is, therefore, apparent that an anti-reductionistic psychology creates more unsolvable problems than a reductionistic one; neither seems to be satisfactory.

Hoped-for reductionism is not naïve; it says neither that "A headache is a neurological process" nor that "It does not exist." A future hoped-for reduction of psychology to neurology or neurophysiology means that psychological phenomena will be explained in terms of those neurosciences, and the neurophysiological conditions for their occurrence will be discovered.

It is questionable whether such a relationship as "Whenever John had a headache, such and such neurophysiological processes took place" could be ever established. Psychoanalysis interprets John's headache in psychogenic terms, that is, it views the headache as an effort to avoid punishment for neglected duties or as a self-inflicted punishment, or as any other primary or secondary gain (Fenichel, 1945). Somatic symptoms appear in this context not as a background or cause of mental disorders, but as their product (cf. Alexander, 1950). Mind and body are always two and not one, no matter what the nature of their interaction.

DUALISM

If mind cannot be reduced to body and body cannot be reduced to mind, the only alternative would seem to be dualism. Dualism has a long past, probably longer than the written history of mankind.

For, as far back as human research goes, humans have been perplexed with the soma-psyche dichotomy. Probably it was the fact of death that gave rise to this perplexity. Were men immortal, were life immortal, perhaps man would never have come across this dichotomy. A rock lasts forever; it neither lives nor dies. But humans do live and die. Here they are, full of energy, and here they still are but not alive; they are mere corpses; something has been radically changed, something is definitely missing. Men and corpses are not one and the same thing.

What makes men move, eat, walk, feel, love, fight, or escape? It is, apparently, something outside the body, for a dead body does not do any of these things. The ancient Israelites called this factor *neshama* (soul), a derivative of *neshima* (breath). Without that Godlike spirit or *neshama,* man was just matter. "For dust thou art, and unto dust shalt thou return."

The nonmaterial, nondust factor was called by the ancient Romans *anima* or soul. Soul was the driving force that made bodies move. Without soul, men were like inanimate objects; one may push and pull corpses like rocks or sand. One would not dare deride or kick a live enemy; one may do it to dead enemies, for their soul has left them and they have turned into inanimate corpses.

Some primitive men ascribed soul to moving objects, such as rivers, winds, rains, stars, moon, and sun. It probably took millennia of experience to learn that inanimate nature is inanimate, that is, does not possess an *anima*. Plants and animals have been believed to be animate, for their life started at a certain point and came at a certain point to a dead end.

The belief in immortality is more plausible, more suggestive than the lack of such a belief. Sun and moon, oceans and rivers, mountains and valleys are for ever. Bodies die, but something lasts forever. The most lasting buildings, the pyramids, were built to accommodate the immortal soul. Do animals have a soul? Some religions accept the idea, others deny it. In regard to humans, the immortality of the soul became a generally accepted belief, and it was not easy to doubt it. One might, in a rebellion against dogmas, supplant soul by mind, consciousness, personality, or the like, but dualism became a common-sense, widely accepted philosophy, irrespective of one's belief or disbelief in the immortality of the soul.

The soma-psyche problem, as presented in the traditional dualistic way, has no solution. By definition, the psyche is something that is not material, something outside matter. The body is material, perishable, born to die; the psyche is nonmaterial and spiritual. There is no bridge, no connection, no common elements between.

Dualism became the fundamental philosophy in the Aristotalian system; dualism is a dogma in the great monotheistic religions, elaborated in the writings of Maimonides, Thomas Aquinas, and Moslem theologians, argued back and forth by the best minds in modern times. Dualism is loudly denounced and tacitly accepted, but always present as an unsurmountable barrier.

All efforts to solve this problem outside religion, either by empirical studies or by philosophical speculations, have led nowhere. One could try, as did Descartes, Geulincx, and others, to accept two systems and invent an arbitrarily set connection system between them, but no one could ever explain the interrelationship between the physical and the mental. If not for the problem of connection, dualism would probably have enjoyed the widest acceptance. But the perplexing fact of communication between mind and body could be neither denied nor explained away. Alcohol changes human moods; moods alter respiration and blood circulation. How it happens is still an enigma.

LOGICAL REDUCTIONISM

Perhaps the problem can be approached in another way. Although, according to everyday observation and common sense, physical and mental processes are entirely different, this does not preclude the presentation of one category of events in terms of the other, provided an adequate level of formalization of the scientific propositions is reached. In other words, no effort need be made to prove that consciousness is a cerebral activity, or that a toothache is a cavity, or a headache is a sort of waves measured by the electroencephelograph, but the logical constructs of a reduced psychology could be, perhaps, presented as or reduced to logical constructs of the reducing neurology or physiology.

Logical reductionism does not assume synonymity of psychological and nonpsychological terms. Its aim is to interpret theoretical psychological propositions derived from observation and experimentation in terms of theoretical propositions of another science. As Nagel (1953) put it:

> The objective of the reduction is to show that the laws or general principles of the secondary science are simply logical consequences of the assumptions of the primary science [the reducing science]. However, if these laws contain expressions that do not occur in the assumptions of the primary science, a logical derivation is clearly impossible. Accordingly, a necessary condition for the derivation is the explicit formulation of suitable relations between such expressions in the secondary science and the expressions occurring in the premises of the primary discipline (p. 541).

Accordingly, efforts should be made to find logical connections between certain empirically confirmed propositions of the two sciences, the one that has to be reduced and the other that will "incorporate" the reduced science. Obviously, "the reduction of chemical law to contemporary physical theory does not wipe out, or transform into a mere appearance, the distinction and the types of behavior which chemistry recognizes" (Nagel, 1953, p. 549; 1961, Ch. 11).

In other words, logical reductionism does not need to prove that mental and somatic process are "the same," provided that one can present the propositions presenting psychological theories as a set of propositions that could be inferred from formal propositions of other sciences (cf. Feigl, 1958; Nagel, 1961; Wolman, 1964).

CHANGE AND IDENTITY

It seems that the discussion concerning reductionism would benefit from a clarification of the concept "the same," "identical," and their synonyms. If headaches were identical with electrical brain currents, if hatreds were identical with glandular secretions, psychology would lose its *raison d'être* as a science distinct from physiology. Watson's point would be well taken; physiology would be a science of partial functions of the various organs, and "behaviorism" could be a science of the "molar" functions of the organism as a whole, and replace the obsolete science of psychology. The identity of empirical data would justify identity in approach and methods of research.[1] Let us suppose that we have accepted Watson's reasoning; what does it mean to say that psychological data are "identical" with physiological data? Can we study human behavior as we study all other events?

Some psychological discussions, inspired by the progress in psychophysics and experimental psychology, have revolved around the problem of *idiographic* as opposed to *nomothetic* sciences. The belief was that phenomena observed and analyzed by natural sciences are repeatable and therefore lead to the formulation of general laws. For instance, the laws of gravitation, thermodynamics, and electromagnetism, are based on innumerable and repetitive cases. History and psychology, however, deal with unrepeatable, unique occurrences, the so-called idiophenomena. Thus, even if a definite correspondence of a reductionistic nature between mental and physical phenomena were proven, still these two classes of phenomena could not be identical.

Yet in contradistinction to Windelband (1921), Dilthey (1924), and others, I believe that this need cause no headache to science: all phenomena are idiophenomena. Whatever happened, happened once; what happened again may be similar to the past, yet not the same. I see no difference in this respect between the various sciences. All sciences that deal with what happens (or happened) are *empirical* or *natural sciences,* physics and history alike, and all sciences strive to generalize, abstract, and discover regularities. Whether their subject matter are idiophenomena or not, all sciences group their factual data, put them into classes on the basis of at least one common denominator and seek general laws applicable to them. Whether the subject matter of sciences are idiophenomena or not, all sciences are nomothetic (Wolman, 1960). Consider just a speck of dust carried by air currents in a room, a drop of water on the window, an experimental animal in a laboratory, or the sound of a whistle. All these are idiophenomena. Not only the battle of Waterloo, but also the sunrise on that day, was an idiophenomenon.

Science is not a copy, photograph, or telephone book of nature. Scientific theory is a system of propositions formed in such a manner that the propositions are expected to correspond to empirical data, explain them, predict as much as possible, and help in discovering new data. Scientific propositions represent reality in an *agreed-on fashion* (cf. Poincaré, 1903; Wolman, 1938, 1948, 1960).

---

[1] When one science applies research methods borrowed from another science, it is *methodological reductionism.* The present essay deals with *theoretical reductionism* only and its three types: the medical, hoped for, and logical.

The question of identity becomes more complex when things mingle, change, or fall apart. Empirically speaking, $H_2O \neq H + H + O$, for everyone knows that water is empirically different from separate hydrogen and oxygen. Yet the scientific proposition $H_2O = H + H + O$ is a valid proposition as far as laws of logic and mathematics go.

Or consider water, ice, and vapor. They are empirically different. Science discovered the connections between them and explained the conditions necessary for the *transition* from one state into the other. Empirically speaking vapor is neither ice nor water. Yet their chemical composition is the same, despite the empirically observable differences. Actually there is not a thing that is exactly the same under all circumstances; thus, the question of sameness and identity has no meaning. Using the totality of spatiotemporal relations, not a thing can be the same under any circumstances. (Schrödinger, 1952; Wolman, 1938). At time t_1 and in space s_1, A is different from what it is at time t_2 and in space s_2:

$$A_{t_1 s_1} \neq A_{t_2 s_2}$$

One may wonder whether the changes follow exactly the pattern established by Aristotle, Maimonides, Hegel, Marx, Bergson, or Broad, or any other general pattern. One may doubt whether it is safe and empirically justified to assume that there is one eternal pattern of *telos,* dialectics, dialectical materialism, creative evolution, or emergence. Perhaps there are many paths and patterns. The fact that a man at twenty is no more the same as he was at five or as an embryo, or that a tree is not a sapling and a sapling is not a seed, should be explained on the basis of whatever empirical evidence and logical rules for theory formation are available. I see no reason to impose theory on fact, nor do I share Hegel's contempt for reality, as expressed in his dictum: *"Desto schlimmer für die Wirklichkeit"* (Too bad for reality).

In cases where things change and are no longer what they were, it seems justified to abandon the term "identical." The fertilized egg A that turned into a zygote, the zygote that became an embryo and then a fetus, neonate, and infant, and presently the twenty-year-old laboratory assistant, the industrious Mr. A, is an example not of identity but of continuity. Although many things changed, there was a continuity in this change. Only egg A turned into Mr. A. Egg B did not develop into Mr. A, nor did egg C, D, or any other. Thus, although Mr. A is *not identical* with the fertilized egg A, his life is a case of continuous change. Certainly this change is more complex than any one simple pattern dialectics, Gestalt, or creative evolution could envisage.

The fact remains that the water that turned into vapor and the egg that turned into a chicken are not what they were before. There are certain rules for the change, although one may doubt the uniformity of these rules. The laws that govern the water are not exactly the same nor *logically inferred* from the laws that govern the steam; the life of the chicken does not necessarily represent the laws inferred from the laws of eggs. In other words, factual changes require formation of new laws that can only *partially* be inferred from the old ones.

Let us consider another case. Ethyl alcohol is composed of two atoms of carbon, one of oxygen, and six of hydrogen; dimethyl ether has exactly the same composition. But, at room temperature, ethyl alcohol is a liquid, whereas dimethyl ether is a gas. Ethyl alcohol boils at 78°C., but dimethyl ether boils at −24°C.

Since F. A. Kekulé's invention of "structural formulas," we know that the compounds, ethyl alcohol and dimethyl ether, are different. They are, respectively:

$$\text{H—C—C—O—H} \qquad \text{H—C—O—C—H}$$

Despite the identity of elements, the two molecules have different *structural* formulas and are, therefore, different. The two molecules have the same number of the same atoms, but the differences in the arrangement of the atoms make the molecules different. To be sure, there are laws common to both ethyl alcohol and dimethyl ether; yet there are certain differences too and, accordingly, different laws have to be formulated.

CONTINUITY

It is an undeniable fact that, under certain conditions, certain bodies change, merge, split, grow, shrink, move, stop, fall apart, and so on. The Montana Indians used to squeeze the skulls of their newborn infants to make them look prettier by the standards of the prevailing fashion. Contemporary women starve themselves to meet the standards set by the Garment Center's fashion designers. When a woman has lost twenty pounds, is she still the same woman or not? When a child has grown up, when an attic has been added to a house, when a man has shaved his beard: are these all still the same?

Obviously, there are degrees of change. When a pot of water is put on a stove, the temperature of the water changes. When the water reaches a boiling point, further changes take place. Logically speaking, as long as at least one element of A_1 persists in A_2, we speak of *continuity*.

There are a great many types and degrees of change and, as mentioned before, there is no reason to prescribe to them one path and one pattern. The fact of continuity in change is evident in many, if not all, phenomena and events in the universe. As amply observed by Greek philosophers and by the Hebrew Ecclesiastes, rivers evaporate and turn into clouds, and clouds give rain and fill rivers with water. Lava erupts and turns into fertile soil, and some fertile soil is eroded or covered by dunes. Species develop and perish, and new worlds develop out of old ones.

This continuous change is expressed in a universal theory, the theory of *monistic transitionism*. Monistic transitionism (1) takes into account the diversity and variability of nature, (2) unites this empirical diversity into an over-all continuous *unity,* (3) and introduces the general idea of continuous changeability of things. Transitionism does not assume uniformity of the universe; it assumes only its continuity. Transitionism does not postulate one law and one pattern of change for all that happens. Transitionism seeks similarities and, whenever they are found, expects similar laws to be discovered.

Monistic transitionism is neither reductionism of any type nor an emergence theory. It simply states that, empirically speaking, heat is not motion; heat and motion are measured by different units and have different impact on things. They act differently; they are different.

Yet heat and motion can be, under certain conditions, transformed into one another. Thus transitionism at the empirical level states that although things are different, some things have many similarities, and certain things can be transformed into other things.

At the level of logical constructs, transitionism maintains that whenever certain groups of phenomena undergo changes, they are no longer the same as they were before. On the basis of similarities, certain rules still apply; as a result of dissimilarities, new and fresh concepts must be formed and new laws discovered.

Obviously, certain phenomena, although empirically different, can be partially reduced to each other. This rule does not apply to all phenomena, for unity does not mean uniformity. Certain sciences can be reduced in a radical sense, while other sciences only in the sense of logical reductionism, that is, interpreted in terms of the laws of other sciences. Perhaps chemistry will be formally reduced to quantum mechanics. Certain areas are, however, not reducible. But even those areas that are not reducible can be presented in a continuum of changes. The issue is not an issue of faith, but of empirical evidence and logical inference.

Possibly Einstein's program will be attained, and the growing physical theory will become a field theory, the concepts of matter being reduced to concentrations of energy (Einstein, 1959). Yet such a future development in physics does not prove that a similar development is feasible or possible in psychology.

TRANSITIONISM IN BIOLOGY

As a student of contemporary psychological theory, I cannot help wondering why psychologists have been more influenced by physics than by sciences that are much closer to psychology, such as biology or biochemistry. Present-day psychological theory is largely patterned after theoretical physics, in most cases avoiding biological patterns (cf. Hinde, 1959; Wolman, 1960).

All sciences, so I believe, are either natural sciences, such as physics, chemistry, geology, history, biology, anatomy, psychology, and all other sciences that deal with bodies and events, or formal sciences, such as logic and mathematics. The natural sciences could be, perhaps, grouped in an order similar to the proposed by Auguste Comte, the order of decreasing abstraction. If the universe could be presented as several concentric circles, the inner circle should represent the organic life as a particular case of inorganic, and mental processes as a part of the organic (cf. Oparin, 1957). For mental life is not "outside" organic life. It is something that happens in living organisms, a certain facet of their functioning that comes to an end when life ends.

The question is not whether biological processes can or cannot be reduced to biochemistry, biochemistry to inorganic chemistry, and mental processes to biological processes, but what can be reduced and to what extent. What cannot be reduced represents, empirically, a case of continuity in change; accordingly, new scientific propositions, representing the new elements and the new constellations, must be coined.

At the empirical level, *certain* biological processes can be interpreted in physicochemical terms. Consider osmosis, oxidation, composition of cells, and so forth. Heme, the essence of hemoglobin, has a definite chemical formula; so have glucose and galactose. The study of nutrition, digestion, respiration, secretion, endocrinology, metabolism, photosyntheses, metabolic tracers, and so on is today largely a matter of chemistry (cf. Baldwin, 1952). In some cases it is a matter of radical reductionism, in some others of logical reductionism, whereas in still other cases, chemistry is not enough. The functions of higher species cannot always be reduced to biochemistry; consider environmentally induced psychosomatic changes (Deutsch, 1953; Wolman, 1960), growth, regeneration, and reproduction.

Lately, the study of genetic processes has gained a great deal of clarity by biochemical research. *Certain* genetic processes are, apparently, reducible to biochemistry. Consider the recent, most spectacular discoveries related to mongolism (Lejeune, 1959). Yet sex itself is hardly a reducible issue. Nor is the very fact of intake of food by higher organisms. Even Pavlov postulated a general unconditioned *instinct of life or reflex of purpose,* the purpose being the preservation of life. Purpose, whether it is related to self-preservation or preservation of species, is not a concept derived from physics or chemistry. It is not reducible; it is a new phenomenon.

Yet even those phenomena that are not reducible do not necessarily create a gulf. In biological sciences, the transition from one evolutionary level to another has taken a peculiar form not known in the inorganic world. Transitionism in biology is based on the facts of phylogenetic and ontogenetic evolution.

PHYLOGENETIC EVOLUTION

The very fact of evolution speaks in favor of monistic transitionism. In biological sciences (psychology is one of them), transitionism is a theory of *continuous transition of organic life from one developmental stage to another*. Each species represents a part of the evolution; A developed into B, B into C, C into D, and so on. Once a species has developed into something new, it is no longer what it was before. Organic life, as explained by Oparin (1957) has developed out of inorganic life. Yet, once it developed, it was no longer inorganic. Thus, instead of *unity* and *identity*, transitionism proposes *unity of continuity*.

The principle of transitionism expands Einstein's formula, $E = mc^2$, into a general theory of physics, physics being seen as the most general science. Biology is a peculiar, "higher level" branch of physics-chemistry, that is, a science that deals with organic matter. A peculiar branch of biology is psychology or the science of behavior of certain organisms. New processes and new relationships require new scientific formulations. Whatever is old in the new processes, can be reduced; whatever is new, cannot be reduced. But both old and new bear witness to the continuity of nature.

The unity of the universe does not contradict the diversity of singular events and bodies. Assuming that all nature is a series of energy fields, the fact remains that each field is different. When field A_1 receives an additional load of energy, it becomes field A_2. Field A_2 is different from field A_1, and so on. The fact that quantum theory does not prove such a continuum, it is, probably as Einstein wrote, because quantum theory is presently an "optimum formulation," but it "offers no useful point of departure for future development" (Einstein, 1959, p. 87).

In biology, transitionism points to the fact that higher species developed out of lower species; some protozoa have probably developed through innumerable changes into mammals; yet mammals are no longer protozoa. Mental processes are believed to be associated with nervous cells; the fewer the cells and the lower the organization of the nervous system, the lower was the level of mental processes. If these are any "mental" processes in protozoa, they are certainly not the same as in mammals (cf. Harlow, 1958).

Logical reductionism could reason as follows: Protozoa are not mammals, yet the same laws of organic matter apply to both. Consider the following example, borrowed from Infeld (1950, p. 11). A radio antenna sends out electromagnetic waves; so does an atom in the sun or in a neon tube. An antenna is not an atom, yet these two different phenomena are governed by the same laws as are formulated in Maxwell's equation.

Yet this is not the case in biological sciences. Consider propagation of species. Scientists could not interpret propagation of species in mammals by using scientific laws derived from empirical findings of division in protozoa. There is no room for reduction here. Mammals reproduce by sexual copulation; do protozoa practice sex? Birds lay eggs; do mammals do the same? Mammals feed their offspring with milk; do insects do the same? No wonder Kinsey and his associates have misinterpreted the sexual life of humans; they have tried to *reduce* human sexuality to zoology, overlooking the fact that sexuality in humans, although rooted in physiology, is one of the most crucial and complex issues in human interindividual relations.

On a new level of development, new processes take place that cannot be reduced to the lower processes. Certainly there are common elements: assimilation of carbon is a general phenomenon for most plants, and oxidation (and respiration) is a general phenomenon for most animals. Yet neither of these facts leads to a general law of biology. Harvey's theory certainly does not apply to those organisms that have no blood. It probably, requires a certain evolutionary development before the organisms develop sensorimotor reactions.

Radical reductionism has been the leading philosophy in the Soviet Union and still prevails in the writings of some writers. After a long and arduous struggle with theoretical and methodological problems (Wolman, 1960), most Russian psychologists seem to have accepted Pavlov and even went beyond Pavlov. Influenced by dialectical materialism (Lenin, 1935), they are opposed to Bekhterev's or Watson's brand of a radical, here-and-now reductionism. Watson (1919) wrote that "states of consciousness, like so-called spiritualist phenomena, cannot be objectively demonstrated, and can therefore never be the object of truly scientific research" (p. vii). Contemporary Russian psychology has accepted the fact of consciousness and of other psychological processes as distinguished from physiological processes and insists that "Man's consciousness can and must be studied by consistently objective methods" (Teplov, 1957, p. 259).

Recent experimental studies in Russia seem to support a transitionistic type of psychological theory. The studies reported by Bykov indicate that certain physiological processes can be reduced to physics, but others cannot. For instance, in an experiment conducted by Balakshina in denervated kidneys with a destroyed hypophysis, the physiological processes in the kidneys could be interpreted in terms of physics (cf. Bykov, 1957, pp. 36ff.). In experiments on pain reception, where speech signals were used, the role of the cerebral cortex in pain sensation was established. Pain sensation is certainly conscious. But several inner organs do not have sensibility to pain and their reaction can be, perhaps, reduced to sheer physiology. Stimulation of exteroceptors has been usually accompanied by a "subjectively perceived sensation." In Russian psychology, this term denotes mental processes. Stimulation of interoceptors was either not perceived subjectively at all or, at least, not accompanied by any definite, localized perception.

Further research contributed to differentiation of what might be called "levels" in the transition from organic to mental. Interoceptive conditioning in man (Ayrapetyants, 1952, 1956; and many others) was proven to be unconscious. As a thorough review of recent Russian literature stated, "Interoceptive conditioning, whether involving conditioned or unconditioned interoceptive stimuli, is readily obtainable and is by its very nature largely unconscious in character" (Razran, 1961, p. 97).

Russian psychologists emphasize that mental processes are not reducible to physiological processes but represent a new, unique, higher level of development. In a paper published in 1956 in the journal *Voprosy Psikhologii,* S. L. Rubinstein expressed this trend of thought: "The discovery of the biochemical nature of physiological phenomena has not resulted in the disappearance of those as specific phenomena. . . . However far-reaching the discoveries of biochemical regularities controlling the formation of cortical connections, reflexes will not cease to be reflexes. . . ." (1957, p. 269).

Since psychic phenomena obey the physiological laws of higher nervous activity they appear as the effect of the operation of physiological laws; similarily, those physiological and biological phenomena which obey the laws of chemistry appear as effects of the operation of chemical laws. But physiological processes represent a new, unique form of manifestation of chemical laws, and it is precisely the discovery of these new specific forms of manifestation that is covered by the laws of physiology. In the same way, the physiological laws of neurodynamics find in psychic phenomena a *new unique form of manifestation which is expressed in the laws of psychology.* In other words, psychic phenomena remain psychic phenomena, even though they appear as a form of manifestation of physiological laws; just as physiological phenomena remain physiological, though as an outcome of biochemical investigation they also appear as a form of manifestation of the laws of chemistry. Such, in general, is the interrelationship of the laws governing the lower and higher forms of movement of matter, the relationship between "lower" and "higher" regions of scientific investigation. The fact that the more general laws governing the lower regions spread to the more specialized regions does not exclude the necessity of discovering the specific laws of these higher regions (pp. 268-269).

A similar stand on this issue was taken by psychoanalysis. Psychological phenomena

are in themselves just as unknowable as those dealt with by the other sciences, by chemistry or physics, for example; but it is possible to establish the laws which those processes obey and follow over long and unbroken stretches their mutual relations and interdependencies. . . . This cannot be effected with-

out framing fresh hypotheses and creating fresh concepts. . . . We can claim
for them the sense value as approximations as belongs to the corresponding
intellectual scaffolding found in the other natural sciences, and we look forward to their being modified, corrected and more precisely determined as
more experience is accumulated and sifted. So too it will be entirely in accordance with our expectations if the basic concepts and principles of the new
science (instinct, nervous energy, etc.) remain for a considerable time no
less indeterminate than those of the older sciences (force, mass attraction,
etc.) (Freud, 1949, p. 36).

Scientific psychology explains mental phenomena as a result of interplay of
primitive physical needs . . . and the influences of the environment on these
needs. . . . Mental phenomena occur only in living organisms; mental phenomena are a special instance of life phenomena. The general laws that are
valid for life phenomena are also valid for mental phenomena; special laws
that are valid only for the level of mental phenomena must be added (Fenichel, 1945, p. 5).

And this is, more or less, what I have been saying (Wolman, 1948; 1960,
pp. 533 ff.). Transitionism is an evolutionary interpretation of monism. At
a certain point of evolution, organisms become capable of receiving stimuli
and responding to them. This ability, noticed already in lower species, undergoes changes. At a high evolutionary level, organisms begin to be aware
of their actions. This awareness or consciousness cannot be found empirically nor inferred logically in lower animals. It is a new phenomenon, a
product of gradual evolution and transition.

Ananyev et al. (1959) emphasized the evolutionary aspect of mentality.
Although on low phylogenetic levels neurological processes are hardly distinguishable from mental-unconscious and preverbal processes, on a level
of verbal conditioning reductionism is no longer possible. Although the
Pavlovian term "unconscious" is not identical with the psychoanalytic "unconscious," both terms indicate a lower level of mentality, onto- and phy-
logenetically, and both terms come closer to the point where, figuratively
speaking, mind and body meet. That they do meet, that there has been a
continuous transition in the afferent–efferent system, is a fundamental
hypothesis of the transitionistic theory.

ONTOGENETIC EVOLUTION

The same transitionistic interpretation applies to ontogenetic processes.
A tree develops out of a seed via sapling, yet a tree is neither sapling nor
seed. A hen develops out of an egg, but a hen is no longer an egg. A man
was an infant but he is an infant no more. The fact that there are amoebas
and mammals, apes and men, seeds and trees, infants and adults supports
the idea of the continuity of nature, as postulated by transitionistic monism,
and serves as a warning against reductionism. Organic life stems from the

inorganic but cannot be interpreted in its entirety in terms of inorganic life; humans stem from lower animals yet their behavior cannot be interpreted in terms of white rats; an adult was a child, yet his actions cannot be interpreted in terms of infancy. Would we, after twenty years, come to visit someone we remember as an infant and expect to find our host in a crib sucking his thumb? Could we chop a tree up to find the seed that started the tree?

When a new life starts and a new nervous system develops, certain early responses observed in the fetus disappear in postnatal life (Carmichael, 1951). Not all parts of the nervous system develop at the same speed, and the nervous system of the neonate is far from maturity.

One wonders how far one should go to find the borderline or the bridge between somatic and mental processes. Since Janet and Freud, unconscious processes have become the subject matter of the science of mental or behavior processes. Unconscious processes are now subject to experimental test (cf. Sears, 1943; Ezriel et al., 1957; etc.). Mental processes start in prenatal life. The earliest reflex responses in humans have been reported between the seventh and eighth weeks, measured from the last menstruation (Hooker, 1954). Yet there is a difference between histological and functional nervous development, and probably between nervous development and mental development. When the nervous cells mature, how many of them are in operational condition; how many of them accept stimuli and discharge responses? Does life start at once? Does mental life start at once at a certain point? Does it start before the embryonic cells for the nervous system separate from the cells for muscle, bones, and so on, or after that separation? (Sperry, 1958).

To be sure, we do not know. We do know that mental processes are definitely associated with nervous cells and tissues. We know that the genes are mainly composed of deoxyribonucleic acid (DNA). We know that heredity is to a large extent an interaction between ribose sugar molecules and DNA (Crick, 1961). We know that many clinical syndromes of mental deficiency are related to hereditary factors. We may hypothesize that, at a certain point of ontogenetic development, genetic, prenatal, or natal physicochemical factors *cause* mental symptoms. Causation, however defined, is one of the possible modes of transition (cf. Planck, 1932, p. 147; Wolman, 1948, 1960, pp. 523ff.).

Yet such a causal soma-psyche connection cannot be proven for a great many, indeed, for the majority of mental disorders. At present, only certain mental disorders are known to be produced by chemical factors, thus permitting a kind of logical reductionism. A majority of mental disorders is most probably caused by interaction with the social environment (Wolman, in press).

Freud was opposed to the radical reductionism on methodological grounds.

We know two things concerning what we call our psyche or mental life: firstly, its bodily organ and scene of action, the brain (or nervous system) and secondly, our acts of consciousness, which are immediate data. Everything that lies between these two terminal points is unknown to us and, so far as we are aware, there is no direct relation between them (Freud, 1949, p. 13).

Therefore, psychoanalysis must develop a set of concepts independent of organic factors.

Yet Freud's view of human behavior, normal and abnormal, leads in the direction of transitionism. Consider the relationship between sexual physical and psychological excitation: "Once it has reached the required level, the somatic sexual excitation is continuously transmitted into psychical excitation" (Freud, 1924, vol. 1, p. 98).

No doubt, Freud's empirical data and logical constructs cannot serve as a final solution of the problem. Freud's remarks on this issue are rather tenuous. But, at the present time "the gap between neurophysiological observations and psychological phenomena must be still bridged with rather tenuous theories" (Jasper, 1958, p. 58).

Freud did not renounce the idea of the organic origin of mental life. At the earliest stage of life, there is only the id. The id, Freud said, contains "everything that is inherited" and "fixed in the constitution." How this organic, inherited endowment is transformed into mental processes, no one knows. Life processes are processes of energy. "We assume," wrote Freud (1949), "that in mental life some kind of energy is at work; but we have no data which enable us to come nearer to a knowledge of it by analogy with other forms of energy" (p. 44). This mental energy is assumed to be a continuation or transformation of physical energy.

Among the psychic functions there is something that should be differentiated (an amount of affect, a sum of excitation), something having all the attributes of a quantity—although we possess no means of measuring it—a something which is capable of increase, decrease, displacement and discharge, and which extends itself over the memory-traces of an idea like an electric charge over the surface of the body (Freud, 1924, p. 75).

Under certain conditions, physical energy becomes transformed into mental and mental into physical.

Freud saw no methodological advantage in the reductionistic assumption that mental processes are physical. But he always believed that mental processes developed out of the organic, and that there is often a "leap" from the mental into the organic world and vice versa.

PSYCHOSOMATICS

If human behavior could be explained in push-and-pull terms, or by neurons and metabolism, a logical reductionism would be justified. When a rock hits a rock, a physicochemical interpretation is proper. When leuco-cytes fight viruses, a biochemical interpretation is possible. But when John hit George, it was because John *perceived* George as an unfair competitor and because John was *motivated* by greediness and hate. John's behavior can be explained in no other terms than of his mental processes. Yet, when John was intoxicated, alcohol, a chemical agent, was an additional deter-minant of his behavior; when John, upset by his own misconduct, developed psychosomatic symptoms, there was an additional organic effect of his guilt feeling.

Transitionism assumes that mental processes are a continuation of and have developed out of biochemical process, just as the latter developed out of the lower-level and more universal physicochemical processes. There is a triple connection between mental and other biological processes. This triple connection is (1) phylogenetic evolution, (2) ontogenetic evolution, and (3) intra-organic processes.

The last category relates to the fact of psychosomatic and somatopsychic transitions. Suppose mental processes are illusions to be eventually reduced to somatic processes. Such an assumption would render psychosomatic symptoms impossible. Psychosomatic medicine, whether it operates with Freud's construct of cathexis or Pavlov's construct of conditioning, is a fairly well-established body of factual observations and theory (cf. Alex-ander, 1950; Deutsch, 1953). The general consensus in that area is that somatic processses in certain disorders are caused by mental processes. Once they have developed, they are no more what they were before; a rain is not a cloud and a tree is not a seed; nor is a bleeding ulcer a mental phe-nomenon even if it was caused by mental tensions.

In addition to the two evolutionary aspects of transitionism, there are several instances in which mental processes turn into organic and vice versa. There is no reason to believe that every single organic process is or turns mental or vice versa. Empirical evidence speaks against such a gen-eral rule. A great many intra-organic processes take place without, as far as we know, being registered consciously or unconsciously. We assume that all mental processes have originated from or are somewhat related to the central or autonomous nervous systems, or both. There are, however, physiological processes not related or not reported to the nerves: consider the growth of bone tissue or of hair. Any somatic organ that is usually served by the nervous system does not cease to report stimuli to the nerv-ous system even when under local anesthesia (Jasper, 1958, p. 59), yet it certainly may stop when the nerves are disrupted.

On the other hand, there are mental processes not related to organic causes. We have already mentioned motivation, perception, and verbal learning, which are only remotely related to organic factors in phylogenetic and ontogenetic evolution. There are many instances when the actions of the individual are merely a product of his interaction with others (Wolman, 1958), and only slightly influenced by his physical constitution. There is, however, a category of events where the transition from mental into physical and vice versa takes place here and now. These are the psychosomatic or somatopsychic phenomena. All "conversion" symptoms belong to the first group; emotional changes caused by alcohol or hallucinogenic drugs belong to the latter.

TOWARD THE FUTURE

At this point, one may compare the difficulties in theoretical psychology to those encountered in theoretical physics. Let us quote relativity theory:

> We cannot build physics on the basis of the matter-concept alone. But the division into matter and field is, after the recognition of the equivalence of mass and energy, something artificial and not clearly defined. Could we not reject the concept of matter and build a pure field physics? What impresses our senses as matter is really a great concentration of energy into a comparatively small space. We could regard matter as the regions in space where the field is extremely strong. . . . There would be no place, in our new physics, for both field and matter, field being the only reality" (Einstein & Infeld, 1961, pp. 242-243).

In Einstein's system, the difference between matter and field is quantitative and not qualitative. Matter represents vast stores of energy, and "energy represents matter." Matter is "where the concentration of energy is great, field where the concentration is small."

This bold program of constructing a field-theoretical physics is in its beginning and, for the present, Einstein has pointed out the necessity of using two realities, field and matter.

Transitionism agrees that what can be reduced, should be reduced. Certainly there is little reason to force in psychology a radical, general, here-and-now reduction at the empirical level. On a formal logical level, transitionism seeks to develop a set of constructs, in psychology and other sciences that deal with living organisms, that would enable us to present mental phenomena not as logical derivative but as a *continuation* of the other organic processes. A programmatic and imaginary formula would, more or less, represent O (organic phenomena) that can in certain conditions of k (conditions of transition) turn into M (mental phenomena) and vice versa. Thus (1) $O_k \rightarrow M$ and (2) $M_{k1} \rightarrow O$.

Einstein did find the formula, whereas in psychology we write imaginary ones because we have not found nor know how to find the right equation.

Yet these imaginary formulas may have a heuristic value. They are not a formal statement, but a program and demand for more distinction between the data and theory, between the language of empirical data and the formal language of theoretical constructs. One may, as has been done briefly in this chapter, offer supporting evidence for the case of transitionism. Yet a formal logical system of transitionism requires well-elaborated systems of explicitly stated theoretical propositions, empirically testable and certifiable in formal terms of logic and mathematics, applicable to psychology as well as to other biological sciences dealing with higher organisms. Formalization of psychological theory without an adequate formalization of other biological sciences may merely increase the gulf instead of closing it.

REFERENCES

ALEXANDER, F. *Psychosomatic medicine.* New York: Norton, 1950.

ANANYEV, B. G., KOSTYUK, G. S., LEONTYEV, A. N., LURIA, A. R., MENCHINSKAYA, N. A., RUBINSHTEYN, S. L., SMIRNOV, A. A., TEPLOV, B. M., & SHEMYAKIN, F. N. (Eds.) *The science of psychology in the U.S.S.R.* Moscow: Akad. Pedag. Nauk, 1959.

AYRAPETYANTS, E. S. Materials on the physiology of the internal analysis in man. *Trud. Inst. Fiziol. Pavlova,* 1956, **5**, 396-406.

AYRAPETYANTS, E. S. *Higher nervous function and the receptors of internal organs.* Moscow: Akad. Nauk USSR, 1952.

BALDWIN, E. *Dynamic aspects of biochemistry.* London: Cambridge Univ. Press, 1952.

BEKHTEREV, V. M. *Objektive Psychologie-Reflexologie.* Leipzig: Teubner, 1913.

BYKOV, W. H. *The cerebral cortex and the internal organs.* New York: Chemical Publishing Co., 1957.

CARMICHAEL, L. Ontogenic development. In S. S. Stevens (Ed.), *Handbook of experimental psychology.* New York: Wiley, 1951.

CRICK, F. M. DNA. In L. I. Gardner (Ed.), *Molecular genetics and human disease.* Springfield, Ill.: Charles C Thomas, 1961.

DEUTSCH, F. (Ed.). *The psychosomatic concept in psychoanalysis.* New York: International Univ. Press, 1953.

DILTHEY, W. *Gesammelte Schriften.* Leipzig: Teubner, 1924.

EINSTEIN, A. Autobiographical notes. In P. A. Schilpp (Ed.), *Albert Einstein, philosopher-scientist.* Vol. 1. New York: Harper, 1959. Pp. 3-95.

EINSTEIN, A., & INFELD, L. *The evolution of physics.* New York: Simon & Schuster, 1942.

EZRIEL, H., FARRELL, B. A. & STENGEL, E. The scientific testing of psychoanalytic findings and theory. *Brit. J. med. Psychol.,* 1951, **24**, 26-51.

FEIGL, H. The "mental" and the "physical." In H. Feigl, M. Scriven, and G. Maxwell (Eds.), *Minnesota studies in the philosophy of science. Vol. II. Concepts, theories, and the mind–body problems.* Univ. Minnesota Press, 1958. Pp. 370-497.

FENICHEL, O. *Psychoanalytic theory of neurosis.* New York: Norton, 1945.

FREUD, S. *Collected papers.* Vol. 1. London: Hogarth Press, 1924.

FREUD, S. *An outline of psychoanalysis.* New York: Norton, 1949.

GRINKER, R. R., & ROBINS, E. P. *Psychosomatic case book.* New York: Blakiston, 1954.

HARLOW, H. F. Behavioral contributions to interdisciplinary research. In H. F. Harlow and C. N. Woolsey (Eds.), *Biological and biochemical bases of behavior.* Madison: Univ. Wisconsin Press, 1958.

HEBB, D. O. *The organization of behavior.* New York: Wiley, 1949.

HINDE, R. A. Some recent trends in ethology. In S. Koch (Ed.), *Psychology: a study of a science.* Vol. 1. New York: McGraw-Hill, 1959.

HOOKER, D. Early human fetal behavior with a preliminary note on double fetal stimulation. *Proc. Ass. Res. nerv. Dis.,* 1954, **33,** 98-113.

HULL, C. L. The problem of intervening variables in motor behavior theory. *Psychol. Rev.,* 1943, **50,** 273-291.

INFELD, L. *Albert Einstein.* (Rev. ed.) New York: Scribner, 1950.

JASPER, H. Reticular-cortical systems and theories. In H. F. Harlow and C. N. Woolsey (Eds.), *Biological and biochemical bases of behavior.* Madison: Univ. Wisconsin Press, 1958.

LEJEUNE, J., GAUTHIER, M., & TURPIN, R. Étude des chromosomes somatiques des neuf enfants mongoliens. *C. Rend. Acad. Sci.,* 1959, **248,** 1721.

LENIN, V. I. Materialism and empirio-criticism. In E. Burns (Ed.), *A handbook of Marxism.* New York: Random House, 1935.

NAGEL, E. Reduction in natural sciences. In P. P. Wiener (Ed.), *Readings in philosophy of science.* New York: Scribner, 1953.

NAGEL, E. *The structure of science.* New York: Harcourt, Brace, 1961.

OPARIN, A. I. *The origin of life on earth.* New York: Academic Press, 1957.

PAVLOV, I. P. *Lectures on conditioned reflexes.* New York: Liveright, 1928.

PLANCK, M. *Where is science going?* New York: Norton, 1932.

POINCARE, H. *La science et l'hypothèse.* Paris: Flammarion, 1903.

PRATT, C. C. *The logic of modern psychology.* New York: Macmillan, 1948.

PRIBRAM, K. H. Toward a science of neuropsychology. In R. A. Patton (Ed.), *Current trends in psychology and the behavioral sciences.* Univ. Pittsburgh Press, 1954.

RAZRAN, G. Observable unconscious and inferrable conscious. *Psychol. Rev.,* 1961, **68,** 81-147.

RUBINSTEIN, S. L. Questions of psychological theory. In B. Simon (Ed.), *Psychology in the Soviet Union.* Stanford, Calif.: Stanford Univ. Press, 1957. Pp. 264-278.

SCHRÖDINGER, E. *Science and humanism.* London: Cambridge Univ. Press, 1952.

SEARS, R. R. Survey of objective studies of psychoanalytic concepts. *Soc. Sci. Rev. Council Bull.,* 1943, No. 51.

SHERRINGTON, C. S. *Man on his nature.* New York: Macmillan, 1941.

SKINNER, B. F. Are theories of learning necessary? *Psychol. Bull.,* 1950, **57,** 193-216.

SPERRY, R. W. Physiological plasticity and brain circuit theory. In H. F. Harlow and C. N. Woolsey (Eds.), *Biological and biochemical bases of behavior.* Madison: Univ. Wisconsin Press, 1958.

TEPLOV, B. M. Objective method in psychology. In B. Simon (Ed.), *Psychology in the Soviet Union.* Stanford, Calif.: Stanford Univ. Press, 1957. Pp. 246-263.

WATSON, J. B. Psychology as the behaviorist sees it. *Psychol. Rev.,* 1913, **20,** 158-177.

WATSON, J. B. *Psychology from the standpoint of a behaviorist.* Philadelphia: Lippincott, 1919.

WINDELBAND, W. *An introduction to philosophy.* London: Allen & Unwin, 1921.

WOLMAN, B. B. The chance: A philosophical study. (Hebrew.) *Tarbitz, Hebrew Univ. Quart.,* 1938, **10,** 56-80.

WOLMAN, B. B. Johann Friedrich Herbart (Hebrew). *Hachinuch Quarterly,* 1942, **15,** 1-23.

WOLMAN, B. B. *Prolegomena to sociology.* (Hebrew.) Jerusalem: Kiryat Sefer, 1948.

WOLMAN, B. B. Instrumental, mutual acceptance and vectorial groups. *Acta Sociol.,* 1958, **3,** 19-28.

WOLMAN, B. B. *Contemporary theories and systems in psychology.* New York: Harper, 1960.

WOLMAN, B. B. Psychoanalysis as an applied science. *Amer. Imago,* 1964, **21,** 153-164.

WOLMAN, B. B. *Mental disorders, their theory and classification.* In press.

SUGGESTED READINGS *

Brief, non-critical reviews of selected works in psychological theory, philosophy of science, methodology of research, and theory-formation.

ARMSTRONG, D. M. *Perception and the physical world.* New York: Humanities Press, 1961.

Analysis of three theories of perception: realism, representationalism, and phenomenalism. The author refutes phenomenalism and representationalism as theories that assume that objects cannot exist independently of the awareness of them. He points out the difficulties encountered by direct realism and suggests a way to overcome them.

AYER, A. J. (Ed.) *Logical positivism.* Glencoe, Ill.: Free Press, 1959.

Papers by members of the Vienna Circle and other logical positivists presenting the viewpoint of logical positivism on meaning and metaphysics, the foundations of knowledge, the nature of logic and mathematics, and on the nature of philosophy itself.

BERGMANN, G. *Philosophy of science.* Madison, Wisc.: Univ. Wisconsin Press, 1957.

This volume, originally intended as *The Logic of Behavior,* deals with the philosophical ideas believed to be indispensable for a detailed analysis of psychology. The entire orientation is toward psychology and the behavior sciences.

BERNARD, C. *An introduction to the study of experimental medicine.* New York: Schuman, 1949.

This ground-breaking work by the famous French physiologist, first published in 1865 is an essay on scientific method as applied to the medicine and related sciences. The first part deals with experimental reasoning, the second describes experimentation with living creatures, and the third analyzes the applications of the experimental method to physiology and medicine. This edition is rounded out by introduction by I. L. Henderson and a biography of Claude Bernard by Paul Bert.

BORING, E. G. *A history of experimental psychology.* (2nd ed.) New York: Appleton-Century, 1950.

* Prepared by the Editors with the assistance of Fredrick Axelberd, Stanley Brechner, Ronald Krate, Murrietta V. Lee, and Peter Riess.

586

The roots of modern experimental psychology are found to lie in the physiology and philosophical psychology of the period from the seventeenth to the nineteenth centuries. The development of nerve physiology in Great Britain, France, and Germany, as well as the trends in philosophical psychology, are examined. In Germany, these two currents are joined in the founding of modern experimental psychology. The establishment of this new discipline in the United States, Germany, and Great Britain is described in terms of the work of the most significant early experimental psychologists. The book concludes with a treatment of such trends in psychology as Gestalt theory, behaviorism, and dynamic psychology, and of recent theories of the functioning of the brain.

BORING, E. G. *Sensation and perception in the history of experimental psychology.* New York: Appleton-Century, 1942.

"This book nor its predecessor (*A History of Experimental Psychology*) of 1929 is a history—an historian's history." In both volumes, the author has written solely to show how psychology came to be as it was in 1942. The chapters are in the following order: sensation and perception; physiology of sensation; visual sensation: beginnings; color and its stimulus; visual phenomena, color theory, visual perception and bidimensional space; visual perception of depth and distance; psychophysics of tone; auditory perception; auditory theory; smell and taste; tactual sensibility; organic sensibility; the perception of time and movement.

BRAITHWAITE, R. B. *Scientific explanation.* Cambridge, Eng.: Cambridge Univ. Press, 1953.

The book opens with four chapters on the roles played by mathematical reasoning and by theoretical concepts and "models" in the structure of a scientific theory. The next three chapters are concerned with the part played by probability in science. The justification of induction as a scientific method and the "status of material and causal laws" are investigated in the next two chapters.

BRIDGMAN, P. W. *The logic of modern physics.* New York: Macmillan, 1927.

Operationism, the doctrine that a concept in science, to be meaningful must be synonymous with a corresponding set of operations received its original statement in this work. Bridgman. The implications of this doctrine for science and the role of models, constructs, explanation, and mathematics in physics, are discussed. Fourteen physical concepts, such as space, force, and motion, are briefly treated from the operational point of view.

BRIDGMAN, P. W. *The nature of physical theory.* Princeton, N.J.: Princeton Univ. Press, 1936.

The author discusses the functions of, the critic and the theorist. "The material for the physicist as critic is the body of physical theory, just as the material of the physicist as theorist is the body of experimental knowledge." Relativity, wave mechanics, operational definitions, and probability are discussed.

BROADBENT, D. E. *Behavior.* New York: Basic Books, 1961.

A history of the activities of the behavior theorists during the last half century, from Watson to the present, followed by a severe criticism. These criticisms include: neglect of natural behavior, premature formulations, and the inadequate treatment of physiology. The author suggests that perhaps the most successful method of attack would be: "to observe, experiment, and build predictive theories for further experimental test."

BRUNSWICK, EGON. *The conceptual framework of psychology*. Chicago, Ill.: Univ. Chicago Press, 1952.

"The efforts, stressed in the present paper, [are] to determine the structural and functional properties of the unit of behavior in abstract terms. Such determination will in turn contribute toward an explicit recognition, not only of the rules and restrictions, but also of the licenses and liberties of the objective, as well as of the molar approach [in psychology]. It will further contribute to the much-needed establishment of psychology as a discipline of distinctive, well-circumscribed internal coherence and formal unity of purpose within the more broadly unitary framework of science at large."

CAMPBELL, N. R. *Foundations of science*. New York: Dover, 1957.

A treatise on physics, of which the main object is "criticism." The author notes that "criticism" does not imply adverse judgment, merely analysis. The volume, completed in 1919, treats two main themes: propositions of science concerning explanation and the nature of laws, theories, and probabilities, and measurement in science.

CHURCHMAN, C. W., & RATOOSH, P. (Eds.) *Measurement: definitions and theories*. New York: Wiley, 1959.

An examination of the problems of measurement which have arisen in physics, psychology, sociology, mathematics, economics, and philosophy. Part I deals with the definitions related to measurement. Parts III and IV illuminate the differences between what measurement means to the physicist and what it means to the social scientist.

COHEN, M. R., & NAGEL, E. *Introduction to logic and scientific method*. New York: Harcourt, 1934.

This volume has for the last thirty years been the standard textbook in logic. The first part, on formal logic, is devoted to propositions, syllogisms, mathematical logic, inferences, and probability. The second part, on applied logic and scientific method, analyzes scientific procedures, and specifically, formation of hypotheses, classification, definition, experimentation, sampling, measurement, and statistics. Two chapters discuss selected problems in historical research, art, and moral judgment. A review of logical fallacies and evolution of the scientific method concludes the volume.

COLBY, K. M. *An introduction to psychoanalytic research*. New York: Basic Books, 1960.

The book describes the general principles of scientific investigation and discusses the distinct traits of scientific observation such as being systematic, recorded, and controlled. Experimental observation is a rather "underdeveloped area of psychoanalysis."

Research in psychoanalysis must be based on systematic observation and search for causal explanation. The problems of theory construction, correlations, and probability are briefly discussed.

DAVID, HENRY P., & BRENGELMANN, J. C. (Eds.) *Perspectives in personality research.* New York: Springer, 1960.

This volume contains contributions from twenty-seven psychologists from eleven countries. "Their chapters range over such themes as person perception, dynamics of perception, phenomenology of behavior, longitudinal study of personality, projective techniques, and religious psychology."

DUHEM, P. *The aim and structure of physical theory.* Princeton, N.J.: Princeton Univ. Press, 1954.

This book is an investigation of the theoretical methods by which physical sciences make progress. The author regards physical theory as a system of logically linked statements and not a series of "incoherent mechanical and algebraic models"; abstraction and generalization, he points out, are the basic tools of physical theory.

ESTES, W. K., KOCH, S., MACCORQUODALE, K., MEEHL, P. E., MUELLER, C. G., SCHOENFELD, W. N., & VERPLANCK, W. S. *Modern learning theory.* New York: Appleton-Century-Crofts, 1954.

The theories of Hull, Tolman, Skinner, Lewin, and Guthrie are systematically evaluated against principles of theory construction. The structure of each theory, its concepts, methodological characteristics, empirical content, and adequacy, are rigorously examined. Special emphasis is placed on determining the dependent and independent variable of each theory, the strictness with which terms are defined, and the relationship between the data language of the empirical foundations and the theoretical formulations.

FEIGL, H., & BRODBECK, M. (Eds.) *Readings in the philosophy of science.* New York: Appleton-Century-Crofts, 1953.

A selection of over fifty essays in the philosophy of science, grouped under the following headings: nature of the scientific method; philosophy of the formal sciences; space, time, and relativity; the logic of scientific explanation and theory construction; causality, determinism, indeterminism, and probability; philosophical problems of biology and psychology; and philosophy of the social sciences. Of special interest to the student of psychology are articles on the logic of psychophysical measurement, the philosophy of science in Gestalt theory, the postulates and methods of behaviorism, the operational analysis of psychological terms, hypothetical constructs, and intervening variables, the mind–body problem in the development of logical empiricism, law and convention in psychology, and on some methodological problems of psychology.

FEIGL, H. & MAXWELL, G. *Scientific explanation, space, and time.* Minneapolis, Minn.: Univ. Minnesota Press, 1962.

This anthology, Vol. III of the *Minnesota studies in the philosophy of science,* examines the general methodological issues of the empirical sciences. The articles center their discussions around these basic topics: (1) the principles of derivability and invariance; (2) "deductive-nomological" explanations; (3) analytic versus synthetic statements; (4) temporal discourse; and (5) geometry, chronometry, and empiricism.

FEIGL, H. & SCRIVEN, M. *The foundations of science and the concepts of psychology and psychoanalysis.* Minneapolis, Minn.: Univ. Minnesota Press, 1956.

The works presented in this volume (the first in the series *Minnesota Studies in the Philosophy of Science*) attempt to enumerate and clarify three major issues of scientific and philosophical importance. The first concern is with the need to distinguish the formal from the factual sciences, either as synthetic or as analytic statements. The second is the need to provide workable and acceptable criteria for factual meaningfulness and the need to evaluate the operationist viewpoint. Lastly, there is the problem of whether science requires metaphysical presuppositions, especially those invoked in the defense of inductive procedures.

FEIGL, H., SCRIVEN, M., & MAXWELL, G. (Eds.) *Concepts, theories, and the mind–body problem.* Minneapolis, Minn.: Univ. Minnesota Press, 1958.

The theme of the second volume of *Minnesota Studies in the Philosophy of Science* is stated in its title. The article by Paul Oppenheim and Hilary Putnam aims to develop a "precise concept of unity of science and to determine to what extent that unity can be attained." Carl Hempel examines the question of whether theoretical terms might be eliminated when structuring an effective scientific theory. Arthur Pap's essay concerns itself with reviewing the terms "disposition concepts" and "extensional logic." Remaining sections deal primarily with the mind–body problem.

FEIGL, H., & SELLARS, W. (Eds.) *Readings in philosophical analysis.* New York: Appleton-Century-Crofts, 1949.

An anthology which selects from articles of recent decades those which the authors consider as contributing to a decisive turn in the history of philosophy, namely, the conception of philosophical analysis. This conception underlying all the selections is derived from two major schools of thought: the Cambridge movement (Moore, Russell), and logical positivism (Wittgenstein, Carnap) in conjunction with the Berlin scientific empiricists (Reichenbach).

FRANK, P. *Philosophy of science.* Englewood, N.J.: Prentice Hall, 1957.

The principal thesis is that science and philosophy belong to one chain and the rupture which occurred between the two in the sixteenth century must be mended if either of them is to continue to progress. The discussion centers primarily on concepts used in the physical sciences and mathematics, but the conclusions are held to apply to the biological and behavioral sciences as well.

GIBSON, Q. *The logic of social enquiry.* New York: Humanities Press, 1960.

The inquiries into the structure and changes in society are becoming so detailed and systematized that they have earned the title of social science. Realizing that the subject matter of these inquiries is different from that of the natural sciences, the author discusses the procedures in social inquiries and the controversies to which they have given rise.

GRINKER, ROY R. (Ed.) *Toward a unified theory of human behavior*. New York: Basic Books, 1956.

This volume discusses a unified theory of behavior and human nature.

The areas covered in the volume range from homeostasis and evolution of dynamic reciprocating mechanisms, through psychological systems, to social systems and culture.

HAMLYN, D. W. *Sensation and perception: a history of the philosophy of perception*. New York: Humanities Press, 1961.

A survey of theories of perception, starting with the pre-Socratic philosophers, through medieval and empiricist philosophy, idealism, sensationalism and associationism, phenomenology, and contemporary views. The main idea of the book is perception and sensation, which have been erroneously connected. The term "perception" belongs to the family of epistemological terms that center around the concept of knowledge.

HANSON, N. R. *Patterns of discovery*. Cambridge, Eng., Cambridge Univ. Press, 1958.

The author is concerned with the development of theory rather than with its testing. "Let us examine not how observation, facts, and data are built up into general systems of physical explanation, but how these systems are built into our observation and our appreciation of facts and data." The author's discussion covers the problems of observation, facts, causality, classical particle physics, and elementary particle physics.

HELSON, H. (Ed.) *Theoretical foundations of psychology*. New York: Van Nostrand, 1951.

"This book is designed to treat the fundamental ideas, concepts, theories and problems which are at the center of the subject" of psychology. Those chapters reviewing the theoretical literature areas discuss: methodological considerations; some problems of nervous function; some neurological correlates of behavior; development and maturation; motivation; feeling and emotion; fatigue and efficiency; perception; learning; thinking; measurement in psychology; intelligence; personality; psychological theory and social psychology; and abnormal psychology.

HEMPEL, C. G. *Fundamentals of concept formation in emipirical science*. Chicago, Ill.: Univ. Chicago Press, 1952.

An account of the bases of concept-formation, dealing with the problems of definition and meaning. The author appeals to the theory of "dispositionals" to solve the problems of explaining (explicating) things in science.

HIRST, R. J. *The problem of perception*. London, Eng.: Allen & Unwin, 1959.

The importance of the person's interaction with a world is upheld and is labeled "publicity assumption." It is held that our perceptions can give us certainty about external objects, although science has presented some evidence to the contrary. To abandon our "significant perceptions" would be to endanger scientific progress. Other related subjects discussed are the mind–body dichotomy, perceptual consciousness, and judgment and examination of selected neurological statements related to the problem of perception.

HOOK, SIDNEY (Ed.) *Psychoanalysis, scientific method and philosophy.* New York: New York Univ. Press, 1959.

The concern of this collective volume is ". . . solely with psychoanalysis as a scientific theory," with no attention given to its "therapeutic implications, individual or social." The papers contributed fall under the following headings: psychoanalysis and scientific method; psychoanalysis and society; psychoanalysis and philosophy; discussion, criticism, and contributions by other participants.

HOOK, S. (Ed.) *The dimensions of mind.* New York: New York Univ. Press, 1960.

The theme of this volume is the relation between mind and body. The presentations are listed under three main problems: the mind–body problem, the brain and the machine, and concept-formation.

JEFFREYS, H. *Scientific inference.* Cambridge, Eng.: Cambridge Univ. Press, 1957.

A treatise on the theory of scientific inference applied to statistical mechanics, quantum theory, and probability. The general point made is that the acceptance of scientific method is based on a theory of epistemological probability.

KOCH, S. (Ed.) *Psychology: a study of a science.* New York: McGraw-Hill, 1963. 6 vols.

Contributions of eighty-six authorities in psychology and related fields, who analyze the methodological, theoretical, and empirical status of psychology and its relation to science in general.

Volume I. *Sensory, perceptual, and physiological formulations.*

Begins with three articles in the area of sensory psychology, which deal with auditory theories, color theory and the relationship between the quantum theory of light and the psychophysiology of vision. An article on stereoscopic vision and one on Lundburg's theory of binocular space perception precede three articles which deal with the systematic psychology of Wolfgang Köhler, the relation of perception to sensation, and Brunswik's probabilistic functionalism. An exposition of adaptation-level theory along with one of neurophysiological theory and a physiological theory of drive conclude this volume.

Volume II. *General systematic formulations, learning, and special processes.*

Presentation of six systematic approaches to the general problem of behavior which emphasize the role of learning; included are the positions of Lewin, Tolman, Guthrie, the Hull-Spence approach, Skinner, and the school which attempts to liberalize and extend the basic concepts of S-R theory. Three articles on specialized areas in learning treat the statistical approach to learning theory, learning set and error factor theories, and rote learning. The final three entries deal with recent trends in ethology, information theory, and linear frequency theory as behavior theory.

Volume III. *Formulations of the person and the social context.*

The volume deals with psychoanalytic theory, client-centered therapy, and personality theory. An article on the perspectives of social psychology is followed by a theory of attitude structure and change, latent structure analysis, and work-emotionality theory of the group as an organization. Also included is an article on an approach to psychological theory in terms of the theory of action and one on the psychogenic study of twins.

Volume IV. *Biologically oriented fields: their place in psychology and in biological science.*

Considers the relation between psychology and such fields as genetics, neurology, physiology, biology, and between psychology and physics and philosophy in the study of vision. Two articles on mind and the brain, as well as more specialized studies on the sense of taste and the relation between neuroelectrical events and sensory perception are included. Four articles consider the relationship between perception and the external world, sensory psychology and behavior, transactional psychology, and other related areas.

Volume V. *The process area, the person, and some applied fields: their place in psychology.*

The first group of articles deals with the relation of perception and motivation to learning and behavior as well as to the problem of defining the stimulus. Three articles treat the relationship between the study of personality and psychology, anthropology, sociology, and social relationships. Two articles are devoted to clinical psychology and deal with its historical and theoretical trends and its relation to psychopathology and research on schizophrenia. The volume concludes with two articles on psychology and human engineering.

Volume VI. *Investigations of man as socius: their place in psychology and the social sciences.*

Three articles from the field of social psychology deal with problems and trends in interdisciplinary relationships, social attitudes and other acquired behavioral dispositions, and the relation of this field to general psychology and other behavioral sciences. Articles treat the relation of psychology to sociology, anthropology, political science, and economics as well as on the more specialized topic of the relation anthropology to studies in perception and cognition and the place of personality, culture, and society in behavioral evolution. Two articles are devoted to the relationship between psychology and linguistics.

KöHLER, W. *The place of value in a world of facts.* New York, Liveright, 1938.

A philosophical examination of science, which raises the question of why scientific procedure implies values at every step and yet does not allow itself to consider the possibilities of these very implications in science's search for answers.

Dr. Köhler discusses theories of value and analysis of requiredness. He compares nature with the phenomenal world, and discusses the problems of isomorphism, memory and transcendence, organic fitness, facts and forces, and man and nature.

LANGE, F. A. *The history of materialism.* (3rd ed.) London, Eng.: Routledge & Kegan Paul; New York: Humanities Press, 1925.

This is a one-volume third edition of the original three-volume (1865) translation by E. C. Thomas. It is a detailed and critical examination of history of materialistic philosophy. The first volume describes the ancient Greek atomists, sensationalists and ethical materialists and analyzes Socrates', Plato's, and Aristotle's reactions against materialism. Roman materialism and the reaction of monotheistic religion, renaissance and seventeenth-century materialism are analyzed in historical sequence, and a description of eighteenth-century materialism in England, France, and Germany completes the first volume. The second volume describes Kant and his impact on philosophy and the relationship between natural science and materialism. The principles of Darwinism, neurophysiology, and psychophysical parallelism are analyzed. An examination of the relationship between ethics, religion, and materialism concludes the volume. In his Introduction, Bertrand Russell describes Lange's book as "a monumental work of the highest value to all who wish to know what has been said by advocates of materialism, and why philosophers have in the main remained unconvinced." The volume includes a brief biography of F. A. Lange.

LAZARSFELD, Q. F., & ROSENBERG, M. (Eds.) *The language of social research*. Glencoe, Ill.: Free Press, 1955.

A reader in the methodology of social research, which presents examples of research that illustrate the systematic analysis of procedural problems. The essays concern themselves with these problems: (1) Are there any general principles of classification and can they be studied with precision? (2) How does one go about establishing categories gathered by the social researcher? (3) What exactly is "multidimensional" classification and how does the "concept of property space" relate to this question? (4) How do we move from concepts to indices?

LEWIS, C. I. *An analysis of knowledge and valuation*. La Salle, Ill.: Open Court, 1962.

Originally, the author notes, this book was intended to discuss ethics. This purpose, however, was altered in view of the need for the premise that "valuation is a form of empirical knowledge." The author proposes this volume as a prolegomena dealing with the problems of meaning and analytic truth, empirical knowledge, and valuation.

LUCE, R. D. & RAIFFA, M. *Games and decisions*. New York: Wiley, 1957.

"This book attempts to communicate the central ideas and results of game theory and related decision-making models unencumbered by their technical mathematical detail." The stress is placed on the concepts of games theory rather than on detailed "solutions" of specific games. The book enumerates the mathematical elements of solving the problems of "maximizing utility" (gain versus risk), subjective probability, conflict of interest, and the conflicts of social decision-making.

MACH, E. *Popular scientific lectures*. (5th ed.) La Salle, Ill.: Open Court, 1943.

The lectures were published in German between 1865 to 1898. While the early lectures deal primarily with problems of physics, the later lectures detail Mach's ideas on the philosophy of science, methods of research, and the nature of scientific inquiry.

MANDLER, G., & KESSEN, W. *The language of psychology*. New York: Wiley, 1959.

The authors believe that a discussion of the language of science must remain and proceed within the bounds of everyday language. The words and terms must refer to, and denote, "real" events. The authors maintain that psychological terms need satisfy the general characteristic of invariance of usage. Certain issues of phenomenology, operationism, induction, and the methodology and structure of theory are discussed.

MARX, MELVIN H. (Ed.) *Psychological theory: contemporary readings.* New York: Macmillan, 1951.

This book includes a collection of forty-seven papers on problems of scientific theory construction in psychology in its first section (Part I) and a group of theoretical papers in the second section (Part II).

Part I, the content section of the book, includes theoretical papers in the following areas: perception, learning, psychodynamics, personality, and social interaction.

MEEHL, PAUL E. *Clinical versus statistical prediction: a theoretical analysis and a review of the evidence.* Minneapolis, Minn.: Univ. Minnesota Press, 1954.

A discussion of a long-standing controversy in clinical psychology is undertaken. The controversy centers around the choice of methodology in the prediction of behavior, "clinical" and "statistical." Clinical judgment and the statistical ordering of data for the purpose of behavior prediction are analyzed and compared. There is, ". . . no convincing reason to assume that explicitly formalized mathematical rules and the clinician's creativity are equally suited for any given kind of task, or that their comparative effectiveness is the same for different tasks. . . ."

MERTON, ROBERT K. *Social theory and social structure.* Glencoe, Ill.: Free Press, 1957.

A revised and enlarged edition of the book published in 1949. Merton proposes his "theories of the middle range," an attempt to cope with the gap existing between empiricism and speculation. These theories should be "intermediate to the minor working hypotheses evolved in abundance during the day-by-day routines of research, and the all-inclusive speculations comprising a master conceptual scheme from which it is hoped to derive a very large number of empirically observed uniformities of social behavior."

MISIAK, H. *The philosophical roots of scientific psychology.* New York: Fordham Univ. Press, 1961.

A concise review of philosophical origins of present-day psychology, starting with early Greek thinkers, through Plato and Aristotle toward modern philosophy. Brief reviews of major philosophical systems and their contributions. The mind–body problem, the impact of British empiricism, sensualism, and associationism on contemporary psychology are analyzed. Nineteenth-century philosophers and the origins of scientific psychology are also discussed.

MURPHY, GARDNER. *Historical introduction to modern psychology.* (Rev. ed.) New York: Harcourt, Brace, 1949.

This is a revised edition of the earlier 1949 book. It brings the modern period of psychology up to date. "The narrative has not been essentially altered as it relates to the period up to and through the work of Wundt and James—very roughly, through the nineteenth century." This period is covered in the first two parts of the book—Part I, on the antecedents of modern psychology, and Part II, on the rise of the research spirit, which describe the early history of psychology before the nineteenth century and the rise of experimental psychology during that century. Part III—contemporary psychological systems—is devoted to some important theoretical systems of the modern period. These include behaviorism, association, Gestalt, field theory, and Freudian psychology and the reaction it evoked. Part IV—some representative research areas—touches on the measurement of intelligence; physiological, child, and social psychology; and personality. Parts III and IV comprise the modern period.

NAGEL, E., SUPPES, P., & TARSKI, A. (Eds.) *Logic, methodology, and philosophy*. Stanford, Calif.: Stanford Univ. Press, 1962.

The papers cover various topics in logic, methodology, and philosophy of science; these topics were divided into eleven sections dealing with mathematical logic, foundation of mathematical theories, philosophy of logic and mathematics, general problems of methodology and philosophy of science, foundations of probability and induction, history of logic, methodology, and philosophy of science, and a methodology and philosophy of the physical, social, biological, psychological, historical, and linguistic sciences.

PATTON, ROBERT, *et al. Current trends in psychological theory: A bicentennial program*. Pittsburgh, Pa.: Univ. Pittsburgh Press, 1961.

This volume is concerned with the "appraisal of advances currently being made in psychological theory," especially in learning, physiological, thinking and problem solving, and personality.

PIAGET, J. *Logic and psychology*. Basic Books, 1953.

An application of the techniques of symbolic logic to the "thought structures" found in intellectual behavior. The algebra of logic and logical calculus are employed as devices for "specifying the structures which emerge in the analysis of the operative mechanisms of thought."

POPPER, K. R. *The logic of scientific discovery*. New York: Basic Books, 1959.

The author presents a new picture of the logical character of scientific discovery. Science, notes the author, is an attempt to construct some comprehensive theory of the world. The issues covered in the book include analysis of theory-formation, empiricism, testability, probability, and corroboration of theories.

POSTMAN, L. (Ed.) *Psychology in the making*. New York: Knopf, 1962.

Histories of eleven selected important research problems which have constituted progress in psychology as a science. The book is divided into three parts: Part I, on biological foundations of behavior, includes writings on cortical localization of function, the mechanisms of hunger and thirst, and the inheritance of behavior. Part II, on perception, learning, and memory, deals with nativism and empiricism in perception, rewards and punishments in human learning, and memory for form. Part III, on individual differences and personality, focuses on the nature and measurement of intelligence, clinical versus statistical prediction in psychology, the sucking behavior of mammals: an illustration of the nature-nurture question, repression, and attempts to understand hypnotic phenomena.

PRATT, C. C. *The logic of modern psychology.* New York: Macmillan, 1939.

The author has eight theses: (1) "Psychology is supposed to be the study of mind, but since no one knows what is meant by mind, it is impossible to define psychology." (2) "Classical psychology and behaviorism and every other possible school or point of view have the same subject matter." (3) "There are two portraits of human nature: one given by intuition and direct description, the other made by systematic and experimental analysis of the conditions correlated with the events initially described." (4) "Exact definitions of psychological concepts are best given by functional equations." (5) "All psychological explanation must move in the direction of physiology." (6) "If physiological knowledge is not available, the construction of psychophysiological hypotheses becomes necessary." (7) "Since so many of the physiological conditions which underlie psychological data are still inaccessible, the correlations or laws of psychology are incomplete and crudely empirical." (8) "Sound theory is necessary before extension and application of knowledge to practical ends can be made with assurance of successful results."

PUMPIAN-MINDLIN, E. (Ed.) *Psychoanalysis as science.* New York: Basic Books, 1952.

Hilgard discusses experimental tests of validity of psychoanalytic proportion. Kubie surveys the problem of developing new and more accurate methods of psychoanalytic measurement. "Psychoanalysis is a field which is related to the biological sciences in that it views man basically as a biological phenomenon. It is related to the social sciences in that it looks upon man as a product of the society in which he lives." For Pumpian-Mindlin these are the crossroads of the psychoanalytic position.

RENSCH, B. *Evolution above the species level.* New York: Columbia Univer. Press, 1960.

Translation from the second, revised edition. Theodosius Dobzhansky in the Foreword describes the work as a new development of the theory of evolution that embraces biology and is "a great synthesis."

Rensch believes that the idea of "randomness" in mutation and natural selection denotes our inability to analyze sufficiently the "extremely complicated but causally determined process of evolution." According to Rensch, evolution is effected by three sets of laws, namely, causal, parallel (psychic), and logical. In a chapter on evolution of phenomena of consciousness, Rensch believes in an evolutional continuum, and ascribes sensation and feelings to all animals inclusive of protozoa.

RUSSELL, B. *Human knowledge: its scope and limitations.* Simon & Schuster, 1948.

Arguments are directed against the thesis that data are private and individual, therefore all knowledge is private and individual, and hence there is no universal knowledge. Russell's philosophy is aimed at discovering the minimum principles required to justify scientific inferences. "As mankind has advanced in intelligence, their inferential habits have come gradually to agreement with the laws of nature, which have made these habits, throughout, more often true than false. The forming of inferential habits which lead to true expectations is a part of the adaption to the environment upon which biological survival depends."

RYLE, G. *The concept of mind.* New York: Barnes & Noble, 1949.

A challenge to the classical distinction between "mind" and "matter" that has existed in philosophy and psychology since Descartes. After criticizing the Cartesian myth and its effect on past and present thought, Ryle presents his theory of mind dealing with the nature of knowledge, the "dispositionals," and "mental acts."

SARBIN, T. R., TAFT, R., & BAILEY, D. E. *Clinical inference and cognitive theory.* New York, Holt, Rinehart & Winston, 1960.

How does the behavior analyst proceed from raw data to refined inferences? The authors analyze the problem of clinical inference, ecological dimensionalism, and cognitive organizations dealing with the character of, and operative probability of modules, inputs and cues. The book includes remarks on intuition, sources of variations in inference, and the validity of clinical inferences.

SCHLICK, M. *Philosophy of nature.* New York: Philosophical Library, 1949.

The author states that "The task of a philosophy of nature is to interpret the meaning of the propositions of natural science; and therefore the philosophy of nature is not itself a science, but an activity which is directed to the consideration of the meaning of the laws of nature." The philosophical issues and problems discussed in the volume include description and explanation, spatial determination, vitalism, causality in physics, construction of theories, and the ideas and foundation of the general and special theories of relativity.

SCHILPP, P. A. (Ed.) *Albert Einstein, philosopher-scientist.* New York: Harper, 1959. 2 vols.

A reprint of the 1949 original edition of the Library of Living Philosophers. It includes Albert Einstein's autobiographical notes in German and in English translation and a discussion of Einstein's contribution by several physicists and philosophers. The problems discussed in the essays cover the relationship between Einstein's theory and epistomology, logical positivism, theory formation, operationism, idealistic philosophy and several problems in theoretical physics and mathematics. The second volume is concluded by Einstein's reply to the essays appearing in the two volumes.

SIDMAN, M. *Tactics of scientific research.* New York: Basic Books, 1960.

"There are three questions of paramount concern in evaluating experimental findings: (a) the scientific importance of the data; (b) their reliability; and (c) their generality." "The soundest empirical test of the reliability of data is provided by replication." The premature acceptance of the premise that the subject matter of psychology is intrinsically variable over and above experimental error "has led to the adoption of experimental designs whose nature effectively prevents further investigation of the problem."

An alternative to the present philosophy and strategy of variability "is that of treating variations as examples of orderliness, rather than of capriciousness, in nature." The author believes that "Appropriate experimental design cannot be legislated, either by logical or by empirical principles."

TORGERSON, W. S. *Theory and method of scaling.* New York: Wiley, 1958.

The viewpoint expressed is that all sciences are developed from a correlation science to a theoretical science, and that the social sciences must strive toward the model of the physical sciences, especially physics. Measurement as pertaining to properties of objects, and not to the objects themselves, is the author's approach. He is most concerned with the theoretical development of scaling procedures.

WEINER, P. P. (Ed.) *Readings in philosophy of science.* New York: Scribner, 1953.

The selections may be subdivided into four parts: foundations of mathematical and physical science, basic biological and psychological concepts, method and problems of the social sciences, and philosophical analyses and syntheses.

WILSON, J. T. (Ed.) *Current trends in psychology and the behavioral sciences.* Pittsburgh, Pa.: Pittsburgh Univ. Press, 1954.

A review of recent (1954 and earlier) interdisciplinary cooperation is presented. One lecture is devoted exclusively to the potential contribution of anthropology to psychology. In the introduction, an example is given of the way in which terms are defined for interdisciplinary investigation. *Stress,* the term used, is defined as the state which leads an individual's system to go beyond its normal boundaries.

WOLMAN, B. B. *Contemporary theories and systems in psychology.* New York: Harper & Row, 1960.

Description and analysis of contemporary schools and systems in psychology, presented in a systematic way, with emphasis on methodological problems, such as research methods, conceptualization, and theory-formation. All theories are grouped according to their historical roots. Part I analyzes the theories that originate in the natural science orientation, stressing Pavlov's system and describing the works of Watson, early behaviorists, Guthrie, Hull, Skinner, Tolman, and others, as well as McDougall and the organismic and holistic systems. Part II starts with Freud, and describes the development of psychoanalytic concepts, as well as the dissident schools of Adler, Jung, Sullivan, Horney, and others. Part III starts with Kant, Dilthey, Spranger and discusses the works of Allport, Gestalt psychology, and Lewin. Part IV presents the author's point of view, and analyzes the problems of scientific method and philosophy of science. The author introduces his own ideas in regard to causation, mind–body controversy, and personality theory.

WOODGER, J. H. *Biology and language.* Cambridge, Eng.: Cambridge Univ. Press, 1952.

This book explores the methodological development of theoretical statements in their relationship to observation and experimentation. In lectures

I and VI the language of science and the classification of biological statements are discussed. Lecture II deals with level of hypothesis, consequence
relation, value of truth tables, and matrices and quantifiers. Lectures III-V
investigate the methodological problems in genetics.

NAME INDEX

Abe, M., 217
Abelé, J., 40
Abraham, Karl, 16
Abt, J. P., 438
Adams, D. K., 91, 196
Adams, Pauline, 287
Adey, W. R., 440
Adler, Alexandra, 347 n., 359
Adler, Alfred, 303, 340–344, 347–360;
   inferiority complex, 349; masculine
   protest, 350–351; style of life, 349
Affani, J., 214
Alexander, F., 142, 566
Allport, Gordon W., 9–10, 54 n., 90, 114,
   121, 285, 293, 301–306, 344–345, 352;
   personality theory, 306–314
Ammons, R. B., 196
Amsel, Abram, 172, 187–203
Ananyev, B. G., 578
Anderson, Harold H., 257, 345
Angoff, W. H., 532
Angyal, A., 305
Anokhin, P. K., 181, 208, 218, 228, 233 n.
Ansbacher, Heinz L., 303, 340–360
Ansbacher, Rowena R., 347 n.
Anscombe, G. E. M., 367
Aquinas, Thomas, 294, 568
Archimedes, 6
Aristotle, 14, 28, 114, 118, 294, 357, 412,
   460, 465, 568, 571
Armstrong, David M., 489–505
Arnold, Magda, 296 n., 300, 303, 372,
   374, 376
Arnold, W. J., 212
Asch, Solomon E., 281, 288, 290, 342,
   351, 370, 513, 516
Ashby, W. Ross, 147, 170, 324
Asratyan, E. A., 139, 208, 212, 221–222
Assagioli, R., 303
Atkinson, Richard C., 254–274
Atreus, 468
Atrides, 468
Augustine, 294, 296 n.
Austin, John, 505
Avakyan, R. V., 216

Ayer, A. J., 399, 467, 478, 486
Ayrapetyants, E. S., 135, 208, 214, 227,
   577

Babkin, B. P., 13, 212
Bach, L. M. N., 434
Back, K., 514
Bacon, Francis, 128
Bakan, D., 54
Baker, C. P., 437
Balakshina, V. L., 576
Baldwin, E., 574
Baldwin, J. Mark, 207
Bales, R. F., 447
Ball, G. G., 212
Balonov, L. Y., 139
Barker, R. G., 8
Barlow, H. B., 444
Baru, A. V., 212
Beach, F. A., 208
Beethoven, Ludwig van, 446
Békésy, G. von, 107
Bekhterev, V. M., 135, 564, 576
Bennett, E. L., 437
Bergmann, G., 54, 188, 190
Bergson, Henri, 17, 114, 294, 571
Beritov, I. S., 208, 212–213, 220, 224,
   229, 236
Berkeley, George, 294, 494
Berkowitz, L., 514
Berlyne, D. E., 34, 172–173, 192
Berman, A. J., 179, 427
Bernard, Claude, 141, 146, 542
Bernstein, A. L., 224
Bertalanffy, L. von, 54, 99, 344
Bertocci, Peter A., 293–314
Beth, E. W., 463, 465, 471
Bevan, William, 88–111
Bilodeau, E. A., 196
Biryukov, D. A., 208, 223
Bitterman, M. E., 208
Black, R. W., 97, 105
Blinkova, T. P., 214
Bois-Reymond, Émile du, 5
Boring, Edwin G., 285, 289, 433

Bousefield, W. A., 237
Bower, W. H., 258, 260
Bowne, B. P., 295–296, 299–300
Boycott, B. B., 212
Bradley, F. H., 450
Brady, J. V., 437
Braithwaite, R. B., 99
Brattgård, S., 436
Breen, R. A., 438
Bregadze, A., 212
Breland, K., 167
Breland, M., 167
Brenman, M., 318 n.
Brentano, Franz, 389
Bridgman, P. W., 14, 59–61, 102
Briggs, G. E., 228 n.
Briggs, M. H., 434
Brightman, E. S., 294, 299
Broad, C. D., 571
Broadbent, D. E., 173, 175
Brogden, W. J., 178, 228 n.
Broglie, Louis de, 18
Bronner, A. F., 318 n.
Brooks, G. W., 359
Brookshire, K. H., 212
Brouwer, L. E. J., 29, 37, 465–466, 469
Brown, J. S., 162, 172, 198, 278
Brown, N., 303
Bruner, J. S., 54, 439–440
Brunswik, Egon, 54–55, 92, 104
Buber, Martin, 119
Buck, Roger, 411 n.
Buhler, C., 303
Bulygin, I. A., 220
Burns, H. W., 59 n.
Burt, G., 438
Burwen, L. S., 280
Bush, R. R., 176, 190, 255–256
Bykov, K. M., 138–139, 214, 576

Caldwell, D. F., 214
Calfee, Robert C., 254–274
Calkins, Mary W., 300, 302
Campbell, B. A., 181, 218
Campbell, C. A., 294–297, 299
Campbell, D. T., 54, 95, 194, 276–277,
    280, 286
Cannon, W. B., 141
Cantril, H., 303, 305
Capek, M., 299
Carnap, R., 91, 439, 441, 445
Cartwright, D., 116, 282
Castell, A., 294
Chassan, J. B., 324
Chernigovsky, V. N., 139
Chesterton, G. K., 454
Chomsky, A. Noam, 559 n.

Chow, K. L., 169
Coan, R. W., 191
Cohen, Morris R., 15, 121, 150
Colby, K. M., 324
Cole, John, 411 n.
Columbus, Christopher, 491
Combs, A., 303, 305
Comte, Auguste, 4, 114, 574
Conant, J. B., 163
Confucius, 119
Constantine the Great, 395
Cooley, C. H., 119
Coombs, C. H., 105–106
Corning, W. C., 436
Cotton, J. W., 175
Cronbach, L. J., 540
Cumming, Robert D., 384–400
Cureton, E. E., 531
Curtis, D. R., 438

Dailey, C. A., 354
Dameron, L. E., 215
D'Arcy, M. C., 303
Darling, L., 208 n.
Darwin, Charles, 10, 207
Dashiell, J. F., 171–172
Davidson, D., 441
Davis, Frederick B., 526–549
Deane, W. N., 359
Deese, J., 13, 152
DeGraaf, Regnier, 129
Delgado, J. M. R., 200, 210
Dembo, T., 8
Denny, R., 432
Descartes, René, 14, 29, 128, 142, 147,
    294, 296 n., 384, 567–568
Deutsch, F., 303, 566
Deutsch, J. A., 170, 174, 182, 434
Deutsch, Morton, 282, 284, 506–524, 574
Deutscher, Max, 504
Dewey, John, 118, 346, 371, 402
Dewey, Thomas E., 412
Diamond, I. T., 169
Dilthey, Wilhelm, 9–10, 570
DiVesta, F. J., 215
Dodwell, P. C., 365
Doob, L., 8
Dollard, John, 8, 173
Dos Passos, John, 143
Douglass, H. R., 537
Dreikurs, R., 355, 359
Duncan, C. P., 437
Duncker, K., 290
Durkheim, Émile, 524
Durov, V. L., 221
Dykman, R. A., 139, 214
Dzhavrishvili, T. D., 224

Ebbinghaus, Hermann, 6, 9, 254
Eccles, J. C., 438
Eddington, H. S., 17–18, 431, 448–449
Edwards, W., 96
Einstein, Albert, 4, 6, 11, 17–18, 60–61, 127, 418, 449, 573, 575, 582
Ellis, Albert, 358
English, Ava C., 346
English, H. B., 346
Eriksen, C. W., 97, 102, 106
Erikson, Erik H., 303
Essman, W. B., 438
Estes, W. K., 13, 151, 155–156, 157 n., 159, 163, 176, 190, 199, 255, 257–258, 260, 267
Estoup, Jean-Baptiste, 552, 554
Eucken, R., 294
Ezriel, H., 579

Farber, I. E., 172, 198
Faris, E., 115
Farrell, B. A., 8
Fechner, G. T., 92, 95, 103, 106
Federn, Paul, 343
Fedorov, N. A., 237
Feigl, H., 6, 54, 348
Fenichel, O., 18
Ferster, C. B., 196, 225, 440
Fichte, J. G., 294
Fisher, C., 319
Fleming, Noël, 495
Fleure, H. J., 218
Foerster, H. Von, 438
Foot, P., 367
Fowler, R. L., 214 n.
Frankl, Viktor, 303, 358
Franquiz, I. A., 296
Frege, Gottlob, 37
French, T., 142
Freud, Sigmund, 13, 15, 17, 20, 256, 283–284, 299, 303, 318–321, 325 n., 327, 337, 343, 351, 385, 450–452, 565, 578–579, 581; in America, 143; emotions, theory of, 375–376; greatest discovery of, 377; on human behavior, 580; lasting contribution to psychology, 366; on mental processes, 366; pleasure principle, 378; psychological theory, 365–383; on radical reductionism, 579; reductionisim, 565; on unconscious, 377–378; on wish mechanisms, 381–382
Fromm, Erich, 303, 343
Fromm-Reichmann, Frieda, 318 n.
Fuller, J. L., 428

Gaito, J., 434
Galambos, R., 210, 214
Galanter, E. H., 97, 346, 428, 431, 444

Galilei, Galileo, 564
Gallup, George, 412
Gambaryan, L. S., 215, 221
Gantt, W. Horsley, 14, 127–147
Gardner, Martin, 423
Garner, W. R., 97, 102, 106
Garnett, A. C., 294
Geach, P., 54 n.
Genet, Jean, 396
Gerard, H. B., 513–514
Gerard, R. W., 324
Gerd, M. A., 221
Geulincx, Arnold, 567–568
Gibson, Eleanor J., 230, 232, 440
Gibson, J. J., 93, 230, 232, 440
Gill, Merton, 450–451
Gilson, E., 294
Ginsberg, R., 261
Gleser, G. C., 540
Glover, E., 333
Gödel, K., 418–419
Goebbels, Joseph P., 120
Goldstein, K., 303
Goltz, F. L., 129
Gorska, T., 179
Goss, A. E., 196–197
Gottheil, E., 514
Gough, H. G., 307
Grant, D. A., 216
Gréco, P., 36, 464, 467–468
Gregory, R. L., 169–170
Grey-Walter, W., 324
Grindley, G. C., 221
Grings, W. W., 215
Grinker, R. R., 566
Grize, Jean-Blaise, 38, 460–472
Grossack, M., 514
Guilford, J. P., 92
Gunin, V. I., 214
Gurevich, B. K., 440
Guthrie, E. R., 8, 11–12, 15, 57–58, 108, 156, 179, 197, 199, 262

Hake, H. W., 97, 102, 106
Hall, C. S., 343
Hall, G. Stanley, 207
Halstead, W., 89
Halverson, H. M., 8
Hansen, Duncan, 265 n.
Harlow, H. F., 13, 212
Harrah, Dave, 411
Harris, J. D., 220
Hartline, H. K., 442
Hartmann, H., 303
Hartshorne, C., 294
Harvey, William, 576
Hebb, D. O., 89–90, 92, 200, 212, 227, 431, 441, 564

Hefferline, R. F., 226
Hegel, Georg Wilhelm Friedrich, 5, 14, 380, 564, 571
Heidenhain, R. P., 129
Heider, F., 279, 282, 284
Helmholtz, Hermann, 29, 103, 465
Helson, Harry, 88 n., 92, 97
Heyman, W., 194
Heyting, A., 466, 469
Henle, Mary, 276–290
Herbart, J. F., 95
Hilbert, D., 461, 465
Hilgard, E. R., 13, 177, 216, 220, 254, 281, 285 n., 305, 321, 324, 449
Hinde, R. A., 220, 565, 574
Hobbes, Thomas, 114, 116
Hobhouse, Leonard, 207
Hochberg, J. E., 286
Hoff, M. E., 435
Honzik, C. M., 13
Hooker, D., 579
Horace, 150
Horney, Karen, 303, 343
Horton, G. P., 8
Hovey, H. B., 218
Howard, Richard, 28 n.
Howison, G., 294
Hsün Tsu, 116
Hudspeth, W., 438
Huffnaker, C. L., 537
Hull, Clark L., 12–13, 15, 151, 172–175, 187, 189, 191–193, 200, 203, 209 n., 254, 256, 276, 278, 365, 412, 566
Hull, Davis, 411 n.
Hume, David, 12, 29, 42, 439, 445
Humphreys, Will, 411 n.
Hunt, E. L., 214
Husserl, E., 53, 117, 384, 387–390, 394–395, 398, 463
Hydèn, H., 434–435

Infeld, Leopold, 582
Irion, A. L., 164, 196–197
Isaacs, Suzanne, 8
Ishihara, I., 182
Ivanov-Smolensky, A. G., 134–135, 141, 220
Iwama, K., 217

Jacobson, A. L., 436
James, William, 58, 294, 298–302, 372, 375, 402, 430–433, 454
Janet, P. M., 17, 579
Janowska, E., 179
Jarvik, M. E., 437–438
Jasper, H., 210, 217, 440, 580–581
Jaspers, K., 462
Jeans, James H., 18

John, E. R., 210, 214, 218, 436
Johnson, H. M., 89
Jones, Ernest, 377–378
Jourard, S., 303
Jung, C. G., 282 n., 299, 303, 443

Kaila, E., 55
Kant, Immanuel, 5, 17, 29, 294, 296 n., 297, 384, 393, 465, 565
Kaplan, Abraham, 319
Karamyan, A. I., 208
Katz, J. J., 89
Kekulé, F. A., 572
Keller, Helen, 137
Kelley, H. H., 515
Kellogg, W. N., 107
Kelly, G. A., 358
Kendler, H. H., 151, 171, 173, 182, 196–197, 203
Kendler, T. S., 197, 203
Kennedy, John F., 412, 565
Kimble, D. P., 436
Kimble, G. A., 13, 153, 162–163
Kimmel, H. D., 214 n.
Kinsey, Alfred C., 576
Kitto, G. B., 434
Kleene, S. C., 466
Klein, G. S., 319
Klineberg, Otto, 114–122
Klopfer, B., 342
Klyavina, M. P., 214
Knapp, H. D., 178
Knudson, A. C., 294
Kobrick, J. L., 194
Koch, H. L., 8
Koch, S., 52, 54 n., 58, 90, 92, 101, 191, 289
Koffka, K., 282 n., 285, 288–289, 345
Köhler, W., 54, 277, 279, 282 n., 285–290, 342
Kol'tsova, M. M., 234–235
Konorski, J., 17, 139, 142, 176, 178, 181, 183, 212 n., 215, 220–221
Koronakos, C., 212
Kotarbiński, Tadeusz, 44–49
Kozak, W., 179
Kraeling, D., 194
Kraft, Marcia S., 438
Krakulis, A. A., 212
Krauss, R. M., 519
Krech, David, 13, 150 n., 437
Krolik, W., 286
Kruger, L., 427
Kubie, Lawrence S., 142, 148, 316–337
Kuhn, T. S., 54 n.
Kukuyev, L. A., 213
Kupalov, P. S., 233

LaBerge, D., 258
Lachman, R., 99, 195, 205
La Mettrie, Julien Offroy de, 564
Landahl, H. D., 438
Lange, G. C., 372, 375
Langman, L., 342
Laplace, Pierre Simon de, 424
Lashley, K. S., 13, 134–135, 139, 168, 211
Laski, Harold, 515
Laurendeau, Monique, 34
Lavoisier, Antoine Laurent, 28, 64
Lawicka, W., 212 n., 234
Lawley, D. N., 537
Lawrence, D. H., 173
LeBon, Gustave, 116
Lecky, P., 303
Leeper, R. W., 370
Leibniz, Gottfried Wilhelm von, 17, 29, 294, 296, 500–501
Lejeune, J., 574
Lenin, V. I., 576
Lettvin, J. Y., 443
Levy, S., 514
Lewin, Kurt, 8, 10, 16, 54, 114, 274, 276–285, 305
Liberman, R., 436
Liddell, Howard, 139, 143
Lilly, John, 138
Lindsley, D. B., 441
Linton, Ralph, 119
Lippitt, R., 16
Lisina, M. I., 214 n.
Livanov, M. N., 210
Locke, John, 42, 144, 294, 296, 384
Lockhart, R. A., 215
Logan, F. A., 163, 192, 194, 254
Loomis, J. L., 517
Lord, F. M., 534, 541
Lorenz, K. Z., 54, 170
Losina-Losinsky, L. K., 218
Lotze, Rudolf Hermann, 294
Loucks, R. B., 178
Lowell, F. C., 34
Luce, R. D., 96
Lukov, B. N., 212
Luria, A. R., 135, 139, 216, 237
Luther, Martin, 347
Lyerly, S. B., 534

McArthur, C. C., 357
McConnell, J. O., 436
McCulloch, W. S., 30–31, 323, 438, 443
McDougall, William, 283–284, 296 n., 300, 307, 370
McGaugh, J. L., 437–438
McGeoch, J. A., 197
McGuigan, J., 93

Mach, Ernst, 12
Macintosh, D. C., 294
MacIntyre, A. D., 379, 384–388, 393, 397
MacKay, D. M., 424, 438, 440
MacLeod, R. B., 117
Macmurray, J., 294
McTaggart, J., 294
Madsen, M. C., 437–438
Magoun, H. W., 208 n., 441
Maier, N. R. F., 16
Maimonides, Moses, 571
Makarov, P. O., 214
Malakhovskaya, D. B., 214
Malcolm, Norman, 505
Malis, L. I., 427, 437
Malmo, R. B., 20
Maltzman, I., 196–197
Malvaux, P., 40
Mandelbrot, Benoit, 550–561
Mandler, G., 203, 212
Marchcafava, P. L., 214
Maritain, Jacques, 294
Marquis, D. G., 177, 220
Marsh, J. D., 319
Marx, Karl, 571
Maslow, A. H., 301, 303, 307, 343, 346, 350
Matalon, B., 36, 468
Maturana, H. R., 443
Mauthner, F., 118
Maxwell, James Clerk, 17, 575
May, Rollo, 358
Mead, George H., 119, 304, 402–408, 524
Medley, D. M., 534, 536
Meehl, P. E., 153
Melden, A. I., 365
Mendel, Gregor, 6, 10
Mencius, 116
Merleau-Ponty, M., 384, 392–396, 398–399
Merton, R. K., 54
Messick, S. J., 98
Meyer, Adolph, 358
Mill, John Stuart, 7, 42, 463
Millard, R. M., 313
Miller, G. A., 346, 426 n., 428, 431, 444, 559 n.
Miller, J. G., 324, 325 n.
Miller, Neal E., 8, 13, 151, 162, 171, 173, 187, 191, 200, 210, 441
Miller, S., 176–177, 220
Milner, P. M., 170, 210, 220, 224, 429
Mizuhara, T., 514
Moleschott, J., 564
Mollenkopf, W. G., 537
Monroe, Ruth, 354

Moreno, J. L., 355, 359
Morf, A., 468
Morgan, C. Lloyd, 168, 207
Morgan, C. T., 210, 214
Morrell, F., 210, 434
Morris, Charles W., 402–408, 471
Morse, Samuel F. B., 554, 561
Mosteller, F., 176, 190, 256, 411 n., 441
Moustakas, C., 303
Mowrer, O. H., 8 ,13, 162–163, 172, 174,
    181–182, 191, 234, 281, 303, 358
Mshvenieradze, V. V., 112
Muensterberg, Hugo, 117
Muenzinger, K. F., 108–110
Müller, Johannes, 103
Murdoch, I., 478, 483, 486
Murphy, Gardner, 114, 215, 229–230,
    235, 303, 343–344
Murray, H., 283, 303
Mysyashchikova, S. S., 220

Nadel, S. F., 121
Naess, Arne, 50–65
Nagel, E., 6, 15, 18, 24–27, 54 n., 342–
    343, 346, 408, 422, 569
Napalkov, A. V., 225
Nevner, Kate, 231
Newton, Isaac, 6, 10–11, 564
Newton, J. E., 136–137
Niebuhr, R., 294
Nietzsche, F., 347
Nikolayeva, N. Y., 178
Nissen, H. W., 208
Nogee, P., 441
Norris, Eugenia B., 216
Northrop, F. S. C., 17
Nunberg, H., 343

Oakeshott, M., 54 n.
Oberndorf, C. P., 318 n.
Obrist, W. D., 438
Olds, J., 200, 210, 224, 429
Oparin, A. I., 574
Oppenheimer, Robert, 99–100
Orbeli, L. A., 208
Osgood, Charles E., 162, 174
Osipov, G. V., 122

Papanek, Helene, 359
Papousek, H., 214
Park, Robert E., 115
Parker, G. H., 139
Parsons, Talcott, 54 n., 447
Pascal, Blaise, 118, 141
Pasteur, Louis, 14
Paterson, Arthur, 139
Paulhan, F., 371
Pauling, Linus, 356

Pavlov, Ivan, 6, 9, 12–14, 17, 20, 76, 127,
    176–177, 200, 212 n., 214, 218, 221,
    233, 411, 565, 574, 576, 581; American
    work associated with, 139; evaluation
    of, 142–144; evolution in, 208; gastro-
    intestinal work of, 129–134; growth
    and extension of work, 128–129, 138–
    147; influence on American psycholo-
    gists, 139–140; as master experimenter,
    143–144; psychiatry and, 134–136; on
    reductionism, 565–566; on schizoki-
    nesis, 141; second signaling system
    of, 136; on speech or language, 234;
    on strong brain centers, 217; system of,
    127–147
Pearlman, C. A., 437–438
Peastral, A., 216, 237
Peirce, Charles S., 402, 404
Penfield, W., 237, 337, 440
Peters, John E., 133 n.
Peters, Richard S., 56, 58, 365–383
Petrinovich, L., 438
Phillips, E. L., 358
Piaget, Jean, 20, 28–43, 54, 460, 463–
    467, 470–472
Pinard, Adrien, 34
Pitts, W. A., 30–31, 323–324, 438, 443
Planck, Max, 18, 143, 579
Plato, 29, 294, 296 n., 357, 564
Plavilstchikov, N. N., 214
Podolski, B., 418
Poincaré, Henri, 11, 29, 37, 269, 465, 570
Polanyi, Michael, 54 n., 411 n.
Polezhayev, E. F., 228
Polikarpov, G. G., 214
Polya, G., 54
Polyakov, K. L., 210, 213
Popper, Karl R., 52, 54 n., 65, 93, 411,
    415, 424
Poschel, B. P. H., 437
Postman, Leo, 150 n., 151, 155–156, 159,
    163, 230, 232
Pratt, C. C., 564
Pratusevich, Yu M., 216
Premack, D., 218
Prentice, W. C. H., 281, 285 n., 286–287
Pribram, K., 170, 346, 426–454, 566
Price, H. H., 474, 478, 486
Pritchard, Joan F., 97
Prost, J., 208 n.
Pumpian-Mindlin, E., 323
Pushkin, Aleksander Sergeevich, 550

Quine, W. O., 37, 445, 464

Rabinovich, M. Y., 224
Radin, Paul, 115
Rank, Otto, 118

Rapoport, Anatol, 68–87, 284, 375–376
Ratliff, F., 442
Razran, Gregory, 13, 15, 138, 207–245, 577
Redfield, R., 115
Reese, W. S., 139
Renouvier, C., 294
Restle, F., 255–256, 261
Reynolds, D. V., 212
Rieff, P., 453
Riesman, David, 432
Riess, B. F., 237
Ritchie, Benbow F., 150–164, 182
Roberts, W. W., 200, 216
Robertson, J. D., 438
Robins, E. P., 566
Robinson, F., 427
Robinson, J., 132
Roby, T. B., 181, 218
Rocheblave-Spenlé, A. M., 118
Rogers, Carl, 303–305
Rokhlin, L. L., 136
Romanes, George, 207
Rose, J. E., 437
Rosen, N., 418
Rosenberg, S., 514
Rosenzweig, M. R., 437
Rosner, B. S., 96–97, 106
Rosvold, H. E., 428
Rotter, J. B., 352
Rousseau, J.-J., 116
Royce, Josiah, 118, 137
Royer, F. L., 136
Rozeboom, W. W., 19
Rubenstein, S. L., 577
Rubin, A. A., 288
Ruff, G .E., 324
Runes, Dagobert D., 460
Rusinov, V. S., 139, 210, 214
Ruskin, John, 216–217
Russell, Bertrand, 29, 37, 465–466, 490
Russell, E. S., 343
Ryle, G., 54 n., 58, 368, 371, 391, 478, 480–482, 486, 491–492

St. Martin, Alexis, 145
Sartre, Jean-Paul, 374–377, 384–400
Saussure, Nicolas Théodore de, 552
Schachter, S., 355, 514
Schastny, A. I., 217
Schelling, T. C., 521–522
Schlaifer, R., 19
Schlosberg, H., 220–222
Schnierla, T. C., 208
Schopenhauer, Arthur, 5, 114
Schrödinger, Erwin, 18, 571
Scriven, Michael, 411–425

Sears, R. R., 8, 321, 579
Sechenov, I. M., 17, 128, 131, 144
Sellars, Wilfrid, 495 n.
Seward, John P., 166–183, 255
Shagass, G., 217
Shakespeare, William, 9
Shannon, Claude, 550–551, 560
Sharpless, S. K., 437–438
Shastin, N. R., 234
Sheffield, F. D., 181, 218
Sherrington, Charles, 129, 131, 142, 144, 147, 334, 443–444, 452, 565
Shiman, Paul, 424
Shoobs, N. E., 359
Shulman, B. H., 355, 359
Shurrager, P. S., 214
Shvarts, L. A., 216, 237
Sigwart, Christopher, 463
Simon, H. A., 422
Simpson, George G., 344
Sjöstrand, F. S., 438
Skinner, B. F., 12, 14–15, 56–57, 90, 93, 127, 138–142, 147, 167, 177, 190–191, 196–197, 219–221, 225, 234, 346, 440, 444, 564
Skipin, G. V., 221
Slonim, A. D., 208, 233
Slutskaya, M. M., 218
Smedslund, J., 36
Smirnov, G. D., 210
Smith, Alexander, 357
Smith, M. Brewster, 305
Smuts, J. C., 342
Snygg, D., 305–306
Sokolov, E. N., 135, 139, 218, 221, 442
Solley, C. M., 215, 230, 235
Solomon, R. L., 139, 211, 214, 219, 517
Spence, G. J. W., 319
Spence, Kenneth W., 13, 90, 151, 173, 187, 190, 192, 194, 200–203, 209 n., 254
Spencer, Herbert, 4, 42, 114, 116
Spelt, D. K., 214
Sperry, R. W., 579
Spiel, O., 359
Spinoza, Baruch de, 376
Staats, A. W., 215
Staats, C. K., 215
Stahl, W. R., 107
Stamm, J. S., 438
Stern, W., 9, 117, 294, 296 n., 299
Stevens, S. S., 60, 92, 96–97, 105–106
Steward, J. P., 58
Straus, Erwin, 127, 142
Strezh, E., 218
Sullivan, H. S., 343
Sumner, William Graham, 115
Sundberg, N. D., 357

608

Suppes, P., 41, 62 n., 257, 261, 266, 272 n., 441
Symonds, P. M., 303
Szeminska, A., 464, 467

Tamai, S., 514
Tarski, A., 461
Taub, E., 179
Tchakotine, S., 214
Tennant, F. R., 294, 298
Teplov, B. M., 576
Thibaut, J. W., 514
Thomas, E. J., 516
Thomson, C. W., 438
Thorndike, E. L., 8, 11–12, 139–140, 151, 172, 220, 281
Thorne, F. C., 358
Thurstone, L. L., 95, 106
Tinbergen, N., 516
Titchener, E. B., 207
Tolman, E. C., 12–13, 15, 51, 54–55, 90, 151–152, 172–174, 181, 202, 209 n., 346, 372
Toman, W., 355
Torgerson, W. S., 98
Traugott, N. N., 139
T'su, C., 217
Turner, C. H., 218
Turner, E. D., 98, 107
Turner, L. H., 211, 214
Tyler, Leona E., 357

Ukhtomsky, A. A., 13, 217, 220
Ullman, M., 354
Underwood, B. J., 196
Undeutsch, U., 212

Vaihinger, H., 346–348
Van Kaam, A. L., 303
Vinogradova, I. S., 216, 221, 237
Vogt, Karl, 564
Volkova, Z. D., 237
von Bertalanffy, see Bertalanffy, L. von
Voronin, L. G., 208, 212, 221, 225

Wadleigh, Elizabeth, 426 n.
Wagner, H. G., 442
Wall, P. D., 438
Wallach, H., 286
Walter, Grey, 127
Walter, W. G., 170
Walton, C., 218
Ward, J., 294

Warnock, George J., 474, 487
Warren, Ann, 438
Warren, J. M., 212
Watson, J. B., 89–90, 115–139, 168, 234, 349, 372, 403, 570, 576
Weber, Max, 54 n., 95
Weiskrantz, L., 435, 438
Weiss, P., 294
Welch, L., 282
Wells, H. G., 127
Wells, H. K., 142
Werboff, J., 214
Wertheimer, M., 286–290, 342
Westbrook, W., 438
White, R., 303
Whitehead, Alfred North, 29, 37, 138, 406, 466
Whitmarsh, C. A., 237
Whorf, Benjamin L., 54, 118
Whyte, Lancelot, 411 n.
Wickens, D. D., 228 n.
Widrow, B., 435
Wiener, Norbert, 444
Wigner, Eugene P., 553 n.
Wild, J., 294
Wilson, C., 303
Winch, P., 54 n.
Windelband, W., 9, 570
Witkin, H. A., 287–288
Wittgenstein, L., 482–487
Wohlwill, J., 34, 36
Wolman, Benjamin B., 3–21, 563–583
Woodbury, C. B., 178
Woodworth, R. S., 171–172, 181, 221–222, 235, 352
Worden, F. G., 319
Wundt, Wilhelm, 9, 412, 463
Wyckoff, L. B., Jr., 173
Wynne, L. C., 219

Yerkes, R. M., 139
Yerofeyeva, M. N., 218
Young, J. Z., 212

Zagona, S. V., 191
Zeliony, G. P., 212, 220
Zener, K., 90
Zernicki, B., 214
Zevald, L. O., 212
Zhukova, G. P., 213
Zipf, George Kingsley, 552, 554, 559–560
Zubkov, A. A., 214

SUBJECT INDEX

abient–adient reactions, 218–219
ablation, method of, 169–170
acetylocholinesterase activity, 437
Achtung, 393
act, collapsing of, 405, 407; consummatory stage of, 403; as impulse, 403; manipulatory stage, 403; Mead's concept of, 403
action, art and, 395–397; emotion and, 370–371, 377, 379–383; goal-oriented, 407–408; human nature and, 380; reflection and, 392; science and, 407–408; singleness of, 443; thought and, 474; *see also* existential psychology
action systems, 447
activation, level of, 441
addition, law of, 462
adiabatic process, 71
adience, 218; in free space, 278
adjectives, 231–232
Adlerian psychology, *see* individual psychology
adolescence, birth and, 31–32
afferent–afferent interaction, 226
afferent–efferent system, 578
afferentiation, reverse, 181
afferent impulses, 279–280
afferent reactions, interaction of, 212
aggression, goals and, 16–17
agitations, emotion and, 371
algebra, 38–39
algorithm, concept of, 550
algorithmic technique, 28
alienation, 56, 348
all-or-none model, 267–268, 270, 272–273
amplitude, as Hullian variable, 194
amygdala, 170
analogy, use of, 91
analysis, logical, 474–487
analysis of variance, 79, 255
analyst, role of, 328–331
analytic incognito, 326, 328–331
anger, 368–370

Anglo-American philosophy, 384-385, 387–389, 393, 399–400
anima, 568
animals, curarized, 211; *dG* conditioning in, 215; experimental, 179, 440 (*see also* dogs; rats); fear reactions in, 220; imagery and image-direction in, 236; language in, 137–138; learning in, 211; rhizotomized, 179; soul of, 568
Anschaulichkeit, 60
anthropology, 5
anthropomorphism, 19
arithmetic operations, child's discovery of, 31–32; *see also* mathematics
ARP learning, 230
art, action and, 395–397; in existential psychology, 395–400; theory and, 397–400
association, two types of, 217
association experiment, 281
association-formation, 228 n.
assumptions, in experimental psychology, 89
astronomy, 6, 11, 14
attitudes, in psychoanalysis, 326
autokinesis, 140
automata, 86
autonomic nervous system, 139, 372, 376

behavior, brain and, 434; capability and, 514; chained patterns of, 196; characteristics of state determined from, contrapredictions in, 412–414; contrient or promotive, 507–513; credence and, 439; definition of, 62; emotions and, 382–383; Freud on, 580; genesis of term, 55–56; hedonic levels of, 13; laws of, 199; meaning of, 56; mind as mode of, 404; "molar" functions and, 570; motivation and, 514–515; nonverbal, 492; perception and, 492, 501–502; physical laws and, 18; predictions of, 412–423; promotive or contrient, 507–513; psychosomatics and, 580–

609

behavior (*cont'd*)
582; self-defeating predictions in, 412; in social interactions, 506–509; in space, 278; "strictly purposive" (Hull), 278; "trusting," 517–518; unpredictability in, 411–425
behavioral data, quantification of, 93–98; statistics and, 77–78
behavioral metascience, 50–65
behavioral phenomena, complexity of, 92; as physical, 89–91
behavioral propositions, 45–47
behavioral system, mathematical laws and, 255
behavioral vectors, 279 n.
behaviorism, 56–59; "act" in, 403; emotions in, 371–372; existential psychology and, 390; and history of psychology, 411; Hullian and neo-Hullian, 187–203; Hull-Spence approach to, 187–203; and individual psychology, 346; inductive versus deductive approaches to, 188–191; language and, 234; Pavlov's influence on, 139–140, 147; perception and, 496; purposive, 346; subjective, 346; term analysis in, 402–403
behavior research, choice-points in, 166–183; drive theory of motivation in, 172; general orientation in, 166–176; neuropsychology in, 168–170; reorientation in, 182–183; specific problem in, 176–182; subjective experience in, 168; units of, 52–54
belief, knowledge and, 502–503; perception and, 499; "true," 503–504
biochemistry, life processes and, 574, 577
biological processes, physicochemical terms for, 574
biology, law of, 576; organismic, 342; versus physics, 18–19; transitionism in, 573–575
birth, adolescence and, 31–32
biunivocal correspondence, 37
"black box," 147, 166–167, 169
bodily perception, 493, 504
brain, behavior and, 434; complex structure of, 86; *dG* conditioning and, 224; electrical recordings from, 440–441; memory storage and retrieval in, 433–445; mind and, 445–449; perception and, 497–498; pleasure and pain centers of, 429
brain cells, division of, 437
brain tissue, lattices in, 89; types of component in, 434
brain waves, 171
brightness scale, 76

calculated risk, 86
canalization, 220
capability, and cooperative process, 514–515
cardiac conditional reflex, 139
cardinal numbers, 466
cardiovascular system, 141
cathexis, 510–512, 522, 581
causality, degree of, 79; perception and, 281, 496
causation, transition and, 579
central nervous system, 319; "crucial microstate" of, 441; models of, 170–171; "nonobservable microstate" of, 440; physiology of, 565; psychoanalysis and, 319; segmental, 131
cerebellum, stimulation of, 178
cerebral cortex, *see* cortex
cerebrum, consciousness and, 564
chance, concept of, 550
change, identity and, 569–572
child, epistemological constructs of, 31–32; genesis of logic and knowledge in, 34–39
children, language requirements of, 234–235; number or numerical behavior in, 467–468
Chinese philosophy, 116, 119
chi-square value, in mathematical models, 266–274
choice, predictability and, 420–421
chronic experiment, 145–146
cognition, 225; in *dD(G)* conditioning, 225; emotion and, 366–370; self in, 296; thought and, 474–475
cognitive attitudes, 216
cognitive change, 360
cognitive-expectancy model, 201
cognitive information, imagery and, 236
cognitive reorganization, 357–358
co-link, in social interaction, 506–507
color, quantification of, 74
color experience, behavior and, 502
communication, free associations and, 333; in social interaction, 520–521
commutative law, 462
comparative judgment, law of, 96
complementarity, 447
compound-stimulus conditioning, 212, 226, 229–230, 235
computers, 170
concept, attainment of, 54; formation of, 255; polymorphous, 479–480
conditioned conditioning, 220
conditioned reflex, 76–77, 127; in dogs, 178 (*see also* dogs); evolution and, 208; free associations and, 332; inhibi-

tion and, 131; neo-Hullian behavior and, 198; primary, 136; vocal, 234
conditioned stimulus, 233; as signal, 136; quantification of, 130
conditioning, associative, 228 n.; compound-stimulus, 212, 226, 229–230, 235; kinesthesis and, 234; Pavlovian, 214; stimulus type, 130, 136, 211, 233; theory of, 13; type II, 220
conditioning-expectancy model, 201
confidence, degree of, 78
conflict, cognition and, 240
Confucian system, 119
conscience, 347
consciousness, 389; cognition and, 296; defined, 564; in existential psychology, 391, 397; neurology and, 451
conscious processes, 328
continuity, change and, 572–573
contra-links, in social interaction, 506–507
contraprediction, 412–415
contrient interdependence, 506–507, 510
converging operations, in existential psychology, 101–103
cooperation, among equals, 509; initiation of, 516–522; responsiveness in, 516
Cooperative Reading Comprehension Test, 537
Cooperative Scaled Scores, 537
cooperative situation, 507
coordination problem, 520–521
correlation, mathematical function and, 79
correspondence rules, 15
cortex, brain-cell division and, 437; consciousness and, 564; imagery and, 236; in monkeys, 169, 442; motor functions of, 200; pain sensation and, 576; in Pavlov's experiments, 133; in physiological experiments, 144; reflexes and, 577; speech areas and, 236; stimulation of, 178; temporal, 169
countertransference, 326, 329
creative evolution, 571
creativity, 213; in individual psychology, 341, 344–345
credence, defined, 439
crowd mentality, 116
cryptography, 552
cybernetics, 85, 168, 323, 334

datum-self, 299
dD(G) learning, 220–226, 241–243
deception, in psychological experiments, 119–120
decision theory, 86

deductive approach, versus inductive, 188–191
deductive mathematics, in psychology, 81–84
defense, neurological aspect of, 452; primary, 453; reflex, 453
déjà vu phenomena, 289, 451
delusions of grandeur, 367
denial, 326
deoxyribonucleic acid (DNA), 434
descriptive mathematics, in psychology, 73–77
determinism, 418; predictability and, 420–424
dG learning or conditioning, 213–220, 222, 235, 239, 241
dialectical materialism, 571, 576
digestion, Pavlov's work on, 129–130; physiology of, 130
digital computers, 170
dimethyl ether, structural formula of, 572
direction, Lewin's definition of, 283; physiological and psychological, 278
displacement, 367
distance quality, 404–405, 407
distribution, defined, 78; in statistical description, 78
DNA, 434
dogs, castrated, 135; dG conditioning in, 215–217; learning in, 145–147, 168, 176–177; motor activity in, 137; Pavlov's experimental use of, 132–134; vocal conditioned reflexes in, 234
dominance, 220–221
dominance–subordination order, 229
d reaction, 211–212, 223
dream metaphor (Adler), 354
dreams, perception and, 504–505; psychoanalysis and, 320–321
drive, 254; biologically conceived, 451
drive satisfaction, 341
drive stimulus, 201
drive tension, 376
drug therapy, 358–359
dualism, history of, 567–568

EEG phenomena, 139, 175
effect, law of, 110, 162, 225
ego, "characterless," 297; formation of, 375; in Gestalt psychology, 288; psychoanalysis and, 326; reappearance of, 303–304; self and, 303
embryogenesis, 31
embryology, internal structure and, 141
emotion, action and, 370; in behaviorist theory, 372; cognition and, 366–368; empirical generalizations about, 379–383; fear as, 381; in Freud's theory,

emotion (cont'd)
  366–370, 375–376; laws of, 376–379;
  origin of, 374; passivity and, 368–370;
  physiology and, 374–375; psychological theories of, 370–373; Sartre's view
  of, 376–377; versus "wishing" and
  "wanting," 373–375
empathy, concept of, 114
empirical-construct theories, 190
empirical generalizations, 10–11
empirical laws, 6–7
empirical observation, logic and, 36
empiricism, 470, 570; logical, 28; personality theory and, 295; radical, 428–429
"empty organism," 166–167
Entfremdung, 56
entropy, 344, 550
environment, perception and, 497–498
epistemic subject, 464–465
epistemological realism, 4–5
epistemology, and experimental method,
  462; general, 460; genetic, 31–34, 42–
  43, 460–472; historical, 42; maze, 63–
  64; perception and, 39; problem of,
  29–33; psychological, 30–31
epoché, religion and, 50
"equal alpha" condition, 256
Eros, 216, 239–240, 244
error, in descriptive mathematics, 81–82;
  in experimental psychology, 104–105;
  standard, 535–546
error variance, 530
ethics, neuropsychology and, 449–454
Euclidean geometry, 460–461
evolution, creative, 571; emergent, 344;
  ontogenetic, 578–580; phylogenetic,
  575–578; psychology and, 207–245
excitation, versus inhibition, 133
existentialism, phenomenological, 384; as
  philosophy of action, 391; Sartre's,
  386–388
existential psychology, of action, 384–
  400; art in, 395–397; perception and
  intention in, 389–394; reflection and
  action in, 391–395; theory and action
  in, 379–380, 386–389
experience, belief and, 499–500, 502–
  503; "boiling over" of, 433; immediate
  and reflective, 403–405; logic and, 35;
  role of in Gestalt psychology, 286
experiment, acute, 144; association, 281;
  chronic, 145–146; controlled, 68–69;
  criteria for, 104; ethics of, 119–120;
  orienting attitudes toward, 103–104;
  personality and, 294; planned, 7; science and, 14; see also experimental
  psychology
experimental laws, 6–7

experimental method, 462; epistemology
  and, 462
experimental neuroses, 133, 146
experimental psychologist, approach and
  viewpoint of, 88–111; goal of, 98; materials of, 98–103; methods of, 103–
  107; quantification and, 94–95; requirements of, 107–108
experimental psychology, 9, 14–15, 25;
  art of, 107–111; conceptualization in,
  104; converging operations in, 101–
  103; deception in, 119–120; measurement levels in, 105–106; nature of
  data in, 100–101; orienting attitudes
  in, 103–104; psychophysical methods
  in, 106–107; in Soviet Union, 208
explanations, 53
exploration, tendency toward, 441–442
exteroceptors, 576

factor analysis, 80
factorial experiment, 255
facts, explanation of, 11
fear, 367–370, 372, 381
feedback, 33, 173, 236, 334; conditioned
  stimulus and, 227; interoceptive, 211;
  interoproprioceptive, 228; positive,
  181; proprioceptive, 180, 211
feelings, 368; brain and, 433
field theory, 9, 114, 280, 573
free association, 326, 331–333
freedom, versus nature, 394
free will, God and, 425
frequency, as Hullian variable, 194
frogs, experimental, 443; in physiological
  research, 144
frustration, 371; goals and, 16–17
functional neuroanatomy, 170

galvanic skin reflex, 237
game theory, 86–87
Gardner's K Series, 537
gas, pressure–volume relationships in,
  71–72
Geisteswissenschaftliche Psychologie, 289
Gemeinschaftsgefühl, 352–353
generality, problem of, 91
generalization, empirical, 5–11; versus
  law, 6–7
genetic epistemology, 42; psychology and,
  460–472
geometry, 38–39; foundations of, 460–
  461
Gestalt psychology, 9, 28, 92, 116, 183,
  202, 227, 230, 276–290, 522, 571; as
  cognitive approach, 282 n.; existentialism and, 390, 399; in individual psychology, 342–343; memory storage

and, 433; misunderstandings about, 285–288; as nativistic theory, 285; present status and tasks ahead, 289–290; self and, 302; translation of into terms of other theories, 276–282

Gestaltungen, 213

glia, in memory function, 435–436

glial tissue, in brain, 434

goal, versus fictional goal, 350; frustration and, 16–17; inducibility in, 510; linking of in social interaction, 506; noninterdependence of, 515; substitutability in, 509

goal reaction, fractional antedating, 278; fractional anticipatory, 173

goal region, "structural pathways to," 278

God, in existentialism, 390–391; free will and, 425

grammar, rules of, 552

G reaction, in learning, 211

group, individual and, 116–117

group behavior, predictability and, 422

group influence, in social interaction, 513

group process, cooperation and competition in, 513–514

habit, 254; versus role, 118–119

habitat, in individual psychology, 354

habit-reversal capacity, 212

habit strength, 198, 277–278

habituation, 240, 442; degree of, 220

hemoglobin, 574

heredity, Pavlov on, 138

heterodynamic conditioning, 220

historical-cognitive-rational level, 239

holism, in individual psychology, 342–343

homeostatic needs, 172

homosexuality, latent, 346

homunculus, within self, 310–311

Hullian system and theory, 172, 174–175, 191–193, 260

Hull-Spence theory, 187–203

human action, science and, 407–408; *see also* act; action

human being, as unique unity, 293; theories about, 295

hunger, 427–428

hypnotic phases, Pavlov's, 132

hypothalamus, injury to, 428

hypotheses, confirming of, 155; incremental, 157–158; kinds of, 153–164; one-trial, 157; physiological, 177

hypothetical constructs, 174

"I," self and, 309–310

id, 307, 326

idealism, personalistic, 299

idealistic positivism, 346–347

identity, change and, 569–572

idiographic sciences, 54; nomothetic, 570

idiophenomena, 9–10, 570

imageless thought, 326

imagery, 229

imagination, in existential psychology, 394–395

immanent truth, 14

incentive hypothesis, 180–182

incognito, analytic, 326–331

incremental hypothesis or model, 157–158, 267–268

indeterminacy, 447–448

individual, creative power of, 340–341; versus group, 116–117; society and, 341

individual psychology, action versus words in, 347; analysis of terms in, 348–352; basic assumptions and methodology of, 342–345; clinical method in, 352–357; cognitive reorganization in, 357–358, 360; creativity in, 344–345; data interpretation in, 355–356; "depth" psychology and, 347; drug therapy in, 358–359; evolution and humanism in, 344; goal and fictional goal in, 350; guessing in, 356–357; masculine protest in, 350–351; milieu therapy in, 359; natural history and, 354–355; open system in, 344–345, 359; operationalism in, 345–348; phenomenology in, 353–354; pragmatic limitation in, 347–348; social interest in, 351–353; social-science orientation of, 342–343; stochastic method and, 357; style of life in, 349–350; teleological explanation and hierarchical organization in, 343; therapy in, 357–359; unconscious in, 349

individual test scores, interpretation of, 540–548

inducibility, in social interaction, 510, 513

inductive reasoning, 188–191, 439

inference, 439, 494

inferiority complex, 349

information, imagery and, 236; verbal idea of, 550

information theory, 85, 175–176, 183; Morse code and, 554; psycholinguistics and, 550–561; word frequencies in, 554–555

inhibition, 131; in learning, 195; Pavlov's concept of, 131; protective, 135

innateness, of cognitive structures, 33

insight, in psychoanalysis, 329

instincts, emotion and, 370

instrumental conditioning, 220

614

instrumentalism, 408
integration, modes of, 226; proprioceptive, 213; suprasummative, 227–228
intelligence tests, 528–533, 543–544
intention, in existentialist psychology, 389–391
interneural reactions, 211
interoceptors, 576–577
interoproprioceptive reaction, 227–228
interpretation, in psychoanalysis, 323
intersubjectivity, 90
interval scale, 105
introspection, 497; classical, 92
IQ, 543–544
irradiation, Pavlov's, 132
irrelevant traits, elimination of, 62
isomers, 448
isothermal process, 71

jealousy, 367–370
just noticeable difference (JND), 76, 96, 106

Kate Nevner octagon, 231
kinesthesis, conditioning and, 234
knowledge, by acquaintance, 490; behavior and, 492; belief and, 502–504; dispositional, 491; law of, 225; neurology of, 439–445; perception and, 489, 500–501; problems of, 29–31; subverbal, 489
Kulturwissenschaften, 9

language, acquisition of by children, 234–235; cognitive-expectancy, 202; as conditioned reaction, 208; function of, 137–138; human function in, 136; logic of, 3; logical structures and, 34; logico-mathematical, 469; Pavlov's concept of, 233–234; thought and, 118; words as signals in, 138
latent-learning experiments, 162
law, behavioral, 199–200; of biology, 576; defined, 69; of effect, 162, 225; versus generalization, 6–7; of knowledge, 225; Lewin-Zeigarnik, 6; physical, 6; of semantic homeostasis, 164; as statement, 282; theory and, 71
leadership, self-perpetuating, 512; social functions of, 512
learning curve, 155–156
learning and learning theory, 13, 195; (*ABC . . . N*) type, 226; behaviorism and, 58; classification of evidence, 211; *dD(G)* type, 220–226; defined, 210; evolution in, 209–210, 240; explanation of, 12–13; *fait accompli* type, 240;

general definition and classification of, 210–214; Gestalt psychology and, 289–290; goal-oriented, 195; H × D formulation and, 198; historical-cognitive-rational level of, 239–240; inhibitory mechanisms in, 195; integrative, 212–213; latent, 13, 162; levels of, 240–243; mathematical, 254–274; measurement in, 526; mechanical level of, 218; memory storage and, 433; modificatory, 211–212; motivationless, 197; neural action and, 209; paired-associate, 255; perception and, 92, 226, 232; phyletic, 233; primitive decremental, 220; punishment in, 109–111; reward, 220; stimulus-response theories of, 155–156, 180, 195; *sy(ABC . . . N)* type, 233–238; trial-and-error, 8; tripartite division of, 238–240; verbal, 197
learning-set, 212
Lewin-Zeigarnik law, 6
libido theory, 13
life, instinct of, 574; organic, 578; origin of, 579
life space functions, 276
life style, 340, 354
linguistics, defined, 551; space symbols and, 559–560
linkage, of goals, 506–507
links, in nervous-system model, 170–171
locomotor-manipulatory-vocal reactions, 241
logic, child's discovery of, 31, 34–39; experience and, 35; mathematics as branch of, 3, 465; metaphysics and, 18; problems of, 29–30; "pure," 38; in psychological terms, 26; psychologism in, 48; science and, 3; use of term, 65
logical analysis, 429; thought and, 474–487
logical behaviorism, 55–56
logical empiricism, 28, 33, 469; analytic and synthetic, 37
logical positivism, 33
logical reductionism, 563, 569, 574–575, 579–582
logico-mathematical language and experience, 36, 469
lung cancer, hypotheses about, 154–155

manic state, 133
Manifest Anxiety Scale (MAS), 198, 201
Markov models, 258, 550
Marxism, in social psychology, 122
masculine protest, 350–351
mass-energy equation, 6, 575

mathematical learning theory, 254–274; main lines of development, 256; new developments in, 255–259

mathematical models, 81–84, 175–176, 190, 257–274, 430; see also model

mathematics, as branch of logic, 3, 465; commutative law in, 462; deductive role of, 70–73; descriptive role of, 68–70; epistemology and, 465–469; organic life and, 574; in psychology, 68–87, 460–461; "pure," 38; see also number

matter, in relativity theory, 582

maturation, internal, 33

"maze dull" and "maze bright" performances, 437

maze epistemology, 63–64

measurement, basic data and, 527–539; chance errors of, 530; covariance in, 535; different examinees in, 545–546; individual test scores in, 540–548; interpretation in, 526–549; mean scores in, 546–548; positive or negative errors in, 534; score differences in, 541–545; scoring procedure in, 534–535; standard error of, 527, 533–542, 546

measurement tests, 528; see also intelligence tests

mechanical analogies, in behavioral research, 170–171

"mechanisms," postulating of, 365

mediating process, 173

mediation theory, in stimulus-response patterns, 171

melancholic state, 133

memistors, 435

memory, 26; linguistics and, 552; physiology of, 433; synaptic conditions and, 437, 452

memory-motive structure, 452–453

memory storage and retrieval, 433–445

mental acts, 481

mentality, evolutionary aspect of, 578

mental life, organic origin of, 579–580

mental process, 483, 486; versus biological, 581–582; prenatal life and, 579

metalogic, 471

metaphors, conditioning and, 216; structural, 327

metaphysics, 4, 460; positivism and, 28

metascience, 469; behavioral, 50–65

methodological reductionism, 18–19, 570 n.

microstate (central nervous system), characteristics of, 439–441

mind, autonomy of, 294; as mode of behavior, 404; objects in, 406; structure of, 445–449

mind–body dichotomy, 564–568

mind–body theories, 293

mindbrain, structural, 445

misperception, 493–494, 499

model, activity versus passivity types, 378–379; all-or-none, 267–268, 270, 272–273; cognitive-expectancy, 201; of emotions, 375–376; in experimental psychology, 98–100; incremental versus all-or-none, 267–268; versus "mathematical model," 274; of nervous system, 170–171; in personalistic psychology, 301; purposive-rule-following, 365; of sense organ, 442; stochastic, 84, 183, 356; of word frequencies and information theory, 556–560; see also mathematical models

modificatory learning, 211–212

molar behavior theory, 279 n.

monism, 431; versus pluralism, 567

monistic transitionism, principles of, 563–583

monkeys, cortex of, 441–442; temporal lobe of, 169

motivation and motives, 26, 115; behavior theory and, 200; continuity and discontinuity in, 309; in cooperative process, 514–515; emotion and, 371, 378; functional anatomy of, 307–308; in Gestalt psychology, 287; Hull's drive theory of, 172; power and, 515; uniqueness in, 307

motor cortex, of brain, 440; see also cortex

Mueller fibers, 436

mutual trust, 517–519

nativism, in Gestalt psychology, 285–286

natural numbers, 465–469

natural philosophy, 384

natural science, 570, 574

Naturwissenschaften, 9

neobehaviorism, 196; language and, 234; neo-Hullian, 187–203

nerve cells, fiber of, 438; phase sequence in, 564

nervous breakdown, 9, 133

nervous development, histological and functional, 579

neuroanatomy, 169; functional, 170

neuro-behaviorism, 427

neurodynamics, psychic phenomena and, 577

neurology, consciousness and, 451; in neo-Hullian behaviorism, 199–201; subjective states and, 565

neurons, 434; imagery and, 236; "new-

neurology (cont'd)
   ness" type, 443; "sameness" type, 443;
   visual, 443
neurophysiology, physico-chemical problems of, 566
neurosis, experimental, 133, 146
neshama, 567
newborn, self in, 302–303
Newtonian physics, 405–406, 412
nomothetic sciences, versus idiographic,
   570
noninterdependence, in social interaction,
   506–508
null hypothesis, 267, 544
numbers, cardinal and ordinal, 466; natural, 32, 465–469; specificity of, 468

Oa learning, 240
object, distance properties of, 403–407
Ob learning, 240–241
observation, versus behavioral viewpoint,
   55–56; intersubjectivity in, 90; public
   versus private, 91
"observe," versus "falsify," 52–53
observer, analyst as, 328
Occamism, 477
Oedipus complex, 347, 355, 385
one-trial hypothesis, 157–158, 163
ontic self, 297–298
ontogenetic evolution, 578–580
"operation," in behavioral descriptions,
   59–60; converging, 101–103; identifiable, 61; rules of, 255
operationism, 56, 59–60; defined, 346; in
   individual psychology, 345–348; theory and, 150
oral character, 348
ordinal numbers, 466
organicism, in individual psychology,
   342–345
orienting reflex, 218, 228, 442
orthogonal factors, 80
overdetermination, in mathematical model, 257

pain sensation, 576
paired-associate learning, 155, 258–259
parameters, of equation, 82
passivity, emotions and, 368–370, 379–
   383
Pasteur effect, 435
perception, 39–42; acquired, 232; behavior and, 492, 496, 501–502; belief and,
   499; bodily, 493; brain and, 497–498;
   causality in, 496; changes in, 215; concordant, 507; defined, 489; emotion
   and, 446; environment and, 497; in ex-

istentialist psychology, 389–391, 394–
   395; field theory of, 280; in Gestalt
   psychology, 287; immediate and mediate, 444, 493–494, 498, 500; indeterminate, 490–491; learning and, 226;
   mediate and immediate, 444, 493–494,
   498, 500; as mental experiment, 496;
   motivation and attitudes in, 287–288;
   objects of, 494; quality of, 501–505;
   "small," 500–501; in social interaction,
   507; speed and, 41; systematic change
   in quality of, 501–502; theory of,
   489–505; time and, 491; transparency
   of, 496; unconscious, 495; veridical,
   492, 494, 499, 504
Perin-Williams data, 189
personality, dynamic continuity of, 306–
   310; Gestalt psychology of, 282–284,
   290; Lewin's account of, 282; proprium
   of, 309–313; psychology of, 293–314;
   quantitative study of, 80; versus self,
   297; structure of, 306, 310; unity of,
   298
personalistic psychology, 293–314; problem-centered, 301
phenomenological existentialism, 384
phenomenology, antipsychologistic, 384;
   in individual psychology, 345–346
philosophy, Anglo-American, 384–385,
   387–389, 393, 399–400; behavioral
   science and, 64–65; disagreement in,
   461–462; history of, 563–564; "natural," 384; neuropsychological considerations in, 426–454; psychology and,
   24–43; "results" in, 462; of science, see
   science, philosophy of; as science of
   science, 4
phoneme frequencies, 561
phonetic vasoconstrictive conditioning,
   237
photosynthesis, 574
phylogenetic evolution, 575–578
physical phenomena, 5–6; behavioral phenomena as, 89
physics, biology and, 18–19; figurative
   language of, 324; as "hard science,"
   553; laws of, 69–70; philosophy of, 4;
   physiological processes and, 576; problem of, 29; psychology and, 573–574;
   representative data in, 94–95; single
   linear dimension of, 98; theory formation and, 11
physiology, acute experiment in, 144;
   chronic experiment in, 145; and neo-
   Hullian behaviorism, 199–201
pleasure principle (Freud), 378
pluralism, 431
pluralistic theory, versus monistic, 567

positive cathexis, in social interaction, 510–512
positivism, idealistic, 346–347; logical, see logical positivism; metaphysics and, 28; radical, 183
power, motivation and, 515
pragmatism, classical, 431–432; Jamesian, 430–431; meaning of, 428; philosophy of science in, 402–408; structural, 426–454
preconscious, role of, 319, 325–336
predication, 237–238
predictability-in-principle, 418
prediction, human behavior and, 412–413; in psychoanalysis, 322
prenatal life, mental processes and, 579
pressure–volume relationships, 71–72
probability, in test trials, 270–271
problem-solving, science as, 402
proprium (Allport), 309–314
protective inhibition, 135
psyche–soma dichotomy, 355, 564, 567–568
psychoanalysis, attitudes in, 326; experimental research in, 15; Freud on, 318; interpretation and prediction in, 322–323; limitations of, 319–325; neurophysiology and, 450–451; Pavlov's relation to, 142; philosophic position of, 335–337; place of in sciences, 316; prediction in, 322–323; and psychological phenomena, 577–578; research areas in, 334; scientific problems of, 316–337; as scientific process, 325–331; as technique, 450; theory of, 15; as therapeutic instrument, 316; transference and countertransference in, 329–331; validation in, 321–322
psychodrama, 359
psycholinguistics, defined, 551–552; information theory and, 550–561
psychological categories, quantification of, 73–74
psychological data, classes of, 100–101; versus physiological, 570
psychological measurement, interpretation in, 526–549; see also measurement
psychological positivism, 166
psychological propositions, 44–49; defined, 45
psychological research, 15–16; mathematical methods in, 85–87; models in, 259–274
psychological science, science of, 20–21
psychological system, defined, 51–52
psychological theory, reductionism in, 563; vagueness in, 150–164

psychology, Adlerian, 340–342; advances in, 25; alien concepts in, 18; cognitive, 168, 202; conceptual structures of, 56; deductive mathematics in, 81–84; divorce from philosophy, 114; empirical, 379; epistemology of, 29–31; evolutionary, 207–245; existentialist, see existentialist psychology; experimental, see experimental psychology; and formalization techniques, 460–461; Freud's theory of, 356–383; genetic epistemology and, 460–472; history of, 411; "individual," 340–342; mathematical learning theory and, 254; mathematics, use in, 68–87, 95; morphisms and, 19; neurophysiology and, 566; "no-evolution" approach to, 208; objectives of, 31; operational approach to, 60, 429; Pavlov's hopes for, 565–566; personalistic, 293–314; philosophy and, 4, 26, 28–43; and philosophy of science, 24–27; physiology and, 566; pure, 464; quantitative, 73–76, 94–95; radical reductionism in, 563–564; Russian, see Soviet Union; as "science of self" (Calkins), 300; social, see social psychology; stimulus-response, see stimulus-response pattern; see also S-R psychology and functions
psychomorphology, 307
psychonervous image-direction, 208
psychophysical function and theory, 6, 92, 95, 97, 107; information theory and, 85
punishment, learning and, 109–111
punishment conditioning, decremental, 219
pure-stimulus act, 173
purpose, reflex of, 574
purposive-rule-following model, 365

quantification, commitment to, 94; degrees or kinds of, 74, 94; science and, 20; studies of, 193
quantum randomizer, 413
quantum theory, 550

radical empiricism, 295, 428
radical realism, 4–5
radical reductionism, 563–567, 576–579
randomness, 356
rationality, defined, 239
rat learning and experiments, 58, 62, 109, 146–147, 166, 437
reaction, afferent, 212; configure of, 236; definition and use of, 210, 239
reaction potential, 254, 277
reaction-time data, 107

realism, epistemological, 4–5; instrumentalism and, 408; objective, 403; radical, 4–5

reality principle, 375–376, 570

reductionism, Freud on, 565; logical, 563, 569, 579; methodological, 18–19, 570 n.; Pavlov on, 565–566; in psychological theory, 563; radical, 563–567, 576–579; theoretical, 570 n.

reflection, action and, 392; role-taking and, 406

reflex-arc theory, 169

reflexes, cortex and, 577; habituation in, 220; inhibition of, 129; orienting, 218; unconditioned, 222; see also conditioned reflex; conditioning

reimorphism, 19

reinforcement, 179–180, 200, 227, 235, 304; in $dD(G)$ conditioning, 218; in neo-Hullian behaviorism, 194–195; secondary, 180, 195; in S-R theory, 172–173; of stimulus event, 152; subject-determined, 263; tension reduction and, 304; testable meaning of, 162; theory of, 13

relativity theory, 40–41, 406–407, 582

repression, of wishes, 381–382

resistance, synapses and, 451–452

response, anticipatory, 278; Hull's meaning for, 278; psychological definition of, 200

response-chains, latency of, 175

response dispersion, 96, 107

response-produced drive induction, 173

restitution, in nerve-cell fiber, 437–438

reverse afferentiation, 181

reverse neural connections, 220

reversibility, 33–34

reward, definitions of, 152–153; magnitude of, 257

reward learning, 220

RNA (ribonucleic acid), 434, 436

role behavior theory, 118–119, 406, 449

Rorschach test, 329

R methods, 107

Russian physiology, 128, 131

salivary secretions, 129–130, 134, 162; inhibition and, 132, 216; meat odor and, 233; semantic conditioning in, 237; at word sounds, 234

satiation, 288

schema, apperceptive, 341

schizokinesis, 141

schizophrenia, pathophysiology of, 136; vertical conditioning in, 216

Schwann cells, 437

science, adolescence of, 128; as behavior, 50–65; defined, 3; empirical versus praxiological, 4, 570; experimentation in, 14; formal, 4; human action and, 407–408; idiographic, 9, 570; instrumentalism and, 408; logic of, 52, 64–65, 99; natural, 570, 574; nomothetic, 54, 570; philosophy of, 4, 17, 64–65, 188, 402–408, 448; pragmatist's philosophy of, 402–408; as problem-solving inquiry, 402; psychoanalysis in, 316; quantification in, 20; realism and, 408; reality and, 570; research and, 3; "science of science," 3, 50, 61; as social activity, 402; total view of, 54; without naïveté, 18

scientific data, as representational, 94–95

scientific thought, roots of, 33; see also thought

scores, in psychological measurement, 536–537, 541–543

second signaling system, 136–138

self, abstract, 304; appropriated, 310–314; datum-self and, 299; evolving sense of, 308; in Gestalt psychology, 302; "knower" in, 310; ontic, 297–298; organization of, 302–306; personality and, 297, 312; propriate, 309; psychological, 295–296, 303–304; as real being, 303; unity of, 296–300; whole, 299

self-awareness, 308

self-concept, 305

self-consciousness, 294, 309, 392, 397

self-defeating predictions, 412

self-esteem, 305, 308

self-experience, 300–302

self-identity, 298

self-observation, 402

self-preservation, 574

self-reinforcement, 262

self-stimulation, 429

self-system, 308

selfups, 412

semantic homeostasis, law of, 164

semanticization, 213, 237–238

semantics, 3

sememes, 213, 238

sensation, 26, 494, 498–500

sensitization, 220

sensory deprivation, neural tissue and, 435

sensory-orienting reactions, 241

sensory preconditioning, 228 n.

servomechanisms, 170

"set," psychological, 442

sex, propagation and, 576

situational invariance, 257

social interaction, capability in, 514–515; communication in, 520–521; cooperation and competition in, 509; coordination problem in, 520–521; defined, 506; dependence and interdependence in, 515–516; developed concept of, 506–516; initiation of cooperation in, 516–522; linked goals in, 506–507; logic and, 33; motivation in, 514–515; mutual trust in, 517–518; noninterdependence in, 507–508; positive cathexis in, 510; psychological aspects of, 506–524

social interest, 353

social psychology, nonphilosophical, 114; philosophical and methodological problems in, 114–122; political systems and, 121–122; in Soviet Union, 121–122; values in, 120–121

social-science orientation, in individual psychology, 342–343

soma–psyche dichotomy, 355, 564, 567–568

somatosomatic reflexes, 220

S-O-R psychology, 171–172

soul, dualism and, 567–568; Plato's view of, 294; as "psychic being," 296 n.

Soviet Union, compound-stimulus studies in, 212; *dG* conditioning in, 215–216; experimental psychology in, 208; extension of Pavlov's work in, 138–139; psychology in, 208, 212–213, 222, 228, 576; radical reductionism in, 576; semantic conditioning in, 237; social psychology in, 121–122

space, behavior in, 278; time and, 405

space symbols, linguistics and, 559–560

spatial operations, discovery of, 32

spatial–temporal relations, 405

species, propagation of, 575–576

speed, concept of, 40; time and, 41

S-R psychology and functions, 104, 109, 151–153, 182, 211, 277; behavior research and, 167; behaviorism and, 202–203; behavior research and, 167; versus cognitive arguments, 201–203; in concept-formation and problem-solving, 197; deductions in, 175; definitions in, 156–161; Gestalt theory and, 276; Hull's system of, 172; language and, 174, 192; learning and, 155–156; in neo-Hullian behaviorism, 193–194; reflex-arc theory and, 169; reinforcement in, 172–173; rewarded but unassociated, 159–161; stimulus generation pattern in, 280–281; *see also* stimulus-response

standard deviation, 527, 541–543

standard error of measurement, 535–538, 546

statistical mechanics, 550

statistics, behavioral data and, 77–78

stimulus-response pattern, 57, 96, 151; versus conditioning-expectancy, 201–202; epistemology and, 101; language and, 202; learning and, 195; and mathematical models, 259–274; mediation theory in, 171–172; reinforcement in, 152; theories of, 179–180, 277; *see also* S-R psychology

stimulus-sampling theory, 257

stimulus-stimulus theories, 211

stochastic models and processes, 84, 183, 356

strategy, predictions and, 420–421

style of life, 304, 349–350, 358

substitutability, in goal attainment, 509–511

success, as goal, 340–341

success learning, 220

superego, 91, 303, 326

suprasummative integration, 227–228

switchboard theory, 169

symbol, cognition through, 475; nonsignificant, 404; significant, 406; thought and, 477–478, 482

symbolic logic, 36

symbolic sampling, 327

symbolization, 213, 233–238; configuring in, 236; learning and, 213; predication and, 237; in psychoanalysis, 337; theory of, 477

symphony, auditory effect of, 446–447

synapse, changes in, 89; resistance and, 451–452

synchronicity, 282 n.

tabula rasa, 429, 438

teleology, 343, 407

telos, 571

temperature scale, 74–75

temporal neocortex, 169

temporal operations, discovery of, 32

"tendency to explore," 441–442

tests, intelligence, 528–533, 543–544

Thanatos, 216, 239

Thematic Apperception Test, 329

theory, criteria for acceptability of, 14; empirical-construct, 190; formation of, 10–12; function of, 6; law and, 71; logical construction of, 26, 72; "loose," 523; of mathematical learning, 254–274; vagueness in, 150–164; verification of, 12–17

thermodynamics, laws of, 71, 344

thought, brain and, 433; concept of, 479; cross-section of, 485; language and, 118; logical analysis and, 474–487; nature of, 474–487; symbols and, 477, 482; versus thinking, 483–485
thumb-sucking, 8
time, absolute, 405; perception and, 491; speed and, 40–41
T maze, 101, 109, 256
topology, 38–39, 274, 278, 283
transference, 329–330, 333–334
transitionism, in biology, 573–575; Freud and, 580; mental processes in, 581; monistic, 563–583
transition matrix, 263, 271
trials, in psychological research, 259–260, 264–265
trusting behavior, 517–518
truth, immanent, 14; meaning of, 432

unconditional reflex, 129–130, 222
unconscious, Freud on, 377–378; mentality of, 578; role of, 325
unconscious processes, 324–328; free associations and, 332–333
uniqueness, personality and, 307
unitas multiplex (Stern), 299, 313

Unlust, 451, 453
utility theory, 86

validation, technique of, 321–322
values, in social psychology, 120–121
variables, intervening, 254; situational, 93
variance, analysis of, 79, 255
verbs, perception and, 489–490
vibrations, frequencies of, 74
visceral reactions, 214, 220, 241, 372
"vision," behavioral, 56
voluntary action, 26
von unten herauf and *von oben herab* psychologies, 230–231

wanting, versus wishing, 373–375
Weber-Fechner law, 6, 76, 95–96
Wechsler Adult Intelligence Scale, 543
we-feeling, 511
wish, repression of, 381–382
word frequencies, 554–560
words, conditioning to, 234–237; in information theory, 554
word-symbols, hierarchical order of, 236–237
world, Newtonian, 405–406; relativistic, 406–407